Oracle Exadata
Expert's Handbook

Oracle Exadata Expert's Handbook

Tariq Farooq
Charles Kim
Nitin Vengurlekar
Sridhar Avantsa
Guy Harrison
Syed Jaffar Hussain

♠Addison-Wesley

New York • Boston • Indianapolis • San Francisco
Toronto • Montreal • London • Munich • Paris • Madrid
Capetown • Sydney • Tokyo • Singapore • Mexico City

For information about buying this title in bulk quantities, or for special sales opportunities (which may include electronic versions; custom cover designs; and content particular to your business, training goals, marketing focus, or branding interests), please contact our corporate sales department at corpsales@pearsoned.com or (800) 382-3419.

For government sales inquiries, please contact governmentsales@pearsoned.com.

For questions about sales outside the U.S., please contact international@pearsoned.com.

Visit us on the Web: informit.com/aw

Library of Congress Control Number: 2015935451

Copyright © 2015 Pearson Education, Inc.

ISBN-13: 978-0-321-99260-4
ISBN-10: 0-321-99260-1
Text printed in the United States on recycled paper at RR Donnelley in Crawfordsville, Indiana
First printing, June 2015

Contents

Preface

Blazingly fast, Exadata is Oracle's complete database machine—with unparalleled performance brought about by engineering hardware and software technologies from Oracle and Sun. Exadata has been widely embraced by enterprise users worldwide, including government, military, and corporate entities.

Authored by a world-renowned veteran author team of Oracle ACEs/ACE directors with a proven track record of multiple bestselling books and an active presence on the Oracle speaking circuit, this book is a blend of real-world, hands-on operations guide and expert handbook for Exadata Database Machine administrators (DMAs).

Targeted for Oracle Exadata DBAs and DMAs, this expert's handbook is intended to serve as a practical, technical, go-to reference for performing administration operations and tasks for Oracle's Exadata Database Machine. This book is a

- Practical, technical guide for performing setup and administration of Oracle's Exadata Database Machine
- Expert, pro-level Exadata handbook
- Real-world, hands-on Exadata operations guide
- Expert deployment, management, administration, support, and monitoring guide and handbook
- Practical, best-practices advice from real-life Exadata DMAs

The authors have written this handbook for an audience of intermediate-level, power, and expert users of the Exadata Database Machine.

This book covers both 11*g* and 12*c* versions of the underlying Exadata software.

Acknowledgments

Tariq Farooq

To begin with, I would like to express my endless gratitude and thanks for anything and everything in my life to the Almighty ALLAH, the lord of the worlds, the most gracious, the most merciful.

I dedicate this book to my parents, Mr. and Mrs. Abdullah Farooq; my amazing wife, Ambreen; and my wonderful kids, Sumaiya, Hafsa, Fatima, and Muhammad-Talha; my nephews, Muhammad-Hamza, Muhammad Saad, Abdul-Karim, and Ibrahim. Without all of their perpetual support, this book would not have come to fruition. My endless thanks to them as I dedicated more than two years of my spare time to this book, most of which was on airplanes and in late nights and weekends at home.

My heartfelt gratitude to my friends at the Oracle Technology Network (OTN), colleagues in the Oracle ACE fellowship, my co-workers and everyone else within the Oracle community, as well as my workplace for standing behind me in my quest to bring this project to completion, especially Jim Czuprynski, Mike Ault, Bert Scalzo, Sandesh Rao, Bjoern Rost, Karen Clark, Vikas Chauhan, Suri Gurram, John Casale, and my buddy Dave Vitalo.

Considering that Exadata was the hot new kid on the Oracle block, I had been contemplating and reaching out to a lot of folks about writing a book on Exadata for over a year, before the stars got aligned and we started working on this project. From inception to writing to technical review to production, authoring a book is a complex, labor-intensive, lengthy, and at times painful process; this book would

not have been possible without the endless help and guidance of the awesome
Addison-Wesley team. A very special thank-you to Greg Doench, the executive editor, and all the other folks at Addison-Wesley, who stood like a rock behind this
project. Kudos to the book review and editorial team at Addison-Wesley for a job
well done. A special thanks to Nabil Nawaz for contributing and helping out with
the authoring process.

Finally, many appreciative thanks to my buddies and co-authors—Charles, Nitin,
Sridhar, Syed, and Guy—for the amazing team effort that allowed us to bring this
book to you, my dear reader. My sincerest hope is that you will learn from this book
and that you will enjoy reading it as much as we did researching and authoring it.

Charles Kim

I dedicate this book to my father, who passed away to be with the Lord earlier this
year. I thank my wonderful wife, Melissa, who always supported my career aspira-
tions no matter how crazy they seemed. Last, I would like to thank my three precious
sons, Isaiah, Jeremiah, and Noah, for always making me smile.

Nitin Vengurlekar

I would like to thank my family, Nisha, Ishan, Priya, and Penny, and especially my
mother, father, and Marlie.

Sridhar Avantsa

Any success that I have had or will have is primarily due to the support, encouragement, and guidance I have received from people I have had the distinct honor,
pleasure, and good luck to have in my life. There are a lot more folks who have had
a profound impact on my life, but the individuals listed here have been my Rocks of
Gibraltar over the years. I dedicate this book to these individuals as a small token
of my appreciation and thanks. I am forever indebted to them for the love, encouragement, and support they have provided over the years.

To my parents, Mr. Avantsa Krishna and Mrs. Avantsa Manga, who for years
denied themselves any pleasures or luxuries to ensure that they provided me with
the education, facilities, and opportunities to build a solid foundation for success
in the future. To my grandfather, Mr. A. V. Rayudu, whose unflinching faith in his
grandchildren helped us to really believe in ourselves.

To my elder brother, Srinivas Avantsa, who understood and knew me better than
I ever did, for guiding and supporting me through my formative years. If not for
him, I might never have made it to college. To my cousin, Nand Kishore Avantsa,
who introduced me to the fascinating world of computer science.

To my wife of the last 19 years, Gita Avantsa, the love of my life and the very best mother my children could ask for. She has stood by me and supported me over the years, through thick and thin, with a smile that always reminds me that "everything is going to be all right." Without her support and understanding, balancing work with writing a book would have been impossible.

To my sons, eight-year-old Nikhil and seven-year-old Tarun, who have put up with me on a daily basis. Your innocence, intelligence, and resiliency never cease to amaze me.

Last, but not least, I want to thank my coauthors for including me in this journey, and my team at Rolta AdvizeX for helping me—among them Rich Niemiec, Robert Yingst, and Michael Messina stand out.

Thank you ever so much, everybody.

Guy Harrison

I dedicate this work to the memory of Catherine Maree Arnold (1981–2010).

Thanks as always to Jenni, Chris, Kate, Mike, and William Harrison who give my life meaning and happiness. Thanks Tariq and Greg for giving me the opportunity to work with Sridhar, Syed, Charles, Sahid, Bert, Michael, Nitin, Nabil, and Rahaman.

Syed Jaffar Hussain

I would like to dedicate this book to my parents, Mr. and Mrs. Saifulla; my wife, Ayesha; my three little champs, Ashfaq, Arfan, and Aahil; and the entire Oracle community.

First and the foremost, I thank the Almighty for giving me everything in life and my parents for giving me wonderful life and making me what I am today. Also, I owe a very big thank-you to my family for allowing me to concentrate on writing assignments and helping me complete the project on time. Beyond a doubt, the project wouldn't have been possible without the tremendous moral support and encouragement of my wife, friends, and colleagues. Thank you, everyone, once again.

I would like to thank my management (Khalid Al-Qathany, Hussain Mobarak AlKalifah, Majed Saleh AlShuaibi), my dearest friends (Khusro Khan, Mohammed Farooqui, Naresh Kumar, Shaukat Ali, Chand Basha, Gaffar Baig, Hakeem, Mohsin, Inam Ullah Bukhari, Rizwan Siddiqui, Asad Khan), my brother Syed Shafiullah, fellow colleagues, well-wishers, supporters, nears, and dears for their immense support and constant encouragement. I can't forget thanking Mr. Vishnusivathej, Nassyam Basha, YV Ravi Kumar, Aman Sharma, and Karan and Asad Khan for helping me while writing this book.

I am also thankful from the bottom of my heart to the official technical reviewers (Sandesh Rao and Javed) for taking some valuable time from their busy schedules to review our book and for providing great input. I can't conclude the list without mentioning the members of the Addison-Wesley team who put this project together.

Nabil Nawaz

I would like to first thank my wife Rabia and the kids for being patient while I was busy contributing to this book and away from family for several weekends—this project ended up taking more time than I expected. I am very lucky to have an understanding family that supported me on my first book!

I am grateful to Charles Kim for inviting me to be part of this amazing book; he also spent time revising the contributions I made and I really appreciate his guidance and all of his help. Charles has been an excellent mentor and is always willing to help anyone learn about technology.

Thank you also to Bane Radulovic from Oracle Support for all of his time to discuss and review the Exadata Stack upgrade process in detail. Without him I would have never been able to contribute to the upgrade chapter.

About the Authors

 **Tariq Farooq** is an Oracle Technologist/Architect/Problem-Solver and has been working with various Oracle Technologies for more than 24 years in very complex environments at some of the world's largest organizations. Having presented at almost every major Oracle conference/event all over the world, he is an award-winning speaker, community leader/organizer, author, forum contributor, and tech blogger. He is the founding president of the IOUG Virtualization & Cloud Computing Special Interest Group and the BrainSurface social network for the various Oracle communities. Tariq founded, organized, and chaired various Oracle conferences including, among others, the OTN Middle East and North Africa (MENA) Tour, the OTN Europe Middle East and Africa (EMEA) tour, VirtaThon (the largest online-only conference for the various Oracle domains), the CloudaThon and RACaThon series of conferences, and the first ever Oracle-centric conference at the Massachusetts Institute of Technology (MIT) in 2011. He was the founder and anchor/show-host of the VirtaThon Internet Radio series program. Tariq is an Oracle RAC Certified Expert and holds a total of 14 professional Oracle Certifications. Having authored over 100 articles, whitepapers, and other publications, Tariq is the coauthor of the *Expert Oracle RAC 12c*, *Building DB Clouds in Oracle 12c*, *Oracle Problem-Solving*, and *Troubleshooting Oracle* books. Tariq has been awarded the Oracle ACE and ACE Director awards from 2010–2015.

Charles Kim is an architect in Hadoop/Big Data, Linux infrastructure, cloud, virtualization, and Oracle Clustering technologies. He holds certifications in Oracle, VMware, Red Hat Linux, and Microsoft and has over 23 years of IT experience on mission- and business-critical systems. Charles presents regularly at Oracle Open-World, VMWorld, IOUG, and various local/regional user group conferences. He is an Oracle ACE director, VMware vExpert, Oracle Certified DBA, Certified Exadata Specialist, and a RAC Certified Expert. His books include *Oracle Database 11g: New Features for DBAs and Developers*, *Linux Recipes for Oracle DBAs*, *Oracle Data Guard 11g Handbook*, *Virtualize Oracle Business Critical Databases*, *Oracle ASM 12c Pocket Reference Guide*, and *Virtualizing Hadoop*. Charles is the current president of the Cloud Computing (and Virtualization) SIG for the Independent Oracle User Group and blogs regularly at DBAExpert.com/blog.

Nitin Vengurlekar is the cofounder and CTO of Viscosity North America where he is responsible for partner relationships and end-to-end solution deployment. Prior to joining Viscosity, he worked for Oracle for more than 17 years, mostly in the RAC engineering group and in RAC product management. He spent his last three years at Oracle as database cloud architect/evangelist in Oracle's Cloud Strategy Group in charge of private database cloud messaging. Nitin is a well-known speaker in the areas of Oracle storage, high availability, Oracle RAC, and private database cloud. He has written or contributed to *Database Cloud Storage*, *Oracle Automatic Storage Management*, and *Oracle Data Guard 11g Handbook,* and has written many papers and contributed to Oracle documentation as well as Oracle educational material. With more than 28 years of IT experience, Nitin is a seasoned systems architect who has successfully assisted numerous customers in deploying highly available Oracle systems.

Sridhar Avantsa started his career with Oracle in 1991 as a developer. Over the years he progressed to become a DBA and an architect. Currently he runs the National Oracle Database Infrastructure Consulting Practice for Rolta AdvizeX (formerly known as TUSC), which he joined in 2006 as a technical management consultant. His specific areas of interest and expertise include infrastructure architecture, database performance tuning, high availability/disaster recovery and business continuity planning, Oracle RAC and Clustering, and the Oracle engineering systems. Sridhar has been an active member of the Oracle community as a presenter and as a member of Oracle Expert Panels at conferences.

Guy Harrison is an Oracle ACE and Executive Director of research and development at Dell Software. He is the author of *Oracle Performance Survival Guide* and (with Steven Feuerstein) *MySQL Stored Procedure Programming* as well as other books, articles, and presentations on database technology. He also writes a monthly column for *Database Trends and Applications* (www.dbta.com).

Syed Jaffar Hussain is an Oracle Database expert with more than 20 years of IT experience. In the past 15 years he has been involved with several local and large-scale international banks where he implemented and managed highly complex cluster and non-cluster environments with hundreds of business-critical databases. Oracle awarded him the prestigious "Best DBA of the Year" and Oracle ACE director status in 2011. He also acquired industry-best Oracle credentials, Oracle Certified Master (OCM), Oracle RAC Expert, OCP DBA 8*i*,9*i*,10*g*, and 11*g* in addition to ITIL expertise. Syed is an active Oracle speaker who regularly presents technical sessions and webinars at many Oracle events. You can visit his technical blog at http://jaffardba.blogspot.com. In addition to being part of the core technical review committee for Oracle technology oriented books, he also coauthored *Oracle 11g R1/R2 Real Application Clusters Essentials* and *Oracle Expert RAC*.

About the Technical Reviewers and Contributors

Dr. Bert Scalzo is a world-renowned database expert, Oracle ACE, author, Chief Architect at HGST, and formerly a member of Dell Software's TOAD dev team. With three decades of Oracle database experience to draw on, Bert's webcasts garner high attendance and participation rates. His work history includes time at both Oracle Education and Oracle Consulting. Bert holds several Oracle Masters certifications and has an extensive academic background that includes a BS, MS, and Ph.D. in computer science, as well as an MBA, and insurance industry designations.

Javid Ur Rahaman has more than 15 years of experience with various Oracle technologies working in the APAC, USA, and African regions. He currently works as a Practice Lead–Oracle Managed Services at Rapidflow Apps Inc., a California-based VCP Specialized Oracle Partner. He contributes to various seminars on Oracle technologies at different forums. Javid's areas of focus include large-scale national and international implementations of Oracle Exadata, Exalogic, Exalyitcs, ODA, RAC, OBIEE, SOA, OTM, Web Center, Oracle Demantra, Cloud Integration with EBS, HCM Cloud Implementation, and EBS among other Oracle technologies. Javid can be followed on his blog http://oraclesynapse.com, on Twitter @jrahaman7.

Nabil Nawaz started his career with Oracle in 1997 and currently works as a senior consultant at Viscosity North America. He has more than 17 years' experience working as an Oracle DBA starting with version 7.1.6; he is an OCP, is Exadata certified; and is also an Oracle ACE associate. His background is quite vast with Oracle and he has had the opportunity to work as a consultant in many large Fortune 500 companies focusing on architecting high availability solutions such as RAC, Dataguard, and most recently Oracle Exadata and Virtualization technologies. Nabil is a native of Dallas, Texas, and resides there with his wife Rabia and three children. Nabil regularly speaks at Oracle Users groups and can be followed at his blog http://nnawaz.blogspot.com/ and on Twitter @Nabil_Nawaz.

Sandesh Rao is an Oracle technologist and evangelist, solving critical customer escalations, and has been part of the Oracle RAC Development organization for the past 8 years, developing several products to help Oracle customers. Sandesh regularly speaks at Oracle OpenWorld, COLLABORATE, and webinars/ seminars as part of the Oracle RAC Special Interest Group on products related to Oracle high availability like RAC, ASM, and Grid Infrastructure. Involved with working on Engineered systems and best practices for the same through tools like exachk, he is also responsible for Diagnosability across the Oracle Database product stack and development of tools in this space. Sandesh has been working with customers, architecting, and designing solutions and solving critical problems and leading four different teams across different products like Database, Enterprise Manager, Middleware, and now the Cloud space for customer private and public clouds. Learn more about Sandesh at http://goo.gl/t6XVAQ.

1

360-Degree Overview of Exadata

Representing the next generation in database computing, an evolution many decades in the making, Exadata is Oracle's flagship database machine. Since its relatively recent inception in 2008, Exadata has become the fastest-adopted product in Oracle's entire history. This unprecedented success saga is attributed to many innovative features that Exadata has folded unto itself by successfully incorporating cutting-edge technologies and getting them to work with each other. This has been accomplished by leveraging the hundreds of man-years of research and development spent within the Oracle Database server family realm.

The goal of this introductory chapter is to familiarize the reader with the Exadata Database Machine by presenting a 360-degree synopsis and overview.

Exadata integrates a lot of next-generation technologies at both the hardware and software layers. Everything is preassembled, precooked, and well tested at the factory and ready to go as soon as it is delivered to your data center; this has been one of the distinguishing factors behind its wild success within the industry.

So how do we begin to describe Exadata?

If there is a common denominator that all categories and tiers of Exadata adopters and users could mutually agree upon in summing up Exadata, it would be "superb performance."

There are other characteristics for which Exadata is also well known: consolidation, Intelligent Storage, Smart Scans, Offloading, Hybrid Columnar Compression (HCC or EHCC), next-generation InfiniBand (IB) as a networking fabric, tons of

PCIe Flash Cache (FC), database cloud computing, and most famously a ready-to-run database machine.

This book attempts to cover all of these topics and a whole lot more by taking the reader on a fun-filled journey of discovery and awareness within the Exadata realm.

Note

The commands executed and the output generated within this book are not restricted to one model or series of Exadata; rather at different places, commands have been executed on different models and versions of the X2 to X4 series, ranging from X2-2, X4-2 Quarter Racks to multiples of X2-8 Full Racks connected with each other via the InfiniBand spine switches. This approach is intentional, in order to present broad coverage of the entire Exadata spectrum throughout the length and breadth of the book.

An Exadata Synopsis

Exadata is a complete and integrated database machine: hardware and software stitched together into a cohesive engineered system. It is ready to go when delivered to your data center: You can start loading data into a precreated database or start creating new databases and using Exadata on Day 1.

To summarize Exadata at a high level, by leveraging the decades of research and development performed within its database server family, Oracle coupled the Oracle Database server software with a superfast networking fabric on an Intelligent Storage layer. Exadata incorporates hundreds of widely adopted best practices right from the factory, at both the hardware and software layers.

Cutting down deployment time was a major goal in the design of Exadata. Oracle wanted to deliver a ready-to-go engineered system on Day 1, with no time needed to glue the various components to each other: Compute to Storage to Network. This is depicted in Figure 1.1 from Oracle documentation.

Many relatively new and innovative technologies ranging from InfiniBand as a choice of networking fabric to large amounts of Flash Cache to the data-cognizant Intelligent Storage Cell software have contributed to Exadata's success.

At the design level, much care was taken to eliminate single points of failure (SPOFs) at each and every layer of the hardware, from entire Storage Cells to power supplies to RAC Compute Nodes and a whole lot more.

On top of the existing innovations, Exadata has gone through rapid, almost annual release cycles to come out with newer, faster, and more cutting-edge versions since version X2 (using Sun as a hardware platform). Exadata V1 was the machine that was built on HP hardware (this version has been all but replaced for the most part by later versions of Exadata based on Sun hardware).

Figure 1.1   A depiction of Exadata from Oracle documentation
that holds very much true as advertised

An Engineered Database Machine

Exadata is an engineered database machine; although it is not an appliance, there are some overlapping characteristics between appliances and Exadata. At the software tier, Oracle leveraged the cluster version of its database server family—Real Application Clusters (RAC)—along with innovating the Storage Cell software at the Storage Tier. Automatic Storage Management (ASM) deployed on the DB Compute Nodes is used to manage the carved-out disks to formulate ASM disk groups.

This is in line with Oracle's current strategy of producing engineered systems on Sun hardware after the acquisition of Sun Microsystems in January 2010, not just at the Oracle Database tier but also at other tiers—for example, middleware, analytics, Big Data, and storage.

This single-vendor approach has for the most part resulted in reducing overall total cost of ownership (TCO) for enterprises by integrating all the hardware and software tiers into a single integrated engineered system.

Note

Exadata is a complete and tightly integrated database machine strictly regimented by Oracle. Custom changes by users are typically not allowed—for example, custom RPMs at the OS tier within the Compute Nodes are not allowed, as they may disturb the internal workings of the machine as a whole.

All changes, patches, upgrades, and so on are tested and certified by Oracle as a whole machine: Compute, Storage, and Network Tiers are engineered to work optimally in a tightly integrated fashion.

How Exadata Changes Your Job Role

Historically and traditionally, Oracle Database administrators (DBAs) are very used to living in their own world, minding the Oracle software realm of database servers, whereas system administrators mind the OS side of the house. With the advent of Exadata, while this approach is still the mainstay option, it has been challenged by a newer alternative approach: DBAs have started to learn the hardware and system administration side of the house and started to incorporate and include all of the involved duties under their management umbrella.

Notwithstanding employing/deploying either of these management and administration approaches, DBAs and system administrators have been compelled to transform their roles into database machine administrators (DMAs), a relatively new term in the industry. In other words, both DBAs and system administrators have had to learn newer technologies in order to effectively and efficiently perform duties as Exadata management and administration personnel.

Tip

Oracle DBAs who are venturing into the Exadata realm for the first time should expand on their system administration skill set and be prepared, mentally and otherwise, to assume a larger job role than they are normally accustomed to. They should transform themselves into database machine administrators (DMAs) as well as database cloud administrators (DCAs).

Oracle Enterprise Manager 12c

Exadata is an engineered conglomerate of sophisticated technologies and stands at the most complex end of the Oracle Database family spectrum; therefore, an advanced and sophisticated administration and monitoring solution is required to manage Exadata: the Oracle Enterprise Manager (OEM) 12c Exadata Plugin is built by Oracle for Oracle technologies to provide this comprehensive end-to-end solution.

OEM has been significantly enhanced and improved in version 12c to provide management, monitoring, administration, and support capabilities for Exadata.

Chapter 9 is dedicated to management of Exadata with OEM 12c. In addition to showing how to perform daily administration tasks on Exadata within OEM 12c, this chapter also covers initial setup, configuration, and discovery of assets and targets by the Exadata Plugin. Figure 1.2 shows a holistic overview of the Exadata machine in OEM 12c.

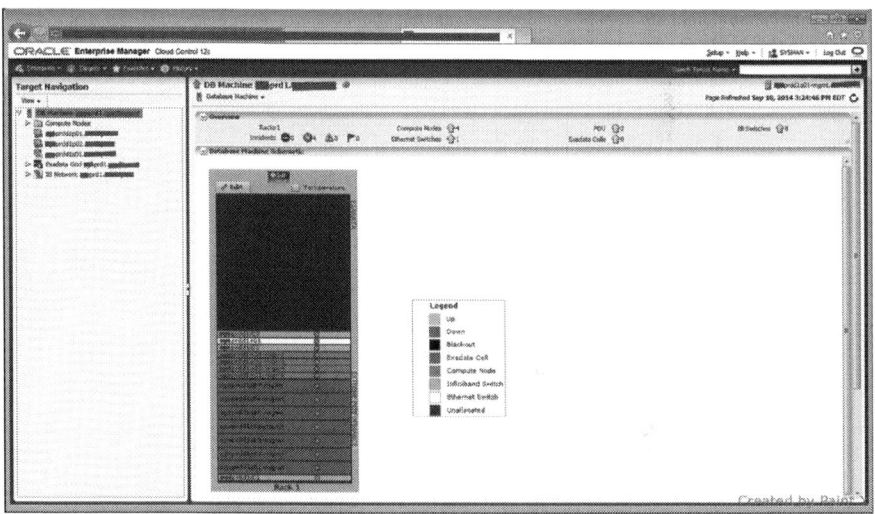

Figure 1.2   Holistic overview of Exadata in Oracle Enterprise Manager 12c

Hardware Architecture

Figure 1.3 depicts the major Exadata building blocks from a hardware perspective, each of which is briefly described in the following sections.

Note

The Exadata R & D team has taken special care to eliminate SPOFs at every tier of the stack. Each of the hardware components and subcomponents has some level of redundancy built in for this purpose.

Server Layer—Compute Nodes

The Exadata Compute Nodes are composed of the Sun X5-2, X4-2, and X4-8 servers respectively (X5-2 is the latest version at the time of writing this book). This is the new naming scheme for the Sun server lineup—for example, the Sun X3-2 server was formerly known as the X4170 server, which is the Compute Tier workhorse that powers the X2-2 Exadata series. This is a moderately sized 2u server with a two-socket configuration; hence the 2 in X2-2, denoting the number of CPU sockets. These servers have been enhanced and improved with each descendant version; currently the X4-2 series has 12-core CPUs and can have up to 512GB of DDR3 memory, and the X5-2 series has 18-core CPUs with up to 768GB of memory.

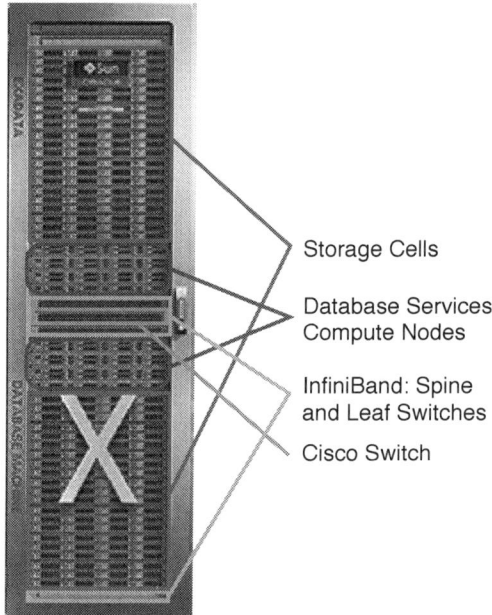

Storage Cells

Database Services:
Compute Nodes

InfiniBand: Spine
and Leaf Switches

Cisco Switch

Figure 1.3   Hardware componentry of an Exadata X4-2 Full Rack

Shared Storage—Storage Cells

The hardware Storage Tier for Exadata is powered by the Sun X4-2 Storage Server. With 3.2TB of Flash Cache, 96GB of memory, 12 CPU cores, 12 SAS (Serial Attached SCSI) disks in a High Capacity or High Performance configuration, dual InfiniBand ports, and up to 72.5GB/s of data bandwidth, this storage server is a little storage beast in a box.

The PCIe Flash cards have been improved and enhanced in both capacity as well as reduction of latency with each descendant version. A comparison section toward the end of this chapter shows the progression of the Flash Cache from Exadata version X2 to version X4.

Networking Fabric—InfiniBand

Exadata employs InfiniBand as a unified high-speed switched fabric for inter-node RAC communication between the RAC cluster nodes as well as between the Compute and Storage Tiers. InfiniBand is also used to link multiple racks of Exadata for horizontal expansion purposes.

For Half and Full Racks of the Xn-2 series, the total number of InfiniBand switches has been reduced in the latest version from Qty: 3 (X2-2, X3-2) to Qty: 2 (X4-2, X5-2). There is no spine switch in X4. A separate spine switch has to be purchased to establish connectivity between multiple racks of Exadata.

Power Distribution Units (PDUs)

Each Exadata machine comes with two redundant Sun power distribution units (PDUs), which can be connected through an Ethernet RJ-45 port for monitoring purposes. The Exadata PDUs can be monitored within Oracle Enterprise Manager by deploying the OEM PDU Plugin.

Cisco Switch

The X2, X3, and X4 Exadata machines come with a 48-port Cisco Catalyst 4948 Ethernet switch for external connectivity with your data center. This provides Ethernet-based external network connectivity for Exadata.

By deploying the Exadata Plugin, Oracle Enterprise Manager can be used to perform monitoring of the Exadata Cisco switch.

2u Custom Network Switch Space

The top 2u's of the Exadata rack can be used by Exadata users to install their custom networking switches.

Software Architecture

The major Exadata building blocks from a software perspective are presented in Figure 1.4. Each of these components is briefly described in the ensuing sections.

Real Application Clusters (RAC)

Real Application Clusters (RAC) is the cluster version of the Oracle Database server family. Grid Infrastructure = Oracle Clusterware + ASM is the heart and soul of Oracle RAC.

Chapter 2 is dedicated to RAC. It covers how to best employ/deploy RAC within the Exadata ecosystem.

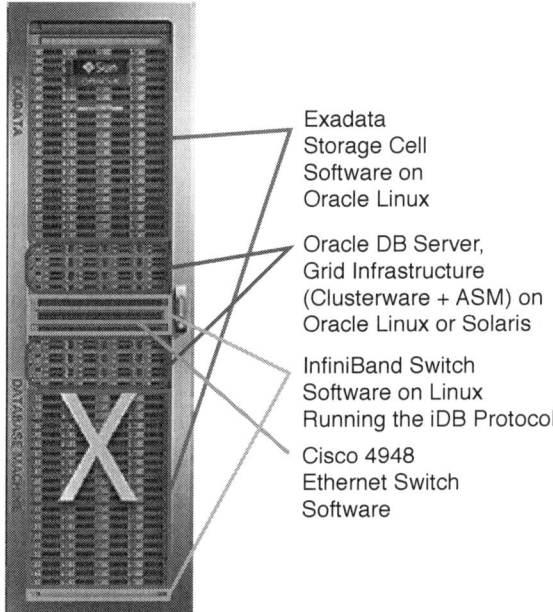

Exadata
Storage Cell
Software on
Oracle Linux

Oracle DB Server,
Grid Infrastructure
(Clusterware + ASM) on
Oracle Linux or Solaris

InfiniBand Switch
Software on Linux
Running the iDB Protocol

Cisco 4948
Ethernet Switch
Software

Figure 1.4   Software componentry of an Exadata X4-2 Full Rack

Note

The RAC DB option is not a mandatory component of Exadata; it is optional. However, seldom is an Exadata machine to be found that is devoid of the RAC option installed and being availed by the users. There are many reasons for this, ranging from horizontal scalability to load balancing to high availability (HA).

It is worthwhile to note here that the authors have not come across a single deployment of Exadata without RAC installed in it. In other words, RAC is pretty much married to Exadata and constitutes the majority software component of Exadata at the Compute Tier.

Automatic Storage Management (ASM)

ASM provides storage-layer capabilities to Exadata. It acts as a file system and volume manager for the disks provided within the Exadata Storage Cells to the database Compute Nodes.

ASM also provides mirroring capabilities for the carved-out ASM disk groups: normal redundancy (double mirroring) or high redundancy (triple mirroring). The optimal setup, configuration, monitoring, and administration of ASM are discussed in detail in the ensuing chapters of this book.

DB Compute Nodes

Users have a choice of deploying either Oracle Linux or Solaris on their Exadata machines at the DB Compute Tier; these are the only operating systems that are supported by Exadata. Both Oracle Linux and Solaris come preinstalled by Oracle on the DB Compute Nodes. When you order your Exadata and after it arrives at your data center, Oracle Support personnel will set up and configure the selected OS as part of the initial deployment process.

Note

From a statistical standpoint, the vast majority of Exadata users employ Linux as the OS of choice. There are a number of reasons for this, ranging from an existing widespread Linux knowledge base among the Oracle user community to Oracle's commitment to R & D of the Linux kernel.

Storage Cell Software

Exadata comes preinstalled with the Storage Cell software. The Storage Cell software provides the secret sauce to the internal workings of Exadata and its now-famous blazing performance. This is the part of Exadata that is responsible for most of the performance enhancements such as Offloading, Smart Scans, Hybrid Columnar Compression, and so on.

Multiple chapters of this book are dedicated to the Storage Cell software, its workings, and how to employ/deploy this tier to best set up and leverage Exadata according to industry-standard best practices.

Models and Configuration Options

This part of the chapter starts off by presenting a brief historical synopsis of Exadata, which is then followed by the various model configurations and finally a section that outlines the notable differences among the various models and versions.

Versions V1 (on HP hardware) and V2 (initial Sun configurations) are not covered in detail as they are all but obsolete within the industry.

Historical Synopsis

Exadata originated on HP hardware but was rapidly replaced by and is currently based on Sun hardware. X*n*-2 versions (X2-2, X3-2, and X4-2) on Linux are the most prevalent and popular configurations in the industry.

Exadata, now in its fifth generation, has gone through rapid changes at the hardware level; notably, the Flash Cache, CPU, and memory have been increased dramatically by an order of magnitude in the descendant versions.

Primarily geared for data-warehousing-type workloads, Exadata was born with the Storage Appliance for Grid Environments (SAGE) project. The first version of Exadata was based on HP hardware in 2008. At that point, Oracle had not yet acquired Sun Microsystems and needed an outside hardware partner (in the form of HP) to build its first-generation Exadata machine: the Exadata X1. After the acquisition of Sun Microsystems, Oracle rapidly transitioned to Sun's hardware platform, in the form of the X2 machine. This was followed by rapid releases of descendant generations of Exadata: the X3, X4, and M6-32 SuperCluster Engineered System.

Exadata can currently be characterized as a complete end-to-end engineered system, geared for running all kinds of Oracle Database workloads: online transaction processing (OLTP), decision support system (DSS)/data warehouse (DW), as well as hybrid workloads (OLTP plus data warehouse).

The next few sections present a high-level anatomy of Exadata from a hardware and software standpoint, the various versions of Exadata, and highlights of the major differences between them. Deep dives into each subject area are presented throughout the book.

Exadata on HP Hardware

The origins of Exadata happened on HP hardware: V1 was announced in September 2008. As mentioned in the previous section, V1 was based on HP hardware. At that point, Oracle had not yet acquired Sun Microsystems.

This initial version of Exadata was based on Qty: 8 HP DL360 G5 servers in a full 42u rack configuration with a total of 64 CPU cores.

V1 came with Qty: 14 HP DL180 G5 Storage Cell servers that contained a total of 112 CPU cores and 5.3TB Flash Cache within them. This machine was intended and designed for high-performance data warehousing.

The Evolution of Exadata

Exadata V2, based on Sun hardware, was announced in September 2009. This happened during the Sun acquisition process, followed by X2, X3, and now X4. This was a natural progression of events, considering that Oracle had acquired Sun and Sun had the resources, products, and decades of R & D to build Exadata machines at a mass production level.

Starting with the X2 series, the following sections present an overview of the various models, configurations, and notable differences and improvements made within the descendant versions from a hardware standpoint. The software components and their optimal setup and configuration are covered in detail throughout this book.

Exadata X2-2

Announced in 2010, the X2-2 was the first widely adopted Exadata model within the industry; it is the most familiar and widely deployed model of Exadata. The X2-2 42u Full Rack is composed of eight moderately sized DB-Compute servers, 14 power-horse Storage Cells running the Exadata Storage Cell software (CELLSRV), three InfiniBand switches, keyboard, video, and mouse (KVM) hardware, dual PDUs, and a Cisco 4948 10GB/s Ethernet switch for external and administrative connectivity.

The Storage Cells come with either 12 x 600GB 15,000 RPM SAS disks in a High Performance configuration or in a 12 x 3TB 7200 RPM High Capacity configuration.

Among other obvious reasons, such as next-generation software and hardware technologies engineered to get maximum performance, the X2-2's popularity can also be attributed to the fact that it is an affordable, extensible, and highly configurable machine and comes in three options: Small (Quarter Rack), Medium (Half Rack), and Large (Full Rack) configurations.

On ASM normal redundancy, a High Capacity X2-2 Full Rack provides 224TB of uncompressed storage capacity. A High Performance X2-8 Full Rack provides 45TB of uncompressed storage capacity on ASM normal redundancy.

The X2-2 series accommodates all kinds of workloads ranging from OLTP to data warehousing to hybrid-type workloads.

Table 1.1 presents an overview of the X2-2's specifications as well as notable components from a hardware standpoint.

Note

The X2-2 Quarter Rack and Half Rack can be expanded all the way up to a Full Rack. Eight X2-2 Full Racks can be interconnected without additional InfiniBand switches.

Table 1.1 Available Exadata X2-2 Series Hardware Configurations

X2-2 Quarter Rack	X2-2 Half Rack	X2-2 Full Rack
2 x database servers	*4 x database servers*	*8 x database servers*
24 CPU cores and up to 288GB memory for database processing (12 CPU cores and up to 144GB memory per database server)	48 CPU cores and up to 576GB memory for database processing (12 CPU cores and up to 144GB memory per database server)	96 CPU cores and up to 1152GB memory for database processing (12 CPU cores and up to 144GB memory per database server)

Compute Nodes

Each database server has

- 2 x six-core Intel Xeon X5675 processors (3.06GHz)
- 96GB memory (expandable to 144GB)
- Disk controller HBA with 512MB battery-backed write cache
- 4 x 300GB 10,000 RPM SAS disks
- 2 x QDR (40Gb/s) ports
- 2 x 10Gb Ethernet ports based on the Intel 82599 10GbE controller
- 4 x 1Gb Ethernet ports
- 1 x Oracle Integrated Lights Out Manager (ILOM) Ethernet port
- 2 x redundant hot-swappable power supplies

Networking:

- 3 x 36-port QDR (40Gb/s) InfiniBand switches (Half/Full Rack)
- 2 x 36-port QDR (40Gb/s) InfiniBand switches (Quarter Rack)
- Ethernet switch for administrative connectivity
- Keyboard, video or visual display unit, mouse (KVM) hardware for local administration

Other hardware:

- 2 x redundant PDUs

3 x Exadata Storage Servers	*7 x Exadata Storage Servers*	*14 x Exadata Storage Servers*
36 CPU cores for SQL processing	84 CPU cores for SQL processing	168 CPU cores for SQL processing
1.1TB Exadata Smart Flash Cache	2.6TB Exadata Smart Flash Cache	5.3TB Exadata Smart Flash Cache
Each Storage Server: 12 x 600GB 15,000 RPM High Performance SAS disks or 12 x 3TB 7200 RPM High Capacity SAS disks	*Each Storage Server:* 12 x 600GB 15,000 RPM High Performance SAS disks or 12 x 3TB 7200 RPM High Capacity SAS disks	*Each Storage Server:* 12 x 600GB 15,000 RPM High Performance SAS disks or 12 x 3TB 7200 RPM High Capacity SAS disks

Uncompressed usable disk data capacity (normal redundancy)

HC disks	HP disks	HC disks	HP disks	HC disks	HP disks
48TB	9.5TB	112TB	22.5TB	224TB	45TB

Exadata X2-8

The X2-8 was announced in 2010 and is a powerhouse symmetric multiprocessing (SMP)-like performer meant for the most demanding of workloads running very, very large database ecosystems.

The X2-8 42u Full Rack is composed of two massive DB-Compute server machines with 160 CPU cores and 4TB of memory, 14 power-horse Storage Cells running the Exadata Storage Cell software (CELLSRV), three InfiniBand switches, KVM hardware, dual PDUs, and a Cisco 4948 10GB/s Ethernet switch for external and administrative connectivity.

The main difference between the X2-2 and X2-8 Full Racks is that the X2-8 has two massive compute servers as opposed to eight moderate compute servers.

On ASM normal redundancy, an X2-8 Full Rack provides 224TB of uncompressed storage capacity in a High Capacity configuration and 45TB in a High Performance configuration.

Table 1.2 presents an overview of the X2-8's specifications as well as notable components from a hardware standpoint.

Note

As opposed to the Exadata X2-2, which comes in Quarter, Half, and Full Rack configurations, the X2-8 comes only in a single Full Rack configuration. Eight X2-8 Full Racks can be interconnected without additional InfiniBand switches.

Table 1.2   Available Exadata X2-8 Database Machine Hardware Configuration

X2-8 Full Rack
2 x massive SMP-like database servers
160 CPU cores and 4TB memory for database processing
(80 CPU cores and 2TB memory per database server)
Compute Nodes
Each database server has
▪ 8 x ten-core Intel Xeon E7-8870 processors (2.40GHz)
▪ 2TB memory
▪ Disk controller HBA with 512MB battery-backed write cache
▪ 8 x 300GB 10,000 RPM SAS disks
▪ 8 x InfiniBand QDR (40Gb/s) ports
▪ 8 x 10Gb Ethernet ports based on the Intel 82599 10GbE controller
▪ 8 x 1Gb Ethernet ports
▪ 1 x ILOM Ethernet port
▪ 4 x redundant hot-swappable power supplies

Continues

Table 1.2   Available Exadata X2-8 Database Machine Hardware Configuration (*Continued*)

Compute Nodes

Networking:

- 3 x 36-port QDR (40Gb/s) InfiniBand switches
- Ethernet switch for administrative connectivity

Other hardware:

- 2 x redundant PDUs

14 x Exadata Storage Servers:

168 CPU cores for SQL processing

5.3TB Exadata Smart Flash Cache

Each Storage Server:

12 x 600GB 15,000 RPM High Performance SAS disks or 12 x 3TB 7200 RPM High Capacity SAS disks

Uncompressed usable disk data capacity (normal redundancy)	
HC disks	*HP disks*
224TB	45TB

Exadata X3-2

Announced at Oracle Open World in September 2012, the X3-2 was the descendant version of the X2-2 series. Because of the massive amounts of Compute Tier memory and Storage Tier Flash Cache, Oracle labeled it the "Exadata X3 In-Memory Database Machine" (not to be confused with the Oracle Times Ten In-Memory Database or the 12*c* In-Memory Database option).

Improving on the X2-2 series, this was again a highly configurable machine, adding an Eighth Rack (the smallest unit you can buy—the logical subset of Quarter Rack) to the Quarter Rack, Half Rack, and Full Rack lineup.

With 128 CPU cores and 2TB of DDR3 memory, the X3-2 42u Full Rack is made up of eight DB-Compute servers, 14 power-horse Storage Cells running the Exadata Storage Cell software (CELLSRV), three InfiniBand switches, dual PDUs, and a Cisco 4948 10GB/s Ethernet switch for external and administrative connectivity.

Other than getting more CPU cores and memory at the Compute Tier, the notable enhancement made in the X3-2 (from the X2-2) was the significant increase in Flash Cache (from 5.3TB to 22.4TB). This was achieved by replacing the Sun PCIe F20 (in X2-2) with the Sun PCIe F40 (in X3-2) Flash Accelerator Card. The KVM hardware was discontinued in the X3-2 (present in the X2-2).

The Storage Cells in the X3-2 can be configured with either 12 x 600GB 15,000 RPM SAS disks in a High Performance configuration or in a 12 x 3TB 7200 RPM High Capacity configuration.

The storage capacity of the X3-2 is identical to that of the X-2: 224TB in a High Capacity or 45TB in a High Performance configuration of uncompressed storage capacity on ASM normal redundancy.

Table 1.3 presents an overview of the X3-2's specifications as well as notable components from a hardware standpoint.

Table 1.3 Available Exadata X3-2 Series Hardware Configurations

X3-2 Eighth Rack	X3-2 Quarter Rack	X3-2 Half Rack	X3-2 Full Rack
2 x database servers	*2 x database servers*	*4 x database servers*	*8 x database servers*
16 CPU cores and 512GB memory for database processing (8 CPU cores per database server are enabled with 256GB memory per database server)	32 CPU cores and 512GB memory for database processing (16 CPU cores and 256GB memory per database server)	64 CPU cores and 1TB memory for database processing (16 CPU cores and 256GB memory per database server)	128 CPU cores and 2TB memory for database processing (16 CPU cores and 256GB memory per database server)

Compute Nodes

Each database server has

- 2 x eight-core Intel Xeon E5-2690 processors (2.9GHz)
- 256GB memory
- Disk controller HBA with 512MB battery-backed write cache
- 4 x 300GB 10,000 RPM disks
- 2 x QDR (40Gb/s) ports
- 4 x 1/10Gb Ethernet ports (copper)
- 2 x 10Gb Ethernet ports (optical)
- 1 x ILOM Ethernet port
- 2 x redundant hot-swappable power supplies

Networking:

- 3 x 36-port QDR (40Gb/s) InfiniBand switches (Half/Full Rack)
- 2 x 36-port QDR (40Gb/s) InfiniBand switches (Eighth/Half Rack)
- Ethernet switch for administrative connectivity

Other hardware:

- 2 x redundant PDUs

Continues

Table 1.3   Available Exadata X3-2 Series Hardware Configurations (*Continued*)

X3-2 Eighth Rack	X3-2 Quarter Rack	X3-2 Half Rack	X3-2 Full Rack
3 x Exadata Storage Servers:	*3 x Exadata Storage Servers:*	*7 x Exadata Storage Servers:*	*14 x Exadata Storage Servers:*
36 CPU cores for SQL processing (18 cores enabled)	36 CPU cores for SQL processing	84 CPU cores for SQL processing	168 CPU cores for SQL processing
12 PCI Flash cards (six cards enabled) with 2.4TB Exadata Smart Flash Cache	12 PCI Flash cards with 4.8TB Exadata Smart Flash Cache	28 PCI Flash cards with 11.2TB Exadata Smart Flash Cache	56 PCI Flash cards with 22.4TB Exadata Smart Flash Cache
18 x 600 GB 15,000 RPM High Performance disks or 18 x 3TB 7200 RPM High Capacity disks (six disks per storage server enabled)	36 x 600GB 15,000 RPM High Performance disks or 36 x 3TB 7200 RPM High Capacity disks	84 x 600GB 15,000 RPM High Performance disks or 84 x 3TB 7200 RPM High Capacity disks	168 x 600GB 15,000 RPM High Performance disks or 168 x 3TB 7200 RPM High Capacity disks

Uncompressed usable disk data capacity (normal redundancy)							
HC disks	*HP disks*	*HC disks*	*HP disks*	*HC disks*	*HP disks*	*HC disks*	*HP disks*
4.5TB	23TB	9.5TB	48TB	22.5TB	112TB	45TB	224TB

Note

The X3-2 Eighth Rack (which is a Quarter Rack with half of it turned off logically), Quarter Rack, and Half Rack can be expanded all the way up to a Full Rack. Eighteen X3-2 Full Racks can be interconnected without additional InfiniBand switches.

Exadata X3-8

Catering to massive SMP mainframe-like workloads, the X3-8 was the next version up for the X2-2 model. It was announced in September 2012 at Oracle Open World at the same time as the X3-2 series.

The X3-8 42u Full Rack is composed of two massive DB-Compute server machines with 160 CPU cores and 4TB of memory (the same CPU and memory as the X2-8 model), 14 power-horse Storage Cells running the Exadata Storage Cell software (CELLSRV), three InfiniBand switches, KVM hardware, dual PDUs, and a Cisco 4948 10GB/s Ethernet switch for external and administrative connectivity.

The X3-8 Storage Cells can be configured with either 12 x 1.2TB 10,000 RPM SAS disks in a High Performance configuration or in a 12 x 4TB 7200 RPM High Capacity configuration.

On ASM normal redundancy, an X3-8 Full Rack provides 300TB of uncompressed storage capacity in a High Capacity configuration and 90TB in a High Performance configuration.

Other than getting more storage (each Storage Cell in the X3-8 came with bigger disks than the X2-8), the major improvement in the X3-8 was the significant increase in Flash Cache (increased from 5.3TB to 44.8TB: an 8.45X increase). This was achieved by replacing the Sun PCIe F20 (in X2-8) with the Sun PCIe F80 (in X3-8) Flash Accelerator Card. As opposed to the X2-8, the KVM hardware was discontinued in the X3-8.

Table 1.4 presents an overview of the X3-8's specifications as well as notable components from a hardware standpoint.

Note

Eighteen X3-8 Full Racks can be interconnected without additional InfiniBand switches. This extensibility is not limited to the X3-8 model only: this interconnected ecosystem can be any combination of the X2, X3, and X4 series.

Table 1.4 Available Exadata X3-8 Database Machine Hardware Configuration

X3-8 Full Rack
2 x massive SMP-like database servers
160 CPU cores and 4TB memory for database processing (80 CPU cores and 2TB memory per database server)
Compute Nodes
Each database server has

- 8 x ten-core Intel Xeon E7-8870 processors (2.40GHz)
- 2TB memory
- Disk controller HBA with 512MB battery-backed write cache
- 8 x 300GB 10,000 RPM SAS disks
- 8 x InfiniBand QDR (40Gb/s) ports
- 8 x 10Gb Ethernet ports based on the Intel 82599 10GbE controller
- 8 x 1Gb Ethernet ports
- 1 x ILOM Ethernet port
- 4 x redundant hot-swappable power supplies

Networking:

- 2 x 36-port QDR (40Gb/s) InfiniBand switches
- Ethernet switch for administrative connectivity

Other hardware:

- 2 x redundant PDUs

Continues

Table 1.4 Available Exadata X3-8 Database Machine Hardware Configuration (*Continued*)

14 x Exadata Storage Servers:

168 CPU cores for SQL processing
56 PCI Flash cards with 44.8TB Exadata Smart Flash Cache
168 x 1.2TB 10,000 RPM High Performance disks or 168 x 4TB 7200 RPM High Capacity disks

Uncompressed usable disk data capacity (normal redundancy)

HC disks	HP disks
300TB	90TB

Exadata X4-2

Announced in December 2013, the X4-2 was the next model up in the descendant versions of the X*n*-2 series.

The configurability options in the X4-2 are identical to those of the X3-2; you can get an X4-2 in one of the following configurations: Eighth Rack, Quarter Rack, Half Rack, or Full Rack.

With 192 CPU cores and 4TB of DDR3 memory, the X4-2 42u Full Rack is composed of eight DB-Compute servers, 14 power-horse Storage Cells running the Exadata Storage Cell software (CELLSRV), two InfiniBand switches, dual PDUs, and a Cisco 4948 10GB/s Ethernet switch for external and administrative connectivity.

Other than getting more CPU cores and doubling the memory at the Compute Tier, 4TB (X4-2) instead of 3TB (X3-2), once again, the most salient improvement made in the X4-2 (from the X3-2) was the significant increase in Flash Cache (from 22.4TB to 44.8TB). This massive increase was achieved by replacing the Sun PCIe F40 (in X3-2) with the Sun PCIe F80 (in X4-2) Flash Accelerator Card.

The Storage Cells in the X3-2 can be configured with either 12 x 1.2TB 10,000 RPM SAS disks in a High Performance configuration or in a 12 x 4TB 7200 RPM High Capacity configuration.

The storage capacity of the X4-2 was increased as compared to the X3-2: 300TB in a High Capacity or 90TB in a High Performance configuration of uncompressed storage capacity on ASM normal redundancy.

Figures 1.5 through 1.8 present an overview of the X4-2's hardware componentry.

Note

The X4-2 Eighth Rack, Quarter Rack, and Half Rack can be expanded all the way up to a Full Rack configuration. Eighteen X3-2 Full Racks can be interconnected without additional InfiniBand switches.

Figure 1.5   The Sun X4-2 Server makes up the Compute layer of the Exadata X4 series.

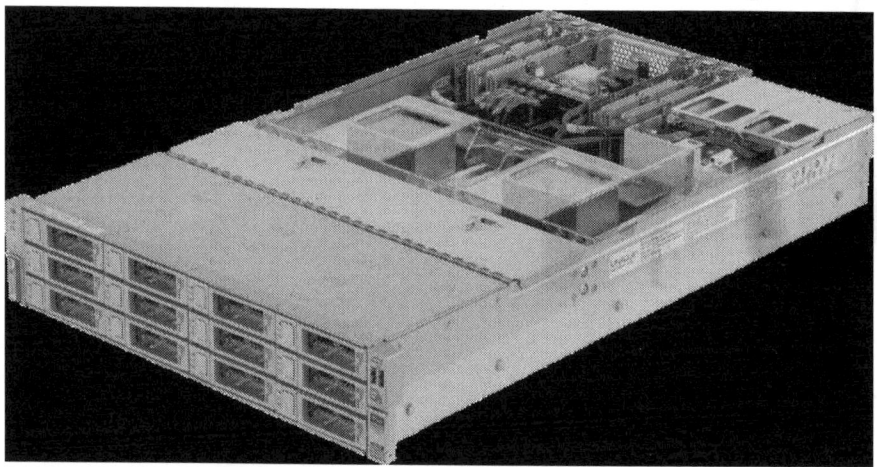

Figure 1.6   The Sun X4-2 Storage Server is also referred to as the Exadata X4-2 Storage Cells.

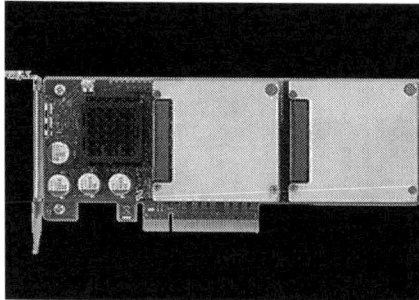

Figure 1.7   With 800GB for Flash Cache, the Sun Flash Accelerator F80 PCIe Card hardware component is the power-horse behind the Exadata X4 series Storage Cells Flash Cache.

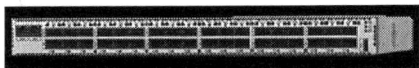

Figure 1.8   With 36 4x ports using standard QSFP connectors, the Sun Datacenter
IB Switch 36 formulates the unified networking backbone of Exadata.

Note

The X4-2 Eighth Rack (which is a Quarter Rack with half of it turned off logically),
Quarter Rack, and Half-Rack can be expanded all the way up to a Full Rack. Eighteen X3-2 Full Racks can be interconnected without additional InfiniBand switches.

Table 1.5 presents an overview of the X4-2's specifications as well as notable
components from a hardware standpoint.

Table 1.5   Available Exadata X4-2 Series Hardware Configurations

X4-2 Eighth Rack	X4-2 Quarter Rack	X4-2 Half Rack	X4-2 Full Rack
2 x database servers	*2 x database servers*	*4 x database servers*	*8 x database servers*
24 CPU cores and up to 1TB memory for data-base processing (12 CPU cores per database server are enabled with up to 512GB memory per database server)	48 CPU cores and up to 1TB memory for database processing (24 CPU cores and up to 512GB memory per database server)	96 CPU cores and up to 2TB memory for database processing (24 CPU cores and up to 512GB memory per database server)	192 CPU cores and up to 4TB memory for database processing (24 CPU cores and up to 512GB memory per database server)

Compute Nodes

Each database server has

- 2 x 12-core Intel Xeon E5-2697 v2 processors (2.7GHz)
- 256GB memory (expandable to 512GB)
- Disk controller HBA with 512MB battery-backed write cache
- 4 x 600GB 10,000 RPM disks
- 2 x QDR (40Gb/s) InfiniBand ports
- 4 x 1/10Gb Ethernet ports (copper)
- 2 x 10Gb Ethernet ports (optical)
- 1 x ILOM Ethernet port
- 2 x redundant hot-swappable power supplies

Networking:

- 2 x 36-port QDR (40Gb/s) InfiniBand switches
- Ethernet switch for administrative connectivity

Other hardware:

- 2 x redundant PDUs

Table 1.5   Available Exadata X4-2 Series Hardware Configurations (Continued)

X4-2 Eighth Rack	X4-2 Quarter Rack	X4-2 Half Rack	X4-2 Full Rack
3 x Exadata Storage Servers:	*3 x Exadata Storage Servers:*	*7 x Exadata Storage Servers:*	*14 x Exadata Storage Servers:*
36 CPU cores for SQL processing (18 cores enabled) 6 PCI Flash cards with 4.8TB (raw) Exadata Smart Flash Cache (six more Flash cards reserved for use on upgrade to Quarter Rack) 18 x 1.2TB 10,000 RPM High Performance disks or 18 x 4TB 7200 RPM High Capacity disks (18 more reserved for use on upgrade to Quarter Rack)	36 CPU cores for SQL processing 12 PCI Flash cards with 9.6TB (raw) Exadata Smart Flash Cache 36 x 1.2TB 10,000 RPM High Performance disks or 36 x 4TB 7200 RPM High Capacity disks	84 CPU cores for SQL processing 28 PCI Flash cards with 22.4TB (raw) Exadata Smart Flash Cache 84 x 1.2TB 10,000 RPM High Performance disks or 84 x 4TB 7200 RPM High Capacity disks	168 CPU cores for SQL processing 56 PCI Flash cards with 44.8TB (raw) Exadata Smart Flash Cache 168 x 1.2TB 10,000 RPM High Performance disks or 168 x 4TB 7200 RPM High Capacity disks

Uncompressed usable disk data capacity (normal redundancy)							
HC disks	*HP disks*	*HC disks*	*HP disks*	*HC disks*	*HP disks*	*HC disks*	*HP disks*
30TB	9TB	63TB	19TB	150TB	45TB	300TB	90TB

Exadata X4-8

Catering to massive SMP mainframe-like workloads, the X4-8 was the next version up for the X3-8 model. It was announced in July 2014.

The X4-8 42u Full Rack is composed of two massive DB-Compute server machines with 240 CPU cores and 12TB of memory, 14 power-horse Storage Cells running the Exadata Storage Cell software (CELLSRV), three InfiniBand switches, KVM hardware, dual PDUs, and a Cisco 4948 10GB/s Ethernet switch for external and administrative connectivity.

The X4-8 Storage Cells can be configured with either 12 x 1.2TB 10,000 RPM SAS disks in a High Performance configuration or in a 12 x 4TB 7200 RPM High Capacity configuration.

On ASM normal redundancy, an X3-8 Full Rack provides 300TB of uncompressed storage capacity in a High Capacity configuration and 90TB in a High Performance configuration.

The major improvement in the X4-8 over the X3-8 is the significant increase in CPU and memory horsepower (15-core CPUs and 12TB of DB-Compute memory). Flash Cache remains the same as in the X3-8: 44.8TB. As in the X3-8, the KVM hardware was discontinued in the X4-8.

Table 1.6 presents an overview of the X4-8's specifications as well as notable components from a hardware standpoint.

Table 1.6   Available Exadata X4-8 Series Hardware Configurations

X4-8 Full Rack

2 x massive SMP-like database servers

240 CPU cores and 4TB memory for database processing (120 CPU cores and 2TB memory per database server)

Compute Nodes

Each database server has

- 8 x 15-core Intel Xeon E7-8895 v2 processors (2.80GHz)
- Up to 6TB memory
- Disk controller HBA with 512MB battery-backed write cache
- 7 x 600GB 10,000 RPM SAS disks
- 8 x InfiniBand QDR (40Gb/s) ports
- 8 x 10Gb Ethernet ports based on the Intel 82599 10GbE controller
- 8 x 1Gb Ethernet ports
- 1 x ILOM Ethernet port
- 4 x redundant hot-swappable power supplies

Networking:

- 2 x 36-port QDR (40Gb/s) InfiniBand switches
- Ethernet switch for administrative connectivity

Other hardware:

- 2 x redundant PDUs

14 x Exadata Storage Servers:

168 CPU cores for SQL processing

56 PCI Flash cards with 44.8TB Exadata Smart Flash Cache

168 x 1.2TB 10,000 RPM High Performance disks or 168 x 4TB 7200 RPM High Capacity disks

Uncompressed usable disk data capacity (normal redundancy)

HC disks	HP disks
300TB	90TB

Note

Eighteen X4-8 Full Racks can be interconnected without additional InfiniBand switches. This extensibility is not limited to the X4-8 model only: this interconnected ecosystem can be any combination of the X2, X3, and X4 series.

Exadata X5-2

Announced in January 2015, the X5-2 is the latest model in the descendant versions of the Xn-2 series (at the time of publishing).

Ranging from more and faster CPUs and memory, capacity-on-demand licensing, virtualization support, and a whole lot more with Oracle VM, the X5-2 series comes loaded with a vast array of new features and options.

- Salient new features, options, and enhancements:
  - Support for Oracle VM (OVM)
  - Capacity-on-demand software licensing
  - Elastic Configuration
  - All-Flash—Extreme Storage Server in High Performance configuration
- Exadata 12.1.2.1 major software enhancements (mandatory for X5-2):
  - Exa-specific Automatic Workload Repository (AWR) enhancements
  - Linux 6 support
  - DBCMLI utility for monitoring and management of Compute Nodes
  - Faster direct-to-wire OLTP protocol
  - Dual-format columnar Flash Cache
  - Snapshotting for very rapid clone operations

The main difference between the configurability options of the X5-2 and the earlier versions (X4-2, X3-2, etc.) is the first-time availability of elastic configurability. Traditionally the Exadata X2-n series has come in an Eighth Rack, Quarter Rack, Half Rack, or Full Rack configuration. The X5-2 is also available in these standard configurations. However, with the X5-2 Elastic Configuration, Oracle has given customers the flexibility of choosing their own custom combination of X5-2 compute and storage servers.

With up to 684 CPU cores and 14.6TB of DDR3 memory, the X5-2 Full Rack can have up to 19 DB-Compute servers and up to 18 Storage Cells running the Exadata Storage Cell software (CELLSRV), two InfiniBand switches, dual PDUs, and an Ethernet switch for external and administrative connectivity.

Other than getting faster and more CPU cores and considerably more memory at the Compute Tier, once again the most salient improvement made in the X5-2 is the induction of the 1.6TB Non-Volatile Memory Express (NVMe) Flash Accelerator card. The F160e PCIe NVMe card powers the High Performance configuration, which replaces the disk-based configuration in the earlier generations of High Performance X2-*n* series with an all-Flash layout.

Table 1.7 presents an overview of the X5-2's standard rack specifications (not Elastic Configuration) as well as notable components from a hardware standpoint.

Table 1.7 Available Exadata X5-2 Series Standard Rack Hardware Configurations

X4-2 Eighth Rack	X4-2 Quarter Rack	X4-2 Half Rack	X4-2 Full Rack
2 x database servers	*2 x database servers*	*4 x database servers*	*8 x database servers*
36 CPU cores and up to 1.5TB memory for database processing (18 CPU cores per database server are enabled with up to 768GB memory per database server)	72 CPU cores and up to 1.5TB memory for database processing (36 CPU cores and up to 768GB memory per database server)	144 CPU cores and up to 3TB memory for database processing (36 CPU cores and up to 768GB memory per database server)	288 CPU cores and up to 6TB memory for database processing (36 CPU cores and up to 768GB memory per database server)
Compute Nodes			

Each database server has

- 2 x 18-core Intel Xeon E5-2699 v3 processors (2.3GHz)
- 256GB memory (expandable to 768GB)
- Disk controller HBA with 1GB Supercap-backed write cache
- 4 x 600GB 10,000 RPM disks
- 2 x QDR (40Gb/s) InfiniBand ports
- 4 x 1/10Gb Ethernet ports (copper)
- 2 x 10Gb Ethernet ports (optical)
- 1 x ILOM Ethernet port
- 2 x redundant hot-swappable power supplies

Networking:

- 2 x 36-port QDR (40Gb/s) InfiniBand switches
- Ethernet switch for administrative connectivity

Other hardware:

- 2 x redundant PDUs

Table 1.7 Available Exadata X5-2 Series Standard Rack Hardware Configurations (*Continued*)

X4-2 Eighth Rack	X4-2 Quarter Rack	X4-2 Half Rack	X4-2 Full Rack
3 x Exadata Storage Servers:	*3 x Exadata Storage Servers:*	*7 x Exadata Storage Servers:*	*14 x Exadata Storage Servers:*
48 CPU cores for SQL processing (24 cores enabled)	48 CPU cores for SQL processing	112 CPU cores for SQL processing	224 CPU cores for SQL processing
High Capacity: 6 PCI Flash cards with 9.6TB (raw) Exadata Smart Flash Cache and 18 x 4TB 7200 RPM disks	High Capacity: 12 PCI Flash cards with 19.2TB (raw) Exadata Smart Flash Cache and 36 x 4TB 7200 RPM disks	High Capacity: 28 PCI Flash cards with 44.8TB (raw) Exadata Smart Flash Cache and 84 x 4TB 7200 RPM disks	High Capacity: 56 PCI Flash cards with 89.6TB (raw) Exadata Smart Flash Cache and 168 x 4TB 7200 RPM disks
High Performance: 12 x 1.6TB NVMe Flash cards	High Performance: 24 x 1.6TB NVMe Flash cards	High Performance: 56 x 1.6TB NVMe Flash cards	High Performance: 112 x 1.6TB NVMe Flash cards
Uncompressed usable disk data capacity (normal redundancy)							
HC disks	HP disks	HC disks	HP disks	HC disks	HP disks	HC disks	HP disks
30TB	8TB	63TB	17TB	150TB	40TB	300TB	80TB

Exadata SuperCluster T4-4

The previous sections gave an overview of the Exadata Xn-2/8 series which is based on the Intel x86 microprocessor architecture. Alternatively, the T4-4 SuperCluster general-purpose engineered system was announced in September 2011 at Oracle Open World and was the first of its kind. Based on the T4 SPARC microprocessor architecture, it is an extremely fast and scalable database machine. In addition to virtualization implemented by Oracle VM for SPARC, an extra level of high availability is also provided by OS-level Solaris Clustering technology.

One similarity that the T4-4 has with the Xn-2 series (X2-2, X3-2, and X4-2) is that it is configurable with Half Rack and Full Rack configurations.

A T4-4 SuperCluster 42u Full Rack is composed of two large DB-Compute server machines with 128 CPU cores (8 x eight-core SPARC T4 microprocessors) and 4TB, six Exadata Storage Cells running the Exadata Storage Cell software (CELLSRV), three InfiniBand switches, dual PDUs, and a Cisco 4948 10GB/s Ethernet switch for external and administrative connectivity.

The T4-4 SuperCluster also comes with an HA-enabled ZFS Storage Cluster Shared Storage Subsystem with 20 x 3TB 7200 SATA disks.

On ASM normal redundancy, a T4-4 Full Rack provides 96TB of uncompressed storage capacity in a High Capacity configuration and 48TB in a High Performance configuration.

Table 1.8 presents an overview of the T4-4's specifications as well as notable components from a hardware standpoint.

Note

The T4-4, T5-5, and M6-32 SuperClusters are general-purpose engineered systems that can run and leverage both database-centric Exadata features such as Hybrid Columnar Compression, Smart Scans, Offloading, and so on, as well as application workloads (for example, Exalogic capabilities).

Table 1.8 Available SuperCluster T4-4 Hardware Configurations

T4-4 Half Rack	T4-4 Full Rack
2 x database servers	4 x database servers
Compute Nodes	

Each database server has

- 4 x eight-core SPARC T4 processors (3.0GHz)
- 64 x 16GB memory
- 6 x 600GB 10,000 RPM disks
- 2 x 300GB solid-state disks
- 4 x dual-port InfiniBand QDR
- 4 x dual-port 10Gb Ethernet

Networking:

- 3 x 36-port QDR (40Gb/s) InfiniBand switches (Half/Full Rack)
- Ethernet switch for administrative connectivity

Other hardware:

- 2 x redundant PDUs

3 x Exadata Storage Servers:	*6 x Exadata Storage Servers:*
36 CPU cores for SQL processing	72 CPU cores for SQL processing
4.6TB Exadata Smart Flash Cache	9.3TB Exadata Smart Flash Cache
Each Storage Server:	Each Storage Server:
12 x 600GB 15,000 RPM High Performance SAS disks or 12 x 3TB 7200 RPM High Capacity SAS disks	12 x 600GB 15,000 RPM High Performance SAS disks or 12 x 3TB 7200 RPM High Capacity SAS disks

Uncompressed usable disk data capacity (normal redundancy)			
HC disks	HP disks	HC disks	HP disks
19TB	9.5TB	96TB	48TB

Table 1.8   Available SuperCluster T4-4 Hardware Configurations *(Continued)*

Highly Available ZFS Storage Cluster Shared Storage Subsystem
Oracle ZFS Storage ZS3-ES Dual Controller

Each storage controller has

- 2 x eight-core 2.4GHz Intel Xeon processors
- 6 x 16GB of memory
- 1 x dual-port InfiniBand host channel adapter
- 2 x 500GB SATA disks
- 4 x 512GB write-optimized solid-state disks
- 2 x 1.6TB read-optimized solid-state disks

Disk shelf:

- 20 x 3TB High Capacity 7200 RPM disks
- 4 x 73GB write-optimized solid-state disks

Exadata SuperCluster T5-8

Based on the T5 SPARC microprocessor architecture, an extremely fast and scalable database machine, the T5-8 SuperCluster engineered system was announced in June 2013 and was the descendant version of the T4-4 SuperCluster engineered system. According to Oracle's claims, the T5-8 SuperCluster has more than 17 world-record benchmarks.

Similar to the Xn-2 Exadata series (X2-2, X3-2, and X4-2), the T5-8 is also configurable with Half Rack and Full Rack configurations.

A T5-8 SuperCluster 42u Full Rack is composed of two massive DB-Compute server machines with 256 CPU cores (8 x 16-core SPARC T5 microprocessors) and 4TB, eight Exadata Storage Cells running the Exadata Storage Cell software (CELLSRV), three InfiniBand switches, dual PDUs, and a Cisco 4948 10GB/s Ethernet switch for external and administrative connectivity.

Similar to the X3-8, the T5-8 Storage Cells can be configured with either 12 x 1.2TB 10,000 RPM SAS disks (High Performance configuration) or 12 x 4TB 7200 RPM (High Capacity configuration) SAS disks. The T5-8 SuperCluster also comes with an HA-enabled ZFS Storage Cluster Shared Storage Subsystem with 20 x 4TB 7200 SATA disks.

On ASM normal redundancy, a T5-8 Full Rack provides 160TB of uncompressed storage capacity in a High Capacity configuration and 48TB in a High Performance configuration.

Table 1.9 presents an overview of the T5-8's specifications as well as notable components from a hardware standpoint.

Figure 1.9 shows the frontal view of a Full Rack T5-8 SuperCluster Engineered System.

Table 1.9   Available SuperCluster T5-8 Hardware Configurations

T5-8 Half Rack	T5-8 Full Rack
2 x database servers	
Compute Nodes	*Compute Nodes*
Each database server has	*Each database server has*
• 128 CPU cores and 2TB of memory for database and application processing (64 CPU cores and 1TB of memory per Compute Node) • 4 x 16-core SPARC T5 processors (3.6GHz) • 64 x 16GB of memory • 8 x 900GB 10,000 RPM disks • 4 x dual-port InfiniBand QDR • 4 x dual-port 10GbE	• 256 CPU cores and 4TB of memory for database and application processing (128 CPU cores and 2TB of memory per Compute Node) • 8 x 16-core SPARC T5 processors (3.6GHz) • 128 x 16GB of memory • 8 x 900GB 10,000 RPM disks • 8 x dual-port InfiniBand QDR • 8 x dual-port 10GbE
Networking:	
• 3 x 36-port QDR (40Gb/s) InfiniBand switches (Half/Full Rack) • Ethernet switch for administrative connectivity	
Other hardware:	
• 2 x redundant PDUs	
4 x Exadata Storage Servers:	*8 x Exadata Storage Servers:*
48 CPU cores for SQL processing	96 CPU cores for SQL processing
12.5TB Exadata Smart Flash Cache	25TB Exadata Smart Flash Cache
Each Storage Server:	Each Storage Server:
12 x 1.2TB 10,000 RPM High Performance SAS disks or 12 x 4TB 7200 RPM High Capacity SAS disks	12 x 1.2TB 10,000 RPM High Performance SAS disks or 12 x 4TB 7200 RPM High Capacity SAS disks
Uncompressed usable disk data capacity (normal redundancy)			

HC disks	HP disks	HC disks	HP disks
80TB	24TB	160TB	48TB

Table 1.9 Available SuperCluster T5-8 Hardware Configurations (*Continued*)

Highly Available ZFS Storage Cluster Shared Storage Subsystem

Oracle ZFS Storage ZS3-ES Dual Controller

Each storage controller has

- 2 x eight-core 2.1GHz Intel Xeon E5-2658 processors
- 16 x 16GB of memory
- 1 x dual-port InfiniBand host channel adapter
- 2 x 900GB SATA disks
- 2 x 1.6TB read-optimized solid-state disk

Disk shelf:

- 20 x 4TB High Capacity 7200 RPM disks
- 4 x 73GB write-optimized solid-state disks

Figure 1.9   Exadata T5-8 SuperCluster Engineered System

Exadata SuperCluster M6-32

Based on the latest M6 SPARC microprocessor architecture (at the time of writing), the M6-32 SuperCluster general-purpose engineered system was announced in September 2013 at Oracle Open World and is the most massive and fastest of the SuperCluster engineered system series.

The M6-32 SuperCluster is geared mainly for massive consolidation within the data center (for example, building out private clouds) and supports databases as well as application-centric workloads.

An M6-32 SuperCluster is composed of a single massive DB-Compute server machine with a whopping 384 CPU cores and 32TB, nine power-horse Exadata Storage Cells running the Exadata Storage Cell software (CELLSRV), three InfiniBand switches, dual PDUs, and a Cisco 4948 10GB/s Ethernet switch for external and administrative connectivity.

Similar to the T5-8 SuperCluster (its predecessor), the M6-32 Storage Cells can be configured with either 12 x 1.2TB 10,000 RPM SAS disks (High Performance configuration) or 12 x 4TB 7200 RPM (High Capacity configuration) SAS disks. The M6-32 SuperCluster also comes with an HA-enabled ZFS Storage Cluster Shared Storage Subsystem with 20 x 4TB 7200 SATA disks.

On ASM normal redundancy, an M6-32 provides 180TB of uncompressed storage capacity in a High Capacity configuration and 54TB in a High Performance configuration.

Table 1.10 presents an overview of the M6-32's specifications as well as notable components from a hardware standpoint.

Note

One M6-32 (rack) can be deployed with mainframe-class RAS (Reliability, Availability and Service), or two M6-32 servers (racks) can be deployed together for redundancy purposes

Table 1.10   Available M6-32 SuperCluster Engineered System Hardware Configuration

M6-32 SuperCluster Engineered System Rack	
1 x massive beastly SMP-like SPARC M6-based database server	
Up to 384 CPU cores and 32TB memory for database processing per rack	
Minimum	*Maximum*
16 x 12-core SPARC M6 processors (3.6GHz)	32 x 12-core SPARC M6 processors (3.6GHz)
512 x 16GB, for 8TB total memory	1024 x 32GB, for 32TB total memory
16 x 900GB 10,000 RPM disks	32 x 900GB 10,000 RPM disks
16 x 10GbE ports	32 x 10GbE ports
8 x I/O base cards	16 x I/O base cards
8 x dual-port InfiniBand QDR	16 x dual-port InfiniBand QDR
2 x quad-port 1GbE, UTP	4 x quad-port 1GbE, UTP

Networking:

- 3 x 36-port QDR (40Gb/s) InfiniBand switches
- Ethernet switch for administrative connectivity

Other hardware:

- 2 x redundant PDUs

Table 1.10   Available M6-32 SuperCluster Engineered System Hardware Configuration (*Continued*)

9 x Exadata Storage X4-2 Servers*

Each Storage Server has

- 2 x six-core Intel Xeon E5-2630 v2 for SQL processing
- 4 x 800GB Exadata Smart Flash Cache
- 12 x 1.2TB 10,000 RPM High Performance disks or 12 x 4TB 7200 RPM High Capacity disks

*Up to 17 additional Exadata Storage Expansion Racks can be added

Uncompressed usable disk data capacity (normal redundancy)

HC disks	HP disks
180TB	54TB

Highly Available ZFS Storage Cluster Shared Storage Subsystem

Oracle ZFS Storage ZS3-ES Dual Controller

Each controller has

- 2 x eight-core 2.1GHz Intel Xeon E5-2658 processors
- 16 x 16GB of memory
- 1 x dual-port InfiniBand host channel adapter
- 2 x 900GB SATA disks
- 2 x 1.6TB read-optimized solid-state disk

Disk shelf:

- 20 x 4TB High Capacity 7200 RPM disks
- 4 x 73GB write-optimized solid-state disk

Figure 1.10 shows the frontal view of the massive M6-32 SuperCluster Engineered System.

Exadata Storage Expansion Racks

First announced in July 2011, Oracle also offers Exadata Storage Expansion Racks in order to add more storage capacity to existing Exadata machines. For storage extensibility, these Storage Expansion Racks can be hooked up to any combination of Exadata and SuperCluster engineered systems.

Exadata Storage Expansion Racks have the same componentry that exists in Exadata engineered systems at the Storage Tier: Exadata Storage Cells. Like Exadata engineered systems, these Storage Expansion Racks are available in High Performance (smaller, faster disks) or High Capacity (larger, relatively slower disks) configurations.

Figure 1.10   M6-32 SuperCluster Engineered System

Table 1.11 presents the three configurable options available for the X4-2 Exadata Storage Expansion Rack.

Table 1.11   Available Exadata X4-2 Storage Expansion Rack Hardware Configurations

4 x Exadata Storage Servers:	9 x Exadata Storage Servers:	18 x Exadata Storage Servers:
48 CPU cores for SQL processing	108 CPU cores for SQL processing	216 CPU cores for SQL processing
16 PCI Flash cards with 12.8TB (raw) Exadata Smart Flash Cache	36 PCI Flash cards with 28.8TB (raw) Exadata Smart Flash Cache	72 PCI Flash cards with 57.6TB (raw) Exadata Smart Flash Cache
48 x 1.2TB 10,000 RPM High Performance disks or 48 x 4TB 7200 RPM High Capacity disks	108 x 1.2TB 10,000 RPM High Performance disks or 108 x 4TB 7200 RPM High Capacity disks	216 x 1.2TB 10,000 RPM High Performance disks or 216 x 4TB 7200 RPM High Capacity disks

Networking:

- 3 x 36-port QDR (40Gb/s) InfiniBand switches (Half/Full Rack)
- 2 x 36-port QDR (40Gb/s) InfiniBand switches (Quarter Rack)
- Ethernet switch for administrative connectivity

Other hardware:

- 2 x redundant PDUs

Uncompressed usable disk data capacity (normal redundancy)					
HC disks	*HP disks*	*HC disks*	*HP disks*	*HC disks*	*HP disks*
48TB	25TB	194TB	58TB	387TB	116TB

Note

The Exadata X4-2 Storage Expansion Quarter and Half Racks can be expanded all the way up to a Full Rack. Any combination of 18 Exadata Database Machine, SuperCluster, and Storage Expansion Racks can be interconnected without additional InfiniBand switches.

Exadata Storage Cells

For storage capacity configurability, as can be observed in Tables 1.1 through 1.9, each Exadata machine and Storage Expansion Rack can be configured as a High Capacity or High Performance unit. This is done at the time of purchase.

The High Performance disks are smaller, faster disks. The High Capacity disks are larger and relatively slower than the High Performance disks. Refer to Tables 1.1 through 1.7 for High Capacity and High Performance disk specifications for each series and version.

Hardware Progression

Figures 1.11 through 1.16 depict the version progression and the hardware improvements made in CPU, memory, Flash Cache, and storage among the descendant versions of Xn-2 (X2-2, X3-2, and X4-2).

As is evident from the graphics, the most significant enhancement was made in the area of Flash Cache. These improvements were also augmented by increases in memory, CPU, and storage.

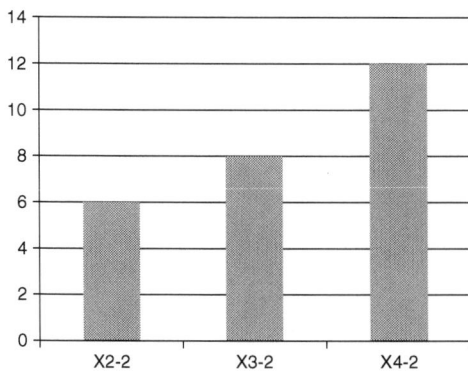

Figure 1.11   Compute power—CPU socket cores progression in Exadata versions (X2-2 to X4-2)

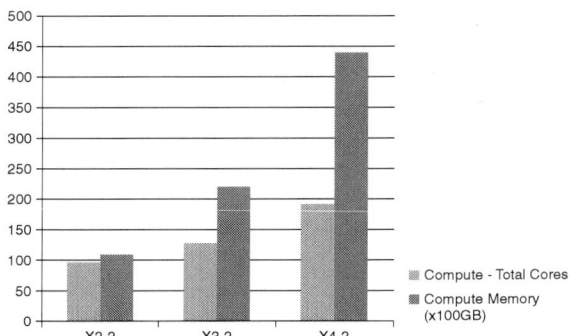

Figure 1.12 Compute power—CPU cores and memory progression in Exadata versions

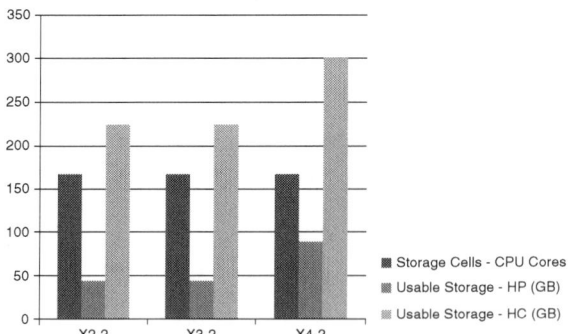

Figure 1.13 Storage—Storage Cells and capacity progression in Exadata versions (X2-2 to X4-2)

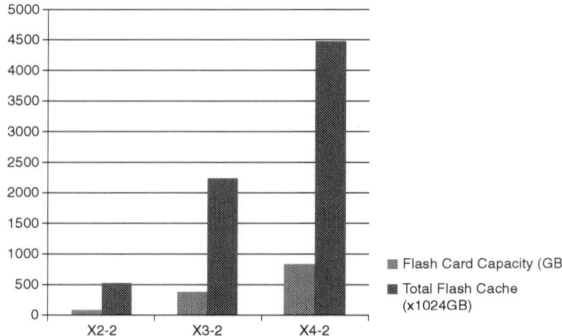

Figure 1.14 Flash Cache—Flash card capacity progression in Exadata versions (X2-2 to X4-2)

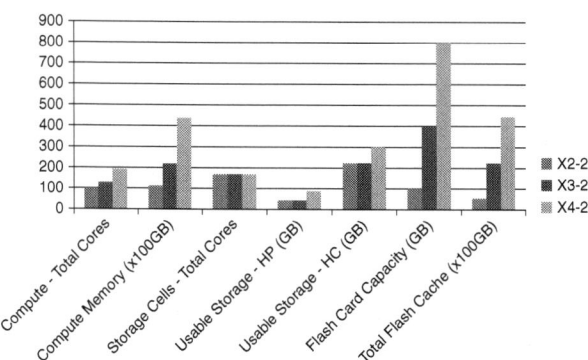

Figure 1.15 Major componentry progression in Exadata versions (X2-2 to X4-2)

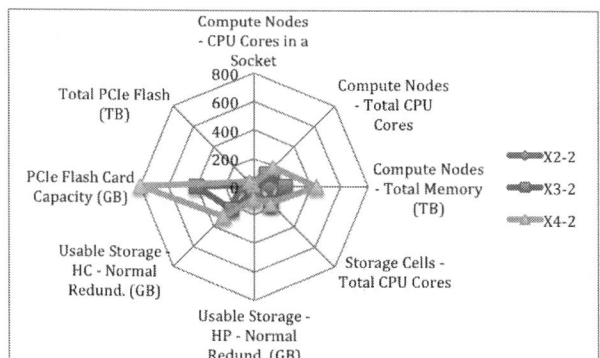

Figure 1.16 Compute power, Flash Cache, and storage capacity progression in Exadata versions (X2-2 to X4-2)

Examining an Exadata Machine

This section lists some basic 101 commands to inspect and view the configurations and settings of an Exadata Database Machine (see Listing 1.1).

Listing 1.1 Basic Commands for Viewing Exadata Configurations and Settings

```
# imageinfo
Kernel version: 2.6.32-400.11.1.el5uek #1 SMP Fri Dec 20 20:31:32 PST 2013 x86_64
Cell version: OSS_11.2.3.2.1_LINUX.X64_130109
Cell rpm version: cell-11.2.3.2.1_LINUX.X64_130109-1
```

```
Active image version: 11.2.3.2.1.130109
Active image activated: 2013-01-13 18:12:13 -0400
Active image status: success
Active system partition on device: /dev/md5
Active software partition on device: /dev/md7

In partition rollback: Impossible

Cell boot usb partition: /dev/sdm1
Cell boot usb version: 11.2.3.2.1.130109

Inactive image version: 11.2.3.2.0.120713
Inactive image activated: 2012-11-30 18:07:15 -0500
Inactive image status: success
Inactive system partition on device: /dev/md6
Inactive software partition on device: /dev/md8

Boot area has rollback archive for the version: 11.2.3.2.0.120713
Rollback to the inactive partitions: Possible

#CellCLI> list physicaldisk detail
        name:                   20:0
        deviceId:               19
        diskType:               HardDisk
        enclosureDeviceId:      20
        errMediaCount:          0
        errOtherCount:          0
        foreignState:           false
        luns:                   0_0
        makeModel:              "HITACHI HUS1560SCSUN600G"
        physicalFirmware:       A700
        physicalInsertTime:     2012-07-25T00:27:07+03:00
        physicalInterface:      sas
        physicalSerial:         K423WL
        physicalSize:           558.9109999993816G
        slotNumber:             0
        status:                 normal

        name:                   20:1
        deviceId:               18
        diskType:               HardDisk
        enclosureDeviceId:      20
        errMediaCount:          0
        errOtherCount:          0
        foreignState:           false
        luns:                   0_1
        makeModel:              "HITACHI HUS1560SCSUN600G"
        physicalFirmware:       A700
        physicalInsertTime:     2012-07-25T00:27:08+03:00
        physicalInterface:      sas
        physicalSerial:         K5325L
        physicalSize:           558.9109999993816G
        slotNumber:             1
        status:                 normalCellCLI> list lun detail


#CellCLI> list griddisk detail
        name:                   DATA_EX01_CD_00_ex01cel01
        asmDiskgroupName:       DATA_EX01
        asmDiskName:            DATA_EX01_CD_00_EX01CEL01
        asmFailGroupName:       EX01CEL01
        availableTo:
        cachingPolicy:          default
        cellDisk:               CD_00_ex01cel01
        comment:
        creationTime:           2012-07-26T02:51:35+03:00
        diskType:               HardDisk
```

```
            errorCount:            0
            id:                    1d4481d8-f6f6-41a4-9354-7382efc87cab
            offset:                32M
            size:                  423G
            status:                active

            name:                  DATA_EX01_CD_01_ex01cel01
            asmDiskgroupName:      DATA_EX01
            asmDiskName:           DATA_EX01_CD_01_EX01CEL01
            asmFailGroupName:      EX01CEL01
            availableTo:
            cachingPolicy:         default
            cellDisk:              CD_01_ex01cel01
            comment:
            creationTime:          2012-07-26T02:51:35+03:00
            diskType:              HardDisk
            errorCount:            0
            id:                    d35a2e5e-cfc7-4d94-aecd-e3bebbf19ff5
            offset:                32M
            size:                  423G
            status:                active

# ibstatus

InfiniBand device 'mlx4_0' port 1 status:
            default gid:     fe80:0000:0000:0000:0021:2800:01ef:6abf
            base lid:        0x5
            sm lid:          0x1
            state:           4: ACTIVE
            phys state:      5: LinkUp
            rate:            40 Gb/sec (4X QDR)

InfiniBand device 'mlx4_0' port 2 status:
            default gid:     fe80:0000:0000:0000:0021:2800:01ef:6ac0
            base lid:        0x6
            sm lid:          0x1
            state:           4: ACTIVE
            phys state:      5: LinkUp
            rate:            40 Gb/sec (4X QDR)

# ibstatus |grep state

            state:           4: ACTIVE
            phys state:      5: LinkUp
            state:           4: ACTIVE
            phys state:      5: LinkUp

# ibhosts

Ca      : 0x0021280001ef6cd2 ports 2 "db02 S 192.168.10.2 HCA-1"
Ca      : 0x0021280001ef684e ports 2 "cel03 C 192.168.10.5 HCA-1"
Ca      : 0x0021280001ef6d36 ports 2 "cel01 C 192.168.10.3 HCA-1"
Ca      : 0x0021280001ef59ea ports 2 "cel02 C 192.168.10.4 HCA-1"
Ca      : 0x0021280001ef6abe ports 2 "db01 S 192.168.10.1 HCA-1"
```

Summary

This chapter gave you a 360-degree overview of Exadata; a synopsis of its historical genesis; the various series, models, and versions available; the major differences among the descendant versions; and a whole lot more to introduce you to Oracle's flagship database machine.

Undoubtedly, Exadata is a game-changer and paradigm shift within the Oracle Database space. Oracle has kept the spirit of innovation alive by integrating best-of-breed next-generation hardware and software. This is reflected by the runaway success of adoption by entities and users, saliently for reasons including but not limited to performance, consolidation, database cloud computing, saving total cost of ownership, and a ready-to-use engineered system on Day 1.

Real Application Clusters (RAC) in Exadata

It is common knowledge that, coupled with next-generation Sun hardware, Exadata is a conglomerate of existing Oracle technologies on the software side of things. Oracle Real Application Clusters (RAC), the parallelized cluster version of the Oracle Database family, plays an integral role in the software picture on Exadata. RAC and Grid Infrastructure (GI: Oracle Clusterware and Automatic Storage Management, or ASM) come preinstalled and preconfigured from the factory with all Exadata machines.

From a technical and contractual standpoint, RAC is not mandatory for Exadata to operate; however, the vast majority of Exadata machines have RAC deployed on them. This is in large part because of the capabilities provided by RAC: high availability, load balancing, and horizontal scalability. For these obvious reasons, it is highly recommended that RAC be an integral part and parcel of the Exadata software stack. Conversely speaking, without RAC, Exadata loses a lot of its high-availability and load-balancing appeal and capability at the Oracle Database server level.

By merit of RAC's features and characteristics, Exadata has become the very backbone of building elastic and self-serviceable Oracle Database Clouds. RAC's significance in Exadata has enabled RAC database administrators to very rapidly transform their previous job roles to Exadata Database Machine administrators (DMAs) by leveraging their existing RAC skills.

This chapter starts out by giving a brief primer on Oracle RAC, followed by its role and relevance within the Exadata family of engineered database machines.

The chapter also focuses on how to optimally configure, leverage, utilize, and troubleshoot RAC within the Exadata realm.

The Significance of RAC in Exadata

Quite simply, without RAC, Exadata does not have high availability and load balancing at the database Compute Tier. In other words, without RAC, Exadata is vulnerable to having a single point of failure (SPOF) at the Oracle Database tier. Without RAC, Exadata loses its ability to eliminate SPOFs at the database Compute Tier. Additionally, horizontal scalability is also limited within Exadata if RAC is not configured; this is the key element that enables Exadata to possess its elastic database cloud characteristics.

A frequently posed question within the industry is: Is RAC on Exadata different from any other RAC implementation on other hardware? From a logical standpoint the answer is no. The RAC architecture is the same on Exadata as it is on non-Exadata. However, multiple enhancements were made for RAC on Exadata, for example, Even Reads, which allowed ASM queries to be spread across multiple failure groups, which were available in 11.2.0.3 on Exadata. These enhancements were later made available for non-Exadata environments in 12.1.0.2. Also, from a hardware standpoint, the RAC experience on Exadata is much faster and smoother by merit of the underlying next-generation hardware, for example, the ultra-high-speed InfiniBand 40GB/s Cluster Interconnect and so on.

By merit of its grid-style architecture coupled with innovative Intelligent Storage Cell software and next-generation hardware throughout the entire Exadata stack, RAC is also one of the key technologies that enable database consolidation within the Exadata Database Machine, along with (Multitenant) Pluggable Databases in 12*c*.

RAC performance on Exadata is greatly enhanced and amplified by Exadata-specific features and next-generation hardware. This performance boost behind RAC on Exadata is supplemented and augmented by Intelligent Storage software at the Storage Cell tier. Exadata Offloading capabilities—for example, Smart Scans, Hybrid Columnar Compression, and so on—most definitely have a positive performance impact on RAC's configuration and capabilities within an Exadata machine. The subsequent chapters of this book explore these performance enhancements at an elaborate level of detail.

Note

The purpose of this chapter is not to present the reader with a deep dive into RAC but rather to give insight to RAC from the perspective of Exadata. RAC configuration best practices and troubleshooting and performance-tuning tips on Exadata are also covered.

An Overview of RAC

RAC was born in Oracle v6 in the form of Oracle Parallel Server (OPS), which was later rebranded as Oracle Real Application Clusters in v9i. Real Application Clusters is the parallelized cluster version of the Oracle Database server family.

In addition to having the ability to scale horizontally without any downtime, RAC gives the Oracle Database server the ability to load-balance Oracle Database workloads among multiple database nodes.

The load-balancing feature of RAC is achieved by fusing the memory areas of the various cluster nodes through a mechanism known as Global Cache Fusion. This mechanism uses various underlying RAC daemons and processes, notably the Lock Management Server (LMS) process, which formulates and constitutes the backbone of Global Cache Fusion.

RAC is well known throughout the Oracle Database industry and is a mature, stable, well-performing, and nth-generation product. Therefore, it was the natural choice for Oracle to adopt RAC as the database clustering product that powers the Exadata series of database machines.

Figure 2.1 depicts a four-node Oracle RAC cluster in an Exadata X4-2 Half Rack Engineered System.

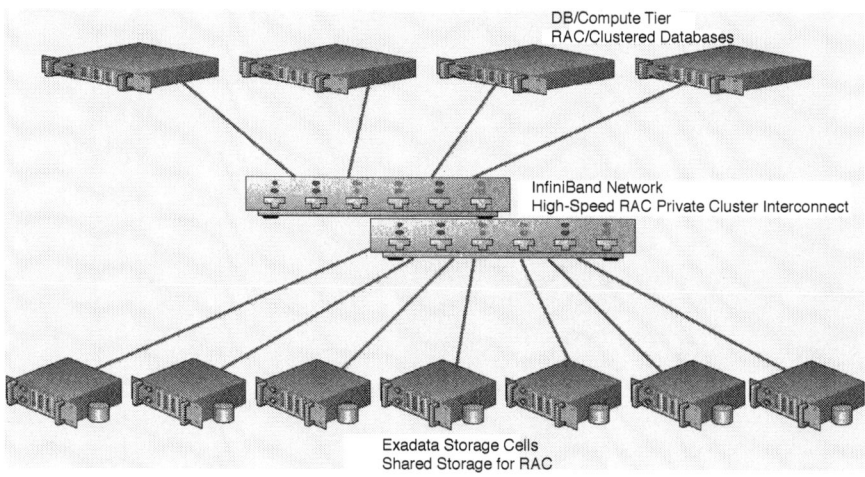

Figure 2.1   Four-node RAC cluster in Exadata X4-2 Half Rack

A Quick Primer on RAC in Exadata

RAC in Exadata from a logical perspective is identical to non-Exadata RAC implementations. However, as alluded to earlier, RAC performance and stability in Exadata are greatly amplified when RAC works in conjunction with Intelligent Storage Cell nodes along with other RAC/ASM enhancements for Exadata. Let's briefly delve into these core subject areas of RAC on Exadata.

Shared storage is a basic requirement for Oracle RAC cluster nodes. It is provided by implementing and utilizing ASM, which works in conjunction with the Storage Cell software within Exadata. Since this storage is intelligent and Oracle data aware, the end result of these complementary technologies is performance-enhanced RAC database clusters within Exadata.

The Private Cluster Interconnect is the networking component that powers Global Cache Fusion, the technology that gives RAC its HA and load-balancing capabilities. The Private Cluster Interconnect is implemented on Exadata by a next-generation low-latency and very high-speed redundant InfiniBand fabric. The choice of InfiniBand as the low-latency Private Cluster Interconnect is one of the major performance drivers on Exadata RAC architectures from a hardware standpoint.

Note

Exadata is a complete and tightly integrated database machine, balanced and tested from the factory by Oracle. RAC is a part of this tightly integrated ecosystem.

Custom RPMs, software, and agents other than OEM at the OS tier within the Compute Nodes are generally not common—their presence has to be verified and validated by Oracle as they may disturb the internal workings of the machine including RAC.

How RAC Affects DBAs

Exadata is a naturally progressive path for Oracle RAC DBAs. Simply put, if you're an experienced RAC DBA moving to Exadata, your learning curve is greatly minimized. This is due to the fact that RAC is *the* database server technology that powers the Compute Tier of Exadata.

It is important to emphasize, though, that undoubtedly there is a learning curve for a RAC DBA when venturing into the Exadata world. Much of this has to do with understanding and embracing the other technologies that make up Exadata in addition to RAC, for example, Storage Cell software, the InfiniBand fabric architecture, and so forth.

Also, it is important for a RAC DBA to learn about the various ways RAC is implemented on Exadata on next-generation InfiniBand hardware and shared storage provided by intelligent Oracle data-cognizant Storage Cells.

The good news, as mentioned previously, is that since RAC formulates the majority of the software componentry behind Exadata, the legacy RAC skills of an Oracle DBA not only come in handy but also provide a great segue to being transformed into the skill set of an Exadata Database Machine administrator (DMA).

Tip

It is recommended that RAC DBAs who are moving to Exadata and transforming their job roles into Exadata DMAs understand and embrace the RAC architecture as it is implemented on Exadata as opposed to legacy non-Exadata hardware.

Setting Up RAC Clusters in Exadata

Figures 2.2 through 2.4 present a few examples of how to partition and carve out RAC clusters in an Exadata environment. Figure 2.2 shows all eight nodes consolidated into a single RAC cluster (Grid Infrastructure) for production. Figure 2.3 shows the partition of the eight DB Compute Nodes into two four-node clusters, one each for online transaction processing (OLTP) and data-warehousing-type workloads or applications respectively. In Figure 2.4 the eight DB Compute Nodes are partitioned into three separate clusters, one each for disaster recovery (DR)/Data Guard, TEST/QA, and development (DEV) environments respectively.

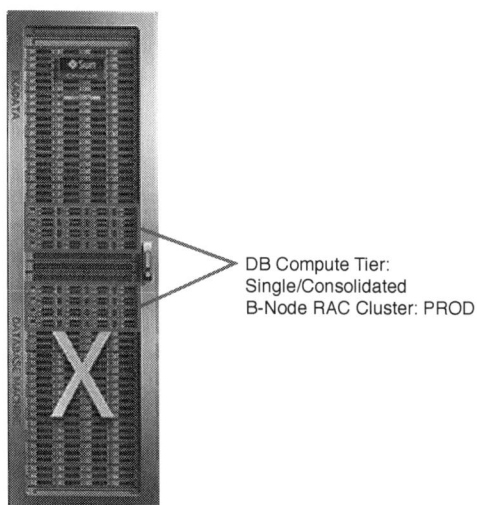

DB Compute Tier:
Single/Consolidated
8-Node RAC Cluster: PROD

Figure 2.2 All nodes consolidated into a single eight-node RAC cluster—
PROD (single Grid Infrastructure)

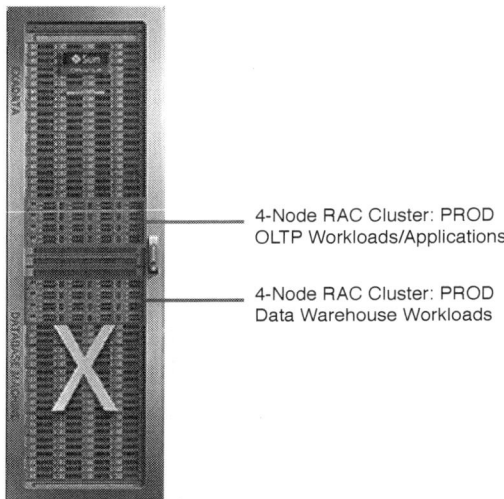

4-Node RAC Cluster: PROD
OLTP Workloads/Applications

4-Node RAC Cluster: PROD
Data Warehouse Workloads

Figure 2.3   Separate four-node RAC clusters for OLTP and data warehouse workloads/
applications—PROD (multiple clusters/Grid Infrastructures)

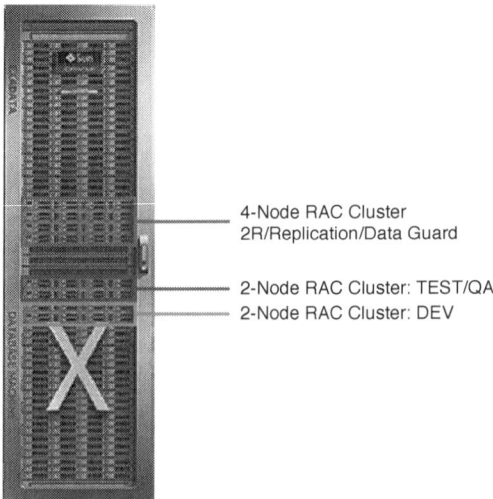

4-Node RAC Cluster
2R/Replication/Data Guard

2-Node RAC Cluster: TEST/QA
2-Node RAC Cluster: DEV

Figure 2.4   Separate four-node RAC clusters for DR/Data Guard/Replication, DEV, and
TEST/QA environments (multiple clusters/Grid Infrastructures)

These example configurations are driven by customer business requirements and related parameters. It is important to mention that these are just examples; actual configurations depend on various parameters such as business, technical, and other requirements.

RAC cluster configurations can be set up either at the time of Exadata's initial deployment or afterward. Cluster nodes can be added or removed in hot mode without any downtime to the end user.

Operational Best Practices

This section outlines some of the salient best practices, tips, and techniques to ensure that your RAC environment within Exadata operates as a well-oiled machine, mitigates problem scenarios, is scalable and sustainable, and gives you the best bang for your buck. These tips are briefly touched upon in this section; some of them are discussed in detail in the subsequent chapters of this book.

Maximum Availability Architecture (MAA)

Implement the Oracle Maximum Availability Architecture (MAA) set of guidelines and best practices to eliminate SPOFs and achieve high availability.

Following are the key components of Oracle MAA from within the Exadata world that have been implemented from the factory with Exadata:

- Oracle RAC—optional
- Oracle ASM
- No SPOF at every component and layer of the Exadata hardware and software stack, for example, redundant power supplies, RAC-clustered DB servers, redundant paths for Network and Storage Tiers, and so on

Following are highly recommended components of Oracle MAA for Exadata that should be implemented to achieve high availability within the Exadata stack:

- Oracle Active Data Guard (ADG) should be implemented—it provides replication of Oracle Databases for Exadata infrastructures while allowing you to open your standby (replicated) databases in read-only mode for reporting, analytics, and so on.
- Set up and configure normal or high redundancy for ASM disk groups (double mirroring or triple mirroring respectively).

- Ether-channeled (bonded) network interfaces should be implemented for outside access of Exadata: public, backup network channels, and so on.

- Set up, configure, and test an effective backup strategy using Oracle Recovery Manager (RMAN). Turn on the Block Change Tracking option to enable faster incremental backups.

- Set up and configure DB block-checking parameters (DB_BLOCK_CHECKING, DB_BLOCK_CHECKSUM, DB_LOST_WRITE_PROTECT) to protect against data block corruption.

- For all production databases within Exadata, turn on ARCHIVELOG and FORCE LOGGING modes to make recovery operations stable and effective.

- Oracle FLASHBACK options are recommended to protect Oracle data against logical corruptions. These options also provide the ability to rewind the RAC databases very easily to a specific point in time.

- Set a minimum or required level of UNDO_RETENTION to protect undo operations as well as flashback operations.

- Set up and configure the applications connecting to RAC/Exadata to seamlessly fail over to the surviving nodes of the cluster as well as the Data Guard standby database in case of failure.

Optimal and Efficient Databases in RAC

The following options, tips, and techniques provide great aid in ensuring efficient and optimal consolidation of Oracle Databases in RAC/Exadata. Categorizing and consolidating Oracle Databases and schemas into similar groups is a common theme in achieving this goal.

Current Versions

Stay current with the latest releases and versions of the Exadata software stack. Potential bugs pose an existential threat to security and stability of the Exadata/RAC system and are routinely fixed in current patches, releases, and versions.

Oracle Support Note ID 888828.1 contains a comprehensive list of the releases and patches of Exadata at all layers: Database, Storage, Network, and so on.

ORAchk and Exachk

Run Exachk (the recommended health-check tool from Oracle) on a periodic basis to check the health of your overall Exadata ecosystem. Exachk can be downloaded from Oracle Support Note ID 1070954.1. ORAchk (Support Note ID 1268927.2), the new health-check tool for the Oracle stack, contains the capabilities of Exachk and should be periodically run to proactively and reactively diagnose issues with the system as a whole. ORAchk is discussed later in this chapter.

Effective Resource Management

Configuring and leveraging resource management options within Oracle at the Database/Compute and Storage Tiers to efficiently manage the various resources within Exadata is crucial to having a balanced and well-tuned system. The two main technologies in this realm to set up are Oracle Database Resource Manager (DBRM) and I/O Resource Manager (IORM).

Resource management technologies put caps on system resources on groups of DB users as well as efficiently manage system resources. Using resource management technologies prevents Oracle programs, queries, and users from running away with your system resources, which can lead to system-wide failures.

CPU and Memory Management

Having adequate amounts of CPU and memory, along with implementing resource limits on them, is a sound and time-tested strategy in setting up RAC-clustered databases on Exadata. This ensures that application workloads run in a stable manner while preventing fatal problems like node evictions and split-brain scenarios in RAC.

Instance Caging (CPU) is a mechanism that is implemented by the CPU_COUNT parameter. It limits the amount of CPU available to an Oracle RAC database. On the other hand, incorrect or insufficient allocation of CPU_COUNT and Instance Caging can lead to RESMGR:CPU quantum wait events. These wait events should be minimized in order to ensure adequate amounts of CPU horsepower to the Oracle RAC database instances.

Automatic Memory Management (AMM) should be set up and configured in a manner that ensures adequate levels of memory for the RAC database instances while putting resource limits on the amount of memory consumption in a Multitenant RAC environment.

HugePages are not compatible with AMM in Linux. This must be taken into account when using AMM. Automatic Shared Memory Management (ASMM) should be used instead. The following Oracle Support Notes cover this subject in greater detail:

- "HugePages and Oracle Database 11g Automatic Memory Management (AMM) on Linux" (ID 749851.1)
- "ASMM versus AMM and LINUX x86-64 HugePages Support" (ID 1134002.1)

Antivirus Software

Antivirus software should not be operational on RAC/Exadata nodes. It can have a fatal impact on the internal workings of Oracle RAC processes, eventually resulting in node evictions.

Third-Party Monitoring Tools and Utilities

Third-party monitoring tools and utilities should be avoided as they have the potential and tendency to interfere with the internal workings of RAC/Exadata. Oracle does not allow these at the cell Storage Tier.

Optimal Tuning of RAC Parameters

Care must be taken when configuring the RAC `init.ora` parameters within Exadata. For example, overallocation of the `LMS_PROCESSES` parameter can lead to excessive CPU consumption, leading to fatal consequences from a cluster stability standpoint. Refer to Oracle Support Note ID 1392248.1, "Auto-Adjustment of LMS Process Priority in Oracle RAC with v11.2.0.3 and Later."

Partitioning and Parallelization

Following the divide-and-conquer approach for achieving maximized performance in RAC/Exadata cluster environments, the golden themes of partitioning and parallelization go hand-in-hand.

Setting up Automatic Degree of Parallelism (`PARALLEL_DEGREE_POLICY= AUTO`) is an excellent approach to enabling parallelism with minimal required effort while enabling automatic parallelism (multithreading) for statement processing in Oracle.

This is a powerful new feature with v11.2 onward. However, care must be exercised in the correct and optimal setup and configuration of the `PARALLEL_` parameters to ensure that they do not have a negative effect on the overall performance of the system. For example, setting `PARALLEL_MAX_SERVERS` to a very high value can potentially starve system memory, resulting in nodes being unresponsive and eventually being evicted from the cluster. This is used in conjunction with the Resource Manager so that sessions don't overconsume the Parallel Slaves.

Partitioning of large DB objects is absolutely crucial to achieving the necessary required performance in RAC/Exadata environments. Partitioning and parallelism often complement each other by reducing overall CPU and memory consumption, achieving optimal performance, and ensuring system stability.

Managing RAC with OEM 12*c*

OEM 12*c* is the end-to-end management, monitoring, administration, and support tool of choice for Exadata environments. With intuitive, easy-to-use functionality, OEM 12*c* is also the best platform for monitoring and managing Oracle RAC in Exadata.

From cluster cache coherency, monitoring RAC clusters, performance tuning, to performing complex administration tasks, OEM has the required capability to efficiently and effectively manage Exadata environments including the RAC componentry.

Chapter 9 is dedicated to Exadata management in OEM 12*c*. A list of the commonly used monitoring, troubleshooting, and performance-tuning pages, tools, and utilities for RAC within OEM 12*c* are presented further in this chapter.

Figure 2.5 illustrates the overall architecture and relationship between OEM and Exadata's various components, including RAC.

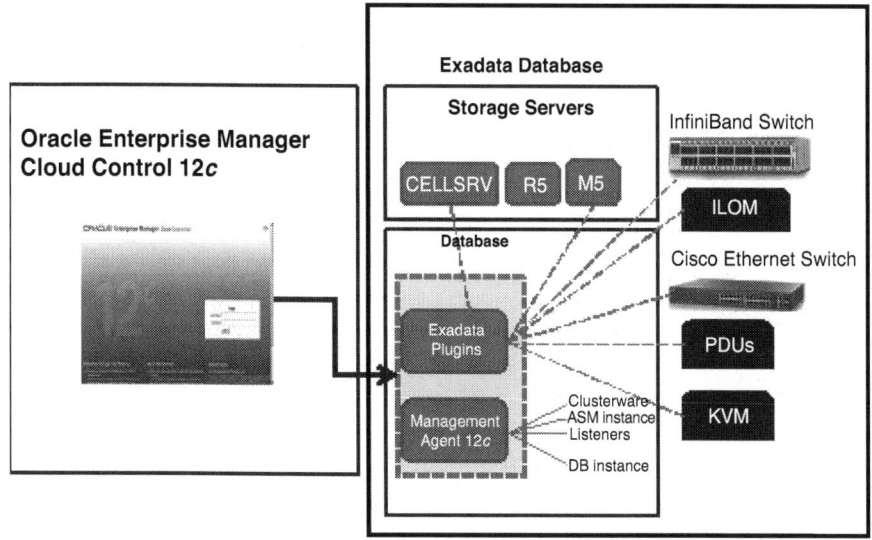

Figure 2.5 Managing Exadata in Oracle Enterprise Manager 12*c*

Common Utilities and Commands

This section surveys some of the common everyday utilities and commands used to inspect, view, and administer RAC and its underlying components in an Exadata Database Machine. These are the exact same commands one would use in a non-Exadata environment.

These commands are broken down into three main categories, each related to its corresponding command-line tool or utility:

- **Oracle Clusterware Control (CRSCTL) utility**—CRSCTL gives you the ability to perform administrative tasks on Oracle RAC Clusterware and its underlying componentry, for example, start, stop, check, enable, disable, health-check, and so on. CRSCTL commands can be run from any node in the cluster. Its use should be restricted to critical Oracle RAC Clusterware operations only; most of the resource management can be performed using SRVCTL.

- **Server Control (SRVCTL) utility**—SRVCTL is used to manage the resources and entities managed by Oracle Clusterware, for example, start, stop, add, remove, enable, and disable the services, databases, and instances, SCAN listeners, NodeApps, ASM, and so on.

- **Miscellaneous**—This includes other command-line utilities and tools to query, inspect, and manage RAC, Clusterware, and so on.

The crsctl query commands in Listing 2.1 show the information related to the Clusterware installed on Exadata.

Listing 2.1 The crsctl query Commands

```
$ crsctl query crs activeversion
Oracle Clusterware active version on the cluster is [11.2.0.4.0]

$ crsctl query crs releaseversion
Oracle High Availability Services release version on the local node is [11.2.0.4.0]

$ crsctl query crs softwareversion
Oracle Clusterware version on node [oe01db01] is [11.2.0.4.0]

$ crsctl query crs softwareversion -all
Oracle Clusterware version on node [oe01db01] is [11.2.0.4.0]
Oracle Clusterware version on node [oe01db02] is [11.2.0.4.0]
Oracle Clusterware version on node [oe01db03] is [11.2.0.4.0]
Oracle Clusterware version on node [oe01db04] is [11.2.0.4.0]
Oracle Clusterware version on node [oe01db05] is [11.2.0.4.0]
Oracle Clusterware version on node [oe01db06] is [11.2.0.4.0]
Oracle Clusterware version on node [oe01db07] is [11.2.0.4.0]
Oracle Clusterware version on node [oe01db08] is [11.2.0.4.0]
```

```
$ crsctl query css votedisk
##  STATE    File Universal Id                      File Name Disk group
--  -----    -----------------                      --------- ---------
 1. ONLINE   7cb8478916a84f10bf7dbb336ca68601 (o/192.168.10.5/DBFS_DG_CD_02_oe01cel01)
[DBFS_DG]
 2. ONLINE   8eb8c6e255534f84bfb1da0194b845bb (o/192.168.10.6/DBFS_DG_CD_02_oe01cel02)
[DBFS_DG]
 3. ONLINE   7f378e868c094fb0bfc38af465fc64f4 (o/192.168.10.7/DBFS_DG_CD_02_oe01cel03)
[DBFS_DG]
Located 3 voting disk(s).

$ crsctl query crs administrator
CRS Administrator List: *
```

The `crsctl` `check` commands in Listing 2.2 check the status of the Clusterware componentry installed on Exadata.

Listing 2.2 The `crsctl` `check` Commands

```
$ crsctl check has
CRS-4638: Oracle High Availability Services is online

$ crsctl check crs
CRS-4638: Oracle High Availability Services is online
CRS-4537: Cluster Ready Services is online
CRS-4529: Cluster Synchronization Services is online
CRS-4533: Event Manager is online
```

The `crsctl` `status` and `crsctl` `get` commands in Listing 2.3 show the status information related to the Clusterware componentry installed on Exadata.

Listing 2.3 The `crsctl` `status` and `crsctl` `get` Commands

```
$ crsctl status serverpool -p
NAME=Free
IMPORTANCE=0
MIN_SIZE=0
MAX_SIZE=-1
SERVER_NAMES=
PARENT_POOLS=
EXCLUSIVE_POOLS=
ACL=owner:oracle:rwx,pgrp:oinstall:rwx,other::r-x

NAME=Generic
IMPORTANCE=0
MIN_SIZE=0
MAX_SIZE=-1
SERVER_NAMES=oe01db01 oe01db02
PARENT_POOLS=
EXCLUSIVE_POOLS=
ACL=owner:oracle:r-x,pgrp:oinstall:r-x,other::r-x

NAME=ora.dbm
IMPORTANCE=1
MIN_SIZE=0
MAX_SIZE=-1
```

```
SERVER_NAMES=oe01db01 oe01db02
PARENT_POOLS=Generic
EXCLUSIVE_POOLS=
ACL=owner:oracle:rwx,pgrp:oinstall:rwx,other::r--

NAME=ora.sri
IMPORTANCE=1
MIN_SIZE=0
MAX_SIZE=-1
SERVER_NAMES=oe01db01 oe01db02
PARENT_POOLS=Generic
EXCLUSIVE_POOLS=
ACL=owner:oracle:rwx,pgrp:oinstall:rwx,other::r--

$ crsctl status serverpool ora.dbm -p
NAME=ora.dbm
IMPORTANCE=1
MIN_SIZE=0
MAX_SIZE=-1
SERVER_NAMES=oe01db01 oe01db02
PARENT_POOLS=Generic
EXCLUSIVE_POOLS=
ACL=owner:oracle:rwx,pgrp:oinstall:rwx,other::r--

$ crsctl get cluster mode status
Cluster is running in "standard" mode

$ crsctl get node role config
Node 'exa1db01' configured role is 'hub'
```

The srvctl config commands in Listing 2.4 show the configuration information related to the resources that Clusterware manages on Exadata.

Listing 2.4 The srvctl config Commands

```
$ srvctl config database -d dbm
Database unique name: dbm
Database name: dbm
Oracle home: /u01/app/oracle/product/11.2.0.4/dbhome_1
Oracle user: oracle
Spfile: +DATA_OE01/dbm/spfiledbm.ora
Domain: at-rockside.lab
Start options: open
Stop options: immediate
Database role: PRIMARY
Management policy: AUTOMATIC
Server pools: dbm
Database instances: dbm1,dbm2
Disk Groups: DATA_OE01,RECO_OE01
Mount point paths:
Services:
Type: RAC
Database is administrator managed

$ srvctl config nodeapps -n oe01db01
-n <node_name> option has been deprecated.
Network exists: 1/174.17.40.0/255.255.255.0/bondeth0, type static
VIP exists: /oe0101-vip/174.17.40.4/174.17.40.0/
255.255.255.0/bondeth0, hosting node oe01db01
GSD exists
ONS exists: Local port 6100, remote port 6200, EM port 2016
```

```
$ srvctl config listener -l LISTENER -a
Name: LISTENER
Network: 1, Owner: oracle
Home: <CRS home>
   /u01/app/11.2.0.4/grid on node(s) oe01db02,oe01db01
End points: TCP:1521
```

The srvctl status commands in Listing 2.5 show the status information related to the resources that Clusterware manages on Exadata.

Listing 2.5 The srvctl status Commands

```
$ srvctl status server -n oe01db01,oe01db02,oe01db03,oe01db04
Server name: oe01db01
Server state: ONLINE
Server name: oe01db02
Server state: ONLINE
Server name: oe01db03
Server state: ONLINE
Server name: oe01db04
Server state: ONLINE


$ srvctl status database -d dbm
Instance dbm1 is running on node oe01db01
Instance dbm2 is running on node oe01db02

$ srvctl status instance -d dbm -i dbm1
Instance dbm1 is running on node oe01db01


$ srvctl status nodeapps
VIP oe01db01-vip is enabled
VIP oe01db01-vip is running on node: oe01db01
VIP oe01db02-vip is enabled
VIP oe01db02-vip is running on node: oe01db02
VIP oe01db03-vip is enabled
VIP oe01db03-vip is running on node: oe01db03
VIP oe01db04-vip is enabled
VIP oe01db04-vip is running on node: oe01db04
VIP oe01db05-vip is enabled
Network is enabled
Network is running on node: oe01db01
Network is running on node: oe01db02
Network is running on node: oe01db03
Network is running on node: oe01db04
GSD is disabled
GSD is not running on node: oe01db01
GSD is not running on node: oe01db02
GSD is not running on node: oe01db03
GSD is not running on node: oe01db04
ONS is enabled
ONS daemon is running on node: oe01db01
ONS daemon is running on node: oe01db02
ONS daemon is running on node: oe01db03
ONS daemon is running on node: oe01db04

$ srvctl status nodeapps -n oe01db01
VIP oe0101-vip is enabled
VIP oe0101-vip is running on node: oe01db01
Network is enabled
Network is running on node: oe01db01
```

```
GSD is disabled
GSD is not running on node: oe01db01
ONS is enabled
ONS daemon is running on node: oe01db01

$ srvctl status asm
ASM is running on oe01db01, oe01db02, oe01db03, oe01db04

$ srvctl status diskgroup -g DATA1
Disk Group DATA1 is running on oe01db01, oe01db02, oe01db03,oe01db04

$ srvctl status listener
Listener LISTENER is enabled
Listener LISTENER is running on node(s): oe01db01, oe01db02, oe01db03,oe01db04

$ srvctl status listener -n oe01db01
Listener LISTENER is enabled on node(s): oe01db01
Listener LISTENER is running on node(s): oe01db01

$ srvctl status scan
SCAN VIP scan1 is enabled
SCAN VIP scan1 is running on node oe01db02
SCAN VIP scan2 is enabled
SCAN VIP scan2 is running on node oe01db01
SCAN VIP scan3 is enabled
SCAN VIP scan3 is running on node oe01db03

$ srvctl status scan -i 1
SCAN VIP scan1 is enabled
SCAN VIP scan1 is running on node oe01db02

$ srvctl status scan_listener
SCAN Listener LISTENER_SCAN1 is enabled
SCAN listener LISTENER_SCAN1 is running on node oe01db02
SCAN Listener LISTENER_SCAN2 is enabled
SCAN listener LISTENER_SCAN2 is running on node oe01db01
SCAN Listener LISTENER_SCAN3 is enabled
SCAN listener LISTENER_SCAN3 is running on node oe01db03

$ srvctl status scan_listener -i 1
SCAN Listener LISTENER_SCAN1 is enabled
SCAN listener LISTENER_SCAN1 is running on node oe01db02

$ srvctl status vip -n oe01db01
VIP oe0101-vip is enabled
VIP oe0101-vip is running on node: oe01db01

$ srvctl status vip -i oe0101-vip-vip
PRKO-2167 : VIP oe0101-vip-vip does not exist.
```

The commands in Listing 2.6 show miscellaneous information related to RAC componentry installed on Exadata.

Listing 2.6   Miscellaneous RAC Componentry Information

```
$ ocrconfig -showbackup

oe01db01    2014/09/08 14:41:23
/u01/app/11.2.0.3/grid/cdata/oe01-cluster/backup00.ocr

oe01db01    2014/09/08 10:41:23
/u01/app/11.2.0.3/grid/cdata/oe01-cluster/backup01.ocr
```

```
oe01db01     2014/09/08 06:41:23
/u01/app/11.2.0.3/grid/cdata/oe01-cluster/backup02.ocr

oe01db01     2014/09/07 02:41:21
/u01/app/11.2.0.3/grid/cdata/oe01-cluster/day.ocr

oe01db01     2014/08/28 14:41:06
/u01/app/11.2.0.4/grid/cdata/oe01-cluster/week.ocr

oe01db01     2013/02/26 17:20:00
/u01/app/11.2.0.4/grid/cdata/oe01-cluster/backup_20130226_172000.ocr

$ olsnodes -s
oe01db01 Active
oe01db02 Active

$ olsnodes -n
oe01db01 1
oe01db02 2

$ ocrcheck
Status of Oracle Cluster Registry is as follows :
 Version                   :       3
 Total space (kbytes)      :   262120
 Used space (kbytes)       :     3036
 Available space (kbytes)  :   259084
 ID                        : 1278623030
 Device/File Name          :   +DBFS_DG
                Device/File integrity check succeeded
Device/File not configured
                Device/File not configured
                Device/File not configured
                Device/File not configured
 Cluster registry integrity check succeeded
ocrcheck     Logical corruption check succeeded

$ ocrcheck -local
Status of Oracle Local Registry is as follows :
 Version                   :       3
 Total space (kbytes)      :   262120
 Used space (kbytes)       :     2684
 Available space (kbytes)  :   259436
 ID                        :  957270436
 Device/File Name          : /u01/app/11.2.0.4/grid/cdata/oe01db01.olr

 Device/File integrity check succeeded
 Local registry integrity check succeeded
 Logical corruption check succeeded
```

Troubleshooting and Tuning RAC

This section gives high-level useful tips and pointers on how to troubleshoot and performance-tune RAC in Exadata. Refer to the earlier "Operational Best Practices" section for architecting a well-oiled Exadata machine.

Start with ORAchk

ORAchk is the new comprehensive health-check tool for the RAC/Exadata stack and can be used for scanning the prevalent issues within RAC/Exadata. Prior to

ORAchk, Exachk was the recommended health-check tool for Exadata—it can be downloaded from Oracle Support Note ID 1070954.1. Exachk can be a great starting point in giving overall directions and pointers toward potential problems, issues, and pain points. With its advent, ORAchk is the latest tool incorporating the functionality of Exachk and RACcheck tools. ORAchk can be downloaded from Oracle Support Note ID 1268927.2, "ORAchk—Health Checks for the Oracle Stack."

Employ the TFA Collector Utility

Released with v11.2.0.4, the Trace File Analyzer (TFA) Collector utility is the new all-encompassing utility that simplifies collection of RAC diagnostic information. TFA greatly simplifies diagnostic data collection, upload, and troubleshooting analysis by Oracle Support. TFA can be downloaded from Oracle Support Note ID 1513912.1, "TFA Collector—Tool for Enhanced Diagnostic Gathering."

Use the Automatic Diagnostic Repository

The Automatic Diagnostic Repository (ADR) is a comprehensive and consolidated platform for storing diagnostic data in a file-based repository. The Automatic Diagnostic Repository Command Interpreter (ADRCI) command-line utility can be used to inspect and view diagnostic information across all RAC/Exadata instances, including incident-related data, alert and trace files and dumps, and so on. ADRCI can also be used to package and compress all related diagnostic data into .zip files for transmission to Oracle Support for further analysis. However, ADR is subsumed by TFA as it collects ADR data as well; if one uses TFA, it already collects ADR data.

Check the Alert and Trace Log Files

Each RAC database instance has its own alert log file. This file is located in the directory specified by the DIAGNOSTIC_DEST init.ora parameter. It can point to further trace files that are linked to specific problems and incidents. Parsing these alert and trace log files is absolutely critical to identifying and troubleshooting problems with RAC/Exadata. If TFA is used to collect and analyze diagnostic data, the RAC DB alert and trace data is already collected within it.

Employ the Three As

Employ the Three As of performance tuning and troubleshooting for performance-related and other general issues:

- **Automatic Workload Repository (AWR) report**—enables you to conduct forensics on the Oracle DB server family
- **Automatic Database Diagnostic Monitor (ADDM) report**—crunches the data in the AWR report and spits out findings and recommendations in human-readable form
- **Active Session History (ASH) report**—enables you to perform tracing and forensics on individual DB sessions

Check the Private Cluster Interconnect

The Private Cluster Interconnect is the central network backbone across which all internode Cache Fusion occurs. Although rare in Exadata (because of the ultrafast InfiniBand network fabric), the Private Cluster Interconnect can be inspected for potential issues. This is a vast subject, some of which is covered in the later chapters of this book.

Enable Tracing and Inspect the Trace Logs

Tracing can be enabled on RAC utilities that are Java based, for example, Database Configuration Assistant (DBCA), Database Upgrade Assistant (DBUA), Cluster Verification Utility, Server Control (SRVCTL) Utility, and so on. These logs can be found in their respective directories (for example, $ORACLE_HOME/cfgtoollogs/dbca) and should be inspected when you are troubleshooting problems and issues.

Cluster Health Monitor

Cluster Health Monitor (CHM) is a very useful tool for troubleshooting problematic scenarios in RAC/Exadata. CHM metrics, which are housed in the Grid Infrastructure Management Repository, can be analyzed for troubleshooting on a RAC cluster. CHM data can be garnered by running the diagcollection.pl script, which is present in the $GRIDHOME/bin directory. However, diagcollection.pl is obsolete in favor of TFA.

Employ Oracle Enterprise Manager 12c

OEM 12c is the standard framework of choice for troubleshooting and performance-tuning RAC/Exadata. The following tools, utilities, reports, and pages can prove to be really helpful in identifying, tracking, and fixing problem scenarios for RAC/Exadata in OEM 12c:

- Performance Home page
- Cluster cache coherency
- Real-time ADDM report
- AWR, ADDM, and ASH reports
- Top activity
- SQL monitoring
- Compare period ADDM
- Compare period (AWR) reports
- Blocking sessions
- SQL tuning, access, and performance advisers
- Emergency monitoring

Miscellaneous Tools and Utilities

In addition to those resources, the following are some useful tools and utilities that can be employed for diagnosing and troubleshooting RAC issues:

- RAC Configuration Audit Tool (RACcheck) (Oracle Support Note ID 1268927.1)
- ProcWatcher—script to monitor and examine Oracle DB and Clusterware processes (Oracle Support Note ID 459694.1)
- OSWatcher Black Box (OSWBB) (Oracle Support Note ID 1531223.1)
- ORATOP—utility for near-real-time monitoring of databases, RAC, and single instances (Oracle Support Note ID 1500864.1)

Useful Oracle Support Resources

The following are some very useful Oracle Support resources for troubleshooting RAC in general as well as in Exadata environments:

- "RAC and Oracle Clusterware Best Practices and Starter Kit (Platform Independent)" (Oracle Support Note ID 810394.1)
- "11gR2 Clusterware and Grid Home—What You Need to Know" (Oracle Support Note ID 1053147.1)

- "Oracle Database (RDBMS) on Unix AIX, HP-UX, Linux, Mac OS X, Solaris, Tru64 Unix Operating Systems Installation and Configuration Requirements Quick Reference (8.0.5 to 11.2)" (Oracle Support Note ID 169706.1)
- "Top 11gR2 Grid Infrastructure Upgrade Issues" (Oracle Support Note ID 1366558.1)
- "Exadata Database Machine and Exadata Storage Server Supported Versions" (Oracle Support Note ID 888828.1)

Summary

The deployment and usage of RAC is not mandatory in Exadata. However, Exadata's full potential and capabilities are not realized without incorporating RAC into the overall Exadata ecosystem. In fact, RAC is *the* software component that provides load balancing at the database tier in addition to providing and enabling database high availability in Exadata by eliminating a single point of failure at the DB Compute Tier.

This chapter gave you insight into RAC in Exadata, starting with a synopsis, followed by a quick primer about RAC, and then a description of its role and relevance in Exadata. Best practices for configuration, setup, and efficient operations along with common everyday commands and troubleshooting and performance-tuning tips were also offered to give a comprehensive overview of RAC in Exadata.

3

The Secret Sauce: Exadata Storage Cells

The core focus of this chapter is to examine the **Exadata Storage Server**, popularly known as **Exadata Cell**, in more detail. Storage Cells are arguably the "secret sauce" or critical element that makes Exadata scale and perform so well. While the previous chapters explained the features and advantages of Exadata in 360-degree view, in this chapter we'll complete the picture by focusing on the highly specialized storage.

DBAs have almost universally acknowledged that historically the Achilles' heel for database performance was disk I/O. The faster the database and/or the more spindles handling database requests, the better the performance. Of course, newer storage technologies such as Flash disk or SSD (solid-state disk) don't fit very nicely into that generalization; however, they are still new enough and remain relatively expensive such that the bulk of storage remains on magnetic disk. Hence I/O performance remains an issue that Exadata storage or cell server attempts to address. This chapter focuses more on the abstract concepts of *what* the cell storages are and *how* they operate in the setup.

An Overview of Exadata Storage Server

An Exadata Database Machine is typically shipped with three preconfigured hardware components: Compute (database) Nodes, cell storage, and ultrafast InfiniBand storage network. The Exadata Storage Server is not simply another storage server.

It is capable of delivering unique features and provides more functionality than any third-party traditional storage server. It plays a significant role in the Exadata Database Machine by provisioning storage capacity and the very unique Exadata features.

Exadata Storage Server is not just another typical storage area network (SAN) storage device or black box that facilitates and fulfills the storage requirements. It has the intelligent Exadata Storage Software that provides the capabilities of Cell Offload processing (Smart Scan), Storage Indexes, Hybrid Columnar Compression (HCC or EHCC), I/O Resource Management (IORM), Smart Flash Cache, fast file creation, and so on. The Exadata software features are covered in detail in other chapters.

In general, each Exadata machine comes in various configurations. The number of database and cell servers purely depends on the Exadata rack capacity you choose. It comes in Eighth, Quarter, Half, and Full Racks. Depending on your choice of configuration, the cell server range can be three, seven, or 14. You have the flexibility to choose the size that best suits your needs, and you can scale up as the demand rises in the future. Figure 3.1 represents the cell server count and capacity of different Exadata racks:

- A Quarter Rack comes with two Compute (DB) Nodes and three storage servers.
- A Half Rack comes with four Compute (DB) Nodes and seven storage servers.
- A Full Rack comes with eight Compute (DB) Nodes and 14 storage servers.

Figure 3.1   The storage server count is based on rack size.

For instance, an Exadata X4 Storage Server has the following software and hardware capacity:

- A mandatory preconfigured Oracle Enterprise Linux (OEL) operating system
- Three default system user configurations: root, celladmin, and cellmonitor
- Intelligent Exadata Storage Server Software
- Two six-core Intel Xeon E5-2630 v2 processors (2.6GHz)
- 12 x 1.2TB SAS disks with High Performance (HP) and 10,000 RPM or 12 x 4TB disks with High Capacity (HC) and 7200 RPM
- 4 x 800GB Sun Flash Accelerator 480 PCI cards
- Dual-port, 2 x InfiniBand, and 4 x QDR (40GB) active-active connectivity
- 96GB memory per server
- 3.2TB Exadata Smart Flash Cache
- CELLSRV, Restart Server (RS), and Management Server (MS) background services

Each Exadata Storage Server is managed and treated individually. The Cell Control Command-Line Interface (CellCLI) utility is used to administrate the local cell, and the Distributed Command-Line Interface (dcli) utility is used to administrate the remote Exadata cell operations. The CellCLI is used to perform most of the administration and management tasks on a local cell server. The dcli utility (noninteractive) has the capability to centralize cell management across all cell servers on an Exadata machine.

Storage Server Architecture

In addition to any traditional storage server components like CPU, memory, network interface controllers (NICs), storage disks, and so on, an Exadata Storage Cell comes preloaded with the OEL operating system and intelligent Exadata Storage Server Software.

Figure 3.2 depicts the typical Quarter Rack Exadata Storage Cell architecture details, two Compute Nodes and three Storage Cells, and how the communication and relation between a Compute Node and Storage Cells are established.

An ASM instance running on the Compute (database) Node communicates with a storage server through an InfiniBand network connection using the special Intelligent Database (iDB) protocol. Additionally, the iDB protocol provides aggregation and failover to the interconnect network bandwidth. An Eighth or Quarter Rack

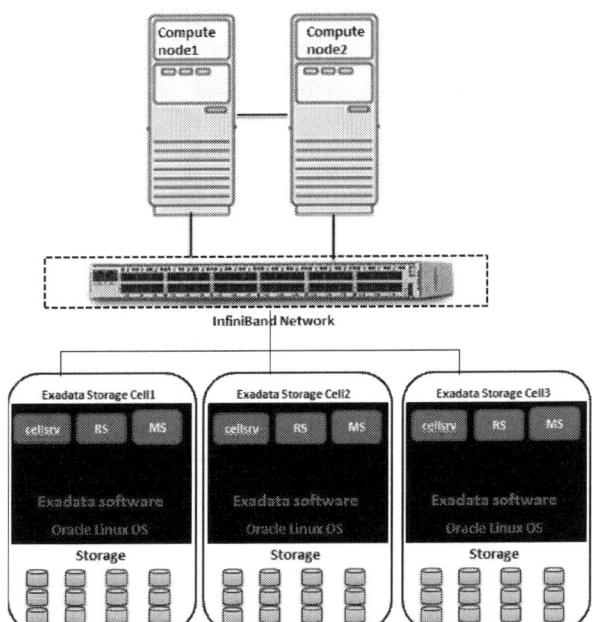

Figure 3.2   Eighth/Quarter Rack Exadata Database Machine compute and cell server architecture

comes with two InfiniBand network switches, known as leaf switches, configured between a cell and Compute Nodes to provide a communication path tolerating any switch failure. A third switch (spine) is provided only in Half and Full Rack capacity.

Each Exadata Storage Server comes with a fixed 12 uniform High Performance (HP) or High Capacity (HC) physical disks, preconfigured OEL operating system, Exadata Storage Software, and three key background services. The storage server can be accessed with three options: local login, secure shell (SSH), and KVM switch.

Cell Software Components and Management

Three key software components that run in the background are responsible for delivering the core functionality of the cell server: Cell Server (CELLSRV), Management Server (MS), and Restart Server (RS).

Cell Server

Cell Server (CELLSRV) is a multithreaded process. Arguably the heaviest among the three processes, it uses the most CPU cycles, and it also uses the special iDB protocol over InfiniBand (Oracle data transfer protocol) for communication between an ASM instance and Storage Cells. It is the primary component running on the cell and is responsible for performing Exadata advanced responsibilities, such as SQL Offloading (Smart Scans), prioritizing and scheduling an I/O on the underlying disks, implementing IORM, and so on.

It is recommended that you set the high limits of soft and hard values for the celladmin user to avoid as few ORA-600 errors as possible. As part of the disk management, when the CELLSRV process discovers that a particular disk is performing poorly, it will notify an ASM instance immediately to take the grid disk offline. Each time a database is started, it gets registered with the cell service on the cell server, and the limit of database connection to each cell service is up to 255.

The following query helps you identify the CELLSRV hang incidents on the cell:

```
# CellCLI> list alerthistory where alertMessage like ".*CELLSRV hang.*" detail
```

To diagnose CELLSRV issues, such as when CELLSRV is hung, consuming a significant amount of CPU and memory, memory leaks, and so on, you can generate a state dump of the CELLSRV process with the following command to troubleshoot the issue:

```
# CellCLI> alter cell events = "immediate cellsrv.cellsrv_statedump(0,0)"
# CellCLI> alter cell events = "immediate cellsrv.cellsrv_statedump(2,0)"
```

The following output is generated upon execution of the command, which can be referred to for further analysis of the current CELLSRV situation:

```
Dump sequence #1 has been written to /opt/oracle/cell11.2.3.0_LINUX.X64_131014.1/log/
diag/asm/cell/cell2/trace/svtrc_31243_80.trc

Cell usdwilo03 successfully altered
Cell cell2 successfully altered
```

Each time a state dump is performed, the sequence count for dump is increased. The trace file name in the preceding example is svtrc_18140_21.trc. The trace file contains detailed information about the cell, that is, cell software version, dump sequence, memory information, cell parameters, statistics, disk owner information, InfiniBand information, and so on. At any point in time, if you want to know the internal working condition of a CELLSRV process, you can generate a state dump to get the complete details.

As mentioned earlier, each cell is managed individually with the CellCLI utility. The CellCLI utility provides a command-line interface to the cell management functions, such as cell initial configuration, cell disk and grid disk creation, and performance monitoring. The CellCLI utility runs on the cell and is accessible from a client computer that has network access to the Storage Cell or is directly connected to the cell. The CellCLI utility communicates with Management Server to administer the Storage Cell.

If you want to manually stop, start, or restart the CELLSRV service on the cell, use the following commands:

```
# CellCLI> alter cell shutdown services cellsrv [FORCE]
```

If you encounter any issue while shutting down the CELLSRV service, use the FORCE option to shut down the service forcefully.

```
# CellCLI> alter cell startup services cellsrv
```

This will start the CELLSRV service on the local cell.

```
# CellCLI> alter cell restart services cellsrv
```

This will stop/start (restart) the CELLSRV service on the local cell.

```
# CellCLI> list cell attributes cellsrvStatus detail
```

This prints the current status of the CELLSRV process on the local cell.

Management Server

Management Server (MS) provides standard cell configuration and management functionality in coordination with CellCLI. It performs the following additional tasks:

- Periodically parses the symbolic links in the /dev/disk/by-path corresponding to the FMOD Flash Disks, to verify their presence and visibility to the underlying OS.
- Tracks down the hardware-level changes on the cell server and notifies the CELLSRV through an ioctl system call.
- Collects, computes, and manages storage server metrics.
- Rebuilds the virtual drives when a disk is replaced.
- Typically, when a disk performs poorly, the associated grid disk and cell disk will be taken offline, and MS service will notify the CELLSRV service.

Apart from these characteristics, MS also triggers the following automated tasks every hour:

- Deletes files older than seven days from the ADR directory, $LOG_HOME, and all metric history.
- Performs alert log file auto-maintenance whenever the file size reaches 10MB in size and deletes previous copies of the alert log when they become seven days old.
- Notifies when file utilization reaches 80%.

The MS service can start-stop-restart and verify the current status with the following commands:

```
# CellCLI> alter cell shutdown services ms
```

This shuts down the MS service on the local cell.

```
# CellCLI> alter cell startup services ms
```

This starts up the MS service on the local cell.

```
# CellCLI> alter cell restart services ms
```

This stops/starts (restarts) the MS service on the local cell.

```
# CellCLI> list cell attributes msStatus detail
```

This prints the current MS service status.

Restart Server

Restart Server (RS) monitors other services on the cell server and restarts them automatically in case any service needs to be restarted. Also, it handles planned service restarts as part of any software updates. The cellrssrm is the main RS process and spans three child processes: cellrsomt, cellrsbmt, and cellesmmt.

The RS service can start-stop-restart and verify the current status with the following commands:

```
# CellCLI> alter cell shutdown services rs
# CellCLI> alter cell startup services rs
# CellCLI> alter cell restart services rs
# CellCLI> list cell attributes rsStatus detail
```

All three component services are automatically started and stopped whenever the cell server is powered off or on. However, sometimes you might need to stop the service(s) manually; for instance, to enable the write-back Flash Cache feature, you need to stop the cell service.

The alter cell shutdown services all [FORCE] command shuts down all services together, and the alter cell startup services all command starts up all services together. All grid disks and related ASM disks will become inactive and go offline respectively upon stopping either all services or just the cell server, and the communication between the cell and ASM/RDBMS instances will be disturbed.

The following commands can be used to verify the current status of all three background processes on the cell:

```
# /etc/init.d/celld status
# /etc/init.d/service cell status

    rsStatus:          running
    msStatus:          running
    cellsrvStatus:     running
```

Configuring Mail Server for Alert Notifications

After the Exadata Database Machine initial deployment, configure the SMTP server settings on each cell to receive notification whenever the storage server generates alerts and warnings. The following piece of code shows an example to configure SMTP server settings on the local cell server:

```
# CellCLI > ALTER CELL realmName=ERP_HO,-
   smtpServer= 'your_domain.com',-
   smtpFromAddr='prd.cell01@domain.com', -
   smtpPwd='password123',-
   smtpToAddr='dba_group@domain.com',-
   notificationPolicy='clear, warning, critical',-
notificationMethod='email,snmp'
```

Once the SMTP settings are configured, use the following command to validate the cell:

```
# CellCLI> ALTER CELL VALIDATE MAIL
```

Displaying Cell Server Details

The following command displays cell server comprehensive details, such as cell services status, cell name, ID, interconnect details, and so on:

```
# CellCLI> list cell detail

name:                   cel01
bbuTempThreshold:       60
bbuChargeThreshold:     800
bmcType:                IPMI
cellVersion:            OSS_11.2.3.2.1_LINUX.X64_130109
cpuCount:               24
diagHistoryDays:        7
fanCount:               12/12
fanStatus:              normal
flashCacheMode:         WriteBack
id:                     1210FMM04Y
interconnectCount:      3
interconnect1:          bondib0
iormBoost:              9.2
ipaddress1:             192.168.10.19/22
kernelVersion:          2.6.32-400.11.1.el5uek
locatorLEDStatus:       off
makeModel:              Oracle Corporation SUN FIRE X4270 M2 SERVER SAS
metricHistoryDays:      7
notificationMethod:     mail,snmp
notificationPolicy:     critical,warning,clear
offloadEfficiency:      53.7
powerCount:             2/2
powerStatus:            normal
releaseVersion:         11.2.3.2.1
upTime:                 376 days, 19:02
cellsrvStatus:          running
msStatus:               running
rsStatus:               running
```

Cell Metrics and Alert History

Cell metrics and alert history provide valuable statistics for optimizing the Exadata storage resources and components on the cell. Using the metricdefinition, metriccurrent, and metrichistory commands, you can display the historical and current metrics of any Exadata component, such as cell disk, Flash Cache, grid disks, I/O, host, and so on:

```
CellCLI> list metricdefinition cl_cput detail
        name:               CL_CPUT
        description:        "Percentage of time over the previous
        metricType:         Instantaneous
        objectType:         CELL
        unit:               %

CellCLI> list metriccurrent where objecttype = 'CELL' detail
        name:               CL_BBU_CHARGE
        alertState:         normal
        collectionTime:     2015-01-14T18:34:40+03:00
        metricObjectName:   usdwilo18
        metricType:         Instantaneous
        metricValue:        0.0 %
        objectType:         CELL

        name:               CL_BBU_TEMP
        alertState:         normal
        collectionTime:     2015-01-14T18:34:40+03:00
```

```
        metricObjectName:       usdwilo18
        metricType:             Instantaneous
        metricValue:            0.0 C
        objectType:             CELL

        name:                   CL_CPUT_CS
        alertState:             normal
        collectionTime:         2015-01-14T18:34:40+03:00
        metricObjectName:       usdwilo18
        metricType:             Instantaneous
        metricValue:            1.6 %
        objectType:             CELL

        name:                   CL_CPUT_MS
        alertState:             normal
        collectionTime:         2015-01-14T18:34:40+03:00
        metricObjectName:       usdwilo18
        metricType:             Instantaneous
        metricValue:            0.0 %
        objectType:             CELL

CellCLI> list metriccurrent cl_cput detail
        name:                   CL_CPUT
        alertState:             normal
        collectionTime:         2015-01-14T18:34:40+03:00
        metricObjectName:       usdwilo18
        metricType:             Instantaneous
        metricValue:            2.0 %
        objectType:             CELL
```

Querying Cell Alert History

Best practices suggest periodically querying the alert history. The alert history notifications are categorized as Informal, Warning, or Critical. The activerequest, alertdefinition, and alerthistory commands display current and historical alert details. In order to display the alert history that occurred on the cell or a particular component, use one of the following commands:

```
CellCLI> list alerthistory detail
        name:                   7_1
        alertDescription:       "HDD disk controller battery in learn cycle"
        alertMessage:           "The HDD disk controller battery is
                                performing a learn cycle. Battery Serial
                                Number : 591  Battery Type        : ibbu08
                                Battery Temperature   : 29 C  Full Charge
                                Capacity  : 1405 mAh  Relative Charge
                                : 100 %  Ambient Temperature   : 24 C"
        alertSequenceID:        7
        alertShortName:         Hardware
        alertType:              Stateful
        beginTime:              2014-10-17T13:51:44+03:00
        endTime:                2014-10-17T13:51:47+03:00
        examinedBy:
        metricObjectName:       Disk_Controller_Battery
        notificationState:      0
        sequenceBeginTime:      2014-10-17T13:51:44+03:00
        severity:               info
        alertAction:            "All hard disk drives may temporarily
                                enter WriteThrough caching mode as part of
```

the learn cycle. Disk write throughput might
be temporarily lower during this time. The
flash drives are not affected. The battery
learn cycle is a normal maintenance activity
that occurs quarterly and runs for
approximately 1 to 12 hours. Note that many
learn cycles do not require entering
WriteThrough caching mode. When the disk
controller cache returns to the normal
WriteBack caching mode, an additional
informational alert will be sent."

```
name:                    7_2
alertDescription:        "HDD disk controller battery back to normal"
alertMessage:            "All disk drives are in WriteBack caching
                         mode.  Battery Serial Number : 591  Battery
                         Type            : ibbu08  Battery Temperature
                         : 29 C  Full Charge Capactiy  : 1405 mAh
                         Relative Charge        : 100 %  Ambient
                         Temperature    : 24 C"
alertSequenceID:         7
alertShortName:          Hardware
alertType:               Stateful
beginTime:               2014-10-17T13:51:47+03:00
endTime:                 2014-10-17T13:51:47+03:00
examinedBy:
metricObjectName:        Disk_Controller_Battery
notificationState:       0
sequenceBeginTime:       2014-10-17T13:51:44+03:00
severity:                clear
alertAction:             Informational.
```

```
# CellCLI> list alerthistory where severity='Critical'
To view alert history of the cell categorized as 'Critical' state

# CellCLI> list alerthistory 4_1 detail
To display more details of the incident mentioned in the above example
```

Querying GV$ Views

The following Exadata-related new V$ dynamic views provide the cell and its wait
events with statistical information that can be used to measure the cell state, IP
address used, and so on:

- **V$CELL**—provides information about cell IP addresses mentioned in the
  cellip.ora file
- **V$CELL_STATE**—provides information about all the cells accessible from the
  database client
- **V$CELL_THREAD_HISTORY**—contains samples of threads in the cell collected
  by the cell server
- **V$CELL_REQUEST_TOTALS**—contains historical samples of requests run by
  the cell

Storage Architecture and Formulation

So far you have learned the fundamental concepts of cell architecture and cell management. It's time now to go for the real treat and discuss the core component of Exadata Cell, that is, the storage layer.

Before we jump in and start discussing the Exadata storage architecture and storage preparation, let's explore the basic differences between non-Exadata and Exadata environments.

A traditional Oracle Database deployment requires three major components: the Oracle Database server, the storage server, and the network layer, as shown in Figure 3.3.

In this particular setup the database is both the "engine" and the "transmission" as it both processes the raw data and delivers information to the user. Here the storage server is merely an I/O facilitator—it simply and blindly serves up requested data blocks to the database. Thus, if the database SQL optimizer decides it must perform a full table scan of a million blocks, both the network and storage server must process or handle one million blocks. Such a request could overwhelm the storage server cache, thus making it less effective for all users. Furthermore, the TCP/IP network protocol packet structure is not well optimized for such simple, massive data transfers—not even with jumbo frames enabled. The general-purpose network packets suffer other limitations, including excessive header overhead waste and processing costs. While this is the most common setup there is, it's nonetheless quite inefficient.

When it comes to Exadata, an Exadata Oracle Database deployment also contains three key hardware components: the database server, the storage server, and the network between them as shown in Figure 3.4.

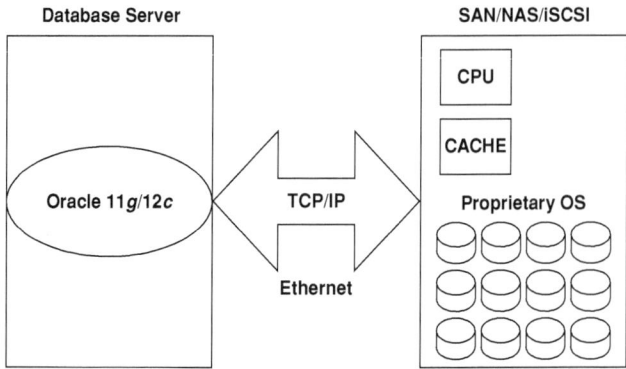

Figure 3.3 Traditional database and storage architecture

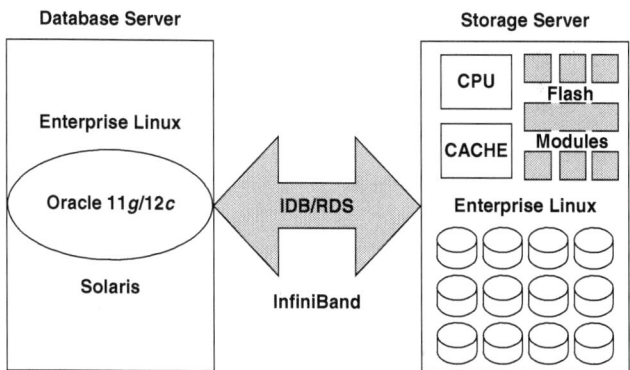

Figure 3.4 Exadata Database Machine architecture

There are four fundamental differences in the Exadata storage hardware architecture in contrast to the non-Exadata architecture, and they make all the difference in the world, especially in relation to storage scalability and performance:

- First and foremost, an Exadata cell contains **Flash Modules** that can be used either as fast disks or as additional cache (more about that later in this chapter).

- Second, the storage server is running Oracle Enterprise Linux as opposed to a proprietary OS—that's going to enable software architectural options otherwise not possible (again to be covered later in this chapter).

- Third, the high-speed, private network between the database and cell servers is based on InfiniBand rather than Ethernet.

- Fourth and finally, all communication between the database and cell servers uses the iDB protocol transmitted via Reliable Datagram Sockets (RDS).

Let's examine that last key difference in more detail since it enables or is directly responsible for some of the cell servers' "special sauce." RDS is a low-overhead, low-latency, and more CPU-efficient protocol that's been around for years (predating Exadata). So merely using the RDS protocol between database and cell servers over InfiniBand is superior to the normal deployment scenario, but while better, it's not what delivers the huge scalability and performance possible via cell servers. It's the iDB and what software architectures it makes possible that deliver most of the performance gains.

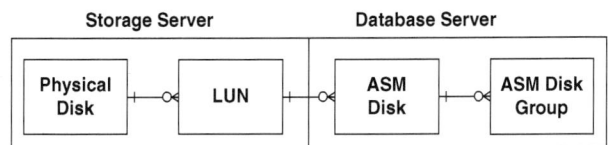

Figure 3.5 Traditional database and storage relationship

Disk Architecture in Non-Exadata

In a traditional Oracle Database deployment using Oracle's ASM, the storage server disk architecture or layout is generally organized as shown in Figure 3.5.

Typically, the physical disks (or partitions) map to logical unit numbers, or LUNs (or devices); those are then used to create Oracle ASM disks for inclusion in ASM disk groups. While ASM is an option in traditional database deployments, Oracle generally recommends it for most new databases—and especially for RAC setups. There are of course several key benefits of using ASM:

- First and foremost, as a storage mechanism it's highly integrated into the Oracle technology stack, and hence it works quite effectively and efficiently.
- Second, it eliminates the need for OS file system and logical volume managers (LVMs).
- Third, ASM offers dynamic load balancing and rebalancing of space when new disks are added or removed—something not possible with LVMs.
- Fourth and finally, it was designed from the ground up to work well with the needs and characteristics of Oracle Database I/O.

Disk Architecture in Exadata

Each Exadata Storage Server ships with 12 SAS physical disks of uniform size, either with the High Performance or the High Capacity configuration, and four Flash cards built in.

The initial two disks are mirrored using RAID (mdadm) and are used for the operating system, swap space, Exadata Storage Server software binaries, and various other Exadata configurations. The df command on the cell shows the following file system structure; right below the output, there is an explanation of the type of mount points and mapped file systems:

```
$ df
Filesystem           1K-blocks      Used Available Use% Mounted on
/dev/md5             10321144   5839912   3956948  60% /
tmpfs                49378532         0  49378532   0% /dev/shm
/dev/md7              3096272    775708   2163284  27% /opt/oracle
/dev/md4              116576      28583     81974  26% /boot
/dev/md11             5160448    205884   4692428   5% /var/log/oracle
```

- / is the root file system.
- /opt/oracle is where the Exadata software is installed.
- /var/log/oracle is where the cells' OS and crash logs are stored.
- The /dev/md5 and /dev/md6 are the system partitions, active and mirror copy.
- The /dev/md7 and /dev/md8 are the Exadata software installation, active and mirror copy.
- The /dev/md11 is mapped with /var/log/oracle.
- At any given point in time, only four multidevice (MD) mount points can be mounted on the cell.

Approximately 29GB of space per disk is used for this purpose. In order to know whether the LUN is the system partition or not, you can use the following command:

```
CellCLI> list lun 0_0 detail
         name:                 0_0
         cellDisk:             CD_00_usdwilo18
         deviceName:           /dev/sda
         diskType:             HardDisk
         id:                   0_0
         isSystemLun:          TRUE
         lunAutoCreate:        TRUE
         lunSize:              1116.6552734375G
         lunUID:               0_0
         physicalDrives:       20:0
         raidLevel:            0
         lunWriteCacheMode:    "WriteBack, ReadAheadNone, Direct, No
                                 Write Cache if Bad BBU"
         status:               normal
```

There are several significant items to note here:

- First, cell servers have both Flash Cache Modules and traditional physical disks.
- Second, there's a new level of disk abstraction called the **cell disk**, which offers the ability to subdivide a LUN into partitions known as **grid disks**.
- Third, cell disks constructed from Flash Cache Modules can be further divided into Flash Cache or grid disks. Of course, physical-disk-based LUNs can map only to grid disks.
- Finally, only grid disks can be mapped to ASM disks.

At the helm of the storage layer on a cell, a physical disk is the first layer of abstraction, and each physical disk is mapped and appears as a LUN. In contrast to other storage boxes, no manual intervention is required to achieve this task as they are created automatically during Exadata Database Machine initial deployment.

The next setup is to configure the cell disk from the existing LUNs. A cell disk is created based on the existing LUN on the cell server. Once the cell disk is created, the disk can be subdivided into one or more grid disks to make them available for an ASM instance as ASM candidate disks.

As standard practice, when a cell disk is subdivided into multiple grid disks, you can then assign different performance characteristics to each grid disk according to business needs. For instance, you can assign a grid disk from a cell disk at the outermost track of a physical disk to gain the highest level of performance, and another grid disk can be assigned to the inner track of a physical disk to achieve moderate performance. The higher-performance grid disks across all cell servers then can be put together into a single disk group to place any hot data, whereas the lower-performance disks can be assembled into a disk group to store archive logs. For example, the higher-performance grid disks can be used for a data disk group and the lower-performance disks can be used to keep archive logs.

In an Oracle Exadata database deployment the cell servers can only use Oracle's ASM; however, the cell server disk architecture or layout is a little more complex with some rather different and unique options for organization. Figure 3.6 represents the relationship between disk storage and its entities.

The major difference between Flash Cache and Flash-based grid disks is quite simple. Flash Cache is autopilot caching of recently accessed database objects.

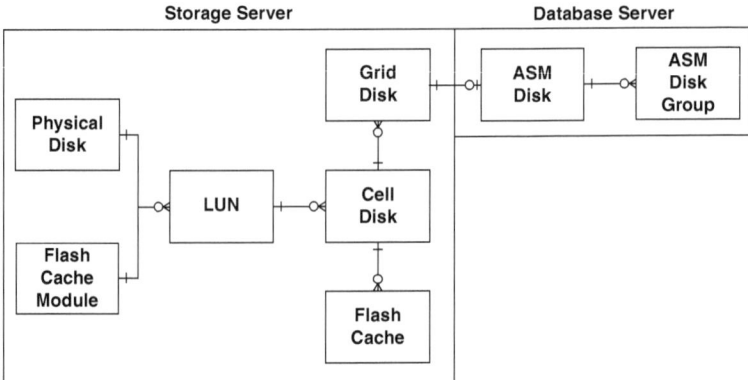

Figure 3.6 Exadata storage (physical, LUN, cell disk, grid disk, and ASM disks) formation flow

Think of it as a supersize System Global Area (SGA) at the storage level. A very similar concept known as **Smart Response Technology (SRT)** exists on some newer Intel CPUs and their chip sets, whereby an SSD can be used as front-end caching of a traditional disk drive. Flash Cache does offer the ability to manually pin database objects into it (much like pinning objects into the SGA). Here's an example of pinning the PARTS table into the Flash Cache:

```
SQL> ALTER TABLE PARTS STORAGE (CELL_FLASH_CACHE KEEP);
```

Flash grid disks, on the other hand, are simply Flash Modules organized into persistent disks for ASM use. In many ways it's like having a fast SSD disk instead of a magnetic disk on your PC. At times there will be database objects that you know will perform better if they are truly Flash based rather than contained on traditional disks (and possibly Flash cached). Hence, there are times when you'll want to create ASM disks and disk groups from Flash Modules to gain the full benefits of that speed. So for those cases you'll want to create cell and grid disks from Flash Cache Modules. The commands for doing so are covered later in this chapter.

System Users for Cell Administration

As mentioned in the beginning of the chapter, each Exadata Storage Server is typically configured with three default users with different roles. Here are the differences between the users and their capabilities:

- **root**—superuser privileges. Used to shut down and start up the storage server.
- **celladmin**—used to perform cell-level administrative tasks such as CREATE, ALTER, MODIFY cell objects, such as cell disks, grid disk, configure notification, and so on, using the CellCLI and dcli utilities
- **cellmonitor**—a monitoring user used to perform cell monitoring tasks. Unlike root and celladmin, it can't be used to CREATE, ALTER, or MODIFY any cell objects.

Following are a few practical examples.

Listing Disk Levels

To list all levels of disks, including physical disks, LUNs, cell disks, and grid disks, use the following commands:

```
Some CellCLI commands
If you want to list all the commands associated with CellCLI utility, use
the following command:
CellCLI> help

 HELP [topic]
   Available Topics:
        ALTER
        ALTER ALERTHISTORY
        ALTER CELL
        ALTER CELLDISK
        ALTER FLASHCACHE
        ALTER GRIDDISK
        ALTER IBPORT
        ALTER IORMPLAN
        ALTER LUN
        ALTER PHYSICALDISK
        ALTER QUARANTINE
        ALTER THRESHOLD
        ASSIGN KEY
        CALIBRATE
        CREATE
        CREATE CELL
```

To list the Flash Cache disks configured on the local cell, run the following command:

```
CellCLI> list lun where disktype = 'flashdisk'
       1_0       1_0      normal
       1_1       1_1      normal
       1_2       1_2      normal
       1_3       1_3      normal
       2_0       2_0      normal
       2_1       2_1      normal
       2_2       2_2      normal
```

To list the LUN details, such as to determine if the LUN is a system LUN or not, LUN size, ID, RAID level, device name, and other information on the local node, execute the following command:

```
CellCLI> list lun detail
        name:                0_0
        cellDisk:            CD_00_usdwilo18
        deviceName:          /dev/sda
        diskType:            HardDisk
        id:                  0_0
        isSystemLun:         TRUE
        lunAutoCreate:       TRUE
        lunSize:             1116.6552734375G
        lunUID:              0_0
        physicalDrives:      20:0
        raidLevel:           0
        lunWriteCacheMode:   "WriteBack, ReadAheadNone, Direct, No
                                Write Cache if Bad BBU"
        status:              normal

        name:                0_1
        cellDisk:            CD_01_usdwilo18
        deviceName:          /dev/sdb
```

```
diskType:               HardDisk
id:                     0_1
isSystemLun:            TRUE
lunAutoCreate:          TRUE
lunSize:                1116.6552734375G
lunUID:                 0_1
physicalDrives:         20:1
raidLevel:              0
lunWriteCacheMode:      "WriteBack, ReadAheadNone, Direct, No
                             Write Cache if Bad BBU"
status:                 normal
```

To list the physical disk details, such as disk name, status, and so forth, on the local cell, run the following command:

```
CellCLI> list physicaldisk detail
        name:                   20:0
        deviceId:               8
        diskType:               HardDisk
        enclosureDeviceId:      20
        errMediaCount:          0
        errOtherCount:          0
        luns:                   0_0
        makeModel:              "HGST     H101212SESUN1.2T"
        physicalFirmware:       A690
        physicalInsertTime:     2014-05-21T04:24:40+03:00
        physicalInterface:      sas
        physicalSerial:         DEAT5F
        physicalSize:           1117.8140487670898G
        slotNumber:             0
        status:                 normal

        name:                   20:1
        deviceId:               9
        diskType:               HardDisk
        enclosureDeviceId:      20
        errMediaCount:          0
        errOtherCount:          0
        luns:                   0_1
        makeModel:              "HGST     H101212SESUN1.2T"
        physicalFirmware:       A690
        physicalInsertTime:     2014-05-21T04:24:40+03:00
        physicalInterface:      sas
        physicalSerial:         DE7ZWF
        physicalSize:           1117.8140487670898G
        slotNumber:             1
        status:                 normal
```

To list the cell disk details, such as device name, creation time, size, and so on, run the following command:

```
CellCLI> list celldisk detail
        name:                   CD_00_usdwilo18
        comment:
        creationTime:           2014-09-24T16:14:52+03:00
        deviceName:             /dev/sda
        devicePartition:        /dev/sda3
        diskType:               HardDisk
        errorCount:             0
```

```
    freeSpace:              0
    id:                     ac757133-886d-465c-b449-8fe35f05519c
    interleaving:           none
    lun:                    0_0
    physicalDisk:           DEAT5F
    raidLevel:              0
    size:                   1082.84375G
    status:                 normal

    name:                   CD_01_usdwilo18
    comment:
    creationTime:           2014-09-24T16:14:53+03:00
    deviceName:             /dev/sdb
    devicePartition:        /dev/sdb3
    diskType:               HardDisk
    errorCount:             0
    freeSpace:              0
    id:                     af978555-022a-4440-9c6c-2c05f776b6cc
    interleaving:           none
    lun:                    0_1
    physicalDisk:           DE7ZWF
    raidLevel:              0
    size:                   1082.84375G
    status:                 normal
```

To list the grid disk details, such as cell disks mapped to the physical disk, size, status, and so on, run the following command:

```
CellCLI> list griddisk detail
    name:                   DG_DBFS_CD_02_usdwilo18
    asmDiskgroupName:       DG_DBFS
    asmDiskName:            DG_DBFS_CD_02_USDWILO18
    asmFailGroupName:       USDWILO18
    availableTo:
    cachingPolicy:          default
    cellDisk:               CD_02_usdwilo18
    comment:
    creationTime:           2014-09-24T16:19:02+03:00
    diskType:               HardDisk
    errorCount:             0
    id:                     7e2d7848-cf81-4918-bb01-d27ef3da3950
    offset:                 1082.84375G
    size:                   33.796875G
    status:                 active

    name:                   DG_DBFS_CD_03_usdwilo18
    asmDiskgroupName:       DG_DBFS
    asmDiskName:            DG_DBFS_CD_03_USDWILO18
    asmFailGroupName:       USDWILO18
    availableTo:
    cachingPolicy:          default
    cellDisk:               CD_03_usdwilo18
    comment:
    creationTime:           2014-09-24T16:19:02+03:00
    diskType:               HardDisk
    errorCount:             0
    id:                     972be19d-5614-4b98-8806-7bdc2faf7630
    offset:                 1082.84375G
    size:                   33.796875G
    status:                 active
```

Configuring Cell Disks

The following command will configure 12 cell disks, one for each LUN, with the default naming convention. This is usually run as part of the initial deployment.

```
# CellCLI> CREATE CELLDISK ALL HARDDISK
```

Alternatively, use the following command to create the cell disks to enable interleaving:

```
# CellCLI> CREATE CELLDISK ALL HARDDISK INTERLEAVING='normal_redundancy'
```

Creating Grid Disks

The following command will create a grid disk at the outermost track layer of a physical disk for high performance:

```
# CellCLI> create griddisk ALL HARDDISK prefix=data, size 500G
```

The next command will create a grid disk at the inner track layer of a physical disk for less I/O-intensive applications:

```
# CellCLI> CREATE GRIDDISK ALL PREFIX=FRA
```

Configuring Flash Grid Disks

The following procedure is used to drop the current Flash Cache and rebuild with the nondefault size:

```
# CellCLI> DROP FLASHCACHE
# CellCLI> CREATE FLASHCACHE ALL SIZE =200G
# CellCLI> CREATE GRIDDISK ALL FLASHDISK
```

Once the Exadata storage configuration is done, the next step is to configure the database hosts to access the grid disks. The cellinit.ora and cellip.ora files must be configured at the Compute Nodes in order to access the grid disk from the cell. The following example shows the contents of each file:

```
#/etc/oracle/cell/network-config/cellinit.ora
Ipaddress=192.168.0.13/24
```

The `cellinit.ora` file contains the database server IP address. Each database server will have its own IP address recorded in the `cellinit.ora` file:

```
/etc/oracle/cell/network-config/cellip.ora
cell="192.168.0.11"
cell="192.168.0.12"
cell="192.168.0.13"
```

The `cellip.ora` file contains the IP addresses of all cells, and all Compute Nodes should have the same entries in order to access storage on the cell servers.

Creating an ASM Disk Group

To show how to create an ASM disk group for your database, let's take the grid disks from cell01 and cell02 to create a data disk group with high-redundancy capabilities:

```
SQL> CREATE DISKGROUP DG_DATA HIGH REDUNDANCY DISK 'o/*/
 DATA_EX01_CD_00_ex01cel01', 'o/*/ DATA_EX01_CD_01_ex01cel01'
, 'o/*/DATA_EX01_CD_02_ex01cel01', 'o/*/ DATA_EX01_CD_00_ex01cel02'
, 'o/*/DATA_EX01_CD_01_ex01cel02', 'o/*/DATA_EX01_CD_02_ex01cel02'
'compatible.asm'='11.2.0.3',      'compatinle.rdbms'='11.2.0.2',
'cell_smart_scan'='TRUE';
```

Managing the Cell Server

Sometimes it becomes necessary, especially before and after patch deployment on the cell as well as on the Compute Nodes, to know the current cell software version and the previous version to which the cell can potentially roll back. In this context, Oracle provides two utilities in /usr/local/bin: `imageinfo` and `imagehistory`.

When the `imageinfo` utility is executed as the root user on the cell server as follows, it will help you get the active cell software details, such as cell kernel version, OS version, active cell image details, cell boot partitions, and so on:

```
# imageinfo

Kernel version: 2.6.32-400.11.1.el5uek #1 SMP Thu Nov 22 03:29:09 PST 2012 x86_64
Cell version: OSS_11.2.3.2.1_LINUX.X64_130109
Cell rpm version: cell-11.2.3.2.1_LINUX.X64_130109-1

Active image version: 11.2.3.2.1.130109
Active image activated: 2013-01-30 19:14:40 +0300
Active image status: success
Active system partition on device: /dev/md5
Active software partition on device: /dev/md7

In partition rollback: Impossible
```

```
Cell boot usb partition: /dev/sdm1
Cell boot usb version: 11.2.3.2.1.130109

Inactive image version: 11.2.3.2.0.120713
Inactive image activated: 2012-12-10 11:59:57 +0300
Inactive image status: success
Inactive system partition on device: /dev/md6
Inactive software partition on device: /dev/md8

Boot area has rollback archive for the version: 11.2.3.2.0.120713
Rollback to the inactive partitions: Possible
```

The imagehistory utility helps you get all the previous software versions installed on the particular cell:

```
#imagehistory

Version                             : 11.2.3.1.1.120607
Image activation date               : 2012-07-25 01:25:34 +0300
Imaging mode                        : fresh
Imaging status                      : success

Version                             : 11.2.3.2.0.120713
Image activation date               : 2012-12-10 11:59:57 +0300
Imaging mode                        : out of partition upgrade
Imaging status                      : success

Version                             : 11.2.3.2.1.130109
Image activation date               : 2013-01-30 19:14:40 +0300
Imaging mode                        : out of partition upgrade
Imaging status                      : success
```

The -h option can be used to list all parameters that are associated with the imageinfo and imagehistory utilities.

To remove the old alerthistory on the cell, you can use the following commands:

```
#CellCLI> drop alerthistory all   -- will drop the complete alerthistory info
#CellCLI> drop alerthistory <9_1> -- will drop a particular incident history
```

Troubleshooting the Cell Server

The following sections discuss and demonstrate some of very important tools and utilities provided on Exadata to collect the diagnostic information on a cell. Most of the diagnostic tools and utilities reside under the /opt/oracle.SupportTool folder.

SunDiag

The sundiag.sh diagnostic collection script exists on each Compute Node and Storage Cell under /opt/oracle.SupportTools. The script can also be downloaded from support.oracle.com. The script helps you gather the required diagnostic information related to problematic disks or any other hardware issues on the cell.

You have to execute the script as root user, as follows:

```
/opt/oracle.SupportTools/sundiag.sh
```

If you would like to gather similar diagnostic information across all cell servers, you will have to execute the script through the dcli utility.

This script generates a timestamped .tar file under /tmp/sundiag_Filesystem which can be uploaded to Oracle Support for analysis.

ExaWatcher

The new ExaWatcher utility located under /opt/oracle.ExaWatcher replaces the traditional OSWatcher utility in Exadata Storage Software 11.2.3.3 and is used for system data collection. The utility is up and running upon system reboot. It collects the statistics for the following components on the cell and keeps the log files under /opt/oracle.ExaWatcher/archive:

- `Diskinfo`
- `IBCardino`
- `Iostat`
- `Netstat`
- `Ps`
- `Top`
- `Vmstat`

In order to produce or extract the reports from the logs generated by the ExaWatcher utility, you will have to use the `GetExaWatcherResults.sh` script. You can collect input at various levels:

- `FromTime` until `ToTime` extracts range reports.
- `ToTime` extracts on or before time reports.
- `AtTime` extracts around the time reports.
- `Hours` extracts time in range reports.

Following are some examples:

```
# ./GetExaWatcherResults.sh --from <time frame> to <time frame>
# ./GetExaWatcherResults.sh --at <time frame> --range 2
```

The second example extracts 2 hours starting with the time defined with the `at` parameter.

The `ExaWatcherCleanup` module is used to automatically manage the file system space used by ExaWatcher. Based on the limits set for space management, the module is responsible for cleaning up the old log files by removing them.

To get more help on how to use the utility, use the following commands:

```
# ExaWatcher.sh --help
# ExaWatcherResults.sh --help
```

Exachk

Exachk is an Oracle Exadata diagnostic tool that comes with different levels of verification and collects hardware, software, firmware, and configuration data on Exadata systems. It is strongly recommended that you include this script as part of your periodic maintenance operation tasks. Also, run the script before any migration, upgrade, or any other major change operations take place.

This script doesn't come with the Exadata machine; you will have to download it (exachk_225_bundle.zip file) from Oracle Support Note ID 1070954.1, which requires login credentials. The Note and the .zip files contain all the information required to use the tool.

CheckHWnFWProfile

The CheckHWnFWProfile utility verifies any hardware and firmware component details and reports if there are any recommended items missing. It is also used to validate the current configuration on the servers. This utility is used without passing any parameters, as shown in the following example:

```
# /opt/oracle.cellos/CheckHWnFWProfile
```

If the current hardware and firmware are to the correct version, it will give the `SUCCESS` output.

To obtain more information on the utilization of this utility use the `-d` option with the command.

Storage Cell Startup and Shutdown

When rebooting or shutting down the Exadata Storage Cell for maintenance or any other valid reason, ensure that you adhere to proper stop/start cell procedure to guarantee a graceful cell shutdown. This section emphasizes the significance of complying with an appropriate cell stop and start procedure and demonstrates the steps in depth.

One of the key responsibilities of a DMA includes graceful shutdown of the cell, be it for a quick reboot or for maintenance. The shutdown shouldn't impact the underlying ASM instance and the active database that is running. That being said, shutting down the cell and its services without affecting the ASM availability largely depends on the current ASM redundancy level. Under any circumstances, it is a best practice to follow this procedure for the graceful shutdown of a cell:

1. Verify that ASM doesn't have any impact by taking the grid disks offline on the cell. Use the following command to verify the result:

   ```
   # CellCLI> list griddisk attributes name,asmdeactivationoutcome
   ```

2. If the result of asmdeactivationoutcome is yes for all the grid disks listed, it is an indication that ASM will not have any impact and it is safe to deactivate all the grid disks, using the next command:

   ```
   # CellCLI> alter griddisk all inactive
   ```

3. Once you turn off all the grid disks on the cell, run the first command to verify the asmdeactivationoutcome output and verify that all the grid disks are now offline, using this command:

   ```
   # CellCLI> list griddisk
   ```

4. Now it is safe to power off/reboot/shut down the cell. As root, shut down the cell using the following command:

   ```
   $ shutdown -h now  -- OS command to shut down the cell server
   ```

   Note

   If you intend to take the cell down for a very long period of time, you will have to adjust the ASM disk's DISK_REPAIR_ATTRIBUTE default value to prevent ASM from dropping the disks automatically upon taking them offline. The default value is set to 3.6 hours; therefore, if you are taking the cell down for 5 hours, for example, use the following command to set the value through an ASM instance:

   ```
   SQL> ALTER DISKGROUP DG_DATA SET ATTRIBUTE 'DISK_REPAIR_TIME'='5H';
   ```

   You will have to adjust all the required disks on the cell.

Once the cell is rebooted or comes online, follow these instructions to bring the services and grid disks back to action:

1. First step of the procedure:

   ```
   # CellCLI > alter griddisk all active
   ```

2. Second step of the procedure:

   ```
   # CellCLI> list griddisk attributes name,asmmodestatus
   ```

3. Last step of the procedure:

   ```
   # CellCLI> list cell detail
   ```

If you have worked on Oracle Database and cluster technologies previously, you probably know that each of them maintains an alert log file where all important events and sequences are written. Similarly, an alert file is maintain by each cell server to record all the important events of the cell, such as when the services started or stopped, disk warning messages, cell and grid disk creation, and so on. It is highly recommended that you review the logs frequently. You can also refer to the OS file to find out when the cell restarted.

Following are some of the most commonly referenced log/trace files and their locations:

- /log/diag/asm/cell/{cell name}/trace
- **MS log**—/opt/oracle/cell/log/diag/asm/cell/{cell name}/trace/ms-odl.log
- **OSWatcher logs**—/opt/oracle.oswatcher/osw/archive
- **OS messages**—/var/log/messages
- **Cell-patching-related logs**—/var/log/cellos

Solving Disk Problems

Yet another major responsibility of a DMA includes determining when and how a faulty (dead, predictive failure, poor performance) disk is identified and getting it replaced on an Exadata Storage Server. Although most of the procedure is automated by Oracle, including identification and notification of an underperforming, faulty, or damaged disk, it is equally important for you to understand the factors and procedures involved in troubleshooting and replacing the disk when it becomes necessary to do so.

When a disk confronts performance issues or any sort of hard failure, an alert is generated by the MS background process on the cell server, and it notifies the CELLSRV background service about the alert. At the same time, if OEM is configured, the message is also pushed to Grid Control, through which you can receive an email or SMS message.

Initially, a set of performance tests is carried out by the MS service on the disk on which the performance degradation has been identified to determine whether the behavior is a temporary glitch or a permanent one. If the disk passes the tests successfully, it is brought back to the active configuration; if not, it is marked as performing poorly and an Auto Service Request (ASR), if configured, is opened for disk replacement.

Whenever a disk failure occurs or a disk goes into predictive status, ASM automatically drops the related grid disks of the failed disk either normally or forcefully. After the disk issues are addressed and the disks are ready to go active, ASM automatically brings related grid disks online as part of the Exadata auto disk management, which is controlled by the _AUTO_MANAGE_EXADATA_DISKS parameter.

Typically the following actions are performed when disk issues are identified on the cell server:

1. When poor performance is detected, the cell disk and physical disk statuses are changed.

2. All grid disks of the particular cell disk are taken offline.

3. The MS service notifies the CELLSRV service about the findings, and in turn, CELLSRV notifies ASM instances to take the grid disk offline.

4. The MS service on the cell then performs a set of confinement checks to determine if the disk needs to be dropped.

5. If the disk passes the performance tests, the MS service notifies the CELLSRV service to turn all the cell disks and all its grid disks online.

6. If the disk fails the performance tests, the cell disk and physical disk statuses are modified, and the disk is removed from the active configuration.

7. The MS service notifies the CELLSRV service about the disk issues. In turn, the CELLSRV service informs ASM instances to drop all the grid disks of the cell.

8. If ASR is configured, a service request is logged to Oracle Support about disk replacement.

9. You will have to either use the spare disk to replace the faulty disk or request a replacement disk from Oracle.

Disk problems can be categorized in two levels: hard failure and predictive failure. A predictive failure is when a disk is flagged as predictive or in a poor performance state. A hard failure is when a disk goes into critical state.

When you have been notified about the critical failure state of a physical disk, through either email or SMS message, your first priority is to identify the damaged physical disk's exact name, position, location, and slot number through the cell alert history or by reviewing the cell logs. Also refer to the ASM alert logs to ensure that ASM turned the damaged disk offline (dropped the disk) and ASM rebalancing is completed before replacing the disk.

To view the disk-related alert history, use the following command on the cell:

```
CellCLI> list alerthistory

         7_1    2014-10-17T13:51:44+03:00        info     "The HDD disk controller battery
is performing a learn cycle. Battery Serial Number : 591  Battery Type         : ibbu08
Battery Temperature    : 29 C  Full Charge Capacity  : 1405 mAh  Relative Charge       :
100 %  Ambient Temperature   : 24 C"

         7_2    2014-10-17T13:51:47+03:00        clear    "All disk drives are in WriteBack
caching mode.  Battery Serial Number : 591  Battery Type         : ibbu08  Battery
Temperature    : 29 C  Full Charge Capactiy  : 1405 mAh  Relative Charge       : 100 %
Ambient Temperature   : 24 C"

# CellCLI> list physicaldisk WHERE diskType=HardDisk AND status=critical detail
# CellCLI> list physicaldisk WHERE diskType=HardDisk AND status like ".*failure.*" detail
# CellCLI> alter physicaldisk disk_name:disk_id drop for replacement
```

Verify that the grid disks of the cell disk are dropped and the rebalancing operations are completed on the ASM instances:

```
SQL> SELECT name,state from v$asm_diskgroup;
SQL> SELECT * FROM v$asm_operation;
```

Three minutes after replacing the faulty physical disk on the cell, all the grid disks and cell disks are automatically re-created, added subsequently to the respective disk group, and then rebalanced.

Enforcing Cell Security

Exadata offers many layers of security setups to meet your business needs. An Exadata cell server by default comes with open storage security, where there are no restrictions applied on accessing grid disks from ASM or database clients. Apart from open security, Oracle Exadata supports two levels of security: ASM-scoped security and database-scoped security. These control the storage access from ASM cluster or database clients.

Security can control which ASM or database clients can access a specific grid disk or pools of grid disks on the cell. With ASM-scoped security, all database clients of that particular ASM cluster can access the grid disks. You can go further and configure database-scoped security to restrict the storage access at the database level.

Even if you intend to deploy database-scoped storage-level security, you will have to first configure ASM-scoped security. The following sections describe step-by-step procedures for how to enforce ASM-scoped and database-scoped security on the cell.

Configuring ASM-Scoped Security

In order to enforce ASM-scoped security on Exadata, follow this procedure:

1. Shut down ASM and all database instances on the Compute Node.

2. Generate a security key using the CREATE KEY command on a cell CellCLI prompt which will be used or copied across all cell servers to enforce the security:

   ```
   CellCLI> CREATE KEY
   ```

3. Create a cellkey.ora file for ASM under /etc/oracle/network-config on the Compute Node, assign the security key against the ASM instance name, and change the permission and ownership as shown:

   ```
   # cellkey.ora
        key=<key generated in the above command>
        asm=<asm db_unique_name>
        realm=<xyz> -- optional
   # chown oracle:dba /etc/oracle/network-config/cellkey.ora
   # chmod 640 /etc/oracle/network-config/cellkey.ora
   ```

4. If you want to change the realm name on the cell, use the following:

   ```
   CellCLI> alter cell realmName=prod_realm
   ```

5. Assign the security key to the ASM instances across all the cell servers where you want to enforce the security:

   ```
   CellCLI> ASSIGN KEY FOR '+ASM'='<security key>'
   ```

6. Add or modify the grid disk's availableTo attribute to add the ASM instance, as follows:

   ```
   CellCLI> list griddisk
   ```

7. After getting the grid disks' names, change the attribute for each grid disk:

   ```
   CellCLI> alter griddisk <grid disk list> availableTo ='+ASM'
   CellCLI> alter griddisk ALL availableTo='+ASM'
   ```

8. Restart the ASM and database instances.

This type of security enables grid disk access to all the database clients of that ASM instance.

Configuring Database-Scoped Security

In order to enforce database-scoped security on Exadata, follow the next procedure:

1. Stop ASM and all database instances on the Compute Node.

2. Generate a separate new security key for each database connecting to the ASM instance with the CREATE KEY command using the CellCLI utility on the cell:

```
CellCLI> CREATE KEY
```

3. Create a cellkey.ora key file under $ORACLE_HOME/admin/<db_name>/ pfile for each database on the Compute Node, assign the key against the database name, and change the permission and ownership as follows:

```
# cellkey.ora
    key=<key generated in the above command>
    asm=<asm db_unique_name>
    realm=<xyz> -- optional
# chmod 640 $ORACLE_HOME/admin/<db_name>/pfile/cellkey.ora
```

4. If you want to change the realm name on the cell, use the following:

```
CellCLI> alter cell realmName=xyz
```

5. Assign the security key to the database on all the cell servers:

```
CellCLI> ASSIGN KEY FOR <DB_NAME1>='<security key1>',
<DB_NAME2>='<security key2>'
```

6. Change the grid disk's availableTo attribute, as follows:

```
CellCLI> list griddisk
```

7. After getting the grid disks' names, change the attribute for each grid disk:

```
CellCLI> alter griddisk <griddisk list> availableTo ='+ASM,
<DB_NAME>,<DB_NAME2>'
CellCLI> alter griddisk ALL availableTo='+ASM,<DB_NAME>,<DB_NAME2>'
```

8. Restart the ASM and database instances.

When you want to further restrict individual databases of that ASM instance to access a different pool of grid disks, you will have to enforce database-scoped security as explained previously.

You can list or view the existing security keys using the following command:

```
# CellCLI> list key
```

Exempting Cell Security

At any given time, you can exempt the cell security that has been imposed earlier. You can bring down the database-scoped security to ASM-scoped security and ASM-scoped security to the default open security. Keep in mind that any change and enforcement require ASM and database downtime.

The following procedure can be used to remove the cell security:

1. Stop ASM and databases.

2. Get the list of grid disk attributes assigned.

3. Exempt the databases from the security and remove Access Control List (ACL) setup using the following commands:

   ```
   CellCLI> alter griddisk griddiskName availableTo='+ASM'
   CellCLI> assign key for <DB_NAME>=''
   ```

4. Remove the cellkey.ora file from the respective database Home location.

5. Finally, verify the grid disks to ensure that the databases are exempted from the security list:

   ```
   CellCLI> list griddisk attributes name,availableTo
   ```

6. The previous steps exempt the databases from database-scoped security. If you want to also remove ASM-scoped security, first use the following commands:

   ```
   CellCLI> alter griddisk all availableTo=''
   CellCLI> alter griddisk griddiskName availableTo=''
   CellCLI> assign key for +ASM=''
   ```

7. Finally, remove the cellkey.ora file from /etc/oracle/cell/network-config.

Summary

To manage any environment effectively, it is always important for a DBA/DMA to understand the underlying architecture and the total functionality of the system. This chapter explained all the essentials and the importance of Exadata Storage Cells in detail. You have learned how to gracefully shut down Storage Cell background services, how to configure cell security, and how to create and manage storage on the cell.

## 4

Flash Cache, Smart Scans, and Cell Offloading

One of the key design goals for the Oracle Exadata Database Machine has always been to build a platform that can deliver extreme performance, reliability, and availability for Oracle Databases across all workloads (OLTP/batch/DSS/DW).

The combination of the Flash Cache on the Storage Cell and the software features embedded into the Storage Cell (Smart Flash Cache) is the key for the Oracle Exadata Database Machine to deliver on this design principle and goal. In this chapter we look at the use and implementation of Flash Cache on Exadata Storage Cells which enables Exadata to deliver extreme performance across all database workloads with reliability.

Concepts of Exadata Flash Cache

The Exadata Smart Flash Cache—a feature of the Exadata Storage Server—is one of the many examples in the Exadata architecture where software and hardware are engineered to work together in order to deliver extreme performance. At the most fundamental level, the Exadata Smart Flash Cache is an intelligent mechanism to replace slow mechanical I/O disk-based operations with rapid Flash memory operations.

Why Flash Cache Is Necessary

The Achilles' heel for any high-performance database has always been I/O, simply because physical I/O is typically the slowest operation that occurs in the database.

Understandably, a key metric or component used when architecting the infrastructure for Oracle Databases has always been I/O per second (IOPS)/megabits per second (MBPS) based on the workload. Storage architects can design and deploy architectures that are capable of handling the demand from a more holistic perspective. The unfortunate part is that Oracle DBAs are at the short end of this transaction, since they are focused at an individual database level. As a result, the DBAs are often held hostage by this difference in viewpoint about I/O performance and response times.

Traditional storage arrays worked around this by placing huge amounts of cache in front of their storage units. This cache was used for two purposes: first to provide a fast, efficient entry point to stage incoming write I/Os to eliminate physical I/O times, and second to cache frequently used blocks to service random read I/O operations. Over time, as technology advanced and changed, this approach has run into some roadblocks.

While the cache worked well for random IOPS, it was not suited for large block or heavy-throughput-based I/O operations like a full table scan. The primary way to get around this was to increase the number of spindles that would service the request and increase the capacity of the data pipe.

The cache worked well for random I/O operations, but the cache does not discriminate on what data blocks and I/O types are cached. This intelligence would be application specific, and therefore the arrays would need to understand and differentiate between database I/Os and file server I/Os.

Array caches provided performance gains since these provided orders-of-magnitude faster I/O operations than physical disks. With the advent of SSD and Flash drives, the traditional array caches lose that benefit and don't add performance value; thus they are not used with front Flash drive and SSD I/O. Furthermore, at this point the bottleneck is moved from physical disks to the actual controllers managing I/O requests.

As seen in the Exadata Database Machine, Oracle's answer to this dilemma is to use Flash PCIe cards that are not limited by disk controller performance or capacity issues. The Exadata Storage Server software allows for simultaneous access and scan of the Flash as well as the disks, maximizing the throughput and bandwidth.

Evolution of Flash Cache in Exadata

Exadata V1, which came out in 2008, was Oracle's primary entry into the "appliance"-based solutions market, aimed at data warehouses. It had zero Flash Cache.

With no Flash Cache, the Exadata V1 was primarily a data-warehouse-only solution. Oracle introduced Flash Cache capabilities in 2009 with Exadata V2, allowing Exadata to become a viable OLTP/batch platform as well.

Table 4.1   Exadata X4-2 Flash Performance Metrics

Metric	X4-2 Full Rack	X4-2 Half Rack	X4-2 Quarter Rack	X4-2 Eighth Rack
Maximum Flash read IOPS	2,660,000	1,330,000	570,000	285,000
Maximum Flash write IOPS	1,960,000	980,000	420,000	210,000
Maximum Flash bandwidth	100GB/s	50GB/s	21.5GB/s	10.7GB/s
Flash Cache capacity (raw)	44.8TB	22.4TB	9.6TB	4.8TB

In 2010, Oracle released Exadata X2. The amount of Flash Cache did not change; rather the improvements were in the storage software layer.

In 2012, Oracle released Exadata X3. The amount of Flash Cache was increased to 1.6TB (4 x 400GB PCIe Flash cards) per cell, for a total of 22.4TB for an X3 Full Rack. The Flash cards were faster, and the Storage Server software supported enhancements such as Flash Cache Compression, Flash Cache Logging, and Flash Cache WriteBack.

Late in 2013, Oracle released Exadata X4. Once again, the amount of Flash Cache was doubled. Each Storage Cell now has a total of 3.2TB (4 x 800GB PCIe Flash cards), for a total of 44.8TB for an X4 Full Rack. The Storage Server software now includes enhancements in Flash Cache algorithms, such as the ability to understand and focus on table and partition scans, and the ability to cache larger objects partially, using both Flash and disk I/O to speed throughput.

Table 4.1 shows the Flash Cache—specific performance metrics with the Oracle Exadata X4 configurations from the Exadata X4 data sheet. These figures are based on assuming 8K block size for I/O.

Note

The Exadata Smart Flash Cache is completely different from and independent of the Oracle 11gR2 Flash Cache option. The database Flash Cache option expands the SGA by extending the buffer cache on high-speed Flash cards.

Storage Server and Flash Cache

A key difference between Exadata at the Storage Tier and other available solutions is the degree and depth to which the Flash cards are integrated into the overall solution. In Exadata, the Flash Cache solution is integrated into the overall solution at the hardware layer, as well as at the software layer. The software layer integration within Exadata goes a level beyond just a pure storage software layer by integrating with the software of the application it is designed to run, that is, with the Oracle Database software. This integrated solution goes beyond just accelerating performance; it includes intelligent Oracle-aware performance acceleration, administration, and management capabilities as well.

In the Exadata Storage Server architecture, there are two features that specifically aim to leverage the Flash hardware: Smart Flash Cache and Smart Flash Logging.

The implementation of these features is what introduces the "smartness" factor to the Flash Cache hardware in the Storage Cells. The Exadata Storage Server software provides the resiliency and redundancy required for a high-performance, mission-critical database.

The Exadata Smart Flash Cache Feature

As with any caching mechanism, the idea is to cache frequently used data blocks. But in order to get to the next level of performance and optimization, the key is to make those caching decisions in an intelligent manner. In other words, know what to cache, what not to cache, and when to cache.

Embedded into the Exadata Storage Server software is the basic understanding and awareness of I/O, specifically as it relates to an Oracle Database. The Storage Server software uses this core understanding and awareness of the Oracle Database to eliminate or reduce dependency on slower mechanical operations by replacing them with high-speed Flash memory operations.

As the database Compute Nodes send I/O requests to the Storage Cells, additional predictive information is embedded into these requests. This includes information such as the nature or type of the I/O, the probability that this data will be requested again in the near term, and so on. The Storage Server software uses this embedded information to determine whether to cache or not cache the data blocks.

For example, random reads and writes against tables are most likely to be cached as they will probably be requested by subsequent I/O requests. Index fast full scans or full table scans, on the other hand, will most likely not be cached since sequentially accessed data requests are generally not repeated.

The second level of intelligence comes from understanding the nature of the I/O request from the database. Armed with this intelligence, the Storage Server software achieves higher efficiencies of Flash Cache usage. Data and index block reads and writes will benefit significantly from a caching mechanism, as that will convert physical I/O to logical, fast memory-based I/O. On the other hand, control file I/O, archive log I/O, RMAN DB backups, mirrored writes, and backup restores see absolutely no benefit from the use of caching.

Most of these features are backward compatible as far as Exadata V2 hardware.

Populating the Flash Cache

So far, we have talked about how Exadata decides what to cache in the Flash Cache and how it delivers performance by servicing read requests from the cache. In this section we talk a bit about how the cache is populated in the first place.

Consider a scenario in which the cell is servicing a read request when the requested block is not in the Flash Cache. In such a case, the Exadata Storage Server reads the data from disk and applies the rules for caching the data. But what about write I/O requests?

By default Flash Cache operates in a mode called Flash Cache Write Through. In this mode, when the database sends write I/O requests, the I/O is sent directly to the physical disks. Upon completion of the I/O requests, Exadata Storage Server sends back the acknowledgment to the database and then applies the rules to determine whether or not to cache the data.

With Exadata Database Machine X3, Oracle introduced the Flash Cache Write-Back mode of operation. In this mode, Exadata treats the I/O much like most SANs do, with Oracle-aware intelligence added in. The overall process is along the lines of the following:

1. The write I/O request is "staged" in the Flash Cache.

2. Once staged in the Flash Cache, Exadata Storage Server sends an acknowledgment back to the database.

3. Asynchronously, Exadata Storage Server software de-stages the write to the physical disk.

4. At this point, Exadata Storage Server applies the rules to decide whether or not the block should be cached.

Tip

Flash Cache WriteBack is not the default mode and needs to be enabled before use. The following commands enable Flash Cache WriteBack:

```
CellCLI> drop flashcache
CellCLI> alter cell shutdown services cellsrv
CellCLI> alter cell flashCacheMode = WriteBack
CellCLI> alter cell startup services cellsrv
CellCLI> create flashcache all
```

To disable Flash Cache WriteBack, use the following commands:

```
CellCLI> alter flashcache all flush
CellCLI> drop flashcache
CellCLI> alter cell shutdown services cellsrv
CellCLI> alter cell flashCacheMode=Writethrough
CellCLI> alter cell startup services cellsrv
CellCLI> create flashcache all
```

> This feature is backward compatible to Exadata V2 X2 models. However, you would need to be at 11.2.0.3.BP 9 for GI and DB and 11.2.3.2 for the Exadata Storage Server.

Keep in mind that with Exadata X3 and X4 models, the amount of Flash Cache has been increased to 1.6TB per cell (versus 400GB per cell) and is four times faster. With WriteBack, we see the combined effect of using SSDs for data and Storage Auto Tiering with disk pools, with the awareness of Oracle Database I/O patterns and processes.

With the introduction of Flash Cache WriteBack and Flash Cache Logging, there is no longer a need to create ASM disk groups on Flash disks for performance reasons. We get the same performance benefits now, without having to resort to a customized configuration of the storage.

- There is improvement in database checkpoint speeds since control file I/O goes through the Flash Cache.

- There are improvements in operations such as merges and sort joins which could cause I/O to the temporary tablespace due to multistep PGA (Program Global Area) operations.

- Flash Cache Logging helps redo-related I/O.

Exadata Smart Flash Logging

Transactionally high-volume systems commonly experience significant database wait times related to online redo log I/O (wait events such as log file sync, log file parallel write, and so on).

One way to resolve these issues might be to reduce commit rate and frequency, which is not always possible. Other solutions include placing the online redo logs on faster disks or in some extreme cases even increasing the priority of the log writer (LGWR) process or even running the process in real-time priority.

Warning

The authors are not endorsing changing the priority of LGWR processes. Such changes must be done with extreme caution and require a lot of testing.

Until the introduction of Smart Flash Logging, Exadata was no exception. Smart Flash Logging incorporates the Flash Cache into the redo log I/O stream. Conceptually, a small amount of the Flash Cache is reserved for online redo-log-related I/O. When the Exadata Storage Server receives a redo log write request, it writes in parallel to the space reserved for Flash Logging as well as the disk. When either request completes, an I/O complete acknowledgment is sent to the database. Under most circumstances, the Flash Cache response completes first, resulting in a very fast redo write response and thus reducing total wait time on log file sync and so on.

This is internally achieved by dedicating an area in the Flash Cache to the Flash Log. The default size of the Flash Log is 512MB, which is more than sufficient in most cases. This size can be changed at creation time. The Flash Log is not a permanent store for redo data, but rather a persistent cache to stage redo I/O until the I/O can be de-staged and written to the actual disk.

In addition, for consolidated deployments, the Exadata IORM has been enhanced to enable or disable Smart Flash Logging for the different databases running on the database machine, reserving Flash for the most performance-critical databases.

Tip

The Flash Log must be created prior to creating the Flash Cache. Under the default configuration method, the remaining space on the Flash cards is used for Flash Cache. Therefore, if you need to change the size, you need to drop the Flash Log and the Flash Cache, re-create the Flash Log to the desired size, and then finally create the Flash Cache to use the remaining space.

The database or the application does not require any modifications in order to use the Smart Flash Log feature. The Smart Flash Log feature is completely transparent to the rest of the stack outside of the Exadata Storage Server.

From an end user perspective, the system behaves in a completely transparent manner, and the user need not be aware that Flash is being used as a temporary store for redo. The only behavioral difference is consistently low latencies for redo log writes.

The best practices and configurations of redo log sizing, duplexing, and mirroring do not change when using Exadata Smart Flash Logging.

The Database and Flash Cache

So far, we have looked at the Flash Cache and its usage from a hardware and system software point of view. This section describes and gives examples of Exadata database-level features that take the efficacy of the Flash Cache to the next level. Specifically, it discusses Smart Scans and Cell Offloading, Storage Indexes, and caching data in the Flash Cache.

In order to simulate these features, we'll build a sample table based on DBA_OBJECTS, but with an additional leading column that is populated by a sequence number generator (see Listing 4.1). There are no indexes created on the table for the sake of simplifying these examples.

Listing 4.1   Table Creation and Data Population

```
-- create the sequence number generator.
create sequence mysequence start with 1 increment by 1 cache 100;

create table my_dbaobjects as
select mysequence.nextval Unique_objid, a.object_id, a.data_object_id,
       a.owner, a.object_name, a.subobject_name, object_type
from dba_objects a;

SQL> desc my_dbaobjects
 Name                                      Null?    Type
 ----------------------------------------- -------- ---------------------------
 UNIQUE_OBJID                                       NUMBER(38)
 OBJECT_ID                                          NUMBER
 DATA_OBJECT_ID                                     NUMBER
 OWNER                                              VARCHAR2(30)
 OBJECT_NAME                                        VARCHAR2(128)
 SUBOBJECT_NAME                                     VARCHAR2(30)
 OBJECT_TYPE                                        VARCHAR2(19)

-- Data Population, execute this multiple times:
Insert into my_dbaobjects
select mysequence.nextval Unique_objid, a.object_id, a.data_object_id,
       a.owner, a.object_name, a.subobject_name, object_type
from dba_objects a
/

-- Row count
SQL> select count(*) from my_dbaobjects;

  COUNT(*)
----------
  37595520

-- Final size
SQL> select sum(bytes)/1024/1024/1024 space_gb from dba_segments where
       segment_name = 'MY_DBAOBJECTS';

  SPACE_GB
----------
2.31005859

-- Object has no indexes whatsoever defined.
```

As we look at each of the specific use cases in the listing, we'll look at specific system statistics that help us understand the interaction between the cells and database layer and the impact of the features and use cases. These are listed below, but keep in mind that there are other statistics that help us understand how the cell I/O works:

- **Cell Flash Cache read hits**—basically identifies the number of I/O requests satisfied directly by the Flash Cache
- **Cell physical I/O bytes eligible for predicate offload**—the number of bytes of I/O that were eligible to be optimized by Smart Scans as a whole, due to predicate filtering, Storage Indexes, or any other aspect

- **Cell physical I/O bytes saved by Storage Index**—bytes of I/O eliminated by the use of Storage Indexes
- **Cell physical I/O interconnect bytes**—total bytes of I/O returned from the cell to the DB node
- **Cell physical I/O interconnects bytes returned by Smart Scan**—bytes of I/O returned by a Smart Scan to the DB node

Smart Scans and Cell Offloading

As described earlier, Smart Scans or Cell Offloading is the phenomenon where the actual work of filtering data based on predicates in the WHERE clause is performed at the Exadata Storage Cells rather than at the DB Compute Nodes (as is the case under the traditional model). However, Cell Offloading occurs only when the WHERE clause structure and predicate filters used are compatible with Cell Offload. To see a list of functions that Exadata supports for Cell Offloading, query the V$ view V$SQLFN_METADATA view (look at the OFFLOADABLE column).

The database parameters that impact Cell Offloading and Smart Scans are listed in Table 4.2. These include both regular parameters and hidden parameters.

Table 4.2 Database Initialization Parameters Impacting Smart Scan and Cell Offloading*

Parameter	Default Value	Description
Regular database initialization parameters		
cell_offload_processing	TRUE	Enable SQL processing offload to cells
cell_offload_decryption	TRUE	Enable SQL processing offload of encrypted data to cells
cell_offload_parameters		Additional cell offload parameters for future use
Hidden database initialization parameters		
_allow_cell_smart_scan_attr	TRUE	Allow checking smart_scan_ capable attribute
_cell_fast_file_create	TRUE	Allow optimized file creation path for cells
_cell_fast_file_restore	TRUE	Allow optimized RMAN restore for cells
_cell_file_format_chunk_size	0	Enable cell file format chunk size in megabytes

Continues

Table 4.2   Database Initialization Parameters Impacting Smart Scan and Cell Offloading* *(Continued)*

Parameter	Default Value	Description
Hidden database initialization parameters		
_cell_index_scan_enabled	TRUE	Enable cell processing of index fast full scan
_cell_offload_capabilities_ enabled	1	Specify capability table to load
_cell_offload_hybridcolumnar	TRUE	Query offloading of HCC tables to Exadata
_cell_offload_predicate_ reordering_enabled	FALSE	Enable out-of-order SQL processing offload to cells
_cell_offload_timezone	TRUE	Enable time-zone-related SQL processing offload to cells
_cell_offload_virtual_columns	TRUE	Enable offload of predicates on virtual columns to cells
_cell_range_scan_enabled	TRUE	Enable cell processing of index range scans
_cell_storidx_mode	EVA	Enable cell Storage Index mode
_disable_cell_optimized_ backups	FALSE	Disable cell optimized backups
_kcfis_cell_passthru_enabled	FALSE	Disable smart I/O filtering on the cell
_kcfis_cell_passthru_fromcpu_ enabled	TRUE	Enable automatic pass-through mode when cell CPU utility is too high
_kcfis_disable_platform_ decryption	FALSE	Disable platform-specific decryption on the Storage Cell
_kcfis_io_prefetch_size	8	Enable smart I/O prefetch size for a cell
_kcfis_kept_in_cellfc_enabled	TRUE	Enable usage of CELLSRV Flash Cache for kept objects
_kcfis_large_payload_enabled	FALSE	Enable large payload to be passed to CELLSRV
_kcfis_nonkept_in_cellfc_ enabled	FALSE	Enable use of CELLSRV Flash Cache for non-kept objects
_serial_direct_read	auto	Enable direct read in serial

*   The "_" parameters are listed here for educational and awareness reasons only. It is not recommended that you change any of the "_" parameters from their default values. Oracle's development team reviews these parameters with every release. Any modification to these "_" parameters must be done in conjunction with and at the request of Oracle Support.

Assuming all the parameters are set up appropriately, the following are some of the reasons the evaluation of the predicate will not be offloaded to the cell:

- When the I/O access path is not based on direct path reads
- While scanning a clustered table or an index-organized table
- When we use ROWID as the sort order in a query
- When performing a fast full scan on compressed indexes or reverse key indexes
- When querying a table with more than 255 columns, unless the table is compressed with HCC
- When the predicate evaluation is on a virtual column
- When there are user-defined hard-coded hints, which may well push Oracle to prevent Cell Offloading capabilities

Let us take a look at some practical examples of Smart Scans, to learn how to identify whether a Smart Scan has occurred or not. The script we'll use is provided in Listing 4.2.

Listing 4.2 Smart Scan Example Script

```
set timing on
spool smart-scan-example.log
set echo on

/* Flush the shared pool and buffer cache prior to each run */
alter system flush shared_pool;
alter system flush buffer_cache;

/* Forcibly disable cell offloading / smart scan */
alter session set cell_offload_processing=false;

select /* NO_OFFLOAD */sum(object_id)/1000000 from my_dbaobjects where
object_id = 1000;

/* Run the same example but with cell-offloading enabled. */
alter session set cell_offload_processing=true;

/* Flush the buffer cache to level the playing field again */
alter system flush buffer_cache;

select /* WITH OFFLOAD */ sum(object_id)/1000000 from my_dbaobjects where
object_id = 1000;
```

If we look at the following output from the example, we can see that the benefit from an elapsed-time perspective is significant: 2.43 seconds compared to .24 seconds, a 90.12% reduction in elapsed time:

```
Elapsed Time (No OFFLOAD)
SQL> select /* NO_OFFLOAD */sum(object_id)/1000000 from my_dbaobjects
where object_id = 1000;
SUM(OBJECT_ID)/1000000
----------------------
                  .512
Elapsed: 00:00:02.43

Elapsed Time (WITH OFFLOAD)
SQL> select /* WITH OFFLOAD */ sum(object_id)/1000000 from my_dbaobjects
where object_id = 1000;

SUM(OBJECT_ID)/1000000
----------------------
                  .512
Elapsed: 00:00:00.24
```

Looking at the following output of the explain plan, we can see why this is the case. The plan looks the same (down to the PATH, the number of bytes read, etc.), but there is a difference in how the predicate is evaluated. In the case where Cell Offloading has occurred, we see the additional clause storage("OBJECT_ID"=1000). This signifies that the actual predicate was applied at the storage level and then passed on to the database where the filter was essentially reapplied.

```
Execution Plan (No OFFLOAD)
----------------------------------------------------------------------------
Id|Operation                      |Name          |Rows|Bytes|Cost(%CPU)|Time
----------------------------------------------------------------------------
 0|SELECT STATEMENT               |              |   1|    5|81884(1)  |0:16:23
 1| SORT AGGREGATE                |              |   1|    5|          |
*2|  TABLE ACCESS STORAGE FULL|MY_DBAOBJECTS| 504| 2520|81884(1)  |0:16:23

----------------------------------------------------------------------------
Predicate Information (identified by operation id):
---------------------------------------------------
   2 - filter("OBJECT_ID"=1000)

Execution Plan (WITH OFFLOAD)
----------------------------------------------------------------------------
Id|Operation                      |Name          |Rows|Bytes|Cost(%CPU)|Time
----------------------------------------------------------------------------
 0|SELECT STATEMENT               |              |   1|    5|81884 (1) |0:16:23
 1| SORT AGGREGATE                |              |   1|    5|          |
*2|  TABLE ACCESS STORAGE FULL|MY_DBAOBJECTS| 504| 2520|81884 (1) |0:16:23
----------------------------------------------------------------------------
Predicate Information (identified by operation id):
---------------------------------------------------
   2 - storage("OBJECT_ID"=1000)
       filter("OBJECT_ID"=1000)
```

Next, let us look at the results from a system statistics perspective for the two runs, as shown in Figure 4.1. When we further analyze the results, we find that

- The "cell Flash Cache read hits" statistics show that in both cases, the Flash Cache did come into play to fulfill the I/O requests. What differed was the extent to which the Flash Cache was used.

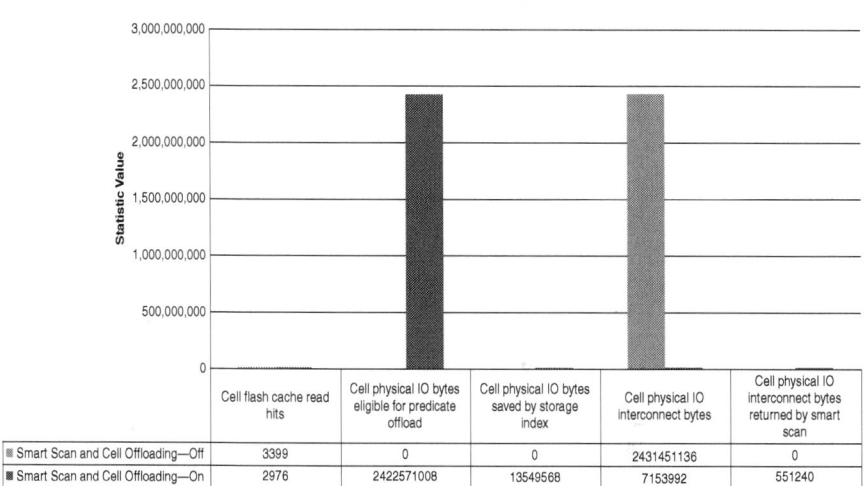

	Cell flash cache read hits	Cell physical IO bytes eligible for predicate offload	Cell physical IO bytes saved by storage index	Cell physical IO interconnect bytes	Cell physical IO interconnect bytes returned by smart scan
▩ Smart Scan and Cell Offloading—Off	3399	0	0	2431451136	0
▩ Smart Scan and Cell Offloading—On	2976	2422571008	13549568	7153992	551240

Figure 4.1   Impact of Smart Scan and Cell Offloading—key statistics

- The statistic "cell physical I/O bytes eligible for predicate offload" tells us that with Smart Scan enabled, approximately 2.26GB worth of I/O was offloaded to the cell.
- The statistic "cell physical I/O interconnect bytes" was reduced from 2.26GB to less than 6.82MB when we enabled Smart Scan.
- The statistic "cell physical I/O interconnect bytes returned by Smart Scan" further tells us that out of a total of 6.82MB of information exchanged between the cell and DB node, Smart Scans accounted for 0.52MB.

In other words, Smart Scans and Cell Offloading eliminated 99.97% of the I/O between Compute Node and storage.

If we take a look at CPU time and DB time, shown in Figure 4.2, we can see the positive impact of the use of Smart Scan. This positive impact stems from the fact that the cell has offloaded the work of filtering data to itself.

- Session CPU time was reduced by 82.73%.
- DB time was reduced by an additional 84.78%.

Figure 4.3 looks at the two sessions, but from the perspective of session wait event and wait time. The reason for the gains in elapsed time and in CPU/DB time

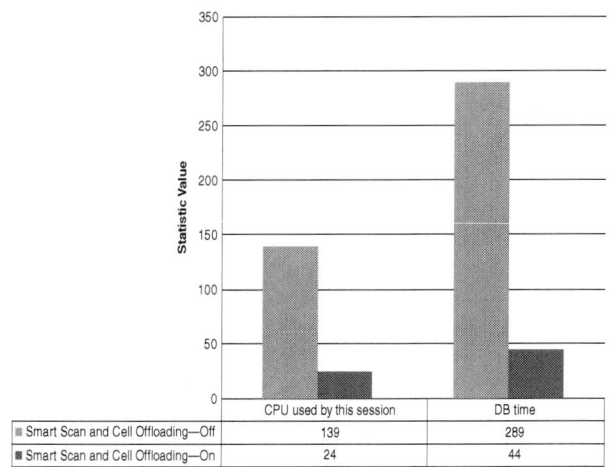

Figure 4.2 Impact of Smart Scan and Cell Offloading—CPU and DB time

is the reduced I/O the Compute Node has to process. As we can see, from a database perspective, the user I/O-related wait time has been reduced by 86.30%.

Looking at the database I/O system statistics shown in Figure 4.4, we can drill down into this further. As we can see, although DB block gets did not significantly

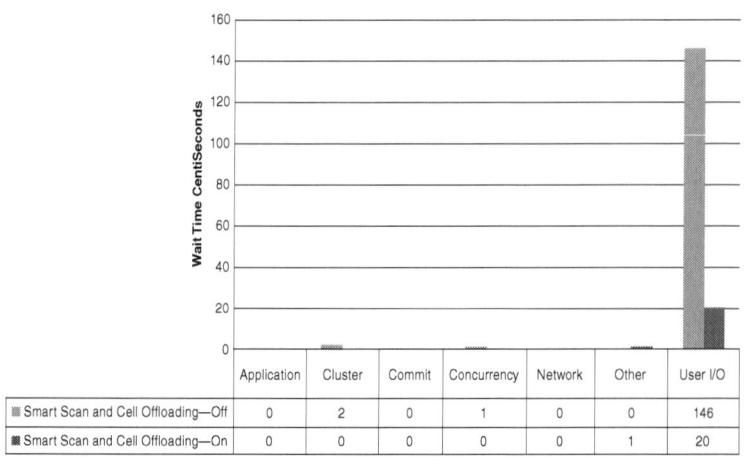

Figure 4.3 Impact of Smart Scan and Cell Offloading—session wait analysis

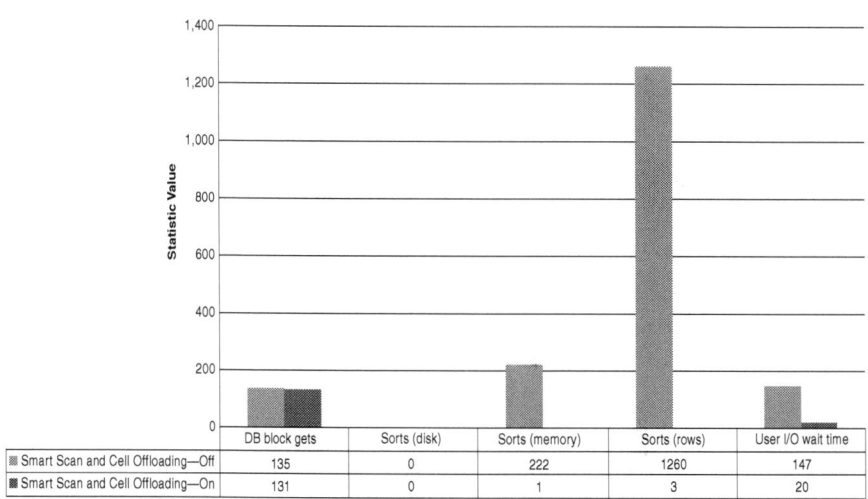

	DB block gets	Sorts (disk)	Sorts (memory)	Sorts (rows)	User I/O wait time
▨ Smart Scan and Cell Offloading—Off	135	0	222	1260	147
▨ Smart Scan and Cell Offloading—On	131	0	1	3	20

Figure 4.4   Impact of Smart Scan and Cell Offloading—miscellaneous I/O statistics

improve, we find that Smart Scans almost completely eliminated sorts; specifically, in this case, Smart Scans eliminated 221 out of 222 sorts.

This example clearly shows how Exadata is able to go beyond just the raw performance capabilities of SSD and memory-based storage by intelligently using its awareness of the Oracle Database execution algorithms and I/O patterns.

We can extend these performance gains to the next level of extreme performance by adding other Oracle features like partitioning, Advanced Compression, and Hybrid Columnar Compression.

This unlocks the capabilities hitherto considered untenable and unrealistic to expect from an Oracle Database. Furthermore, Exadata delivers the promise of extreme performance at a relatively low TCO when compared with other solutions that are capable of delivering extreme performance at this level.

Storage Indexes

Storage Indexes are a new feature currently unique to Exadata. Unlike Smart Scans and Cell Offload processing, Storage Indexes are an intelligent storage implementation based on prior knowledge of the Oracle Database internals.

In some ways, the name "Storage Indexes" is actually a misnomer. Indexes by definition are designed to identify the location of a certain data key within the entire dataset. Storage Indexes are actually focused on eliminating areas on storage (blocks) as possible locations where the data might exist.

Oracle builds these metadata-based data maps online, and they are completely transparent to the database and application. These maps are stored on the Flash Cache. This is unlike storing regular indexes, which are stored on tablespaces. They are not persistent objects or part of the data dictionary.

At a fundamental level, the process of building this metadata is clean and simple. The solution's brilliance lies in the very fact of the simplicity of its approach and its seamless integration with the Oracle Database. Following are the salient points of the solution's design and implementation:

- Storage Indexes are constructed and maintained online as data transactions occur:
  - Storage Indexes are constructed as entire chunks of storage are read.
  - These Storage Indexes are transient in nature and are stored on the Flash Cache.
  - A Storage Index maintains statistics on up to eight columns.
  - The columns chosen are based on usage, distribution, and data characteristics.
- Storage Indexes are maintained at a storage region level:
  - Each region is approximately 1MB in size.
  - Three data elements are maintained at a column level: MIN Value, MAX Value, and NULL Exists.

When a query that is calling for a full table scan on an object is received by the Exadata Storage Server, it looks for the existence of a Storage Index based on the predicate column. The Exadata Storage Server scans through the Storage Index and identifies the regions where the predicate value falls within the MIN/MAX for the region. Physical I/O is then targeted at only the identified regions.

We can expand on this basic foundation and state the following:

- The smaller the set of storage regions identified as candidates, the more I/O saved.
- The more ordered and clustered the data for a column, the smaller the set of regions that will be identified.

The database parameters that impact Storage Indexes are listed in Table 4.3.

Listing 4.3 illustrates the workings of a Storage Index in a more practical manner.

Table 4.3   Database Initialization Parameters Impacting Storage Indexes*

Parameter	Default Value	Description
*Hidden database initialization parameters***		
`_kcfis_disable_platform_decryption`	FALSE	Disable platform-specific decryption on the Storage Cell
`_kcfis_storageidx_diag_mode`	0	Enable debug mode for Storage Index on the cell
`_kcfis_storageidx_disabled`	FALSE	Disable Storage Index optimization on the Storage Cell

*   The "_" parameters are listed here for educational and awareness reasons only. It is not recommended that you change any of the "_" parameters from their default values. Oracle's development team reviews these parameters with every release. Any modification to these "_" parameters must be done in conjunction with and at the request of Oracle Support.

**   There are no direct parameters available for DMAs or DBAs to use. This functionality is enabled at a system level.

Listing 4.3   Smart Scan Example Script

```
set timing on
spool stor-idx-example.log
set echo on

/* Flush the shared pool and buffer cache prior to each run */
alter system flush shared_pool;
alter system flush buffer_cache;

/* Disable storage indexes */
alter session set "_kcfis_storageidx_disabled"=TRUE;

set autot on
select /* NO_STORAGE_INDEX */ sum(object_id)/1000000 from my_dbaobjects
where unique_objid between 10000000 and 10001000;
set autot off;
set echo off;

/* Enable storage indexes */
alter session set "_kcfis_storageidx_disabled"=FALSE;
alter system flush buffer_cache;
select /* WITH_STORAGE_INDEX */ sum(object_id)/1000000 from my_dbaobjects
where unique_objid between 10000000 and 10001000;
```

Once again, let us execute the script and review the output. The script queries only on `unique_objid` this time, the data value derived from a sequence number generator.

First, let us look at the effect of Storage Indexes on pure query execution and elapsed times:

```
Elapsed Time (No STORAGE INDEX)
SQL> select /* NO_STORAGE_INDEX */sum(object_id)/1000000 from
my_dbaobjects where unique_objid between 10000000 and 10001000;

SUM(OBJECT_ID)/1000000
----------------------
            36.126654
Elapsed: 00:00:00.23

Elapsed Time (WITH STORAGE INDEX)
SQL> select /* WITH_STORAGE_INDEX */ sum(object_id)/1000000 from
my_dbaobjects where unique_objid between 10000000 and 10001000;

SUM(OBJECT_ID)/1000000
----------------------
            36.126654
Elapsed: 00:00:00.28
```

With Storage Indexes enabled, the same query completed in .28 seconds versus .23 seconds, a reduction of only 17% on total elapsed time. Keep in mind that Smart Scans are still enabled in both cases, and therefore related performance gains apply to both cases.

The query plan does not necessarily change when we enable or disable Storage Indexes, which is in line with our earlier statement that the use of Storage Indexes is an Exadata Storage Server decision made at runtime. What does change are some of the statistics of the SQL execution. In particular, using Storage Indexes eliminated sorts and reduced the recursive calls from 52 to 1:

```
Auto Trace Statistics (No STORAGE INDEX)
Statistics
-----------------------------------------------------------
        52  recursive calls
         1  db block gets
    296599  consistent gets
    296502  physical reads
     22356  redo size
       543  bytes sent via SQL*Net to client
       524  bytes received via SQL*Net from client
         2  SQL*Net roundtrips to/from client
        11  sorts (memory)
         0  sorts (disk)
         1  rows processed

Auto Trace Statistics (WITH STORAGE INDEX)
Statistics
-----------------------------------------------------------
         1  recursive calls
         1  db block gets
    296493  consistent gets
    296489  physical reads
     21680  redo size
       543  bytes sent via SQL*Net to client
       524  bytes received via SQL*Net from client
```

```
2  SQL*Net roundtrips to/from client
0  sorts (memory)
0  sorts (disk)
1  rows processed
```

Next, let us look at the session statistics shown in Figure 4.5 to see if we can shed further light on this matter.

This data tells us that

- Enabling or disabling did not impact Cell Offloading capabilities.
  - We can see from the statistic "cell physical I/O interconnect bytes returned by Smart Scan" that query offload worked exactly the same way.
  - The statistic "cell Flash Cache read hits" once again shows that the Flash Cache was used, just with fewer hits, as it needed fewer blocks with Storage Indexes enabled.
- Specifically, Storage Indexes saved 224MB of I/O. This is above and beyond the gains from Smart Scans.
- Use of Storage Indexes did save an additional 36.31% of I/O between the cells and the Compute Nodes (the value of cell physical I/O bytes between the two runs).

If we look at CPU and DB time, shown in Figure 4.6, we see the impact Storage Indexes have on the Compute Node. Keep in mind that in both the test cases, Smart Scan was enabled.

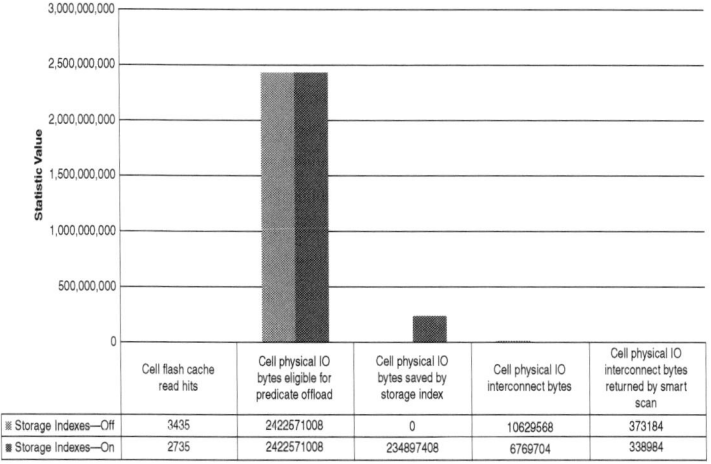

	Cell flash cache read hits	Cell physical IO bytes eligible for predicate offload	Cell physical IO bytes saved by storage index	Cell physical IO interconnect bytes	Cell physical IO interconnect bytes returned by smart scan
Storage Indexes—Off	3435	2422571008	0	10629568	373184
Storage Indexes—On	2735	2422571008	234897408	6769704	338984

Figure 4.5 Impact of Storage Indexes—key system statistics

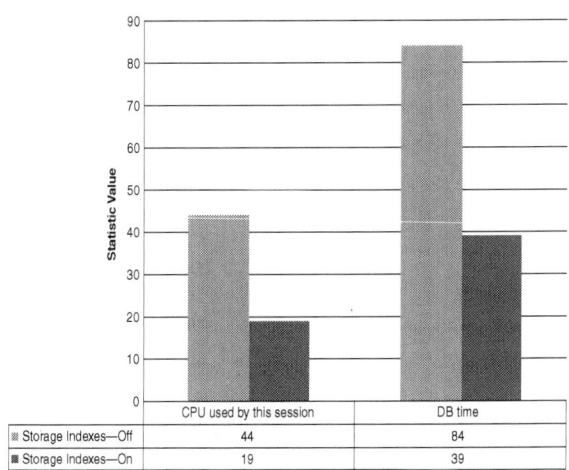

	CPU used by this session	DB time
▣ Storage Indexes—Off	44	84
▣ Storage Indexes—On	19	39

Figure 4.6   Impact of Storage Indexes—CPU and DB time

With the use of Storage Indexes over Smart Scan, we were able to reduce the overall CPU time and DB time above and beyond the savings from the use of Smart Scans and Cell Offloading:

- Session CPU time was reduced by an additional 56.82%.
- DB time was reduced by an additional 53.57%.

Figure 4.7 looks at the two sessions, but from the perspective of session wait event and wait time. Once again, keep in mind that Smart Scan is already enabled. What we see here is the incremental benefit of using Storage Indexes; we eliminated an additional 42.42% of the I/O-related wait time.

Looking at a few more database I/O system statistics, we can drill down into this further. As we can see in Figure 4.8, with the use of Storage Indexes:

- We see a 55% reduction in DB block gets.
- Sorting is almost completely eliminated.
- There is a 42% reduction in I/O wait time.

This clearly shows that Storage Indexes, when used properly, can provide efficiencies above and beyond those of just regular Cell Offloading.

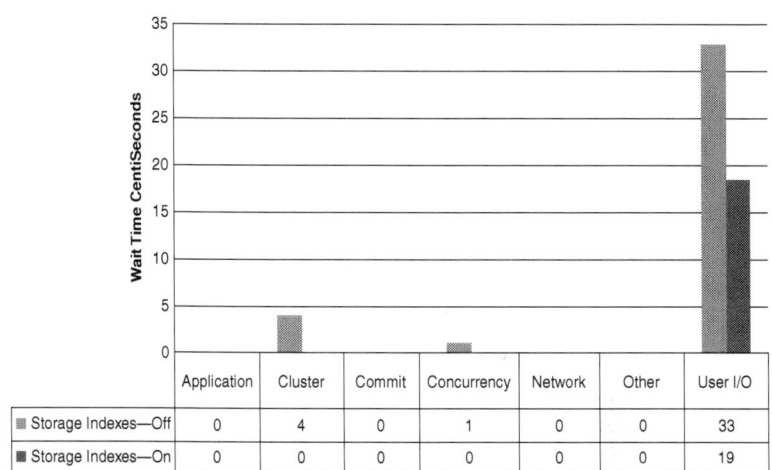

Figure 4.7 Impact of Storage Indexes—session wait time analysis

However, there is a very fundamental reason why the Storage Indexes proved so useful in this case. Consider the impact of sorting the data by a key during data load. This in turn would imply that the rows for a specific key are localized to a smaller region of the table in terms of physical storage. This implies that

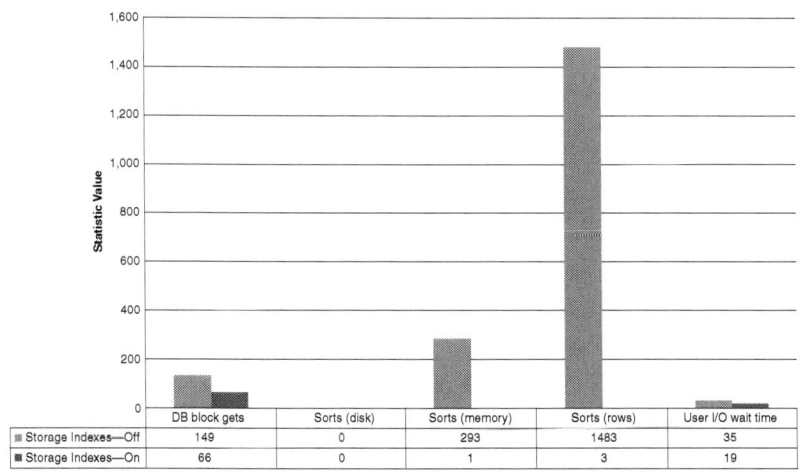

Figure 4.8 Impact of Storage Indexes—miscellaneous I/O statistics

a given key value would be found in fewer and more localized Storage Index regions. As a result, Storage Indexes using sorted data will prove to be more efficient at eliminating wasteful I/O when compared to using an unsorted key value for retrieval.

Compare the query we used for Storage Indexes with the query used earlier for Smart Scans. Keep the following points in mind when we compare the data between the two runs, shown in Figure 4.9:

- When we loaded the data, a sequence number generator was used to populate UNIQUE_OBJID.
- Since the data loaded using a key, the data was sorted by UNIQUE_OBJID for all intents and purposes.
- For both queries and test runs, Smart Scan and Storage Index capabilities were enabled.
- The OBJECT_ID column, on the other hand, is a repeated value and fairly well distributed across the entire table.
- In this example the query filtered on the column UNIQUE_OBJID.
- In the previous section, when we discussed Smart Scans, we queried the database by OBJECT_ID.

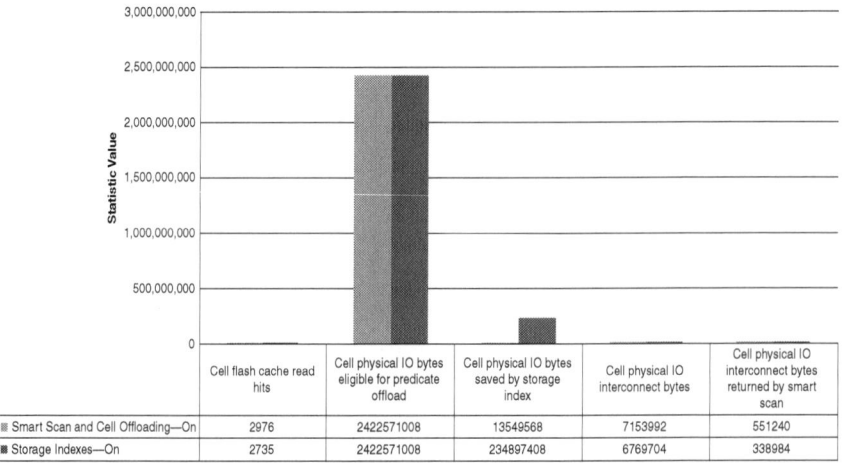

	Cell flash cache read hits	Cell physical IO bytes eligible for predicate offload	Cell physical IO bytes saved by storage index	Cell physical IO interconnect bytes	Cell physical IO interconnect bytes returned by smart scan
▥ Smart Scan and Cell Offloading—On	2976	2422571008	13549568	7153992	551240
▦ Storage Indexes—On	2735	2422571008	234897408	6769704	338984

Figure 4.9 Impact of data localization on Storage Indexes

We can quite clearly see that

- The number of bytes eligible for offloading is exactly the same.
- However, when we look at "cell physical I/O bytes saved by Storage Index," we find that for the query by UNIQUE_OBJID we saved almost 17 times more I/O (12.9MB versus 224MB).
- As a result, we see that the UNIQUE_OBJID query was slightly more efficient in terms of bytes shipped between cells and the Compute Nodes, a 5% improvement.

Understand that these numbers will change from query to query based on the data spread, data load nature, and so on. However, the core concepts will still apply, and when used appropriately, Storage Indexes can prove to be extremely efficient, especially in DW and DSS environments.

Caching Data in the Flash Cache

Another potential use of the Flash Cache is as an additional data caching area outside of the database SGA. With Exadata, an additional available feature is to force data objects to be cached in the Flash Cache. In other words, the data objects are cached on the PCIe Flash cards on the Exadata Storage Cells. This can be defined at an individual object level (tables, indexes, partitions, LOB segments, etc.). The syntax for defining or setting up object-level Flash Cache caching rules follows:

```
ALTER TABLE owner.object_name STORAGE (CELL_FLASH_CACHE cache-type)
```

The cache-type attribute defines the nature and algorithm to apply for caching object data in the Flash Cache:

- **DEFAULT**—The default cell Flash Caching algorithms are applied and controlled by the Exadata Storage Server.
- **NONE**—An object is never to be cached on the Flash Cache.
- **KEEP**—The object, once loaded, will remain in the Flash Cache.

When specifying the KEEP option for the object, each cell will cache its portion as requested. Over time, the data will be fully cached. Once an object is cached in the Flash Cache attribute of KEEP, it will not be aged out.

By design, the default behavior for sequential scans is to bypass the Flash Cache; this is not the case when KEEP is specified. If KEEP has been specified for an object, and it is accessed via an offloaded Smart Scan, the object is kept in and scanned from cache. Another advantage of the Flash Cache is that when an object that is kept in the cache is scanned, the Exadata software will simultaneously read the data from both Flash and disk to get a higher aggregate scan rate than is possible from either source independently.

Listing 4.4 illustrates the workings of cell Flash Cache in a more practical manner. The script will have three runs, the first run with no specific configuration for cell Flash Cache enabled. After the first run, we will enable cell Flash Cache at KEEP. For the second run we will prime the Flash Cache, and we will see the actual benefits in the third run.

Listing 4.4   Cell Flash Cache Example Script

```
set timing on
spool cfckeep-example.log
set echo on

/* Flush the buffer cache prior to each run */
alter system flush buffer_cache;
select /* NO_KEEP */sum(object_id)/1000000 from my_dbaobjects;

/* Flush the buffer cache, enable flash cache keep and rerun the query
a second time*/
alter system flush buffer_cache;
alter table my_dbaobjects storage (cell_flash_cache keep);
select /* RUN1_KEEP */ sum(object_id)/1000000 from my_dbaobjects;

/* Flush the buffer cache, enable flash cache keep and rerun the query
a third time*/
alter system flush buffer_cache;
select /* RUN2_KEEP */ sum(object_id)/1000000 from my_dbaobjects;
```

First, let us look at the effect of cell Flash Cache Keep on pure query execution and elapsed times. Keep in mind that we have enabled both Smart Scans as well as Storage Indexes.

```
Elapsed Time (Cell Flash Cache -default value)
SQL> select /* NO_KEEP */sum(object_id)/1000000 from my_dbaobjects;
SUM(OBJECT_ID)/1000000
----------------------
          1364497.24

Elapsed: 00:00:02.43
Elapsed Time (Cell Flash Cache - Keep - Run 1)
SQL> select /* RUN1_KEEP */ sum(object_id)/1000000 from my_dbaobjects;

SUM(OBJECT_ID)/1000000
----------------------
          1364497.24

Elapsed: 00:00:02.60
Elapsed Time (Cell Flash Cache - Keep - Run 2)
SQL> select /* RUN2_KEEP */ sum(object_id)/1000000 from my_dbaobjects;
```

```
SUM(OBJECT_ID)/1000000
----------------------
          1364497.24
Elapsed: 00:00:01.96
```

- The first run with CELL_FLASH_CACHE set to DEFAULT uses all the default settings.

- The second run with CELL_FLASH_CACHE set to KEEP took just a little longer, 7% to be exact. The overhead is due to necessary actions for warming and priming the cell Flash Cache.

- By the time we run this for the third time, the table has been cached in the cell Flash Cache and we see a reduction of almost 20% in elapsed time when compared to the original.

When we look at the execution plans, we do not really find any difference in the plan per se. If we look at the system statistics, shown in Figure 4.10, we find that the number of hits from the cell Flash Cache increased by a factor of 3 once the data was fully cached in the Flash Cache.

However, the same query run in the section for Smart Scans shows us the positive impact of Cell Offload and Storage Indexes. When we enabled the use of cell Flash Cache Keep, however, we find that Storage Indexes were not being used anymore. This would lead us to believe that using cell Flash Cache Keep can potentially impact the Storage Server's decision on whether or not Storage Indexes will be maintained and used.

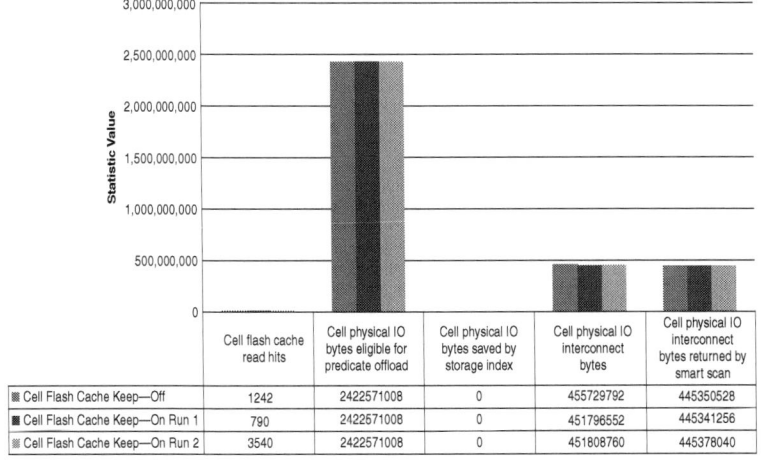

	Cell flash cache read hits	Cell physical IO bytes eligible for predicate offload	Cell physical IO bytes saved by storage index	Cell physical IO interconnect bytes	Cell physical IO interconnect bytes returned by smart scan
Cell Flash Cache Keep—Off	1242	2422571008	0	455729792	445350528
Cell Flash Cache Keep—On Run 1	790	2422571008	0	451796552	445341256
Cell Flash Cache Keep—On Run 2	3540	2422571008	0	451808760	445378040

Figure 4.10   Impact of Cell Flash Cache Keep—key system statistics

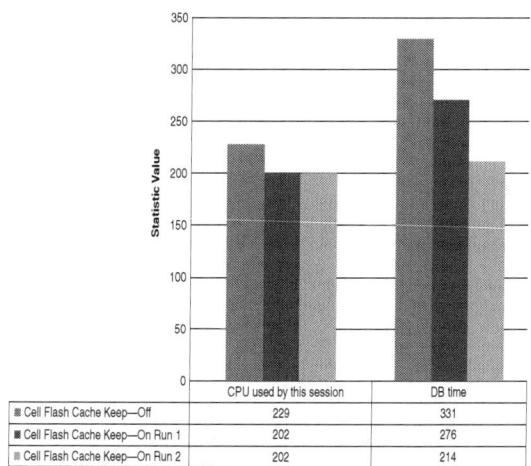

	CPU used by this session	DB time
▨ Cell Flash Cache Keep—Off	229	331
▨ Cell Flash Cache Keep—On Run 1	202	276
▨ Cell Flash Cache Keep—On Run 2	202	214

Figure 4.11   Impact of Cell Flash Cache Keep—CPU and DB time

Once again, looking at this from a database resource viewpoint, we can compare the CPU and DB time, as shown in Figure 4.11:

- The CPU time for the session was reduced by 11%.
- We see a more significant improvement when we look at this from a DB time viewpoint, with an improvement of almost 35%.

Let us next look at the session wait event (see Figure 4.12). As expected:

- Between the runs with the default setting and the first run after we enabled Flash Cache Keep, we find the user I/O wait time did not change significantly.
- However, once enable and the data was actually cached, the user I/O wait time dropped 84% when comparing Flash Cache Keep and Flash Cache enabled.

Looking at a few more database I/O system statistics, shown in Figure 4.13, we can drill down into this further. As we can see, with the use of Storage Indexes:

- There is a 70% reduction in DB block gets.
- Sorting is almost completely eliminated.
- There is an 85% reduction in user I/O wait time.

This clearly shows that once primed, cell Flash Cache can provide significant bene-fits and efficiencies, when used properly.

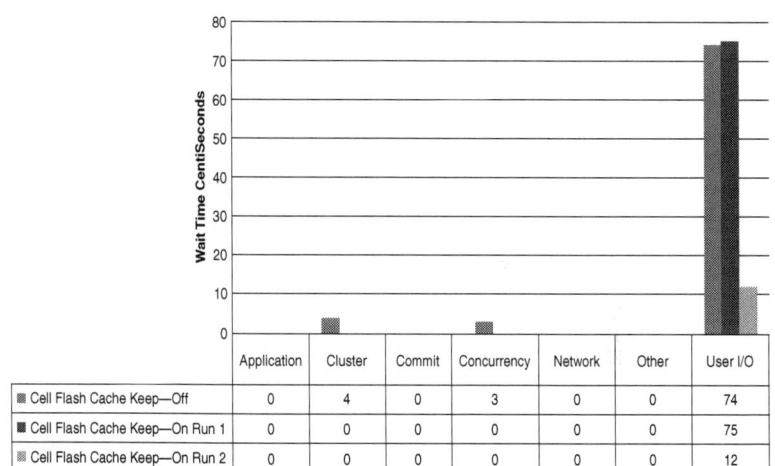

	Application	Cluster	Commit	Concurrency	Network	Other	User I/O
Cell Flash Cache Keep—Off	0	4	0	3	0	0	74
Cell Flash Cache Keep—On Run 1	0	0	0	0	0	0	75
Cell Flash Cache Keep—On Run 2	0	0	0	0	0	0	12

Figure 4.12   Impact of cell Flash Cache Keep—session wait time analysis

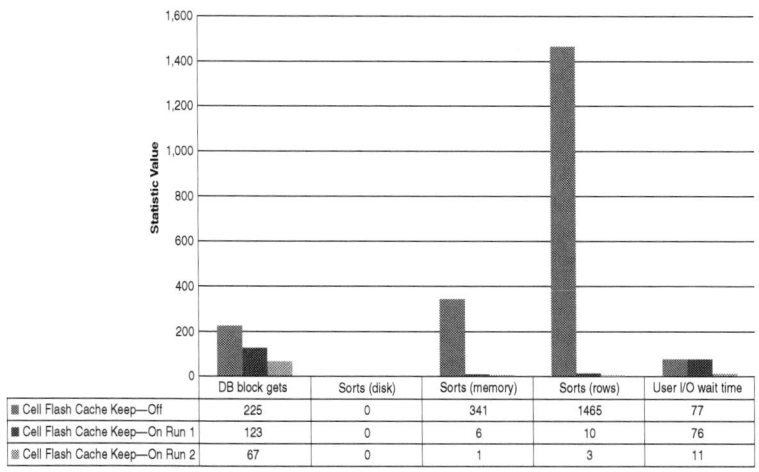

	DB block gets	Sorts (disk)	Sorts (memory)	Sorts (rows)	User I/O wait time
Cell Flash Cache Keep—Off	225	0	341	1465	77
Cell Flash Cache Keep—On Run 1	123	0	6	10	76
Cell Flash Cache Keep—On Run 2	67	0	1	3	11

Figure 4.13   Impact of cell Flash Cache Keep—miscellaneous I/O statistics

Summary

With the Exadata Database Machine, Oracle has successfully developed a system with a combination of hardware and software that has knowledge of Oracle internals.

In this chapter, we talked about how Oracle has incorporated SSD/Flash technology into the hardware and at the same time seamlessly integrated it with the inner workings of the database.

We saw how to view, measure, and understand the impact of the Flash Cache technology on the day-to-day operations of the database.

Exadata in general, and the Flash Cache specifically, is not the panacea of all performance and capacity-planning issues. Flash Cache provides us with yet another tool when it comes to performance tuning. When it is combined with knowledge of our application, we can ensure that we are getting the most out of Exadata. When used in conjunction with other features like compression, partitioning, parallelism, and so on, the possibilities are even greater.

## 5

Exadata Compression: HCC Demystified

With his first paper in 1969, Edgar F. Codd, while working at IBM's San Jose Research Center, launched the field of relational databases.[1] Based on his research, Codd created the first relational database management system (RDBMS) called SYSTEM-R. Until this point in time, most information-storing systems were based on tree structured files. He is rightly considered the father of relational databases. Oracle started off as and is still at the core of a relational database, so the constructs that Codd defined and laid out still apply to this day.

At the core, Codd said, "R is a relation on these n sets if it is a set of n-tuples each of which has its first element from S_1, its second element from S_2, and so on. . . . Each row represents an n-tuple of R. . . . The totality of data in a data bank may be viewed as a collection of time-varying relations. These relations are of assorted degrees. As time progresses, each n-ary relation may be subject to insertion of additional n-tuples, deletion of existing ones, and alteration of components of any of its existing n-tuples."

In other words, each table is a representation of the relation R and each row is a representation of an n-tuple. Oracle extended this definition to how the database was physically stored as well—that is, until the introduction of Hybrid Columnar Compression (HCC or EHCC) with Exadata V2. This chapter focuses on helping you understand Oracle's implementation of HCC.

---

1. See Edgar Codd's original 1970 paper, "A Relational Model of Data for Large Shared Data Banks," in *Communications of the ACM* 13, no. 6 (June 1970). It is available online at www.seas.upenn.edu/~zives/03f/cis550/codd.pdf.

Columnar Storage Models

Traditionally, relational databases use what is called an N-ary Storage Model (NSM). NSM stores records contiguously in their entirety and uses offsets to identify the start of each record (or row). Figure 5.1 shows an example.

The alternative to this approach is the Decomposition Storage Model (DSM), which was introduced in 1985 by George Copeland and Setrag Khoshafian.[2] In this approach, each attribute is stored individually as a set of relations or a key-value pair. The key is used to join the individual attribute relations to construct a row, as shown in Figure 5.2.

When we look at the two models from a **data access** point of view, we find that within DSM, each entry is binary in nature, with one value per surrogate. Therefore, the indexing options and combinations are really limited to either the ID or the value. When compared to NSM, the number of indexing options depends upon the access paths, and there could be multiple indexes with differing columns, orders of columns, and so on.

When we look at it from a **storage space** point of view, we find that clearly there is a certain amount of storage being wasted as the surrogate key is repeated for each attribute. However, it is not necessary for every attribute to have a value for a

ID	Column 1	Column 2	Column 3	Column 4
1	R1V1	R1V2	R1V3	R1V4
2	R2V1	R2V2	R2V3	R2V4
3	R3V1	R3V2	R3V3	R3V4
4	R4V1	R4V2	R4V3	R4V4

Figure 5.1 Traditional *n*-ary storage model

ID	Column 1
1	R1V1
2	R2V1
3	R3V1
4	R4V1

ID	Column 2
1	R1V2
2	R2V2
3	R3V2
4	R4V2

ID	Column 3
1	R1V3
2	R2V3
3	R3V3
4	R4V3

ID	Column 4
1	R1V4
2	R2V4
3	R3V4
4	R4V4

Figure 5.2 Example of relational data decomposed to a key-value pair

2. The link to the paper by Copeland and Khoshafian: "A Decomposition Storage Model," www3.in.tum.de/teaching/ws0506/MMDBMS/download/decomposition-storage-model.pdf.

given surrogate key or ID. The data type and data size of the surrogate key column are what will define the actual space consumption.

Now when we look at it from an **index storage** point of view, we see that DSM generally tends to provide significant savings as there are not really too many ways to index a key-value pair. Using various indexing techniques such as clustering or inverted B-tree, the storage savings can be reduced even further.

As a base expectation, in most cases Copeland and Khoshafian estimated that DSM would increase data storage space by a factor of between 1 and 4 and reduce the index storage space by a factor of 1 to 2.

Some of the other considerations that go into a DSM model include data manipulation language (DML) performance and query performance.

In DSM, modifying a single attribute of a single surrogate or ID requires three writes: one to the data store itself, one to the index on the surrogate, and one to the index on the attribute.

With the NSM model, there is one write to the actual data block and additional writes to the indexes being maintained on that given attribute.

When we extend these updates to cover multiple IDs for a given attribute, the DSM model provides efficiencies due to the fact that in a block of storage, we can store a much larger number of key-value pairs as compared to rows per block. Therefore, each individual ID update is a memory operation with a single write-back to save multiple writes.

NSM, on the other hand, requires a much larger number of blocks that need to be touched and therefore be written down.

When it comes to query performance, the key is the number of filter attributes and the number of display attributes.

The common IDs across all the individual filters define the actual row IDs. The row IDs are then used to access the remaining key-value pairs to get the attributes required to display all the results.

In the DSM model, the universe of IDs that meet the filter criterion is the intersection point of all the individual sets of IDs determined by applying the appropriate filter against the attributes in each key-value pair. Those IDs are then used to access the display attributes from the remaining key-value pairs in the decomposed storage to retrieve the data and build or "stitch" the row together for display.

In the NSM model, the access path is defined by the indexing strategy, but once a row has been identified, filtering on the remainder of the filter attributes and retrieving the data for the display attributes are done inline.

The amount of comparative I/O really depends on the number of filter attributes, the number of display attributes, and the dataset size. Furthermore, in the DSM model, parallelism is applied or achieved across attribute stores, whereas in the NSM model, parallelism is achieved across datasets.

Another important aspect to consider in the DSM versus NSM design debate is the structure of the memory cache. Should the memory cache be maintained at an attribute store level or should it be maintained at a row level?

As a result of these distinct pros and cons of NSM and DSM, hybrid approaches have tended to be successful. In the following sections we discuss some of those being used in systems today.

The PAX Model

PAX, which stands for Partition Attributes Across, was first introduced by Anastassia Ailamaki from Carnegie Mellon University and David DeWitt, Mark Hill, and Marios Skounakis from the University of Wisconsin–Madison in 2001.[3]

The key difference between PAX and the classic DSM model is in the physical storage of the attribute key-value pair. In PAX, all the data for a given set of rows is maintained and retained locally for a given block. In other words, instead of storing multiple rows of data row by row within a block, the same data is stored for the rows within a block, but it is stored column by column.

This is a hybrid model, storing data via a column but at the granularity of a data block. This eliminates the overhead of extra I/O for row stitching, while providing the benefits of a column store.

Fractured Mirrors

The idea of Fractured Mirrors was published in 2002 in the VLDB paper "A Case for Fractured Mirrors" by Ravi Ramamurthy, David DeWitt, and Qi Su.[4] The fundamental assumption of this approach is that most organizations will replicate their data for HA or disaster recovery (DR) purposes. Why not have different storage models for each replica? Based upon the query and its characteristics, it can be redirected to the appropriate data store.

Obviously, there needs to be a translation or synchronization layer that is capable of intelligently deciding where and how to redirect requests, keeping the two data stores in sync, with the ability to translate between the two different formats.

Fine-Grained Hybrids

In fine-grained hybrid approaches, individual tables are stored in a mixed row and column format. Columns that are accessed as a group are stored in NSM format, while the other column data is stored using the DSM principle. Further, at a

---

3. Anastassia Ailamaki, David J. DeWitt, Mark D. Hill, and Marios Skounakis, "Weaving Relations for Cache Performance," www.vldb.org/conf/2001/P169.pdf.
4. Ravishankar Ramamurthy, David J. DeWitt, and Qi Su, "A Case for Fractured Mirrors," www .vldb.org/conf/2002/S12P03.pdf.

physical level, this can be implemented at the granularity of a disk block, within a table, across tables, and so on.

In such an approach, the decision of whether to go with rows or columns for an attribute drives the success of the implementation. The decision about whether to use row or column storage format is based on implementation-specific knowledge of data access, data relationships, and query workload.

Oracle Implementation of DSM—Hybrid Columnar Compression

The design and implementation of Oracle Hybrid Columnar Compression (HCC) are based on the PAX model, with the additional twist of including compression. In HCC, Oracle uses compression to increase the amount of data or the number of rows that can be stored within a given block.

Compression within Oracle Databases

Before going further, it would be prudent to visit Oracle's implementation of compression within the context of the database. Fundamentally speaking, there are two ways to achieve compression.

The first approach is based on values being stored. This approach is also called **tokenization**. What tokenization effectively does is replace every value in a column that is repeated with a token. The token-to-value matrix is stored elsewhere and is used to perform the translation during runtime.

The second approach is based on using a standard compression algorithm such as BZIP or LZIP to actually compress the data, based on bit strings being stored.

The Concepts of HCC

As we said earlier, Oracle HCC is an extension of the PAX model in that data is stored in row format as well as columnar format, hence the inclusion of the word *hybrid* in the name of the technology. Additionally, Oracle has added bitwise compression to be able to store more data within a given block.

An extremely good source of information about how Oracle actually implements HCC is their patent filing papers: Patent Number US 8,583,692 B2, patented on November 12, 2013. There are also numerous posts, documents, and books out there that dive deeper into the internals. The salient points of the implementation are as follows:

- HCC partitioning is applied at a segment level. Therefore it can apply at a table level, partition level, or even a sub-partition level.

- HCC works at what is called a compression unit (CU). A CU spans multiple physical database blocks, primarily to take advantage of large I/Os to retrieve a full CU at a time.

- From an organizational point of view, a CU logically has two sections:

  - An **uncompressed** section that stores metadata about the CU, such as where one column ends and another begins, the type of compression, and so on

  - A **compressed** section where the actual data is maintained

- Oracle's HCC can be implemented in one of two types:

  - **Warehouse compression**, or **COMPRESS FOR QUERY**, is optimized to save storage space and intended for data warehouse applications.

  - **Online archival**, or **COMPRESS FOR ARCHIVE**, is optimized for maximum compression levels and intended for use with Information Lifecycle Management (ILM) and historical data and data that does not change.

- Within each compression type, we can further specify a compression level (LOW or HIGH), which defines the compression algorithm that will be used.

We will use a simple example to demonstrate some of the key aspects of HCC. The sample code to generate the test case in this example is provided in Listing 5.1.

Listing 5.1   SQL Code to Construct and Load an Example Table with Data

```
CREATE SEQUENCE MYSEQUENCE START WITH 1 INCREMENT BY 1 CACHE 100;

CREATE TABLE MY_DBAOBJECTS AS
SELECT MYSEQUENCE.NEXTVAL UNIQUE_OBJID, A.OBJECT_ID, A.DATA_OBJECT_ID,
       A.OWNER, A.OBJECT_NAME, A.SUBOBJECT_NAME, OBJECT_TYPE
FROM DBA_OBJECTS A;

DESC MY_DBAOBJECTS ;

-- DATA POPULATION, EXECUTE THIS MULTIPLE TIMES:
DECLARE
  I PLS_INTEGER := 0;
BEGIN
  FOR I IN 1 .. 50
LOOP
INSERT INTO MY_DBAOBJECTS
SELECT MYSEQUENCE.NEXTVAL UNIQUE_OBJID, A.OBJECT_ID, A.DATA_OBJECT_ID,
       A.OWNER, A.OBJECT_NAME, A.SUBOBJECT_NAME, OBJECT_TYPE
FROM DBA_OBJECTS A;
COMMIT;
END LOOP;
END;
/
```

The following SQL code creates the same table using OLTP compression:

```
CREATE TABLE MY_DBAOBJECTS_OLTP_COMP (
    UNIQUE_OBJID CONSTRAINT MY_DBAOBJECTS_OLTP_COMP_PK PRIMARY KEY,
    OBJECT_ID, DATA_OBJECT_ID,OWNER, OBJECT_NAME, SUBOBJECT_NAME, OBJECT_TYPE)
COMPRESS FOR OLTP AS
SELECT * FROM MY_DBAOBJECTS;
```

The SQL code to create the same table using HCC with QUERY LOW compression follows:

```
CREATE TABLE MY_DBAOBJECTS_QUERY_LOW (
    UNIQUE_OBJID CONSTRAINT MY_DBAOBJECTS_QUERY_LOW_PK PRIMARY KEY,
    OBJECT_ID, DATA_OBJECT_ID,OWNER, OBJECT_NAME, SUBOBJECT_NAME, OBJECT_TYPE)
COMPRESS FOR QUERY LOW AS
SELECT * FROM MY_DBAOBJECTS ;
```

The SQL code to create the same table using HCC with QUERY HIGH compression follows:

```
CREATE TABLE MY_DBAOBJECTS_QUERY_HIGH (
    UNIQUE_OBJID CONSTRAINT MY_DBAOBJECTS_QUERY_HIGH_PK PRIMARY KEY,
    OBJECT_ID, DATA_OBJECT_ID,OWNER, OBJECT_NAME, SUBOBJECT_NAME, OBJECT_TYPE)
COMPRESS FOR QUERY HIGH AS
SELECT * FROM MY_DBAOBJECTS ;
```

The SQL code to create the same table using HCC with ARCHIVE LOW compression follows:

```
CREATE TABLE MY_DBAOBJECTS_ARCHIVE_LOW (
    UNIQUE_OBJID CONSTRAINT MY_DBAOBJECTS_ARCHIVE_LOW_PK PRIMARY KEY,
    OBJECT_ID, DATA_OBJECT_ID,OWNER, OBJECT_NAME, SUBOBJECT_NAME, OBJECT_TYPE)
COMPRESS FOR ARCHIVE LOW AS
SELECT * FROM MY_DBAOBJECTS ;
```

And the following SQL code creates the same table using HCC with ARCHIVE HIGH compression:

```
CREATE TABLE MY_DBAOBJECTS_ARCHIVE_HIGH (
    UNIQUE_OBJID CONSTRAINT MY_DBAOBJECTS_ARCHIVE_HIGH_PK PRIMARY KEY,
    OBJECT_ID, DATA_OBJECT_ID,OWNER, OBJECT_NAME, SUBOBJECT_NAME, OBJECT_TYPE)
COMPRESS FOR ARCHIVE HIGH AS
SELECT * FROM MY_DBAOBJECTS ;
```

Compression Ratios

As we can see from the queries used to build the tables, the only change made was in the compression clause used when creating the tables. Each table contained

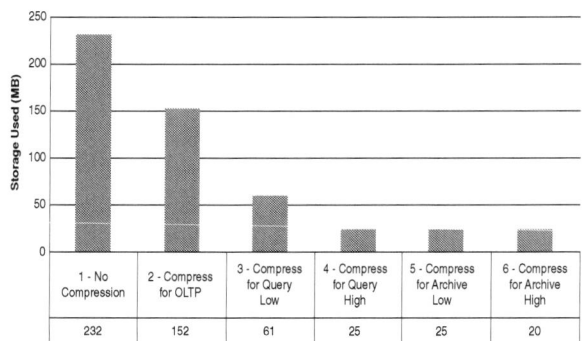

Figure 5.3   Compression ratios by compression type

Table 5.1   Compression Ratios by Compression Type

Compression Type	Size (MB)	Savings (%)	Ratio
Uncompressed	232	0.0%	1.0
OLTP compression	152	34.5%	1.5
HCC QUERY LOW	61	73.7%	3.8
HCC QUERY HIGH	25	89.2%	9.3
HCC ARCHIVE LOW	25	89.2%	9.3
HCC ARCHIVE HIGH	20	91.4%	11.6

3,691,125 rows. Each of these tables had a primary key on it, the size of which did not change with the compression type used, for obvious reasons.

Keep in mind that the exact compression ratio depends a lot upon the data and how compression friendly the data is. In our case, we used DBA_OBJECTS as the basis, and the data is text and numbers. For this reason we see extremely high compression ratios. The actual results are shown in Figure 5.3 and Table 5.1.

There are a couple of points of note here:

The compression ratio seen from QUERY HIGH and ARCHIVE LOW is comparable; in our case, it's exactly the same. The reason is the type of compression algorithm used:

- QUERY LOW uses the LZO algorithm for compression.
- Both QUERY HIGH and ARCHIVE LOW use the ZLIB algorithm for compression.

- ARCHIVE HIGH uses the BZIP2 algorithm for compression.
- The LZO algorithm provides the least compression but is most efficient with respect to CPU.
- The BZIP2 algorithm provides the highest levels of compression but is also more CPU intensive.
- The ZLIB algorithm is a compromise between the BZIP2 and LZO compression algorithms.
  - In terms of CPU usage, ZLIB uses more CPU than LZO, but less than BZP2.
  - In terms of compression ratios, ZLIB has higher compression ratios compared to LZO but lower compression ratios compared to BZIP2.

Compression Types and Compression Units

Figure 5.4 is a logical representation of a CU. The image does not specifically show block headers and so on, but they are maintained for each block. The initial piece of CU is a header that maintains the metadata associated with its contents. Among others, it contains the starting point of each column within the CU.

A given column's data can span several blocks, and for that reason the CU header is structured similarly to chained rows within regular tables, with a pointer to the top of each column. Therefore, ROWID for an HCC organized table must refer to the CU and not the block itself.

For normal tables, ROWID consists of the following:

- File number or relative file number
- Block number
- Row number

In the case of HCC, the file number and block number actually relate to the CU itself. We can use DBMS_ROWID.RELATIVE_FNO_NUMBER and DBMS_ROWID.ROWID_BLOCK_NUMBER to see how many rows are in each CU, an example of which can be seen in the query below.

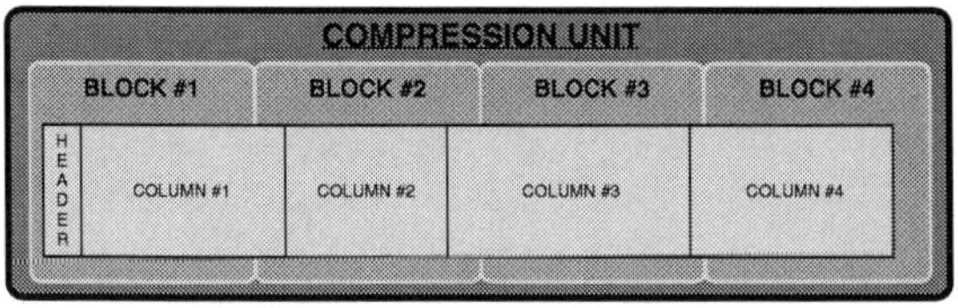

Figure 5.4 Logical structure of a compression unit under HCC

To see how many blocks were actually in use, not just allocated, we used the Oracle-provided PL/SQL package DBMS_SPACE.UNUSED_SPACE.

```
SELECT COUNT(*) FROM (
SELECT DISTINCT DBMS_ROWID.ROWID_RELATIVE_FNO(ROWID),
DBMS_ROWID.ROWID_BLOCK_NUMBER(ROWID) FROM TABLE_NAME);
```

Table 5.2 combines the results of the query to identify rows per CU, alongside physical space usage.

Figure 5.5 is a graphical representation of the data rows per CU by compression type.

Figure 5.6 is a graphical representation of the blocks per CU by compression type.

We can clearly see that the number of rows packed into each CU increases as we go from QUERY LOW to ARCHIVE HIGH. Second, the storage space per CU also increases as we go from QUERY LOW to ARCHIVE HIGH. However, between the

Table 5.2   CU Usage Statistics by Compression Type

HCC Type	# of CU	Blocks Used	Rows/CU	Blocks/CU
HCC ARCHIVE HIGH	126	2413	29294.6	19.15
HCC ARCHIVE LOW	656	3074	5626.7	4.69
HCC QUERY HIGH	824	3094	4479.5	3.75
HCC QUERY LOW	1926	7506	1916.5	3.90

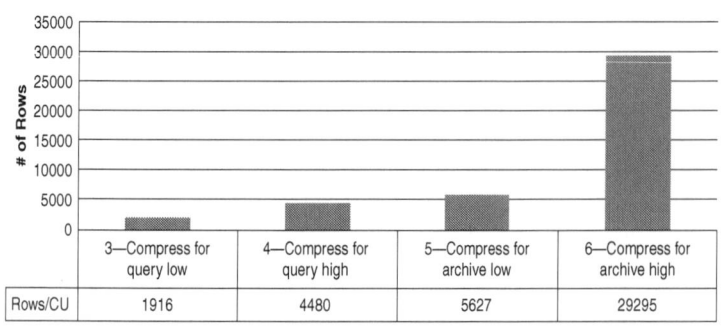

Figure 5.5   Rows per CU by HCC type

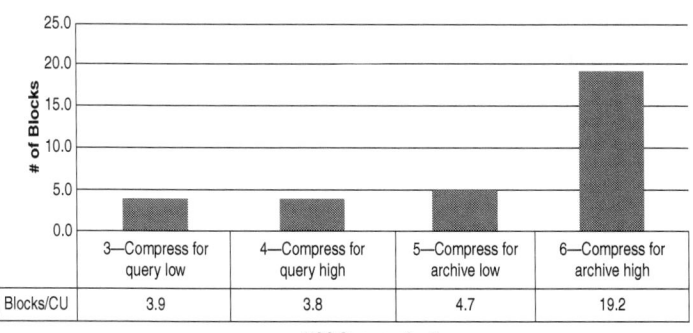

Figure 5.6   Blocks per CU by HCC type

two, the density of a CU (rows per CU) rises at a much steeper gradient than the space usage of a CU (blocks per CU). For this reason, the compression efficiency improves at each level as we go from QUERY LOW to ARCHIVE HIGH.

Note

Testing done by various experts has shown that for Warehouse compression the maximum number of blocks per CU is four, and for Archive compression the number of blocks per CU can go as high as 32. The number of rows per CU seems to hit a limit of 32,000.

HCC and Performance

In order to understand the precise impact HCC would have on performance, we need to look at read versus write I/O as well as large versus small I/O. In this section, we will test and evaluate the impact based upon the following scenarios:

- Large block writes such as during data bulk load operations
- Large block reads such as during a full table scan
- Single block read such as during data access via the primary key (PK)

Using the same example, we can compare the CPU utilization for these operations. It is important to note that these are not absolute numbers; rather they are indicative of what one can expect. The actual performance numbers will vary based upon the compressibility of the data and the nature of the data.

Bulk Load Operations

An important point to keep in mind with respect to HCC data compression for data inserts and loads is that it only occurs during operations that support DIRECT PATH WRITE operations such as INSERT APPENDS or direct load or CREATE TABLE AS SELECT.

The data was loaded using a CREATE TABLE AS SELECT statement, an example of which follows:

```
CREATE TABLE MY_DBAOBJECTS_QUERY_LOW (
    UNIQUE_OBJID CONSTRAINT MY_DBAOBJECTS_QUERY_LOW_PK PRIMARY KEY,
    OBJECT_ID, DATA_OBJECT_ID,OWNER, OBJECT_NAME, SUBOBJECT_NAME, OBJECT_TYPE)
COMPRESS FOR QUERY LOW AS
SELECT * FROM MY_DBAOBJECTS ;
```

Figures 5.7 through 5.9 show the relative CPU load, I/O load, and execution time for the data-loading table creation scripts. At first glance these graphs seem to contradict each other.

For execution time, shown in Figure 5.7, results are as expected:

- HCC ARCHIVE HIGH took the most time and QUERY LOW took the least.
- COMPRESS FOR OLTP was the second worst, but a significant improvement from ARCHIVE HIGH.
- The results for the remaining were fairly closely bunched together and in the expected order.
- QUERY HIGH and ARCHIVE LOW took about the same time, since they use the same compression algorithm.

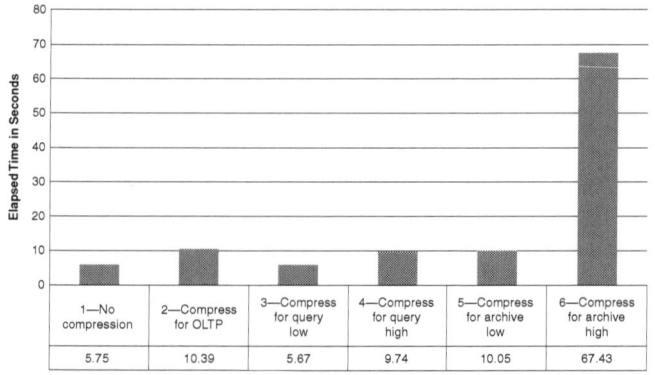

	1—No compression	2—Compress for OLTP	3—Compress for query low	4—Compress for query high	5—Compress for archive low	6—Compress for archive high
	5.75	10.39	5.67	9.74	10.05	67.43

Figure 5.7   Bulk load operations performance—elapsed time by HCC type

From an I/O perspective, shown in Figure 5.8, the results are as expected:

- No compression had the most I/O and ARCHIVE HIGH had the least.
- OLTP compression performed less I/O than no compression.
- OLTP compression performed more I/O when compared to any form of HCC.
- QUERY HIGH and ARCHIVE LOW, once again, were very close to each other in terms of the amount of I/O performed.

But from a CPU load perspective, shown in Figure 5.9, the results are unexpected:

- OLTP compression was the worst option.
- No compression had about the same CPU load as any other HCC compression.

If we look at the data from a wait time perspective, shown in Table 5.3, we find that these numbers are more aligned with what we see in the DB load graph. So why is this?

What is happening here is that the HCC compression-related work is being off-loaded completely to the cell, and therefore the database times are low. This is not the case for OLTP compression.

Figure 5.10 looks at some of the HCC-related statistics that the database gathers and shows the number of CUs involved in each operation. Notice how similar these numbers are to what we computed as the number of CUs earlier.

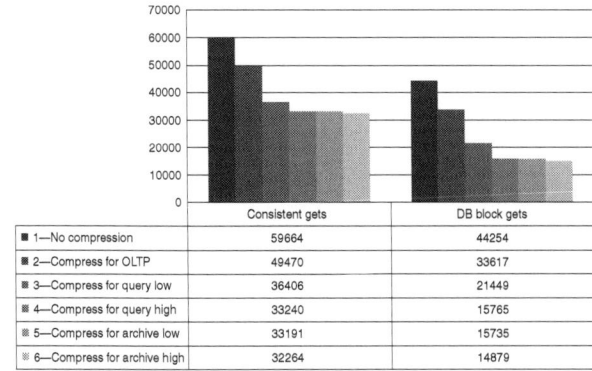

	Consistent gets	DB block gets
■ 1—No compression	59664	44254
■ 2—Compress for OLTP	49470	33617
▨ 3—Compress for query low	36406	21449
▨ 4—Compress for query high	33240	15765
▨ 5—Compress for archive low	33191	15735
▨ 6—Compress for archive high	32264	14879

Figure 5.8   Bulk load operations performance—I/O load by HCC type

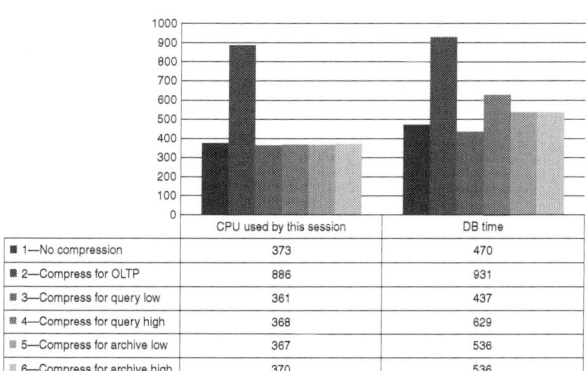

	CPU used by this session	DB time
■ 1—No compression	373	470
▨ 2—Compress for OLTP	886	931
▨ 3—Compress for query low	361	437
▨ 4—Compress for query high	368	629
▨ 5—Compress for archive low	367	536
▨ 6—Compress for archive high	370	536

Figure 5.9   Bulk load operations performance—CPU and DB time by HCC type

Table 5.3   Bulk Load Operations Performance—Wait Time Analysis by HCC type

	Application Wait Time (Csec)	Cluster Wait Time (Csec)	Other Wait Time (Csec)	User I/O Wait Time (Csec)	Grand Total Wait Time (Csec)
1—No Compression	0	10	1	102	113
2—COMPRESS FOR OLTP	0	7	0	36	43
3—COMPRESS FOR QUERY LOW	0	3	1	19	23
4—COMPRESS FOR QUERY HIGH	0	2	0	14	17
5—COMPRESS FOR ARCHIVE LOW	0	1	1	5	7
6—COMPRESS FOR ARCHIVE HIGH	0	2	0	3	5

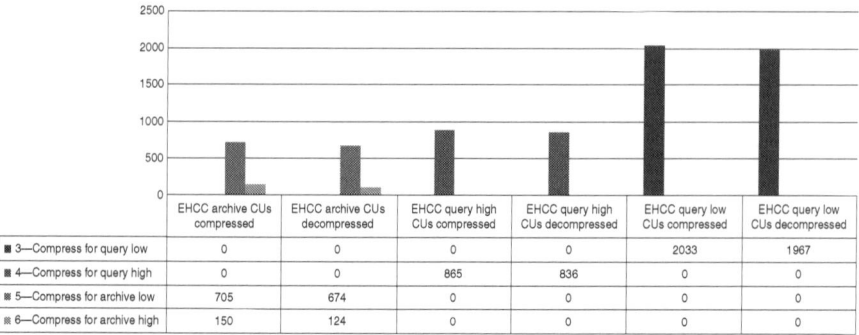

	EHCC archive CUs compressed	EHCC archive CUs decompressed	EHCC query high CUs compressed	EHCC query high CUs decompressed	EHCC query low CUs compressed	EHCC query low CUs decompressed
■ 3—Compress for query low	0	0	0	0	2033	1967
▨ 4—Compress for query high	0	0	865	836	0	0
▨ 5—Compress for archive low	705	674	0	0	0	0
▨ 6—Compress for archive high	150	124	0	0	0	0

Figure 5.10   Bulk load operations performance—key statistics by HCC type

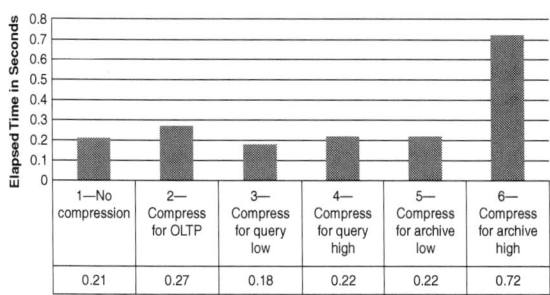

Figure 5.11   Bulk I/O operations performance—elapsed time by HCC type

Bulk Read I/O Operations

In this particular case, we use SQL that will force a full table scan. Following is an example of the specific SQL used. The reason we specify `COUNT(OBJECT_TYPE)` is to completely eliminate the possibility of using an index fast full scan.

```
SELECT COUNT(OBJECT_TYPE)
FROM MY_DBAOBJECTS_QUERY_HIGH ;
```

Figures 5.11 through 5.13 show the relative CPU load, I/O load, and execution time for a SQL operation involving a full table scan. These reflect behaviors similar to what we saw in the previous section.

Looking at execution time, shown in Figure 5.11, the results are once again not from very far from expectations:

- HCC ARCHIVE HIGH took the most time and QUERY LOW took the least.
- COMPRESS FOR OLTP was the second worst, but a significant improvement from ARCHIVE HIGH.
- The results for the remaining were fairly closely bunched together and in the expected order.
- QUERY HIGH and ARCHIVE LOW took about the same time, since they use the same compression algorithm.

From an I/O perspective, shown in Figure 5.12, we see these results:

- No compression performed the maximum amount of I/O. (Notice that full table scan was still fast since we took advantage of Cell Offloading and caching.)
- ARCHIVE HIGH had the least amount of I/O.

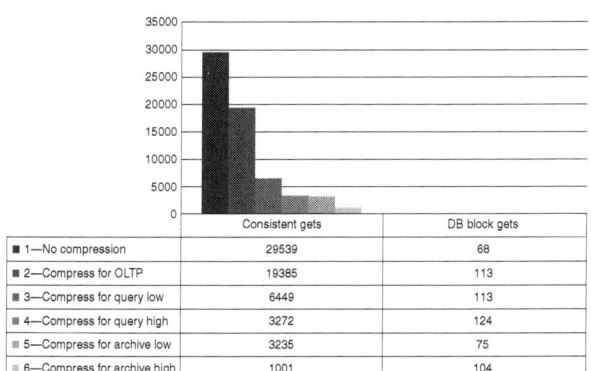

	Consistent gets	DB block gets
■ 1—No compression	29539	68
▩ 2—Compress for OLTP	19385	113
▩ 3—Compress for query low	6449	113
▩ 4—Compress for query high	3272	124
▩ 5—Compress for archive low	3235	75
▩ 6—Compress for archive high	1001	104

Figure 5.12   Bulk I/O operations performance—I/O load by HCC type

- OLTP compression performed more I/O when compared to any form of HCC.
- QUERY HIGH and ARCHIVE LOW, once again, were very close to each other in terms of the amount of I/O performed.

But from a database time/CPU time perspective, shown in Figure 5.13, we see the following unexpected results:

- ARCHIVE HIGH seems to be the most resource intensive.
- OLTP compression seems to be the second most resource intensive.
- All the remaining options seem to be in the same ballpark.

If we take a closer look at elapsed time, we see the following:

- The ratio for ARCHIVE HIGH is about 3.5 times longer than that for the other options.
- With CPU/DB time, however, the ratio is closer to 1.5 times longer.

When we looked at the numbers for event wait time, we saw that Oracle did not record any time as being waited; that's because time waited was too small to be recorded, perhaps smaller than a centisecond.

What this seems to suggest is that during read operations, ARCHIVE HIGH does require slightly more DB CPU but not in the same ratio as other options, and still most of the work of decompression is being done at the cell level.

Figure 5.14 once again just pulls some HCC-specific statistics, especially to see how many CUs were actually uncompressed during the read operation. As

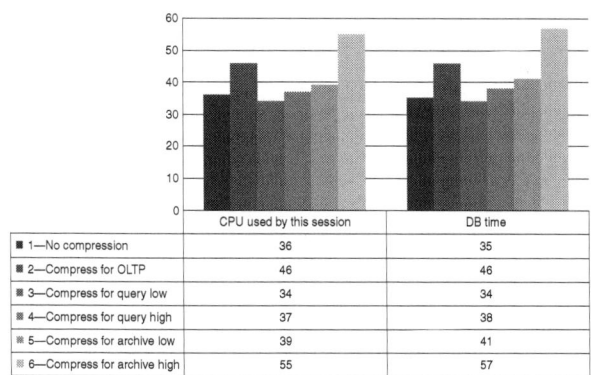

	CPU used by this session	DB time
1—No compression	36	35
2—Compress for OLTP	46	46
3—Compress for query low	34	34
4—Compress for query high	37	38
5—Compress for archive low	39	41
6—Compress for archive high	55	57

Figure 5.13 Bulk I/O operations performance—CPU and DB time by HCC type

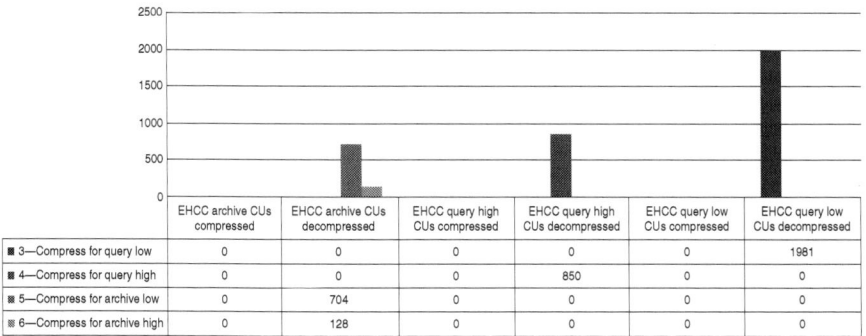

	EHCC archive CUs compressed	EHCC archive CUs decompressed	EHCC query high CUs compressed	EHCC query high CUs decompressed	EHCC query low CUs compressed	EHCC query low CUs decompressed
3—Compress for query low	0	0	0	0	0	1981
4—Compress for query high	0	0	0	850	0	0
5—Compress for archive low	0	704	0	0	0	0
6—Compress for archive high	0	128	0	0	0	0

Figure 5.14 Bulk I/O performance—key HCC statistics by HCC type

expected, ARCHIVE HIGH had to work with the least CU, followed by ARCHIVE LOW, QUERY HIGH, and finally QUERY LOW.

Small I/O Operations

To provide an example of a smaller, more standard operation, we'll pull just a single row based on the PK. We do have to hint the query to force index usage. The following SQL is used for the test:

```
SELECT /*+ INDEX (A MY_DBAOBJECTS_ARCHIVE_HIGH_PK ) */ *
FROM MY_DBAOBJECTS_ARCHIVE_HIGH  A WHERE UNIQUE_OBJID=72334;
```

Figures 5.15 through 5.17 show the relative CPU load, I/O load, and execution time for a SQL operation involving access via the PK. These reflect similar but not identical behavior to what we saw in the earlier section.

Looking at execution time for single-row access based on PK is not really very meaningful given that the spread is less than .003 second. However, the broad pattern is largely being maintained here as well, but with variations that are to be expected and can be explained:

- HCC ARCHIVE HIGH took the most time.

- No compression and COMPRESS FOR OLTP are seemingly at par and the best performing overall.

- The remaining HCC compression types were identical for all intents and purposes.

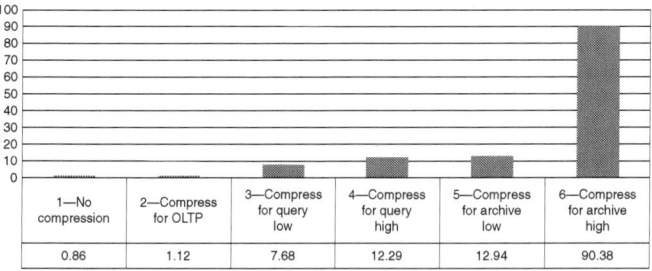

	1—No compression	2—Compress for OLTP	3—Compress for query low	4—Compress for query high	5—Compress for archive low	6—Compress for archive high
	0.86	1.12	7.68	12.29	12.94	90.38

Figure 5.15   Single-block I/O—elapsed time by HCC type

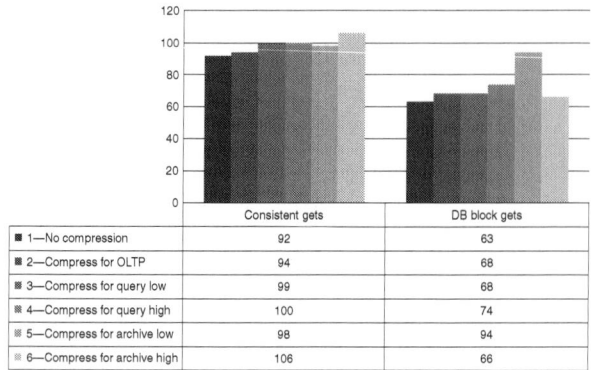

	Consistent gets	DB block gets
■ 1—No compression	92	63
■ 2—Compress for OLTP	94	68
■ 3—Compress for query low	99	68
▨ 4—Compress for query high	100	74
▨ 5—Compress for archive low	98	94
▨ 6—Compress for archive high	106	66

Figure 5.16   Single-block I/O—I/O load by HCC type

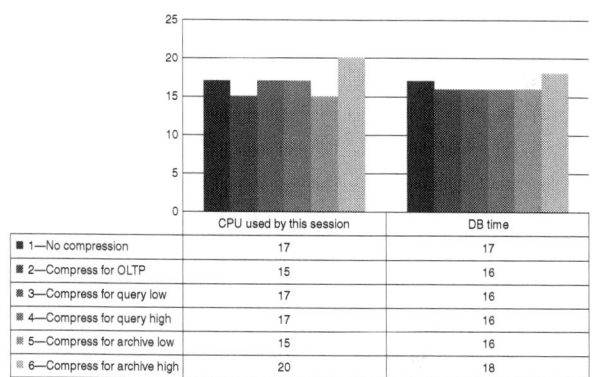

Figure 5.17 Single-block I/O—CPU and DB time by HCC type

I/O-wise, the results are all very close, as you can see in Figure 5.16. This is because the access is PK based. Not much else need be said there.

CPU-wise, the results were again very close for the same reasons, as you can see in Figure 5.17.

Figure 5.18 once again just pulls some HCC-specific stats, and we see that we had to uncompress exactly one block to get the rows we were looking at, which is what we would have expected.

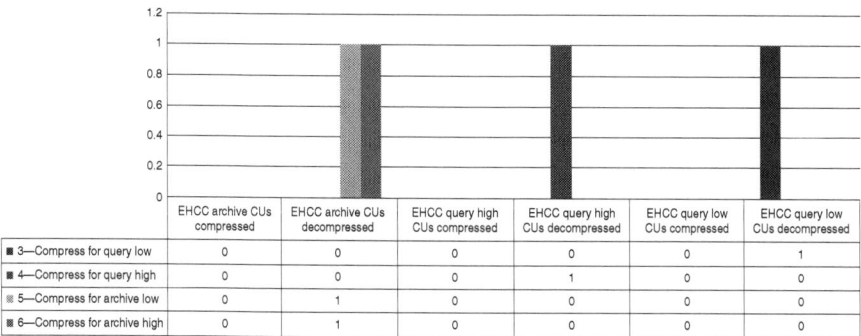

Figure 5.18 HCC access via PK—system statistics showing CU decompression

HCC and DML

A useful DBMS PL/SQL to be aware of when working with HCC is the DBMS_
COMPRESSION package. This package provides access to different functionality
and introspection related to compression. Included here is the output of describe
DBMS_COMPRESSION:

```
PROCEDURE GET_COMPRESSION_RATIO RETURNS NUMBER
 Argument Name                   Type                    In/Out Default?
 ------------------------------- ----------------------- ------ --------
 SCRATCHTBSNAME                  VARCHAR2                IN
 OWNNAME                         VARCHAR2                IN
 TABNAME                         VARCHAR2                IN
 PARTNAME                        VARCHAR2                IN
 COMPTYPE                        NUMBER                  IN
 BLKCNT_CMP                      BINARY_INTEGER          OUT
 BLKCNT_UNCMP                    BINARY_INTEGER          OUT
 ROW_CMP                         BINARY_INTEGER          OUT
 ROW_UNCMP                       BINARY_INTEGER          OUT
 CMP_RATIO                       NUMBER                  OUT
 COMPTYPE_STR                    VARCHAR2                OUT
 SUBSET_NUMROWS                  NUMBER                  IN     DEFAULT

FUNCTION GET_COMPRESSION_TYPE RETURNS NUMBER
 Argument Name                   Type                    In/Out Default?
 ------------------------------- ----------------------- ------ --------
 OWNNAME                         VARCHAR2                IN
 TABNAME                         VARCHAR2                IN
 ROW_ID                          ROWID                   IN

PROCEDURE INCREMENTAL_COMPRESS
 Argument Name                   Type                    In/Out Default?
 ------------------------------- ----------------------- ------ --------
 OWNNAME                         VARCHAR2(30)            IN
 TABNAME                         VARCHAR2(128)           IN
 PARTNAME                        VARCHAR2(30)            IN
 COLNAME                         VARCHAR2                IN
 DUMP_ON                         NUMBER                  IN     DEFAULT
 AUTOCOMPRESS_ON                 NUMBER                  IN     DEFAULT
 WHERE_CLAUSE                    VARCHAR2                IN     DEFAULT
```

When performing nondirect path row inserts or updates to existing data in an
HCC organized table, the data is not stored in columnar format, rather in row format. When a row is inserted, the row itself is inserted into a portion of the CU that
is reserved for row-oriented column stores. Listing 5.2 illustrates the point, compressing the table in QUERY LOW format.

Listing 5.2   Example of Regular Inserts to an HCC Organized Table

```
SQL> DESC EXABOOK.MY_DBAOBJECTS_QUERY_LOW
 NAME                                      NULL?         TYPE
 ----------------------------------------- --------      ----------------------
 UNIQUE_OBJID                              NOT NULL      NUMBER(38)
 OBJECT_ID                                               NUMBER
 DATA_OBJECT_ID                                          NUMBER
 OWNER                                                   VARCHAR2(30)
```

```
OBJECT_NAME                                          VARCHAR2(128)
SUBOBJECT_NAME                                       VARCHAR2(30)
OBJECT_TYPE                                          VARCHAR2(19)

SQL> INSERT INTO MY_DBAOBJECTS_QUERY_LOW (UNIQUE_OBJID, OBJECT_ID,
         DATA_OBJECT_ID, OWNER, OBJECT_NAME, SUBOBJECT_NAME, OBJECT_TYPE)
    VALUES ( 10000000, 555555 , 666666,
                'EXBOOK','SINGLEROWINSERT',NULL,'SINGLE ROW');

1 ROW CREATED.

SQL> COMMIT»»»»

COMMIT COMPLETE.

SQL> SELECT ROWID FROM MY_DBAOBJECTS_QUERY_LOW WHERE UNIQUE_OBJID=10000000;

ROWID
------------------
AAASHJAAHAAC0PRAAA

SQL > SQL> DEFINE ROWID_QRY='AAASHJAAHAAC0PRAAA';

SQL> SELECT DECODE(DBMS_COMPRESSION.GET_COMPRESSION_TYPE('EXBOOK',
'MY_DBAOBJECTS_QUERY_LOW','&ROWID_QRY'),
1,  'COMP_NOCOMPRESS',
2,  'COMP_FOR_OLTP',
4,  'COMP_FOR_QUERY_HIGH',
8,  'COMP_FOR_QUERY_LOW',
16, 'COMP_FOR_ARCHIVE_HIGH',
32, 'COMP_FOR_ARCHIVE_LOW') COMPRESSION_TYPE
FROM DUAL;

COMPRESSION_TYPE
---------------------
COMP_NOCOMPRESS
```

When we update a row that is currently compressed, the row is converted from a compressed columnar format into a row format. In other words, the row data is migrated into a different section of the CU. Therefore, one would expect the ROWID also to be changed as a result. Listing 5.3 illustrates this point. The row with UNIQ_OBJID = 10003 was randomly chosen for this test.

Listing 5.3 Example of an Update to an HCC Organized Table

```
SQL> SELECT ROWID, A.* FROM MY_DBAOBJECTS_QUERY_LOW A
WHERE UNIQUE_OBJID= 10003;

ROWID              UNIQUE_OBJID OBJECT_ID DATA_OBJECT_ID OWNER OBJECT_NAME
       SUBOBJECT_NAME OBJECT_TYPE
------------------ ------------ --------- -------------- ----- -----------
----- -------------- -----------
AAASHJAAHAACZSUAKQ    10003       10175                   SYS
KU$_PHTABLE_VIEW                 VIEW


SQL> SELECT ROWID, DBMS_ROWID.ROWID_RELATIVE_FNO(ROWID) ROWID_FILE_NO,
 DBMS_ROWID.ROWID_BLOCK_NUMBER(ROWID)ROWID_BLOCK_NUMBER
 FROM MY_DBAOBJECTS_QUERY_LOW WHERE UNIQUE_OBJID=10003;
```

```
ROWID               ROWID_FILE_NO ROWID_BLOCK_NUMBER
----------------- ------------- ------------------
AAASHJAAHAACZSUAKQ           7              734356

SQL> DEFINE ROWID_QRY='AAASHJAAHAACZSUAKQ';

SQL>   SELECT DECODE(DBMS_COMPRESSION.GET_COMPRESSION_TYPE('EXABOOK',
'MY_DBAOBJECTS_QUERY_LOW','&ROWID_QRY'),
  2   1,  'COMP_NOCOMPRESS',
  3   2,  'COMP_FOR_OLTP',
  4   4,  'COMP_FOR_QUERY_HIGH',
  5   8,  'COMP_FOR_QUERY_LOW',
  6  16,  'COMP_FOR_ARCHIVE_HIGH',
  7  32,  'COMP_FOR_ARCHIVE_LOW') COMPRESSION_TYPE
  8* FROM DUAL;
OLD    1: SELECT DECODE(DBMS_COMPRESSION.GET_COMPRESSION_TYPE('EXABOOK',
'MY_DBAOBJECTS_QUERY_LOW','&ROWID_QRY'),
NEW    1: SELECT DECODE(DBMS_COMPRESSION.GET_COMPRESSION_TYPE('EXABOOK',
'MY_DBAOBJECTS_QUERY_LOW','AAASHJAAHAAC0PRAAB'),

COMPRESSION_TYPE
--------------------
COMP_FOR_QUERY_LOW

SQL> UPDATE MY_DBAOBJECTS_QUERY_LOW SET SUBOBJECT_NAME = 'UPDATED COLUMN'
WHERE UNIQUE_OBJID=10003;

1 ROW UPDATED.

SQL> COMMIT;

COMMIT COMPLETE.

SQL> SELECT ROWID, DBMS_ROWID.ROWID_RELATIVE_FNO(ROWID) ROWID_FILE_NO,
DBMS_ROWID.ROWID_BLOCK_NUMBER(ROWID) ROWID_BLOCK_NUMBER
FROM MY_DBAOBJECTS_QUERY_LOW WHERE UNIQUE_OBJID=10003;

ROWID               ROWID_FILE_NO ROWID_BLOCK_NUMBER
----------------- ------------- ------------------
AAASHJAAHAAC0PRAAB           7              738283

SQL> DEFINE ROWID_QRY='AAASHJAAHAAC0PRAAB';

SQL> SELECT DECODE(DBMS_COMPRESSION.GET_COMPRESSION_TYPE('EXABOOK',
'MY_DBAOBJECTS_QUERY_LOW','&ROWID_QRY'),
  2   1,  'COMP_NOCOMPRESS',
  3   2,  'COMP_FOR_OLTP',
  4   4,  'COMP_FOR_QUERY_HIGH',
  5   8,  'COMP_FOR_QUERY_LOW',
  6  16,  'COMP_FOR_ARCHIVE_HIGH',
  7  32,  'COMP_FOR_ARCHIVE_LOW') COMPRESSION_TYPE
  8* FROM DUAL;

OLD    1: SELECT DECODE(DBMS_COMPRESSION.GET_COMPRESSION_TYPE('EXABOOK',
'MY_DBAOBJECTS_QUERY_LOW','&ROWID_QRY'),
NEW    1: SELECT DECODE(DBMS_COMPRESSION.GET_COMPRESSION_TYPE('EXABOOK',
'MY_DBAOBJECTS_QUERY_LOW','AAASHJAAHAAC0PRAAB'),

COMPRESSION_TYPE
--------------------
COMP_NOCOMPRESS

SQL> SELECT * FROM MY_DBAOBJECTS_QUERY_LOW
WHERE ROWID= AAASHJAAHAACZSUAKQ;

NO ROWS SELECTED
```

As expected, once the row has been updated, the ROWID for the row is changed because the block number associated with the row has changed as well.

However, much to our chagrin, there are applications out there that track actual ROWIDs rather than tracking by primary key. Those applications would need to be modified to use HCC.

The following listings provide an example of the same table. Listing 5.4 has the underscore parameter set to FALSE, and we see that we cannot access the row using the old ROWID. In Listing 5.5, with the parameter set to TRUE, we are able to access the data row with the old ROWID as well as the new one.

Notice that there is an underscore parameter, "_KDZ_HCC_TRACK_UPD_RIDS", which is set to FALSE by default. This parameter enables the ability to track ROWIDs for rows in HCC organized tables even after the row has been migrated.

Note

This example is for educational purposes only. It is not recommended that you change the "_" parameter. As a matter of fact, rather than changing the parameter, it's better to change the code so that it does not require changing the "_" parameter.

Listing 5.4 Example with ROWID Tracking for HCC Disabled

```
SQL> ALTER SYSTEM SET "_KDZ_HCC_TRACK_UPD_RIDS"=FALSE;

SYSTEM ALTERED.

SQL> SELECT * FROM MY_DBAOBJECTS_QUERY_HIGH WHERE ROWID='AAASHLAAHAAC1HLAAA';

UNIQUE_OBJID   OBJECT_ID DATA_OBJECT_ID OWNER  OBJECT_NAME
SUBOBJECT_NAME OBJECT_TYPE
------------ ---------- -------------- ------ --------------------
-------------- ---------------
      79944       7521           9658 SYSTEM LOGMNR_I2TABSUBPART$
P_LESSTHAN100  INDEX PARTITION

SQL> UPDATE MY_DBAOBJECTS_QUERY_HIGH SET OBJECT_TYPE='MODIFIED' WHERE
UNIQUE_OBJID=79944;

1 ROW UPDATED.

SQL> SELECT ROWID FROM MY_DBAOBJECTS_QUERY_HIGH WHERE UNIQUE_OBJID=79944;

ROWID
-----------------
AAASHLAAGAAC8R+AAB

SQL> SELECT * FROM MY_DBAOBJECTS_QUERY_HIGH WHERE ROWID='AAASHLAAHAAC1HLAAA';

NO ROWS SELECTED

SQL> ROLLBACK;
```

Listing 5.5 Example with ROWID Tracking for HCC Enabled

```
SQL> ALTER SYSTEM SET "_kdz_hcc_track_upd_rids"=TRUE;

SYSTEM ALTERED.

SQL> SELECT * FROM MY_DBAOBJECTS_QUERY_HIGH WHERE ROWID='AAASHLAAHAAC1HLAAA';


UNIQUE_OBJID  OBJECT_ID DATA_OBJECT_ID OWNER  OBJECT_NAME
SUBOBJECT_NAME OBJECT_TYPE
------------ ---------- -------------- ------ --------------------
-------------- ---------------
       79944       7521           9658 SYSTEM LOGMNR_I2TABSUBPART$
P_LESSTHAN100  INDEX PARTITION

SQL> UPDATE MY_DBAOBJECTS_QUERY_HIGH SET OBJECT_TYPE='MODIFIED'
WHERE UNIQUE_OBJID=79944;

1 ROW UPDATED.

SQL> SELECT ROWID FROM MY_DBAOBJECTS_QUERY_HIGH WHERE UNIQUE_OBJID=79944;

ROWID
------------------
AAASHLAAGAAC8R+AAB

SQL> SELECT * FROM MY_DBAOBJECTS_QUERY_HIGH WHERE ROWID='AAASHLAAHAAC1HLAAA';

UNIQUE_OBJID  OBJECT_ID DATA_OBJECT_ID OWNER  OBJECT_NAME
SUBOBJECT_NAME OBJECT_TYPE
------------ ---------- -------------- ------ --------------------
-------------- ---------------
       79944       7521           9658 SYSTEM LOGMNR_I2TABSUBPART$
P_LESSTHAN100  INDEX PARTITION

SQL>ROLLBACK;
```

HCC and Locking

Oracle has for the longest time maintained locking at the lowest level possible, at the row level. However, that is no longer the case with HCC. When a table is created to take advantage of HCC, irrespective of the type, locking is now managed and maintained at the CU level.

What this means is that if a session updates a row that is currently stored using an HCC compression type, the session lock is taken at the CU level. In other words, another session that tries to update a second row in the same CU will be blocked by the first session and will have to wait on an enq: TX - row lock contention wait event. It is important to note that though the lock is effectively on a CU, the wait event reported is still a row-level lock.

The following test shows that with HCC, Oracle locks a CU and not a row:

1. Identify two individual rows that are stored in the same CU. See the example below.
2. From the first session, issue an update to the first row but do not commit.
3. From a second session, issue an update to the second row.
4. Query blockers and waiter views to see the locker and blocker relationship.

Figures 5.19 through 5.22 show an example of this:

- Session #1: SID 886, SERIAL# 6977 is the first session to lock a row in the CU with an update.

- Session #2: SID 1372, SERIAL# 257 is the second session that will attempt to update a second row in the CU.

We again use the DBMS_ROWID PL/SQL package to identify the two rows that were using HCC compression and were stored in the same CU:

```
14:33:24 SQL> SELECT ROWID FROM MY_DBAOBJECTS_QUERY_HIGH
WHERE DBMS_ROWID.ROWID_RELATIVE_FNO(ROWID)=7 AND
DBMS_ROWID.ROWID_BLOCK_NUMBER(ROWID)= 743499 AND ROWNUM < 3;

ROWID
------------------
AAAShLAAHAAC1HLAgI
AAAShLAAHAAC1HLAgJ
```

Figure 5.19 shows that the first session, SID 886, was successfully able to update the first row and complete without any issue. However, we have not yet committed the transaction.

```
14:30:03 SQL> select sid, serial# from v$session where sid=sys_context('USERENV','SID');

   SID    SERIAL#
--------- ---------
   886      6977

14:30:12 SQL> update MY_DBAOBJECTS_QUERY_HIGH set object_type='MODIFIED-ROW' where rowid='AAAShLAAHAAC1hLAgI';

1 row updated.

14:30:23 SQL> 14:30:23 SQL>
14:31:05 SQL>
14:31:05 SQL>
14:31:05 SQL>
14:31:05 SQL> []
```

Figure 5.19   Session #1—update and lock of row number within a CU

```
14:30:07 SQL> select sid, serial# from v$session where sid=sys_context('USERENV','SID');

     SID    SERIAL#
---------- ----------
    1376       257

14:30:14 SQL> update MY_DBAOBJECTS_QUERY_HIGH set object_type='MODIFIED-ROW' where rowid='AAAShLAAHAAC1hLAgJ';
[]
```

Figure 5.20   Session #2: attempting to update a second row in the same CU

Figure 5.20 shows the second session, attempting to update a second row within the same CU. As a result, it waits for an update to complete before returning us to a SQL prompt.

In a third session, looking at wait events and the chain of blockers and waiters, Figure 5.21 shows SID 1376 waiting on an enq: TX - row lock contention event.

When we look further to see the blockers and waiters, we find that SID 886 is blocking SID 1376, as shown in Figure 5.22. As soon as the first session SID 886 issues a commit, the second session will proceed to update the subsequent row.

Clearly we can see that though the locks are showing up at the row level, Oracle internally is escalating the lock to a CU level.

```
         Oracle                                                                             Sec
sh
Sid,Serial User              OS User  Svr-Pgm   Wait Event                     State-Seq   Wt Module
ue            P1             P2   P3
--- ------- --------------   -------  -------   -----------------------------  ---------   -- -------
1376,   257 EXABOOK          oracle   3365-TNS  enq: TX - row lock contention  Wtng- 66     5 SQL*Plus
04          1415053318       262153 ####
1277,   461 EXABOOK          oracle   3206-TNS  N msg to clnt                  Shrt-1096    0 SQL*Plus
38          1650815232       1    0
```

Figure 5.21   Enqueue wait event experienced by Session #2

```
14:33:11 SQL> select sid, serial# from v$session where sid=sys_context('USERENV','SID');

     SID    SERIAL#
---------- ----------
    1277       461

14:33:18 SQL> @rac-baw
                                                                                         Last
                Logn Ora  SQL/Prev                 OS                                    Call
BW I#, Sid, Ser,S Time User Hash     Module         User  Svr-Pgm  Machine  HR Resource  Elap Ctim Locked Object
BLOCK      REQUEST
----- ---- ----- ---- ---- -------- ----------     ----- -------- -------- -- ---------- ---- ---- --------------
> 1,  886, 6977-I 1418 EXABOO 0       SQL*Plus       oracle 3956-TNS oe01db01  6 TX:393217-2145 181s 181s -1)0-0-0
  1    0
< 1, 1376,  257-A 1418 EXABOO 3030898684 SQL*Plus    oracle 3365-TNS oe01db01  6                173s 173s 75851)7-743499-2057
  0    6
```

Figure 5.22   Session #1 blocking Session #2

Practical Uses of HCC

HCC is a very powerful database feature that is available only on specific platforms from Oracle. Apart from Exadata, HCC is also supported when using the Oracle ZFS Storage Appliance and Oracle Pillar storage platforms.

HCC does provide significant storage savings and potential I/O benefits depending upon the types of queries and amounts of data queried. That being said, one also needs to understand the implications and ramifications of using HCC, specifically:

- Row insertion using direct path writes triggers the HCC algorithm; otherwise the data is stored in columnar format.
- Rows migrate from a compressed columnar format to a row format when updated.
- Row updates cause CU-level locking, which, depending upon the type of HCC, can be up to 32,000 rows.

The two most common use cases of HCC are in data warehousing environments and Information Lifecycle Management.

HCC provides a huge benefit, especially in terms of storage space savings, in the ILM space. It is not uncommon to find regulatory guidelines and requirements that necessitate organizations holding up to seven or 11 years of data for compliance but rarely if ever using that data. Apart from storage with respect to the data, index maintenance and other management overhead are also incurred as a result.

It is a common practice with Exadata and HCC to use range partitioning to partition data by age and apply different compression algorithms to partitions by age:

- The most recent or active data is maintained either in OLTP compressed format or in uncompressed format.
- Data that is queried often but not always active is stored using HCC, either COMPRESS FOR QUERY (LOW or HIGH) or COMPRESS FOR ARCHIVE LOW.
- The older and historic data is stored using HCC COMPRESS FOR ARCHIVE HIGH.

When coupled with the 12c partitioning enhancement, which allows the DBA to selectively identify partitions that will maintain indexes or not, the space savings are considerable.

Data warehousing environments by definition fall into "write once—read all the time" usage case. Additionally, data warehouses make heavy use of Oracle partitioning in order to manage the data volumes for read and provide filtering, but they perform mostly large bulk I/O operations. Furthermore, data warehouses tend to store data for longer durations for trending and planning purposes, rather than regulatory purposes. All these aspects make HCC a great fit for a DW environment.

Summary

Oracle introduced Hybrid Columnar Compression as a new feature with Exadata and has since then expanded the platforms that can support HCC to include ZFS Storage Appliance as well as the Pillar storage stack. HCC was primarily introduced to support DW use cases and provides significant benefit in that area. This chapter explained the fundamentals of HCC and its different flavors. It then took a deeper look at the impact of using HCC under different circumstances.

That being said, this chapter is not exhaustive in nature about the performance implications. It's important to test individual use cases to understand the specific behavior of HCC. What this chapter provided is the basic framework of how HCC works and what aspects to look at. It is important to keep in mind that HCC complements other Exadata-specific performance features such as Smart Scan, Cell Offloading, and Storage Indexes.

## 6

Oracle Database 12c and Exadata

The objective of any new Oracle version release is to improve manageability, performance, and efficiency. As data growth rapidly increases, maintaining and lowering storage costs also becomes a key objective. This chapter covers many key features that address these customer requirements. Many features illustrated in this chapter are Exadata, but it covers non-Exadata-specific features as well. The generic, non-Exadata-specific features covered, we believe, are ones that provide huge benefits for Exadata customers.

12c Partitioning Features

There are several new partitioning features, all aimed at reducing management overhead, providing higher availability, and simplifying maintenance. These include partial indexes, partition move, and partition index maintenance.

Partial Indexes

Most Exadata DBAs want to squeeze the most out of their Exadata storage and improve overall efficiency. In Oracle Database 12c, DBAs can create local and global indexes on a subset of the partitions of a table. Creating these partial indexes provides more flexibility since index segments are built only for the necessary partitions. More importantly, deferring index creation for newly created partitions is especially important since generally newer partitions incur bulk inserts.

With partial indexes there is effectively no corresponding index segment for these index partitions. These unusable indexes consume no storage and thus reduce the overall storage footprint.

Partial indexes are enabled by using the INDEXING OFF attribute of the partitioned table and creating indexes with the Partial attribute. Following is an example where we create a test table from the V$BH view. We create indexes only on the older partitions; the newer partitions, Buffer3 and Buffer4, have indexing turned off. Note that the default for the table is INDEXING ON.

```
SQL> CREATE TABLE NISHAS_BUFFERS
INDEXING ON
PARTITION BY RANGE (class#)
(PARTITION buffer1 VALUES LESS THAN (10) INDEXING ON,
 PARTITION buffer2 VALUES LESS THAN (20) INDEXING ON,
 PARTITION buffer3 VALUES LESS THAN (30) INDEXING OFF,
 PARTITION buffer4 VALUES LESS THAN (40) INDEXING OFF)
as select file#,block#,status,class# from v$bh;
```

Notice in the following that user_tab_partitions show that indexing is disabled for the stated partitions:

```
SQL> select table_name, partition_name, indexing from
     user_tab_partitions
TABLE_NAME            PARTITION_NAME         INDEX
-------------------   --------------------   -----
NISHAS_BUFFERS        BUFFER4                OFF
NISHAS_BUFFERS        BUFFER3                OFF
NISHAS_BUFFERS        BUFFER2                ON
NISHAS_BUFFERS        BUFFER1                ON
```

Now let's create a local index on this partitioned table:

```
SQL> create index nishas_buffer_idx on nishas_buffers(file#) local indexing partial
SQL> select index_name, partition_name, status from user_ind_partitions
INDEX_NAME                            PARTITION_NAME         STATUS
-----------------------------------   --------------------   --------
NISHAS_BUFFER_IDX                     BUFFER4                UNUSABLE
NISHAS_BUFFER_IDX                     BUFFER3                UNUSABLE
NISHAS_BUFFER_IDX                     BUFFER2                USABLE
NISHAS_BUFFER_IDX                     BUFFER1                USABLE
```

Notice that index partitions marked with INDEXING OFF are listed with the status of UNUSABLE. Changing a table attribute at the partition level to INDEXING OFF automatically causes the corresponding partitions for local indexes to become unusable. In contrast, changing the attribute from INDEXING OFF to INDEXING ON rebuilds the index and marks the index partition as USABLE. This provides the capability to automatically rebuild the index:

```
SQL> select index_name, partition_name, num_rows, status
from user_ind_partitions;
INDEX_NAME                          PARTITION_NAME       NUM_ROWS STATUS
---------------------------------- -------------------- ---------- ------
NISHAS_BUFFER_IDX                   BUFFER2                   449 USABLE
NISHAS_BUFFER_IDX                   BUFFER1                 16455 USABLE
NISHAS_BUFFER_IDX                   BUFFER4                     0 UNUSABLE
NISHAS_BUFFER_IDX                   BUFFER3                     0 UNUSABLE
```

Let's run some queries to determine if the index is being used or not (after indexing is set to OFF). The following example indicates that the index Partition 1 and 2 are being used, per the explain plan:

```
SQL>select count(*) from nishas_buffers where class# < 30
COUNT(*)
----------
16904
Execution Plan
----------------------------------------------------------
Plan hash value: 2875086163

--------------------------------------------------------------------------------
----------------------------

| Id  | Operation               | Name              | Rows  | Bytes | Cost (%C
PU)| Time     | Pstart| Pstop |

--------------------------------------------------------------------------------
----------------------------

|   0 | SELECT STATEMENT        |                   |     1 |     3 |    11
(0)| 00:00:01 |       |       |

|   1 |  SORT AGGREGATE         |                   |     1 |     3 |
   |          |       |       |

|   2 |   PARTITION RANGE ITERATOR|                 | 10009 | 30027 |    11
(0)| 00:00:01 |     1 |     2 |

|   3 |    INDEX FAST FULL SCAN | NISHAS_BUFFER_IDX | 10009 | 30027 |    11
(0)| 00:00:01 |     1 |     2 |
```

Now let's try to execute a query on a partition where the index does not exist:

```
SQL> select count(*) from nishas_buffers where class# > 30

  COUNT(*)
----------
       597


Execution Plan
----------------------------------------------------------
Plan hash value: 2217647015

--------------------------------------------------------------------------------
--------------------------

| Id  | Operation               | Name         | Rows  | Bytes | Cost (%CPU)|
```

```
Time       | Pstart| Pstop |

-------------------------------------------------------------------------------
------------------------
|   0 | SELECT STATEMENT        |                   |   1 |    3 |    7   (0)|
00:00:01 |       |       |
|   1 |  SORT AGGREGATE         |                   |   1 |    3 |            |
         |       |       |
|   2 |   PARTITION RANGE SINGLE|                   | 605 | 1815 |    7   (0)|
00:00:01 |   4 |     4 |
|*  3 |    TABLE ACCESS FULL    | NISHAS_BUFFERS |  605 | 1815 |    7   (0)|
00:00:01 |   4 |     4 |
```

Now if we run a query that pulls data across all the partitions, the optimizer will do interesting things. Notice that the optimizer leverages the index where it can and does a full table scan where an index doesn't exist:

```
SQL> select count(*) from nishas_buffers where class# between 10 and 40
COUNT(*)
----------
      1982


Execution Plan
----------------------------------------------------------
Plan hash value: 2976918285

-------------------------------------------------------------------------
| Id  | Operation               | Name              | Rows | Bytes | Cost (
%CPU)| Time      | Pstart| Pstop |

-------------------------------------------------------------------------
|   0 | SELECT STATEMENT        |                   |    1 |    3 |  14
 (0)| 00:00:01 |       |       |
|   1 |  SORT AGGREGATE         |                   |    1 |    3 |
     |       |       |       |
|   2 |   VIEW                  | VW_TE_2           |   24 |      |  14
 (0)| 00:00:01 |       |       |
|   3 |    UNION-ALL            |                   |      |      |
     |       |       |       |
|   4 |     PARTITION RANGE SINGLE |                |    1 |   14 |   1
 (0)| 00:00:01 |     2 |     2 |
|*  5 |      INDEX RANGE SCAN   | NISHAS_BUFFER_IDX |    1 |   14 |   1
 (0)| 00:00:01 |     2 |     2 |
|   6 |     PARTITION RANGE ITERATOR|               |   23 |  345 |  13
 (0)| 00:00:01 |     3 |     4 |
|   7 |      TABLE ACCESS FULL  | NISHAS_BUFFERS    |   23 |  345 |  13
 (0)| 00:00:01 |     3 |     4 |
```

```
Predicate Information (identified by operation id):
---------------------------------------------------

   5 - access("NISHAS_BUFFERS"."CLASS#">=10 AND "NISHAS_BUFFERS"."CLASS#"<20)


SQL> select table_name, partition_name, indexing from user_tab_partitions;

TABLE_NAME                       PARTITION_NAME                     INDEX
------------------------------   ------------------------------     -----
NISHAS_BUFFERS                   BUFFER1                            ON
NISHAS_BUFFERS                   BUFFER2                            ON
NISHAS_BUFFERS                   BUFFER4                            OFF
```

Partition Index Maintenance

Before Oracle Database 12c, invoking a drop or truncate partition resulted in an explicit global index maintenance operation; that is, it left the global indexes in unusable status. In 12c, these specific DML operations do not render the global indexes unusable.

The index maintenance can be deferred and executed at a later time. The global index maintenance can be deferred to off-peak times without impacting the index availability, thus making the drop and truncate partition and sub-partition maintenance operations less resource intensive at the point in time of the partition maintenance operation. Additionally, in 12c, partition maintenance operations can be performed on multiple partitions as part of a single operation. Allowing multiple partition maintenance operations to be executed as a single task provides more efficient partition maintenance using fewer system resources.

The next example illustrates the benefit of asynchronous global index maintenance. It shows that the maintenance of global indexes can be decoupled from the drop and truncate partition operation, without making the global index unusable, and delayed to a user-defined window. With this example dropping a partition in Oracle Database 12c is notably faster than a partition in pre-12c databases. The drop operation is faster because it is a metadata-only operation.

List the existing indexes:

```
SQL> SELECT index_name, status, orphaned_entries
from user_indexes WHERE index_name like 'NISHAS%'
INDEX_NAME                         STATUS     ORP
---------------------------------  --------   ---
NISHAS_BUFFER_IDX                  N/A        NO
NISHASBUFFERS_GLOBAL_PART_IDX      N/A        NO
```

List the table partitions and indexing:

```
SQL> select table_name, partition_name, indexing from user_tab_partitions
TABLE_NAME                       PARTITION_NAME                     INDEX
------------------------------   ------------------------------     -----
NISHAS_BUFFERS                   BUFFER4                            OFF
NISHAS_BUFFERS                   BUFFER3                            OFF
NISHAS_BUFFERS                   BUFFER2                            ON
NISHAS_BUFFERS                   BUFFER1                            ON
```

Let's query the NISHAS_BUFFERS table and review the plan table:

```
SQL> select count(*) from nishas_buffers where class# = 10;

COUNT(*)
----------
3184

Execution Plan
----------------------------------------------------------
Plan hash value: 1324872353


----------------------------------------------------------------------
| Id  | Operation            | Name  | Rows  | Bytes | Cost (%CPU)| Time     | Pstart| Pstop |
----------------------------------------------------------------
|   0 | SELECT STATEMENT     |       |       |     1 |     3 |     9   (0)| 00:00
:01 |       |       |
|   1 |  SORT AGGREGATE      |       |     1 |     3 |       |
    |       |       |
|   2 |   PARTITION RANGE SINGLE|    |  3184 |  9552 |     9   (0)| 00:00
:01 |     2 |     2 |
|*  3 |INDEX FAST FULL SCAN | NISHASBUFFERS_GLOBAL_PART_IDX |  3184 |
9552 |     9   (0)| 00:00
:01 |     2 |     2 |


SQL> alter table nishas_buffers drop partition for (20) update indexes;

Elapsed: 00:00:00.04    → very fast !

SQL> select table_name, partition_name, indexing from user_tab_partitions;

TABLE_NAME                 PARTITION_NAME                INDEX
-------------------------- ---------------------------   -----
NISHAS_BUFFERS             BUFFER1                       ON
NISHAS_BUFFERS             BUFFER2                       ON
NISHAS_BUFFERS             BUFFER4                       OFF


SQL> select index_name,partition_name,status,
orphaned_entries
from user_ind_partitions;

INDEX_NAME                    PARTITION_NAME       STATUS    ORP
----------------------------  -------------------  --------  ---
NISHAS_BUFFER_IDX             BUFFER2              USABLE    NO
NISHAS_BUFFER_IDX             BUFFER1              USABLE    NO
NISHASBUFFERS_GLOBAL_PART_IDX P5                   USABLE    YES
NISHASBUFFERS_GLOBAL_PART_IDX P4                   USABLE    YES
NISHASBUFFERS_GLOBAL_PART_IDX P3                   USABLE    YES
NISHASBUFFERS_GLOBAL_PART_IDX P2                   USABLE    YES
NISHASBUFFERS_GLOBAL_PART_IDX P1                   USABLE    YES
```

The orphaned rows in NISHASBUFFERS_GLOBAL_PART_IDX (P1) are to be expected because the drop partition is a metadata-only operation. Next we will perform an offline cleanup of the index. This can performed using various methods:

```
dbms_part.cleanup_gidx
     exec dbms_part.cleanup_gidx('nitin', 'nishas_buffers');
alter index NISHAS_BUFFER_IDX coalesce cleanup
alter index rebuild
```

Note, however, that if the number of orphaned entries is large, as would be typical in a production Exadata environment, the recommended method is to use the dbms_part.cleanup_gidx method.

Partition Move

In pre-12c databases, migrating partitions or tablespace data files off to a different, lower storage tier required a read-only state for the actual move, thus it required an outage. In Oracle Database 12c, ALTER TABLE MOVE PARTITION is a new feature or optimization that permits the partition to be moved while allowing non-blocking online DML operations to continue uninterrupted on the partition that is being moved. Additionally, global indexes are maintained during the move partition, so a manual index rebuild is no longer required. Essentially, this optimization eliminates the read-only state for the actual MOVE PARTITION command.

Using our earlier created partition table NISHAS_BUFFERS and its associated index partitions, we will illustrate the ALTER TABLE MOVE PARTITION feature by running an update operation while the move operation continues in the background. The resulting partition and its index should remain intact and usable.

Let's see how many rows are in this:

```
SQL> select count(*) from nishas_buffers;
COUNT(*)
----------
294992
```

In addition, we will create a local index just for illustration:

```
create index nishas_buffer_idx on nishas_buffers(file#) local ;

SQL> select count(*) from nishas_buffers where class# < 20;
COUNT(*)
----------
270464
SQL> select partition_name,  tablespace_name from user_tab_partitions
PARTITION_NAME          TABLESPACE_NAME
------------------- ------------------------------------
BUFFER4                 USERS
BUFFER3                 USERS
BUFFER2                 USERS
BUFFER1                 USERS

SQL> SELECT index_name, status, tablespace_name from user_ind_partitions;
INDEX_NAME                              STATUS    TABLESPACE_NAME
-------------------------------------- -------- -----------------
NISHAS_BUFFER_IDX                       USABLE    USERS
```

```
NISHAS_BUFFER_IDX                        USABLE    USERS
NISHAS_BUFFER_IDX                        USABLE    USERS
NISHAS_BUFFER_IDX                        USABLE    USERS
NISHASBUFFERS_GLOBAL_PART_IDX            USABLE    USERS
NISHASBUFFERS_GLOBAL_PART_IDX            USABLE    USERS
NISHASBUFFERS_GLOBAL_PART_IDX            USABLE    USERS
NISHASBUFFERS_GLOBAL_PART_IDX            USABLE    USERS
NISHASBUFFERS_GLOBAL_PART_IDX            USABLE    USERS
```

Now let's move a partition. In order to illustrate this correctly, we need to build a script that updates the partition asynchronously with the move operation. This script starts the timer, executes the updates against the partitioned table, and displays the end time:

```
sqlplus /nolog << EOF
  connect nitin/nitin
  spool moveit_update.log
  select 'Update starts at '|| to_char(sysdate,'hh24:mi:ss') from dual;
  update nishas_buffers set block#=2,status='kirananya' where file#=1;
  commit;
  select 'Update ends at ' ||to_char(sysdate,'hh24:mi:ss') from dual;
  spool off
  exit;
EOF
```

This script executes the ALTER MOVE PARTITION against the partitioned table while the update is occurring in the background:

```
sqlplus /nolog << EOF
  connect nitin/nitin
  spool moveit.log
  SELECT 'Online move starts at ' ||to_char(sysdate,'hh24:mi:ss')
from dual;
  ALTER TABLE nishas_buffers move partition for (30) tablespace
SATA_EXPANSIONCELL_STORAGE1
online update indexes SELECT 'Online move ends at '
||to_char(sysdate,'hh24:mi:ss') from dual;
  spool off
  exit;
EOF
```

After the move is completed, here's the state and status of the partitions:

```
select partition_name,  tablespace_name from user_tab_partitions
PARTITION_NAME          TABLESPACE_NAME
------------------      ----------------------------------------
BUFFER3                 USERS
BUFFER2                 USERS
BUFFER1                 USERS
BUFFER4                 USERS
BUFFER3                 USERS
BUFFER1                 USERS
BUFFER4                 SATA_EXPANSIONCELL_STORAGE1
BUFFER2                 SATA_EXPANSIONCELL_STORAGE1
```

And now the index status:

```
SQL> SELECT index_name, status, tablespace_name from user_ind_partitions
INDEX_NAME                              STATUS    TABLESPACE_NAME
-----------------------------------     --------  --------------------
NISHAS_BUFFER_IDX                       USABLE    USERS
NISHAS_BUFFER_IDX                       USABLE    USERS
NISHAS_BUFFER_IDX                       USABLE    USERS
NISHAS_BUFFER_IDX                       USABLE    USERS
NISHASBUFFERS_GLOBAL_PART_IDX           USABLE    USERS
NISHASBUFFERS_GLOBAL_PART_IDX           USABLE    USERS
NISHASBUFFERS_GLOBAL_PART_IDX           USABLE    USERS
NISHASBUFFERS_GLOBAL_PART_IDX           USABLE    USERS
NISHASBUFFERS_GLOBAL_PART_IDX           USABLE    USERS
```

New 12c Optimizer Features

With each new release of Oracle Database there's always the promise of a better future and a positive direction for the optimizer, and 12c is no exception. In this section we introduce the marquee feature of Adaptive Query Optimization. There are two distinct sub-features of Adaptive Query Optimization: the Adaptive Plans feature, which focuses on improving the initial execution of a query, and the Adaptive Statistics feature, which provides additional statistical and environmental information to improve subsequent executions. Within the Adaptive Plans feature there are two key optimizations: join method and parallel data distribution (for parallel query operations).

Adaptive Plans

The Oracle Optimizer examines multiple access methods, such as full table scans or index scans, and different join methods such as nested loops and hash joins, all in an effort to determine the best plan for a SQL statement. There are several factors and considerations that influence the generation of an execution plan, including the size of the datasets, system resources (I/O, CPU, and memory), and the number of rows returned.

However, we all know that the optimizer makes wacky decisions when it comes to building accurate execution plans. A large part of this is due to miscalculations and estimations during initial plan generation. In Oracle Database 12c the Adaptive Plans feature allows these miscalculations to be self-remedied by enabling the optimizer to make runtime adjustments to execution plans and discover additional information that can lead to better statistics.

You may recall that the Oracle Optimizer, or more specifically the plan generator, breaks down a parsed SQL query block into subplans and generates execution plans for each of these subplans. The optimizer's plan estimator estimates and generates a subplan for each query block from the innermost query block first, then finally generates the outer query block representing the entire query. Using this approach, the optimizer can generate appropriate plans at a subplan level and adjust dynamically at runtime.

When automatic optimization is enabled, the statistics collector component of the optimizer gathers information about the execution and buffers a subset of returned rows from the query. Using this information, the optimizer in-band can dynamically choose a more appropriate subplan. Once a decent subplan is produced, the collector stops buffering rows and gathering statistics. At this point standard row processing occurs. For subsequent executions of the child cursor, the optimizer continues to use the same plan, until the plan is either invalidated or aged out of the library cache.

An example of this type of dynamic runtime change is switching from a nested loop join to a hash join. This runtime adjustment can be made if the initially determined cardinality estimate was determined to be inaccurate. The optimizer then switches to a better approach (after some rows have been processed). The optimizer can switch only from a nested loop join to a hash join and vice versa. However, if the initial join method chosen is a sort merge join, no adaptation will take place.

Parallel query (PQ) execution is used in parallel sorts, aggregations, and join operations. To efficiently execute PQ operations, the optimizer uses various data distribution methods, such as broadcast distribution or hash distribution. However, as stated previously, wrong assumptions can be made based on statistics or due to environment. In Oracle Database 12c, the statistics collectors front-end the producer side of the operation, which allows the Adaptive Query Optimization for PQ to make the final decision on the data distribution method until execution time. If the actual number of rows is less than twice the degree of parallelism (DOP), which is the default threshold, the data distribution method switches from the default of hash to broadcast.

To enable the Adaptive Plans feature, OPTIMIZER_FEATURES_ENABLE is set to 12.1.0.1 or later, and the OPTIMIZER_ADAPTIVE_REPORTING_ONLY initialization parameter is set to the default of FALSE. When OPTIMIZER_ADAPTIVE_REPORTING_ ONLY is set to TRUE, adaptive optimizations run in reporting-only mode. With this setting, the information required for an adaptive optimization is gathered, but no action is taken to change the plan. In this scenario Adaptive Query Optimization will take a passive approach: monitor the initial execution of a given SQL statement and determine variability between the actual execution statistics and the original plan estimates. The execution statistics are recorded and used for subsequent statement executions. This is done to determine if a new plan will be chosen for subsequent execution.

Automatic Re-optimization

Another Oracle Database 12c feature similar in nature to Adaptive Query Optimization is Automatic Re-optimization. The key difference between the two features is that Adaptive Plans assist in determining the best initial subplan, whereas Automatic Re-optimization changes a plan on subsequent executions after the initial execution. For example, in cases of suboptimal join orders, Adaptive Query Optimization does not support adapting the join order during execution.

With Automatic Re-optimization, the optimizer uses the information gathered after the first execution of a SQL statement to determine if Automatic Re-optimization would be effective. If the gathered execution information shows significant differences from the optimizer estimates, the optimizer looks for a replacement plan on the next execution. The optimizer can re-optimize a query several times, each time learning more and further improving the plan. There are several forms of Automatic Re-optimization.

Oracle Database 11gR2 introduced the cardinality feedback feature. In 12c this feature is rebranded as Statistics Feedback; however, Statistics Feedback also automatically improves plans for repeated queries that have cardinality misestimates. At the end of the first SQL execution, the optimizer compares its initial cardinality estimates to the actual number of rows returned by each operation in the plan during execution. If estimates differ significantly from actual cardinalities, the optimizer stores the correct estimates for subsequent use. This estimate difference and remediation (via feedback) can be seen in the plan table. In addition to improving subsequent estimates, the optimizer also creates a SQL plan directive so that other SQL statements can benefit from the information obtained during this initial execution.

Dynamic Adaptive Statistics

As part of the execution of a SQL query, the optimizer compiles the SQL and generates an execution plan. The execution plan depends on many environmental variables, such as availability of statistics to generate an appropriate plan. If the available statistics are not "decent," dynamic statistics need to be used.

Dynamic statistics are gathered by dynamic sampling. In pre-12c, dynamic sampling was invoked only if one or more of the tables in the query did not have statistics; however, dynamic sampling gathered basic statistics on these tables before optimizing the statement. In 12c, the optimizer automatically decides if dynamic statistics will be useful for other SQL statements referencing those objects and if dynamic sampling is the right approach. If it is, the optimizer also determines what dynamic sampling level will be used.

Dynamic statistics are persistent and may be used by other queries. The scope of the statistics gathered by dynamic sampling now includes the JOIN and GROUP BY clauses. Dynamic statistics are automatically stored persistently in the statistics repository, making them available to other queries. This feature goes hand-in-hand with the incremental statistics feature, which has been enhanced in 12c. In releases prior to 12c, if any DML occurred on a partition, the optimizer generally considered statistics on that partition to be stale. Subsequently, tools such as DBMS_STATS must be used to regather the statistics to accurately aggregate the global statistics (i.e., incremental statistics). This regathering of statistics has significant performance and management overhead.

In Oracle Database 12c, incremental statistics can automatically calculate global statistics for a partitioned table even if the partition or sub-partition statistics are stale and locked.

Incremental Statistics

In Oracle Database versions prior to 12c, incremental statistics considered partition-level statistics to be stale if any DML occurred on the partition. In Oracle Database 12c the incremental staleness threshold can be set to allow incremental statistics to use partition statistics even if some DML has occurred. Additionally, in Oracle Database 12c, incremental statistics can automatically calculate global statistics for a partitioned table even if the partition or sub-partition statistics are stale and locked.

To set up incremental statistics for a partitioned table, set the INCREMENTAL setting to TRUE, and ensure that the GRANULARITY and ESTIMATE_PERCENT settings for the specific table are using the default setting.

First we enable incremental statistics:

```
EXEC DBMS_STATS.set_table_prefs('nitin', 'nishas_buffers', 'INCREMENTAL', 'TRUE');
```

Then we reset to default setting values:

```
EXEC DBMS_STATS.set_table_prefs('nitin', 'nishas_buffers', 'GRANULARITY', 'AUTO');

EXEC DBMS_STATS.set_table_prefs
('nitin', 'nishas_buffers', 'ESTIMATE_PERCENT', DBMS_STATS.AUTO_SAMPLE_SIZE);
```

The statistics will now be gathered incrementally for the partitioned table by issuing the gather table statistics command.

Execute gather table statistics using the default values:

```
EXEC DBMS_STATS.gather_table_stats('nitin', 'nishas_buffers');
```

Or you can override the defaults and specify granularity and sample sizes:

```
EXEC DBMS_STATS.gather_table_stats('nitin', 'nishas_buffers', granularity
=> 'AUTO', estimate_percent => DBMS_STATS.AUTO_SAMPLE_SIZE);
```

To check the current setting of INCREMENTAL for a given table, use DBMS_STATS .GET_PREFS as follows:

```
SELECT DBMS_STATS.GET_PREFS('INCREMENTAL', 'nitin', 'nishas_buffers') FROM dual;
DBMS_STATS.GET_PREFS('INCREMENTAL','NITIN','NISHAS_BUFFERS')
------------------------------------------------------------------------TRUE
```

Incremental statistics, by default, kick in when a single row is altered in a partitioned table; then statistics for that partition are considered stale and must be gathered again before they can be used to generate global-level statistics. Now in 12c you can set the following INCREMENTAL_STALENESS setting. When setting INCREMENTAL_STALENESS to USE_STALE_PERCENT, the partition-level statistics are used as long as the percentage of rows changed is less than the value of the STALE_PERCENTAGE preference (10% by default). Alternatively it can be set to USE_LOCKED_STATS, which means if statistics on a partition are locked, they will be used to generate global-level statistics regardless of how many rows have changed in that partition since statistics were last gathered. You can specify USE_ STALE_PERCENT and USE_LOCKED_STATS together:

```
EXEC DBMS_STATS.SET_TABLE_PREFS (null, 'nitin', 'incremental_staleness',
'use_stale_percent, use_locked_stats');
```

Note that incremental statistics do not apply to the sub-partitions. Statistics will be gathered normally on the sub-partitions and on the partitions. Only the partition statistics will be used to determine the global- or table-level statistics.

Workload Statistics

Along with database statistics enhancements, Oracle Database 12c also automatically gathers system statistics at startup. Typically the CPU and I/O characteristics tend to become static over time, unless a system configuration has been made, for example, CPU has been added or upgraded. In these scenarios, it is recommended that you gather system statistics only when a physical change occurs in your environment. There are two types of statistics: no-workload and workload. Generally, the database initializes the no-workload statistics to default values at the first instance startup. For workload-based statistics, it is recommended that you capture statistics for the interval of time when the system is running the common workload.

The major difference between workload statistics and no-workload statistics is the method by which statistics are gathered. No-workload statistics are collected by submitting random reads against the database data files, whereas workload statistics are continuously gathered as online database activity occurs. Note that workload statistics are more accurate and thus, if collected, will override no-workload statistics.

To gather workload-based statistics, leverage the DBMS_STATS.GATHER_SYSTEM_STATS package to capture statistics. This should be executed when the database has the most typical workload. Workload statistics include the following:

- Single-block (sreadtim) and multiblock (mreadtim) read times
- Multiblock count (mbrc)
- CPU speed (cpuspeed)
- Maximum system throughput (maxthr)
- Average parallel execution throughput (slavethr)

Database internal routines compute sreadtim, mreadtim, and mbrc by comparing the number of physical sequential and random reads at intervals defined by the user (begin and end workload). The database collects and deploys these values through counters that change as the buffer cache completes synchronous read requests.

Since the counters are in the buffer cache, they include not only I/O delays but also waits related to latch contention and task switching. Thus, workload statistics depend on system activity during the workload window. If the system is I/O bound, the statistics promote a less I/O-intensive plan after the database uses the statistics. When workload statistics are gathered, the optimizer uses the mbrc value gathered for workload statistics to estimate the cost of a full table scan.

As with any database system, Exadata systems also need accurate system statistics to be gathered. This ensures that the optimizer is aware of Smart Scan throughput and bandwidth, allowing the optimizer to make accurate and optimal execution plans in an Exadata environment. The following command gathers Exadata-specific system statistics:

```
EXEC DBMS_STATS.GATHER_SYSTEM_STATS ('EXADATA');
```

When gathering workload statistics, the database may not gather the mbrc and mreadtim values if no table scans occur during serial workloads, as is typical of OLTP systems. However, full table scans occur frequently on DSSs. These scans may run in parallel and bypass the buffer cache. In such cases, the database still gathers the sreadtim because index lookups use the buffer cache.

If the database cannot gather or validate gathered mbrc or mreadtim values, but has gathered sreadtim and cpuspeed, the database uses only sreadtim and cpuspeed for costing. In this case, the optimizer uses the value of the initialization parameter DB_FILE_MULTIBLOCK_READ_COUNT to cost a full table scan. However, if DB_FILE_MULTIBLOCK_READ_COUNT is 0 or is not set, the optimizer uses a value of 8 for calculating cost. For workload statistics gathering to work correctly, ensure that JOB_QUEUE_PROCESSES is set to a nonzero value, allowing DBMS_JOB jobs and Oracle Scheduler jobs to execute.

Use the DBMS_STATS.GATHER_SYSTEM_STATS procedure to gather workload statistics. The GATHER_SYSTEM_STATS procedure refreshes the data dictionary or a staging table with statistics for the elapsed period. To set the duration of the collection, first set up and build a workload capture stats table:

```
EXEC DBMS_STATS.CREATE_STAT_TABLE('NITIN', 'workload_stats', 'USERS');
```

Specify the START parameter to indicate the beginning of the workload window and INTERVAL time. In our example we use the default of 60 minutes:

```
EXEC DBMS_STATS.GATHER_SYSTEM_STATS('START', NULL, 'workload_stats');
```

To stop the workload window, use the following:

```
EXEC DBMS_STATS.GATHER_SYSTEM_STATS('STOP', NULL, 'workload_stats');
```

The optimizer can now use the workload statistics to generate execution plans that are effective during the normal daily workload:

```
SELECT PNAME, PVAL1 FROM   SYS.AUX_STATS$
WHERE  SNAME = 'SYSSTATS_MAIN';
```

When the reported workload returns, DBAs can import the appropriate statistics into the data dictionary from the previously defined statistics table:

```
  EXEC DBMS_STATS.IMPORT_SYSTEM_STATS(stattab => 'workload_stats'
,    statid  => 'OLTP'
);
END;
/
```

No-Workload Statistics

The no-workload statistics capture characteristics of the I/O subsystem. By default, the database uses no-workload statistics and the CPU cost model. No-workload statistics are initialized to defaults at the first instance startup.

The `DBMS_STATS.GATHER_SYSTEM_STATS` procedure can be used to gather no-workload statistics manually. No-workload statistics include I/O transfer speed (`iotfrspeed`), I/O seek time (`ioseektim`), and CPU speed (`cpuspeednw`).

Note that there is an overhead on the I/O system during the gathering process of no-workload statistics. In some cases the no-workload statistics do not get set or picked up correctly. If you have concrete data points for these system statistics, they can be set manually as follows:

```
EXEC DBMS_STATS.GATHER_SYSTEM_STATS(gathering_mode => 'NOWORKLOAD');

COL PNAME FORMAT a15
SQL> SELECT PNAME, PVAL1 FROM SYS.AUX_STATS$ WHERE SNAME = 'SYSSTATS_MAIN';
PNAME               PVAL1
--------------- ----------
CPUSPEED
CPUSPEEDNW          1378
IOSEEKTIM             10
IOTFRSPEED          4096
MAXTHR
MBRC                  84
MREADTIM
SLAVETHR
SREADTIM
```

Information Lifecycle Management

Oracle's implementation of Information Lifecycle Management (ILM) really started in 11g. At the time it was based on partitioning being the keystone feature underneath.

The basic concept of any ILM strategy is to manage data from cradle to grave, with data classification being the key component. Data management along with data classification allows you to tag and identify the current stage in the life of the dataset and its eventual evolution. For example, a telecom company may archive customer call detail records near-site after four months. These decisions are generally made for business or industry compliance reasons; however, some businesses leverage ILM strategies to reduce the cost of storage. Data retrieval for archived data, with or without a service level agreement (SLA), must also be considered. Different vendors use various technologies to archive and perform management; these can vary from static tiered storage to dynamic data classification (rules and policy driven) based. Additionally, the granularity of data management can be as coarse as the storage-layer volumes or as granular as rows relating to specific content.

Oracle Database 12c implements an ILM strategy using cornerstone features such as Oracle Advanced Compression and tiered storage. Specifically, three new ILM-related features have been rolled into the ILM suite: Advanced Compression Option (ACO), Automatic Data Optimization (ADO), and Heat Map. Heat Map provides visibility into how, when, and where data is accessed and how access patterns change over time. It tracks at the row and segment levels. Data modification times are tracked at the row level and aggregated to the block level. Modification times, full table scan times, and index lookup times are tracked at the segment level.

ADO automatically moves and compresses data using user-defined policies driven by Heat Map metrics.

The reason the Heat Map and ADO are a good, tight fit is that, as opposed to static policies that define and map data classification to a specific tier, ADO/Heat Map not only defines the tier placement policy but also associates it with a compression factor. This provides space efficiency and optimization.

The different types of compression options help move data through its lifecycle:

Hot → Active → Less active → Historical

This data migration and evolution are completely transparent to the user.

For cold or historic data within the OLTP tables, use either Warehouse or Archive HCC. This ensures that data that is infrequently or never changed is compressed to the highest levels. Note that Advanced Row Compression is the only compression format supported for row policies.

To implement ILM with storage tiering and compression, DBAs can create ADO policies for data compression and data movement. Oracle commonly uses the term Smart Compression to refer to the ability to leverage Heat Map metrics to map compression policies, and compression levels, with user data. These ADO policies, along with Heat Map metrics, are evaluated and executed automatically in the background during the defined maintenance window. Optionally, DBAs can manually evaluate and execute ADO policies to generate a plan of when to move and compress data. ADO policies can be specified at the segment or row level for tables and table partitions.

The two key aspects of the ADO policy are the "when" and "what" of the data. For example, the "what" describes data access, such as no data reference (no reads) or no modification. The "when" describes the time since this data access occurred, for example, after three days of no access or three months of no modification. DBAs can also create custom conditions extending the flexibility of ADO to define when to move or compress data, as defined by the specific business or compliance requirements.

To activate ADO and Heat Map tracking, the following must be enabled at the system level:

```
ALTER SYSTEM SET HEAT_MAP = ON;
```

When Heat Map is enabled, the Oracle Database tracks all user segment accesses in-memory, using an activity-tracking module. Note that segment objects in the System and Sysaux tablespaces are not tracked.

Now let's generate a workload on some user tables:

```
update nitin.nishas_buffers set class# = 5;
```

Next, let's look at the Heat Map metrics using the V$ views. The following metrics are for tablespace Heat Map:

```
SELECT SUBSTR(TABLESPACE_NAME,1,20) tablespace_name,
SEGMENT_COUNT
FROM DBA_HEATMAP_TOP_TABLESPACES
ORDER BY SEGMENT_COUNT DESC;

TABLESPACE_NAME      SEGMENT_COUNT
-------------------- -------------
USERS                          11
```

The following is used to determine which objects are hot:

```
SQL> SELECT SUBSTR(OWNER,1,20),
SUBSTR(OBJECT_NAME,1,20),
OBJECT_TYPE, SUBSTR(TABLESPACE_NAME,1,20),
SEGMENT_COUNT
FROM DBA_HEATMAP_TOP_OBJECTS where owner
not like '%SYS'  ORDER BY SEGMENT_COUNT DESC

SUBSTR(OWNER,1,20)   SUBSTR(OBJECT_NAME,1 OBJECT_TYPE
-------------------- -------------------- -----------------
SUBSTR(TABLESPACE_NA SEGMENT_COUNT
-------------------- -------------
NITIN                NISHAS_BUFFERS       TABLE
USERS                           2
.
.
.
```

In the following example, a segment-level ADO policy defines row-level compression (Advanced Row Compression) after 34 days of no modifications. This policy is created to automatically compress partitions after there have been no modifications for 34 days:

```
ALTER TABLE nishas_buffers ILM
ADD POLICY ROW STORE COMPRESS ADVANCED SEGMENT
AFTER 34 DAYS OF NO MODIFICATION
```

In the next example, we create a segment-level compression policy for data after six months of no modifications:

```
ALTER TABLE nishas_buffers MODIFY PARTITION buffer1 ILM
ADD POLICY COMPRESS FOR ARCHIVE HIGH SEGMENT
AFTER 6 MONTHS OF NO MODIFICATION;
```

Is it assumed that we created a tablespace to house all the archive data to the expansion cabinet storage. This example illustrates the creation of archive data tablespace:

```
create tablespace SATA_EXPANSIONCELL_STORAGE1 datafile size 100G;
```

Now we set a policy to move the archive to this archived tablespace on the expansion storage:

```
SQL> ALTER TABLE nishas_buffers MODIFY PARTITION buffer2 ILM
ADD POLICY TIER TO SATA_EXPANSIONCELL_STORAGE1;
```

We use the following to see what ADO policies we have in place:

```
SELECT SUBSTR(policy_name,1,24) POLICY_NAME, policy_type, enabled
FROM USER_ILMPOLICIES;
POLICY_NAME              POLICY_TYPE    ENABLED
------------------------ -------------- -------
P1                       DATA MOVEMENT  YES
P21                      DATA MOVEMENT  YES
P41                      DATA MOVEMENT  YES
P61                      DATA MOVEMENT  YES
```

Application Continuity

Before 12c, application developers were required to deal explicitly with outages of the underlying software, hardware, and communications layers if they wanted to mask outages from end users. There have been many Oracle features that detected and reacted to failed connections. These include Transparent Application Failover (TAF), Fast Application Notification (FAN), and Fast Connection Failover (FCF). However, none of these features conveyed the correct outcome of the last transaction back to the application or recovered the in-progress request from an application perspective. If handled incorrectly, this could result in duplicate purchases and/or the multiple submission or processing of payments for the same invoice.

The Oracle Database 12c feature Application Continuity (AC), an application-independent feature, was introduced to handle these connection failures. AC attempts to recover incomplete requests from an application perspective and masks underlying system, network, and hardware failures and storage outages from the end user. As of this writing, AC is supported and available for Oracle JDBC Thin Driver, Oracle Universal Connection Pool (UCP), and Oracle WebLogic Server.

The AC protocol ensures that end user transactions are executed no more than once. When successful, the only time that an end user should see an interruption in service is when there is no point in continuing. When replayed, the execution appears to the application and client as if the request was delayed. This provides overall efficiency as it results in fewer calls to the application's error-handling logic. Without AC, the application would have to raise an error; however, this leaves the transaction in a state of flux since the user does not know if the transaction should or should not be reentered.

A sister feature of AC is Transaction Guard. Transaction Guard provides a generic tool for applications to use for "at-most-once" execution in case of planned or unplanned outages and repeated submissions. With Transaction Guard, applications implement a logical transaction ID (LTXID) to determine the outcome of the last transaction open in a database session following an outage. Without using Transaction Guard, applications that attempt to retry operations following outages can cause logical corruption by committing duplicate transactions.

One of the fundamental problems for recovering applications after an outage is that the commit message that is sent back to the client is not durable; that is, if there is a break between the client and the server, the client sees an error message indicating that the communication failed. However, this error does not inform the application whether the submission executed any commit operations or if a procedural call ran to completion, executing all expected commits and session state changes, or if it failed partway through, or, more problematic, is still running disconnected from the client.

If the end user cannot determine if the last transaction submission was committed, may commit at some point, or has not run to completion, the application may attempt to replay the transaction. This may cause duplicate transaction submissions because the software might try to reissue already persisted changes.

There is some confusion about how Transaction Guard and Application Continuity differ. In actuality, Transaction Guard is used by Application Continuity and is automatically enabled; however, Transaction Guard can be used and enabled independently. Transaction Guard prevents transactions from being replayed by Application Continuity. If the application has implemented an application-level replay, it requires the application to be integrated with Transaction Guard to provide idempotence.

Multitenant Architecture

Customers have been consolidating and reducing their database footprint to reduce IT costs by simplifying consolidation. There are numerous methods that DBAs can use to do this. Virtualization is one such approach. However, with CPU speed improving as well as becoming increasingly dense with more cores per socket, instance and schema consolidation is becoming increasingly popular.

Overview

Oracle Database 12c introduces another approach that marries the instance and schema models. Oracle Multitenant, more commonly known as Pluggable Database (PDB), is a new feature in Oracle Database 12c that helps customers drive consolidation and simplify provisioning, upgrades, and data transportability. The key benefit of this higher density is that many databases (PDBs) share the memory footprint and background processes. A small footprint per PDB allows DBAs to consolidate a large number of PDBs on a particular platform, as opposed to single databases that use the old architecture. This is the same benefit that schema-based consolidation brings. But there are significant barriers to adopting schema-based consolidation, as it causes ongoing operating problems. The new architecture removes these adoption barriers and operating problems.

PDB: A New Consolidation Model

By consolidating databases as PDBs, DBAs can manage many databases as one; for example, tasks like backup and Data Guard management are performed at the container database (CDB) level. An existing database can be simply adopted, with no change required by the application. Additionally, high-availability features such as RAC and Active Data Guard fully complement PDB.

There are several inherent key benefits for PDB-based consolidation, such as the capability to rapidly provision and clone a database. Patching is simplified as well, for example, when patching the CDB results in patching all of its many Pluggable Databases. This may or may not be a good thing. To isolate the patching to a single PDB, it is recommended that you establish a CDB with the patched Oracle version, then unplug or plug the PDB to be patched into the patched CDB.

Oracle Multitenant is such a big marquee feature that it cannot be easily covered in this chapter or in this book, but this chapter does cover how it fits in an Exadata environment.

For those who have done consolidation via virtualization platforms such as VMware or OVM, you know it's fairly straightforward and involves a simple "drag and drop" methodology. Similarly, consolidation of many databases as separate database instances on a platform is also fairly straightforward. However, there are a few reasons why schema consolidation is efficient:

- The schema consolidation model has consistently provided the most opportunities for reducing operating expenses, since you have only a single big database to maintain, monitor, and manage.

- Though schema consolidation allows the best ROI (regarding capital and operating expenses), you are sacrificing flexibility for compaction. Consolidation and isolation move in opposite directions. The more you consolidate, the fewer capabilities you have for isolation; in contrast, the more you try to isolate, the more you sacrifice the benefits of consolidation.

- Custom (homegrown) apps have been best-fit use cases for schema consolidation, since application owners and developers have more control over how the application and schema are built.

With the Oracle Database 12c feature Pluggable Database (PDB), you now have more incentive to lean toward schema consolidation. PDB *begins* to eliminate the typical issues that come with schema consolidation, such as namespace collisions, security, and granularity of recovery.

But before we go any further, a very, very high-level primer on a couple of terms is necessary:

- **Root Container Database**—Also known as the root CDB (cdb$root), this is the real database (if you will), and the name you give it will be the name of the instance. The CDB database owns the SGA and running processes. There can be many CDBs on the same database server (each with its own PDBs). But the cool thing is that there can be more than one CDB, allowing DBAs to have a database instance consolidation model coupled with schema consolidation. For best scalability, mix in RAC and leverage all the benefits of RAC Services, Quality of Service (QoS) Management, and workload distribution. The seed PDB (PDB$SEED) is an Oracle-supplied system template that the CDB can use to create new PDBs. You cannot add or modify objects in PDB$SEED.

- **Pluggable Database**—PDBs are sub-containers that are serviced by CDB resources. The true beauty of the PDB is its mobility; that is, you can plug and unplug 12c databases into and out of CDBs. You can create like-new PDBs from existing PDBs, such as full snapshots.

PDB Creation

Now let's look at the important and interesting new screens of 12c Database Installer and create a RAC PDB on Exadata Half Rack.

The Oracle Universal Installer (OUI) installation of RDBMS and creation of the database are fairly routine. However, there a few key screens that are specific to multitenancy PDB. In step 11 of the Oracle 12c Installer, shown in Figure 6.1, we specify "Create as Container database." Checking the box allows us to create our first PDB database in the CDB. In this example we specified "yoda" as the CDB name and the PDB is "pdbobi."

In the next screen we obviously choose ASM as the storage location, as shown in Figure 6.2.

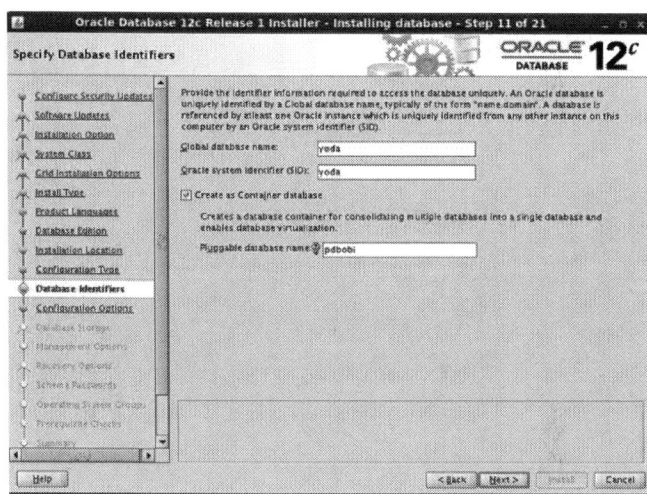

Figure 6.1 Create Database screen. We selected "Create as Container database."

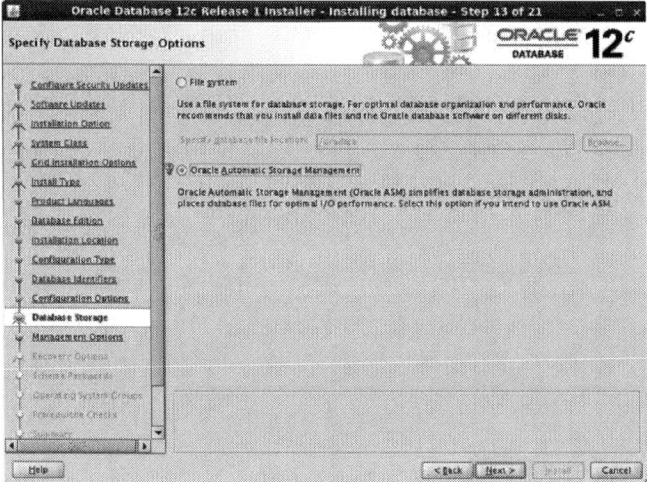

Figure 6.2 Select ASM for the storage layer.

The rest of the steps and screens are fairly standard. But here's an excerpt from the database alert that shows the magic underneath:

```
create pluggable database PDB$SEED as clone using
'/u02/app/oracle/product/12.1.0/dbhome_1/assistants/dbca/templates/pdbseed.xml'
source_file_name_convert =
('/ade/b/3593327372/oracle/oradata/seeddata/pdbseed/temp01.dbf',
'+PDBDATA/YODA/DD7C48AA5A4404A2E04325AAE80A403C/DATAFILE/pdbseed_temp01.dbf',
'/ade/b/3593327372/oracle/oradata/seeddata/pdbseed/system01.dbf',
'+PDBDATA/YODA/DD7C48AA5A4404A2E04325AAE80A403C/DATAFILE/system.271.823892297',
'/ade/b/3593327372/oracle/oradata/seeddata/pdbseed/sysaux01.dbf',
'+PDBDATA/YODA/DD7C48AA5A4404A2E04325AAE80A403C/DATAFILE/sysaux.270.823892297')
file_name_convert=NONE  NOCOPY

Mon Aug 19 18:58:59 2013
….
….
Post plug operations are now complete.
Pluggable database PDB$SEED with pdb id - 2 is now marked as NEW.


create pluggable database pdbobi as clone  using
'/u02/app/oracle/product/12.1.0/dbhome_1/assistants/dbca/templates/samples
chema.xml'  source_file_name_convert =
('/ade/b/3593327372/oracle/oradata/seeddata/SAMPLE_SCHEMA/temp01.dbf',
'+PDBDATA/YODA/DD7D8C1D4C234B38E04325AAE80AF577/DATAFILE/pdbobi_temp01.dbf',
'/ade/b/3593327372/oracle/oradata/seeddata/SAMPLE_SCHEMA/example01.dbf',
'+PDBDATA/YODA/DD7D8C1D4C234B38E04325AAE80AF577/DATAFILE/example.275.823892813',
'/ade/b/3593327372/oracle/oradata/seeddata/SAMPLE_SCHEMA/system01.dbf',
'+PDBDATA/YODA/DD7D8C1D4C234B38E04325AAE80AF577/DATAFILE/system.276.823892813',
'/ade/b/3593327372/oracle/oradata/seeddata/SAMPLE_SCHEMA/SAMPLE_SCHEMA_users01.dbf',
'+PDBDATA/YODA/DD7D8C1D4C234B38E04325AAE80AF577/DATAFILE/users.277.823892813',
'/ade/b/3593327372/oracle/oradata/seeddata/SAMPLE_SCHEMA/sysaux01.dbf',
'+PDBDATA/YODA/DD7D8C1D4C234B38E04325AAE80AF577/DATAFILE/sysaux.274.823892813')
file_name_convert=NONE  NOCOPY

Mon Aug 19 19:07:42 2013
….
….
****************************************************************
Post plug operations are now complete.
Pluggable database PDBOBI with pdb id - 3 is now marked as NEW.
****************************************************************
Completed: create pluggable database pdbobi as clone  using
'/u02/app/oracle/product/12.1.0/dbhome_1/assistants/dbca/templates/samples
chema.xml'  source_file_name_convert =
('/ade/b/3593327372/oracle/oradata/seeddata/SAMPLE_SCHEMA/temp01.dbf',
'+PDBRECO/YODA/DD7D8C1D4C234B38E04325AAE80AF577/DATAFILE/pdbobi_temp01.dbf',
'/ade/b/3593327372/oracle/oradata/seeddata/SAMPLE_SCHEMA/example01.dbf',
'+PDBRECO/YODA/DD7D8C1D4C234B38E04325AAE80AF577/DATAFILE/example.275.823892813',
'/ade/b/3593327372/oracle/oradata/seeddata/SAMPLE_SCHEMA/system01.dbf',
'+PDBRECO/YODA/DD7D8C1D4C234B38E04325AAE80AF577/DATAFILE/system.276.823892813',
'/ade/b/3593327372/oracle/oradata/seeddata/SAMPLE_SCHEMA/SAMPLE_SCHEMA_users01.dbf',
'+PDBRECO/YODA/DD7D8C1D4C234B38E04325AAE80AF577/DATAFILE/users.277.823892813',
'/ade/b/3593327372/oracle/oradata/seeddata/SAMPLE_SCHEMA/sysaux01.dbf',
'+PDBRECO/YODA/DD7D8C1D4C234B38E04325AAE80AF577/DATAFILE/sysaux.274.823892813')
file_name_convert=NONE  NOCOPY

alter pluggable database pdbobi open restricted
Pluggable database PDBOBI dictionary check beginning
Pluggable Database PDBOBI Dictionary check complete
Database Characterset is US7ASCII
….
….
```

```
XDB installed.

XDB initialized.
Mon Aug 19 19:08:01 2013
Pluggable database PDBOBI opened read write
Completed: alter pluggable database pdbobi open restricted
```

PDB Creation, Cloning, and Dropping

Once the Oracle Database 12*c* software is installed, any future database management (specifically PDB) can be performed using the DBCA (shown in Figure 6.3), which has been extended to support PDB. The operations can also be executed using SQL commands. Let's illustrate some examples.

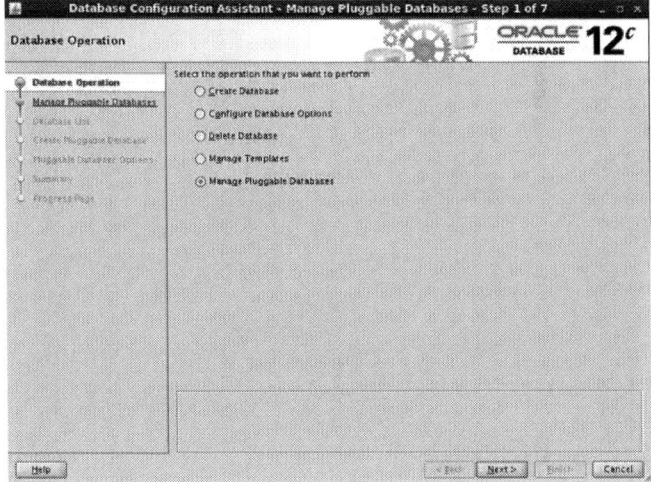

Figure 6.3   Manage existing Pluggable Databases

In this example we create a PDB (PDBvader) from an existing PDB (PDBOBI):

```
CDB$ROOT@YODA> create pluggable database PDBvader from PDBOBI;
```

Or we could create it into a different disk group:

```
CDB$ROOT@YODA> create pluggable database PDBvader from PDBOBI;
FILE_NAME_CONVERT=('+PDBRECO/YODA/DD7D8C1D4C234B38E04325AAE80AF577/DATAFILE',
'+PDBDATA');

Pluggable database created.
```

```
CDB$ROOT@YODA> select pdb_name, status from cdb_pdbs;

PDB_NAME    STATUS
----------  -------------
PDBOBI      NORMAL
PDB$SEED    NORMAL
PDBVADER    NORMAL

And

CDB$ROOT@YODA> select CON_ID,DBID,NAME,TOTAL_SIZE from v$pdbs;

    CON_ID        DBID    NAME              TOTAL_SIZE
----------  ----------  -------------      -------------
         2  4066465523  PDB$SEED               283115520
         3   483260478  PDBOBI                 917504000
         4   994649056  PDBVADER                       0
```

Note that the TOTAL_SIZE column shows 0 bytes. Recall that all new PDBs are created and placed in a MOUNTED state.

Through the following illustration we see that when the PDB is opened, the TOTAL_SIZE is reflected correctly.

Set to the correct container:

```
CDB$ROOT@YODA> alter session set container=pdbvader;

Session altered.
```

Open the container:

```
CDB$ROOT@YODA> alter pluggable database open;

Pluggable database altered.
```

List the container's data files:

```
CDB$ROOT@YODA> select file_name from cdb_data_files;

FILE_NAME
-------------------------------------------------------------------------
+PDBDATA/YODA/E46B24386A131109E043EDFE10AC6E89/DATAFILE/system.280.823980769
+PDBDATA/YODA/E46B24386A131109E043EDFE10AC6E89/DATAFILE/sysaux.279.823980769
+PDBDATA/YODA/E46B24386A131109E043EDFE10AC6E89/DATAFILE/users.281.823980769
+PDBDATA/YODA/E46B24386A131109E043EDFE10AC6E89/DATAFILE/example.282.823980769
```

Now the size is reflected correctly!

```
CDB$ROOT@YODA> select CON_ID,DBID,NAME,TOTAL_SIZE from v$pdbs;

    CON_ID        DBID    NAME                           TOTAL_SIZE
----------  ----------  ----------------------------    ----------
         4   994649056  PDBVADER                          393216000
```

Incidentally, that long identifier, E46B24386A131109E043EDFE10AC6E89, in the Oracle Managed File (OMF) name is the GUID or globally unique identifier for that PDB. This is not the same as a container unique identifier (CON_UID). The CON_UID is a local identifier, whereas the GUID is universal. Keep in mind that we can unplug a PDB from one CDB and plug it into another CDB, so the GUID provides this uniqueness and streamlines portability.

Note that the scope of PDBVADER is set to its own container files; it can't see PDBOBI files at all. If we connect back to cdb$root and look at v$datafile, we see that cdb$root has a scope for all the data files in the CDB. The following query illustrates this scope:

```
CDB$ROOT@YODA> select name from v$datafile order by con_id

NAME
-----------------
+PDBDATA/YODA/DATAFILE/undotbs1.260.8238921551
+PDBDATA/YODA/DATAFILE/sysaux.257.8238920631
+PDBDATA/YODA/DATAFILE/system.258.8238921091
+PDBDATA/YODA/DATAFILE/users.259.8238921551
+PDBDATA/YODA/DD7C48AA5A4404A2E04325AAE80A403C/DATAFILE/system.271.8238922972
+PDBDATA/YODA/DD7C48AA5A4404A2E04325AAE80A403C/DATAFILE/sysaux.270.8238922972
+PDBDATA/YODA/DD7D8C1D4C234B38E04325AAE80AF577/DATAFILE/example.275.8238928133
+PDBDATA/YODA/DD7D8C1D4C234B38E04325AAE80AF577/DATAFILE/users.277.8238928133
+PDBDATA/YODA/E456D87DF75E6553E043EDFE10AC71EA/DATAFILE/obiwan.284.8246833393
+PDBDATA/YODA/DD7D8C1D4C234B38E04325AAE80AF577/DATAFILE/system.276.8238928133
+PDBDATA/YODA/DD7D8C1D4C234B38E04325AAE80AF577/DATAFILE/sysaux.274.8238928133
+PDBDATA/YODA/E46B24386A131109E043EDFE10AC6E89/DATAFILE/sysaux.279.8239807694
+PDBDATA/YODA/E46B24386A131109E043EDFE10AC6E89/DATAFILE/users.281.8239807694
+PDBDATA/YODA/E46B24386A131109E043EDFE10AC6E89/DATAFILE/example.282.8239807694
+PDBDATA/YODA/E46B24386A131109E043EDFE10AC6E89/DATAFILE/system.280.8239807694
```

For completeness, let's look at a couple of different ways to create a PDB. The beauty of PDB is not just mobility (plug and unplug), which we'll show later, but that we can create or clone a new PDB from a gold-image PDB. That's real agility and a Database as a Service (DBaaS) play. So let's create a new PDB in a couple of different ways.

First, let's create a PDB from SEED:

```
CDB$ROOT@YODA> alter session set container=cdb$root;

Session altered.

CDB$ROOT@YODA> CREATE PLUGGABLE DATABASE pdbhansolo
admin user hansolo identified by hansolo roles=(dba);

Pluggable database created.


CDB$ROOT@YODA> alter pluggable database pdbhansolo open;

Pluggable database altered.
```

```
CDB$ROOT@YODA> select file_name from cdb_data_files;

FILE_NAME
----------------------------------------------------------------------------
+PDBDATA/YODA/E51109E2AF22127AE043EDFE10AC1DD9/DATAFILE/system.280.824693889
+PDBDATA/YODA/E51109E2AF22127AE043EDFE10AC1DD9/DATAFILE/sysaux.279.824693893
```

Notice that it contains just the basic files to enable a PDB. The CDB will copy from the PDB$SEED the System and Sysaux tablespaces and instantiate them in the new PDB.

In our next example, let's clone from an existing PDB (PDBOBI in this case):

```
CDB$ROOT@YODA> alter session set container=cdb$root;

Session altered.

CDB$ROOT@YODA> alter pluggable database pdbobi close;

Pluggable database altered.

CDB$ROOT@YODA> alter pluggable database pdbobi open read only;

Pluggable database altered.

CDB$ROOT@YODA> CREATE PLUGGABLE DATABASE pdbleia from pdbobi;

Pluggable database created.

CDB$ROOT@YODA> alter pluggable database pdbleia open;

Pluggable database altered.

CDB$ROOT@YODA> select file_name from cdb_data_files;

FILE_NAME
----------------------------------------------------------------------------
+PDBDATA/YODA/E51109E2AF23127AE043EDFE10AC1DD9/DATAFILE/system.281.824694649
+PDBDATA/YODA/E51109E2AF23127AE043EDFE10AC1DD9/DATAFILE/sysaux.282.824694651
+PDBDATA/YODA/E51109E2AF23127AE043EDFE10AC1DD9/DATAFILE/users.285.824694661
+PDBDATA/YODA/E51109E2AF23127AE043EDFE10AC1DD9/DATAFILE/example.286.824694661
+PDBDATA/YODA/E51109E2AF23127AE043EDFE10AC1DD9/DATAFILE/obiwan.287.824694669
```

Notice that the OBI tablespace that we created in PDBOBI came over as part of this clone process.

We can drop this PDB if it's no longer needed:

```
CDB$ROOT@YODA> alter session set container=cdb$root;

Session altered.

CDB$ROOT@YODA> drop pluggable database pdbvader including datafiles;
drop pluggable database pdbvader including datafiles
*
ERROR at line 1:
ORA-65025: Pluggable database PDBVADER is not closed on all instances.
```

```
CDB$ROOT@YODA> alter pluggable database pdbvader close;

Pluggable database altered.

CDB$ROOT@YODA> drop pluggable database pdbvader including datafiles;

Pluggable database dropped.
```

Unplug/Plug Operations

Oracle Multitenant is unique in accomplishing the positive attributes of alternative consolidation methods while avoiding their drawbacks. One of the key elements of the Pluggable Database feature is unplug/plug capabilities. In fact, unplug/plug is one method to migrate into a CDB platform. The requirement is that the source database must first be a 12c database.

With this feature, a PDB can be unplugged from one CDB and plugged into another to allow DBAs the option of performing maintenance on an individual PDB; for example, an individual PDB can be provisioned, patched, cloned, consolidated, restored, or moved without impacting other PDBs in the same CDB. Unplug/plug requires that a manifest file be created; this can be performed at the command line or via DBCA.

To create the manifest file, we must first close the source database:

```
alter pluggable database endor close immediate;
alter pluggable database endor unplug into '/u01/app/oracle/oradata/endor.xml'
```

Before we plug in, we need to verify the compatibility of the source-target database:

```
set serveroutput on
DECLARE compatible BOOLEAN := FALSE;
BEGIN compatible := DBMS_PDB.CHECK_PLUG_COMPATIBILITY
(pdb_descr_file => '/u01/app/oracle/oradata/endor.xml');
if compatible then
DBMS_OUTPUT.PUT_LINE('Is pluggable Endor compatible? YES');
else DBMS_OUTPUT.PUT_LINE('Is pluggable Endor compatible? NO');
end if; END;
Is pluggable PDB1 compatible? YES
```

If all looks good, we proceed to plug into the CDB:

```
create pluggable database pdb_plug_nocopy using
'/u01/app/oracle/oradata/pdb1.xml'  NOCOPY tempfile reuse;
```

The source (unplugged) data files are now part of the plugged-in PDB. A file with the same name as the temp file specified in the XML file exists in the target location. Therefore, the TEMPFILE_REUSE clause is required.

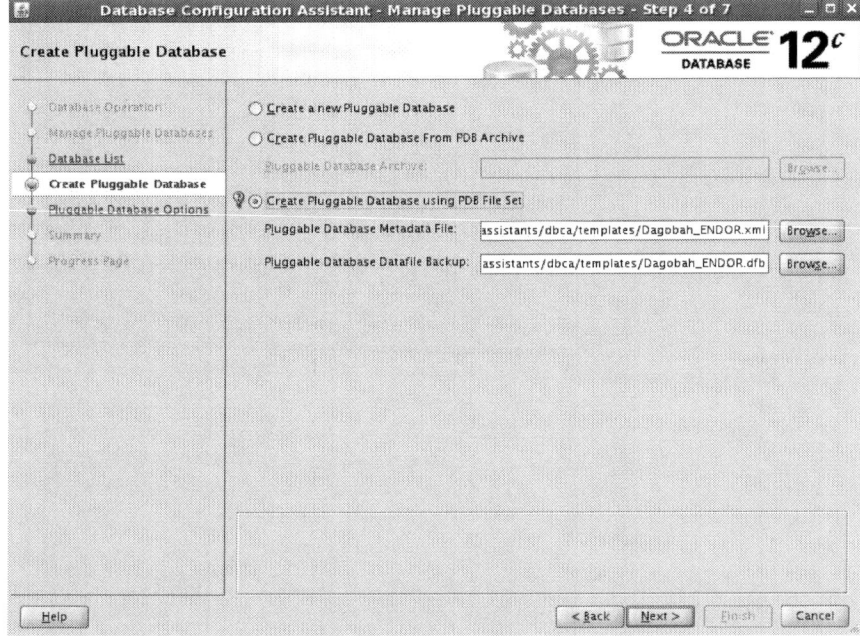

Figure 6.4   Create a Pluggable Database using an existing PDB file set

Figure 6.4 illustrates a similar method using DBCA.

In this example we used a NOCOPY method; there is also the option to plug in using the COPY and AS CLONE MOVE methods.

RAC and PDB

There are benefits of deploying PDB with RAC Services. Although the key ingredient is the service, RAC provides the final mile for scalability and availability. It's best not to implement PDB without RAC. Database (RAC) Services integration with PDBs provides seamless management and availability.

Initially, we have only the PDB$SEED:

```
SQL> select * from v$pdbs;


CON_ID      DBID      CON_UID GUID       NAME
OPEN_MODE   RES OPEN_TIME
```

```
CREATE_SCN TOTAL_SIZE
----------------------------------------- ---------- ----------
2 4080865680 4080865680 F13EFFD958E24857E0430B2910ACF6FD PDB$SEED
READ ONLY   NO   17-FEB-14 01.01.13.909 PM
1720768   283115520
```

Let's create a PDB from the SEED:

```
SQL> CREATE PLUGGABLE DATABASE pdbhansolo admin user hansolo
identified by
hansolo roles=(dba);

Pluggable database created.

Now we have the new PDB listed.

SQL> select * from v$pdbs;

CON_ID      DBID        CON_UID      GUID       NAME
OPEN_MODE   RES OPEN_TIME
CREATE_SCN TOTAL_SIZE
---------- ---------- ---------- ------------------------------- 

2           4080865680 4080865680 F13EFFD958E24857E0430B2910ACF6FD PDB$SEED
READ ONLY   NO   17-FEB-14 01.01.13.909 PM
1720768   283115520
            3 3403102439 3403102439 F2A023F791663F8DE0430B2910AC37F7
PDBHANSOLO     MOUNTED         17-FEB-14 01.27.08.942 PM
1846849         0
```

Notice that it's in MOUNTED status. Even if we restart the whole CDB, the new PDB will not come up in OPEN READ WRITE mode. If we want to have the PDB available on startup, here's how we go about making that happen.

When we create or plug in a new PDB, a default service gets created. As with previous versions, it is highly recommended not to connect to a service. Oracle took this one step further and forced users to create a user-generated service. So let's associate a user service with that PDB. Notice that there's a -pdb flag in the add service command:

```
$ srvctl add service -d dagobah -s hoth -pdb pdbhansolo

[oracle@rac02 ~]$ srvctl config service -d dagobah -verbose
Service name: Hoth
Service is enabled
Server pool: Dagobah
Cardinality: 1
Disconnect: false
Service role: PRIMARY
Management policy: AUTOMATIC
DTP transaction: false
AQ HA notifications: false
Global: false
Commit Outcome: false
Failover type:
Failover method:
TAF failover retries:
```

```
TAF failover delay:
Connection Load Balancing Goal: LONG
Runtime Load Balancing Goal: NONE
TAF policy specification: NONE
Edition:
----> Pluggable database name: pdbhansolo
Maximum lag time: ANY
SQL Translation Profile:
Retention: 86400 seconds
Replay Initiation Time: 300 seconds
Session State Consistency:
Preferred instances: Dagobah_1
Available instances:
```

And the Service is registered with the listener

```
[oracle@rac02 ~]$ lsnrctl stat

LSNRCTL for Linux: Version 12.1.0.1.0 - Production on 17-FEB-2014 13:34:41

Copyright (c) 1991, 2013, Oracle.  All rights reserved.

Connecting to (ADDRESS=(PROTOCOL=tcp)(HOST=)(PORT=1521))
STATUS of the LISTENER
------------------------
Alias                     LISTENER
Version                   TNSLSNR for Linux: Version 12.1.0.1.0 - Production
Start Date                17-FEB-2014 12:59:46
Uptime                    0 days 0 hr. 34 min. 54 sec
Trace Level               off
Security                  ON: Local OS Authentication
SNMP                      OFF
Listener Parameter File   /u01/app/12.1.0/grid/network/admin/listener.ora
Listener Log File         /u01/app/oracle/diag/tnslsnr/rac02/listener/alert/log.xml
Listening Endpoints Summary...
  (DESCRIPTION=(ADDRESS=(PROTOCOL=ipc)(KEY=LISTENER)))
  (DESCRIPTION=(ADDRESS=(PROTOCOL=tcp)(HOST=172.16.41.11)(PORT=1521)))
  (DESCRIPTION=(ADDRESS=(PROTOCOL=tcp)(HOST=172.16.41.21)(PORT=1521)))
  (DESCRIPTION=(ADDRESS=(PROTOCOL=tcps)(HOST=rac02.viscosityna.com)(PORT=5500))(Security=
(my_wallet_directory=/u02/app/oracle/product/12.1.0/db/admin/Dagobah/xdb_wallet))
(Presentation=HTTP)(Session=RAW))
Services Summary...
Service "+ASM" has 1 instance(s).
  Instance "+ASM3", status READY, has 2 handler(s) for this service...
Service "Dagobah" has 1 instance(s).
  Instance "Dagobah_1", status READY, has 1 handler(s) for this service...
Service "DagobahXDB" has 1 instance(s).
  Instance "Dagobah_1", status READY, has 1 handler(s) for this service...
---->Service "Hoth" has 1 instance(s).
  Instance "Dagobah_1", status READY, has 1 handler(s) for this service...
 Service "pdbhansolo" has 1 instance(s).
  Instance "Dagobah_1", status READY, has 1 handler(s) for this service...
Service "r2d2" has 1 instance(s).
  Instance "Dagobah_1", status READY, has 1 handler(s) for this service...
The command completed successfully
[/sql]
```

Now let's test this. Close the PDB and also stop the CDB:

```
SQL> alter session set container=cdb$root;

Session altered.

SQL> alter pluggable database pdbhansolo close;
```

```
[oracle@rac02 ~]$ srvctl stop database -d dagobah

[oracle@rac02 ~]$ lsnrctl stat

LSNRCTL for Linux: Version 12.1.0.1.0 - Production on 18-FEB-2014 15:36:49

Copyright (c) 1991, 2013, Oracle.  All rights reserved.

Connecting to (ADDRESS=(PROTOCOL=tcp)(HOST=)(PORT=1521))
STATUS of the LISTENER
------------------------
Alias                     LISTENER
Version                   TNSLSNR for Linux: Version 12.1.0.1.0 - Production
Start Date                18-FEB-2014 12:57:30
Uptime                    0 days 2 hr. 39 min. 19 sec
Trace Level               off
Security                  ON: Local OS Authentication
SNMP                      OFF
Listener Parameter File   /u01/app/12.1.0/grid/network/admin/listener.ora
Listener Log File         /u01/app/oracle/diag/tnslsnr/rac02/listener/alert/log.xml
Listening Endpoints Summary...
  (DESCRIPTION=(ADDRESS=(PROTOCOL=ipc)(KEY=LISTENER)))
  (DESCRIPTION=(ADDRESS=(PROTOCOL=tcp)(HOST=172.16.41.11)(PORT=1521)))
  (DESCRIPTION=(ADDRESS=(PROTOCOL=tcp)(HOST=172.16.41.21)(PORT=1521)))
Services Summary...
Service "+APX" has 1 instance(s).
  Instance "+APX3", status READY, has 1 handler(s) for this service...
Service "+ASM" has 1 instance(s).
  Instance "+ASM3", status READY, has 2 handler(s) for this service...
The command completed successfully


[oracle@rac02 ~]$ srvctl start database -d dagobah

[oracle@rac02 ~]$ lsnrctl stat

LSNRCTL for Linux: Version 12.1.0.1.0 - Production on 18-FEB-2014 15:37:39

Copyright (c) 1991, 2013, Oracle.  All rights reserved.

Connecting to (ADDRESS=(PROTOCOL=tcp)(HOST=)(PORT=1521))
STATUS of the LISTENER
------------------------
Alias                     LISTENER
Version                   TNSLSNR for Linux: Version 12.1.0.1.0 - Production
Start Date                18-FEB-2014 12:57:30
Uptime                    0 days 2 hr. 40 min. 9 sec
Trace Level               off
Security                  ON: Local OS Authentication
SNMP                      OFF
Listener Parameter File   /u01/app/12.1.0/grid/network/admin/listener.ora
Listener Log File         /u01/app/oracle/diag/tnslsnr/rac02/listener/alert/log.xml
Listening Endpoints Summary...
  (DESCRIPTION=(ADDRESS=(PROTOCOL=ipc)(KEY=LISTENER)))
  (DESCRIPTION=(ADDRESS=(PROTOCOL=tcp)(HOST=172.16.41.11)(PORT=1521)))
  (DESCRIPTION=(ADDRESS=(PROTOCOL=tcp)(HOST=172.16.41.21)(PORT=1521)))
  (DESCRIPTION=(ADDRESS=(PROTOCOL=tcps)(HOST=rac02.viscosityna.com)(PORT=5500))(Security=
(my_wallet_directory=/u02/app/oracle/product/12.1.0/db/admin/Dagobah/xdb_wallet))
(Presentation=HTTP)(Session=RAW))
Services Summary...
Service "+APX" has 1 instance(s).
  Instance "+APX3", status READY, has 1 handler(s) for this service...
Service "+ASM" has 1 instance(s).
  Instance "+ASM3", status READY, has 2 handler(s) for this service...
Service "Dagobah" has 1 instance(s).
  Instance "Dagobah_1", status READY, has 1 handler(s) for this service...
```

```
Service "DagobahXDB" has 1 instance(s).
  Instance "Dagobah_1", status READY, has 1 handler(s) for this service...
---->Service "Hoth" has 1 instance(s).
  Instance "Dagobah_1", status READY, has 1 handler(s) for this service...
 Service "pdbhansolo" has 1 instance(s).
  Instance "Dagobah_1", status READY, has 1 handler(s) for this service...
Service "r2d2" has 1 instance(s).
  Instance "Dagobah_1", status READY, has 1 handler(s) for this service...
The command completed successfully


SQL> select NAME,OPEN_MODE from v$pdbs;

NAME                          OPEN_MODE
----------------------------- ----------
PDB$SEED                      READ ONLY
--> PDBHANSOLO                READ WRITE
```

Now we can connect to this PDB using the EZCONNECT string:

```
sqlplus hansolo/hansolo@rac02/hoth
```

So let's see this relationship between the service (Hoth) Pluggable Database (pdbhansolo):

```
$crsctl stat res ora.dagobah.hoth.svc -p
NAME=ora.dagobah.hoth.svc
TYPE=ora.service.type
ACL=owner:oracle:rwx,pgrp:oinstall:rwx,other::r--
….
….
DELETE_TIMEOUT=60
DESCRIPTION=Oracle Service resource
GEN_SERVICE_NAME=Hoth
GLOBAL=false
GSM_FLAGS=0
HOSTING_MEMBERS=
INSTANCE_FAILOVER=1
INTERMEDIATE_TIMEOUT=0
LOAD=1
LOGGING_LEVEL=1
MANAGEMENT_POLICY=AUTOMATIC
MAX_LAG_TIME=ANY
MODIFY_TIMEOUT=60
NLS_LANG=
NOT_RESTARTING_TEMPLATE=
OFFLINE_CHECK_INTERVAL=0
PLACEMENT=restricted
PLUGGABLE_DATABASE=pdbhansolo
PROFILE_CHANGE_TEMPLATE=
RELOCATE_BY_DEPENDENCY=1
[/sql]
```

The key here is that the RAC Service of PDBHANSOLO (nondefault) becomes an important aspect of PDB auto-startup. Without the use of the nondefault service the PDB does not open read/write automatically. So where does RAC fit in here?

Well, if you have, for example, a six-node RAC cluster, you can have some PDB services not start on certain nodes. This effectively prevents access to those PDBs from certain nodes; thus, you can have a certain predefined workload distribution.

Exadata Software Updates

In this section, we touch on the new features of the Exadata Storage Server software. Generally it is difficult to discuss new features for such a dynamic layer as Exadata. However, we cover some of the key features of Exadata 11.2.3.3 and 12.1.1.1.

With the advent of Exadata 11.2.3.3, Exadata Smart Flash Cache Compression provides the capability to compress user data, in-band, as it is loaded into the Flash Cache. This is transparent to the application. With compression, more data can be kept in Flash, which potentially increases the logical capacity of the Flash Cache. In Exadata 11.2.3.3, Oracle Exadata Storage Server software automatically caches objects read by table and partition scan workloads in Flash Cache based on how frequently the objects are read.

We touched on Multitenant-PDB in the previous section; with Exadata 12.1.1.1, IORM has been extended to support the Oracle Database 12c Multitenant architecture and PDBs. In the latest Exadata version, IORM along with DBRM now supports PDB to ensure that defined policies are met, even when multiple databases, CDBs, or PDBs share the same cluster domain.

But the biggest feature of Exadata, in 11.2.3.3 and 12.1.1.1, is the introduction of network resource management. Network resource management automatically and transparently prioritizes critical database network messages. This prioritization is implemented throughout the Exadata stack, from the Database Node, database InfiniBand adapters, Exadata Storage Server software, Exadata Storage Cell InfiniBand adapters, and InfiniBand switches. The main purpose behind this feature is to improve messaging latency for Oracle components that are latency sensitive. These main latency-sensitive messages such as RAC Cache Fusion messages, critical background internode communication, are prioritized over batch, reporting, and backup messages. To minimize the impact of log file sync outliers, log file write operations are given the highest priority to ensure low latency.

Summary

As with any new Oracle version, improved manageability, performance, and efficiency were the key objectives. Oracle Database 12c is no exception. This chapter covered the marquee features that address customers' efforts to standardize, consolidate, and automate database services. Oracle Database 12c introduced big-ticket features such as Automatic Data Optimization, Heat Map monitors, as well as several high-availability features and enhancements to existing technologies such as Oracle partitioning that enable continuous database access. Oracle Database 12c also introduced key new features for application high availability, for example, Application Continuity, that complement Oracle RAC which masks application failures.

7

Exadata Networking: Management and Administration

Oracle Exadata Database Machine is shipped with three major preconfigured hardware components: storage servers (cell), database servers (compute), and ultrafast InfiniBand storage network. The network configuration in Exadata plays a significant role, and the prerequisites are far more complex and larger than for any non-Exadata setup. The goal of this chapter is to present you with a broad picture of the fundamentals of the network layer and its functionality in Exadata Database Machine. The chapter also outlines the prerequisites and essential requirements and explains the role played by the InfiniBand network. You will also learn how to manage and troubleshoot the IB switches using command-line tools and utilities or OEM/ILOM GUI.

Exadata Network Components

A DMA has very little control over network component management and configuration. Although DMAs have a very limited role to play in network management, it is essential for them to understand its prerequisites and gain thorough knowledge of the network requirements, the key components, and the InfiniBand switch to be able to resolve any issues that could arise from the network layer.

We will explore some of the important technical details and architecture design details of Exadata network components, the InfiniBand switch, and network setup in an Exadata environment. You will understand the architecture involved in Exadata setup and the key role played by InfiniBand.

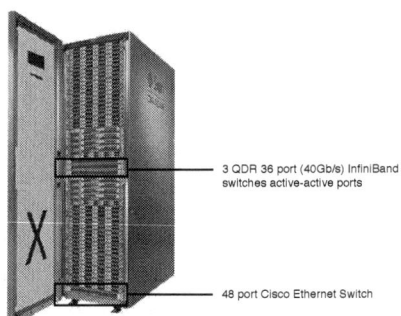

3 QDR 36 port (40Gb/s) InfiniBand
switches active-active ports

48 port Cisco Ethernet Switch

Figure 7.1   A full-capacity Exadata rack with three InfiniBand switches

An Oracle Exadata X4-2 Full Rack is typically equipped with the following ultra-fast high-bandwidth network components:

- At least 2 x QDR (40Gb/s) InfiniBand switches with dual active-active ports (PCIe 3.0)
- Half and Full Racks, which also come with an additional InfiniBand switch, a spine switch, for storage expansion, external connectivity, and so forth
- 1GB or 10GB Ethernet data center connectivity
- At least one pair of InfiniBand ports per server

Figure 7.1 depicts the network components and their location in an Exadata Full Rack.

The Role of the InfiniBand Network

Being able to deliver breakthrough application performance in any type of environment requires a solid networking foundation. InfiniBand delivers high performance, low latency, and great scalability services for high-performance computing environments. All Oracle engineered systems leverage and heavily depend on the InfiniBand technology because of its node interconnects, its use as a bridge between Storage and Database Nodes, and for storage expansion to provide superior network performance. The following specifies the role and the current model of InfiniBand in an Exadata:

- New InfiniBand switch firmware (2.1.3)
- Dual ports (active-active)
- High-performance 40Gb/s (bidirectional)

- Two leaf switches and one spine switch for Half and Full Racks only
- Low-latency and high-bandwidth network access between storage and database servers and for interconnect
- Unified network fabric for cluster interconnect, storage network, rack expansion, and external connectivity, for example, RMAN backups
- Uses Zero-loss Zero-copy Datagram protocol (ZDP)
- Minimal CPU consumption in transforming data
- Fault-tolerant network capabilities through network redundant switches
- Redundant power and cooling
- Data throughput of 2.3TB/s (bidirectional)

Network Architecture

This section will help you understand the network architectural details: how the spine and leaf switches communicate with each other, what ports are used for which type of network, and how the cell and Compute Nodes communicate.

Figure 7.2 illustrates the network connectivity and communication involved in a typical Full Rack Exadata Database Machine.

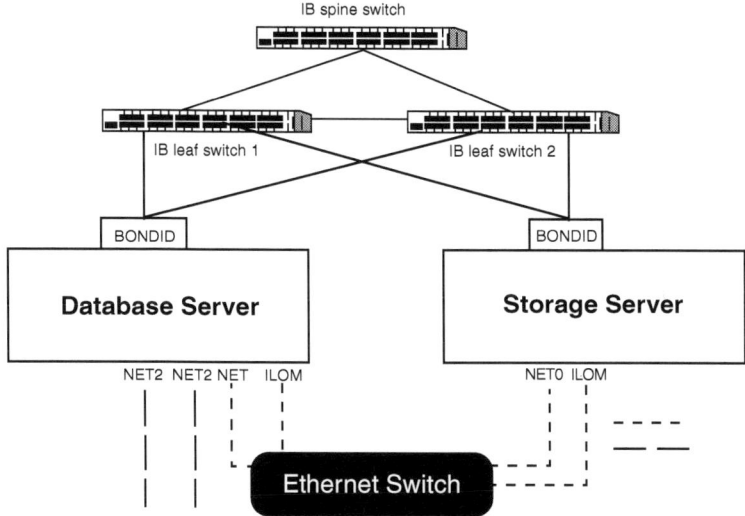

Figure 7.2   InfiniBand switch connectivity and ports

The following explains the network design architectural details showcased in Figure 7.2 and what type of networks are involved in the setup.

A Half or Full Rack Exadata Database Machine has three InfiniBand switches: one spine switch and two leaf switches. In Figure 7.2, each IB leaf switch is connected to a spine switch through a single network link, and each leaf switch is connected through seven inter-switch links.

The Full Rack has a client access network connection with a standard Ethernet network. Either you can connect it as a single network (NET1/NET2), or you can configure it as a bonded network, which is configured using the default NET1 and NET2 interfaces.

The management network is configured to the NET0 and ILOM on standard network interfaces.

Network Setup Requirements

A typical RAC configuration primarily requires public, private, virtual (VIP), and three SCAN network IPs for a standard network. Similarly, an Exadata Database Machine typically requires three different networks: management, client access, and IB.

This section explores the basic network connectivity configuration in detail. You will understand and acquire thorough knowledge about network configuration and how to manage and troubleshoot common network problems.

Each database (Compute Node) server on an X4-2 machine is composed of the following network components and interfaces:

- Dual 10GB Ethernet SFP and ports
- 4 x 1/10GbE Base-T Ethernet ports (NET0, NET1, NET2, and NET3)
- Dual active-active port InfiniBand 4x QDR (40GB/s) PCIe-3.0
- Ethernet port for ILOM remote management

The following components are part of the client access network:

- One Ethernet (NET1) port access per database server for management network and client access network
- One Ethernet (NET2) port access per database server for additional networks
- One Ethernet (NET3) port access per database server for additional networks

The NET1, NET2, and NET1-2 ports provide client network access to RAC VIP and SCAN IPs. The NET3 port supports and is used for backup and other external needs.

Each database server IP is specified in the `cellinit.ora` file on the local server. The `cellip.ora` file on the local server contains Storage Cell IPs. There are three types of networks involved in the setup:

- The **management network** connects to the servers, ILOM, and switches in the rack to perform the administrative work for all Exadata hardware components, such as Compute Nodes and Storage Cells.
- The **client access network** uses the existing client network for public client connection to the database server. It is connected to the NET1, NET2, or bonded NET1-2 network port on the Compute Nodes using the eth1 and eth2 interfaces.
- The **InfiniBand network** uses the InfiniBand switch rack and acts as a bridge between the database server and cell storage, RAC interconnect, storage expansion, and rack expansion and allows for high-speed backups. Each cell and Compute Node is connected to the InfiniBand networks through the InfiniBand interfaces.

Each Storage Cell on an X4-2 machine typically has the following network components and interfaces:

- 2 x InfiniBand 4x QDR (40GB/s) PCIe-3.0 active-active ports
- Embedded 10 or 1Gb Ethernet ports for management connectivity
- 1Gb Ethernet port for ILOM

Each Exadata Database Machine comes with a range of default IP addresses, 192.168.1.1 through 192.168.1.203, and with the subnet mask 255.255.255.0. It is recommended that you run the `checkip.sh` script to ensure that the Exadata factory IPs do not conflict with your existing IPs.

A typical X4-2 Full Rack machine requires the following large number of IP addresses:

- 49 IPs for the management network
- 19 IPs for the client access network
- 8 IPs for each additional network (NET2, NET3)
- 44 private IPs for the InfiniBand network

Before initial configuration, the hostnames and IP addresses associated with the management network, the client access network, and additional networks, and all public, SCAN, and VIP addresses, must be registered with the Domain Name System (DNS).

Troubleshooting Tools and Utilities

Although Oracle OEM Cloud Control 12c provides great monitoring capabilities to all Exadata components, including InfiniBand, it is equally important to have adequate knowledge of some of the commonly used tools and utilities to quickly verify and manage network configuration details on the Exadata machine. This section focuses on some of the commonly used tools and utilities for administering, diagnosing, and verifying InfiniBand network utilization in Exadata.

Ensure that you cover the following areas as part of your regular InfiniBand monitoring procedure: IB switch, IB fabric, and IB port.

Physical Link Monitoring

We will discuss here how to review and monitor current InfiniBand network settings and configuration.

The `ibstatus` command queries and retrieves the current InfiniBand driver basic information on the local node:

```
# ibstatus

Infiniband device 'mlx4_0' port 1 status:
        default gid:     fe80:0000:0000:0000:0021:2800:01ef:6abf
        base lid:        0x5
        sm lid:          0x1
        state:           4: ACTIVE
        phys state:      5: LinkUp
        rate:            40 Gb/sec (4X QDR)

Infiniband device 'mlx4_0' port 2 status:
        default gid:     fe80:0000:0000:0000:0021:2800:01ef:6ac0
        base lid:        0x6
        sm lid:          0x1
        state:           4: ACTIVE
        phys state:      5: LinkUp
        rate:            40 Gb/sec (4X QDR)
```

The status for both ports should be ACTIVE, and the physical state (cable connection) should be LinkUp. If the rate is less than 40Gb, you will have to examine the cables for damage or other problems.

To verify the current status of IB on the local node, use the following filtered command as root user:

```
# ibstatus |grep state

        state:           4: ACTIVE
        phys state:      5: LinkUp
        state:           4: ACTIVE
        phys state:      5: LinkUp
```

The `ibhosts` command displays information about the nodes (compute and cell) connected to the switch:

```
[root ~]# ibhosts

Ca       : 0x0021280001ef6cd2 ports 2 "db02 S 192.168.10.2 HCA-1"
Ca       : 0x0021280001ef684e ports 2 "cel03 C 192.168.10.5 HCA-1"
Ca       : 0x0021280001ef6d36 ports 2 "cel01 C 192.168.10.3 HCA-1"
Ca       : 0x0021280001ef59ea ports 2 "cel02 C 192.168.10.4 HCA-1"
Ca       : 0x0021280001ef6abe ports 2 "db01 S 192.168.10.1 HCA-1"
```

To display the existing IB and network interface configuration details on the local node, use the following command:

```
# ifconfig ib0:ib1

ib0        Link encap:InfiniBand  HWaddr
           80:00:00:48:FE:80:00:00:00:00:00:00:00:00:00:00:00:00:00:00
           UP BROADCAST RUNNING SLAVE MULTICAST  MTU:65520  Metric:1
           RX packets:12159586 errors:0 dropped:0 overruns:0 frame:0
           TX packets:13108639 errors:0 dropped:11 overruns:0 carrier:0
           collisions:0 txqueuelen:256
           RX bytes:8276811902 (7.7 GiB)  TX bytes:6817160403 (6.3 GiB)

ib1        Link encap:InfiniBand  HWaddr
           80:00:00:49:FE:80:00:00:00:00:00:00:00:00:00:00:00:00:00:00
           UP BROADCAST RUNNING SLAVE MULTICAST  MTU:65520  Metric:1
           RX packets:16427 errors:0 dropped:0 overruns:0 frame:0
           TX packets:0 errors:0 dropped:0 overruns:0 carrier:0
           collisions:0 txqueuelen:256
           RX bytes:14692746 (14.0 MiB)  TX bytes:0 (0.0 b)
```

IB interface configuration details are stored in /etc/sysconfig/network-scripts/ ifcfg-ib0 and ifcfg-ib1.

Sometimes it becomes essential to monitor and validate InfiniBand network topology and the current state of all IB network links on a cell or Compute Node in Exadata. The following `verify-topology` command validates the IB network layout. This utility can be executed on a cell or Compute Node as root user:

```
# /opt/oracle_SupportTools/ibdiagtools/verify-topology -t fattree
```

You can verify the topology details using the `verify-topology` command. The following example demonstrates how to verify the topology for a Half Rack Exadata Database Machine:

```
# /opt/oracle_SupportTools/ibdiagtools/verify-topology -t halfrack
```

To perform IB hardware component failure sensor checks manually, log in to a switch as root user and execute the following command:

```
# showunhealthy
```

```
# env_test
```

To query an IB port's health status, execute the `ibqueryerrors.pl` command either from the Compute Nodes or a switch every 60 to 120 seconds and keep the results for future comparison.

To verify the subnet manager (SM) master information, and the switch's information, use the following commands:

```
# sminfo

sminfo: sm lid 2 sm guid 0x10e035c5dca0a0, activity count 26769024
        priority 5 state 3 SMINFO_MASTER

# ibswitches

Switch  : 0x0010e035c5dca0a0 ports 36 "SUN DCS 36P QDR n3-
          ibb01.domain.com" enhanced port 0 lid 2 lmc 0
Switch  : 0x0010e035c604a0a0 ports 36 "SUN DCS 36P QDR n3-
          iba01.domain.com" enhanced port 0 lid 1 lmc 0
```

The `ibnetdiscover` command discovers the node-to-node connectivity:

```
# ibnetdiscover

# Topology file: generated on Sun May 18 15:06:42 2014
#
# Initiated from node 0010e0000129699c port 0010e0000129699d

vendid=0x2c9
devid=0xbd36
sysimgguid=0x10e035c5dca0a3
switchguid=0x10e035c5dca0a0(10e035c5dca0a0)
Switch 36 "S-0010e035c5dca0a0" # "SUN DCS 36P QDR n3-tst-ibb01 " enhanced port 0 lid 2 lmc 0
[1] "H-0010e00001295420"[2](10e00001295422)# "cel-es02 C 20.168.166.14 HCA-1" lid 10 4xQDR
[2] "H-0010e0000129699c"[2](10e0000129699e)# " cel-es01 C 20.168.166.13 HCA-1" lid 8 4xQDR
[4] "H-0010e0000129768b0"[2](10e000012968b2) # " cel-es03 C 20.168.166.15 HCA-1" lid 12 4xQDR
[8] "H-0010e00001294cd0"[2](10e00001294cd2)# "rp-od01 S 20.168.166.11 HCA-1" lid 4 4xQDR
[10]"H-0010e0000128d288"[2](10e0000128d28a) # " rp-od02 S 20.168.166.12 HCA-1" lid 6 4xQDR
[13] "S-0010e035c604a0a0"[14] # "SUN DCS 36P QDR n3-tst-iba01 " lid 1 4xQDR
```

The `ibcheckstate -v` command performs a quick check of all ports on all nodes:

```
# Checking Switch: nodeguid 0x0010e035c5dca0a0
Node check lid 2:  OK
Port check lid 2 port 1:   OK
Port check lid 2 port 2:   OK
Port check lid 2 port 4:   OK
Port check lid 2 port 7:   OK
Port check lid 2 port 10:  OK
Port check lid 2 port 13:  OK
Port check lid 2 port 14:  OK
Port check lid 2 port 15:  OK
Port check lid 2 port 16:  OK
Port check lid 2 port 17:  OK
Port check lid 2 port 18:  OK
Port check lid 2 port 31:  OK

# Checking Switch: nodeguid 0x0010e035c604a0a0
Node check lid 1:  OK
```

```
Port check lid 1 port 1:   OK
Port check lid 1 port 2:   OK
Port check lid 1 port 4:   OK
Port check lid 1 port 7:   OK
Port check lid 1 port 10:  OK
Port check lid 1 port 13:  OK
Port check lid 1 port 14:  OK
Port check lid 1 port 15:  OK
Port check lid 1 port 16:  OK
Port check lid 1 port 17:  OK
Port check lid 1 port 18:  OK
Port check lid 1 port 31:  OK

# Checking Ca: nodeguid 0x0010e0000128d288
Node check lid 5:  OK
Port check lid 5 port 1:   OK
Port check lid 5 port 2:   OK


## Summary: 7 nodes checked, 0 bad nodes found
##          34 ports checked, 0 ports with bad state found

# ibdiagnet
```

When `ibdiagnet` is executed, it scans the IB fabrics and extracts all relevant information regarding the connectivity and devices on the node (cell or compute), and the output directories by default are written to /tmp. It also performs validation for duplicate node and port GUIDs in the IB fabric. The following demonstrates some examples with the desired output:

```
# /opt/oracle_SupportTools/ibdiagtools/ibdiagnet

Loading IBDIAGNET from: /usr/lib64/ibdiagnet1.2
-W- Topology file is not specified.
    Reports regarding cluster links will use direct routes.
Loading IBDM from: /usr/lib64/ibdm1.2
-W- A few ports of local device are up.
    Since port-num was not specified (-p option), port 1 of device 1 will be
    used as the local port.
-I- Discovering ... 7 nodes (2 Switches & 5 CA-s) discovered.


-I---------------------------------------------------
-I- Bad Guids/LIDs Info
-I---------------------------------------------------
-I- No bad Guids were found
-I---------------------------------------------------
-I- Links With Logical State = INIT
-I---------------------------------------------------
-I- No bad Links (with logical state = INIT) were found
-I---------------------------------------------------
-I- PM Counters Info
-I---------------------------------------------------
-I- No illegal PM counters values were found
-I---------------------------------------------------
-I- Fabric Partitions Report (see ibdiagnet.pkey for a full hosts list)
-I---------------------------------------------------
-I-    PKey:0x7fff Hosts:10 full:10 partial:0
-I---------------------------------------------------
-I- IPoIB Subnets Check
-I---------------------------------------------------
```

```
-I- Subnet: IPv4 PKey:0x7fff QKey:0x00000b1b MTU:2048Byte rate:10Gbps SL:0x00
-W- Suboptimal rate for group. Lowest member rate:40Gbps > group-rate:10Gbps
-I-------------------------------------------------
-I- Bad Links Info
-I- No bad link were found
-I-------------------------------------------------
-------------------------------------------------------------
-I- Stages Status Report:
    STAGE                              Errors  Warnings
    Bad GUIDs/LIDs Check               0       0
    Link State Active Check            0       0
    Performance Counters Report        0       0
    Partitions Check                   0       0
    IPoIB Subnets Check                0       1

Please see /tmp/ibdiagnet.log for complete log
-------------------------------------------------------------

-I- Done. Run time was 1 seconds

# ibdiagnet -c 1000
```

The preceding command verifies the IB network quality and detects errors on any fabric links.

To verify network-related issues on the InfiniBand network, use the `infinicheck` tool located in the /opt/oracle.SupportTools/ibdiagtools directory. The following example shows how to use the tool with various parameters:

```
# infinicheck
# infinicheck -z
infinicheck -g
infinicheck -d -p
```

Log Files Collection

It is also recommended that you verify the OS-level logs pertaining to the network components and IB switches to identify the cause of any issue. Following is a list of log files that need attention or review in case any issues are diagnosed:

- /var/log/messages
- /var/log/opensm.log
- /var/log/opensm-subnet.lst

Run the following utilities to collect more diagnostic data:

- /usr/local/bin/nm2version
- /usr/local/bin/env_test
- /usr/local/bin/listlinkup

Integrated Lights Out Manager

This section provides details for how to monitor and manage InfiniBand switches through the Oracle ILOM interface from the web.

Log on to the ILOM through the browser using the IP or hostname assigned to the switch you want to monitor or configure. Following is an example:

```
https://10.1.10.131/iPages/i_login.asp
```

Next, enter the login credentials of the switch interface, username, and password, as shown in Figure 7.3.

The main page has tabs for System Information, System Monitoring, Configuration, User Management, Maintenance, and Switch/Fabric Monitoring Tools, as shown in Figure 7.4.

These tabs provide access to the various features of ILOM:

- **System Information**—provides information and current status of the components, ILOM versions, Fault Management, firmware version, and so on.

- **System Monitoring**—can view event logs, display the list of sensors.

- **Configuration**—allows configuration of the SMPT server details, which is necessary in order to receive alert messages about the switch. Additionally, you can configure the time zone, clock, DNS, and network settings, as well as edit and set rules for alert management and so on.

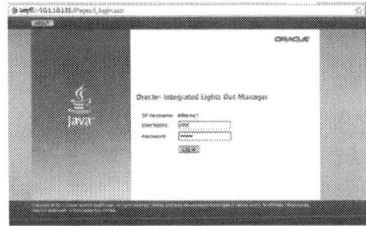

Figure 7.3   ILOM login page

Figure 7.4   ILOM main page with options

- **User Management**—provides access to Active Session for listing details for users who are currently connected to the switch, and to User Account for adding, deleting, and modifying local ILOM user accounts and SSH keys.

- **Maintenance**—provides options for upgrading firmware, backing up and restoring, resetting service processor (SP), and storage snapshot technologies.

- **Switch/Fabric Monitoring Tools**—provides the options for System Info, Sensor Info, IB Performance, IB Port Map, and Subnet Manager, as shown in Figure 7.5. The IB Performance tab displays details about Link Status and includes a usage graph, as shown in Figure 7.6.

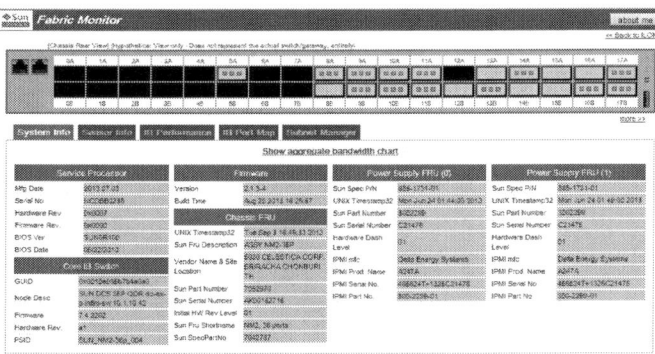

Figure 7.5 Fabric monitoring

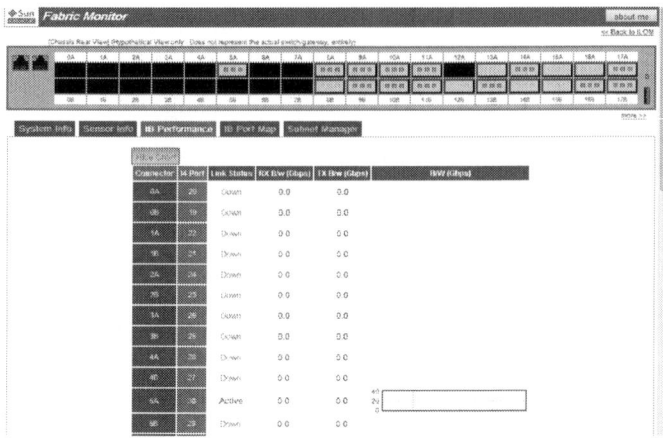

Figure 7.6 InfiniBand performance

To disable HTTP/HTTPS access to the switches, go to the Configuration tab, Web Server, and uncheck the Enabled box. To reenable HTTP/HTTPS access to the switches, you need to use the command-line interface (CLI), in paths /SP/services/ http and /SP/services/https.

OEM Cloud Control 12c

With OEM Cloud Control 12c, one can monitor, define metrics, and configure alerts to receive a notification whenever there is an issue identified with regard to IB switches. When a database machine is discovered through OEM Cloud Control 12c, all InfiniBand switches are discovered automatically under the IB network group along with other components on the servers.

Let's discuss how Exadata network interfaces and switches are monitored and managed with OEM Cloud Control 12c.

First, launch the OEM Cloud Control 12c web interface through the web browser and log in.

To display all targets that can be identified and configured with OEM Cloud Control, select the All Targets option from the Targets drop-down list. All important components are listed under the Servers, Storage and Network category, as shown in Figure 7.7.

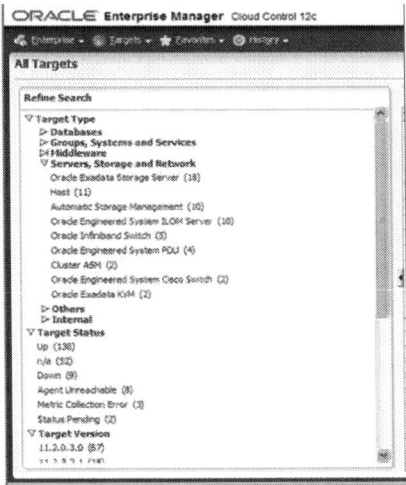

Figure 7.7   OEM All Targets display screen

When the Oracle InfiniBand Switch option is selected from the list, all details with regard to the InfiniBand switches are displayed, as shown in Figure 7.8. This includes Target status, which appears as 5 because there are two Full/Half Exadata Racks configured with the OEM. It also includes Target version, Platform, and OS details.

The three InfiniBand switches (one spine and two leaf for a Full Rack machine) are listed when a Compute Node is selected, as shown in Figure 7.9. Switch current statistics and status are displayed on the right side. This is the main screen to review for throughput, status, and port usage.

The InfiniBand switch drop-down list (on the right side) provides options like Monitoring, Control, and Configuration and options for other historical details, as shown in Figure 7.10.

For example, if you choose the Configuration option, you can select the Last Collect option, which allows you to view the configuration details of the switch version, a configuration summary, and HCA port configuration details, as shown in Figure 7.11.

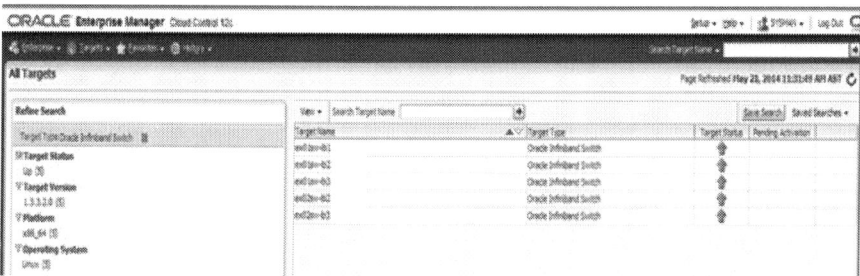

Figure 7.8 OEM with Targets list

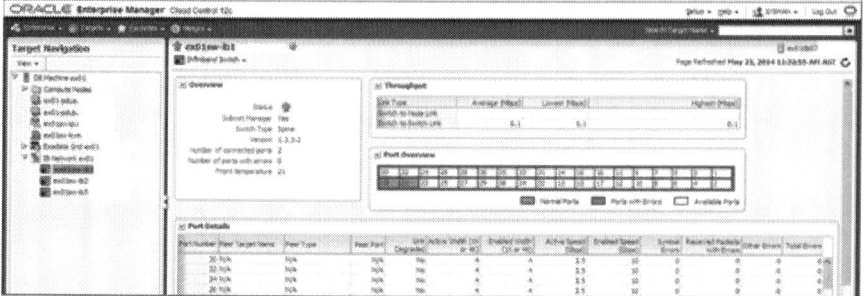

Figure 7.9 OEM with InfiniBand list

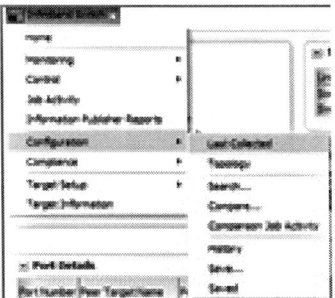

Figure 7.10 InfiniBand switch drop-down menu with options

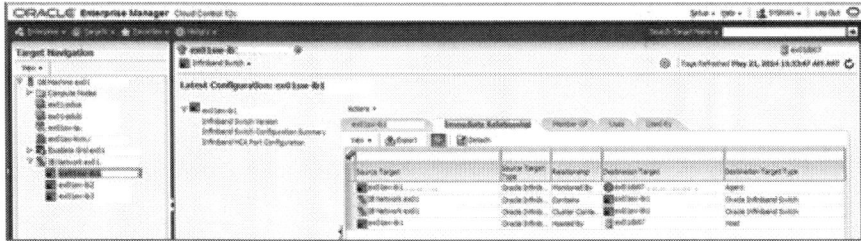

Figure 7.11 Latest configuration details screen

Summary

This chapter provided a thorough description of Exadata network components, IB switch configuration, and different types of networks for managing and accessing the database server and Storage Cells. It also covered the important topics of monitoring and managing IB switches and ports with ILOM and OEM Cloud Control 12c web interfaces. Most importantly, it described the steps for collecting and reviewing the logs to diagnose network- or IB-switch-related issues.

## 8

Backup and Recovery and Data Guard

Oracle Data Guard provides the best data protection and data availability solution for mission-critical databases. Data Guard works on the principle of keeping a standby database in sync with the primary database. Myriad best practices and techniques have been provided by Oracle's Maximum Availability Architecture (MAA) team and industry experts that address backup and recovery and Data Guard when it comes to performance, scalability, and reliability. Best practices are tweaked with each release of Oracle products and as technology evolves. Compliance with best practices can help mitigate potential performance and infrastructure issues that plague a lot of companies.

This chapter disseminates fundamental backup and recovery considerations and configuring Data Guard with best practices in mind for the Exadata. The goal is to demonstrate a number of options for performing backups on the Exadata. It also demonstrates options for instantiating Data Guard on the Exadata.

Tip

On the Exadata, the ZFS Storage Appliance (ZFSSA) is strongly recommended for performing backups against dedicated 40Gb low-latency InfiniBand connections. All the backups are performed with Oracle's RMAN utility to a shared backup file system on the ZFSSA. This discipline also allows you to separate and isolate backup storage from database storage. In the event of a catastrophe on the Exadata, you will be able to restore the databases to another Exadata machine or even non-Oracle bare-metal servers. DMAs will want this peace of mind as they consider upgrading or updating the Exadata software stack on the Database Compute Nodes or the Storage Cells.

Backing up a database on the Exadata and ZFS Storage Appliance may be perceived as challenging when compared to traditional database environments. This chapter reveals a soup-to-nuts guide for performing database backups using Oracle Recovery Manager.

RMAN Disk-to-Disk Backups

Starting with Oracle Database 10*g*, Oracle Recovery Manager (RMAN) provides the capability to take incremental backups and update the baseline level 0 image backup. To use this functionality, we have to perform a special "backup as copy" of the database to copy the binary image of the database to the file system or ASM Fast Recovery Area (FRA). In the event of catastrophic failure of the primary disks, we can then switch to the copy and start the database from the image copy.

When it comes to performing database backup on the Exadata, we have choices. In fact, we have more choices than we think. Although we want to promote the ZFS Storage Appliance for the Exadata, we can also leverage other vendors such as EMC and NetApp to perform our backups. With the 10GigE availability, we can easily serve up a Direct NFS (dNFS) mount point to the Compute Nodes and perform backups to third-party storage vendors.

Using Oracle technology, we also have the option to perform backups on the Exadata Expansion Storage Rack and back up to an EXA_DATA2 disk group. We can perform full image copies of the database and switch the data file or tablespace or even the database to the image copy for local high-availability protection. We can stagger our incremental updates to sustain a one- or two-day (or even longer) recovery window. If we want to back up to tape media, we can leverage Oracle Secure Backup and send our backups to offsite storage.

In the absence of additional hardware, we can leverage the Oracle Database File System (DBFS) on the Exadata Compute Nodes for RMAN disk-to-disk (D2D) backups. DBFS is free, and many companies choose to leverage DBFS until they can find or afford an alternative target for backups. DBFS or the Oracle 12*c* ASM Cluster File System (ACFS) can be configured for RMAN disk backups and GoldenGate trail files.

You can leverage the backup as a copy and update the baseline image copy with incremental backups (aka Incremental Forever) on a nightly basis to allow incrementally updated backups to be converted to full backups. Conceptually, you will rarely need to perform a full level 0 image copy of the database again. Updated incremental backup image copies are essential when it comes to reducing restore times, deploying snapshot technology, and creating clones of production snapshot data.

Settings for RMAN Backups on the Exadata

With RMAN, we can perform image copy backups or backup set backups. More companies choose RMAN backup set implementations simply because this technology is what they are comfortable with. Instead, consider image copy backups with incremental updates on the Exadata and imagine a world where you do not have to perform a full backup again. Depending on which method we choose, we can tune the RMAN backup processes with the following hidden underscore (_) parameters:

- **_backup_disk_bufcnt**—number of buffers used to process backup sets
- **_backup_disk_bufsz**—size of the buffers used to process backup sets
- **_backup_file_bufcnt**—number of buffers used to process image copies
- **_backup_file_bufsz**—size of the buffers used to process image copies

Table 8.1 depicts the best-practice recommendations for the number of buffers and buffer size to perform backup sets and image copies for RMAN backups over IB or 10GigE connections to the Exadata over dNFS.

The following are additional recommended guidelines:

- Use two to four RMAN channels per tray of disks.
- Load-balance RMAN channels across shares and controllers.
- Load-balance RMAN channels across Exadata Compute Nodes.

Table 8.1 RMAN Backup Settings

Type of Backup	_backup_ disk_ bufcnt	_backup_ disk_ bufsz	_backup_ file_ bufcnt	_backup_ file_ bufsz
Backup set backup	64	1048576		
Backup set restore	64	1048576		
Image copy backup			64	1048576
Image copy restore	64	1048576	64	1048576
Restore validate	64	1048576	64	1048576

rman2disk Shell Script

In this chapter, we introduce a revised rman2disk.ksh script that is custom tailored for Exadata and can be incorporated to automate your backups. Whether you want to perform backup set backups, backup as image copy backups, incremental backups, or incrementally updated backups, this single script can address all your requirements. You can download the rman2disk.ksh script and many other Data Guard–related scripts from http://dbaexpert.com/dg/dgmenu/.

The rman2disk.ksh shell script has numerous prerequisites and requirements. First and foremost, a couple of directories need to be added to the Optimal Flexible Architecture (OFA)-compliant directory structure. In the $ORACLE_BASE/admin/ $ORACLE_SID directory, we need to add a log directory and a symbolic link called bkups that points to the backup destination for the database. Here's how the directory structure should look in $ORACLE_BASE/admin/$ORACLE_SID:

```
$ ls -ltr
total 40
drwxr-xr-x   2 oracle oinstall   4096 Oct 16 16:24 exp
drwxr-xr-x   2 oracle oinstall   4096 Oct 16 16:24 adump
drwxr-xr-x  52 oracle oinstall   4096 Oct 23 12:12 cdump
lrwxrwxrwx   1 oracle oinstall     18 Nov 14 08:58 bkups -> /zfs/ /DBATOOLS/bkups
drwxr-xr-x  11 oracle oinstall  20480 Nov 21 13:00 bdump
drwxr-xr-x   2 oracle oinstall   4096 Nov 22 09:48 udump
lrwxrwxrwx   2 oracle oinstall   4096 Nov 22 09:57 log-> /zfs/ /DBATOOLS/log
```

In the example above, pay particular attention to the log and bkups symbolic link. The log directory houses all the RMAN backup scripts generated by the rman2disk korn shell script and the log files associated from the executed RMAN script. If you are leveraging the ZFSSA for backups, these two directories (log and bkups) should reside on the ZFSSA and the symbolic links should point to the ZFSSA target directories. For RMAN backups with multiple channels, we need to place bkup1, bkup2, bkup3, bkup4, bkup5, bkup6, bkup7, bkup8, and so on to alternate ZFS mount points.

In a nutshell, the rman2disk korn shell script creates an RMAN script and executes it. The RMAN script is specified in the format

```
rman2disk.ksh_[date]_[time]_[level].sql
```

Examine the naming convention of the files that are created in the log directory. As you will see in the sample directory listing, the file names have some design so that we can quickly identify the backup script that it generated and the log of the executed RMAN output:

```
rman2disk.ksh_20Nov08_2116_0.sql
rman2disk.ksh_20Nov08_2116_Level0.log
rman2disk.ksh_21Nov08_0726_1.sql
rman2disk.ksh_21Nov08_0726_Level1.log
rman2disk.ksh_22Nov08_0139_baseline.sql
```

```
rman2disk.ksh_22Nov08_0139_Levelbaseline.log
rman2disk.ksh_22Nov08_0943_1.sql
rman2disk.ksh_22Nov08_0943_Level1.log
rman2disk.ksh_22Nov08_0948_1.sql
rman2disk.ksh_DBTOOLS1.log
rman2disk.ksh_22Nov08_0948_Level1.log
rman2disk.ksh_22Nov08_1050_1.sql
rman2disk.ksh_22Nov08_1050_Level1.log
rman2disk.ksh_DBTOOLS1.history.log
```

First, the .sql files are the generated RMAN scripts. You can see from our sample file listing that there are three kinds of .sql files:

- `_0.sql` to denote level 0 backup sets
- `_1.sql` to denote incremental level 1 backups
- `_baseline.sql` script to denote RMAN database copy backups

The second kind of file is the log file. There are log files for each day of the backup. In addition, there is a history file that provides high-level statistics about all the backups performed. You should purge log files on a regular basis, such as after 90 days, but not the history log file. The history log file just stores high-level information about the database backups such as when it started, when it ended, and what parameters were passed for the backups. The history log file will be handy for reviewing previous backup trends. The history file is specified in the format

```
rman2disk.ksh_[ORACLE_SID].log
```

Here's a small excerpt of the history log file:

```
Performing backup with arguments: -l 1 -d DBTOOLS1 -m  -n 2
Performing backup with arguments: -r
Spfile Backup:
Previous BASELINE Tag: DBTOOLS1_baseline_22Nov08_0139
#------------------------------------------------------------------
# Backup Started: Sat Nov 22 10:50:19 EST 2008
#------------------------------------------------------------------
Catalog:
#------------------------------------------------------------------
# Backup Completed Successfully for DBTOOLS1 on Sat Nov 22 10:51:01 EST 2008
#------------------------------------------------------------------
DB Backup Size is:  8.80469
Archive Backup Size is:  5.02344
Performing backup with arguments: -l 1 -d DBTOOLS1 -m  -n 2
Performing backup with arguments: -r
Performing backup with arguments: -z
Spfile Backup:
Archive log mode: Y
```

The `rman2disk.ksh` script starts by establishing ORACLE_BASE. ORACLE_BASE is set to the directory structure two levels up from $ORACLE_HOME. In our example, ORACLE_BASE is set to /apps/oracle:

```
# --------------------
# Start of .ORACLE_BASE
export BASE_DIR=/apps/oracle
export ORACLE_BASE=/apps/oracle
export RMAN_CATALOG=RMANPROD
BACKUP_DEST=asm
```

The .ORACLE_BASE file is expected to be located in the $HOME directory for the Oracle Linux/Unix account.

rman2disk Template Files

Each of the template files serves a different purpose. For example, the rman2disk .sql.cold template performs a cold backup. The rman2disk.sql.compressed template performs a compressed RMAN backup. It's pretty obvious that the rman2.sql.noncompression file performs no compression. Based on the options specified in the command-line argument of the rman2disk.ksh script, different template files are sourced and modified accordingly to generate the RMAN script to execute.

The rman2disk.sql.cold template file simply performs shutdown immediate and startup mount commands prior to issuing the backup database command. Once the backup of the database, archive log, control file, and pfile/spfile is complete, the script issues an alter database open command to open the database for general availability.

The RMAN scripts use the following numerous template files:

```
-rw-r--r--  1 oracle oinstall 1232 Nov 22 01:37 rman2disk.sql.baseline
-rw-r--r--  1 oracle oinstall 1275 Nov 22 01:37 rman2disk.sql.cold
-rw-r--r--  1 oracle oinstall  963 Nov 22 15:57
rman2disk.sql.cold.noarchivelog
-rw-r--r--  1 oracle oinstall 1529 Nov 22 01:37 rman2disk.sql.compression
-rw-r--r--  1 oracle oinstall 1370 Nov 22 01:37 rman2disk.sql.for_recover
-rw-r--r--  1 oracle oinstall 1506 Nov 22 01:37 rman2disk.sql
```

The rman2disk.sql script performs the standard RMAN backup set of the database.

Using rman2disk

This section provides some usage examples for the rman2disk.ksh shell script.

Following is a regular usage of rman2disk.ksh with RMAN backup sets. This example performs a full level 0 backup:

```
/apps/oracle/general/sh/rman2disk.ksh -d DATABASE -l 0 -c catalog >
/tmp/rman2disk_DATABASE.0.log 2>&1
```

The next example shows an incremental backup:

```
/apps/oracle/general/sh/rman2disk.ksh -d DATABASE -l 1 -c catalog >
/tmp/rman2disk_DATABASE.1.log 2>&1
```

Following are the various options available for the `rman2disk.ksh` script to perform backup sets, image copy backups, and incremental backups. The set of examples provide the syntax options to perform a level 0 backup leveraging an RMAN catalog. The second syntax provides the options to perform an incremental level 1 RMAN backup:

```
#  1.  Perform a full level 0 backup
#       /apps/oracle/general/sh/rman2disk.ksh -d DATABASE -l 0 -c catalog >
/tmp/rman2disk_DATABASE.0.log 2>&1
#  2.  Perform a level 1 incremental backup
#       /apps/oracle/general/sh/rman2disk.ksh -d DATABASE -l 1 -c catalog
> /tmp/rman2disk_DATABASE.1.log 2>&1
```

Next, let's look at how to perform an RMAN database image copy backup and take a subsequent incremental backup for recovery to the image copy backup with the `rman2disk.ksh` script:

```
#  1.  Perform a baseline level 0 backup
#       /apps/oracle/general/sh/rman2disk.ksh -d DATABASE -l baseline >
/tmp/rman2disk_DATABASE.baseline.log 2>&1
#  2.  Perform an incremental backup
#       /apps/oracle/general/sh/rman2disk.ksh -d DATABASE -l 1 -r merge >
/tmp/rman2disk_DATABASE.1.log 2>&1
```

Here are a couple of important usage notes that you will be interested in. First, the `-r` option can be used only with image copy backups. Second, the `-r` option must find a baseline tag in the $SH directory; otherwise, the script will perform a full level 0 copy.

If you do not specify the `-c` (for catalog) option, the RMAN backup will not take advantage of the RMAN repository and will only leverage the control file. If you specify the `-c` option, for security reasons you should create a .rman.pw password file in the same directory where you extracted the `rman2disk.ksh` shell script with the Linux/Unix permission of 600. The RMAN catalog can be designated in the .ORACLE_BASE file.

Let's look into the details of the `rman2disk.ksh` parameter. The following code example displays all the command-line arguments for the `rman2disk` shell script:

```
while getopts :l:d:c:n:m:r:z: arguments
do
  case $arguments in
    c) CATALOG=${OPTARG}
       export CATALOG=$(echo $CATALOG |tr '[A-Z]' '[a-z]')
       ;;
```

```
    d) DB=${OPTARG}
       ;;
    l) BACKUP_LEVEL=${OPTARG}
       ;;
    n) NUMBER_OF_DAYS_TO_RETAIN=${OPTARG}
       ;;
    m) BACKUP_MODE=${OPTARG}
       export BACKUP_MODE=$(echo $BACKUP_MODE |tr '[A-Z]' '[a-z]')
       ;;
    r) RECOVERY_MODE=${OPTARG}
       export RECOVERY_MODE=$(echo $RECOVERY_MODE |tr '[A-Z]' '[a-z]')
       ;;
    z) COMPRESSION_MODE=${OPTARG}
       export COMPRESSION_MODE=$(echo $COMPRESSION_MODE |tr '[A-Z]' '[a-z]')
       ;;
    *) echo "${OPTARG} is not a valid argument\n"
       echo "Usage is: rman2disk.ksh -d $DB -l [0 or 1 or baseline]
[-m cold] [-n # of days to retain archivelogs] [-r merge]"
       exit -1
       ;;
  esac
done
```

Following is a detailed explanation of all the parameters:

- The -l option specifies the backup level. Valid options are 0 and 1.
- The -d option specifies the database name. The database must be listed in the /etc/oratab file.
- The -c option specifies whether you want to use the RMAN catalog to store the backup metadata. If the -c option is not specified, the script does not leverage the RMAN catalog and defaults to the nocatalog syntax.
- The -n option specifies the number of days of archive logs to retain. If the parameter is not specified, the number of days defaults to 2:

```
[ "$NUMBER_OF_DAYS_TO_RETAIN" = "" ] && export
NUMBER_OF_DAYS_TO_RETAIN=2
```

- The -m option specifies the backup mode. Acceptable values for backup mode are cold and hot.
- The -r mode option can be used only with the image copy backup command. The -r option must find a baseline tag in the $SH directory. If the baseline tag is not found in the $SH directory, what is equivalent to a full level 0 copy database is performed. As an extra feature, the baseline is established at the database level:

```
export PREVIOUS_BASELINE_TAG=$(cat $SH/rman2disk.tag.baseline.${ORACLE_SID})
```

The history of all the baseline tags is preserved in a file called echo $TAG |tee -a $SH/rman2disk.tag.history. The history of all the baselines is kept at a global level. Every time you issue an rman2disk.ksh script

with the −1 baseline option, the baseline tag name is recorded in both the
TAG file and the TAG history file:

```
export TAG=${ORACLE_SID}_${BACKUP_LEVEL}_${ORADATE}
echo $BASELINE_TAG > $SH/rman2disk.tag.baseline.${ORACLE_SID}
echo $TAG |tee -a $SH/rman2disk.tag.history
```

- The −z option specifies the compression mode. Compression in normal circumstances yields incredible disk-saving opportunities. For example, for a
  customer who houses compressed BLOBs inside the database, the compression option produced unexpected results, resulting in backup times that were
  orders of magnitude higher than noncompressed backup sets with compression savings of just 20 to 30%. For another customer, the compression option
  shrank their backups by 90% of the allocated database size.

Compression can produce incredible results for some databases. In this particular
example, you can see a 1.91TB database compressed down to 289.18GB in size:

```
SESSION          Compress                                    Time
    KEY INPUT_TYPE   Ratio IN_SIZE    OUT_SIZE  START_TIME    Taken
------- ---------- -------- --------- --------- ------------ ---------
  11613 DB INCR       6.80    1.91T    289.18G  19-feb 18:00  04:58:15
  11609 ARCHIVELOG    1.00    4.68G      4.68G  19-feb 16:01  00:01:33
  11605 ARCHIVELOG    1.00   93.95G     93.95G  19-feb 07:00  00:24:39
```

Creating RMAN Backups

Often DBAs think that backing up multiterabyte databases is not a viable option
because backups take too long and they are worried about the amount of time
it would take to restore or recover the database in the event of a disaster. With
RMAN image copy backups, full backups can be a rare event, and in the event of a
SAN loss or loss of groups of disks, you can "switch to copy" and run your databases
off of the image copy that's been updated on a nightly basis. If you architect a solution where the image copy backups go to another SAN, you can even survive a SAN
failure.

The rman2disk.ksh shell script provides the full capability to perform image
copy backups and performs incremental updates. The template file needed for the
RMAN backup set is rman2disk.sql.

Note

Backup as copy plus incremental update (Incremental Forever) of the database is
a poor man's equivalent to EMC's sync and split technology with their business
continuity volumes (BCVs) or Hitachi's shadow images (SI) technology.

Before we start taking backups of the database, we need to create database services specifically dedicated to RMAN backups with the `srvctl` command. In our example, we have a Half Rack Exadata and will create database services called bkup1 to bkup8 for the DBATOOLS database (one for each node).

```
$ srvctl create service -d DBATOOLS -s bkup1  -r DBATOOLS1 -a
DBATOOLS2,DBATOOLS3,DBATOOLS4
$ srvctl create service -d DBATOOLS -s bkup2  -r DBATOOLS2 -a
DBATOOLS1,DBATOOLS3,DBATOOLS4
$ srvctl create service -d DBATOOLS -s bkup3  -r DBATOOLS3 -a
DBATOOLS1,DBATOOLS2,DBATOOLS4
$ srvctl create service -d DBATOOLS -s bkup4  -r DBATOOLS4 -a
DBATOOLS1,DBATOOLS2,DBATOOLS3
$ srvctl create service -d DBATOOLS -s bkup5  -r DBATOOLS1 -a
DBATOOLS2,DBATOOLS3,DBATOOLS4
$ srvctl create service -d DBATOOLS -s bkup6  -r DBATOOLS2 -a
DBATOOLS1,DBATOOLS3,DBATOOLS4
$ srvctl create service -d DBATOOLS -s bkup7  -r DBATOOLS3 -a
DBATOOLS1,DBATOOLS2,DBATOOLS4
$ srvctl create service -d DBATOOLS -s bkup8  -r DBATOOLS4 -a
DBATOOLS1,DBATOOLS2,DBATOOLS3

$srvctl start service -d DBATOOLS -s bkup1
$srvctl start service -d DBATOOLS -s bkup2
$srvctl start service -d DBATOOLS -s bkup3
$srvctl start service -d DBATOOLS -s bkup4
$srvctl start service -d DBATOOLS -s bkup5
$srvctl start service -d DBATOOLS -s bkup6
$srvctl start service -d DBATOOLS -s bkup7
$srvctl start service -d DBATOOLS -s bkup8
```

For a Full Rack, we will create database services called bkup1 to bkup16. Just as in the previous example, we essentially create two services per node and two repeating preferred and available instances.

Following is an example of a level 0 RMAN compressed backup set. Notice that we are leveraging eight channels with `backup_disk_bufcnt` and `_backup_disk_bufsz` hidden pairs of parameters. Depending on whether you are performing image copy backups or backup set backups, you will leverage different underscore (_) parameters. For RMAN backup sets, we need to set the buffer size to 1MB and the number of buffers to 64:

```
run
{
allocate channel d1 type disk connect 'sys/oracle123@exa-scan/bkup1'
format '/zfs/DBATOOLS/bkups1/%U';
allocate channel d2 type disk connect 'sys/oracle123@exa-scan/bkup2'
format '/zfs/DBATOOLS/bkups2/%U';
allocate channel d3 type disk connect 'sys/oracle123@exa-scan/bkup3'
format '/zfs/DBATOOLS/bkups3/%U';
allocate channel d4 type disk connect 'sys/oracle123@exa-scan/bkup4'
format '/zfs/DBATOOLS/bkups4/%U';
allocate channel d5 type disk connect 'sys/oracle123@exa-scan/bkup5'
format '/zfs/DBATOOLS/bkups5/%U';
allocate channel d6 type disk connect 'sys/oracle123@exa-scan/bkup6'
format '/zfs/DBATOOLS/bkups6/%U';
```

```
allocate channel d7 type disk connect 'sys/oracle123@exa-scan/bkup7'
format '/zfs/DBATOOLS/bkups7/%U';
allocate channel d8 type disk connect 'sys/oracle123@exa-scan/bkup8'
format '/zfs/DBATOOLS/bkups8/%U';

set limit channel d1 kbytes = 32000000;
set limit channel d2 kbytes = 32000000;
set limit channel d3 kbytes = 32000000;
set limit channel d4 kbytes = 32000000;
set limit channel d5 kbytes = 32000000;
set limit channel d6 kbytes = 32000000;
set limit channel d7 kbytes = 32000000;
set limit channel d8 kbytes = 32000000;


sql 'alter system set "_backup_disk_bufcnt"=64';
sql 'alter system set "_backup_disk_bufsz"=1048576';

backup as backupset incremental level 0 section size 32g
tag=DBATOOLS_bkup_0z_02Feb13_0300 filesperset 1 (database) ;


sql "alter system archive log current";
sql "alter system switch logfile";
sql "alter system switch logfile";

change archivelog all validate;

sql "alter database backup controlfile to trace";

backup as backupset skip inaccessible (archivelog all not backed up 2 times);
backup tag=DBATOOLS_CTL_02Feb13_0300 format '' (current controlfile);
backup backupset from tag DBATOOLS_CTL_02Feb13_0300 format
'/u01/app/oracle/admin/DBATOOLS/bkups/%d.%s.%p.%t.CTL';

delete noprompt archivelog until time 'sysdate - 2' backed up 2 times to
device type disk;

release channel d1;
release channel d2;
release channel d3;
release channel d4;
release channel d5;
release channel d6;
release channel d7;
release channel d8;

}
```

Notice the two alter system commands with the underscore parameters. These two parameters are needed for RMAN backup set backups.

Let's look at what the syntax looks like to perform RMAN restores. To restore the database, we need to set up the same underscore parameter prior to issuing the restore command:

```
run
{
...
allocate channel d7 type disk connect 'sys/oracle123@exa-scan/bkup7'
format '/zfs/DBATOOLS/bkups7/%U';
allocate channel d8 type disk connect 'sys/oracle123@exa-scan/bkup8'
format '/zfs/DBATOOLS/bkups8/%U';
```

```
sql 'alter system set "_backup_disk_bufcnt"=64';
sql 'alter system set "_backup_disk_bufsz"=1048576';

restore database;
..
release channel d7;
release channel d8;
}
```

We have two main driver files that are needed for image copy backups: the
rman2disk.sql.baseline script to perform the level 0 image copy backup and
the rman2disk.sql.for_recover script to perform the incremental updates to
the database image copy. The rman2disk.sql.baseline script simply performs
a full image copy backup of the database to the dNFS.

Here's a snippet from the rman2disk.sql.baseline script:

```
run
{
...
allocate channel d7 type disk connect 'sys/oracle123@exa-scan/bkup7'
format '/zfs/DBATOOLS/bkups7/%U';
allocate channel d8 type disk connect 'sys/oracle123@exa-scan/bkup8'
format '/zfs/DBATOOLS/bkups8/%U';

sql 'alter system set "_backup_disk_bufcnt"=64';
sql 'alter system set "_backup_disk_bufsz"=1048576';

backup as copy incremental level 0 tag='FOREVER' (database);
..
release channel d7;
release channel d8;
}
```

If you do not have multiple mount points for the RMAN backups, the RMAN scripts
are designed to follow a symbolic link from the $ORACLE_BASE/admin/$ORACLE_
SID directories as directory paths may not exist from one server to another.

Now let's look at a code example from rman2disk.sql.for_recover:

```
run
{
...
allocate channel d7 type disk connect 'sys/oracle123@exa-scan/bkup7'
format '/zfs/DBATOOLS/bkups7/%U';
allocate channel d8 type disk connect 'sys/oracle123@exa-scan/bkup8'
format '/zfs/DBATOOLS/bkups8/%U';

sql 'alter system set "_backup_file_bufcnt"=64';
sql 'alter system set "_backup_file_bufsz"=1048576';
sql 'alter system set "_backup_disk_bufcnt"=64';
sql 'alter system set "_backup_disk_bufsz"=1048576';

recover copy of database with tag 'FOREVER';

BACKUP INCREMENTAL LEVEL 1 FOR RECOVER OF COPY WITH TAG 'FOREVER'
format '/u01/app/oracle/admin/###_ORACLE_SID_###/bkups/%d.%s.%p.%t.L1.4R.DB'
DATABASE;
```

```
. .
release channel d7;
release channel d8;
}
```

This script performs two main tasks. First, it performs a recovery of the image copy (updates it with the last incremental backup). Then, a level 1 incremental backup is taken with the sole purpose of being recovered against the image copy later on.

Tip

If we stagger the incremental update (recover copy of database with TAG) command prior to performing our level 1 incremental backup, we can achieve another 24 hours (or more) of protection on the primary production database from end user errors or even corruptions. Many customers do not have the luxury of keeping flashback logs for 24 hours. If we delay our incremental update, we can switch the data file/tablespace/database to copy or even restore the data file/tablespace/database from the ZFS file system and be able to achieve a higher level of SLA.

RMAN Backup Schedule

A properly architected D2D backup schedule should look the same for every day of the week since we are incrementally updating our database image. DMAs who struggle with this concept can perform a full level 0 backup to disk on a monthly or quarterly basis depending on their requirements and comfort level for RMAN disk image copies and Incremental Forever backup strategy. You should also architect offsite retention of your backups. You can sweep your backup file system to tape on a daily or weekly basis. Your D2D RMAN backup schedule will look something like this:

- Sunday: Level 1 Merge with Level 0 => it is LEVEL 0
- Monday: Level 1 Merge with Level 0 => it is LEVEL 0
- Tuesday: Level 1 Merge with Level 0 => it is LEVEL 0
- Wednesday: Level 1 Merge with Level 0 => it is LEVEL 0
- Thursday: Level 1 Merge with Level 0 => it is LEVEL 0
- Friday: Level 1 Merge with Level 0 => it is LEVEL 0
- Saturday: Level 1 Merge with Level 0 => it is LEVEL 0

Conceptually, we do not need to perform another full backup again, but you should take a full image copy at least once per month or quarter depending on your database's rate of change and the amount of space it has. Once you take the RMAN image copy of the database, you can place the following for the crontab entry:

```
#
# ---------------------------------------------------------------------
# -- RMAN Daily Incremental Updates
# ---------------------------------------------------------------------
00 00 * * * /home/oracle/general/sh/rman2disk.ksh -d DBATOOLS -l 1 -r
merge > /tmp/rman2disk.DBATOOLS.1.log 2>&1
```

For RMAN backup sets, the backup schedule looks significantly different. You should perform a level 0 backup every Saturday or Sunday evening. The traditional backup schedule looks something like this:

- Sunday: Level 0
- Monday: Level 1
- Tuesday: Level 1
- Wednesday: Level 1
- Thursday: Level 1
- Friday: Level 1
- Saturday: Level 1

Before you purge any previous full level 0 backups, make sure that you have a successful current level 0 backup. You should architect enough storage to be able to house two full backup sets plus a week or two of archive logs and incremental backups. The cronjob entries should look like the following example (obviously, the database name will be different):

```
# ---------------------------------------------------------------------
# -- RMAN Weekly Backups
# ---------------------------------------------------------------------
00 00 * * 6 /home/oracle/general/sh/rman2disk.ksh -d DBATOOLS -l 0 >
/tmp/rman2disk.DBATOOLS_L0.log 2>&1

#
# ---------------------------------------------------------------------
# -- RMAN Daily Incremental Backups
# ---------------------------------------------------------------------
00 00 * * 0-5 /home/oracle/general/sh/rman2disk.ksh -d DBATOOLS -l 1 >
/tmp/rman2disk.DBATOOLS_L1.log 2>&1
```

For compressed backups, you can add a -z y option to the rman2disk.ksh syntax. An example of a compressed backup looks like this:

```
00 00 * * 6 /home/oracle/general/sh/rman2disk.ksh -d DBATOOLS -l 0 -z y >
/tmp/rman2disk.DBATOOLS_L0z.log 2>&1
```

Container and Pluggable Databases

In Oracle Database 12*c*, backing up a CDB is identical to backing up a non-container database. When we perform a full level 0 backup of the CDB, all the PDBs are automatically backed up together with the CDB. When we perform an OS authenticated RMAN target connection, we are essentially connecting to the root container (also called CDB) with the AS SYSDBA authentication. We will not even try to cover the features of CDB/PDB in this section, but there are some key features that you will want to consider when performing backups on the Exadata.

You can perform a backup of one or more PDBs simply by issuing this syntax:

```
RMAN TARGET /
BACKUP PLUGGABLE DATABASE my_pdb, your_pdb;
```

If you log in to a specific PDB, you can back up the individual PDB:

```
RMAN TARGET=sys@my_pdb
BACKUP DATABASE;
```

We can create a special database account referred to as a common user which is new to Oracle Database 12*c* and exists only in the Multitenant environment. Common users are special database accounts starting with C## or c## that exist in the root CDB and all the PDBs plugged into the CDB and all future PDBs. A new role is also available in Oracle Database 12*c* called SYSBACKUP. The SYSBACKUP role has the following system privileges:

```
1* select * from dba_sys_privs where grantee = 'SYSBACKUP'
SQL> /

GRANTEE       PRIVILEGE               ADM     COM
-----------   ----------------------  ---     ---
SYSBACKUP     ALTER SYSTEM            NO      YES
SYSBACKUP     AUDIT ANY              NO      YES
SYSBACKUP     SELECT ANY TRANSACTION NO      YES
SYSBACKUP     SELECT ANY DICTIONARY  NO      YES
SYSBACKUP     RESUMABLE              NO      YES
SYSBACKUP     CREATE ANY DIRECTORY   NO      YES
SYSBACKUP     UNLIMITED TABLESPACE   NO      YES
SYSBACKUP     ALTER TABLESPACE       NO      YES
SYSBACKUP     ALTER SESSION          NO      YES
SYSBACKUP     ALTER DATABASE         NO      YES
SYSBACKUP     CREATE ANY TABLE       NO      YES
SYSBACKUP     DROP TABLESPACE        NO      YES
SYSBACKUP     CREATE ANY CLUSTER     NO      YES

13 rows selected.
```

As an example, let's create a common user called C##DBABACKUP and grant the user the new SYSBACKUP role for purposes of performing backups for CDB and PDB. We first create a user account called C##DBABACK:

```
1   CREATE USER C##DBABACK
2   PROFILE DEFAULT
3   IDENTIFIED BY oracle123
4   DEFAULT TABLESPACE USERS
5   TEMPORARY TABLESPACE TEMP
6   ACCOUNT UNLOCK
7*  CONTAINER=ALL
SQL> /

User created.
```

Next we grant connectivity to all the PDBs and the SYSBACKUP role:

```
SQL> GRANT CONNECT TO C##DBABACK CONTAINER=ALL;

Grant succeeded.

SQL> GRANT SYSBACKUP TO C##DBABACK CONTAINER=ALL;

Grant succeeded.
```

Notice the special syntax CONTAINER=ALL which indicates that this statement applies to the root CDB and all PDBs plugged into the CDB. Now we can log in as the new C##ORABACK user and perform backups on our CDB and PDB:

```
$ rman

Recovery Manager: Release 12.1.0.1.0 - Production on Mon Feb 3 19:18:25 2014

Copyright (c) 1982, 2013, Oracle and/or its affiliates.  All rights reserved.

RMAN> connect target "c##dbaback/oracle123 as sysbackup"

connected to target database: CDB1 (DBID=811637436)
```

We can perform backups of the CDB, one or more PDBs, or just the root CDB. Since Exadata is the best consolidation platform on the market, you are strongly encouraged to learn the multitenant features of CDB and PDB.

Data Guard

DBAs must have intimate knowledge of their company's recovery point objective (RPO) and recovery time objective (RTO). The Data Guard configuration needs to be directly correlated to meeting the company's RPO and RTO requirements. You need to implement fundamental best practices and configure, monitor, and maintain a Data Guard environment suited for your RPO and RTO.

Patches

First and foremost, as part of best-practice compliance, you should apply the latest bundle patch (BP) at an N-1 BP release cycle specific to your Exadata. For the latest BP, check the following Oracle Support Notes:

- "Oracle Recommended Patches—Oracle Database" (ID 756671.1)
- "Exadata Database Machine and Exadata Storage Server Supported Versions" (ID 888828.1)

Oracle Data Guard Standby-First Patch Apply was introduced in Oracle Database 11*g* Release 2 Enterprise Edition (11.2.0.1) and provides support for certified software patches. With the Oracle Data Guard Standby-First Patch Apply support feature, we can have different software releases between the primary and physical standby databases for applying and validating Oracle patches in rolling fashion with zero risk. For additional details, review the section later in this chapter dedicated to Data Guard Standby-First Patch Apply.

Session Data Unit

As we deal with wide area network (WAN) connectivity between the primary database and the standby database, we often have the need to adjust the session data unit (SDU) to gain additional performance and throughput. We will want to adjust the SDU when the transferred data is fragmented into separate packets or large amounts of data are being transferred.

You have two options for setting the SDU. You can set the default SDU to be 32K in the SQLNET.ORA file, which applies to every database, or in the listener/tnsnames.ora files for each database (discussed in the next section). Here's an example of setting the parameters in the SQLNET.ORA file:

```
/u01/app/oracle/product/11.2.0.3/dbhome_1/network/admin/sqlnet.ora

# -- This will set SDU to 32k for all the databases
# --
DEFAULT_SDU_SIZE=32767
TCP.NODELAY=YES
```

In this example, we enabled SDU at 32K and also disabled the Nagle algorithm with the TCP.NODELAY option which is covered later in this chapter. One thing to note is that DBAs and system administrators may object to setting the SDU at the global level. (Be advised that setting this in the SQLNET.ORA file will impact all databases that use that ORACLE_HOME file.) The maximum value for SDU is 64K; setting the SDU to higher values does consume more memory on the Exadata Compute Nodes.

Bandwidth-Delay Product

In addition to SDU, you need to calculate the bandwidth-delay product (BDP) to determine the appropriate size for the receive and send buffer sizes. BDP is calculated as

Network bandwidth * Round-trip latency * 3

To calculate BDP, you need to know what kind of network you have between the primary database and your DR site. The following matrix defines the common high-speed WAN connection bandwidths:

- **T1**—1.544Mb/s
- **T3**—43.232Mb/s (equivalent to 28 T1s)
- **OC3**—155Mb/s (equivalent to 84 T1s)
- **OC12**—622Mb/s (equivalent to four OC3s)
- **OC48**—2.5Gb/s (equivalent to four OC12s)

Once we calculate BDP, we can plug in the SEND_BUF_SIZE and RECV_BUF_SIZE parameters in the TNSNAMES.ORA and LISTENER.ORA files. Round-trip time (RTT) is measured as the number of milliseconds (ms) for a network communication to travel from the primary database to the standby database and back and the response time in milliseconds from the PING command. As a preliminary step, first configure the dg_bdp.conf configuration file and specify the kind of WAN that is deployed at your company and the network RTT:

```
WAN=OC3

# --
#  PING RESPONSE measured in milliseconds
RTT_RESPONSE=44
```

Once you modify the dg_bdp.conf file, you can execute the corresponding shell script not only to derive BDP but also to autogenerate the corresponding TNSNAMES.ORA and LISTENER.ORA files:

```
#!/bin/ksh
# -- Script Name:  dg_bdp.ksh
# --

[ "$CONF" = "" ] && export CONF=$PWD/dg.conf
[ ! -f "$CONF" ] && { echo "Configuration file: $CONF is missing."; echo
"Exiting."; exit 1; }
. $CONF
. $PWD/dg_bdp.conf

#
[ "$WAN" = "T1" ] && export SPEED=1.544
[ "$WAN" = "T3" ] && export SPEED=43.232
[ "$WAN" = "OC3" ] && export SPEED=155
[ "$WAN" = "OC12" ] && export SPEED=622
[ "$WAN" = "OC48" ] && export SPEED=2500

BANDWIDTH=$(echo $SPEED \* 1000000 |bc)
LATENCY=$(echo "scale=5;$RTT_RESPONSE / 1000" |bc)
BDP=$(echo "$BANDWIDTH * $LATENCY * 3 / 8" |bc)
export BDP_NODECIMAL=$(echo "$BDP" |awk -F"." {'print $1'})

echo "BANDWIDTH is:  $BANDWIDTH"
echo "LATENCY is:  $LATENCY"
echo "BDP = $BDP_NODECIMAL"


cat $PWD/dg_generate_bdp.txt |sed -e "s/###_PRIMARY_DATABASE_###/$PRIMARY_DB/g" \
                    -e "s/###_STANDBY_DATABASE_###/$STANDBY_DB/g" \
                    -e "s/###_PRIMARY_DB_###/$PRIMARY_DB/g" \
                    -e "s/###_STANDBY_DB_###/$STANDBY_DB/g" \
                    -e "s/###_PRIMARY_DB_INSTANCE_###/$PRIMARY_DB_INSTANCE/g" \
                    -e "s/###_STANDBY_DB_INSTANCE_###/$STANDBY_DB_INSTANCE/g" \
                    -e "s=###_PRIMARY_ORACLE_HOME_###=$PRIMARY_ORACLE_HOME=g" \
                    -e "s=###_STANDBY_ORACLE_HOME_###=$STANDBY_ORACLE_HOME=g" \
                    -e "s/###_PRIMARY_VIP_###/$PRIMARY_VIP/g" \
                    -e "s/###_DR_VIP_###/$DR_VIP/g" \
                    -e "s/###_PRIMARY_HOST_###/$PRIMARY_HOST/g" \
                    -e "s/###_STANDBY_HOST_###/$STANDBY_HOST/g" \
                    -e "s/###_PRIMARY_PORT_###/$PRIMARY_PORT/g" \
                    -e "s/###_BDP_###/$BDP_NODECIMAL/g" \
                    -e "s/###_STANDBY_PORT_###/$STANDBY_PORT/g"


# --
#
echo "Option #2:"
echo "You can add the following to:"
echo "${PRIMARY_HOST}: $PRIMARY_ORACLE_HOME/network/admin/sqlnet.ora "
echo "${STANDBY_HOST}: $STANDBY_ORACLE_HOME/network/admin/sqlnet.ora "
echo ""
echo "# -- This will set SDU to 32k for all the databases"
echo "# --"
echo "DEFAULT_SDU_SIZE=32767"
```

As you can see, the supplied script supports T1, T3, OC3, OC12, and OC48 configurations and is hard-coded. If you need any other WAN bandwidths to be supported, feel free to customize the dg_bdp.ksh script. Executing the dg_bdp.ksh script autogenerates for both the TNSNAMES.ORA and LISTENER.ORA entries with the appropriate SEND_BUF_SIZE and RECV_BUF_SIZE values as determined by the BDP algorithm:

```
$ ./dg_bdp.ksh
BANDWIDTH is:  155000000
LATENCY is:    .04400
BDP = 2557500
```

As of Oracle Database 11*g*, we should set SEND_BUF_SIZE and RECV_BUF_SIZE to be 3X BDP or 10MB, whichever is greater, to accommodate the new streaming protocol for redo transport. You should compare the SEND_BUF_SIZE and RECV_BUF_SIZE parameters with your operating system TCP settings. If your BDP calculations turn out to be larger than your TCP maximum socket size, you may want to increase your net.ipv4.tcp_wmem and net.ipv4.tcp_rmem parameters:

```
net.ipv4.tcp_wmem = 4096   16384     4194304
net.ipv4.tcp_rmem = 4096   87380     4194304
```

This example shows the minimum, default, and maximum values. You will never need to change the minimum or the default value for these parameters. The maximum value should be at least 2X your BDP. /proc/sys/net/core/rmem_max and /proc/sys/net/core/wmem_max should also be set to 2X your BDP calculation.

Network Queue Size

In the world of Linux, you have two network queues: the interface transmit queue and a network receive queue that should be adjusted for better performance. The default txqueuelen for Oracle Linux 5 and Red Hat 5 is 1000ms. A txqueuelen of 1000 may be inadequate for long-distance, high-throughput pipes and thus should be modified to a higher value as shown here:

```
/sbin/ifconfig eth0 txqueuelen 10000
```

For the receiver side, there is a similar queue for incoming packets. This queue builds up in size when an interface receives packets faster than the kernel can process them. If this queue is too small, we begin to lose packets at the receiver, rather than on the network. You can benefit from setting this kernel parameter to 20,000:

```
echo "sys.net.core.netdev_max_backlog=20000" >>/etc/sysctl.conf
sysctl -p
```

You can reload the kernel parameters dynamically with the sysctl -p option. More importantly, you need to keep in mind that txqueuelen network interface changes on the primary database server and the sys.net.core.netdev_max_backlog kernel parameter changes on the standby database server need to happen in pairs and should be adjusted together.

Disabling TCP Nagle Algorithm

The parameter TCP.NODELAY, in the SQLNET.ORA file, activates and deactivates Nagle's algorithm, automatic concatenation of the number of small buffer messages to increase network efficiency. TCP.NODELAY alters the way packets are delivered on the network, thereby possibly impacting performance.

Under certain conditions for some applications using TCP/IP, Oracle Net packets may not get flushed immediately to the network, especially when large amounts of data are streamed. To mitigate this issue, you can specify no delays in the buffer flushing process. This is not a SQL*Net feature, but rather an ability to set the persistent buffering flag at the TCP layer.

To prevent delays in buffer flushing in the TCP protocol stack, disable the TCP Nagle algorithm by setting TCP.NODELAY to YES (the default value) in the SQLNET.ORA file on both the primary and standby systems:

```
TCP.NODELAY=YES
```

Enabling Network Time Protocol

Network Time Protocol (NTP) is a networking protocol that enables you to synchronize the clock among all the servers. Just as NTP is a requirement for all Exadata implementations to keep all the clocks between Compute and Storage Nodes in sync, you should synchronize your system time between your primary and standby database servers by enabling the NTP daemon. Enable NTP with the –x option to allow for gradual time changes, also referred to as slewing. This slewonly option is mandatory for RAC but is also recommended for Data Guard configurations. To set up NTP with the –x option, you need to modify the /etc/sysconfig/ntpd file and add the desired flag to the OPTIONS variable, then restart the service with the service ntpd restart command:

```
# Drop root to id 'ntp:ntp' by default.
OPTIONS="-x -u ntp:ntp -p /var/run/ntpd.pid"
```

You can check your current NTP configuration by checking the process status and filtering on the ntp daemon. You should see the –x option specified:

```
$ ps -ef |grep ntp |grep -v grep
ntp       6496     1  0 Mar10 ?        00:00:00 ntpd -x -u ntp:ntp -p
/var/run/ntpd.pid
```

Block Change Tracking

If you are performing any level of incremental backups, you need to enable block change tracking (BCT) to track changed blocks on the database since the last backup. Enabling BCT will significantly reduce your backup window for incremental backups as RMAN leverages the BCT file to identify specific blocks that must be backed up. On the primary database, issue the following if your database storage is on ASM:

```
alter database enable block change tracking using file '+DATA_EXAP';
```

You can now enable block change tracking on the physical standby database to quickly identify the blocks that have changed since the last incremental backup. (DBAs may not be aware of this, but enabling BCT on the standby database requires a license for Oracle Active Data Guard [ADG].) You can view the file name, status, and size of the BCT file with the following query:

```
SQL> select filename, status, bytes from v$block_change_tracking;

FILENAME                                            STATUS      BYTES
--------------------------------------------------- ----------  ----------
+DATA_EXAP/visk/changetracking/ctf.294.744629595    ENABLED     11599872
```

From time to time, you should make sure change tracking is being used for RMAN backups:

```
  1  SELECT count(*)
  2  FROM v$backup_datafile
  3* where USED_CHANGE_TRACKING = 'NO'
SQL> /

  COUNT(*)
----------
         0
```

Fast Recovery Area

The Fast Recovery Area (FRA), formerly known as the Flash Recovery Area, is a location on the file system or ASM disk group that houses all the recovery-related files. FRA can hold control files, archived logs, flashback logs, RMAN backup sets/ image backups, and incremental backups required to recover a database. You should always set the parameter DB_RECOVERY_FILE_DEST to be the disk group dedicated for recovery such as +RECO_EXAD. You should also set the accompanying parameter DB_RECOVERY_FILE_DEST_SIZE with the appropriate value to accommodate your recovery-related files.

As a general rule, configure the FRA and define your local archiving parameters as follows:

```
LOG_ARCHIVE_DEST_1='LOCATION=USE_DB_RECOVERY_FILE_DEST'
```

As part of best practices, you should always enable Flashback Database on primary and standby databases for easy reinstantiation after a failover. With Flashback Database enabled, you do not have to rebuild the primary database after a database failover. You can reinstate the failed primary database. Also, Flashback Database provides the mechanism to expeditiously rewind the database after an erroneous batch update, a bad data load, user error(s), or a malicious set of activities on the database.

Oracle MAA recommends that DB_FLASHBACK_RETENTION_TARGET should be set to a minimum of 60 minutes if all you are trying to achieve is the reinstantiation of the primary database after a failover; however, if you require the additional protection from user errors and corruptions, you will need to extend that time. Oracle MAA best practices also recommend a minimum of six hours for the retention period. You need to determine what that retention period is based on your business requirements. The longer you set the flashback retention time, the more disk space you will need.

You should also enable Flashback Database on the standby database to minimize downtime resulting from logical corruptions.

Automatic Archive Switch

Oracle natively provides the mechanism to force a log switch even if the database is idle or has very little redo log activity. This capability is not known to a lot of DBAs, and they often write a shell script to force a log switch if the redo logs have not switched in a specified time frame. Instead of writing a shell script, you can set the ARCHIVE_LAG_TARGET parameter.

The ARCHIVE_LAG_TARGET parameter forces a log switch after a specified time interval in seconds. By default the ARCHIVE_LAG_TARGET parameter is set to 0, indicating that the primary database does not perform a time-based redo switch. The recommended setting for this parameter is 1800 seconds (30 minutes), which informs the primary database that it must switch log files every 30 minutes during times of low or no activity:

```
ALTER SYSTEM SET ARCHIVE_LAG_TARGET=1800 sid='*' scope=both;
```

Parallel Execution Message Size

Parallel execution message size (PEMS) specifies the size of messages for parallel execution (formerly known as parallel query, parallel DML, parallel recovery, or replication). Best-practice recommendation is to set PEMS to 16K (16,384) or as high as 64K (65,535). PEMS is used by all parallel query operations and retrieves memory from the shared pool. The actual value might be automatically lowered to the inter-process communication (IPC) limit for the OS.

Be aware that this larger value has a direct relationship to a larger shared pool requirement. Larger values can result in significant performance improvement of parallel recovery at the cost of additional memory use.

Starting from Oracle Database 11g Release 2, this parameter is set to 16K right out of the box:

```
SQL> select name, value, isdefault from v$parameter
where name like 'parallel_execut%';

NAME                                     VALUE      ISDEFAULT
---------------------------------------- ---------- ---------
parallel_execution_message_size          16384      TRUE
```

Database Cache Size

On the standby database, you can set DB_KEEP_CACHE_SIZE and DB_RECYCLE_CACHE_SIZE to zero and allocate additional memory to DB_CACHE_SIZE to a larger value than on the primary database. Additionally, you can shrink SHARED_POOL_SIZE on the standby database since managed the recovery process (MRP) does not require much shared pool memory.

Furthermore, you should incorporate two spfiles and flip the tuned initialization parameters back and forth as database role transitions occur. You can have a tuned set of parameters for production usage and another set of parameters for media recovery.

Standby Redo Logs

Standby redo logs (SRLs) are recommended for all Data Guard database configurations. Even though SRLs are not required for maximum performance mode, they will improve redo transport speed, data recoverability, and apply speed.

You must create at a minimum the same number of SRL groups as there are online redo log (ORL) groups on the primary database. As a best practice, you should create one more SRL group than the number of ORL groups per instance. For example, if the primary database has five redo logs per instance and is a three-node RAC, we will need to create six standby redo logs per instance. In total, we will need to create 18 standby redo logs.

Another important factor is that SRLs should be of the same size and should not be multiplexed. In anticipation of the primary database possibly becoming the standby database as a result of a database switchover or failover, you should create

SRLs on the primary database as well. The same rules apply when creating SRLs on the primary database in terms of the number of SRLs to be created. SRLs should be placed on the fastest disk group.

Another important tip is that you can create SRLs on the primary database and create the physical standby database using the DUPLICATE TARGET DATABASE FOR STANDBY FROM ACTIVE DATABASE command so that RMAN will duplicate the SRLs automatically on the physical standby database. To automate the creation of SRLs, you can download and execute the http://www.dataguardbook.com/Downloads/dgmenu/dg_generate_standby_redo.ksh script. This script generates two SQL scripts, one for the primary database (cr_standby_redo_p.sql) and one for the standby database (cr_standby_redo_s.sql). You can identify the different scripts by the _p.sql and _s.sql suffixes.

Here's an example of the output from a two-node RAC configuration generated from the ./dg_generate_standby_redo.ksh script:

```
Max Redo Group:      4
Redo Size:           2000
Redo Count:          3
Thread Count:        2
# --
# -- On the Primary Database:  VISK
# --
alter database add standby logfile thread 1 group 5
('+DATA_EXAD/VISK/onlinelog/stdby_redo_05a.rdo') size                2000m;
alter database add standby logfile thread 1 group 6
('+DATA_EXAD/VISK/onlinelog/stdby_redo_06a.rdo') size                2000m;
alter database add standby logfile thread 1 group 7
('+DATA_EXAD/VISK/onlinelog/stdby_redo_07a.rdo') size                2000m;
alter database add standby logfile thread 2 group 8
('+DATA_EXAD/VISK/onlinelog/stdby_redo_08a.rdo') size                2000m;
alter database add standby logfile thread 2 group 9
('+DATA_EXAD/VISK/onlinelog/stdby_redo_09a.rdo') size                2000m;
alter database add standby logfile thread 2 group 10
('+DATA_EXAD/VISK/onlinelog/stdby_redo_10a.rdo') size                2000m;
# --
# -- On the Standby Database:  VISKDR
# --
alter database add standby logfile thread 1 group 11
('+DATA_EXAD/VISKDR/onlinelog/stdby_redo_11a.rdo') size              2000m;
alter database add standby logfile thread 1 group 12
('+DATA_EXAD/VISKDR/onlinelog/stdby_redo_12a.rdo') size              2000m;
alter database add standby logfile thread 1 group 13
('+DATA_EXAD/VISKDR/onlinelog/stdby_redo_13a.rdo') size              2000m;
alter database add standby logfile thread 2 group 14
('+DATA_EXAD/VISKDR/onlinelog/stdby_redo_14a.rdo') size              2000m;
alter database add standby logfile thread 2 group 15
('+DATA_EXAD/VISKDR/onlinelog/stdby_redo_15a.rdo') size              2000m;
alter database add standby logfile thread 2 group 16
('+DATA_EXAD/VISKDR/onlinelog/stdby_redo_16a.rdo') size              2000m;
# --
# --
# --
# --
Execute SQL Script:  cr_standby_redo_p.sql on VISK
Execute SQL Script:  cr_standby_redo_s.sql on VISKDR
```

This shell script determines that the maximum redo group number is 4 and starts to create the standby redo group from number 5. In addition, the script knows that the redo log size is 2000MB in size and creates the standby redo logs of the same size. Also, the script determines the number of threads and creates groups for each corresponding thread in the designated disk group in ASM.

The generated SRL script is fully qualified with database, directory names, and file name. You can change the `ALTER DATABASE ADD STANDBY LOGFILE` command to include just your disk group name.

The supplied shell script adheres to the best-practices equation for the number of SRLs:

# of SRLs = (# of ORLs + 1) x # of threads

The equation simply states that the number of SRLs needs to be the number of ORLs plus one per RAC instance. Even though SRLs are not required for maximum performance, it is recommended that you still create SRLs.

Force Logging

We can enable the force logging option for the database to ensure that changes made in the database will be captured and written for recovery in the redo logs. As a best practice, you should enable force logging on the primary database at the database level with the following command:

```
SQL> alter database force logging;
```

Before making the critical decision to enable or not to enable force logging, you should be aware that temporary tablespaces and temporary segments are never logged. Also, if you enable force logging on the primary database while the database is open, force logging will not be enabled until all of the current nologging activities are complete.

For heavy ETL (extract, transform, load) jobs on the Exadata, you may opt to enable force logging at the tablespace level instead of at the database level. You need to strategically name nologging tablespaces with special names (i.e., NOLOG_DATA and NOLOG_INDEX). You should at maximum have one or two nologging tablespaces. You may have materialized views or temporary tables used for reports that may gain additional performance if you enable nologging at the tablespace level. If you enable nologging for these tablespaces, you should also enable monitoring with alert notifications for the remaining tablespaces that require force logging to be enabled. You can create an exception table or a .conf configuration file that lists the tablespaces that can have nologging enabled. All other tablespaces that show up as nologging should have alert escalations for responsible recipients.

If force logging mode is not at the database level, you need to proactively check for force logging and unrecoverable activities. You should download the `http://www.dataguardbook.com/Downloads/dgmenu/dg_check_force_logging.sql` and `dg_check_unrecoverable.sql` scripts to see if nologging activities have occurred in the past at the data file level and examine tablespaces to see if they are in nologging mode.

Flashback Logging

As of Oracle Database 11*g* Release 2, Oracle provides substantial performance enhancements to the stack that reduce the impact of flashback logging on the primary database, load operations, and initial flashback allocations. You should also enable Flashback Database on the standby database to minimize downtime resulting from logical corruptions.

As of Oracle Database 11*g* Release 2, we can enable Flashback Database while the database is online. For some DBAs who do not want to turn on Flashback Database, this can provide a little more flexibility for enabling or disabling flashback for critical database operations or in a controlled scenario. You can now enable flashback logging (`alter database flashback on;`) prior to a critical operation and turn it off (`alter database flashback off;`) afterward without a database outage. DBAs who have to deal with limited space for the FRA and have to disable flashback logging from time to time due to limited space and uncontrolled batch jobs can now reenable it when crisis situations clear up.

As a best practice, we should enable flashback logging for every database, especially prior to planned maintenance such as database switchover. If flashback is enabled on the primary and standby, we do not have to rebuild the physical standby database if something goes wrong during the switchover exercise. Flashback technology will simply reverse the issue encountered during the switchover. By ensuring flashback logging on both primary and standby databases, we will be able to sleep better at night knowing that we have another level of protection. For additional details on flashback logging best practices, refer to Oracle Support Note ID 565535.1, "Flashback Database Best Practices."

Real-Time Apply

Always enable Real-Time Apply (RTA) so that changes are applied as soon as the redo data is received. With the availability of SRLs, when the remote file server (RFS) process on the standby database server receives redo, the RFS process writes the redo data to the SRL. The Redo Apply automatically applies the redo data directly from the SRL. You can use the `dg_start.sql` script to enable the RTA feature of the physical standby:

```
alter database recover managed standby database using current logfile disconnect;
```

RTA is the default if you created your configuration with Data Guard Broker (DG Broker).

Timeout and Reopen Options

Always make sure that you have `net_timeout` and `reopen` options set. A `net_timeout` of 30 seconds is the default in Oracle Database 11*g* and 180 seconds in Oracle Database 10*g* Release 2. If you have a reliable network, you can set this to 10 to 15 seconds. Oracle does not recommend setting this option below 10 seconds as you will experience failed reconnects and possibly performance problems.

The `reopen` option controls the wait time before Data Guard will allow the primary database to attempt a reconnect. The default is 300 seconds (5 minutes). You will want to set this to 30 seconds or even 15 seconds to allow Data Guard to reconnect as soon as possible. With the setting of 5 minutes, DBAs often perceive that Data Guard is not working right after it comes back online.

Redo transport compression is another important attribute to consider but requires the Oracle Advanced Compression license. Compression can significantly increase your throughput in the WAN for redo stream transport. If you have throughput or high latency issues in your WAN, you should consider licensing the Advanced Compression option. Starting in Oracle Database 11*g* Release 2, redo transport compression can be enabled with all protection modes.

Review the following Oracle Support Note for details: "Redo Transport Compression in a Data Guard Environment" (ID 729551.1).

Note

You can enable compression by setting the `COMPRESSION=ENABLE` attribute of the `LOG_ARCHIVE_DEST_x` parameter or by editing the database property with the Broker as shown here:

```
DGMGRL> EDIT DATABASE 'visk' SET PROPERTY 'RedoCompression' = ENABLE;
```

Do not use `MAX_CONNECTIONS` starting in Oracle Database 11*g*. Although this parameter was introduced in Oracle Database 10*g* Release 2, it is no longer used in Oracle Database 11*g*. Using this option on Oracle Database 11*g* will impede redo transport performance.

DBAs often delay applying redo stream on the physical standby database to mitigate potential human-induced errors or other hardware-inflicted issues with the

DELAY attribute. Instead of using the DELAY attribute, enable Flashback Database on both the primary and standby databases.

Archive Generation Rate

You need to know the number of archive logs that you are generating. Many DBAs calculate just the average archive log generation per day. In addition, you need to calculate the archive generation during a specified peak window to determine how your batch jobs will behave. Knowing how to address high bursts of archive log generation will help you to determine if you can meet your RPO and RTO objectives. Companies are often behind by several hours in the morning after a big batch job occurred in the middle of the night.

Knowing what kind of throughput numbers you need for archive generation is the beginning point of designing the kind of network you need for your WAN. Also, depending on your throughput requirements, you may want to separate out your public network (RAC VIP and client connections) with redo transport traffic. You can design public network traffic to flow in and out of an eth1 network interface and disaster recovery traffic to flow in and out of an eth3 network interface. For details on how to direct Data Guard network traffic through a different network, review Oracle Support Note ID 960510.1, "Data Guard Transport Considerations on Oracle Database Machine (Exadata)."

To determine your archive log generation rate throughout the day, you can execute the following script (http://dataguardbook.com/Downloads/SQL/dg_archive_rates.sql):

```
cat dg_archive_rates.sql
set lines 255
set pages 14

SELECT
    TO_CHAR(TRUNC(FIRST_TIME),'Mon DD')                        "Date",
    TO_CHAR(SUM(DECODE(TO_CHAR(FIRST_TIME,'HH24'),'00',1,0)),'9999')   "00",
    TO_CHAR(SUM(DECODE(TO_CHAR(FIRST_TIME,'HH24'),'01',1,0)),'9999')   "01",
    TO_CHAR(SUM(DECODE(TO_CHAR(FIRST_TIME,'HH24'),'02',1,0)),'9999')   "02",
    TO_CHAR(SUM(DECODE(TO_CHAR(FIRST_TIME,'HH24'),'03',1,0)),'9999')   "03",
    TO_CHAR(SUM(DECODE(TO_CHAR(FIRST_TIME,'HH24'),'04',1,0)),'9999')   "04",
    TO_CHAR(SUM(DECODE(TO_CHAR(FIRST_TIME,'HH24'),'05',1,0)),'9999')   "05",
    TO_CHAR(SUM(DECODE(TO_CHAR(FIRST_TIME,'HH24'),'06',1,0)),'9999')   "06",
    TO_CHAR(SUM(DECODE(TO_CHAR(FIRST_TIME,'HH24'),'07',1,0)),'9999')   "07",
    TO_CHAR(SUM(DECODE(TO_CHAR(FIRST_TIME,'HH24'),'08',1,0)),'9999')   "08",
    TO_CHAR(SUM(DECODE(TO_CHAR(FIRST_TIME,'HH24'),'09',1,0)),'9999')   "09",
    TO_CHAR(SUM(DECODE(TO_CHAR(FIRST_TIME,'HH24'),'10',1,0)),'9999')   "10",
    TO_CHAR(SUM(DECODE(TO_CHAR(FIRST_TIME,'HH24'),'11',1,0)),'9999')   "11",
    TO_CHAR(SUM(DECODE(TO_CHAR(FIRST_TIME,'HH24'),'12',1,0)),'9999')   "12",
    TO_CHAR(SUM(DECODE(TO_CHAR(FIRST_TIME,'HH24'),'13',1,0)),'9999')   "13",
    TO_CHAR(SUM(DECODE(TO_CHAR(FIRST_TIME,'HH24'),'14',1,0)),'9999')   "14",
    TO_CHAR(SUM(DECODE(TO_CHAR(FIRST_TIME,'HH24'),'15',1,0)),'9999')   "15",
    TO_CHAR(SUM(DECODE(TO_CHAR(FIRST_TIME,'HH24'),'16',1,0)),'9999')   "16",
    TO_CHAR(SUM(DECODE(TO_CHAR(FIRST_TIME,'HH24'),'17',1,0)),'9999')   "17",
    TO_CHAR(SUM(DECODE(TO_CHAR(FIRST_TIME,'HH24'),'18',1,0)),'9999')   "18",
```

```
        TO_CHAR(SUM(DECODE(TO_CHAR(FIRST_TIME,'HH24'),'19',1,0)),'9999')    "19",
        TO_CHAR(SUM(DECODE(TO_CHAR(FIRST_TIME,'HH24'),'20',1,0)),'9999')    "20",
        TO_CHAR(SUM(DECODE(TO_CHAR(FIRST_TIME,'HH24'),'21',1,0)),'9999')    "21",
        TO_CHAR(SUM(DECODE(TO_CHAR(FIRST_TIME,'HH24'),'22',1,0)),'9999')    "22",
        TO_CHAR(SUM(DECODE(TO_CHAR(FIRST_TIME,'HH24'),'23',1,0)),'9999')    "23"
FROM V$LOG_HISTORY
    GROUP BY TRUNC(FIRST_TIME)
    ORDER BY TRUNC(FIRST_TIME) DESC
/

set lines 66
```

Sample output from this query looks like this:

```
Date     00     01     02     03     04     05     06     07     08     09     10     11     12

13     14     15     16     17     18     19     20     21     22     23
------- ---- ---- ---- ---- ---- ---- ---- --- --- ---- ---- ---- ---- ---
- ---- ---- ---- ---- ---- ---- ---- ---- ---- ----
Feb 28     1      0      0      1      2      1      4      9      5      6      7      9      8
8      0      0      0      0      0      0      0      0      0      0
Feb 27     2      1      1      2      2      1      1      5      1      1      2      0      1
0      0      0      5      0      0      0      3      5      0      0
Feb 26    12      5     12      2      5      5      1      8      4      4      6      4      2
2      1      1      5      3      2      1      3      3      1      6
Feb 25     8      3      4      4      5      3      7      8      5      7      8      9      3
8     11      9     12     12      8      6      6     10     10     12
Feb 24    12     10     13      7      3      3      7      9      8      8      8      3      5
6      3      8      4      9     14     12      9      8     10     12
Feb 23    16     25     23     20     15     11      5     11      6      8
2      7      7      9      3      8      9     11     13     13      7      8      8     14
Feb 22     4      3      3      1      3      3      4      9      4      4      7      9      7
3      8      9      8      5     10      9      4      4     16     16
Feb 21     0      0      1      2      1      2      3      8      4      3      5      4      7
5      4      7     10      7      5      6      5     10      6      5
Feb 20     6     20     14      0      0      1      5      8      4      1      2      0      2
6      0      0      5      0      1      1      2      6      0      0
Feb 19     8      2      3      1      6      3      3      8      3      5      6      4      4
1      2      1      5      0      0      0      2      5      7     12
Feb 18     6      4      3      2      4      3      6      8      7      6      9     11      8
10      7     10     12      9      8      6      2      8     11      7
Feb 17     6      4      3      2      4      4      5      8      9      7     10      9      9
8      8      8     15      7     11      8      5      9      8      9
Feb 16     5      4      6      2      6      3      3      6      3      8      8     11     12
10     11     11     12      9      9      7      6      9      8      9
Feb 15     5      3      2      4      5      4      5      9      7      5      9     11      7
9      7      9     12      9      8     10      7      4     10     11
Feb 14     0      0      0      0      0      0      0      0      0      0      0      0      0
0      5     10     12      9      8      8      6      9      9      6

15 rows selected.
```

It is no longer uncommon to see 1GB, 2GB, or even 4GB redo logs on the Exadata with multiterabyte databases and applications that have high transaction volumes. Ideally, a log switch should not occur more than once per 20 minutes during peak activity. You should consider sizing your redo logs accordingly to fit an archive switch within the specified window.

Standby File Management

The standby file management initialization parameter dictates if file additions and deletions on the primary database are replicated to the physical standby database. As a best practice, the STANDBY_FILE_MANAGEMENT parameter should always be set to TRUE on the physical standby database. However, with the STANDBY_FILE_ MANAGEMENT option set to TRUE, you will not be able to perform the following commands:

- ALTER DATABASE RENAME
- ALTER DATABASE ADD or DROP LOGFILE
- ALTER DATABASE ADD or DROP STANDBY LOGFILE MEMBER
- ALTER DATABASE CREATE DATAFILE AS

If you need to issue these commands, you will need to reset STANDBY_FILE_ MANAGEMENT, perform your maintenance, and reenable it after completion of maintenance tasks.

Data Guard Standby-First Patching

Starting with Oracle Database 11*g* Release 2 (11.2.0.1), we are allowed to patch the standby database environment before applying patches to the primary database environment. There are certain times when you are allowed to apply certain patches on the standby database without patching the primary database. Our goal is to apply patches on the target standby database environment first and eventually patch the primary database. Data Guard Standby-First Patch Apply is certified under the following conditions without impacting the integrity of the Data Guard configuration:

- Patch Set Update (PSU) (i.e., Database version 11.2.0.3 PSU2 to 11.2.0.3 PSU5)
- Security Patch Update (SPU), formerly known as Critical Patch Update (CPU)
- Oracle Grid Infrastructure patches or software updates
- Patch Set Exception (PSE)
- Oracle Exadata Database Machine bundled patch or Quarter Database Patch for Exadata (QDPE) (i.e., Database version 11.2.0.3.5 to 11.2.0.3.9)
- Oracle Exadata Storage Server software update (i.e., Exadata Cell 11.2.2.4.2 to 11.2.3.1.1)

- Operating system changes that do not have dependencies on Oracle Database software
- Oracle Exadata Database Machine hardware or network changes

There are some caveats. The maximum time between the standby database patching and the primary database patching should not exceed one month. MAA recommends validation on the standby database for no more than 48 hours. Data Guard Standby-First Patch Apply is supported for patches that are less than one year apart or patches that are six versions apart from each other. Data Guard Standby-First Patch Apply cannot be considered for major releases and patches. Refer to "Oracle Patch Assurance—Data Guard Standby-First Patch Apply" (Oracle Support Note ID 1265700.1) for complete details.

Active Data Guard

ADG provides a near-real-time read-only database for reporting purposes. In addition to a read-only database that continuously applies redo stream or archive logs, ADG is a licensed option that provides these additional benefits:

- BCT on the standby database for speedy backups. By allowing BCT on the physical standby site, you can truly offload your backups to the physical standby site.
- Automatic block repair so that corrupted blocks can be automatically repaired using the good copy from either the primary or the standby database without user intervention or application awareness.

ADG provides great ROI with these features. New features in ADG available in Oracle Database 12c Release 1 make ADG more appealing for reporting databases. As of Oracle 12.1, Oracle allows the use of sequences on the standby database and DML on global temporary tables for ADG configurations. Another added benefit of Oracle Database 12c ADG is Real-Time Cascade where the physical standby can cascade redo in real time as it is being written to the standby redo logs. Prior to Oracle Database 12c, redo cascading continued after the standby log file had been archived locally.

Note
As of Oracle Database 12c, in a RAC configuration, we need to shut down only one instance (we no longer have to shut down all the instances of the database) for a switchover to a physical standby database.

Far Sync

Oracle Database 12*c* has a new Data Guard feature called Far Sync which can offload the redo transport overhead, including compression overhead (the Oracle Advanced Compression license is needed), from the primary database. With Far Sync, we can configure an Oracle Data Guard Far Sync instance which is actually a remote Oracle Data Guard destination that accepts redo from the primary database and sends the redo stream to other participants in the Oracle Data Guard ecosystem. A Far Sync instance has a PFILE/SPFILE, control file, standby redo logs, and a password file. A Far Sync instance receives redo into SRLs, and archives logs to local archived redo logs. This is where the resemblance to a physical standby ends. A Far Sync instance *cannot* do the following:

* Have database data files
* Be opened for database access
* Run Redo Apply
* Become a primary database
* Become a standby database

Creating a Far Sync instance is similar to creating a physical standby database except we do not have to perform data file copies of restores. We create a special Far Sync Instance Control with this syntax:

```
SQL> ALTER DATABASE CREATE FAR SYNC INSTANCE CONTROLFILE AS
'/tmp/DBA/FarSynccontrol01.ctl';
```

From a design perspective, we can create a local Far Sync instance on the local data center in synchronous mode (maximum protection or maximum availability), and then the Far Sync instance can forward all the redo stream to the rest of the Data Guard configuration in asynchronous mode (maximum performance). If you are interested in implementing Oracle 12*c*'s new Data Guard feature called Far Sync, you have to be licensed for Oracle Active Data Guard.

Archive Log Retention Policy

You should set your RMAN archive log retention policy so that archive logs are not deleted on the primary database until confirmation is made that they are either received or applied on the standby database. From RMAN on the primary database instance, issue one of the following commands:

```
configure archivelog deletion policy to shipped to all standby;
configure archivelog deletion policy to applied on all standby;
```

On the standby database, from RMAN, issue the following command:

```
configure archivelog deletion policy to applied on standby;
```

We want to make sure that we do not purge any archive logs until they are applied. For performance implications, archival history count should be less than 10,000. You should set the `control_file_record_keep_time` parameter accordingly.

Data Corruptions

Table 8.2 lists the best-practice configuration settings on the primary and the physical standby databases for corruption detection, prevention, and automatic block repair.

There are some things you'll want to keep in mind regarding these parameters:

- Best practice is to set `DB_BLOCK_CHECKSUM=FULL` on both the primary and standby databases. Oracle MAA team testing has shown that setting this parameter to `FULL` incurs less than 5% overhead on the system, while setting the parameter to `TYPICAL` incurs 1% to 5% overhead on the system.

- Performance overhead is incurred on every block change; thus, you need to performance-test `DB_BLOCK_CHECKING`. With higher rates of insertions or updates, this parameter becomes more expensive for block checking. Oracle recommends setting `DB_BLOCK_CHECKING` to `FULL` on the primary database, but you need to assess if the performance overhead is acceptable and adjust to your business needs.

- With `DB_LOST_WRITE_PROTECT`, primary database performance impact is negligible (see the next section).

- Starting with Oracle Database 11.2, you can use Active Data Guard to enable automatic block repair.

As a best practice, you can set `DB_BLOCK_CHECKSUM` to `FULL`, so both disk corruption and inmemory corruption are detected and the block is not written to disk,

Table 8.2   Initialization Parameters for Data Corruption

Primary Database	Physical Standby Database
`DB_BLOCK_CHECKSUM=MEDIUM` or `DB_BLOCK_CHECKSUM=FULL`	`DB_BLOCK_CHECKSUM=FULL`
`DB_BLOCK_CHECKING=FULL`	`DB_BLOCK_CHECKING=OFF`
`DB_LOST_WRITE_PROTECT=TYPICAL`	`DB_LOST_WRITE_PROTECT=TYPICAL`

thus preserving the integrity of the physical standby database. This parameter has minimal effect on Redo Apply performance.

You should set LOST_WRITE_PROTECT to TYPICAL to prevent corruptions due to stray or lost writes on the primary database from being propagated and applied to the standby database. By setting LOST_WRITE_PROTECT, the database server can record buffer cache block reads in the redo log so that lost writes can be detected. Setting this parameter has a negligible effect on the standby database.

For additional details, refer to Oracle Support Note ID 1302539.1, "Best Practices for Corruption Detection, Prevention, and Automatic Repair in a Data Guard Configuration."

Data Guard Instantiation

There are several options when it comes to instantiating a physical standby database. A popular approach that emerged with Oracle Database 11g is the Duplicate Target Database For Standby Database syntax. This syntax has become widely used for instantiating physical standby databases for smaller databases. RMAN provides rapid Exadata-to-Exadata physical standby instantiation over InfiniBand connectivity because prior RMAN backup or a backup staging area is not needed before instantiating the physical standby. InfiniBand can sustain the throughput to copying multiterabyte databases. If you are creating a physical standby on another Exadata over InfiniBand or over 10GigE on the same network, the Duplicate Target Database For Standby From Active Database option is your best solution. Internal MAA performance tests have reported the following results using RMAN active database duplication:

- 2.9TB/hour using a single IB connection and one RMAN session
- 0.4TB/hour using a single1GigE connection

The traditional method of building a physical standby database typically involves the following steps:

1. Perform an RMAN backup of the primary database.
2. Create the standby control file.
3. Copy the backup of the database, standby control file, or spfile to the standby database server.
4. Restore the spfile and standby control file.
5. Restore the database from the RMAN backup.
6. Configure both primary and standby databases with Data Guard–related initialization parameters.
7. Start the MRP.

For complete details on how to build a physical standby database with the traditional method listed above, download the Create Standby Database PDF file from DBAExpert.com: http://dbaexpert.com/dg/DGToolkit-CreateStandbyDatabase.pdf. This document provides detailed scripts and automated scripts to transfer RMAN backup sets from one ASM disk group in a RAC environment to another ASM disk group in another RAC environment. Since the Exadata is a 100% ASM configuration, this document is for you!

As of Oracle Database 11g, Oracle provides the capability to create a physical standby database from an active copy over the network of a database without requiring a backup. With this technique, you can reduce the amount of work required to create a physical standby database, especially if your source and target databases happen to be at the same data center.

Before you start this process, make sure that you create the SRLs on the primary database.

You can leverage a comprehensive korn shell script called `dg_duplicate_database.ksh` to autogenerate the `Duplicate Target Database For Standby From Active Database` command.

At the heart of the shell script is the `sed` script that parses the duplicate database template file called dg_duplicate_database_template.txt and replaces the variable holders with values derived from the dg.conf file. Executing the `http://dbaexpert.com/dg/dgmenu/dg_duplicate_database.ksh` script yields the following output based on the dg.conf configuration file. In addition, the script produces instructions that serve as a step-by-step process to build your Data Guard environment:

```
# ----------------------------------------------------------------------
# -- Set ORACLE Environment
# ----------------------------------------------------------------------
export ORACLE_SID=VISKDR1
export PATH=/usr/local/bin:$PATH
. oraenv
```

Either configure your listener under ORACLE_HOME for the standby (typically using NETCA, the Oracle Net Configuration Assistant) or make additions to the Grid Infrastructure listener.ora to add your entries. Let's configure listener.ora with the physical standby information and reload listener:

```
SID_LIST_LISTENER =
  (SID_LIST =
    (SID_DESC =
      (SID_NAME = PLSExtProc)
      (ORACLE_HOME = /u01/app/oracle/product/11.2.0.3/dbhome_1)
      (PROGRAM = extproc)
    )
    (SID_DESC =
      (GLOBAL_DBNAME = VISKDR)
```

```
        (SID_NAME = VISKDR)
        (ORACLE_HOME = /u01/app/oracle/product/11.2.0.3/dbhome_1)
      )
  )

$ lsnrctl reload LISTENER

# ----------------------------------------------------------------------
# -- Add the following to your tnsnames.ora file on both the primary and
standby database on your SCAN
# ----------------------------------------------------------------------
VISK =
  (DESCRIPTION =
    (ADDRESS_LIST =
      (ADDRESS = (PROTOCOL = TCP)(HOST = exap-scan)(PORT = 1521))
    )
    (CONNECT_DATA =
      (SERVER = DEDICATED)
      (SERVICE_NAME=VISK)
    )
  )

VISKDR =
  (DESCRIPTION =
    (ADDRESS_LIST =
      (ADDRESS = (PROTOCOL = TCP)(HOST = exapdr-scan)(PORT = 1521))
    )
    (CONNECT_DATA =
      (SERVER = DEDICATED)
      (SERVICE_NAME=VISKDR)  (UR=A)
    )
  )

# ----------------------------------------------------------------------
# -- Create password file on the standby database server:
# ----------------------------------------------------------------------
orapwd file=/u01/app/oracle/product/11.2.0.3/dbhome_1/dbs/orapwVISKDR1
entries=25 password=oracle123

# ----------------------------------------------------------------------
# -- Create the following initialization file for the VISKDR1 instance:
# -- /u01/app/oracle/product/11.2.0.3/dbhome_1/dbs/initVISKDR1.ora
# ----------------------------------------------------------------------
cat <<EOF > /u01/app/oracle/product/11.2.0.3/dbhome_1/dbs/initVISKDR1.ora
db_name=VISK
db_unique_name=VISKDR
cluster_database=false
EOF

# ----------------------------------------------------------------------
# -- Execute the following RMAN script on the standby database server
# --
# -- First startup nomount the database with either SQL*PLUS or RMAN>
# ----------------------------------------------------------------------
echo "startup nomount;

# ----------------------------------------------------------------------
# --
# ----------------------------------------------------------------------
rman <<EOF
connect target sys/oracle123@VISK;
connect auxiliary sys/oracle123@VISKDR;
run {
allocate channel prmy1 type disk;
allocate channel prmy2 type disk;
allocate channel prmy3 type disk;
allocate channel prmy4 type disk;
allocate auxiliary channel stby type disk;
```

```
duplicate target database for standby from active database
spfile
parameter_value_convert 'VISK','VISKDR'
set 'db_unique_name'='VISKDR'
set 'db_file_name_convert'='+DATA_EXAP/VISK','+DATA_EXAP/VISKDR'
set log_file_name_convert=
'+DBFS_DG/VISK','+DBFS_DG/VISKDR','+DATA_EXAP/VISK','+DATA_EXAP/VISKDR'
set control_files='+DBFS_DG/VISKDR/control.ctl'
set log_archive_max_processes='5'
set fal_client='VISKDR'
set fal_server='VISK'
set standby_file_management='AUTO'
set log_archive_config='dg_config=(VISK,VISKDR)'
set log_archive_dest_1='service=VISK LGWR ASYNC
valid_for=(ONLINE_LOGFILES,PRIMARY_ROLE) db_unique_name=VISK'
set cluster_database='FALSE'
set parallel_execution_message_size='32768'
set db_lost_write_protect='TYPICAL'
set db_block_checking='TRUE'
set db_block_checksum='FULL'
nofilenamecheck
;

sql channel prmy1 "alter system set log_archive_config=''dg_config=(VISK,VISKDR)''";
sql channel prmy1 "alter system set log_archive_dest_2= ''service=VISKDR
LGWR ASYNC valid_for=(online_logfiles,primary_role)
db_unique_name=VISKDR''";
sql channel prmy1 "alter system set log_archive_max_processes=5";
sql channel prmy1 "alter system set fal_client=VISK ";
sql channel prmy1 "alter system set fal_server=VISKDR";
sql channel prmy1 "alter system set standby_file_management=auto";
sql channel prmy1 "alter system set log_archive_dest_state_2=enable";
sql channel prmy1 "alter system set parallel_execution_message_size=8192
scope=spfile sid=''*''";
sql channel prmy1 "alter system archive log current";

sql channel stby "alter database recover managed standby database
using current logfile disconnect";
}
EOF
```

Before we begin our duplicate database process, we establish our Oracle environment by setting ORACLE_SID and source the oraenv file from the /usr/local/ bin directory. Next, we set the minimal set of Oracle initialization parameters in the init${STANDBY_DB}.ora file and startup instance in nomount mode. In this particular example, spfile from the primary database is copied from the primary database to the standby database ORACLE_HOME. In addition, standby redo logs that already exist on the primary database are cloned during the duplicate database process. Unfortunately, the output of this duplicate database command is too long to display in this chapter. Visit the following URLs to see the output:

- To download the duplicate database script: http://DBAExpert.com/dg/dup.rman
- To peruse the log file: http://DBAExpert.com/dg/dup.txt

Note

fal_client is deprecated as of Oracle Database 11.2, so we do not need to set it.

Configuring Data Guard Broker

As another best practice, you should leverage Data Guard Broker (DG Broker) for maintaining your Data Guard environment. DG Broker is the management framework for Data Guard. DG Broker serves as the foundation for OEM Cloud Control (CC) 12c. DG Broker presents a single integrated view of a Data Guard configuration that allows DBAs to connect through any database in the configuration and propagate changes to both the primary and standby database configurations. If you are planning to leverage OEM 12c to monitor and maintain Data Guard, you are strongly encouraged to learn the internals behind DG Broker.

Numerous improvements to DG Broker are available with Oracle Database 12c. We consider the Resumable Switchover feature to be one of the most important features. In previous releases of Oracle, we deleted and re-created the broker configuration when a switchover failed. We then resolved the issues with the SQL command line. With the Resumable Switchover feature, we can now resolve the problem and perform one of the following:

- Reissue the switchover command as DG Broker will resume where it last failed.
- Switch back to the primary database until the problem is resolved.
- Switch over to another physical standby in a multiple-physical-standby configuration.

The VALIDATE DATABASE command is also improved in Oracle Database 12c to perform extensive validation checks to ensure that the DG environment is ready for a switchover/failover operation. DG Broker also can be configured to generate warning messages when the transport or apply lag exceeds the defined RPO.

Let's start with creating the required DG Broker configuration files with the alter system syntax for DG_BROKER setup (initialization parameters). DG Broker maintains configuration files at each database to keep track of the Data Guard–wide settings and intended states for each database in the configuration. DG Broker maintains two copies of the configuration for redundancy controlled by the DG_BROKER_CONFIG_FILE1 and DG_BROKER_CONFIG_FILE2 parameters:

```
# --
# -- Execute the following on the Primary Database:  VISK
alter system set dg_broker_config_file1='+DATA_EXAP/VISK/broker1.dat'
scope=both sid='*';
alter system set dg_broker_config_file2='+DBFS_DG/VISK/broker2.dat'
scope=both sid='*';
alter system set dg_broker_start=true scope=both sid='*';

# --
# -- Execute the following on the Standby Database:  VISKDR
```

```
alter system set dg_broker_config_file1='+DATA_EXAP/VISKDR/broker1.dat' scope=both sid='*';
alter system set dg_broker_config_file2='+DBFS_DG/VISKDR/broker2.dat' scope=both sid='*';
alter system set dg_broker_start=true scope=both sid='*';
```

We need to generate LISTENER.ORA entries for DG Broker. The only reason this step is important is because the database listener has a special attribute for the Broker for the GLOBAL_DBNAME parameter:

```
2
# -- Primary Database Server
# --
LISTENER_VISK =
.
..

SID_LIST_LISTENER_VISK =
  (SID_LIST =
    (SID_DESC =
    (SDU=32767)
      (GLOBAL_DBNAME = VISK_DGMGRL)
      (ORACLE_HOME = /u01/app/oracle/product/11.2.0.3/dbhome_1)
      (SID_NAME = VISK1)
    )
  )
# -- Standby Database Server
# --
LISTENER_VISKDR =
.
..

SID_LIST_LISTENER_VISKDR =
  (SID_LIST =
    (SID_DESC =
    (SDU=32767)
      (GLOBAL_DBNAME = VISKDR_DGMGRL)
      (ORACLE_HOME = /u01/app/oracle/product/11.2.0.3/dbhome_1)
      (SID_NAME = VISKDR1)
    )
  )
```

Now, let's proceed to create the Broker configuration with the command-line interface (dgmgrl) by setting up VISK as the primary database and VISKDR as the physical standby:

```
create configuration VISK_DGCONFIG as primary database is "VISK" connect
identifier is VISK;
add database "VISKDR" as connect identifier is VISKDR maintained as physical;
enable configuration;
```

Fast-Start Failover (FSFO) allows DG Broker to fail over automatically to a standby database when a failure occurs on the primary database. No manual intervention is required as FSFO issues a failover to the physical standby database. As an optional step, if you intend to use FSFO, you can enable an FSFO configuration:

```
edit database 'VISK' set property 'LogXptMode'='SYNC';
edit database 'VISKDR' set property 'LogXptMode'='SYNC';
edit database 'VISK' set property FastStartFailoverTarget='VISKDR';
edit database 'VISKDR' set property FastStartFailoverTarget='VISK';
edit configuration set protection mode as maxavailability;
enable fast_start failover;
show fast_start failover;
```

As you can see from the preceding examples, setting up the DG Broker configuration including FSFO is relatively straightforward. We cannot stress enough the importance of understanding the command-line interface and architecture for DG Broker.

The Observer is a third-member quorum that ensures that a failover only occurs when certain conditions are met. Ideally, the Observer should be placed in another data center away from both the primary and standby databases. The Observer can be installed on any system and does not have to match your OS or bit level. The only requirement is that the Oracle Client is of the same release or higher than the database version. You can only have one Observer per a Data Guard FSFO configuration. The DG Toolkit provides the shell script to launch the observer in the Data Guard Broker Submenu. You will see an option to start the Observer process on another server. In addition to creating the TNSNAMES and LISTENER.ORA entries, the shell script will also generate the script to start the Observer process on another server, preferably on a different data center from the primary and standby database:

```
#!/usr/bin/ksh
dgmgrl <<___EOF >/tmp/observer_'hostname'.log
connect sys/oracle123@VISK_PRI
start observer
___EOF
```

A scenario where a fast-start failover will happen is when the Observer and the standby database both lose connectivity with the production database for a specified time interval that surpasses the value designated in the FastStartFailoverThreshold, and the Observer and the standby database are still communicating.

OEM Cloud Control 12c

The best tool in the industry to monitor, maintain, and even instantiate the Data Guard environment is OEM Cloud Control (CC) 12c. OEM CC 12c provides wizards to set up a physical standby; if DG Broker has not been established in your database ecosystem, OEM CC 12c configures it as part of the physical standby instantiation. OEM CC 12c also focuses on setting up the Observer and setting up monitoring with metrics for alert notifications.

You will quickly realize that the wizard format for creating a physical standby with OEM 12c is extremely simple to follow. From the primary database Home page, select Availability from the top menu option and click on the Add Standby Database option. Next, answer all the questions to create a physical standby. For additional details on OEM CC 12c for Exadata, please review Chapter 9.

Switchover Considerations

By far the easiest way to perform a switchover is to leverage DG Broker. Switchovers can be performed using OEM, the Data Guard Broker command-line interface, or SQL*Plus statements.

With a single command on the primary database, you can perform a graceful switchover to your standby database. There is no RAC auxiliary instance to shut down and restart for a physical standby switchover, no restart of the old primary, and no manual startup of the apply process. The DG Toolkit provides this simple interface in the Launch the Data Guard Broker submenu:

```
Execute the following on the VISK:  switchover to VISK_DR1
from DGMGRL>
```

Even though you are not executing SQL*Plus, you still need to perform all the prerequisite checks for configuration completeness, check for the Broker completeness, and perform preparatory steps prior to executing the switchover command. A majority of these checks can be accomplished with the DG Toolkit in the Data Guard Broker submenu.

Here are some best-practice considerations you should be aware of prior to performing a graceful switchover to the standby database:

- Reduce the number of ARCH processes to the minimum needed for both remote and local archiving.
- Terminate all sessions on the primary database.
- Online redo logs on the target physical standby need to be cleared before the standby database can become the primary database. Although this will automatically happen as part of the SWITCHOVER TO PRIMARY command, it is recommended that the logs be cleared prior to the switchover:

```
SELECT DISTINCT L.GROUP#
FROM V$LOG L, V$LOGFILE LF
WHERE L.GROUP# = LF.GROUP#
AND L.STATUS NOT IN ('UNUSED', 'CLEARING','CLEARING_CURRENT');
```

- If that query produces output, on the target physical standby issue the following statement for each GROUP# returned:

```
ALTER DATABASE CLEAR LOGFILE GROUP <ORL GROUP # returned
from the query above>;
```

- For Oracle Database 11.1 and earlier, check to see if the standby has ever been open in read-only mode:

```
SELECT VALUE
FROM V$DATAGUARD_STATS
WHERE NAME='standby has been open';
```

- Disable jobs on the primary database so it will not submit additional jobs and block further job submissions:

```
ALTER SYSTEM SET job_queue_processes=0 SCOPE=BOTH SID='*';
EXECUTE DBMS_SCHEDULER.DISABLE( <job_name> );
```

For additional details pertaining to switchover steps, review Oracle Support Note ID 751600.1.

Switchover Tracing

You can trace the switchover activities by turning on the Data Guard tracing level on primary and standby to see exactly where the switchover activities are. This comes in handy for overall Data Guard–related troubleshooting. LOG_ARCHIVE_ TRACE is an optional parameter but very useful for viewing details of the switchover. Set the Data Guard trace level to 8192 on both the primary and the target physical standby databases:

```
ALTER SYSTEM SET log_archive_trace=8192;
```

A LOG_ARCHIVE_TRACE value of 8192 provides the greatest level of auditing and will include tracking Redo Apply activity on the physical standby. The higher value indicates a greater level of tracing and is inclusive of the lower-value trace options. A LOG_ARCHIVE_TRACE of 1 tracks archiving of redo log files. A LOG_ARCHIVE_ TRACE setting of 2 tracks the archive status per archived redo log destination and includes LOG_ARCHIVE_TRACE of 1. Other levels that you may be interested in are level 128, which tracks the FAL (fetch archive log) server process activity; 1024, which tracks the RFS process activity; and 4096, which tracks Real-Time Apply activity.

You can issue the tail -f command on the alert logs on both the primary and standby databases.

Guaranteed Restore Point

Just as you perform a guaranteed restore point (GRP) prior to upgrading a database or application, you should perform a GRP before a switchover. To perform a GRP, you can execute the following command:

```
CREATE RESTORE POINT <guaranteed_restore_point_name> GUARANTEE FLASHBACK DATABASE;
```

To revert the database back to its original state, you can flash back to the GRP with the following command:

```
STARTUP MOUNT FORCE;
FLASHBACK DATABASE TO RESTORE POINT <guaranteed_restore_point_name>;
```

Summary

In this chapter, we reviewed RMAN disk-to-disk (D2D) backup as it is the best line of defense for Exadata database protection. We reviewed RMAN backup set backups and image copy backups.

When it comes to instantiating a physical standby for the Exadata, whether your goal is to establish a disaster recovery site or to even create a reporting database server, you have options for how you can create your physical standby database. You can instantiate a Data Guard environment using the traditional backup and restore and recover database syntax from RMAN, or you can skip some steps with the `Duplicate Target Database For Standby From Active Database` syntax. Monitoring and maintaining a physical standby has never been easier with OEM 12c Cloud Control. With wizards, you can instantiate Data Guard environments and fully monitor and maintain your entire primary and physical standby database environments.

We learned in this chapter the significance of performing RMAN backups to disk and leveraging the `rman2disk` shell scripts with template files. We also reviewed pertinent RMAN best practices for performing backups on the Exadata. We covered Data Guard best practices and concluded the chapter with switchover considerations.

9

Managing Exadata with OEM 12*c*

Oracle Enterprise Manager Cloud Control 12*c* (popularly known as OEM 12*c*) provides centralized, comprehensive, and end-to-end monitoring, management, administration, and support capabilities for all key Oracle systems. Some non-Oracle systems can also be managed with OEM 12*c*. Exadata can best be monitored and managed through OEM 12*c* as it is tightly integrated with all the software and hardware components of Exadata: storage, networking, and database componentry. With OEM 12*c*, you can manage all stages of the Exadata lifecycle from deployment to administration to management to support. OEM 12*c* supports all Exadata Database Machines ranging from V2 to the latest X4 configurations, including Eighth Rack, Quarter Rack, Half Rack, Full Rack, and so on.

This chapter presents a quick overview and gives you a brief look at some of the important concepts that are required for effective management of Exadata and its key components in OEM 12*c*. This chapter illustrates the step-by-step procedures for setup and discovery of Exadata Database Machines and provides how-to examples for monitoring, managing, and administering Exadata and its key components with OEM 12*c*.

For the purpose of this chapter, it is assumed that you already have a preconfigured and fully functional OEM Cloud Control 12*c* environment in place. If you don't have the setup ready yet, proceed with the typical OEM 12*c* installation and configuration process, and ensure that the environment is ready with OEM in order to test all the scenarios discussed in this chapter.

The fundamental architecture for OEM remains the same whether you are monitoring Exadata or non-Exadata environments. Exadata monitoring and management rely on the OEM 12*c* Plugins architecture—specifically, the Exadata Plugin is needed for monitoring, managing, and administering the Exadata components. If you are looking for a quick and easy OEM deployment, get the Oracle Enterprise Manager Setup Automation kit for Exadata (refer to Oracle Support Note ID 1440951.1 for more details). The OMS kits includes all the important components needed for Exadata monitoring and management in OEM 12*c*.

At the time of writing, the latest OEM 12*c* version is 12cR4, or v12.1.0.4, which requires Exadata Plugin version 12.1.0.6 or higher.

Exadata Targets Discovery

In a typical OEM and Exadata environment, the following sequence is followed for the Exadata targets discovery:

1. Deploy OEM 12*c* agents across all Compute Nodes.
2. Discover Exadata Database Machines through OEM 12*c*.
3. Customize and automate notification and monitoring tasks.

When you deploy the OEM 12*c* agents, ensure that you deploy them on each Compute Node. Deploying the agents provides the ability to monitor the targets remotely. No additional software is required on cells, switches, InfiniBand, PDU, KVM, and ILOM for monitoring.

The Exadata Database Machine discovery phase runs through some prerequisites before executing any discovery scripts. SSH user equivalence for cells and IB is set. You need to assign primary and backup agents to each component. Newly added hardware components can be rediscovered. You can discover the database machine through a guided discovery process or by specifying the individual target-monitoring option. As part of the Storage Cell discovery process, it reads storage server IPs and hostnames from the output and finally completes the process by customizing and automating metric collections and notifications.

Exadata Monitoring Architecture

To monitor an Exadata Database Machine and its key components within OEM 12*c* requires a fully configured Enterprise Manager 12*c* setup, and an OEM 12*c* agent and Exadata Plugin must be deployed on each database server. The Oracle Management Agent maintains and is responsible for managing Oracle software targets, such as Clusterware, ASM instances, DB instances, listeners, and so on. The Exadata Plugin provides support to monitor the key components, such as storage, InfiniBand, Cisco switches, and so on.

OEM 12c provides Exadata monitoring capabilities for the following components:

- Database servers
- Storage servers
- InfiniBand switches
- Cisco switches
- Keyboard, video, and mouse (KVM)
- Power distribution units (PDUs)
- Integrated Lights Out Manager (ILOM)
- Exadata patching

Figure 9.1 represents the overall architecture and relationship between OEM, the Exadata, and its components.

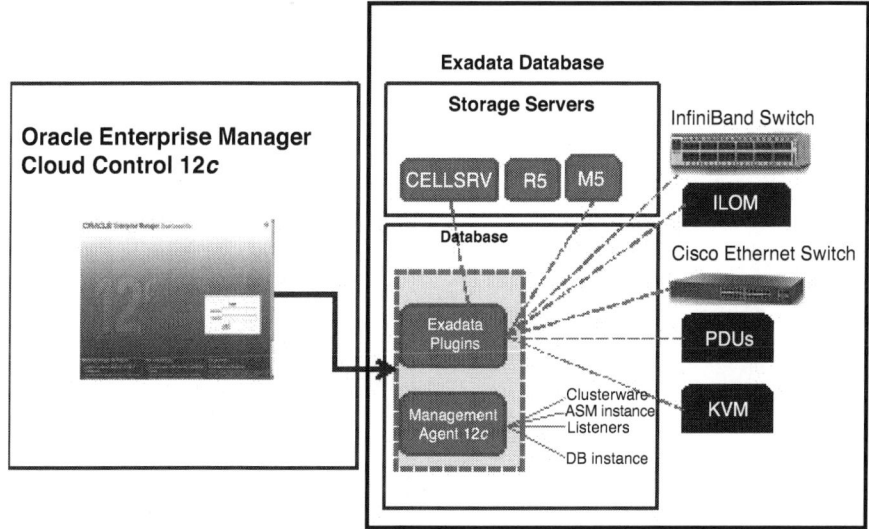

Figure 9.1 OEM and Exadata machine components monitoring architecture

Oracle Exadata Plugins

An Oracle Management Agent is responsible for monitoring and managing RDBMS and ASM instances, cluster resources, listeners, and other resources on the database server, whereas Exadata Plugins are critically important for monitoring and managing Exadata key components, such as storage, InfiniBand, switches, PDU, KVM, and so on.

The Exadata Plugin delivers a consolidated view of the Exadata Database Machine within OEM 12*c*. Each individual plugin connects to its associated monitoring targets using different methods to gather monitoring data. For example, CellCLI connects over SSH, gathers the required information, and so on.

Following are the Exadata component plugins that are typically required to monitor Exadata within OEM 12*c*. These are configured by default when the discovery process is complete:

- **Avocent MergePoint Unity switch**—This plugin provides the ability to monitor KVM targets, and it also provides the current status of the KVM and the event occurrences related to the Factory Defaults Set, Fan Failure, Aggregated Target Device Status, Power Supply Failure, Power Supply Restored, Reboot Started, and Temperature Out of Range on the KVM target.

- **Cisco switch**—With this plugin, the OEM agent runs remote SNMP get calls to gather metric data, which includes port status and switch vitals, for example, CPU, memory, power, and temperature. In addition, performance metrics are collected, for example, ingress and egress throughput rates.

- **ILOM targets**—With this plugin, the OEM agent executes remote `ipmitool` calls to each Compute Node's ILOM target. This execution requires oemuser credentials to run `ipmitool`. The agent collects sensor data as well as configuration data (firmware version and serial number).

- **Oracle ILOM**—This plugin monitors the Oracle ILOM card in a database server for hardware events and records sensor data.

- **InfiniBand switch**—The InfiniBand Switches OEM agent runs remote SSH calls to collect switch metrics, and the InfiniBand switch sends SNMP traps (push) for all alerts. This collection does require SSH equivalence for nm2user. This collection includes various sensor data, including fan, voltage, and temperature as well as port metrics. The plugin does the following:

```
ssh nm2user@<ibswitch> ibnetdiscover
```

It reads the names of components connected to the IBM switch and matches the Compute Node hostnames to the hostnames used to install the agent.

- **PDU and KVM**—Both active and passive PDUs are monitored with the Exadata Power Distribution Unit Plugin. The agent runs SNMP get calls against each PDU. Metric collection includes power, temperature, and fan status. The same steps and metrics are gathered for the KVM.

Prerequisite Checks

For an error-free setup, it is always recommended that you run thorough prerequisite verification to ensure that all the critical requirements for installation are met. In this section, you will learn and understand the procedure to deploy the Exadata Plugins and know the prerequisites to run through prior to the deployment.

Before you get started with the plugins deployment procedure, ensure that you have a dedicated ILOM user ID. You also need to verify software, component versions, firewall configuration, name resolution, and so on.

A dedicated ILOM user ID is extremely critical for communicating with an ILOM server process, hence it is recommended that you create an ILOM user ID and assign the aucro role before you proceed with deployment of the plugin. Following are the instructions for creating an ILOM user ID:

1. Log in as root in the server processor, and go to the /SP/users location.

2. Execute `create oemuser` from the command line to create the user. Enter the desired password upon prompt.

3. When the cursor is back at the command prompt, go to the new user's directory and set the role as demonstrated here:

```
# cd oemuser
# set role= 'aucro'
# set 'role' to 'aucro'
```

4. Verify the user ID with the following example and repeat the preceding steps on all Compute Nodes:

```
# ipmitool -I lan -H <ilom_hostname> -U oemuser -P oempass -L
    USER sel list last 5
```

Manual Deployment

Under certain circumstances, you might need to choose manual Exadata Plugin deployment on each of the Database Nodes. For instance, when there is no agent deployed as part of the automation kit, or the latest version is not pushed through OMS on a new or fresh installation, you will have to deploy the agent manually. You will also need to do manual deployment when upgrading the existing configuration to the latest release. The `emctl listplugins agent` command will help you get the current version of the plugins and indicate on which node they are deployed.

Exadata Database Machine Discovery

This section will take you through the Exadata Database Machine discovery journey and explain the procedure with the help of some important screen shots.

Prerequisite Checks

To avoid falling into various configuration mismatches before discovering the Exadata Database Machine, verify the prerequisites by executing the following exadataDiscoveryPreCheck.pl precheck script across all database servers. You'll need to download the script from Oracle Support Note ID 1473912.1. Then export the $ORACLE_HOME environment on the node and initiate the script on the database server:

```
$ $ORACLE_HOME/perl/bin/perl exadataDiscoveryPreCheck.pl

*************************************************************
* Enterprise Manager Exadata Pre-Discovery checks          *
*************************************************************
Running script from /home/oracle/dba
Script used is ./exadataDiscoveryPreCheck.pl

Obtaining setup information...
----------------------------
 Log file location
 -----------------
Default log location is /tmp/exadataDiscoveryPreCheck_2014-05-23_16-48-11.log

Do you want to use this log file location? [Y/N]
```

The script will run in interactive mode where you will have to input appropriate values to proceed further. The script then starts running all built-in checks and displays the messages.

Launching Exadata Discovery

Once the prerequisites are met, you can start the discovery process. Before launching the discovery process, you will have to deploy the Oracle Management Agent on the Database Node.

Following is the step-by-step procedure for deploying the agent and discovering Exadata Database Machines:

1. In OEM 12c go to Setup, Add Target, Add Targets Manually, and select Add Host Targets, as shown in Figure 9.2. In this example we are doing an Exadata discovery for a Half Rack, so add all four Compute Nodes with the same platform, Linux x86-64, then click Next.

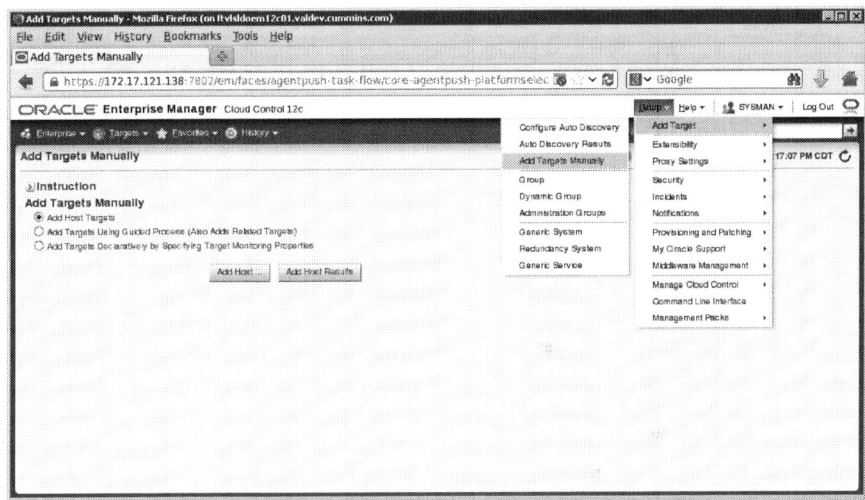

Figure 9.2 Add targets manual process screen

2. Go to OEM 12*c*, Setup, and then add the targets manually, as shown in Figure 9.3.

3. Click Next to deploy the agent, which is shown in Figure 9.4.

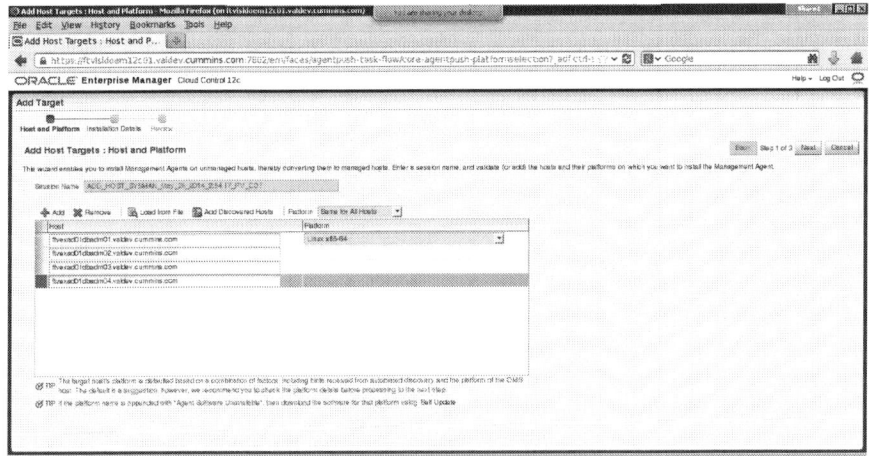

Figure 9.3 Targets list screen

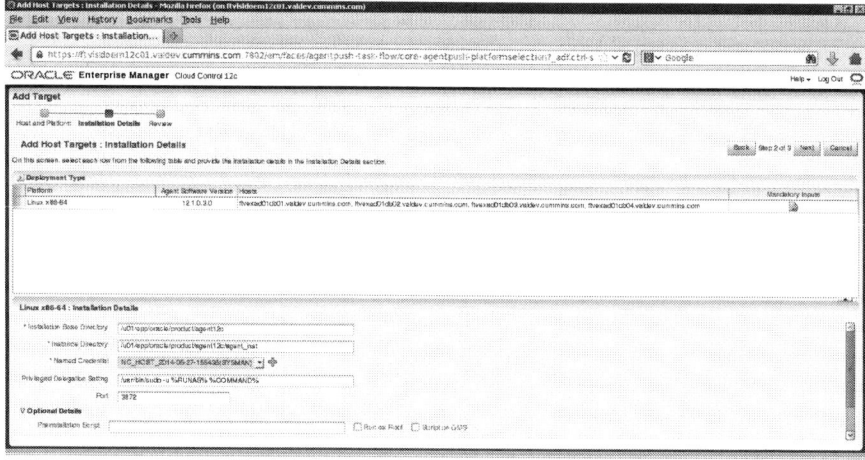

Figure 9.4   Agent deployment screen

Note

You may ignore the message shown in Figure 9.5 when deploying the agents. The requiretty flag is set in the sudoers file on the remote host, and as a result, the user will not be able to run `sudo` over SSH. You can also ignore this warning and continue, in which case the `root.sh` and any pre-installation or post-installation scripts specified with run as root enabled will not be run and you will have to run them manually after installation. Then click Deploy Agent in the upper right.

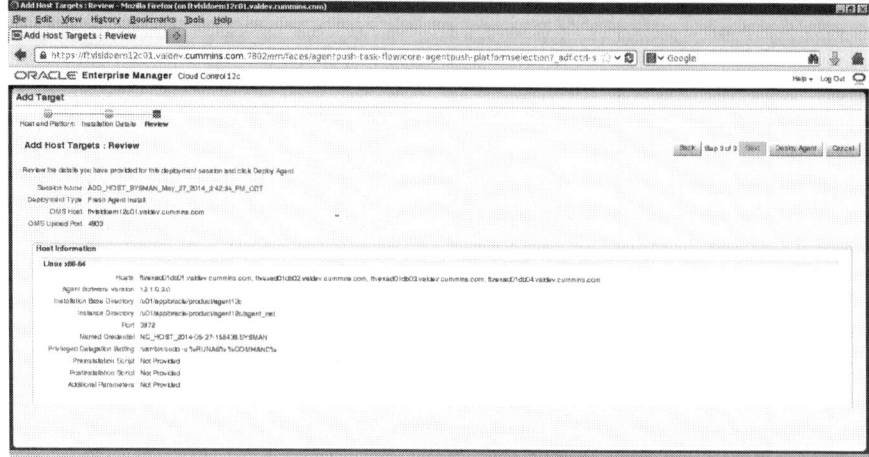

Figure 9.5   Add target review screen

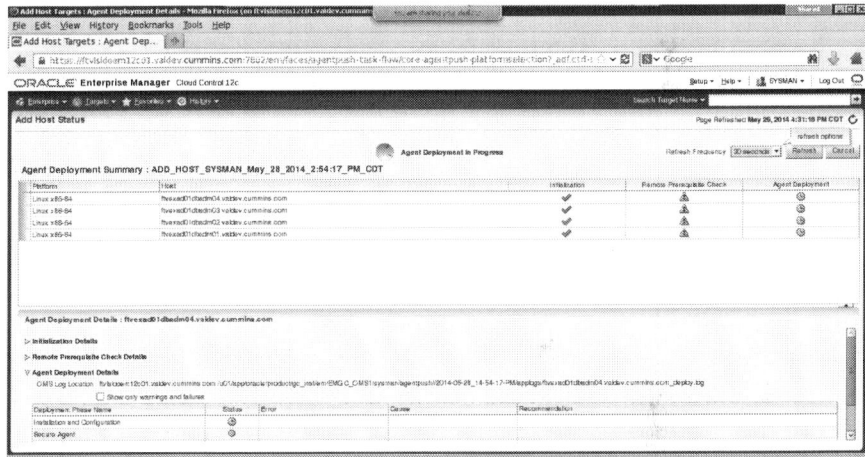

Figure 9.6   Deployment summary screen

You will get a screen like the one shown in Figure 9.6 with the agent deployment in progress.

As the deployment completes, the clock icons become checkmarks, as shown in Figure 9.7.

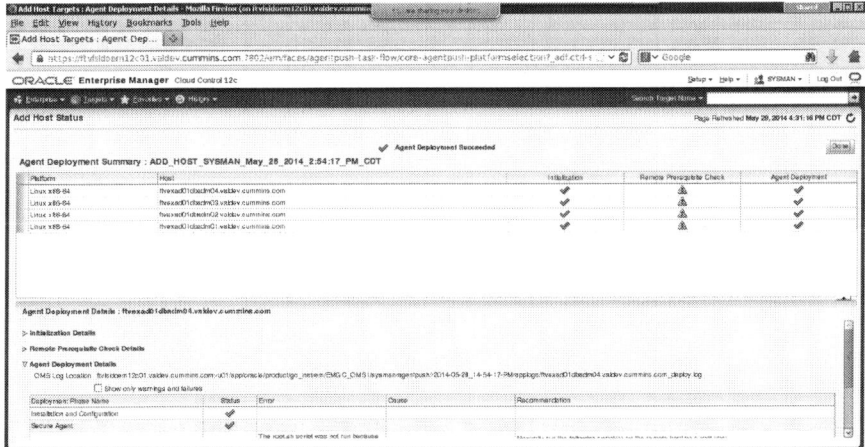

Figure 9.7   Post-deployment screen

4. Run root.sh, shown in Listing 9.1, as root under the agent Home from the
    agent target node (DB Compute Node). Then restart the agent as the Oracle
    account.

Listing 9.1 Root.sh output

```
# ./root.sh
Finished product-specific root actions.
/etc exist

Creating /etc/oragchomelist file...
Finished product-specific root actions.

[oracle@ftvexad01dbadm01 bin]$ ./emctl stop agent
Oracle Enterprise Manager Cloud Control 12c Release 3
Copyright (c) 1996, 2013 Oracle Corporation.  All rights reserved.
Stopping agent ..... stopped.
[oracle@ftvexad01dbadm01 bin]$ ./emctl start agent
Oracle Enterprise Manager Cloud Control 12c Release 3
Copyright (c) 1996, 2013 Oracle Corporation.  All rights reserved.
Starting agent .......... started.
[oracle@ftvexad01dbadm01 bin]$ ./emctl status agent
Oracle Enterprise Manager Cloud Control 12c Release 3
Copyright (c) 1996, 2013 Oracle Corporation.  All rights reserved.
---------------------------------------------------------------
Agent Version     : 12.1.0.3.0
OMS Version       : 12.1.0.3.0
Protocol Version  : 12.1.0.1.0
Agent Home        : /u01/app/oracle/product/agent12c/agent_inst
Agent Binaries    : /u01/app/oracle/product/agent12c/core/12.1.0.3.0
Agent Process ID  : 2350
Parent Process ID : 1891
Agent URL         : https://ftvexad01dbadm01.valdev.cummins.com:3872/emd/main/
Repository URL    : https://ftvlsldoem12c01.valdev.cummins.com:4903/empbs/upload
Started at        : 2014-05-29 18:01:00
Started by user   : oracle
Last Reload       : (none)
Last successful upload                       : 2014-05-29 18:01:05
Last attempted upload                        : 2014-05-29 18:01:05
Total Megabytes of XML files uploaded so far : 0
Number of XML files pending upload           : 1
Size of XML files pending upload(MB)         : 0
Available disk space on upload filesystem    : 86.65%
Collection Status                            : Collections enabled
Heartbeat Status                             : Ok
Last attempted heartbeat to OMS              : 2014-05-29 18:01:04
Last successful heartbeat to OMS             : 2014-05-29 18:01:04
Next scheduled heartbeat to OMS              : 2014-05-29 18:02:04

---------------------------------------------------------------
Agent is Running and Ready
```

Now we need to do a Guided Discovery for the remaining components on Exadata:

1. In the Add Targets Manually page shown in Figure 9.8, select the Add
    Targets Using Guided Process. Choose Oracle Exadata Database Machine
    from the drop-down and click the Add Using Guided Discovery button. Select
    Exadata as the Target Type. Then click Add Using Guided Process.

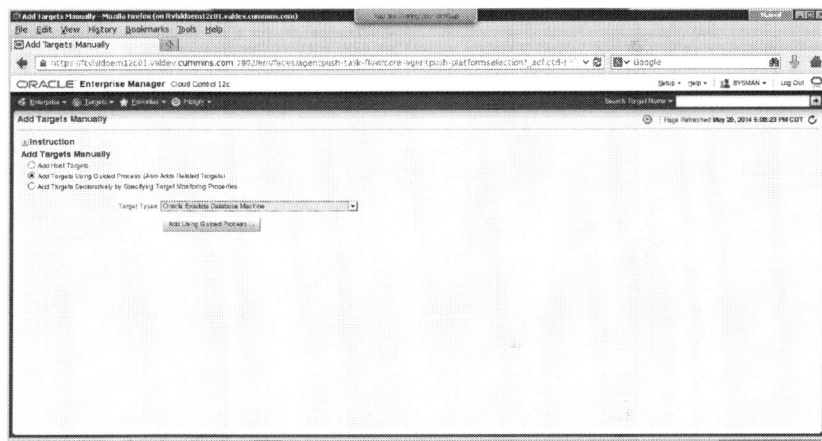

Figure 9.8   Guided process for add targets screen

2. Click on the first choice, Discover a new Database Machine and its hardware components as targets. Then click Discover Targets. Select the option Discover a new Database Machine.

3. Input the Agent URL from Compute Node 1 as well as the Oracle Database Home and below add the hostname for the database Compute Node, click Set Credential, and then click Next, as shown in Figure 9.9.

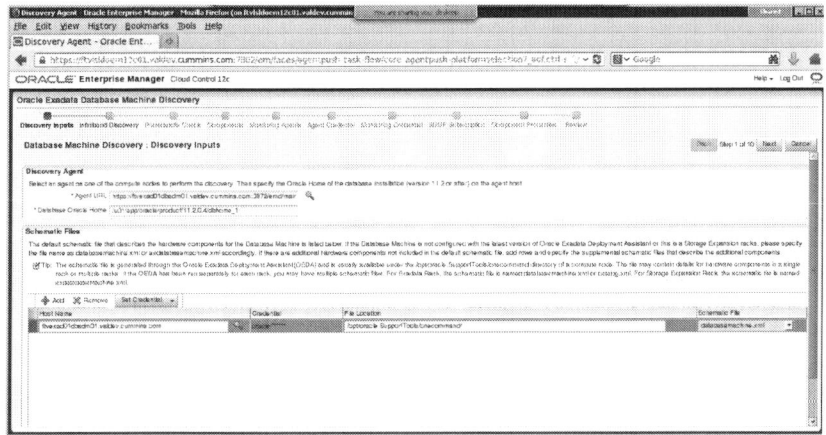

Figure 9.9   Discovery inputs screen

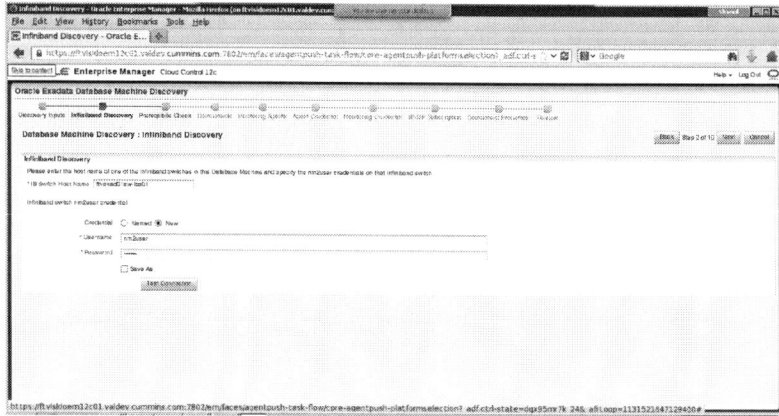

Figure 9.10   InfiniBand discovery screen

4. Enter the InfiniBand switch hostname and the nm2user credential, as shown in Figure 9.10, and then click Next.

5. Review the Prerequisite check and then click Next.

6. Review the Discovery Components and then click Next.

7. Review the Monitoring and Backup Monitoring Agents for each component, and then click Next.

8. Enter the Oracle account credentials, as shown in Figure 9.11, and then click Next.

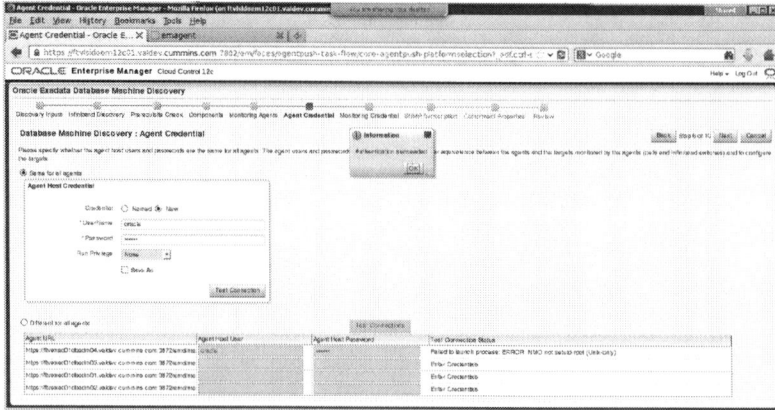

Figure 9.11   Agent credentials screen

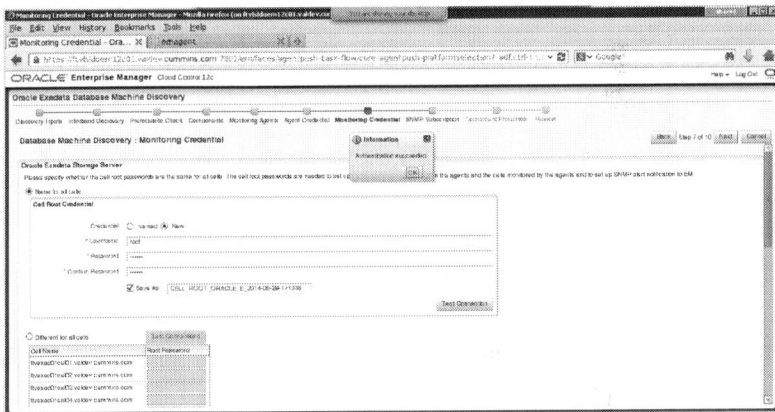

Figure 9.12 Monitoring credential for storage server screen

9. Enter the root password for the Storage Cell Nodes, as shown in Figure 9.12, and then click Next.

10. Enter the credentials as shown in Figure 9.13 and then click Next.

11. Ensure that both Storage and InfiniBand sections are unchecked for SNMP traps, as shown in Figure 9.14, and then click Next.

12. Review all components and then click Next.

13. Do a final review, shown in Figure 9.15, and then click Submit.

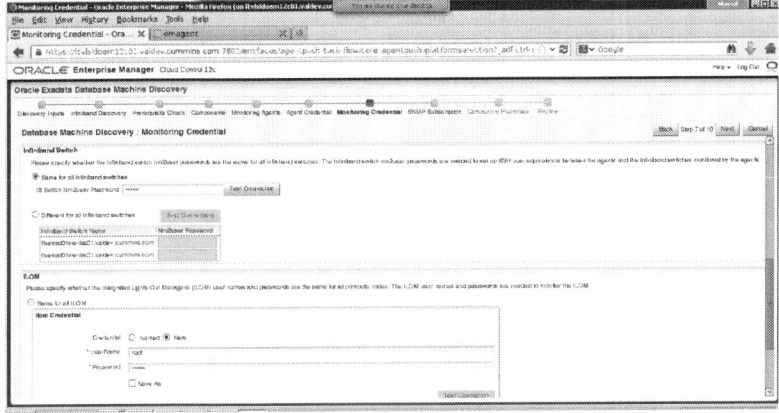

Figure 9.13 Monitoring credential for InfiniBand screen

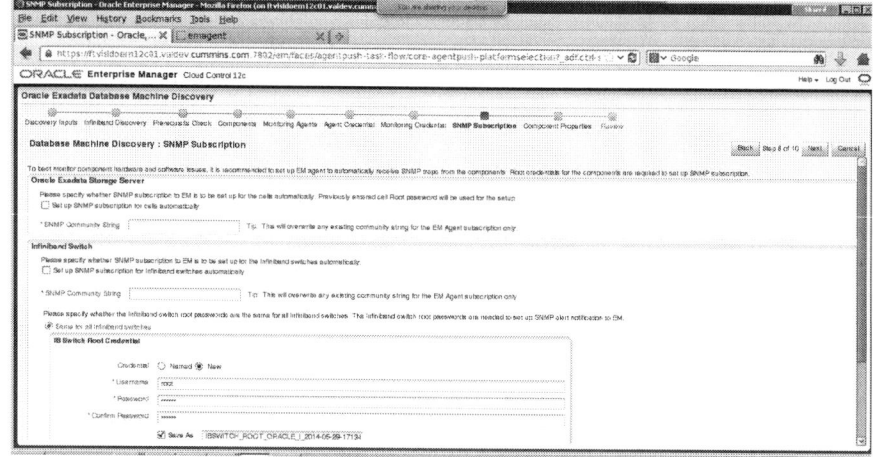

Figure 9.14   SNMP subscription screen

Figure 9.16 shows us that the target promotion completed successfully. The Target Creation Summary continues in Figure 9.17.

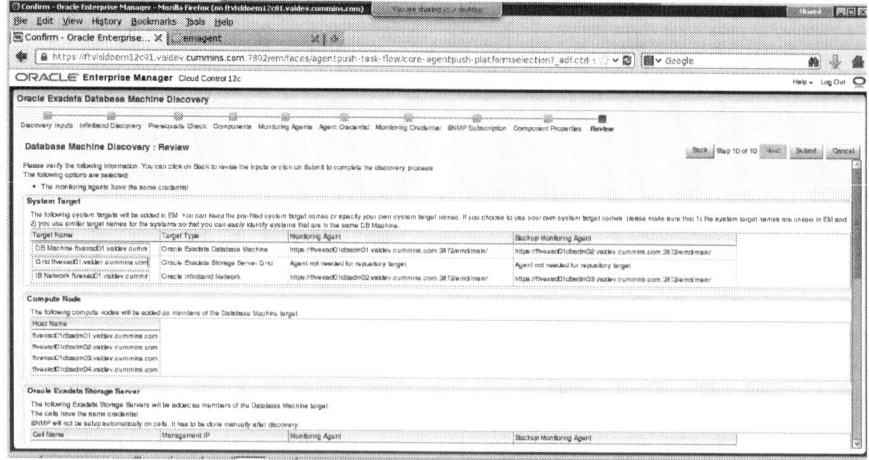

Figure 9.15   Configuration review screen

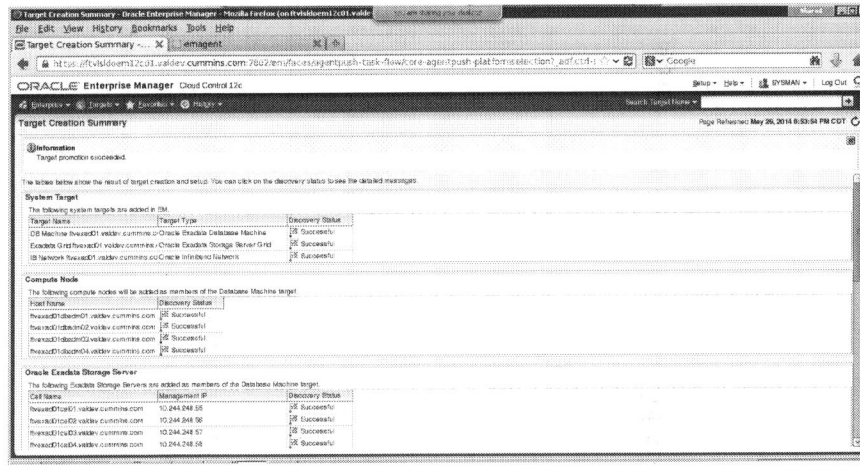

Figure 9.16   Post-discovery screen

At the bottom of the screen there is a DB Machine Home Page, shown in Figure 9.18. This is the final screen of the Exadata discovery process.

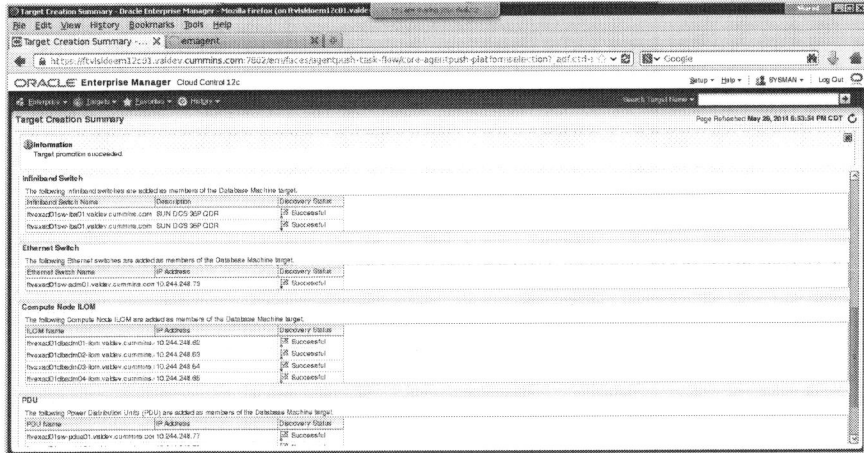

Figure 9.17   Post-discovery screen (*continued*)

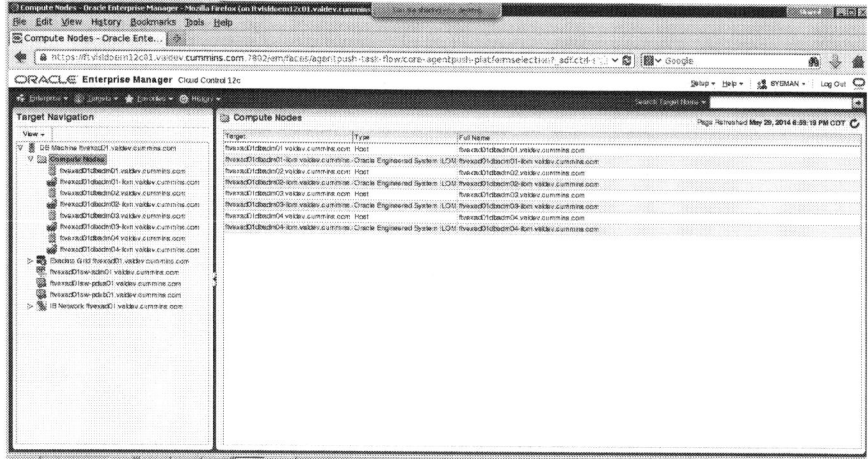

Figure 9.18   Main monitoring screen

Post-Discovery Procedure

On completion of the Exadata Database Machine discovery procedure, run through these important post-discovery tasks:

- Configure SNMP for Storage Cells, Cisco Ethernet switch targets, PDU targets, InfiniBand switch targets, KVM targets, and ILOM.
- Verify the ILOM server and InfiniBand switch targets configuration.

The preceding discovery process discovers the Database Machine in OEM 12*c*; however, to monitor clusters, databases, and other resources, you must run through another discovery process and configure them to be able to monitor through OEM 12*c*.

Exadata Components

Upon successful OEM configuration, database machine discovery, and discovering clusters, RDBMS, and other resources, you need to understand the important components that should be monitored in OEM 12*c* for the Exadata Database Machine.

The following sections provide example how-to procedures for monitoring, managing, and administering Exadata Storage Cells and Compute Nodes (database servers) in OEM 12*c*. Note that only brief examples are covered here, as this is a vast subject.

Monitoring and Management

Once you log in to OEM 12*c* using the required credentials, choose the Exadata option from the Targets drop-down list, which gives you the list of database machines configured under this OEM. Figure 9.19 shows a three Eighth Rack database machine rack configuration; you can also see the status of those machines and their associated components.

Figure 9.20 gives a glimpse of an Eighth Rack database machine in OEM 12*c*. The overview on the top of the image gives details of the database machine components' health status for cell, Compute Nodes, IB switches, PDUs, and Ethernet switches.

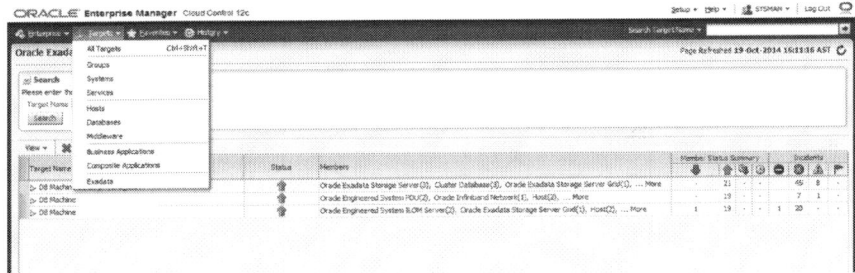

Figure 9.19   Choose target screen

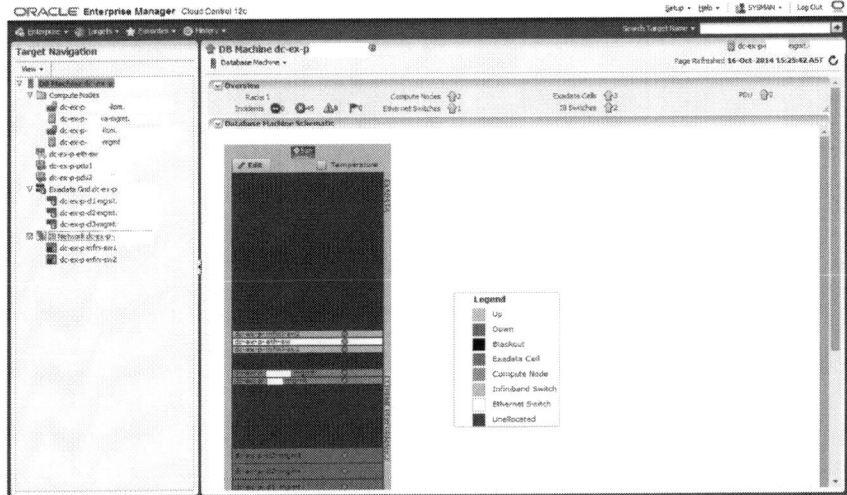

Figure 9.20   DB machine main screen

You can choose the individual target that you want to monitor or administer. For example, to view and manage the Compute Nodes, select the Compute Node options and choose any individual Compute Node. Similarly, you can select individual cells under the Exadata Grid option.

Figure 9.21 presents the overall summary of a Compute Node, where you can view CPU, memory, file system, and network utilization trends on the Compute Node.

Select the Exadata Grid option to look at the complete usage details of the storage server. Figure 9.22 displays cell(s) current health status, total storage capacity details, ASM disk group utilization, workload distribution, and resource consumption statistics.

Administration

To monitor and administer an individual cell, select the desired cell under the Exadata Grid, and from the Exadata Storage Server drop-down on the right, choose the operation option that you need to perform, as shown in Figure 9.23.

From the Administration option, you can manage I/O resources or execute any CellCLI-related operations. This is a very powerful capability in OEM 12c. For example, to execute any CellCLI command, choose the Execute or schedule any Cell Command as shown in Figure 9.24.

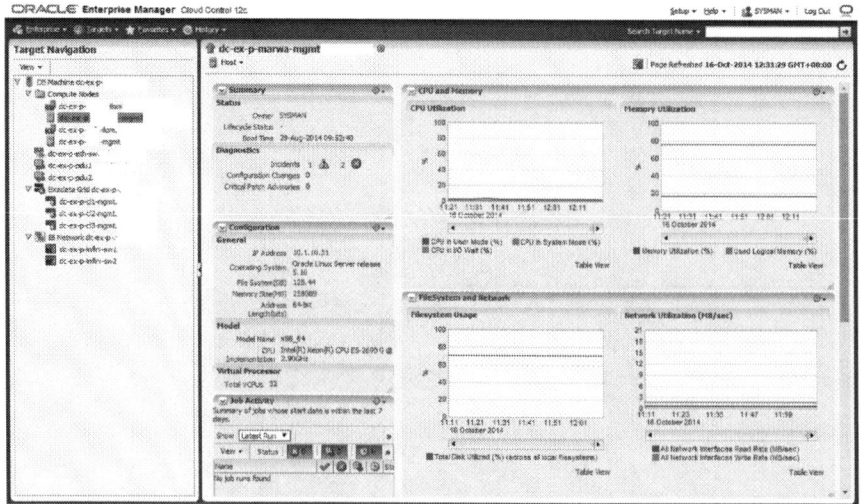

Figure 9.21   Overall summary screen

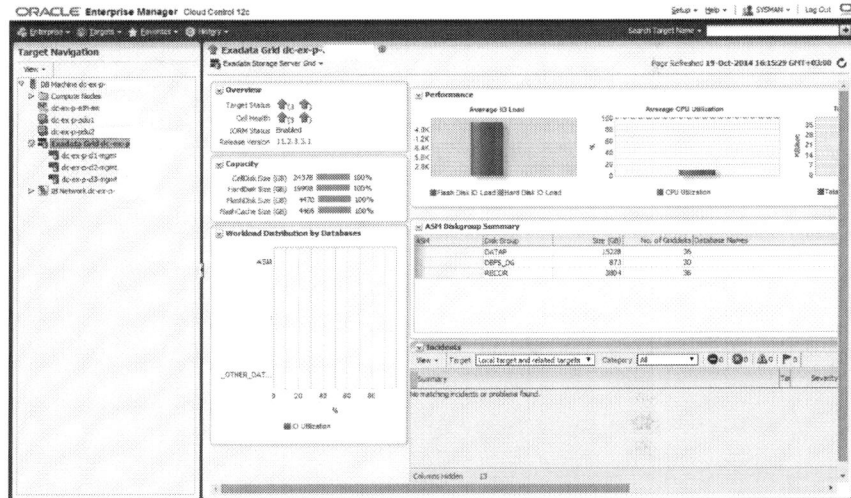

Figure 9.22   Storage server overview screen

In order to monitor or view cell metrics, its collections settings, alert history, and status history, choose the correct option from the available monitoring options.

Metric and collection settings can be managed and thresholds can be set by selecting the Metric and Collection Settings (Figure 9.25). The Other Collected Items tab

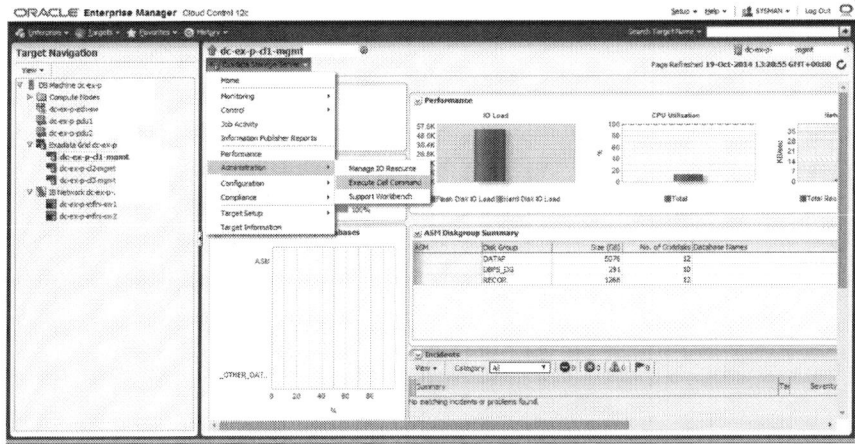

Figure 9.23   Exadata Server admin screen

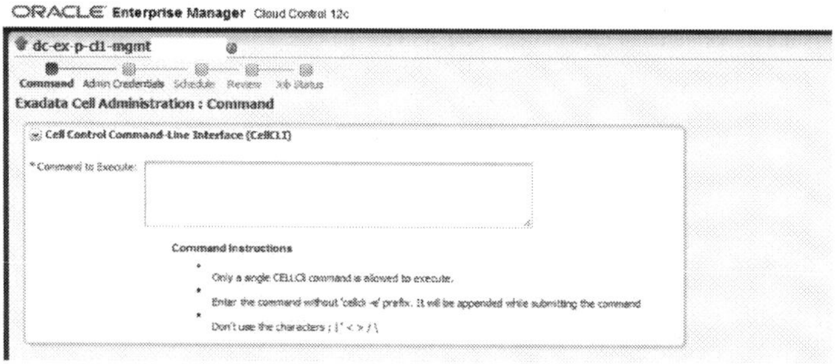

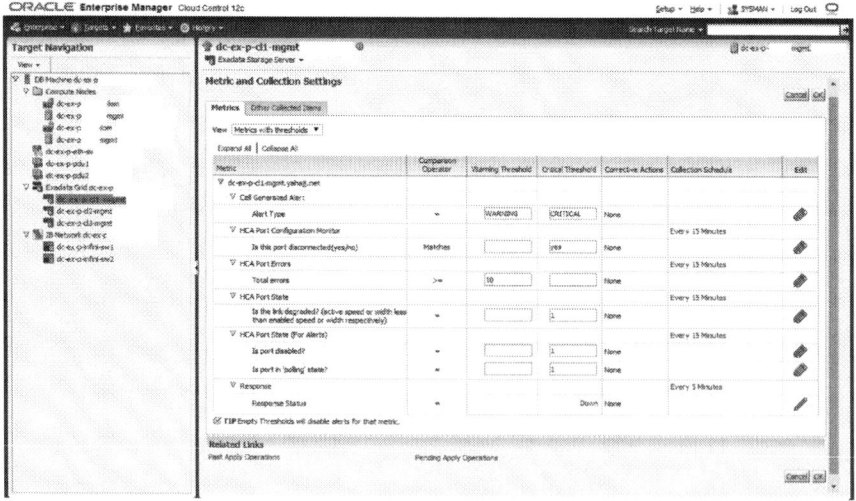

Figure 9.24   Executing a `CellCLI` command through the OEM screen

Figure 9.25   Metric and Collection Settings screen

presents collection schedule details for cell disk, cell Flash disk, InfiniBand host channel adapter (HCA) configuration, capacity metrics, and so on.

To remove a target or add additional groups, as shown in Figure 9.26, choose the Target Setup option from the drop-down list.

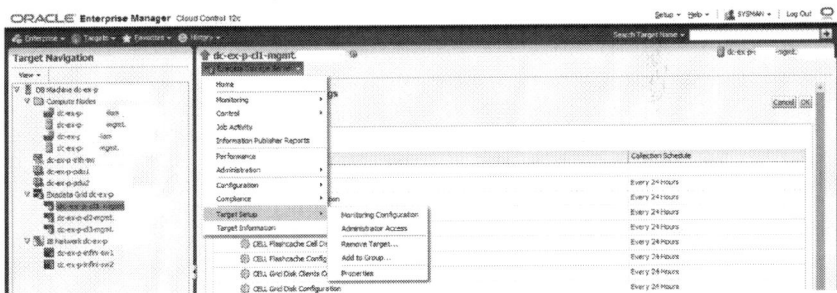

Figure 9.26   Remove/Add target option

Summary

OEM 12*c* is a powerful and comprehensive end-to-end tool that allows you to effectively and efficiently monitor and manage the Exadata Database Machine in an easy and intuitive GUI interface. This chapter gave a quick overview of monitoring, management, and administration of Exadata in OEM 12*c*. Exadata setup and discovery along with plugin componentry were illustrated in detail. Examples for monitoring, management, and administration of Exadata componentry were also presented.

10

Migrating to Exadata

While the Exadata Database Machine does run what looks like a standard Oracle 11gR2 or 12c database, it is more than just a database. The Exadata Database Machine includes proprietary storage, high-performance computing networks, and Oracle Database features proprietary to the hardware. Add to that the fact that Exadata supports only OEL and Solaris, and migrating to Exadata means potentially a cross-platform migration as well as a database upgrade.

That is a lot of moving parts in one single migration, which in turn leads to a lot of possibilities for things not to go as expected. As a result, migrations onto Exadata have a fair share of surprises waiting to surface and catch us off guard.

This chapter helps you plan and prepare for the overall process of successfully deploying Exadata within the organization.

Exadata Implementation Lifecycle

As we all know, Exadata Database Machine is capable of delivering extreme performance with a lot of database-aware features and technologies built into the platform and infrastructure. This extreme performance and database-aware intelligent software do have a cost. Therefore, the implementation of Exadata into an organization requires a more rigorous approach to sizing and evaluation before being brought in house. The traditional phases in the Exadata implementation lifecycle are as follows:

- **Phase I: Architectural Strategy**—This phase represents the task of defining the overall ongoing architectural strategy with respect to running Oracle Database.

- **Phase II: Planning and Design**—During this phase we plan the actual deployment of and migration to the target environment decided upon.

- **Phase III: Migration Testing**—This phase is for testing the implementation to validate that all functional as well as performance requirements are met.

- **Phase IV: Production Migration and Cutover**—This phase covers the migration and cutover of the actual databases from their current environment to the Exadata platform.

- **Phase V: Post-Cutover Support and Administration**—This phase marks the culmination of the migration effort. At this point, the Exadata environment is fully integrated into the day-to-day administration, monitoring, alerting, and incident management process.

The remainder of this chapter focuses primarily on the first three phases. Phase IV and Phase V are really specific to each implementation and are covered in detail elsewhere in the book.

Phase I: Architectural Strategy

Phase I literally starts with the inception of the idea. It begins with identifying, testing, and comparing the potential options available and culminates with the final decision as it relates to the Oracle Database platform strategy.

Projects and initiatives where Exadata is among the short-listed options tend to be strategic in nature, supporting highly critical systems, with demanding performance, availability, and supportability requirements. As a platform, Exadata is being adopted across a wide range, if not all, industry verticals, deployed to handle all workload types (OLTP to DSS to DW systems) and deployed as a platform capable of delivering consolidation. Projects where Exadata is being evaluated or implemented fall into one (or more) of the three following general categories:

- Building a platform to support Oracle infrastructure consolidation projects and plans

- Building a platform for deploying DBaaS

- Deploying a platform designed to meet and/or exceed demanding organizational performance and availability SLAs

The primary milestones and tasks in this effort are:

1. Understand the organizational purpose and needs driving the effort.
2. Identify the available technological options and short-list the finalists.
3. Define the metrics to evaluate and rank these options.
4. Perform the tests on each short-listed option and select the final architecture.

The first key aspect is to be able to identify the organizational and business requirements and success criteria that are driving the process. These factors can be based on the following:

- Organizational goals (cut data center operating costs, for example)
- Business goals (such as managing to expected growth in sales)
- Business needs (such as being able to deliver on customer-facing SLAs as promised)
- Managing to capacity growth (due to mergers and acquisitions)

Obviously, these would be areas that the current system or architecture may fall short of meeting or is not capable of meeting. It is extremely important to tie a dollar value to these requirements, such as lost revenue or additional cost overheads incurred.

These organizational requirements then need to be translated into technical requirements, which will be used further along in the process for evaluation, selection, and implementation of the architecture.

One business goal is to provide a highly available system with minimum or even no downtime. This would then be further translated into technical requirements such as

- A more concrete definition of availability (99.9% or 99.99%)
- A goal of downtime associated with patching and maintenance
- RPO/RTO in case of catastrophic disasters

The business may very well need to meet some SLAs of a contractual nature, such as:

- Staged data will be loaded and processed within a specified and agreed-upon time window.
- Data extracts will be provided on a fixed schedule.
- Reports will be processed and generated within a specific SLA.
- Response times associated with end user experience or small, single atomic transactions are very aggressive, making the systems extremely sensitive to even the smallest deviation in performance.

These business-level SLAs would need to be translated into technical IT infrastructure-level SLAs and requirements, based on volume and anticipated and expected growth. For example:

- I/O capacity and scaling, either IOPS (I/O per second) or throughput (megabytes per second)
- CPU capacity and scaling, in terms of CPU utilization targets

Once we have understood and documented the business needs and converted them into infrastructure targets and goals, we have the foundation to short-list the potential options. What the potential options are can vary depending on the project or purpose but could include

- Purpose-built architectures such as Netezza/Teradata or Greenplum
- Other converged architecture offerings from other vendors
- Storage options such as tiered storage or pure Flash/SSD-based storage in a more traditional architectural setup

The evaluation criteria need to be uniform and easily measurable across all options, so that we can compare apples to apples. Targeted tuning and configuration of the database specific to each option is fine as long as it does not change the test or its nature or the result.

Some of the evaluation criteria that would apply across all the options are not associated with performance per se but rather have more to do with whether the option fits within the organization. The IT structure and strategy are listed here:

- Effort and ease of migration to the target system
- Ability of the solution to scale and grow with the business
- Cost of staffing or training required to build a team that would be able to administer and manage the environment in an efficient way

If the options go beyond using Oracle as the database platform of choice, the criteria would need to include

- Time and effort required to migrate the database from one platform to another
- Time and effort required to migrate the application onto the target platform
- Time and effort required to load the data into the target system
- Cost of building the team to support the potentially new platform

The evaluation criteria need to be based on the ability to perform the same test in a repeatable fashion across all the options. The tests need to be defined and designed so as to quantify and test the various technical requirements and SLAs defined previously, in a repeatable fashion with a baseline to use for comparison. These tests would therefore be the basis of the proof-of-concept (POC) or proof-of-value (POV) testing.

The features that specifically need to be evaluated fall into two categories: the features that are enabled by default and the feature set we specifically would like to implement. As a part of the design and planning phase, we should test for the various combinations of features, as is reasonable and sensible. The purpose is to understand the pros and cons associated with each feature. This testing should include financial aspects as well, such as licensing costs, conversion costs, and outage costs. For example, the tests should be repeated to gauge the benefits of features such as

- Use of HCC (though HCC does not have an additional cost under Exadata)
- Use of Advanced Compression (this is an additionally licensable option)
- Potential elimination of indexing, taking advantage of Exadata options and features, where applicable
- Use of IORM, primarily from a consolidation viewpoint

Furthermore, there may be multiple options and configurations for each option from a physical hardware viewpoint. The final testing should be performed against a hardware configuration that reflects what would be implemented if the option were chosen. In the case of the Exadata, this would basically be limited to

- The size of the rack: Eighth, Quarter, Half, or Full (with either two sockets or eight sockets per server model)
- High Capacity disks versus High Performance disks in the Storage Cells

When performing the final comparison of the various options, each option would be scored against each test criterion, taking into account the final weightage given to the criterion. The POV would be based on evaluating the test results against the more subjective or qualitative criteria and costs associated with the actual live implementation of this technology.

These costs include hardware, licensing, migration, and staffing costs, as well as the potential savings the option would directly influence or improve. As an example, the savings could include eliminating penalties due to missed SLAs or reduction in resource time spent on tasks, and so on.

Sizing the Specific Exadata Solution

Sizing the solution is especially key to a successful migration and implementation, to ensure that we have sufficient capacity, both I/O- and CPU-wise. Sizing and capacity planning would follow the standard methodology as with any traditional platform. Basic data needed from each database or database server would include

- I/O rates
- Memory utilization (used by the SGA as well as by the PGA)
- Storage volume requirements
- CPU utilization

For all of these areas we need to understand the current resource utilization of all the databases targeted for migration to the Exadata. The Exadata environment would need to be sized based on the sum of the resources consumed across all the targeted databases.

I/O Sizing

We can gather information regarding I/O rates and volumes for each individual database from the AWR data maintained within the database, assuming that we have the required Oracle licensing to support our use of that data. Listing 10.1 is an example of that. In the following query:

Total IOPS = Read IOPS + Write IOPS

Total MBPS = Read MBPS + Write MBPS

Listing 10.1 SQL Script to Pull the Actual I/O Activity Number

```
SET LINES 132 PAGES 60
COL stat_name FORMAT a50 HEADING "Event Name"
COL tot_read_io_reqs_per_sec FORMAT 9999999999.999 HEADING "Read IOPS"
COL tot_mb_read_io_reqs_per_sec FORMAT 9999999999.999 \
    HEADING "Multi Block|Read IOPS"
COL tot_write_io_reqs_per_sec FORMAT 9999999999.999 HEADING "Write IOPS"
COL tot_mb_write_io_reqs_per_sec FORMAT 9999999999.999 \
    HEADING "Multi Block|Write IOPS"
COL tot_read_iobytes_per_sec FORMAT 9999999999.999 HEADING "Read MBPS"
COL tot_write_iobytes_per_sec FORMAT 9999999999.999 HEADING "Write MBPS"

WITH base AS(
SELECT
    sn.snap_id,
    TO_CHAR(BEGIN_INTERVAL_TIME,'YYYY-MM-DD HH24:MI') snap_start,
(EXTRACT(DAY FROM (sn.end_interval_time - sn.begin_interval_time))*86400)
+
(EXTRACT(HOUR FROM (sn.end_interval_time -sn.begin_interval_time))*3600)
+
```

```
(EXTRACT(MINUTE FROM (sn.end_interval_time - sn.begin_interval_time))*60)
(EXTRACT(SECOND FROM (sn.end_interval_time - sn.begin_interval_time))*01)
  seconds_in_snap,
sw.stat_name, sw.value Statvalue
FROM    SYS.DBA_HIST_SYSSTAT sw,
        SYS.DBA_HIST_SNAPSHOT sn
WHERE   sw.snap_id=sn.snap_id
AND     sw.dbid=sn.dbid
AND     sw.instance_number = sn.instance_number
AND     begin_interval_time > TRUNC(SYSDATE -5)
AND     stat_name IN (
              'physical read total IO requests',
              'physical read total multi block requests',
              'physical write total IO requests',
              'physical write total multi block requests',
              'physical read total bytes',
              'physical write total bytes'
              )
order by sw.stat_name, BEGIN_INTERVAL_TIME
)
SELECT snap_start,
  ROUND(SUM(DECODE(stat_name,'physical read total IO requests',
                   (curr_value - pre_value),0))
        /seconds_in_snap,3) tot_read_io_reqs_per_sec,
  ROUND(SUM(DECODE(stat_name, 'physical read total multi block requests',
              (curr_value - pre_value),0))
              /seconds_in_snap,3) tot_mb_read_io_reqs_per_sec,
  ROUND(SUM(DECODE(stat_name, 'physical write total IO requests',
              (curr_value - pre_value),0))
              /seconds_in_snap,3) tot_write_io_reqs_per_sec,
  ROUND(SUM(DECODE(stat_name, 'physical write total multi block requests',
              (curr_value - pre_value),0))
              /seconds_in_snap,3) tot_mb_write_io_reqs_per_sec,
  ROUND(SUM(DECODE(stat_name, 'physical read total bytes',
              (curr_value - pre_value),0))
              /seconds_in_snap,3) tot_read_iobytes_per_sec,
  ROUND(SUM(DECODE(stat_name, 'physical write total bytes',
              (curr_value - pre_value),0))
              /seconds_in_snap,3) tot_write_iobytes_per_sec
FROM (
SELECT  snap_start, stat_name, seconds_in_snap,
        Statvalue curr_value,
        LAG(Statvalue,1,0) OVER( PARTITION by stat_name
                                 ORDER BY snap_start,stat_name) pre_value
FROM base
GROUP BY  snap_start, stat_name, statvalue, seconds_in_snap
)
GROUP BY snap_start, seconds_in_snap
ORDER BY snap_start;
```

We would need to account for the sum of the I/O rates and volumes across all the databases targeted for migration. These numbers need to be matched with the physical I/O rates and volume capabilities of Exadata to determine whether we require a Full, Half, Quarter, or Eighth Rack. Exadata-specific features, such as Flash Cache, Flash Log, Smart Scans, Cell Offloading, and Storage Indexes, will reduce the actual physical I/O performed. Predicting the percentage of reduction due to these features is not an exact science; therefore, it is prudent to be conservative when projecting the estimated benefits.

Memory Sizing

When it comes to sizing the servers from a memory perspective, we would follow the standard methodology, which includes accounting for the following items:

- Memory allocated to the SGA
- OS-level Oracle background process accounting for the background processes, active sessions, and inactive sessions
- OS-level memory requirements

When it comes to accommodating future projected growth, there are always two options. The first is to design the solution so that there is room for growth as the business scales. The second option is to design the solution so that it includes the projected business growth over the expected term of the hardware and the overall solution. Most often, the final approach is a hybrid of the two options, including the first few years into the current sizing as well as the ability to grow beyond that as needed.

We can use the same query as in Listing 10.1, modifying it to look at PGA and UGA statistics.

CPU Sizing

You can use the script in Listing 10.1 to look at CPU utilization from a database perspective by looking for the statistic "CPU used by this session," or you can do the same from an OS perspective using the output from sar or similar utilities. The OS-level statistics, in general, would be more appropriate, the one caveat being that in cases where multiple databases are running on a server, we cannot distinguish the CPU usage between databases.

From a CPU perspective, we need to take into account DB Node CPU savings due to Cell Offloading. A good indicator of how much savings to expect would be based upon the CPU utilized under the I/O waits category. If we are using Advanced Compression or HCC, there is some CPU overhead we need to account for. Chapter 5 presented data points to gauge the savings based on the compression type used.

A commonly used approach to translate current system CPU utilization numbers to the equivalent of the CPUs used on the Exadata is to use the rating data from benchmarks conducted and published by the Standard Performance Evaluation Corporation (SPEC). The current benchmark, called SPEC CPU2006, is described on their website (www.spec.org/benchmarks.html):

> Designed to provide performance measurements that can be used to compare compute-intensive workloads on different computer systems, SPEC CPU2006 contains two benchmark suites: CINT2006 for measuring and comparing compute-intensive integer performance, and CFP2006 for measuring and comparing compute-intensive floating point performance.

Storage Volume Sizing

From a storage perspective, we need to plan the capacity for space requirements as well as from a performance requirements and capability perspective. There are two main decision points here: the ASM redundancy level to implement and the type of disk to choose (High Performance versus High Capacity).

When deciding how much usable and raw capacity is needed, we need to account for

- Total space required for each database, including tablespace used for storing non-user data, such as System or Sysaux or Undo or Temp and so on
- Redo log space (both online and standby if applicable), the default for which under Exadata is 4GB
- Space required for archive log destination for each database (in Exadata the archive logs are written to the flashback area, which is on ASM)
- Whether or not we plan on using DBFS for OS-level file systems on the Exadata

ASM Cluster File System (ACFS) is also supported on Exadata, starting with Oracle Grid Infrastructure version 12.1.0.2. Note that ACFS does not support Exadata Cell Offloading, IORM, Flash Cache, Flash Logging, and so on. We **do not** recommend using ACFS for database storage use, rather for ancillary use, such as for GoldenGate trail files which need to be available across all nodes.

In terms of choosing ASM redundancy levels, the choice boils down to the fault tolerance and redundancy we expect and need. Fundamentally, normal redundancy basically supports the loss of one cell at a time, while high redundancy survives the loss of up to two cells. Loss of cells could be either loss of cells entirely (kernel panic causing a reboot, for example), or loss of sufficient spindles within a cell, or could even be caused by applying patches to the cells in a rolling fashion.

In terms of choosing the type of spindles used within the Storage Cells, it is a matter of understanding the trade-off between physical I/O performance expected and the actual usable space. The Exadata Storage Cells, as we have seen, have a total of 1.6TB of Flash Cache, which can be used to cache reads and writes as well if enabled. This should be one of the focal points during the POC testing and evaluation. As a general note, for DW and database consolidation workloads, using High Capacity disks is industry best practice.

The other aspect of this choice is the impact on future growth and expansion. Within an Exadata rack, Oracle does not allow us to mix and match the Storage Cells by disk type. Either all cells have High Performance disks or they all have High Capacity disks. The only option, if we need to mix and match, is to use a storage expansion cabinet and connect that to the Exadata rack.

Built into the Oracle SQL Performance Analyzer there is an additional simulation function called Oracle Exadata Simulation. This functionality can be accessed via OEM as well as from the command line. The overall process and logic are as follows:

1. Create a SQL set with the statement(s) to test (using DBMS_SQLTUNE.CREATE_SQLSET and LOAD_SQLSET).

2. Execute the simulator to estimate against the SQL set created in step 1 to gauge and understand the potential impact the Exadata platform and its architecture could have. We can either use OEM or use the manual process to execute the simulator.

The process followed by the simulator is as follows; these examples are straight out of the tcellsim.sql script:

1. Create a SQL Performance Analyzer tuning task using the SQL_PA.CREATE_ANALYSIS_TASK, and pass it the SQL set created previously:

```
:aname := dbms_sqlpa.create_analysis_task(sqlset_name =>
'&&sts_name',              sqlset_owner => '&&sts_owner');
```

2. Execute the task using DBMS_SQLPA.EXECUTE_ANALYSIS_TASK specifying the EXECUTION_TYPE = 'test execute' and the EXECUTION_PARAMS setting for CELL_SIMULATION_TASK = FALSE:

```
dbms_sqlpa.execute_analysis_task(task_name => :aname,
execution_type => 'test execute',
execution_name => 'cell_simulation_DISABLED',
execution_params => dbms_advisor.arglist('cell_simulation_enabled',
'FALSE'));
```

3. Execute the task using DBMS_SQLPA.EXECUTE_ANALYSIS_TASK specifying the EXECUTION_TYPE = 'test execute' and the EXECUTION_PARAMS setting for CELL_SIMULATION_TASK = TRUE:

```
dbms_sqlpa.execute_analysis_task( task_name => :aname,
execution_type => 'test execute',
execution_name => 'cell_simulation_ENABLED,
execution_params =>dbms_advisor.arglist('cell_simulation_enabled',TRUE));
```

4. Compare the performance across the two executions using the EXECUTION_TYPE= "compare" and metric "io_interconnect_bytes":

```
dbms_sqlpa.execute_analysis_task(:aname, 'compare',
execution_params => dbms_advisor.arglist('comparison_metric',
'io_interconnect_bytes'));
```

5. Generate a report to compare analysis of the two executions using `DBMS_SQLPA.REPORT_ANALYSIS_TASK`:

```
selectdbms_sqlpa.report_analysis_task(:aname,'text', top_sql => 10)
aspa_summary from dual;
```

The report generated uses `io_interconnect_data` as the basis to measure the impact Exadata would have on the performance of the query and reports the potential improvement under Exadata. The point is that using this simulator, we can also get an understanding of the impact of moving a database to Exadata and use this information for sizing and capacity planning.

Phase II: Planning and Design

By the time we have completed the first phase, we know the platform of choice and the feature sets of the platform we would consider implementing and enabling. Phase II marks the transition from the "proof" phase to the actual implementation of the platform.

Given that this book is about Exadata, there is an inherent assumption from this point forth that Exadata is the selected platform of choice. However, the concept is easily expandable to cases where Exadata is not the final choice.

The primary goals for the team during this phase are related to the actual implementation, deployment, and migration to the Exadata platform selected. The team would need to define specifics around

- Finalizing the list of current databases targeted for the migration.
- Designing the overall configuration of and connectivity to the Exadata Database Machine.
- Identifying the Exadata-specific features that will be used and implemented, either at a global level or at an application or database level.
- For any third-party applications, determining the application-specific impact of migrating to Exadata. This would also include ensuring vendor compatibility and support for Exadata.
- Reviewing the various options available to actually migrate the database and select the migration approach best suited to the environment.
- Building the testing and validation plan. The testing would focus on both the database as well as the application. Testing should include functional as well as performance aspects. The goal here is to minimize the risks post-migration.

Custom versus Third-Party Applications

From a purely technical viewpoint, both custom and vended applications should work just fine even if the database is migrated onto Exadata. However, migrating databases associated with third-party vended applications introduces certain additional nuances and subtleties.

All vendors have a basic requirement for support that their applications are run on "certified" hardware or software stacks. Vendor certification implies that the vendor has tested the application under the configuration and will actively support its clients with upgrades, bug fixes, and resolutions. Prior to migrating the application database to Exadata, it is prudent to get confirmation from the vendor regarding Exadata certification to ensure ongoing support. Additionally, Exadata places very specific requirements around database versions supported, which may change when applying bundle patches, for example. While it is not mandatory, Exadata often assumes Oracle RAC. We therefore need to clearly understand the vendor support and certification of the application deployed against an Oracle RAC database.

Vended applications quite often have specific installation requirements beyond the database itself. These could be fairly standard requirements, which do not violate the support agreement, such as supporting NFS shares (using the Oracle dNFS capabilities) or opening custom ports. On the other hand, if the application requires installation of specific software or packages, we might be looking at a potential issue. Remember, the Exadata is a tightly controlled system, at both the hardware and software levels. Applying future patches or updates can potentially break these dependencies or even potentially impact ongoing support by Oracle.

With third-party applications, the ability to modify application code is not available. Once again, this applies whether the database is on Exadata or not. However, it is crucial that we understand the implications, especially when looking to use Exadata-specific features. Examples of tuning that is designed to take advantage of Exadata features and functionality are listed below. These methods are especially useful when it comes to tuning third-party applications.

- Loading data in a specific order so as to favor the use of Storage Indexes
- Using the `CELL_FLASH_CACHE` option to force caching the object on the cell Flash Cache
- Implementing the proper combination of DBRM and IORM to manage I/O by session
- Using the appropriate compression scheme to reduce I/O

The key point here is that porting databases associated with third-party applications introduces some additional nuances and twists. It is important that we understand, quantify, and plan around the potential impacts of these nuances.

Choosing Exadata Features to Implement

During the POC/POV stage we were focused on proving the value of the specific Exadata features in terms of performance gains or storage gains in broad terms. During the planning phase we go one step further to define the rules and use cases, which will govern the actual implementation and deployment of these features.

This phase requires clear and in-depth understanding of which databases are targeted for migration to the Exadata, how the application uses and accesses the data residing in each of these databases, and the performance characteristics, workload characteristics, and interdependencies between each of these. Specific examples of such a focused feature set to include within the evaluation would be:

- In the case of consolidation where multiple databases may reside on the Exadata, we need to define the exact rules and profiles required for IORM.
- We need to understand whether or not CPU caging is required, especially from a consolidation perspective.
- We need to decide how and under what circumstances to use a given type of compression.
- The combination of partitioning and the right type of compression can provide a very cheap and effective way of managing storage utilization for large tables that contain active data as well as historical data. Combined with the Oracle Database12c feature of selective indexing, this can provide significant storage savings.
- In the case of OLTP workloads, we want to use Smart Scans and Storage Indexes in a very controlled and deliberate manner. However, under DW loads, we want to leverage Smart Scans and Storage Indexes in a prominent manner.
- Understand the database I/O to see if features such as Flash Cache Logging or Flash Cache WriteBack may provide performance boosts.

Accounting for the Paradigm Change

With Exadata, we now have a single machine that contains all the components included in the solution. These components used to be seen as separate entities, and in legacy environments they were managed by distinct groups or departments. These components are

- Networking—primarily InfiniBand
- Storage—the Storage Cells
- Servers—both Compute Nodes and Storage Nodes

With Oracle Clustering or Grid Infrastructure combined with the Exadata Database Machine, these components are tied together very closely. The earlier paradigm, where the DBA was responsible for the database, the system administrator managed the servers, the network administrator managed the network, and so on, does not apply. The DBA now needs to understand the interdependencies and the inner workings of these components when it comes to Exadata. That is why, for Exadata specifically, the industry now talks in terms of a database machine administrator (DMA).

An example of the implications discussed here is patching. Most Exadata patching activity is performed as root, DBAs are evolving into DMAs, and therefore it is completely logical to expect the DMAs to have root-level access to the Exadata Database Machine. Introducing a new role with privileged access, however, implies additional work, especially as it relates to security audit and regulatory compliance (HIPPA, PII, SOX, etc.). Therefore, the final solution and/or process must balance both of these aspects, to come up with an optimal, effective, and manageable solution.

There is no one way to solve this dilemma; it all depends upon the security standards, processes, and policies that are in place and how we can bring the two together. In some cases, the security and compliance procedures have been amended to support the DBA having root access, most often using sudo to access specific functionality. In other cases, the system administrators are specifically trained on Exadata, not from the perspective of managing the database, but from the perspective of managing the infrastructure. This is especially the case where security and auditing software is running. The key point here is that this is an important issue that needs to be accounted for and planned for up front.

Determining Migration Strategies

There are many options available for performing the actual migration of the databases onto the Exadata platform. The question really is how one decides which of these methods to use. The following are some of the main elements that help drive the final decision:

- **Architectural characteristics**—The hardware and architectural specifics of the current environment will play a very large role in the overall decision process. There are numerous factors that define the viability and applicability of various migration options to a given environment. These include processor architecture or endianness, OS platforms and versions, database versions and options in use, as well as connectivity between the two environments.

- **Downtime considerations**—How much downtime do we have to migrate a given database? It is important to understand that we cannot totally eliminate downtime, but only reduce or minimize the downtime available for the migration.

- **Data reorganization and restructuring needs**—Often, in order to get the most benefit from Exadata, we might need to restructure the data during the data load process.

- **Cost**—This factor in most cases is tied to the downtime requirements. The additional cost could be due to the cost of software licensing for replication software (GoldenGate) or buying temporary hardware or storage to facilitate the migration.

- **Complexity**—Depending on the downtime needs and other data synchronization and dependency needs, the migration process may take on extra complexity. As an example, GoldenGate extra configuration can add complexity in terms of setup as well as maintenance. The higher the number of databases simultaneously involved in the migration, the more the complexity due to synchronization requirements.

All database migration options can be placed into one of two categories: physical database migration or logical database migration.

A physical migration process is one where the physical database structure is exactly the same, including tablespace names, the number of data files, the user objects' definitions and parameters, and even the object IDs. A logical migration is defined as being consistent in terms of the data stored in the database, irrespective of any similarities or differences in the physical aspects of the database.

Under the options for physical migration, the technical options are

- Use of Oracle Data Guard or standby database technologies
- Use of RMAN backup and restore, including data file conversion

Under the options for logical migration, the technology options available are

- Use of Oracle Data Pump
- Use of custom data movement strategies
- Use of replication tools such as GoldenGate

Physical database migrations tend to be much more straightforward and easier as there are fewer moving parts involved. The Exadata platform is based upon the Intel x86 64-bit hardware; that is, the endianness CPU architecture is little endian. This results in a fair number of limitations.

Physical migration techniques by no means imply that we cannot perform database structure tuning specifically to take advantage of Exadata features. However, what this does imply is that these tuning activities will be performed on the target database on Exadata, either as part of the migration steps or at a later date.

Data Pump–Based Migration

A Data Pump–based approach provides us with a high degree of flexibility, especially if we need to make data structure changes or physical storage changes. Data Pump, with its rich feature set and functionality, allows us to

- Modify the physical storage characteristics to meet Exadata best practices.
- Reorder data as a part of the export action in preparation to take advantage of Exadata Storage Cell features such as Smart Scans, Storage Indexes, and so on.
- Migrate logical sections of the data. This is extremely useful for consolidation of databases.
- Ignore endianness differences. Data Pump is impervious to any changes to the endian characteristics between the source and target architectures.
- Eliminate the requirement for a separate step to upgrade the database.

On the other hand, the major downsides of a Data Pump–based approach are due to the inherently sequential nature of the process:

- In general, the downtime required for migration tends to be significant.
- The larger the dataset size, the longer the downtime, and at certain sizes it almost becomes unviable as an option.
- We will need a significant level of effort and resources, if we were to design and engineer "incremental" data load functionality into the data extraction and load process.

Some recommendations when using Data Pump as the migration process are:

- Use the PARALLEL option within Data Pump to improve overall speed.
- Stage the dump files within ASM's Flash recovery area.
- Alternatively, directly import from the source using the NETWORK option.
- Research the bugs involving your specific DB versions and use the NETWORK option in conjunction with the PARALLEL options.

Using CTAS/IIS to Migrate Data

Conceptually speaking, the advantages and disadvantages of Data Pump options translate to the option of using CTAS/IIS to migrate data almost one to one. The difference, if any, is the degree of the impact, which stems from the fact that we own writing and executing the code to migrate and validate the data on the target site.

Since we can completely own the data movement coding and process, we enhance our flexibility and ability to

- Modify data structures on the fly
- Modify logical organization of data on the fly
- Build more environment- and data-aware intelligence into the process such as parallelization, better control of incremental loads, and so on.

On the other hand, being responsible for the code can also have a negative impact, especially upon the timeline:

- The overall timeline is impacted due to the fact that we need to develop the code, almost from scratch.
- Not only do we have to develop the code, we also have to redo the development process for each database being migrated.
- We need to develop a complete and thorough process to test and validate the data movement.

If you do end up having to choose this option to migrate the data, some recommendations to consider for improving performance are:

- Pull data over DB links, preferably over the IB network, for better throughput and speed.
- If using flat files, use SQL against external tables to access files. This automatically implies the use of an NFS mount storage option or the use of DBFS on Exadata to stage the flat file.
- Use PARALLEL DML feature along with the INSERT APPEND.
- If possible, turn off archive logging to improve speed.

Using Data Replication Tools

Using data replication tools and software, such as Oracle GoldenGate or Quest SharePlex, conceptually gives us all the benefits associated with the Data Pump or CTAS or IIS, while at the same time providing a solution for disadvantages:

- These tools inherently provide the technology and procedure to capture just the changes after the initial data instantiation.
- Downtime is reduced because the incremental data changes are being pushed to Exadata as they occur on the source, thereby eliminating most of the work that would be performed during the outage.

Tools such as GoldenGate or SharePlex include all the automation required to set up, keep current, as well as monitor the replication stream for errors and delays. Not having to develop the code saves us a lot of coding and testing-related validation time.

However, the added flexibility and functionality come at a price. GoldenGate and SharePlex are licensed options that can prove to be expensive when you consider the size of the Exadata environments. Even so, data-replication-based migration strategies have the least downtime among all other options.

Data Guard–Based Migration—Physical and Logical

Data Guard–based migration has an inherent assumption that the platform architecture between the source and target does not change. Starting with 10*g*, Oracle does support physical standby databases across platforms. Data Guard also supports standby databases across very specific platforms. See Oracle Support Note ID 413484.1 for more details about which source and target systems are currently supported.

Using physical standby as the migration strategy implies the following:

- Initial downtime is limited to switchover/activation time.

- The source system is left as is and therefore provides a fast, smooth alternative for rollback if needed.

- Depending upon the version of the source database, a database upgrade might be needed to ensure compatibility with Exadata supported versions. The upgrade is performed post-switchover/activation of the database on Exadata and will impact downtime further.

- All structural changes to take advantage of Exadata features will be performed on the database on Exadata post-switchover/activation and upgrade. This would also add to the total downtime.

From a rollback perspective, it is important to understand that Exadata-specific changes or feature enabling implies that the rollback operation is now much more complicated and beyond simple switchovers and failovers. The challenge lies in bringing data changes performed post-release back onto the source platform.

Alternatively, one can use the Oracle MAA architecture along with the transient logical standbys to get around some of these limitations.

Using Transportable Tablespaces with RMAN Convert

Transportable tablespaces and databases allow us to migrate databases from one server to another by copying the actual data files from one server to another and then just importing the applicable metadata into the target database. The limitation with this approach, however, is that there needs to be a consistent platform between source and target databases. As far as migrations to Exadata are concerned, that assumption is, most often, not the case.

In order to get around these limitations, we can use the RMAN functionality for CONVERT TABLESPACE and CONVERT DATABASE, when the data files are being moved between systems that have the same endian characteristic. However, when moving between systems with different endian characteristics, we need to use the RMAN CONVERT DATAFILE functionality.

The overall approach when using CONVERT TABLESPACE and CONVERT DATAFILE is as follows:

- Place the tablespace(s) in read-only mode.
- Use RMAN to back up the data files as a copy.
- Export the metadata associated with the tablespaces.
- Use RMAN to convert the data file format to match that of the new database. This can be done on the source or on the target.
- Make the converted data file available on the target.
- Use standard Transportable Table Space (TTS) procedures and import the metadata and the tablespaces into the target database.

With CONVERT DATABASE the basic concept remains the same except that instead of doing it one tablespace at a time, we can perform the task at a database level. Again, the actual convert operation can occur on either the source or target platform. As a part of the CONVERT DATABASE execution, a "transport script" is also generated which can be used to import the data files and so on into the target database.

In order for this approach to work with the required efficiency, there are a number of factors to consider:

- The size of the data files and database directly impacts the overall speed for obvious reasons.
- This option requires additional temporary storage, to store the data file copies in the source platform format as well as in the target platform format.
- Using CONVERT DATAFILE on the target (Exadata) is the most scalable, for the following reasons:
  - It allows us access to multiple nodes to parallelize the convert process and takes advantage of the Storage Cell I/O capabilities.
  - It uses the RMAN convert functionality and directly places the converted data files on the ASM disk group.

- Using CONVERT DATABASE does place a minimum version requirement on the source database; it needs to be at least 11.1.0.7. However, if we were to use CONVERT DATAFILE, we do not have an upgrade requirement.

- In terms of finding a landing spot to store the data files for the convert process, the two primary options are to either use an NFS mount to the Compute Nodes or to use DBFS.

Keep in mind that this is still a physical migration, so we would need to account for post-migration tasks to tune the database structures to take advantage of Exadata features to the fullest.

This process does involve significant downtime due to the volume of data that is moving during the outage. We can limit this downtime significantly if we modify the procedure such that we stage the bulk of the data file conversion beforehand and use the actual outage window to apply only incremental changes. This process or methodology is called Transportable Tablespace Downtime Using Cross Platform Incremental Backup and is clearly explained in detail in Oracle Support Note ID 1389592.1. The idea here is that instead of copying and converting data files between the system architectures, we convert the backups. So the process, at a high level, is as follows:

1. **Prepare phase** (source data remains online):
   - Transfer data files to the destination system.
   - Convert data files, if necessary, to the destination system endian format.

2. **Roll forward phase** (source data remains online; repeat this phase as many times as necessary to catch destination data file copies up to the source database):
   - Create an incremental backup on the source system.
   - Transfer the incremental backup to the destination system.
   - Convert the incremental backup to the destination system endian format and apply the backup to the destination data file copies.

3. **Transport phase** (source data is read-only):
   - Make tablespaces in the source database read-only.
   - Repeat the roll forward phase one final time. This step makes the destination data file copies consistent with the source database.
   - Export the metadata of objects in the tablespaces from the source database using Data Pump.
   - Import the metadata of objects in the tablespaces into the destination database using Data Pump.
   - Make tablespaces in the destination database read-write.

Using ASM Disk Add/Remove to Migrate to Exadata

The ASM rebalance technique for migration to Exadata, as the name suggests, uses the built-in ASM rebalance feature to move the data blocks from the legacy storage to the Exadata storage. The overall procedure is as follows:

1. Make the Exadata storage visible to the legacy server.
2. Add the disks from the Exadata Storage Cell to the disk groups and remove the legacy LUNs.
3. Wait for the ASM rebalance operation to complete.
4. Once completed, shut down the database on the legacy servers and restart it on the Exadata server.
5. Add the database to the Oracle Cluster Registry and add listeners, services, and so on.

While this procedure allows for the fastest possible migration process, there are some inherent challenges and restrictions. In a nutshell, this is not necessarily a well-documented step-by-step process; it requires significant expertise with Linux and InfiniBand:

- The inherent assumption is that we are going from Linux to Linux.
- Source database ASM version restrictions also apply.
- The current disk groups need to be set up for normal or high redundancy.
- The existing disk groups should be created with an allocation unit (AU) size of 4MB at least. If not, we would need to move the data from the current disk groups to the newly created disk group.
- The source servers need to be configured with InfiniBand cards and have the RDS/OpenFabrics Enterprise Distribution (OFED) drivers installed and configured appropriately.
- All database structure configurations for Exadata-specific features need to be done post-migration.

Phase III: Migration Testing

This phase is dedicated to testing the various processes and procedures that have been defined during the earlier two phases. A successful Exadata migration and implementation is not just about migrating the database; it is also about the less glamorous tasks of preparing the environment and team for ongoing operation support. There are three primary aspects that need to be planned out, fully tested, and implemented: a database backup and recovery strategy, a monitoring and alerting strategy for the Exadata system as a whole (database + storage + hardware), and the Exadata patching strategy. This will allow us to integrate the Exadata environment into the ongoing operational management and maintenance workflow.

All these aspects are covered in much more detail elsewhere in the book. For that reason, this chapter just looks at these from the narrow viewpoint of Exadata migration alone.

Backup and Recovery Strategy

Prior to go-live, we need to have a comprehensive backup and recovery process and strategy in place. With Exadata, RMAN remains the primary database backup tool of choice. So this really boils down to how to configure RMAN for backups.

Primarily there are three options available:

- Perform RMAN backups to disks, with the disk storage being the Flash recovery area on the ASM disks.
- Perform RMAN backups to an NFS mount point, mounted using Oracle's dNFS.
- Perform RMAN backups to tape, using media management software to facilitate tape communication and management.

Using the space in the ASM disk groups is probably not optimal, primarily because we are allocating premium Exadata storage for backups; we could put the space to much better use. Also, this solution by itself does not take into account taking backups offsite for DR perspectives.

On the other hand, backups to an NFS mount are now becoming more prevalent, especially in conjunction with high-speed NFS-compliant and cost-effective solutions focused on backups and storage such as the EMC Data Domain devices or the Oracle ZFSSA. Connectivity to the Exadata servers over InfiniBand greatly improves performance and throughput as well. The architecture and design also have to take into account the task and responsibility of taking backups offsite. If relying completely upon an NFS-based backup solution, we need to take into account managing backup and aging as well. ZFS replication between two ZFSSAs is the most commonly used method to move backups offsite.

The primary reason to go the Media Management Layer (MML) route is to adapt and deploy the organization-wide standard backup infrastructure. At this point, the backup group has to ensure that the existing infrastructure and architecture will meet, if not exceed, the expectations from the DBA group from a backup and recovery time perspective. Using an MML, the tasks of sending backups offsite, backup aging, and retention tasks can be handed over to the backup MML management group.

Exadata Monitoring and Alerting

Oracle Enterprise Manager 12c is a very robust tool with plugins specific to Exadata that deliver a significant capability of monitoring and alerting on all aspects of Exadata, the hardware as well as the databases themselves.

Another very useful tool to deploy is the Oracle ASR gateway, which allows for early detection of hardware issues on the Exadata. The ASR gateway is connected to the Oracle servers; it tracks hardware issues and reports any failures directly to Oracle Support to be resolved.

In the arsenal of the DMA, there are other tools that prove useful during as well as for the ongoing administration of an Exadata environment (these are covered in Chapter 17 in further detail):

- **Oracle Exachk utility**—This tool is critical and probably the most useful data collection and analysis tool off the shelf.

- **Oracle Trace File Analyzer (TFA) Collector**—This tool is aimed at being a comprehensive approach to collecting, packaging, and analyzing all the log files needed for the failure diagnostics.

Exadata Patching

Post-go-live, one of the most critical and potentially complicated tasks one needs to perform with the Exadata is the ongoing patching of the Exadata Database Machine. There is an entire chapter dedicated to the process of patching, so we will not go into those details here. Instead, we will focus on the Exadata patching aspects one needs to consider and plan for during the journey to migrate databases onto the Exadata.

As we all understand very well, we will be patching Exadata post-migration as a part of the ongoing operational support. The goal during the migration phase, to the extent possible, is to define the fundamental aspects of the process and procedure. This will form the building blocks for the ongoing operation support.

The first step is to put in place the generic workflow of patching consistent with the existing organization policies, standards, and expectations. This includes items such as

- **Patch promotion lifecycle**—Define the order in which the patch is applied and promoted through the various environments before being applied to production.

- **Patch testing and validation**—As the patch is promoted from one environment to the next, define the testing process, incubation time, and other such details.

- **Patch deployment documentation**—Prior to applying a patch, the DBA team would need to research and understand the patch components, the order in which to apply them, as well as the exact steps to perform. These should be documented in a standard operating procedure as the patch is promoted through the lifecycle.

- **Documentation**—As we promote a patch through the various environments, we should document the procedure.

Last but not least, it is our recommendation that prior to cutover and go-live, we apply the latest Quarterly Full Stack Patch Bundle. This is also the best place to validate the procedures and documentation defined previously.

Exadata Migration Best Practices

The first three phases of migration as defined earlier in this chapter, done right, should address and minimize the impact and volume of any last-minute surprises. The migration options available are numerous, and with the knowledge and information gathered during the design phase, we should be able to pick the most suitable option. Following are some additional items that are important to account for or implement during migrations:

- DB character set changes impact the way in which VARCHAR2 columns are actually stored. The testing process should account for validating whether CHAR or BYTE semantics should be implemented in such cases.

- Beware of the myth "Drop all indexes when moving to Exadata." This is not a valid statement.

  At the bare minimum we should always retain the PK indexes and any indexes associated with foreign keys to avoid transaction maintenance locks on child tables associated with ensuring data integrity during DML.

  For other indexes use the index usage monitoring feature or the VISIBLE/INVISIBLE index feature to verify if a given index is a candidate for elimination.

  The driving decision-making factor in such cases is whether the use of Smart Scans is better for overall performance than index range scans.

- Put in the modifications to the database design and structure to get the maximum benefit from the Exadata machine and its features as early in the cycle as possible.

- The better the quality of application and stress testing, the better the results and chances of success. Time spent on testing both functionality and performance is time well spent. Shortcuts to testing have always resulted in much more work and cost after the fact.

    Real Application Testing (RAT) is a very useful way to qualify and quantify the impact of any database change on database performance. It allows us to compare the execution profile of the same workload, before and after making any changes. RAT is an extremely useful utility, especially in Oracle environments that demand consistent high performance.

- Mismatching the type of compression to use with the actual use case can have a serious impact on performance and requires additional downtime to resolve.

- Prior to going live on Exadata, perform at least one run-through of the patching process.

- Prior to going live on Exadata, perform a full suite test of the Exadata-related DR processes and procedures. The test scope should include the application suite functionality being validated in a DR scenario, as well as a full test of the database recovery procedures.

- Use the Exadata simulation functionality available under the SQL Performance Analyzer to identify SQL statements that will improve, understand the extent of improvement one can expect, and, most importantly, understand which SQL statements, if any, will regress in terms of performance. This is especially useful in cases of as-is migration such as with third-party-vendor applications.

- Last but not least, use Exachk on a periodic basis to make sure the Exadata Database Machine is working at its optimal level. Additionally, run Exachk before and after patching activity or hardware-replacement-related activities.

Summary

In this chapter, we covered the methodology and technical choices, and reviewed the options that we should consider, when migrating to Exadata. To reiterate, the most important phase is the planning and design phase. This phase literally represents the foundation upon which the implementation will be built.

That being said, the testing phase is a close second. The extent, quality, and completeness of the testing performed directly impact the amount of time and effort as well as the quality of the result.

There are many possible ways to perform the actual migration, each having its distinct advantages and disadvantages. Therefore, it is key to pick a migration method and option best suited to the organization's needs.

11

Upgrading and Patching Exadata and ZFS Storage Appliance

Exadata, Oracle's flagship engineered platform, is made up of several hardware components that require regular updates and patching. It is crucial to keep your Exadata system current with the latest updates. By keeping your Exadata system up-to-date, not only are you keeping your system current with Oracle's recommended patches, but you also benefit from many resolved issues and bugs, overall stability, and also avoid potential problems.

Oracle Support (https://support.oracle.com) has a master note (ID 888828.1), "Exadata Database Machine and Exadata Storage Server Supported Versions," containing a list of all supported software and patches available for Exadata, starting with version 11.2. The note is kept up-to-date with useful information, directions, and links to the latest recommended patches as they become available. Review the top section, "Latest Releases and Patching News," regularly for the most recent information, and please bookmark this note as well for easy access.

We often negotiate outage windows to perform upgrades on our Exadata Compute and Storage Nodes. As we collaborate with Oracle's Platinum Support engineers, we are dependent on the schedules they mandate. The scheduled dates provided by Oracle are often not negotiable, and we have to become the liaisons between Oracle and the business owners. At times, the schedules offered by Oracle Support engineers are not acceptable to the business owners. As a result, you as the DMA may have to perform the upgrade on the Exadata machine. This chapter is meant to be a reference guide as you plan for and perform the upgrade on the Exadata platform and ZFS Storage Appliance (ZFSSA).

Planning an Exadata and ZFS Upgrade

Why even upgrade or patch your Oracle Exadata Database Machine and Oracle ZFS Storage Appliance? As the saying goes, "If it ain't broke, don't fix it!" Perhaps everything has been running smoothly on your Exadata and ZFS system for several months with no issues—this would be an ideal situation. However, for the vast majority of Exadata and ZFS customers it is critical to keep a schedule for maintaining your Exadata and ZFS current with the latest patches and software from Oracle Support since eventually you may encounter a bug or issue that has been resolved with the updates from Oracle Support.

If you don't patch your Exadata and ZFS on a regular schedule, or at all, you are really missing out on numerous bug fixes and enhancements that would greatly benefit the overall stability and performance of your system. Not only that, if you wait a long time between updates, it will take more time and patches to bring Exadata and ZFS up to the current supported version. Oracle ACS (Advanced Customer Support) also requires customers to be at a current supported bundle patch level; otherwise they may not even consider touching the environment (though this can be negotiated with ACS on a case-by-case basis).

Table 11.1 displays the Certified Platinum Configuration provided by Oracle for Exadata that is required for Oracle ACS to upgrade your environment.

Patching Exadata and ZFS is definitely not something that a DBA should do too frequently; it is a task you would not just jump into. Careful planning and consideration are needed before undertaking a complex endeavor like this. Upgrading your Exadata and ZFS requires a specialized skill set and is normally done by Oracle ACS and consulting companies such as Viscosity North America and a handful of others. Keep in mind that when upgrading your Exadata and ZFS, you are not only upgrading the cell Storage Nodes or Compute Nodes or even the databases to the latest bundle patch level version; it is all of that and much more. With regard to Exadata, you need to evaluate the full scope of what you are going to upgrade. Is it an Eighth Rack, Half Rack, Quarter Rack, or Full Rack?

The larger the Exadata rack system you have, the more time you will need to allow for upgrading since you have more nodes to deal with; a larger rack also introduces more risk. For example, in the small Eighth (Exadata X3) and Quarter Racks (Exadata X2-2, X3-2, X4-2) you have only two Compute Nodes, three Cell Nodes, and two InfiniBand switches to upgrade. In comparison, a Full Rack (Exadata X2-2, X3-2, X4-2) has eight Compute Nodes and 14 Cell Nodes. Fortunately upgrading some of these components can be done in parallel, which should save valuable time. At first you might be overwhelmed since patching the Exadata system requires updating several hardware components such as the Storage Nodes, Compute Nodes, InfiniBand switches, and so on. This chapter goes into great detail about how you can update the software on the entire Exadata stack and not just the

Table 11.1 Certified Platinum Configuration for Exadata, Current as of October 2014

Hardware (Required)	Operating System (Required/Optional as Noted)	Oracle Database (Required)	Programs (Required/ Optional as Noted)
X2-2 or X2-8 (Exadata Storage)	Oracle Linux 5.5–5.10 (required) or Oracle Solaris 11 option for X2-2 only (required)	11.2.0.3 July 2014 or later or 11.2.0.4 July 2014 or later Quarterly Full Stack Download or 12.1.0.2	Exadata Storage Server 11.2.3.3.1 or later if used in conjunction with Oracle Database 11.2.0.3 or 11.2.0.4 (required) or 12.1.1.1.0 or later (recommended for Oracle Database 11.2.0.3 or 11.2.0.4, required for 12c)
X3-2 or X3-8 with X3-2 Storage (Exadata Storage)	Oracle Linux 5.8–5.10 (required) or Solaris 11 option for X3-2 only (required)	11.2.0.3 July 2014 or later or 11.2.0.4 July 2014 or later Quarterly Full Stack Download or 12.1.0.2	Exadata Storage Server 11.2.3.3.1 or later (required) or 12.1.1.1.0 or later (recommended for Oracle Database 11.2.0.3 or 11.2.0.4 and required for 12c)
X4-2 (Exadata Storage)	Oracle Linux 5.9 or 5.10 (required) or Solaris 11 (required)	11.2.0.3 July 2014 or later or 11.2.0.4 July 2014 or later Quarterly Full Stack Download or 12.1.0.2	Exadata Storage Server 11.2.3.3.0 or later (required) or 12.1.1.1.0 or later

core components. It also explains what components are mandatory to upgrade and which are optional.

If you have downtime in a non-production Exadata or ZFS system that is at the same software level as your production environment, document and test your entire upgrade plan and note the timings before planning the production upgrade. Please add some buffer time when requesting downtime for the production upgrade. The extra time will benefit you in case you run into issues during the upgrade process. Suppose your environments vary, for example, an Exadata Eighth or Quarter Rack in non-production and a Half Rack or Full Rack in production; the different sizing will dictate the upgrade timing. You may also decide to go the rolling upgrade route with no downtime, which is also an option to consider. Once again, as a best practice please execute your upgrade in a non-production Exadata or ZFS system as just stated.

Also consider upgrading every single component in the entire Exadata stack to have the most current supported software from Oracle Support. As far as patch set levels go, you should apply the latest patch bundle to your non-production environment and test your Exadata or ZFS stack against your application(s) to ensure that there are no issues that would prevent you from doing the upgrade. Once you have certified the latest bundle patch set in your non-production environment, you may proceed with planning and implementing the same patch set in production.

Also, create an Oracle Service Request (SR) just prior to your upgrade window; this will notify Oracle Support in advance just in case you need to reach out to them for support for any issues you may encounter during the upgrade process.

Patch Release Cycle

As stated earlier, review the following Oracle Support Note as it is updated frequently and lists the latest supported patch bundle versions for Exadata: "Exadata Database Machine and Exadata Storage Server Supported Versions" (ID 888828.1). Oracle Support has also noted that the patch release frequency is subject to change at any time without notice. Table 11.2 from Oracle Support depicts the patch release frequency for Exadata.

Note

This book covers the Oracle ZFS 7000 series and you are encouraged to regularly check the following Oracle Support Note for the latest ZFS patch information: "Sun Storage 7000 Unified Storage System: How to Upgrade the Appliance Kit Software and Service Processor BIOS/ILOM Firmware" (ID 1513423.1), which in turn references the following URL: https://wikis.oracle.com/display/FishWorks/Software+Updates. See Table 11.3.

Table 11.2   Patch Release Frequency for Exadata

Software	Patch Release Frequency
Quarterly Full Stack Download	Quarterly
Exadata Storage Server	Quarterly to semiannually
Database Server	Grid Infrastructure/RDBMS Bundle Patches 12.1.0.2—Quarterly (1)
	12.1.0.1—Quarterly (1)
	11.2.0.4—Monthly
	11.2.0.3—Quarterly (2)
	11.2.0.2—No further bundle patches (3)—Error Correction Support ended October 31, 2013
	11.2.0.1—No further bundle patches (4)—Error Correction Support ended April 30, 2012
InfiniBand switch	Semiannually to annually

Table 11.3 Latest Patch Releases for ZFS Appliance

Product	Minimum Version	Recommended Minimum Version	Latest Version
ZS4-4	2013.1.3.0	2013.1.3.0	2013.1.3.0
ZS3-4, ZS3-2	2013.1.2.13*	2013.1.2.13	2013.1.3.0
7420, 7320, 7120	2013.1.2.13*	2013.1.2.13	2013.1.3.0
7410, 7310, 7210, 7110	2011.1.9.2*	2011.1.9.2	2011.1.9.2

* 7420, 7320, and 7120 systems support both 2011.1 and 2013.1 releases. For these systems, the minimum software version from which you can update to 2013.1.3.0 is 2011.1.4.2.

Quarterly Full Stack Download

The Exadata Quarterly Full Stack Download Patch (QFSDP) mentioned in Table 11.2 is the recommended way to upgrade all Exadata components; there is no need to download all patch files separately for each component. Oracle has simplified the process for their customers by introducing the QFSDP as a convenience to download the full set of the most current updates; it will be released on a quarterly schedule along with the Patch Set Updates (PSUs).

QFSDP releases contain the latest software for the following components:

- **Infrastructure**
  - Exadata Storage Server
  - InfiniBand switch
  - Power Distribution Unit
- **Database**
  - Oracle Database and Grid Infrastructure PSU
  - Oracle JavaVM PSU (as of October 2014)
  - OPatch, OPlan
- **Systems Management**
  - EM Agent/OMS/Plugins

Patching Tools and Processes

Across the full suite of Oracle products there have been many tools over the years for applying patches and upgrading software and firmware. In the Exadata stack upgrade, the tools described in the following sections are used to apply patches to various components.

OPatch

OPatch is a Java-based utility mainly used to patch the Oracle Home binary software. Most DBAs are very familiar with this common tool if they ever have had to patch the Oracle Home software. OPatch has many sub-programs that can take many arguments. It is platform specific, and the latest OPatch utility can be downloaded via patch number 6880880 from My Oracle Support. OPatch can be unzipped in the Oracle Home, which will create this directory:

```
$ORACLE_HOME/OPatch.
```

Execute the following command from the appropriate Oracle Home to verify the OPatch version:

```
$ORACLE_HOME/OPatch/opatch version
OPatch Version: 12.1.0.1.2

OPatch succeeded.
```

In the Exadata upgrade process the OPatch tool is not used any differently than it is in a non-Exadata environment. OPatch is used to apply the necessary patches to the Grid and Database Homes. The main utilities of OPatch include applying, rolling back, and conflict-checking the subject patch. You can also issue a report of the installed components and patches.

The most common OPatch command options are

- $ 'opatch apply ...'—applies the patch to the Oracle Home
- $ 'opatch rollback ...'—rolls back the patch from the Oracle Home
- $ 'opatch lsinventory'—shows inventory on an Oracle Home
- $ 'opatch version'—shows the version of the OPatch being used
- $ 'opatch prereq ...'—invokes some prerequisite checks

Invoking OPatch without arguments or with the –help sub-command returns a list of valid sub-commands to the user:

```
Usage: opatch [ -help ] [ -r[eport] ] [ command ]
opatch -help apply
opatch -help lsinventory
opatch -help nappl
opatch -help nrollback
opatch -help rollback
opatch -help query
opatch -help version
opatch -help prereq
opatch -help util
```

Optionally, you can set the environment variable OPATCH_DEBUG=TRUE before applying a patch. This is the maximum logging level supported by OPatch. You can then analyze the log files generated in respective locations to review the specific OPatch operation performed.

patchmgr

The patchmgr tool is used to update the Exadata Storage software on the Cell Nodes and also to update the software on the InfiniBand switches.

Later in this chapter, you will learn how to patch the Exadata Cell Nodes and the InfiniBand switches.

Before using patchmgr, you should know that the Cell Nodes will reboot during the patch or rollback process. Also, you should not do the following with patchmgr running:

- Start more than one instance of patchmgr
- Interrupt the patchmgr session
- Alter the state of the ASM instances during patch or rollback
- Resize the screen as it may disturb the screen layout
- Reboot cells or alter cell services during patch or rollback
- Open log files in the editor in write mode or try to alter them

> **Note**
>
> Prepare a file named cell_group that has one cell hostname or IP address per line for each cell to be patched.

Following is the usage for this tool for cell patching and/or rollback. The patchmgr command with the -h (help) option displays the man page equivalent for the patchmgr command:

```
./patchmgr -cells cell_group
        [-patch_check_prereq | -rollback_check_prereq [-rolling] [-ignore_alerts]]
        [-patch | -rollback [-rolling] [-ignore_alerts]]
        [-cleanup]
```

The cell patching will fail if the list file referenced by the -cells parameter is not specified.

The -cleanup parameter cleans up all patch files and temporary content on all cells. Before cleaning up, it collects logs and information for problem diagnostics and analysis. Cleaning up patch files can be done manually if the patch fails by removing the /root/_patch_hctap_ directory on each cell.

The -ignore_alerts parameter ignores any active hardware alerts on the Exadata cell and proceeds with the patching.

The -patch option applies the patch, including firmware updates, wherever possible (BIOS, disk controller, and if possible disk drives) to all cells in the cell list file.

The -patch_check_prereq parameter checks on all the cells to determine if the patch can be applied to the cells. Obviously, the -rollback option rolls back the patch. The -rollback_check_prereq parameter executes the prerequisite check on all the cells to determine if the cells can be rolled back for the specified patch. The -rolling option applies the patch or executes the rollback in rolling fashion, one cell at a time, based on the EXA_PATCH_ACTIVATE_TIMEOUT_SECONDS (default 36,000 seconds) environment variable which defines the timeout value waiting for the grid disks to be activated.

The following options are supported for InfiniBand switch upgrade and/or downgrade:

```
./patchmgr -ibswitches [ibswitch_list_file]
        <-upgrade | -downgrade> [-ibswitch_precheck] [-force]]
```

The -ibswitches [ibswitch_list_file] parameter specifies the name of the IB switch list file. This file contains one switch hostname or IP per line. If the [ibswitch_list_file] file name is not provided, patchmgr executes the command on all IB switches identified by running the -ibswitches command.

The -upgrade option upgrades the IB switch in the list file. The -downgrade option downgrades the IB switches listed in the list file. The -force parameter continues the upgrade or downgrade even after encountering noncritical failures. Last, the -ibswitch_precheck parameter executes the pre-update validation checks on the IB switch(es).

OPlan

OPlan is a tool that simplifies the patch installation process by providing step-by-step patching instructions specific to your environment. OPlan eliminates the need to identify the patching commands required by automatically collecting the configuration information for the target Oracle Home and then generating instructions specific to the Oracle Home to patch it.

The instructions cover both patch application and rollback steps. The OPlan utility can be downloaded from Oracle Support via patch 11846294; the available product and patch support is shown in Table 11.4. Issue the following command to create the instructions to apply the patch:

```
$ORACLE_HOME/oplan/oplan generateApplySteps <bundle patch location>
```

Table 11.4   Product and Patch Support Available from OPlan

Product Family	Product	Patch Type	Release	Platform
Oracle Database	Oracle Exadata Database Machine*	Recommended bundle patches*	11.2.0.2	Linux x86-64, Solaris x86-64
	Oracle GI/RAC running on normal clusters	GI PSU and DB PSU	11.2.0.2	Linux x86-64, Solaris x86-64, Solaris SPARC (64-bit)
Oracle Database	Oracle Exadata Database Machine*	Recommended bundle patches	11.2.0.3*	Linux x86-64, Solaris x86-64, Solaris SPARC (64-bit)
	Oracle GI/RAC running on normal clusters	GI PSU and DB PSU	11.2.0.3	Linux x86-64, Solaris x86-64, Solaris SPARC (64-bit)
Oracle Database	Oracle Exadata Database Machine	Recommended bundle patches	12.1.0.1/12.1.0.2	Linux x86-64, Solaris x86-64, Solaris SPARC (64-bit)
	Oracle GI/RAC running on normal clusters	GI PSU and DB PSU	12.1.0.1/12.1.0.2	Linux x86-64, Solaris x86-64, Solaris SPARC (64-bit)

*   Support available for recommended bundle patches (Bundle Patch 2 and onward)

The patch installation instructions specific to your target are available as HTML and text format in these locations:

```
$ORACLE_HOME/cfgtoollogs/oplan/<TimeStamp>/InstallInstructions.html
$ORACLE_HOME/cfgtoollogs/oplan/<TimeStamp>/InstallInstructions.txt
```

Here's an example of the steps generated from the `generateApplySteps` command listed above:

```
Stop the resources running from Database Home
On hostname stop the resources running out of the oracle home Database Home
As a oracle user on the host hostname run the following commands:
[oracle@hostname]
$ rm -f /tmp/OracleHome-hostname_OraDb11g_home1.stat
[oracle@hostname] $ ORACLE_HOME=/u01/app/oracle/product/11.2.0/dbhome_1
/u01/app/oracle/product/11.2.0/dbhome_1/bin/srvctl stop home -o
/u01/app/oracle/product/11.2.0/dbhome_1 -n hostname -s
/tmp/OracleHome-hostname_OraDb11g_home1.stat

Apply Patch to Database Home
On hostname Apply the patch to oracle home Database Home
```

```
As an oracle user on the host hostname run the following commands:
[oracle@hostname]$
/u01/app/oracle/product/11.2.0/dbhome_1/OPatch/opatch napply -local
 /tmp/OPlan-patches/crs_automation/bp3/10387939 -invPtrLoc
 /u01/app/oracle/product/11.2.0/dbhome_1/oraInst.loc -oh
 /u01/app/oracle/product/11.2.0/dbhome_1
[oracle@hostname]$
/u01/app/oracle/product/11.2.0/dbhome_1/OPatch/opatch napply -local
/tmp/oplan-patches/crs_automation/bp3/10157622/custom/server/10157622
-invPtrLoc /u01/app/oracle/product/11.2.0/dbhome_1/oraInst.loc -oh
/u01/app/oracle/product/11.2.0/dbhome_1
```

In case of errors running OPlan to produce the patching commands, the detailed logs are available under the $ORACLE_HOME/cfgtoollog/Oplan directory.

OPlan has some basic restrictions. First, shared Oracle Home configurations are not supported. Also, Data Guard configurations are not supported. OPlan can be used to create patch plans for Oracle Homes running Oracle Data Guard configurations, but OPlan does not consider such an environment usable as a Data Guard Standby-First Patch Apply alternative.

Oracle Data Guard Standby-First Patch Apply is supported only for *certified* interim patches and patch bundles (e.g., Patch Set Update, or Database Patch for Exadata) for Oracle Database 11.2.0.1 and later, on both Oracle engineered systems (e.g., Exadata, SuperCluster) and non-engineered systems. A patch and patch bundle that is Data Guard Standby-First certified will state so in the patch README.

The following types of patches are candidates to be Data Guard Standby-First certified:

- Database Home interim patches
- Exadata bundle patches (e.g., monthly and quarterly database patches for Exadata)
- Database patch set updates

Oracle patch sets and major release upgrades do not qualify for Data Guard Standby-First Patch Apply. For example, upgrades from 11.2.0.2 to 11.2.0.3 or 11.2 to 12.1 do not qualify.

Oracle Patch Types

An Oracle patch set is released infrequently and contains fixes for most known issues for the release and may potentially also introduce some new features. A patch set is cumulative, and when installed it changes the fourth digit of the product release banner—for example, 10.2.0.5 is the fourth patch set for 10.2, and 11.2.0.4 is the most recent patch set for 11.2. The Oracle patch set must be installed via the Oracle Universal Installer (OUI) in either GUI or silent mode and is usually considered an upgrade. At the time of this writing, 11.2.0.4 is the latest release for 11gR2 and 12.1.0.2 is the latest release for 12c Release 1.

Starting with 11gR2, Oracle patch set releases are now full releases and no longer require a base release to be in place first; for example, 11.2.0.2 can be installed directly without having to install 11.2.0.1 first. The patch sets for Grid Infrastructure and RDBMS are also delivered separately since they are full releases.

Prior to Oracle Database 11gR2, even though the Grid and RDBMS base releases were provided on separate media as downloadable .zip files, the patch sets for both products were delivered as one; that is, they were the same patch set and could be applied to the Clusterware as well as the RDBMS Database Home.

Patch Set Updates

An Oracle Patch Set Update (PSU) is applied on top of a certain patch set release. These patches are released on a quarterly schedule (January, April, July, October) and contain fixes for known critical issues for the patch set. PSUs do not include changes that would alter the behavior of the software such as database optimizer plan changes. Oracle Support highly recommends that customers keep their software up-to-date to be proactive and to avoid potential issues by applying the latest PSU.

All PSUs are installed using the OPatch tool, and they are not considered an upgrade. Independent PSUs are released for both the Database and Clusterware or Grid Infrastructure installations. Clusterware PSUs (pre-11.2) are referred to as CRS PSUs. Grid Infrastructure PSUs are referred to as GI PSUs. Both Clusterware and Grid Infrastructure and Database PSU patches are cumulative. Clusterware PSU refers to CRS PSU for pre-11gR2 and GI PSU for 11gR2.

PSUs are usually cumulative and all-encompassing, meaning that you can apply higher-version PSUs directly to the binaries without having to apply a lower-version one first. For example, the 11.2.0.4.3 GI PSU can be applied to an 11.2.0.4 Home without having to apply GI PSU 11.2.0.4.1 first. Oracle associates a version number to the patch. The fifth-place number of the database version is incremented for each PSU and ranges from 1 to 4. For example, the initial PSU is version 11.2.0.4.1, the second PSU for Release 11.2.0.4 is 11.2.0.4.2, and so on.

One item to note is that starting with 11gR2, GI PSUs contain both GI PSU and Database PSU for a particular quarter. For example, 11.2.0.2.3 GI PSU contains both the 11.2.0.2.3 GI PSU and the 11.2.0.2.3 Database PSU.

Here are examples of PSUs applied to a 12c Release 1 Grid and Database Home:

```
$ORACLE_HOME/OPatch/opatch lsinventory -details|grep -i "Clusterware Patch Set Update"
Patch description:  "Oracle Clusterware Patch Set Update 12.1.0.1.1"

$ORACLE_HOME/OPatch/opatch lsinventory -details|grep -i "database Patch Set Update"
Patch description:  "Database Patch Set Update : 12.1.0.1.3 (18031528)"
```

Critical Patch Updates and Security Patch Updates

An iterative, cumulative patch consisting of security fixes was formerly known as a Critical Patch Update (CPU). As of October 2012, CPU patches have been called Security Patch Update (SPU) patches. The patches are still released as part of the overall Oracle CPU program.

SPU patches are cumulative, which means fixes from previous Oracle security alerts and Critical Patch Updates are included. It is not required to have previous security patches applied before applying a new SPU patch. However, you must be on the stated patch set level for a given product Home before applying the SPU patches for that release. Also note that SPUs have been superseded, as well, as explained in the next section.

Oracle Patching Standard

All of the patching name acronyms and types can be very confusing for Oracle's customers. PSUs and SPUs are an example of this; they are released each quarter by Oracle Support and contain the same security material. Oracle recommends the PSU as it provides additional critical bug fixes. Starting with Oracle Database version 12.1.0.1, Oracle will provide just PSU patches instead of CPUs to meet the criteria for security patching; SPU patches will no longer be available. Oracle has moved to this streamlined model due to the fame of the PSU patches. PSUs have been part of Oracle Support's new standard for patching since they were released in 2009.

Refer to the following Oracle Support Note for more information: "Database Security Patching from 12.1.0.1 Onwards" (ID 1581950.1).

One-Off Patches

Occasionally you may run into a scenario where you need to ask Oracle Support to provide a custom one-off patch that would be merged with your existing installed patch set software. Typically this would be needed for your Database or Grid Home for a very specific bug encountered; in general this would not be a common occurrence since most issues would be addressed in the PSU or the latest patch set.

We actually faced this scenario when doing an Exadata upgrade of the Compute Nodes and we had to escalate the issue with Oracle Support. After some time a senior engineer from Oracle had to make custom changes while we were in the middle of our downtime.

Exadata High Availability Upgrades

A traditional database upgrade can be done in place; however, it requires complete downtime for the whole database environment. In other words, for the entire duration of the upgrade, the system would be down and unavailable for users and the applications. In a critical 24x7 shop, staying online is of utmost importance and being down is not an option; in fact, every single second of downtime can translate to a loss of thousands of dollars. A rolling upgrade minimizes downtime as generally only one node is patched at a time; a non-rolling upgrade would bring down all of the same components, such as the Storage Cell Nodes, to be patched simultaneously.

Table 11.5 shows the Exadata components that can be upgraded with a rolling method. Fortunately most Oracle suites of products are MAA certified, including Exadata and ZFS. Oracle MAA is Oracle's best-practices blueprint based on Oracle HA technologies, extensive validation performed by the Oracle MAA development team, and the accumulated production experience of customers who have successfully deployed business-critical applications on Oracle. The goal of MAA is to achieve the optimal HA architecture at the lowest cost and complexity.

Having an Exadata Data Guard environment is ideal since you can test the entire upgrade or patch process there first. You can greatly reduce risk and downtime by having this type of environment in place. Once the standby environment has been upgraded, you can switch over to the new primary.

You should use the Data Guard transient logical standby rolling upgrade process for database patch sets and major releases.

You can upgrade the following components with no impact to your primary Exadata environment:

- Exadata Storage Server software
- InfiniBand switch software
- Database Server Exadata OS and firmware
- Database Server Grid Infrastructure Home

Table 11.5   Rolling Upgrade Components

Component to Update	Rolling Patch
Database—patch set	Yes (with Data Guard or GoldenGate)
Quarterly patch	Yes
Grid Infrastructure	Yes
Exadata Database Compute Node	Yes
Exadata Cell Storage Node	Yes
InfiniBand switch	Yes

There is no dependency between the primary and standby environments for them. Be sure to review the README file for each patch to ensure that it is Data Guard Standby-First certified. The following types of patches are candidates to be Data Guard Standby-First certified:

- Database Home interim patches
- Exadata bundle patches (e.g., monthly and quarterly database patches for Exadata)
- Database patch set updates

Reviewing Settings with Exachk

Exachk is an excellent tool provided by Oracle Support to review the configuration settings of your Exadata system across the stack, which includes the storage servers, Database Compute Nodes, InfiniBand switches, and the Ethernet network. There are several categories of checks that the tool reviews:

- ASM
- CRS/Grid Infrastructure
- Database and ASM initialization parameters
- Database Upgrade Module with pre- and post-upgrade functions
- Hardware and firmware
- Several database configuration settings vital to RAC
- Several OS configuration settings vital to RAC
- MAA scorecard
- OS kernel parameters
- OS packages

The tool is nonintrusive. When the tool completes its data gathering and examination, it creates a detailed HTML report and a .zip file which should be provided to Oracle Support for further analysis if an SR needs to be logged. The HTML report encompasses benefit/impact, risk, and action/repair information. In many cases it also references publicly available documents with additional information about the problem and explains how to resolve it. For more detailed information, see Oracle Support Note ID 1070954.1.

Exachk should be executed after the initial Exadata deployment, and also on a regular schedule such as monthly or bimonthly, and before and after any system configuration change and definitely before an Exadata upgrade! Ensure that you are able to resolve all issues discovered on your Exachk run and note any issues that you believe can be ignored before starting your Exadata upgrade.

Exadata Full Stack Upgrade

This section provides a step-by-step guide for upgrading your entire Exadata full stack.

Following is the approximate duration of an upgrade to the Exadata/ZFS full stack. Keep in mind that if your Exadata is current, it may take only about five to eight hours to upgrade the core components instead of the 14.25 hours listed below. This estimate represents a system that is about 2.5 years old without any patches being applied to it.

Exadata Component	Upgrade Duration (Hours)
Storage Cell Nodes (parallel)	1.5
DB Node upgrade to 11.2.2.4.2 (parallel)	1
DB Node upgrade to 11.2.3.3 (parallel)	2
Three InfiniBand switches (script does serial)	1.5
Grid Home update	2
DB Home install	1.5
Patch to latest PSU (11.2.0.4.2) (parallel)	2
KVM console	0.5
PDUs	0.25
Cisco switch	0.5
ZFS	1.5
Total Exadata stack upgrade time	**14.25**

Exadata Upgrade Path

Figure 11.1 illustrates the eight major components that need to be upgraded and also the suggested order, or upgrade path, to implement the upgrade.

The top section of Figure 11.1 shows the minimum recommended core components to upgrade for an Exadata Database Machine, and the bottom section shows the components that do not need to be part of the full stack upgrade plan and can be upgraded individually later.

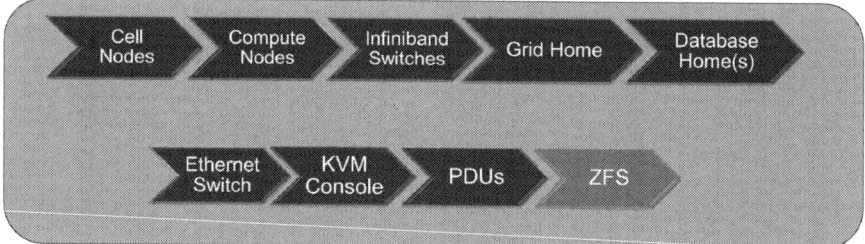

Figure 11.1   Recommended Exadata/ZFS full stack upgrade path

At a minimum, you should patch the Storage Cell Nodes, Database Compute Nodes, and then the Grid/DB Homes together. Finally, it is also a good idea to patch the InfiniBand switches to take advantage of the latest firmware updates for the interconnect.

This chapter outlines an Exadata upgrade path going from an old Exadata image version 11.2.2.3.5 released in 2011 to version 11.2.3.3 released in 2013 and also upgrading the Database and Grid Home from version 11.2.0.2 to 11.2.0.4.2.

Exadata Software Image Versions

The Exadata server software binaries and OS kernel are maintained as images; when you install or upgrade a Cell Node or Compute Node, a new Exadata image is installed.

You can query your current active image by running the `imageinfo` and `imagehistory` commands. The following output displays an upgraded Exadata Cell Node to 11.2.3.3:

```
$ imageinfo
Kernel version: 2.6.39-400.126.1.el5uek #1 SMP Fri Sep 20 10:54:38 PDT 2013 x86_64
Cell version: OSS_11.2.3.3.0_LINUX.X64_131014.1
Cell rpm version: cell-11.2.3.3.0_LINUX.X64_131014.1-1

Active image version: 11.2.3.3.0.131014.1
Active image activated: 2014-01-10 20:11:28 -0600
Active image status: success
Active system partition on device: /dev/md6
Active software partition on device: /dev/md8

In partition rollback: Impossible

Cell boot usb partition: /dev/sdm1
Cell boot usb version: 11.2.3.3.0.131014.1

Inactive image version: 11.2.2.3.5.110815
Inactive image activated: 2011-09-07 13:46:03 -0500
```

```
Inactive image status: success
Inactive system partition on device: /dev/md5
Inactive software partition on device: /dev/md7

Boot area has rollback archive for the version: 11.2.2.3.5.110815
Rollback to the inactive partitions: Possible

[root@exadcel01 ~]# imagehistory
Version                          : 11.2.2.3.5.110815
Image activation date            : 2011-09-07 13:46:03 -0500
Imaging mode                     : fresh
Imaging status                   : success

Version                          : 11.2.3.3.0.131014.1
Image activation date            : 2014-01-10 20:11:28 -0600
Imaging mode                     : out of partition upgrade
Imaging status                   : success
```

The upgrade path described in this chapter is used to upgrade the following components:

- Cell, InfiniBand switches 11.2.2.3.5 > 11.2.3.3
- Database Node image 11.2.2.3.5 > 11.2.2.4.2 > 11.2.3.3
- Grid Infrastructure Home 11.2.0.2 > 11.2.0.2
- BP 12 > 11.2.0.2
- One-off patch 14639430 > 11.2.0.4.2
- Database Home 11.2.0.2 > 11.2.0.4.2

Note

The InfiniBand switch as well as the ILOM for the InfiniBand switch will be updated automatically from the 11.2.3.3 patch set.

As shown in Figure 11.2, the image version for Exadata software is explained by each of its digits. At the time of this writing, the latest Exadata image software release is version 12.1.1.1.1

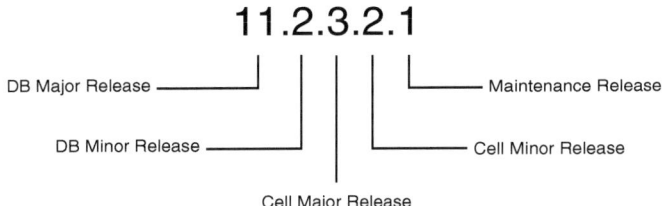

Figure 11.2 Exadata software image version

Checking Your Current Release Version

Table 11.6 provides some of the menu paths and commands you need to run to view the current version of the component that you need to upgrade. Knowing the correct version of your component is the first step when planning an upgrade. You can use this information to determine your upgrade path.

The following is example output showing the current InfiniBand switch version:

```
[root@exaib1 ~]# version
SUN DCS 36p version: 2.1.3-4
Build time: Aug 28 2013 16:25:57
SP board info:
Manufacturing Date: 2011.03.23
Serial Number: "NCD6C0452"
Hardware Revision: 0x0006
Firmware Revision: 0x0000
BIOS version: SUN0R100
BIOS date: 06/22/2010
```

The following is example output showing the current Cisco switch version:

```
ciscoswitch>show version
Cisco IOS Software, Catalyst 4500 L3 Switch Software (cat4500-IPBASEK9-M),
Version 15.0(2)SG8, RELEASE SOFTWARE (fc2)
Technical Support: http://www.cisco.com/techsupport
Copyright (c) 1986-2013 by Cisco Systems, Inc.
Compiled Mon 02-Dec-13 17:00 by prod_rel_team
Image text-base: 0x10000000, data-base: 0x12095E08
ROM: 12.2(31r)SGA2
Dagobah Revision 226, Swamp Revision 5
ciscoswitch uptime is 21 weeks, 4 days, 14 hours, 58 minutes
System returned to ROM by reload
System restarted at 22:43:15 CST Sat Feb 22 2014
System image file is "bootflash:cat4500-ipbasek9-mz.150-2.SG8.bin"
```

Figure 11.3 shows the current version of the KVM switch from the console. Figure 11.4 shows the current version of ZFS from the console.

Table 11.6 Component Versions

Component	Command or Path
Cell Storage Node	imageinfo
DB Compute Node	imageinfo
Database/Grid Homes	opatch lsinventory
InfiniBand switch	show version
Ethernet switch	show version
KVM	Appliance settings > Version
PDU	From web console, Module Info
ZFS	From web console, Maintenance > System > Version

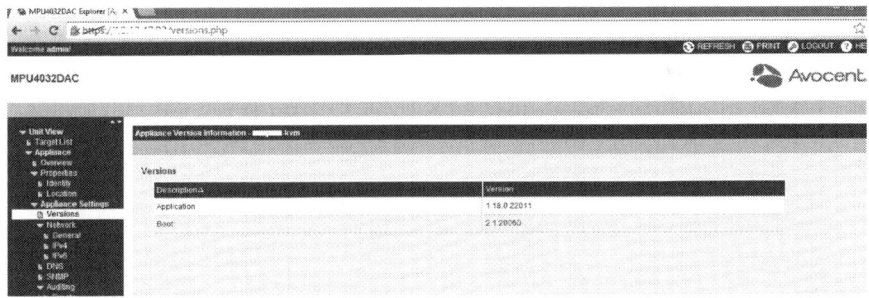

Figure 11.3 KVM version

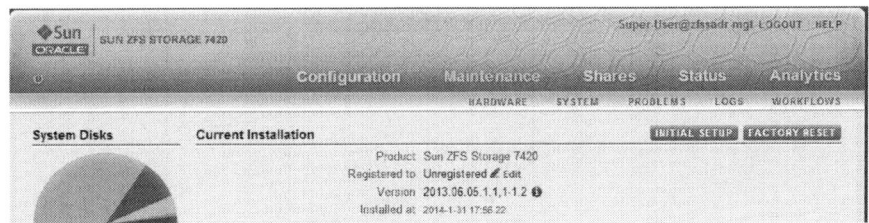

Figure 11.4 ZFS version

Downloading Patches for Exadata and ZFS

Based on the upgrade path outlined earlier, we need to download and stage the following patches. Download all the following patches to Database Node 1. You need to ensure that the root account from Database Compute Node 1 has SSH equivalence to all Storage Cell Nodes and also has an accessible cell_group file listing all related hosts.

- **Patch 17938410**—Exadata 11.2.3.3.0 Patchmgr plug-ins download
- **Patch 16278923**—Exadata image for 11.2.3.3.0 for Cell and Database Nodes and switches
- **Patch 13513611**—Exadata image for 11.2.2.4.2 Database Nodes
- **Patch 16486998**—dbnodeupdate.sh
- **Patch 17809253**—Exadata Compute Node 11.2.3.3.0 Base Repository ISO
- **Patch 12982245**—BP12 patch update to 11.2.0.2 GI Home
- **Patch 14639430**—One-off patch for 11.2.0.2 GI Home

- **Patch 13390677**—11.2.0.4 Database (download the first three files)
- **Patch 17838803**—11.2.0.4 Database PSU patch for Exadata (December 2013—11.2.0.4.2)
- **Patch 6880880**—OPatch p6880880_112000_Linux-x86-64.zip
- **Patch 14363313**—ZFS BIOS and SP firmware on the Sun Fire X4470 server
- **Patch 15750578**—ZFS Storage software update 2011.1.4.2
- **Patch 17945242**—ZFS Storage software update 2013.1.1.1
- **Patch 16523441**—PDU metering unit firmware and HTML interface v1.06
- **Patch Cisco switch update**—cat4500-ipbasek9-mz.150-2.SG8.bin
- **Patch KVM**—FL0620-AVO-1.18.0.22011.fl
- **TFTP RPM**—tftp-server-0.49-2.0.1.x86_64.rpm (needed for Cisco switch update)

Upgrading the Cell Nodes

The Cell Nodes or the Storage Cell Nodes are the first Exadata component to upgrade and probably one of the most important. As you know, the Storage Cell Nodes store all of the data for the ASM disk groups and is also responsible for the major performance features of Exadata such as Smart Scan, HCC, Flash Cache, Storage Indexes, and so on.

Cell Node Upgrade Preliminary Steps

It is best practice to create fundamental preliminary steps to include in your upgrade plan when updating your Storage Cell Nodes. You will want to create RMAN backups of all your databases on the Exadata system. For example, you may want to take a full level 0, level 1 incremental and archive log backup just before you shut down all of your databases.

You need to ensure that any critical issues do not exist on the Cell Nodes such as with the cell disks, grid disks, and physical disks. The status of the output should be active, normal, or online. If the status is other than that, you will need to resolve the disk issue(s) before the upgrade. If you do get a bad status, in most cases you may need to replace a bad disk. Ideally your data is safe and the Cell Node is using normal or high redundancy, which means you would have a copy of the data block in another disk on another Cell Node.

In order to run the `dcli` command from the Cell Node as root, you need to ensure that you have a file with all of the cell storage hostnames listed so the `dcli` command can issue the `cellcli` command across all Cell Nodes listed in the file.

The following cell commands can be executed from the Exadata Compute Node to detect disk errors prior to the upgrade or patch activities:

```
$ dcli -g cell_group -l root cellcli -e "LIST CELL"
$ dcli -g cell_group -l root cellcli -e "LIST CELLDISK"
$ dcli -g cell_group -l root cellcli -e "LIST GRIDDISK"
$ dcli -g cell_group -l root cellcli -e "LIST PHYSICALDISK"
```

As a precautionary step, check ASM disk group status against all disk groups. This command verifies the disk integrity, performs metadata checks, and cross-checks all of the file extent maps and allocation tables for consistency:

```
ASMCMD> ALTER DISKGROUP diskgroup_name CHECK ALL;
```

As another pre-verification check, verify that no rows are returned from gv$asm_operation, as follows. If something is running in ASM, such as a disk group rebalance, you have a row returned and need to let the operation complete before proceeding.

```
SQL> select * from gv$asm_operation;
no rows selected
```

Note

After you replace a disk, ASM automatically rebalances the data blocks for the associated disk groups that had data on the disk replaced. If the ASM rebalance takes much longer than normal, you can stop the compact phase of the ASM rebalance by setting the _DISABLE_REBALANCE_COMPACT parameter to TRUE. Setting the initialization parameter _DISABLE_REBALANCE_COMPACT=TRUE disables the compacting phase of the disk group rebalance for all disk groups. The third phase of ASM rebalancing is compacting (ASM version 11.1.0.7 and later). This phase tries to move the data blocks to the exterior tracks of the disk, and during this phase of the rebalance, the column EST_MINUTES will keep showing 0.

Last, you should have extra spare disks for your Storage Cell Nodes on site in case you need to replace one before or during the upgrade process.

Cell Node Patch Preparation

Before you can begin the patch, you need to unzip the following patch from Database Compute Node 1 as root: 16278923: Exadata 11.2.3.3.0 (Oracle Support Note ID 1487339.1). Actually, the Exadata image software patch in this example was applied to both the Storage Cell Nodes and the Database Compute Nodes to be consistent, and the patch for the InfiniBand switch software is also included. The process for upgrading the Database Compute Nodes and InfiniBand switches is covered later in the chapter.

After unzipping the file, perform the following steps to prepare for the patch:

1. Review the README for patch 16278923.
2. If doing a non-rolling upgrade, shut down all databases on the Compute Nodes.
3. If doing a rolling upgrade, issue the patchmgr prerequisite check (-patch_ check_prereq). Also, set the Oracle ASM disk repair timer for all disk groups to its default value of 3.6 hours for the duration of the patch.
4. Download any patchmgr plugins attached to Oracle Support Note ID 1487339.1, and install them as documented in the note.

Cell Node Patching

Once the preparations have been completed, we can proceed with the actual upgrade of the Storage Cell Nodes by completing the following steps. Note that when upgrading the Cell Nodes, it is simple to go directly to the latest version in this release; there are no intermediate patches that need to be applied first.

1. Keep the hot spare disk as a hot spare, and *do not* add it to the RAID configuration on each Database Compute Node. Run the following command on each Compute Node, which will save about six to eight hours on each node upgrade:

```
$ touch /opt/oracle/EXADATA_KEEP_HOT_SPARE_ON_YUM_UPDATE
```

2. As the root account on the Database Node, change to the patch_11.2.3.3.0.131014.1 directory where the .zip file p16278923_112330_Linux-x86-64.zip was unzipped.

3. It is recommended that you reset the server to a known state using the following command:

```
$ ./patchmgr -cells cell_group -reset_force
```

4. Issue the following Cell Node patching command to upgrade to Exadata version 11.2.3.3.0. Use the -rolling option if you plan to use rolling updates to update one Cell Node at a time while keeping the databases online. Each Cell Node may take about one and a half to two hours to apply. If the rolling option is not used, all Cell Nodes will be patched in parallel. Also note that the Cell Nodes will be rebooted as part of the patching process.

```
$ ./patchmgr -cells cell_group -patch
```

5. Monitor patch activity using less -rf patchmgr.stdout from another terminal session or window to see raw log details from the patchmgr utility.

Use the following `-cleanup` option to clean up all the temporary patch or rollback files on the cells. This option cleans the stale patch and rollback states. Use this option before retrying a halted or failed run of the patchmgr utility.

```
./patchmgr -cells cell_group -cleanup
```

6. Once the patching of the Storage Cell Nodes is complete, run the `imageinfo` and `imagehistory` commands as previously mentioned in this chapter; you should have similar results.

7. Run the following status commands as a post-check to ensure that the Storage Cell Node disks are fine. The output should be active, normal, or online.

```
$ dcli -g cell_group -l root cellcli -e "LIST CELL"
$ dcli -g cell_group -l root cellcli -e "LIST CELLDISK"
$ dcli -g cell_group -l root cellcli -e "LIST GRIDDISK"
$ dcli -g cell_group -l root cellcli -e "LIST PHYSICALDISK"
```

Updating the Compute Nodes

As you follow the process covered in this section, refer to the following Oracle Support Note: "Configuring Exadata Database Server Routing" (ID 1306154.1). Some details from the note are listed in this section for your reference. These steps are required to prepare for the update of the Database Compute Nodes.

The procedure listed here configures network routing on database servers in Exadata Database Machine so that packets arriving via a given interface will have their responses sent out using that same interface (instead of always sending via the default gateway). The default route for the system typically uses the client access network and the gateway for that network. All outbound traffic that is not destined for an IP address on the management or private networks is sent out via the client access network. This poses a problem for some connections to the management network in some customer environments.

After making these changes, run the following command to restart network services:

```
$ dcli -g dbs_group -l root 'service network restart'
```

The Exadata Database Compute Node update is divided into three steps:

1. Upgrade the image on the DB Nodes to 11.2.2.4.2, then to 11.2.3.3.0.

2. Update ILOM, which is done automatically; no separate steps are required.

3. Update the InfiniBand drivers.

Image 11.2.2.4.2 Update

First, let's cover the steps to update the Exadata image software on the Database Compute Nodes from version 11.2.2.3.5 to 11.2.3.3.0. This image upgrade is not a direct version upgrade as we did with the Storage Cell Nodes; rather we need to apply an intermediate patch first (11.2.2.4.2), and then we can upgrade the Database Compute Nodes to 11.2.3.3.0.

Go to section 3.1 in the README for Oracle patch 16278923, which we just used for updating the Storage Cell Nodes to 11.2.3.3.0. There is a table with three rows that states that if your Database Compute Node is on a release earlier than 11.2.2.4.2 and has an Oracle release 5.5 or later, you need to update the database server to Oracle Exadata Storage Server Software 11*g* Release 2 (11.2) 11.2.2.4.2 using patch 13513611. You can ignore the fact that it mentions the term *storage* which may be confusing.

If your system meets these criteria, it applies to our versioning. You can confirm the current image version by running the `imageinfo` command as shown earlier in this chapter, and the Linux version can be verified with the following command:

```
$ cat /etc/oracle-release
Oracle Linux Server release 5.9
```

We continue to update the database server to Oracle Exadata Storage Server Software 11*g* Release 2 (11.2) 11.2.2.4.2 using patch 13513611. Follow the procedure in section 8.1 of the patch 13513611 README to update the servers.

Let's edit the /etc/security/limits.conf file to update or add the following limits for the database owner (`orauser`) and the grid infrastructure user (`griduser`). Your deployment may use the same operating system user for both and it may be named oracle user. Adjust the following as needed:

```
########## BEGIN DO NOT REMOVE Added by Oracle ###########
orauser    soft    core       unlimited
orauser    hard    core       unlimited
orauser    soft    nproc      131072
orauser    hard    nproc      131072
orauser    soft    nofile     131072
orauser    hard    nofile     131072
orauser    soft    memlock    <value of x listed below>
orauser    hard    memlock    <value of x listed below>
griduser   soft    core       unlimited
griduser   hard    core       unlimited
griduser   soft    nproc      131072
griduser   hard    nproc      131072
griduser   soft    nofile     131072
griduser   hard    nofile     131072
griduser   soft    memlock    <value of x listed below>
griduser   hard    memlock    <value of x listed below>

########### END DO NOT REMOVE Added by Oracle ###########
```

```
let -i x=($((`cat /proc/meminfo | grep 'MemTotal:' | awk '{print $2}'` * 3
/ 4))); echo $x
```

If you have any NFS mount points, comment out the entries in the /etc/fstab file and then unmount the share. In the following example, we unmount the NFS share from the ZFS Storage Appliance:

```
$ umount /zfs/backup1 /zfs/backup2 /zfs/backup3
```

Next, as root, unzip the db_patch_11.2.2.4.2.111221.zip file. It will create the db_patch_11.2.2.4.2.111221 directory. Change to the db_patch_11.2.2.4.2.111221 directory. Execute the ./install.sh script as follows to apply the 11.2.2.4.2 Exadata image; run this command on each node:

```
./install.sh -force
```

The install.sh shell script submits the patch process in the background to prevent interruption of the patch in case the login session gets terminated due to a network connection break. The database host reboots as part of the patch process after a while. The final results of dopatch.log are as follows:

```
Exit Code: 0x00
[INFO] Power cycle using /tmp/firmware/SUNBIOSPowerCycle

Wait 180 seconds for the ILOM power cycle package to take effect. Then
start the power down.
```

Last, issue the imageinfo command to verify that the version has been updated to 11.2.2.4.2.

Image 11.2.2.3 Update

Next, let's update the Exadata Database Compute Nodes to release 11.2.3.3.0. Keep in mind that in the steps detailed in this section, we will not be using YUM. In a secure environment, the Exadata system most likely does not have outside network access. For this reason we will download the ISO .zip file that was listed earlier in this chapter: patch 17809253—Exadata Compute Node 11.2.3.3.0 Base Repository ISO. This can be used to apply the 11.2.3.3.0 image update to the Exadata Database Compute Node.

These are the final steps to apply 11.2.3.3 on each Exadata Database Compute Node:

1. Follow the steps in section 4 of the following document to patch: "Exadata YUM Repository Population and Linux Database Server Updating" (Oracle Support Note ID 1473002.1).

2. Stop the CRS on each node, and then use the dbnodeupdate.sh script with
the local .zip file:

```
$ crsctl stop crs -all (-f optional)
$ ./dbnodeupdate.sh -u -l p17809253_112330_Linux-x86-64.zip
```

3. After completing the previous step, continue with phase 2 of the one-time
setup by running the following command:

```
$ ./dbnodeupdate.sh -u -p 2
```

It is OK to rerun the command if your session becomes disconnected or an
RPM doesn't install (indicated by an error).

4. Issue the completion (post-patching) steps using the dbnodeupdate.sh utility:

```
$ ./dbnodeupdate.sh -c
```

5. Repeat the preceding steps for each Database Compute Node.

Note

It's common for step 3 (the step with the -u p 2 option) to hang. The -c option
may fail if so. The error message will confirm this error:

```
ERROR: Unable to determine hardware type, reset ILOM and retry, exiting.
```

Troubleshooting Image 11.2.2.3 Update

As you wait for the image update to complete, you can check the processes as follows and confirm that they are applying an image. You will want to wait until the
process is complete.

1. Run $ dmidecode -s system-product-name.
   - If output is Not Available, also execute $ ipmitool bmc reset cold.
   - If output is SUN FIRE X4170 M2 SERVER, retry ./dbnodeupdate.sh -c
     and ignore the following steps.
2. Confirm that ILOM is up (executing $ ipmitool bmc restarted it).
3. Shut down the node for 5 minutes: $ shutdown -h now.
4. After 5 minutes or more, start the node from the ilom $ start /SYS.
5. Once the node is up, repeat step 2.
6. Review the logfile $ tail -f /var/log/cellos/vldrun.each_boot.log.

The last line should read something similar to this:

```
2014-02-22 04:43:53 -0600  the each boot completed with SUCCESS
```

Run the `imageinfo` command to verify that the Database Compute Node has been upgraded to 11.2.3.3.0:

```
# imageinfo

Kernel version: 2.6.39-400.126.1.el5uek #1 SMP Fri Sep 20 10:54:38 PDT 2013 x86_64
Image version: 11.2.3.3.0.131014.1
Image activated: 2014-01-11 01:42:52 -0600
Image status: success
System partition on device: /dev/mapper/VGExaDb-LVDbSys1
```

Updating InfiniBand Switches

Now update the Exadata InfiniBand switches. Starting with release 11.2.3.3.0, the patchmgr utility is used to upgrade and downgrade the InfiniBand switches. From Database Node 1 go to the following directory where the patch is located: cell_11233_image/patch_11.2.3.3.0.131014.1/. The command to upgrade both switches serially one by one in a rolling fashion as the root account is as follows. The total time to apply the patch is about 30 minutes per InfiniBand switch.

```
$ ./patchmgr -ibswitches -upgrade
```

The InfiniBand version is now 2.1.3.4. At this point if you're following the process provided in this chapter in order, you should be done with patching the Exadata image to 11.2.3.3.0 on the Storage Cell Nodes and DB Compute Nodes, and patching the InfiniBand switches to version 2.1.3.4.

Updating Grid Home

Next let's review the steps to upgrade the Grid, synonymous with Oracle Clusterware Home, from 11.2.0.2 to 11.2.0.4.2. These steps are very similar in a non-Exadata environment as well. As a precautionary step, you should verify that there are no grid disk, physical, or ASM disk group issues before upgrade; check ASM disk groups with the command `alter diskgroup <diskgroup name> check all`. Execute the same set of commands as run previously when upgrading the Storage Cell Nodes:

```
$ dcli -g cell_group -l root cellcli -e "LIST CELL"
$ dcli -g cell_group -l root cellcli -e "LIST CELLDISK"
$ dcli -g cell_group -l root cellcli -e "LIST GRIDDISK"
$ dcli -g cell_group -l root cellcli -e "LIST PHYSICALDISK"
ASMCMD> ALTER DISKGROUP diskgroup_name CHECK ALL;
SQL> select * from gv$asm_operation;
no rows selected
```

1. Refer to "Exadata Database Machine 11.2.0.4 Grid Infrastructure and Database Upgrade for 11.2.0.2 BP12 and Later" (Oracle Support Note ID 1565291.1).

2. Apply the OPatch update to the Grid and DB Home on each node: patch 6880880, download p6880880_112000_Linux-x86-64.zip (for 11.2).

3. In Oracle Support Note ID 1565291.1, review the 11.2.0.4 upgrade prerequisites for Grid Infrastructure software. In our case we are on version 11.2.0.2 bundle 10. The prerequisite states that there are two requirements to upgrade to 11.2.0.4: 11.2.0.2 BP12 or later and a fix for bug 14639430.

4. Download these two patches and apply them to the Grid Home on each Database Compute Node using OPatch: patch 12982245 (BP12 patch update to 11.2.0.2 GI Home) and patch 14639430 (one-off patch for 11.2.0.2 GI Home).

5. Apply this to Grid Home and DB Home on each node: BUG 12982245— TRACKING BUG FOR 11.2.0.2 EXADATA DATABASE RECOMMENDED PATCH 12 (BP12); file name: p12982245_112020_Linux-x86-64.zip.

   Create an ocm.resp file, and run as root:

   ```
   $ORACLE_HOME/OPatch/ocm/bin/emocmrsp
   ```

   Then apply the patch as root:

   ```
   $ORACLE_HOME/OPatch/opatch auto
   /u01/app/oracle/exadata_patch/04_BP12_GI_HOME/12982245 -ocmrf
   /tmp/ocm.rsp
   ```

   Finally, run the catbundle script from the Database Home for each database:

   ```
   SQL> @rdbms/admin/catbundle.sql exa apply
   ```

6. Apply the following to only the Grid Home: BUG 17484294—PSE FOR BASE BUG 14639430 ON TOP OF 11.2.0.2.4 FOR LINUX X86-64 [226] (PSE #2243; file name: p14639430_112024_Linux-x86-64.zip).

   Apply the patch as root:

   ```
   $ORACLE_HOME/OPatch/opatch auto
    /u01/app/oracle/exadata_patch/05_One_Off_GI_HOME -oh
   /u01/app/11.2.0.2/grid -ocmrf /tmp/ocm.rsp
   ```

7. Ensure that the required files for patching the Grid Home and Database Home are staged: Oracle Database 11*g* Release 2 (11.2.0.4) Patch Set 3 (patch 13390677); patch 17838803—11.2.0.4 Database Patch for Exadata (December 2013—11.2.0.4.2).

8. Upgrade the Grid Infrastructure to 11.2.0.4 using the OUI. Do not shut down Clusterware, ASM, or any databases. Follow and perform the 11.2.0.4 Grid Infrastructure software installation and upgrade using the OUI.

Create a new Grid Home:

```
$ dcli -g dbs_group -l root 'mkdir -p /u01/app/11.2.0.4/grid;
$ chown -R oracle:dba /u01/app/11.2.0.4'
```

11.2.0.4 Clusterware Upgrade and Update

Execute $ ./runInstaller with the full stack up and running. At step 10 of the OUI upgrade, do not execute the scripts but first perform the following steps in order. Last, change the SGA memory settings for ASM to at least 1040MB for the parameter SGA_TARGET.

You should get the screen shown in Figure 11.5 once the Grid Clusterware upgrade has finished.

This book does not cover the screen-by-screen examples for the Grid Infrastructure and database software update as the processes are not any different from non-Exadata environments. For the complete Grid Infrastructure upgrade screen shots and examples, visit www.dbaexpert.com/blog/grid-infrastructure-installation/.

As a best practice, you need to apply the latest bundle patch set 11.2.0.4.2 to the Grid Infrastructure Home using the napply option before running rootupgrade.sh

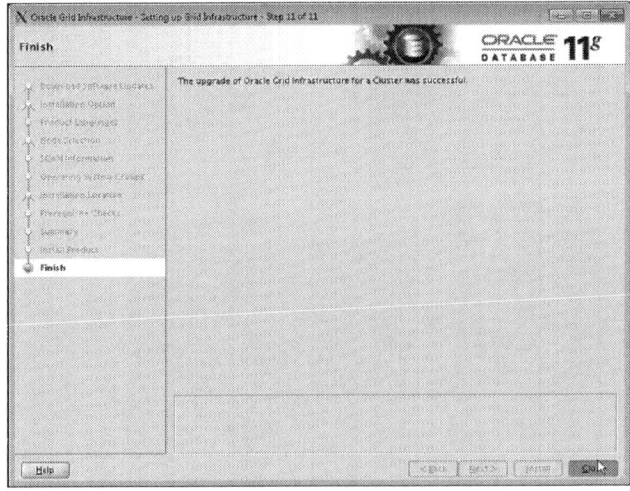

Figure 11.5 Upgrade Grid Infrastructure to completion

on all nodes in the cluster. In this example, you are applying 11.2.0.4 BP2 (patch 17838803) since you want to apply the latest PSU, not BP1 as it says in the note. Once the PSU is on the file system, you need to execute rootupgrade.sh on server 1 and wait for it to finish. Only then run rootupgrade.sh on the remaining database servers serially. Once the rootupgrade.sh process is complete, the Clusterware and ASM will run from the new Grid Home and new version 11.2.0.4.2.

As a verification procedure, leverage the OPatch executable and check the output to confirm that Grid Home has been upgraded successfully:

```
$ORACLE_HOME/OPatch/opatch lsinventory
Oracle Interim Patch Installer version 11.2.0.3.6
Copyright (c) 2013, Oracle Corporation.  All rights reserved.


Oracle Home       : /u01/app/11.2.0.4/grid
Central Inventory : /u01/app/oraInventory
   from           : /u01/app/11.2.0.4/grid/oraInst.loc
OPatch version    : 11.2.0.3.6
OUI version       : 11.2.0.4.0
Log file location : /u01/app/11.2.0.4/grid/cfgtoollogs/opatch/opatch2014-
05-26_23-56-18PM_1.log

Lsinventory Output file location : /u01/app/11.2.0.4/grid/cfgtoollogs/opatch/lsinv/
lsinventory2014-05-26_23-
56-18PM.txt


-------------------------------------------------------------------------
Installed Top-level Products (1):

Oracle Grid Infrastructure 11g                                11.2.0.4.0
There are 1 product(s) installed in this Oracle Home.


Interim patches (3) :

Patch  17839474     : applied on Sat Feb 22 13:21:28 CST 2014
Unique Patch ID:  17003208
Patch description:  "DISKMON PATCH FOR EXADATA (DEC2013 - 11.2.0.4.2) : (17839474)"
   Created on 1 Dec 2013, 21:24:06 hrs PST8PDT
   Bugs fixed:
     17839474


Patch  17629416     : applied on Sat Feb 22 13:20:59 CST 2014
Unique Patch ID:  17003208
Patch description:  "CRS PATCH FOR EXADATA (DEC 2013 - 11.2.0.4.2) : (17629416)"
   Created on 01 Dec 2013, 04:05:15 hrs PST8PDT
   Bugs fixed:
     17065496, 17551223, 16346413


Patch  17741631     : applied on Sat Feb 22 13:19:55 CST 2014
Unique Patch ID:  17003208
Patch description:  "DATABASE PATCH FOR EXADATA (DEC 2013 - 11.2.0.4.2) : (17741631)"
   Created on 28 Nov 2013, 22:49:01 hrs PST8PDT
Sub-patch  17628006; "DATABASE PATCH FOR EXADATA (NOV 2013 - 11.2.0.4.1):
  (17628006)"
   Bugs fixed:
     17288409, 17265217, 17465741, 16220077, 17614227, 16069901, 17726838
     16285691, 13364795, 17612828, 17443671, 17080436, 17446237, 16837842
     16863422, 17332800, 17501491, 17610798, 17602269, 16850630, 17313525
     14852021, 17783588, 13866822, 17546761, 12905058
```

```
Rac system comprising of multiple nodes
  Local node = exapdb01
  Remote node = exapdb02
  Remote node = exapdb03
  Remote node = exapdb04

-------------------------------------------------------------------------

OPatch succeeded.
```

Once the Grid Infrastructure environment is complete, we can proceed to install the Oracle Database 11.2.0.4 software. First, we need to create the new Database Homes on each of the Database Nodes. We can leverage dcli to create the new $ORACLE_HOMEs on all the Database Nodes with a single command:

```
dcli -g dbs_group -l root 'mkdir -p /u01/app/oracle/product/11.2.0.4/dbhome_1;
chown -R oracle:dba /u01/app/oracle/product/11.2.0.4/'
```

Install the new Oracle Database 11.2.0.4 software via patch 13390677—11.2.0.4 Database. You need to download the first three files, which are for the database install. Follow the instructions for the patch to install 11.2.0.4 on a RAC cluster using the OUI: http://docs.oracle.com/cd/E11882_01/install.112/e24326/toc.htm.

PSU Patch to Database Home

To apply the PSU patch to the Database Home, complete the following steps:

1. Unizip and apply patch 17838803—11.2.0.4 Database PSU Patch for Exadata (December 2013—11.2.0.4.2).

2. Follow the Oracle Support Note to upgrade the database to 11.2.0.4.

3. Complete the "Checklist for Manual Upgrades to 11gR2" (Oracle Support Note ID 837570.1).

4. After the database upgrade completes, run exabundle: @?/rdbms/admin/catbundle.sql exa apply (see the README for 17838803).

Upgrading Ethernet Switches

The Ethernet Cisco switch is not something that is typically upgraded; however, the steps are covered in this section. Once you upgrade the Ethernet switch, it allows SSH connectivity and you can optionally disable telnet as well. You may reference the following Oracle Support Note: "Configuring SSH on Cisco Catalyst 4948 Ethernet Switch" (ID 1415044.1).

Installing and Configuring tftp for Linux

You need to download, install, and configure tftp for Linux:

1. First, download the RPM from http://public-yum.oracle.com/repo/OracleLinux/ OL5/latest/x86_64/getPackage/tftp-server-0.49-2.0.1.x86_64.rpm to stage the RPM.

2. Next, install the RPM by executing the rpm command with the -ihv option as root:

   ```
   $ rpm -ihv tftp-server-0.49-2.0.1.x86_64.rpm
   ```

3. Once the RPM is installed, restart the services and ensure that they are running:

   ```
   $ service xinetd restart
   ```

4. Confirm that tftp is running on the Exadata node:

   ```
   $ chkconfig --list|grep -i ftp
   tftp:          on
   ```

On the Exadata Linux node do the following steps to configure tftp:

1. Create a directory as root named /tftpboot with permission of 777:

   ```
   mkdir /tftpboot
   chown nobody:nobody /tftpboot
   chmod 777 /tftpboot
   ```

2. Set up the configuration file for tftp and set the disable parameter to no as shown below. Also update the server_args parameter to be set as follows with the -c option:

   ```
   server_args = -s /tftpboot/ -c
   ```

   Following is a configuration file example:

   ```
   [root@exa01 tftpboot]# cat /etc/xinetd.d/tftp
   # default: off
   # description: The tftp server serves files
   #        using the trivial file transfer
   #        protocol.  The tftp protocol is often used to boot diskless
   #        workstations, download configuration files to
   #        network-aware printers,
   #        and to start the installation process for
   #        some operating systems.
   service tftp
   {
           disable = no
           socket_type            = dgram
           protocol               = udp
           wait                   = yes
   ```

```
        user                  = root
        server                = /usr/sbin/in.tftpd
        server_args           = -s /tftpboot/ -c
        per_source            = 11
        cps                   = 100 2
        flags                 = IPv4
}
```

3. Now restart the tftp service on the Exadata node to load the new configuration:

```
service xinetd restart
```

4. Validate that the service for tftp is on:

```
[root@exa01 ~]# chkconfig --list|grep -i ftp
tftp:         on
```

Note
You will not see the tftp process running on the node until a session from the Cisco switch is invoked.

Confirming Available Space

Before we continue, we need to confirm that we have available space. You need to telnet to the switch and enter the root password. Execute the enable command and you will be prompted again for the root password. Verify that free space is available on Cisco 4948 Flash. Log in to Cisco 4948 via telnet with superuser privileges. After logging in, issue the show file systems command to display the available space:

```
cisco4948-ip# show file systems
File Systems:
Size(b) Free(b) Type Flags Prefixes
* 60817408 45204152 flash rw bootflash:
- - opaque rw system:
- - opaque rw tmpsys:
- - opaque ro crashinfo:
524280 523664 flash rw cat4000_flash:
- - opaque rw null:
- - opaque ro tar:
- - network rw tftp:
- - opaque ro profiler:
- - opaque wo syslog:
524280 513891 nvram rw nvram:
- - network rw rcp:
- - network rw http:
- - network rw ftp:
- - opaque ro cns:
```

This sample output shows approximately 45MB of free space in bootflash. As only 20MB are required, this switch passes the prerequisite check for space available. You can also display the contents of bootflash using the dir command as shown below. As an example, here it shows a default IOS (Internetwork Operating System) firmware file stored:

```
exadsw-ip#dir bootflash:
Directory of bootflash:/

 1  -rwx   14569696  Jan 29 2010 19:27:27 -06:00  cat4500-ipbase-mz.122-46.SG.bin
 2  -rw-       4053  Jan 30 2014 08:55:30 -06:00  cisco4948-ip-confg-before-ssh

60817408 bytes total (46243400 bytes free)
```

Including the Boot Firmware

By default, the current configuration may not be set up to boot from a specific firmware file. As a best practice, update the current configuration to include the boot firmware file name. In the previous section, we identified the default IOS firmware file stored in bootflash. Next, save the current configuration, write to NVRAM, and also save it in bootflash with a unique name.

```
cisco4948-ip# copy running-config startup-config all
```

List the file system with the startup configuration file (the saved configuration is in bold):

```
exadsw-ip#dir nvram:
Directory of nvram:/

509  -rw-    3082            <no date>  startup-config
510  ----       5            <no date>  private-config
  1  ----       0            <no date>  rf_cold_starts
  2  ----      55            <no date>  persistent-data
  3  -rw-       0            <no date>  ifIndex-table.gz
```

Copy the config file from NVRAM to the bootflash location:

```
cisco4948-ip# copy running-config bootflash:cisco4948-ip-confg-before-ssh
```

List the file system with the startup configuration file (the original file is in bold):

```
exadsw-ip#dir bootflash:
Directory of bootflash:/

1  -rwx   14569696  Jan 29 2010 19:27:27 -06:00  cat4500-ipbase-mz.122-
46.SG.bin       2  -rw-       4053  Jan 30 2014 08:55:30 -06:00
cisco4948-ip-confg-before-ssh
```

Now, take a backup of this configuration on the remote tftp file server. Copy the current configuration from the switch to the Exadata node using tftp. Connect to the switch:

```
[root@exa01 ~]# telnet exadsw-ip
Trying 10.43.47.101...
Connected to exadsw-ip.
Escape character is '^]'.

User Access Verification

Password:
exadsw-ip> enable
Password:
```

Next, invoke the copy of the Cisco switch config to the Exadata node:

```
exadsw-ip#copy bootflash:cisco4948-ip-confg-before-ssh tftp:
Address or name of remote host []? 10.43.47.101
Destination filename [cisco4948-ip-confg-before-ssh]?
!!
4053 bytes copied in 0.016 secs (253313 bytes/sec)
```

After this command is entered, the switch prompts for the tftp server name and file name to use when saving to the remote tftp server. Those outputs aren't shown here.

Verify that the file has been copied to the Exadata DB Node:

```
[root@exa01 ~]# ls -l /tftpboot
total 4
-rw-rw-rw- 1 nobody nobody 4053 Jan 30 11:09 cisco4948-ip-confg-before-ssh
```

Transfer the new Cisco IOS SSH-capable firmware to the switch's bootflash.

Copy the new firmware file into the Cisco 4948 Flash file system and verify its integrity in bootflash. In this example, our tftp server is named tftp-server and we have staged the updated IOS firmware on the tftp server at cat4500-ipbasek9-mz.150-2.SG8.bin. On the Exadata node, copy the firmware file to the /tftpboot directory.

```
[root@exa01 ~]# telnet exadsw-ip
Trying 10.43.47.101...
Connected to exadsw-ip.
Escape character is '^]'.
```

Verifying User Access

The following steps will verify the user access on the Cisco switch:

```
Password:
exadsw-ip>enable
Password:
exadsw-ip#copy tftp: bootflash:
Address or name of remote host []? 10.43.47.101
Source filename []? cat4500-ipbasek9-mz.150-2.SG8.bin
Destination filename [cat4500-ipbasek9-mz.150-2.SG8.bin]?
```

```
Accessing tftp://10.43.47.133/cat4500-ipbasek9-mz.150-2.SG8.bin...
Loading cat4500-ipbasek9-mz.150-2.SG8.bin from 10.43.47.133 (via Vlan1):
!!!!!!!!!!!!!!!!!!!!!!!!!!!!!!!!!!!!!!!!!!!!!!!!!!!!!!!!!!!!!!!!!!!!!!!!!
[OK - 18095100 bytes]

18095100 bytes copied in 80.624 secs (224438 bytes/sec)


Directory of bootflash:/
exadsw-ip#dir bootflash:
    1  -rwx    14569696  Jan 29 2010 19:27:27 -06:00  cat4500-ipbase-mz.122-46.SG.bin
    2  -rw-        4053  Jan 30 2014 08:55:30 -06:00  cisco4948-ip-confg-before-ssh
    3  -rwx    18095100  Jan 30 2014 11:20:37 -06:00  cat4500-ipbasek9-mz.150-2.SG8.bin

60817408 bytes total (28148172 bytes free)
```

Run the verify command to verify and validate that the download was successful and complete:

```
exadsw-ip#verify bootflash:cat4500-ipbasek9-mz.150-2.SG8.bin
CCCCCCCCCCCCCCCCCCCCCCCCCCCCCCCCCCCCCCCCCCCCCCCCCCCCCCCCCCCCCCCCCCCCCCCCCC
CCCCCCCCCCCCCCCCCCCCCCCCCCCCCCCCCCCCCCCCCCCCCCCCCCCCCCCCCCCCCCCCCCCCCCCCCC
CCCCCCCCCCCCCCCCCCCCCCCCCCCCCCC
CCCCCCCCCCCCCCCCCCCCCCCCCCCCCCCCCCCCCCCCCCCCCCCCCCCCCCCCCCCCCCCCCCCCCCCCCC
CCCCCCCCCCCCCCC
CCCCCCCCCCCCCCCCCCCCCCCCCCCCCCCCCCCCCCCCCCCCCCCCCCCCCCCCCCCCCCCCCCCCCCCCCC
CCCCCCCCCCCCCCC
CCCCCCCCCCCCCCCCCCCCCCCCCCCCCCCCCCCCCCCCCCCCCCCCCCCCCCCCCCCCCCCCCCCCCCCCCC
CCCCCCCCCCCCCCC
CCCCCCCCCCCCCCCCCCCCCCCCCCCCCCCCCCCCCCCCCCCCCCCCCCCCCCCCCCCCCCCCCCCCCCCCCC
CCCCCCCCCCCCCCCCCCCCCCCCCCCCCCC

Verifying file integrity of bootflash:cat4500-ipbasek9-mz.150-2.SG8.bin
Embedded hash not found in file bootflash:cat4500-ipbasek9-mz.150-2.SG8.bin.
File system hash verification successful.
```

Now prepare Cisco 4948 to boot with new IOS firmware. Use the following to update the configuration with a config-register value of 0x2102 and a new IOS firmware boot file that we just downloaded. 0x2102 instructs the boot process to ignore any breaks, sets the baud rate to 9600, and boots into ROM if the main boot process fails for some reason:

```
cisco4948-ip# configure terminal
Enter configuration commands, one per line. End with CNTL/Z.
cisco4948-ip(config)# config-register 0x2102
cisco4948-ip(config)# no boot system
cisco4948-ip(config)# boot system bootflash:cat4500-ipbasek9-mz.150-2.SG8.bin
cisco4948-ip(config)#
cisco4948-ip(config)# (type <control-z> here to end)
cisco4948-ip# show running-config | include boot
boot-start-marker
boot system bootflash:cat4500-ipbasek9-mz.150-2.SG8.bin
boot-end-marker
cisco4948-ip#
```

Save the configuration into NVRAM:

```
cisco4948-ip# copy running-config startup-config all
cisco4948-ip# write memory
Building configuration...
Compressed configuration from 6725 bytes to 2261 bytes[OK]
```

Boot the Cisco 4948 switch with the new IOS firmware. When the reload command is issued, as follows, the switch reboots and there is an outage on the management network for all connected devices (including all Storage Cells, database servers, ILOMs, and InfiniBand switches) for a minute or two while the switch reboots. A management network outage should not cause an application outage as the databases should all remain available and functioning normally.

```
cisco4948-ip# reload
```

You will be asked to confirm if you wish to continue and reboot the Cisco switch.

Note

If the switch does not come back online, refer to the section "Force Booting the Cisco Switch." This step requires physical access.

With the switch successfully reloaded, reconnect using telnet and configure SSH as shown in the following procedure. The username command in the following example is required and shows the choice of username admin and password of welcome1 to configure a user. This is a required statement, but the username and password can be any username or password (it is recommended that you choose a better password than welcome1). After telnet login, use the enable command to get superuser privileges again and proceed with the following configurations:

```
cisco4948-ip# configure terminal
Enter configuration commands, one per line. End with CNTL/Z.
cisco4948-ip(config)# crypto key generate rsa
% You already have RSA keys defined named cisco4948-ip.us.oracle.com.
% Do you really want to replace them? [yes/no]: yes
```

Choose the size of the key modulus in the range of 360 to 2048 for your general-purpose keys, as follows. Choosing a key modulus greater than 512 may take a few minutes.

```
How many bits in the modulus [512]: 768
% Generating 768 bit RSA keys, keys will be non-exportable...[OK]
```

```
cisco4948-ip(config)#
cisco4948-ip(config)# username admin password 0 welcome1
cisco4948-ip(config)# line vty 0 4
cisco4948-ip(config-line)# transport input all
cisco4948-ip(config-line)# exit
cisco4948-ip(config)# aaa new-model
cisco4948-ip(config)#
cisco4948-ip(config)# ip ssh time-out 60
cisco4948-ip(config)# ip ssh authentication-retries 3
cisco4948-ip(config)# ip ssh version 2
cisco4948-ip(config)# (type <control-z> here to end)
```

Verify that the SSH configuration is working and configured properly using the show ip ssh command:

```
cisco4948-ip# show ip ssh
SSH Enabled - version 2.0
Authentication timeout: 60 secs; Authentication retries: 3
```

This switch should now be available for SSH logins using username admin and password welcome1 (this is the default password) via SSH v2 (which is typically the default for most SSH clients).

After configuring SSH and accessing and verifying it, some sites may want you to disable telnet access to the switch (leaving only SSH access available). This is optional as the switch can allow access via SSH and telnet simultaneously. To disable telnet access, connect to the switch using SSH (since telnet will be disabled as part of this procedure) and enter these commands:

```
cisco4948-ip# configure terminal
Enter configuration commands, one per line. End with CNTL/Z.
cisco4948-ip(config)#
cisco4948-ip(config)# line vty 0 4
cisco4948-ip(config-line)# transport input ssh
cisco4948-ip(config-line)# exit
cisco4948-ip(config)# (type <control-z> here to end)
```

If there are more input lines in your operational Cisco firmware, apply SSH to the remaining lines as well. Verify the number of transport lines in show running output:

```
cisco4948-ip(config)# line vty 5 15
cisco4948-ip(config-line)# transport input ssh
cisco4948-ip(config-line)# exit
cisco4948-ip(config-line)# end
```

After this change is in place, telnet on the switch is disabled and may be verified. SSH connectivity should be the only allowed connection method.

Finally, with all configuration changes complete, save the current configuration, write to NVRAM, and also save the configuration in bootflash with a unique name for easy reference:

```
cisco4948-ip# copy running-config startup-config all
cisco4948-ip# copy running-config bootflash:cisco4948-ip-confg-with-ssh
cisco4948-ip# write memory
Building configuration...
Compressed configuration from 6725 bytes to 2261 bytes[OK]
```

The configuration is complete. The bootflash on the 4948 is large enough to hold both the original IOS version and the updated SSH-capable IOS version, so no cleanup is required.

Force Booting the Cisco Switch

You will need to perform these steps only if and when the Cisco switch does not start after applying the firmware update. These steps require physical access to the Cisco switch:

1. Find out which com port your prolific USB-to-serial cable is connected to on your laptop. You can confirm this from the Device Manager (in Windows).
2. Connect to the console port of the Cisco switch, not the mgt port. This is the top port on the far right on the x2 Cisco switch.
3. The console cable will be a cat5 on one end. Plug this end into the device. You can use a console-to-USB converter to plug it into your laptop.
4. 9600 8,1 is usually your connect speed. Use a terminal program such as putty and note your com port and set the baud rate.
5. Push Return and you should see the prompt.
6. Type in `enable` to get a prompt.
7. Issue the boot command to start up the switch.

Upgrading the KVM Switch

Upgrade the Avocent MergePoint Unity KVM Switch by downloading updates available from Avocent. The minimum recommended firmware version is 1.2.8. For KVM upgrade, which is straightforward, simply go to the web interface, use tftp to copy file FL0620-AVO-1.18.0.22011.fl to KVM, and then update the firmware file. You can download updates from www.avocent.com/Pages/GenericTwoColumn .aspx?id=12541.

Upgrading PDUs

The PDUs are part of Exadata and ZFS and are responsible for supplying redundant power to the systems. In some cases this component is neglected, but it should not be. Keeping the firmware of the PDU updated should be part of your full Exadata stack and ZFS upgrade.

Reference the Oracle Support Note README for "Oracle Power Distribution Unit (PDU)—Patch 16523441—Metering Unit Firmware and HTML Interface v1.06." The downloaded .zip file contains three update files:

- MKAPP_Vx.x.dl—metering unit firmware
- HTML_Vx.x.dl—HTML interface files
- pdu_eth_110324.mib—mib file

If the .zip file also contains a text file, review it for any additional information about the firmware updates. Exercise caution when updating the firmware. You must update both the metering unit firmware and the HTML interface pages. Failure to update the HTML pages causes certain pages of the interface not to display, which renders the web interface unusable.

1. On a system connected to the network, type the metering unit IP address in a web browser's address line to connect to the PDU metering unit. Ask your network administrator for the IP address of the PDU metering unit.

2. Click on the Net Configuration link and log in as an admin user as prompted. By default, both the admin username and password are admin.

3. Scroll down the page until you see the Firmware-Update heading.

4. Click on the Browse button and locate the MKAPP_Vx.x.dl file you downloaded previously.

5. Click the Submit button to update the metering unit firmware. After updating the firmware, you are prompted to update the HTML interface.

6. Click on the Browse button again, log in as an admin user, and locate the HTML_Vx.x.dl file you downloaded previously.

7. Click the Submit button to update the HTML interface.

8. Click on the Module Info link to verify the firmware revision level and confirm that you updated the firmware and HTML interface successfully.

ZFS Upgrade

Now let's review the steps for upgrading the ZFS Storage Appliance model 7420. Oracle recommends that Firefox or the Chrome Internet browser be used rather than Internet Explorer when updating the ZFS.

Note
Oracle Support will provide help to do the ZFS upgrade. This is a mandatory requirement to upgrade the Service Processor SP/ILOM and BIOS.

Ensure that the following files are downloaded for the ZFS upgrade from Oracle Support from the Patches tab: p14363313_14_Generic.zip BIOS and SP firmware. Oracle Support uses the contents of the .zip file to apply an update to the ZFS. To start the ZFS SA firmware update, go to the ZFS maintenance page and select SYSTEM, and click Available updates. Click the + symbol next to Available updates and upload the two ZFS support bundle files. Upload the .gz file for each support bundle. It will say it is unpacking; this will not apply the ZFS file, only stage it. This step can be prepped prior to an outage window.

The file is staged on Exadata Database Node 1 for BIOS/ILOM update for the ZFS: /u01/app/oracle/exadata_patch/ZFS_BIOS_ILOM_UPDATE/p14363313_14_Generic.zip.

Create a support bundle before the upgrade; Oracle Support is required to assist in the actual upgrade.

ZFSSA Configuration and Upgrade

Confirm that each DB Node's /etc/fstab file has the `actimeo=0` parameter set accordingly:

```
192.168.10.23:/export/backup1 /zfs/backup1 nfs
rw,bg,hard,nointr,noacl,rsize=131072,wsize=1048576,tcp,vers=3,timeo=600, actimeo=0
```

The ZFSSA configuration process involves the following three requirements:

1. Stand-alone 7420 is based on X4470 hardware.
2. Current appliance OS is 2011.1.3.
3. Current BIOS level is 09030115.

ZFS Update Stage 1

In the first stage of the ZFSSA update, we upgrade to the 2011.1.4.2 code and subsequently upgrade to the latest code, 2013.1.1.1.

First, read and understand the document "Sun Storage 7000 Unified Storage System: How to Upgrade the Appliance Kit Software and Service Processor BIOS/ILOM Firmware" (Oracle Support Note ID 1513423.1). This document outlines six steps. You need to follow steps 1 through 5 to upgrade from 2011.1.3 to 2011.1.4.2 (you can skip step 6, the BIOS upgrade, as this will be done once the upgrade to 2013 code is completed).

The document also references a release matrix that contains links to download the following OS upgrade patches:

- 2011.1.4.2—https://updates.oracle.com/Orion/Services/download/p15750578_201110_Generic.zip?aru=16672629&patch_file=p15750578_201110_Generic.zip
- 2013.1.1.1—https://updates.oracle.com/Orion/Services/download/p17945242_20131_Generic.zip?aru=17067413&patch_file=p17945242_20131_Generic.zip

Once you understand the process, download the 2011.1.4.2 and 2013.1.1.1 upgrade images.

Next, upgrade from the current code, 2011.1.3, to 2011.1.4.2 using the upgrade document. Once the upgrade is complete, repeat the same procedure to upgrade from 2011.1.4.2 to 2013.1.1.1.

Once the upgrade is complete, you can move to stage 2 of the update.

ZFS Update Stage 2

After both upgrades in stage 1 are complete, begin stage 2 by logging a new SR against the serial number of the 7420 appliance. This schedules an Oracle TSC (Technical Solutions Center) engineer to remotely upgrade SP/ILOM and BIOS. (It's recommended that you log an SR as soon as the schedule is known.)

Let TSC know the current BIOS level, 09030115, and advise that it's an appliance that will be upgraded once the appliance is running 2013.1.1.1 code.

Next, download the BIOS image to the client that will be used for the remote WebEx or shared shell session. Find the image by searching for patch ID 14363313—SP 3.0.16.13.a r74558 BIOS 09.05.01.02 patchId 14363313.

Oracle TSC remotely upgrades SP/ILOM and BIOS image from 09030115 to version SP 3.0.16.13.a r74558 BIOS 09.05.01.02 patchId 14363313. Once the upgrade is complete, they will apply BIOS settings to the BIOS using the remote session.

Once both stage 1 and stage 2 are complete, the ZFS Storage Appliance is fully up-to-date.

Updating ZFS BIOS

This section covers the steps Oracle Support or a certified partner runs to update ZFS BIOS. They are listed here for your review only. For the BIOS update, upload the pkg file from within the p14363313_14_Generic.zip file, ILOM-3_0_16_13_a_ r74558-Sun_Fire_X4470.pkg.

```
# ssh zfssadr-ilom
The authenticity of host 'zfssadr-ilom (10.43.47.132)' can't be established.
RSA key fingerprint is d1:6b:ea:ac:28:c2:2a:10:30:79:92:a8:0f:18:18:8a.
Are you sure you want to continue connecting (yes/no)? yes
Warning: Permanently added 'zfssadr-ilom,10.43.47.132' (RSA) to the list
of known hosts.
Password:
Oracle(R) Integrated Lights Out Manager
Version 3.0.16.13.a r74558
Copyright (c) 2012, Oracle and/or its affiliates. All rights reserved.

-> stop -f SYS
Are you sure you want to immediately stop /SYS (y/n)? y
Stopping /SYS immediately

-> start SYS
Are you sure you want to start /SYS (y/n)? y
Starting /SYS

-> stop /SP/console
Are you sure you want to stop /SP/console (y/n)? y

-> start /SP/console
Are you sure you want to start /SP/console (y/n)? y

Serial console started.  To stop, type ESC (
```

1. Hit Ctrl-E, then Ctrl-S to get into the BIOS.
2. Go to the PCIPnP menu and disable all PCIe slots and also the I/O Allocation Slot [0-9].
3. Enable the I/O Allocation for the Cluster in BIOS settings.
4. In the Boot Settings menu, enable the Expert Mode, and issue Ctrl-U to invoke it.
5. In the Boot Settings Configuration, enable Persistent Boot Mode.
6. Hit Esc to go to the top-level menu and then save the changes and exit.
7. Go into the BIOS menu and check Boot device priority. Check for the HHDP0 as the first and HHDP1 as the second boot entry/mirrored system disk.
8. Verify the new BIOS version by clicking the Sun logo in the upper left corner. It should be American Megatrends Inc. 09050102 07/03/2012.
9. From the ZFS Management Host, bring online all controllers and issue the shell command to run the following command:

```
# zpool online dr-pool c0t5000CCA01B1DF4A0d0
```

10. Check the hardware status by running the following command:

```
fmadm faulty
```

11. From the ZFS Management web interface, go to Maintenance Hardware to verify that no problems exist.

Summary

In summary, we hope this chapter provided clear guidance on the steps required to do a full Exadata stack upgrade and also for the ZFS Appliance upgrade. The steps required are lengthy and we do recommend that you cross-reference the steps provided here with the READMEs from Oracle Support for the specific patch or upgrade steps you will be executing in your environment. As stated in the beginning of this chapter, please test the upgrade in a non-production environment and document your own notes and lessons learned to ensure that you will have a successful production upgrade. Good luck with your Exadata and ZFS upgrade endeavors!

## 12

ZFS Storage Appliance for Exadata

Storage requirements are exploding across the Oracle industry, often beyond DBA control. We are constantly asked to maximize existing resources and do more with less, and the reality is that data volumes are increasing exponentially. What kind of options do we have to maximize our storage on the Exadata? Whether you have adopted normal redundancy or high redundancy for your High Capacity or High Performance SAS disks, you will want to squeeze every megabyte out of the Exadata Storage Server.

How can we do that? The best answer is the ZFS Storage Appliance (ZFSSA). This chapter demonstrates how you can couple the ZFS Storage Appliance with the Exadata to fully maximize space utilization by tiering storage on the Exadata and ZFSSA.

This chapter provides insight into optimal RMAN backup settings, dNFS settings, and quick scripts used to drive throughput on the ZFSSA across all the Compute Nodes. You will also learn about the power of implementing snapshots and clones to provision databases on the fly.

This chapter is primarily aimed at database architects, DMAs, and managers who support databases on the Exadata and are interested in stretching the storage footprint on the Exadata. This chapter is also for DMAs who are interested in optimal backup strategies and snapshot/cloning features available with the Exadata on the ZFSSA.

ZFSSA is not just for the Exadata. This chapter also reveals additional use cases for the ZFSSA that are relevant for your IT infrastructure.

ZFS Family Line

In September 2013, Oracle added the ZS3-2 and ZS3-4 line of appliances to their ZFS Storage Appliance family line and updated their 7420M2 with internal SAS. The ZS3 ships with OS8 code. The 7420M2 model ships with the older OS7 (2011.1.7) code but can be updated to OS8 at your convenience. For the latest information on either the ZS3-2 or ZS3-4, you can peruse the following URLs:

- **ZS3-2**—www.oracle.com/us/products/servers-storage/storage/nas/zs3-2/overview/index.html
- **ZS3-4**—www.oracle.com/us/products/servers-storage/storage/nas/zs3-4/overview/index.html

Here are the pertinent highlights that you should be aware of for the ZS3-*x* Storage Appliances:

- ZS3-2 can reach 768TB in capacity with eight PCIe slots and 15TB cache.
- ZS3-4 can reach 3500TB in capacity with 14 PCIe slots and 25TB cache, 2TB of DRAM.
- Both offer a full range of connectivity (10Gb E, 40Gb IB, 16Gb FC).

When we talk about storage in the context of this chapter, we are referring to the Sun ZFS Storage 7000 Appliances. Previously, the similar line of storage appliances was called Sun Storage 7000 Unified Storage System and consisted of the 7110, 7210, 7310, and 7410 models. The Sun Storage 7000 Unified Storage System evolved into the Sun ZFS Storage 7000 Appliances, which consist of the 7120, 7320, 7420, and 7720 models. The current line of ZFS Storage Appliances consists of the ZS3-2 and ZS3-4. Here are some highlights of the 7120, 7320, 7420, and 7720 ZFS Storage Appliance product lines:

- **Sun ZFS Storage 7120**
  - High-capacity storage at entry-level pricing
  - Up to 120TB raw capacity
  - 24GB DDR3 DRAM
  - 96GB Write Flash
- **Sun ZFS Storage 7320**
  - High-availability storage with Flash-enabled hybrid storage pools
  - Optional cluster for high availability

* Up to 192TB raw capacity
* Up to 144GB DRAM
* Up to 4TB Flash-enabled read cache
* Up to 288GB Flash-enabled write cache

- **Sun ZFS Storage 7420**
  * High-performance, high-capacity, high-availability unified storage
  * Consists of either a single storage controller or two storage controllers in a high-availability cluster configuration
  * Up to 24 Sun disk shelves
  * Up to 1.15PB (petabytes) raw capacity
  * Up to 1TB DDR3 DRAM
  * Up to 4TB Flash-enabled read cache
  * Up to 1.7TB Flash-enabled write cache

- **Sun ZFS Storage 7720**
  * Industry-leading density and simplicity
  * High-availability, high-density, rack-scale configuration
  * Two storage controllers in a high-availability cluster configuration installed in a Sun Storage 7700 cabinet
  * 12 drive cages
  * Up to 720GB raw capacity
  * Up to 1TB DDR3 DRAM cache
  * Up to 4TB Flash-based read cache
  * Up to 432GB Flash-based write cache

Note
For a detailed overview and information on hardware configuration, review the following web site: http://docs.oracle.com/cd/E22471_01/html/821-1792/ maintenance__hardware__overview__7420_7720.html.

The ZFSSA line of products is evolving and changing each year. The ZFSSA 7420 model can scale up to 2.59PB of raw capacity, can accommodate up to two controllers with up to 2TB read Flash Cache per storage controller, and can hold up to 292GB write Flash Cache per disk shelf. Most importantly, the ZFSSA 7420 accepts up to Quad Gigabit Ethernet UTP, Dual 10GigE, QDR InfiniBand HCA, and 8Gb FC HBA. What we are interested in the most is the Dual 10GigE and QDR InfiniBand HCA to drive performance of our space utilization on the ZFSSA.

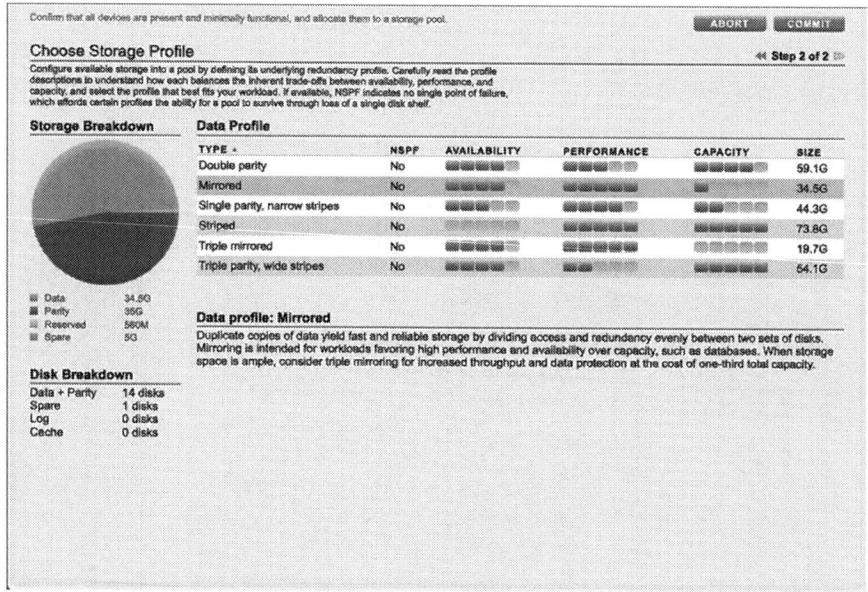

Figure 12.1   Choosing a storage profile

Once you purchase the ZFSSA for the Exadata, you have to choose a data protection option based on performance and capacity according to your business requirements, as shown in Figure 12.1. If you want the best protection and performance, choose the mirrored option. If you are leveraging the ZFSSA for just backups, you may opt not to do mirroring and choose double parity instead. Similarly, if you choose to place only archived data files (not active data files), you can choose the double parity option also.

On the Exadata, the only protocol that we want is NFS. Once shares are allocated from the ZFSSA, we can Direct NFS–mount the shares on the Exadata.

Increased Storage Capacity

Oracle Exadata and ZFSSA are optimized at the data protection layer to provide the best solution for storage capacity in the industry. Oracle leverages the QDR IB fabric technology to deliver 40Gb of extreme low-latency bandwidth per port between the Database Compute Nodes and the ZFSSA over Oracle dNFS. dNFS is an optimized NFS client configured for Oracle Databases that provides a high-bandwidth solution for data transfer over the standard NFS protocol. Oracle RMAN is the perfect solution for backup and recovery of Oracle Databases on the Exadata. With the ZFSSA, the administration and maintenance of the database backups are simplified and enhanced through native ZFSSA features such as snapshots and clones. Backups can also be parallelized in all the Database Nodes and ZFSSA controllers and IB interfaces for ultimate scalability and throughput. ZFSSA also provides options to leverage the Incremental Forever backup architecture to reduce the backup window and restore time. Last, Oracle incorporates the native Exadata features such as deduplication and EHCC to the ZFSSA.

One of the biggest business drivers for moving to the Exadata is database consolidation. As we consolidate databases and notice that we need additional capacity, what do we do if we hit 80 or 90% space utilization on the DATA_DG disk group? Better yet, what do we do if our company is interested in purchasing the Exadata and we realize our database footprint is larger than what Oracle provides on the full Exadata? Obviously, purchasing additional storage servers is an option to increase your capacity footprint, but many companies are opting to purchase a ZFSSA simply for cost effectiveness.

Not only do we have to calculate the size of the databases housed on the Exadata, we have to take into consideration the space required for database backups. We can perform backups to the RECO_DG disk group or to the DB file system. Neither of these solutions allows for the backup to leave the Exadata ecosystem, nor do they take into consideration the complete loss of storage or failures at the disk levels beyond ASM normal or high redundancy.

On the Exadata, we can perform backups over the network. Network backups can be over 1GigE, 10GigE, or 40GigE InfiniBand. In this chapter, we cover only 10GigE and InfiniBand (more on the InfiniBand side). We can perform D2D backups from the Exadata to the ZFSSA over extremely low-latency 40GigE InfiniBand leveraging Oracle's dNFS. The ZFSSA provides deduplication and Exadata HCC support. For larger customers, we can leverage image copy backups and perform Incremental Forever backups.

Reclaiming Resources and Space from DBFS

Once you have the ZFSSA in place, you can completely eliminate the DBFS (database file system) from the Exadata. Not only are you eliminating the Clusterware resource from the Exadata but also the database that houses the DBFS contents. If the Exadata has a huge DBFS requirement, the tablespace that houses the DBFS table must be moved from the SYSTEM_DG to either the DATA_DG or the RECO_DG. Removing the DBFS database can free up quite a bit of valuable space from the DATA_DG or the RECO_DG.

Information Lifecycle Management

ZFSSA storage costs are low compared to adding Storage Cells to existing Exadata. On each ZFSSA, disk space is scalable up to 1.72PB of disk drives (1720TB), and Flash storage is scalable up to 10TB. Our goal is to leverage high-transactional data on a DATA_DG disk group as Tier 1 storage. We can move less active data that is over one or two years old (or even three to six months old) from Tier 1 to Tier 2 storage (RECO_DG). Ultimately, we can move data that is older than two to three years from Tier 2 to Tier 3 (ZFSSA).

As we move data from Tier 1 to Tier 2 storage, we can leverage Warehouse compression for Tier 2 storage. If your goal is to achieve the highest level of performance, you do not want to compress the contents of your DATA_DG at all. As you move data from Tier 1 to Tier 2, you can leverage various compression options. We also want to take advantage of any partitioning strategy to move data from different tiers of storage. As we move from Tier 1 to Tier 2, we can leverage HCC compression in Warehouse compression mode. You should choose Warehouse compression LOW if load time service levels are more critical than query performance. Furthermore, we can achieve a deeper level of HCC (ARCHIVE HIGH) as we move data from Tier 2 to Tier 3 storage. With the ARCHIVE compression mode, our goal is to sacrifice performance for maximum storage gains. You should use ARCHIVE compression only if the tables or partitions are rarely accessed.

As we take into consideration Tier 3 storage, we can architect for situations where Oracle data files can be made read-only. For tables that are partitioned and have archiving requirements, older partitions become great candidates for read-only tablespaces where we can skip read-only data files during RMAN backups. Our strategic goal is to back up the read-only tablespaces once and be able to forget about them for any future backups. After three years, we can even convert data to external tables or external Data Pump files.

ZFSSA Browser User Interface

The most important tool for the ZFSSA administrator is the Browser User Interface (BUI). The BUI is the graphical interface to the ZFSSA and allows for administration, configuration and maintenance, reporting, and performance visualization. If you are new to the ZFSSA, you are strongly encouraged to leverage the BUI.

You can log in to the BUI by directing your browser to either the IP address or the hostname designated in your DNS for the NET-0 port (also known as the management port). During the initial configuration of the ZFS, you will plug your laptop directly to the console port and configure the hostname and IP address. The default port designation for the BUI is 215, and to access the login page, you can leverage either https://ipaddress:215 or https://hostname:215.

Alternatively, you can log in directly to the management port via SSH to the CLI. You can use any terminal emulator that supports SSH2 protocol to log in to the ZFSSA. Initially, you will log in using the root-privileged account. As your organization matures and develops standards to log in to the ZFSSA, you can create multiple roles and accounts.

The ZFSSA CLI is designed to provide mirrored capabilities and functionality of the BUI. The CLI also provides a rich and powerful scripting ecosystem to automate tasks and to build repetitive processes.

Creating NFS Shares

On the ZFSSA, we can create NFS shares to serve directories and files with Exadata Compute Nodes over the IB network. We can create NFS shares from the ZFSSA in the BUI or from the command line. This section demonstrates the simplicity of creating shares with both approaches. We start with the BUI method. Once you log in to your ZFSSA, click on the Shares link at the top. Your screen will change to display all the projects and file systems, as shown in Figure 12.2.

Click on the + sign to the left of Filesystems. The Create Filesystem window will pop up for you to edit, as shown in Figure 12.3.

In this window, associate the file system to a project (take the default if you do not have projects created yet) and name your share. Click on the Apply button when you are finished. You have successfully created your first NFS share.

We can achieve the exact same result from the command line. Whether you prefer to use the BUI or the CLI, you should learn how to manage the ZFSSA from

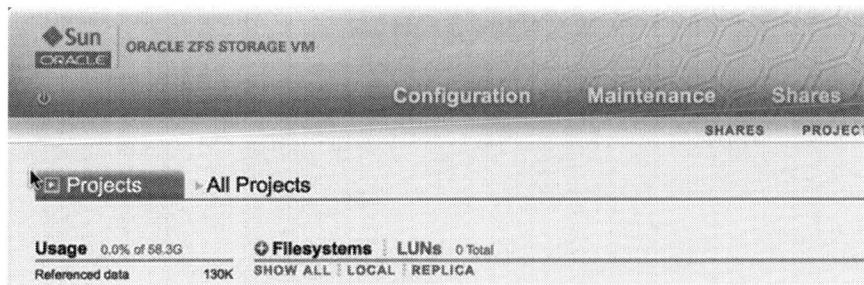

Figure 12.2 Displaying projects and file systems for shares

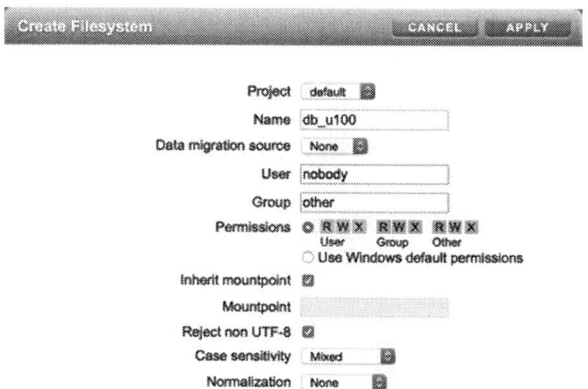

Figure 12.3   Settings for creating the file system

the CLI. There may be situations when the BUI is not available to you, especially in environments where you have to traverse through a series of firewalls or have issues with port availability. From the CLI, you can easily create shares:

```
zfs1:> shares
zfs1:shares> select default
zfs1:shares default> filesystem db_u200
zfs1:shares default/db_u200 (uncommitted)> commit
```

After you create your share, set the appropriate permissions and security settings:

```
zfs1:shares default> select db_u200
zfs1:shares default/db_u200> set aclinherit=discard
                aclinherit = discard (uncommitted)
zfs1:shares default/db_u200> set sharenfs="rw,anon=0"
                sharenfs = rw,anon=0 (uncommitted)
zfs1:shares default/db_u200> set root_permissions=755
            root_permissions = 755 (uncommitted)
zfs1:shares default/db_u200> commit
```

That completes the setup. Let's look at all the properties of the new share that we just created:

```
zfs1:shares default/db_u200> show
Properties:
                aclinherit = discard
                   aclmode = discard (inherited)
                     atime = true (inherited)
            casesensitivity = mixed
                  checksum = fletcher4 (inherited)
```

```
            compression = off (inherited)
                  dedup = false (inherited)
          compressratio = 100
                 copies = 1 (inherited)
               creation = Tue Feb 05 2013 22:36:49 GMT+0000 (UTC)
                logbias = latency (inherited)
             mountpoint = /export/db_u200 (inherited)
          normalization = none
                  quota = 0
             quota_snap = true
               readonly = false (inherited)
             recordsize = 128K (inherited)
            reservation = 0
       reservation_snap = true
               rstchown = true (inherited)
          secondarycache = all (inherited)
                 shadow = none
                 nbmand = false (inherited)
               sharesmb = off (inherited)
               sharenfs = rw,anon=0
                snapdir = hidden (inherited)
               utf8only = false
                  vscan = false (inherited)
               sharedav = off (inherited)
               shareftp = off (inherited)
              sharesftp = off (inherited)
              sharetftp = (inherited)
                   pool = Default
         canonical_name = Default/local/default/db_u200
               exported = true (inherited)
               nodestroy = false
             space_data = 130K
        space_unused_res = 0
         space_snapshots = 0
         space_available = 58.3G
            space_total = 130K
             root_group = other
        root_permissions = 755
              root_user = nobody
                 origin =
```

Preparing Exadata for Direct NFS

Before we can mount any file system over the network, we have preliminary system administration tasks that need to be performed on all the Exadata Compute Nodes. To start, we must start the portmap, NFS, and NFSLOCK services. In addition, we must enable the services with the chkconfig command to be persistent across server reboots. To start the services, execute the service command from the sbin directory and pass two arguments: the name of the service followed by what you want it to do (start, stop, or status).

Following are the exact commands to execute to enable the NFS services:

```
# cat zfs.1
export PATH=$PATH:/usr/local/bin:/sbin
dcli -l root -g /home/oracle/dbs_group /sbin/chkconfig portmap on
dcli -l root -g /home/oracle/dbs_group /sbin/service portmap start
```

```
dcli -l root -g /home/oracle/dbs_group /sbin/chkconfig nfs on
dcli -l root -g /home/oracle/dbs_group /sbin/service nfs start
dcli -l root -g /home/oracle/dbs_group /sbin/chkconfig nfslock on
dcli -l root -g /home/oracle/dbs_group /sbin/service nfslock start
```

Upon execution, you should see results similar to the following:

```
# ksh ./zfs.1
exaddb01: Starting portmap: [  OK  ]
exaddb02: Starting portmap: [  OK  ]
exaddb01: Starting NFS services:  [  OK  ]
exaddb01: Starting NFS quotas: [  OK  ]
exaddb01: Starting NFS daemon: [  OK  ]
exaddb01: Starting NFS mountd: [  OK  ]
exaddb01: Starting RPC idmapd: [  OK  ]
exaddb02: Starting NFS services:  [  OK  ]
exaddb02: Starting NFS quotas: [  OK  ]
exaddb02: Starting NFS daemon: [  OK  ]
exaddb02: Starting NFS mountd: [  OK  ]
exaddb02: Starting RPC idmapd: [  OK  ]
exaddb01: Starting NFS statd: [  OK  ]
exaddb02: Starting NFS statd: [  OK  ]
```

After the services are started and enabled, you can leverage the `chkconfig` command again followed by the `--list` option (double dashes) and confirm that the services are configured to restart as part of the server reboot process. In particular, we want these services to restart in run levels 3, 4, and 5:

```
# /usr/local/bin/dcli -l root -g /home/oracle/dbs_group
/sbin/chkconfig --list |egrep -i "nfs|port"
exaddb01: nfs      0:off   1:off   2:on    3:on    4:on    5:on    6:off
exaddb01: nfslock  0:off   1:off   2:on    3:on    4:on    5:on    6:off
exaddb01: portmap  0:off   1:off   2:on    3:on    4:on    5:on    6:off
exaddb02: nfs      0:off   1:off   2:on    3:on    4:on    5:on    6:off
exaddb02: nfslock  0:off   1:off   2:on    3:on    4:on    5:on    6:off
exaddb02: portmap  0:off   1:off   2:on    3:on    4:on    5:on    6:off
```

Next, we want to enable dNFS on all the Exadata Compute Nodes. You can leverage the dcli to simply enable Oracle dNFS on all of the Compute Nodes simultaneously:

```
$ dcli -l oracle -g /home/oracle/dbs_group make -f $ORACLE_HOME/rdbms/lib/ins_rdbms.mk
dnfs_on
```

In this example, we use dcli to run a set of commands on all or a subset of Compute Nodes in parallel. dcli can save you an enormous amount of time and can help mitigate human errors that often occur when running the same command multiple times on each individual Compute Node.

Another requirement for dNFS is that the /etc/hosts.allow and /etc/hosts.deny files must have permissions for read-write at the owner level and read-only for group and world access:

```
# /usr/local/bin/dcli -l root -g /home/oracle/dbs_group
chmod 644 /etc/hosts.allow
# /usr/local/bin/dcli -l root -g /home/oracle/dbs_group
chmod 644 /etc/hosts.deny
```

We leverage the dcli executable again to confirm that our commands executed successfully:

```
# /usr/local/bin/dcli -l root -g /home/oracle/dbs_group
ls -l /etc/hosts.allow /etc/hosts.deny
exaddb01: -rw-r--r-- 1 root root 161 Jan 12  2000 /etc/hosts.allow
exaddb01: -rw-r--r-- 1 root root 347 Jan 12  2000 /etc/hosts.deny
exaddb02: -rw-r--r-- 1 root root 161 Jan 12  2000 /etc/hosts.allow
exaddb02: -rw-r--r-- 1 root root 347 Jan 12  2000 /etc/hosts.deny
```

Next, we must modify the Linux kernel parameters in the /etc/sysctl.conf file. The first parameter, net.core.wmem_max, resides in the middle of the file. Notice the line that is commented out; that is the original value that was configured with the Exadata:

```
Modify Kernel Parameters (in the middle of the file):
#net.core.wmem_max = 2097152
# -- Modified per ZFS
net.core.wmem_max = 4194304
```

The new value is what we want to configure for dNFS with the ZFSSA. In addition to the net.core.wmem_max parameter, we will also configure the net.ipv4.tcp_wmem and net.ipv4.tcp_rmem parameters to 4Mbs. Since these are new parameters, we can add them to the end of the sysctl.conf file:

```
# -- At the end of the file
# --
# -- Added for ZFS
net.ipv4.tcp_wmem=4194304
net.ipv4.tcp_rmem=4194304
```

The Exadata Compute Nodes do not need to be restarted. Once the kernel parameters are set, we can dynamically reload them with the sysctl -p command:

```
# /usr/local/bin/dcli -l root
-g /home/oracle/dbs_group /sbin/sysctl -p
exaddb01: net.ipv4.ip_forward = 0
exaddb01: net.ipv4.conf.default.rp_filter = 1
exaddb01: kernel.sysrq = 1
exaddb01: kernel.softlockup_panic = 1
exaddb01: kernel.core_uses_pid = 1
exaddb01: kernel.shmmax = 4398046511104
exaddb01: kernel.shmall = 1073741824
exaddb01: kernel.msgmni = 2878
exaddb01: kernel.msgmax = 8192
```

```
exaddb01: kernel.msgmnb = 65536
...
...
...
...
```

You can also pass the −a option with the sysctl command to display all the run-time kernel parameter settings.

Again, we can leverage dcli to execute the kernel reload across all Exadata Compute Nodes. In a Quarter Rack, this may not be a big deal, but as you start supporting Half Racks or even a Full Rack Exadata, dcli will be an important tool for you to master.

Once the kernel parameters are set and all ancillary preliminary requirements are satisfied, we can proceed to the database component. To enable dNFS, we must execute the make command with the dnfs_on option:

```
$ make -f ins_rdbms.mk dnfs_on
rm -f /u01/app/oracle/product/11.2.0/dbhome_1/lib/libodm11.so;
cp /u01/app/oracle/product/11.2.0/dbhome_1/lib/libnfsodm11.so
/u01/app/oracle/product/11.2.0/dbhome_1/lib/libodm11.so
```

You will need to repeat the dNFS settings on every Exadata Compute Node.

Another pair of services that you need to check for are cpuspeed and irqbalance. On the Exadata, these services are disabled by default, which optimizes through-put for some network devices. The services cpuspeed and irqbalance can reduce NFS throughput over 10Gb Ethernet. If these services are not being used, or their use is less valuable than maximizing NFS performance over 10Gb Ethernet, the services can be manually disabled after boot or dynamically disabled with the chkconfig and service commands:

```
# chkconfig cpuspeed off
# service cpuspeed stop
# chkconfig irqbalance off

# /sbin/chkconfig --list |egrep -i "cpu|irq"
irqbalance        0:off    1:off    2:on    3:on    4:on    5:on    6:off

# /sbin/service irqbalance status
irqbalance (pid 6756) is running...
```

Configuring and Mounting the NFS Share

On the Exadata, dNFS is the preferred solution over the Linux kernel-managed NFS. Instead of leveraging the operating system kernel NFS client, we can con-figure Oracle Database(s) to access NFS V3 servers using an Oracle internal dNFS client. This optimizes the I/O access path to the NFS server, which provides improved scalability and reliability.

We will have to configure dNFS on the Exadata Compute Nodes:

```
$ cat /etc/oranfstab
server: zfssa-dr-h1
path: 192.168.10.23
path: 192.168.10.25
export: /export/backup1 mount: /zfs/backup1
export: /export/backup2 mount: /zfs/backup2
```

Next, we manually NFS-mount the /dNFS share with the following settings:

```
# mount -t nfs -o rw,bg,hard,nointr,noacl,rsize=131072,wsize=1048576,tcp,vers=3,timeo=600
192.168.10.25:/export/dNFS /dNFS
```

For complete NFS options and settings, consult the following Oracle Support Note: "Mount Options for Oracle Files When Used with NFS on NAS Devices" (ID 359515.1).

Snapshots

Snapshots are point-in-time read-only copies of the file system or LUN. Snapshots initially do not consume any space, but as the active share data content changes, the previous unreferenced blocks will be kept as part of the snapshot (copy-on-write). Over time, if the active data volumes change, the snapshot can grow as big as the file system at the time the snapshot was created.

Shares support the ability to roll back to a previous snapshot. When you perform a rollback, newer snapshots and clones of the snapshot are destroyed. To create a new snapshot of a share, you can simply leverage the BUI. From the BUI, drill down into the share properties and click on the + sign next to the Snapshots label on the header of the Snapshot section. When you click on the + sign, the Create Snapshot window pops up. Designate a name for your snapshot and click the Apply button, as shown in Figure 12.4.

As a general rule, you should determine a strategy for naming your snapshots since there can potentially be an unlimited number of them. This allows you to apply purging rules or find them easily if you have hundreds of snapshots.

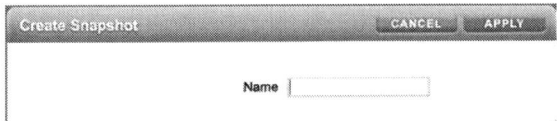

Figure 12.4   Creating a snapshot in ZFS

Snapshot Architecture

We have full flexibility and control over the number of snapshots that we can take. We even have the flexibility to automate our snapshots just by clicking a few screens. Proper architecture and implementation of snapshots significantly reduces your storage requirements, especially for your lower environments (DEV, QA, TEST). In addition to saving money and storage, time to refresh these lower environments significantly decreases. Just as important, refresh technology is simplified because an up-to-date image copy of the database becomes available in lower environments by simply sharing and NFS-mounting a share of the snapshot to the target hosts.

Another architectural consideration may be to perform snapshots of your backup file systems on a regular basis such as daily or nightly or even more often, such as every hour for the archive log destination. For RAC databases on the Exadata, we can specify multiple destinations for archive logs. One location where the archive logs can go is the RECO_DG disk group, and the second copy of the archive logs can go to the ZFSSA file system. This architecture not only simplifies your archive log backup strategy without inducing load on the Exadata Compute Nodes but also adds another level of protection by completely segmenting off all backups away from the Exadata nodes.

As we perform snapshots on the ZFSSA, we also need to be conscientious about removing snapshots. All changes made to the snapshot location (add, delete, or modify) incur additional storage on the ZFSSA. It is imperative that we also design a purge strategy to remove older snapshots.

For example, we can have a snapshot architecture that performs snapshots on a daily basis on the backup file system. We can have another rule that removes all snapshots that are older than 60 days. Exercise caution as improper management of snapshots can easily fill up the remaining storage on the ZFSSA.

Snapshot Deployment Strategy

Let's look at practical use cases for snapshot deployments with Oracle backup and recovery considerations. We need to implement the Incremental Forever backup strategy to fully leverage snapshots of Oracle Databases with the ZFSSA. This backup strategy encompasses an image copy backup of the databases, performs incremental backups, and applies incremental backups to the image copy to sustain a baseline image copy of the database that is perpetually updated to mirror the production database on a nightly basis. For complete details of this technology, refer to Chapter 8.

A lot of companies house multiple copies of their production database for development, QA, and TEST databases. Worse, companies even have multiple copies such as DEV2, DEV3, and DEV4 and QA1, QA2, and so on. Snapshot deployment technology saves tremendous storage costs and simplifies provisioning of these databases.

Clones

A clone is a writable copy of a snapshot share. Similar to a snapshot, a clone does not consume any space initially, but as new changes occur on the cloned copy, the size of the clone grows relative to the changes on the cloned copy. Space is shared between snapshots and clones. There can be multiple clones per snapshot. The caveat is that when you destroy a snapshot, you also destroy all the clones associated with the snapshot. Let's quickly run through the process of creating a clone of a snapshot from the BUI, as shown in Figure 12.5. If you look carefully at the bottom right corner of Figure 12.5, you can also see that we have the capability to roll back to a snapshot or even destroy a snapshot.

To create a clone of a snapshot, simply click on the Create Clone + sign in the Clones section from the BUI. The Create Clone window appears, as displayed in Figure 12.6, for you to provide some basic information.

As with the snapshot, you must designate a name for the snapshot clone. The name of the clone cannot have a # or similar metadata characters. A snapshot clone

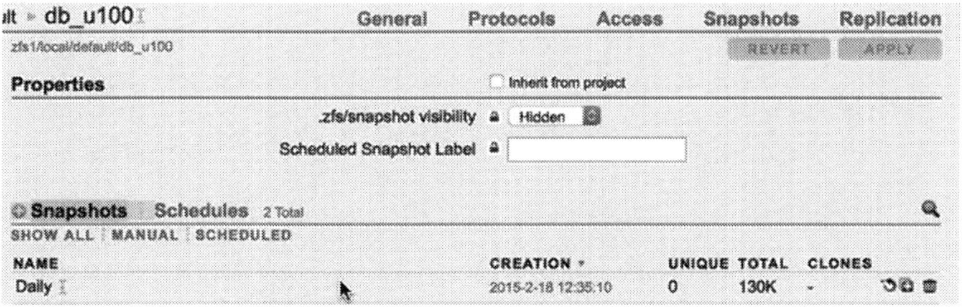

Figure 12.5   Snapshot and clone details

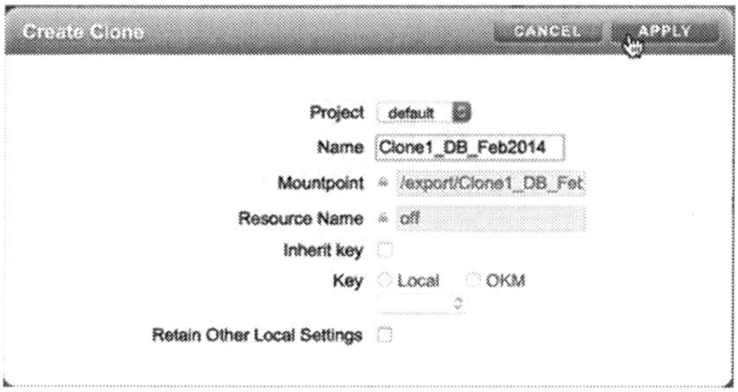

Figure 12.6   Settings for creating a clone

is considered to be a snapshot for all practical purposes when it comes to administration. You can have practically an unlimited number of clones for a snapshot.

Snapshots and Clones with Data Guard

On the other side of a Data Guard configuration, if you place physical standby data
files on the ZFSSA, you can create snapshots and clones of the physical standby
database and rapidly provision cloned databases for DEV, QA, hot fix testing, or
stress testing purposes.

The process for creating cloned databases from a snapshot is quite simple and
extremely fast:

1. Stop the managed recovery process (MRP) to place the standby database in a
   consistent state.

2. From the ZFSSA BUI, take a snapshot of the project or file system where the
   physical standby resides.

3. Once the snapshot is taken, resume MRP on the physical standby database.

4. From the snapshot taken, create a clone of the file systems from the BUI.

5. Next, dNFS-mount the cloned file system to the new database server at the
   physical standby site.

6. Finally, open the cloned physical standby database in read-write mode.

Unlike the snapshot standby feature of Oracle Database 11*g*, we do not have to
worry about running out of space for the archived logs or the amount of time it
will take to flashback the database. Another beauty of this architecture is that we
can create multiple snapshots and potentially an unlimited number of clones. The
number of snapshots and clones that we create is dependent on the amount of space
available on the ZFSSA. Also imagine multiple components of the application that
can be tested at the same time. How often do you hear that part of the QA team has
to wait for the other part of the QA team to finish so that they do not step on each
other? Also, imagine application releases being tested simultaneously with multiple clones of the database to deliver a faster application release cycle.

If you also happen to be running a DEV environment next to a physical standby,
you can have full production-size DEV databases for testing. If you do not modify
that much data in your DEV environment, which is what we would expect, the
actual space consumption would only be the size of the changes that you make. You
can also refresh DEV and QA environments exponentially faster. What would normally take hours or days can now be done in minutes.

Best-Practice Settings on ZFS Share

The default options for the ZFSSA share provide an adequate start, but we need to consider some best practices for RMAN backups and restorability, as shown in Figure 12.7. First, we want to set the database record size property to 128KB. The record size attribute controls the block size used by the file system. The default block size is not sufficient to hold large files. Valid values for this property can be from 512 to 128KB set to any power of 2 value.

The property setting for synchronous write bias controls the behavior for servicing synchronous writes. For purposes of performing RMAN image copy backups and backup sets, set the Synchronous write bias to Throughput. For incremental backups and incremental updates to image copies, set the Synchronous write bias to Latency.

Latency is the default value for the ZFSSA which leverages the log devices to provide faster response times. Database file placement on the ZFSSA requires the synchronous setting (Throughput) for heavier bandwidth.

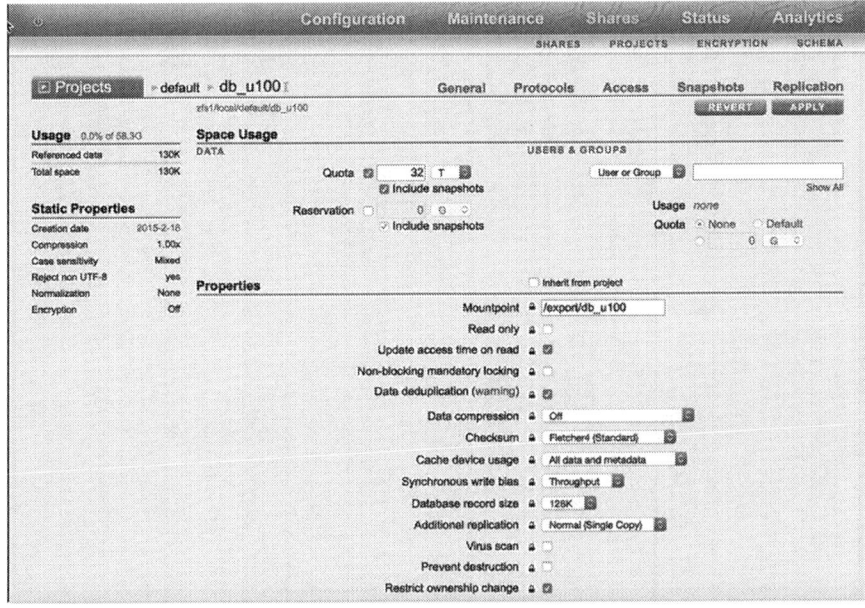

Figure 12.7   Property options for shares

Cache devices are configured as part of the storage pool. The property setting for Cache device usage controls whether cache devices are leveraged for the share. This property setting (secondary cache) needs to be set to None for backup sets, and for incrementally applied backups or database clone operations, Cache device usage needs to be set to All. Cache devices can provide an extra layer of caching for faster tiered access.

By default, data compression is not enabled on the ZFSSA. Data compression specifies whether the share can compress the data before being written to disk (storage pool). The Data compression property needs to be set to Off for performance-optimized systems and to LZJB for capacity-optimized systems. Obviously, data compression allows for greater storage capacity at the expense of additional CPU overhead. As with any kind of setting that can lead to possible performance degradation, you should test the settings for each compression option and recognize which setting produces the optimal performance overhead versus capacity savings. Our end goal is to leverage the ZFSSA for optimal Oracle Exadata backup and restore. Here are the other compression options on the ZFSSA:

- **LZJB (lzjb)**—This is the fastest option. It's a simple run-length encoding that works only for sufficiently simple inputs but doesn't consume much CPU.
- **GZIP-2 (gzip-2)**—This is a fast option. It's a lightweight version of the gzip compression algorithm.
- **GZIP (gzip)**—This is the default option. It is the standard gzip compression algorithm.
- **GZIP-9 (gzip-9)**—This provides the highest achievable compression using gzip. It consumes a significant amount of CPU and can often yield only marginal gains.

For RMAN backups from Exadata to the ZFSSA, we use LZJB if we want to enable compression from the Storage Tier. Gzip compression or replication can be considered for shares used to support business requirements.

We also need to specify the number of shares per pool as 1 for management-optimized systems. We need to specify the number of shares per pool as 8 for performance-optimized systems.

Just like any storage vendor, Oracle ZFSSA can also set quotas and minimum reservations. We can specify in our reservations to include snapshots as part of the quota.

Notice that we have the capability to set data deduplication on or off. Deduplication is the process of eliminating duplicate copies of data. In a standard deduplication process, data can be deduplicated at the level of files, blocks, or bytes. ZFSSA performs block-level deduplication since it is the finest level of granularity that makes sense for a general-purpose storage system. Chunks of blocks are checksummed using a hash function to uniquely identify data and prevent duplicate data from being stored. We want to enable deduplication because we store database files or backup image files that contain duplicate data.

Other Industry Use Cases

The ZFS Storage Appliance is not just for the Exadata. We can leverage it anywhere we can leverage an NAS appliance. Oracle E-Business Suite has a requirement for a shared apps tier. We can create shares on the ZFSSA to be presented to the E-Business Suite application server. E-Business Suite also has a requirement for a share on the database server to be shared with the application server. Again, a share can be presented from the ZFSSA.

One thing you will hear about ZFSSA more than anything else is that it can expand and protect Oracle Database Appliance (ODA). On the ODA, we get far more than additional capacity and a place to back up the database. Oracle also provides full HCC support on the ZFSSA.

If the disks and controllers are purchased to accommodate IOPS and throughput, we can run production databases on the ZFSSA. The workload of mission-critical databases can run on the ZFSSA if proper capacity-sizing exercises are performed.

Other use cases for the ZFSSA include the following:

- Plug and play with your existing environment on 10GigE as NFS Appliance.
- Run RAC or non-RAC databases over fiber channel (not just over dNFS).
- Rapidly provision physical standby or active standby with snapshots and clones.
- Rapidly clone databases with snapshots.

What a lot of customers are not aware of is that ZFSSA can also be leveraged with Oracle VM and VMware to support Oracle virtualization efforts. Whether you are virtualizing the middle tier or the complete Oracle stack including the database, the ZFSSA is fully integrated and certified with both virtualization technologies.

Learning on the Simulator

You can download the ZFS Storage Appliance simulator for Oracle's Virtual Box to test, configure, and prototype by visiting Oracle's website: www.oracle.com/technetwork/server-storage/sun-unified-storage/downloads/sun-simulator-1368816.html.

If you are new to the ZFSSA, you are strongly encouraged to download the virtual simulator for training purposes. The ZFSSA simulator VM is configured with 2048MB of memory and 125GB of dynamically allocated disk space. Exercise wise virtualization and make sure that your system has adequate resources (memory, disk space) to support the VM.

Summary

This chapter exposed the practicality and the usefulness of the ZFS Storage Appliance to anyone who is interested in expanding the storage options and footprint on the Exadata. We looked at how to set up direct NFS for the ZFS Storage Appliance and to drive performance in backups. We revealed the power of creating snapshots and cloning databases instantly and discussed how to take advantage of Data Guard databases to instantiate another copy of the database on the fly. We reviewed various RMAN strategies for you to take back to your enterprise and covered some best practices to leverage on the ZFSSA.

13

Exadata Performance Tuning

Exadata offers massive improvements in throughput and scalability for many applications. In most scenarios, these performance improvements can be achieved simply by "dropping in" an application. However, even the most zealous Exadata advocates would concede that tuning and troubleshooting are required to deliver the final mile of performance. Furthermore, Exadata is not a cheap solution, so it's important to be certain we configure the database machine for the maximum performance gains.

This chapter provides an overview of Exadata performance tuning, combining the general principles of Oracle Database tuning with the Exadata-specific technologies covered in detail elsewhere in this book.

Oracle Performance Tuning

Exadata is first and foremost an Oracle Database, and an understanding of general Oracle Database tuning is an essential prerequisite for tuning Exadata.

Many books have been written on Oracle performance tuning, and indeed complete books have been written on nuances of performance tuning such as SQL tuning, I/O tuning, and so on. Therefore, this section does not provide a full overview of this broad topic but a concise summary.

There are at least two valid and complementary approaches to Oracle performance optimization:

- Systematically tune each layer of the software stack, starting with application and database schema design, optimization of application SQL code, elimination of bottlenecks, optimization of memory, and finally optimization of physical I/O. This systematic approach leads to the most optimal results overall but requires the most time and often needs to start early in the application and database design cycle.
- Identify the slowest and most time-consuming operations and optimize these. This is typically a troubleshooting approach that can deliver performance gains quickly but may leave fundamental performance issues unaddressed.

Experienced Oracle practitioners learn both techniques and employ them as circumstances dictate. Building a high-performance Oracle Database from the ground up is the most certain path toward performance nirvana. But all too often we are required to find immediate performance improvements on an application or database we did not design, or when we don't have the luxury of rebuilding our system from scratch.

Systematic Oracle Performance Tuning

The systematic approach to tuning an Oracle system is dictated by the reality of how applications, databases, and operating systems interact. At a very high level, database processing occurs in layers as follows:

1. Applications send requests to the database in the form of SQL statements (including PL/SQL requests). The database responds to these requests with return codes and/or result sets.
2. To deal with an application request, the database parses the SQL and performs various overhead operations (security, scheduling, and transaction management) before finally executing the SQL. These operations use operating system resources (CPU and memory) and may be subject to contention between concurrently executing database sessions.
3. Eventually, the database processes (create, read, or change) some of the data in the database. The exact amount of data that needs to be processed can vary depending on the database design (indexing, for instance) and the application (wording of the SQL, for instance).
4. Oracle will first attempt to access the data in memory, though of course not all of the required data will be in memory. The chance that a block is in memory is determined mainly by the frequency with which the data is requested

and the amount of memory available to cache the data. When we access database data in memory, it's called **logical I/O**. In a RAC system we may access data in memory from another member of the cluster.

5. If the block is not in memory, it must be accessed from disk, resulting in real **physical I/O**. Physical I/O is by far the most expensive of all operations, and consequently the database goes to a lot of effort to avoid performing unnecessary I/O operations. However, some disk activity is inevitable.

Activity in each of these layers influences the demand placed on the underlying layer. For instance, if a SQL statement is submitted that somehow fails to exploit an index, it will require an excessive number of logical reads, which in turn will increase contention and eventually involve a lot of physical I/O. It's tempting when you see a lot of I/O or contention to deal with the symptom directly by tuning the disk layout. However, if you sequence your tuning efforts so as to work through the layers in order, you have a much better chance of fixing root causes and improving performance at lower layers.

In summary, problems in one database layer can be caused or cured by configuration in a higher layer. The logical steps in Oracle tuning are therefore:

1. Reduce application demand to its logical minimum by tuning SQL and PL/SQL and optimizing physical design (partitioning, indexing, etc.).

2. Maximize concurrency by minimizing contention for locks, latches, buffers, and other resources in the Oracle code layer.

3. Having normalized logical I/O demand in the preceding steps, minimize the resulting physical I/O by optimizing Oracle memory.

4. Now that the physical I/O demand is realistic, configure the I/O subsystem to meet that demand by providing adequate I/O bandwidth and evenly distributing the resulting load.

Oracle Performance Troubleshooting

Performance troubleshooting takes a more pragmatic approach to improve performance for specific issues, in a limited time frame, and often for systems for which we have little or no ability to change the application design. The troubleshooting approach can be summarized as finding what's slow and making it faster. There is a wide range of troubleshooting techniques, but seasoned Oracle tuning practitioners typically start by examining the "wait" profile of a system:

1. Using the Oracle views that implement the wait and time model interface (V$SYSTEM_EVENT, V$SYS_TIME_MODEL, and related tables), identify the

resources (CPU, I/O, etc.) or bottlenecks (locks, latches, etc.) that are consuming the most resources, then use whatever techniques are available (database parameter changes, OS configuration tweaking, human sacrifices) to reduce those wait times.

2. Using the Oracle views that implement information about SQL statement execution (V$SQL and related tables), identify the SQL statements that are consuming the most database resources or that have the highest elapsed time and tune these using techniques such as indexing, baselines, or SQL rewrites.

Oracle Enterprise Manager contains most of the information required to perform performance troubleshooting, though some command-line junkies prefer to use the wait interface. For those who do, Listing 13.1 shows a script (Time_model_qry.sql) that summarizes global waits since the database has started.

Listing 13.1   Top Ten Waits and Time Model Categories

```
SQL> l
  1  WITH waits
  2      AS (  SELECT event,SUM (total_waits) AS total_waits,
  3                   ROUND (SUM (time_waited_micro) / 1000000, 0)
  4                       AS time_waited_seconds
  5               FROM gv$system_event
  6              WHERE wait_class <> 'Idle'
  7           GROUP BY event
  8           UNION
  9             SELECT stat_name, NULL AS waits,
 10                    ROUND (SUM (VALUE) / 1000000, 0)
                          AS time_waited_seconds
 11               FROM v$sys_time_model
 12              WHERE stat_name IN ('DB CPU', 'background cpu time')
 13           GROUP BY stat_name)
 14  SELECT event,
 15         total_waits,
 16         time_waited_seconds,
 17         ROUND (time_waited_seconds * 100 /
 18             SUM (time_waited_seconds) OVER (),2)
 19             AS pct_time
 20      FROM (SELECT w.*,RANK () OVER (
 21                ORDER BY time_waited_seconds DESC) time_rank
 22              FROM waits w)
 23      WHERE time_rank <= 10
 24* ORDER BY 3 DESC
SQL> /
```

EVENT	Total Waits	Time Waited (s)	Pct
control file sequential read	84,364,933	94,116	29.08
DB CPU		69,513	21.48
cell single block physical read	9,944,146	37,987	11.74
cell smart table scan	52,059,906	30,534	9.44
Streams AQ: qmn coordinator waiting for slave to start	5,153	27,998	8.65

```
background cpu time                         25,857   7.99
Disk file Mirror Read          13,256,135   17,052   5.27
DFS lock handle                 2,394,441    8,311   2.57
db file parallel write          3,276,183    6,210   1.92
enq: TM - contention               17,262    6,031   1.86
```

Finding SQLs that consume the most elapsed time can be done using the script (Top_sql.sql) provided in Listing 13.2.

Listing 13.2   Top Ten SQL Statements

```
SQL> l
  1    SELECT sql_id, child_number,elapsed_time_sec, sql_text
  2       FROM ( SELECT sql_id, child_number,  substr(sql_text,1,90) sql_text,
  3               SUM (elapsed_time/1000000) elapsed_time_sec,
  4               SUM (cpu_time) cpu_time,
  5               SUM (disk_reads) disk_reads,
  6               RANK () OVER (ORDER BY SUM (elapsed_time) DESC)
  7                 AS elapsed_rank
  8           FROM gv$sql
  9          GROUP BY sql_id, child_number, sql_text)
 10    WHERE elapsed_rank <= 5
 11* ORDER BY elapsed_rank
SQL> /

                 Child
SQL_ID              no Elapsed Time (s) SQL Text
--------------- ----- ---------------- ----------------------------
bunfu3xcs0634        0      182,559.17 SELECT l.total n_logs, l.mb si
                                       ze_mb,       DECODE(d.log_mod
                                       e,'ARCHIVELOG',(l.unarchived*1

faz5nc0wt4qg4        0       64,186.13 BEGIN    FOR i IN 1..1 LOOP    F
                                       OR r IN (SELECT latency_ms, co
                                       unt(*)  FROM EXA_TXN_DATA_SSD

4v52dj4c5ds0p        0       64,138.46 SELECT LATENCY_MS, COUNT(*) FR
                                       OM EXA_TXN_DATA_SSD WHERE CATE
                                       GORY='A' GROUP BY LATENCY_MS

98txwdrsb0acf        1       18,208.88 SELECT se.event,         NVL2 (
                                                       qec.name,
                                       qec.topcategory || ' - ' || q

4dvx8jkw0g505        2       14,578.22 SELECT NVL2 (          qec.na
                                       me,          qec.topcategory
                                       || ' - ' || qec.subcategory,
```

Oracle Enterprise Manager provides views that show similar information and add historical context as well as graphical displays. Figure 13.1 shows the OEM Top Activity screen, which combines a top-level historical breakdown of wait times together with a summary of top SQL and sessions.

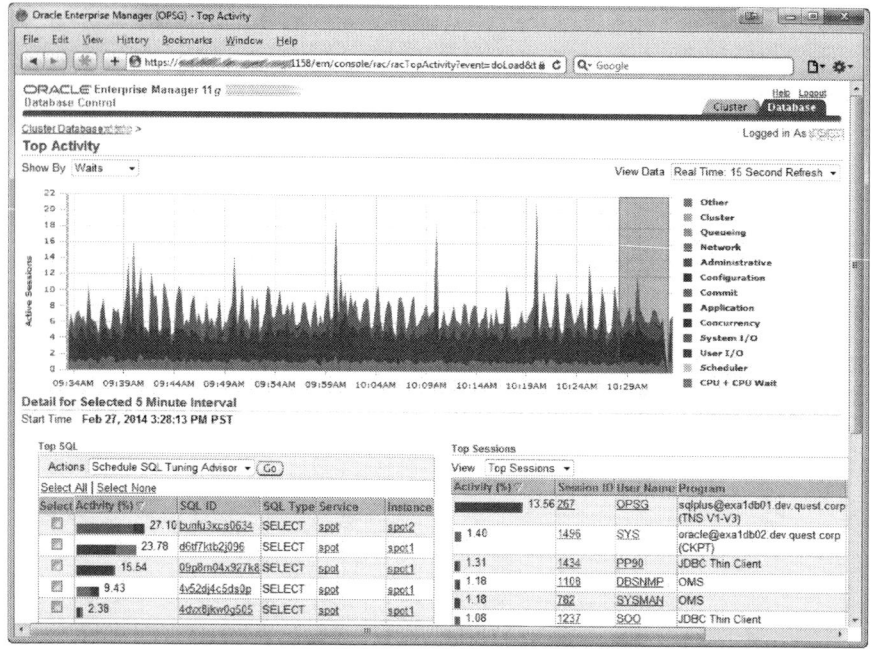

Figure 13.1   Oracle Enterprise Manager performance view

Application Design for Exadata

The overall design of an application has a critical effect on database performance. A well-designed application does the following to ensure an equitable load on the database:

- Eliminates unnecessary requests from the application to the database server:
  - By eliminating any unnecessary SQL execution requests
  - By eliminating unnecessary SQL parse requests through bind variables and effective cursor management
- Reduces network overhead and unnecessary network round trips:
  - By exploiting the array fetch and insert interface
  - By using stored procedures when appropriate
- Reduces application-driven lock contention through sensible transaction design and locking strategies

All of these principles are as valid in an Exadata context as for any other Oracle Database configuration. However, reducing network overhead takes on particular significance in an Exadata system—ironically, because of the very high I/O bandwidth provided by the Exadata architecture.

InfiniBand networking together with Smart Scan technology and other Exadata-specific technologies allows the Database Storage Nodes to forward very large result sets to the Database Compute Nodes. However, if the client application uses poor application programming techniques—in particular fails to employ array fetch—this data will bottleneck between the Database Compute Nodes and the application layer.

Figure 13.2 illustrates the network configuration of a typical Exadata application. The InfiniBand network between Storage Cells and Database Compute Nodes is typically of higher bandwidth than that between the database and the application

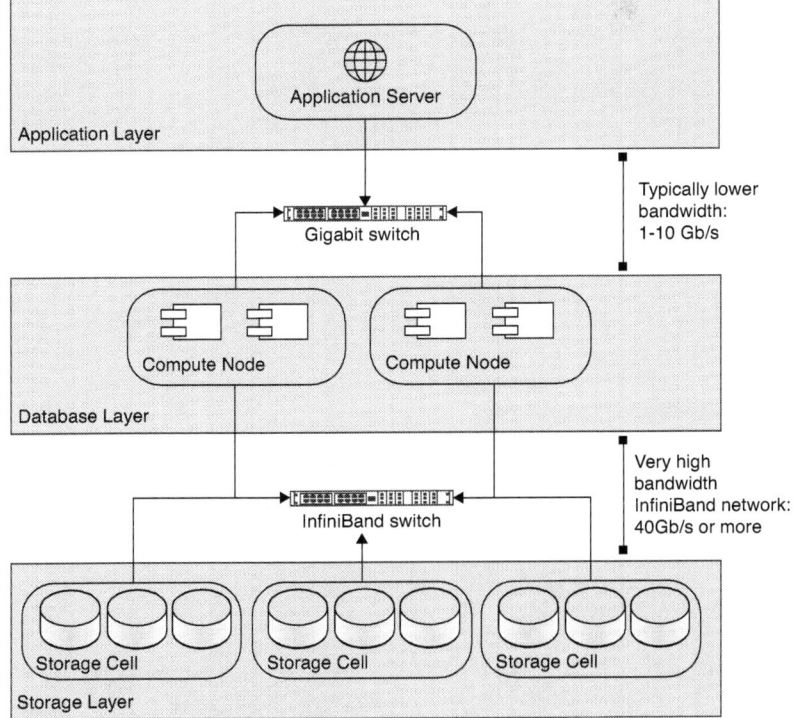

Figure 13.2 Exadata application architecture

server or a client tool (SQL*Plus, Business Intelligence tool, etc.). Furthermore, an application that fails to follow best practices often wastes network bandwidth by fetching rows one at a time rather than in batches.

It's therefore critical that applications that aim to exploit the Exadata high I/O capacity employ the Oracle array interface. The techniques to do so vary from language to language—for instance, in Java the setFetchSize method is used to control the array size.

Another useful technique to reduce I/O bottlenecks between application and Exadata is to use PL/SQL packages to perform bulk processing. Since PL/SQL packages execute within the database server, they avoid network traffic between the application and the server and may be effective when processing large datasets.

Note
All the standard application design principles—using bind variables, data caching, and array interface—apply to Exadata applications.

Exadata's extraordinary I/O bandwidth may overtax the bandwidth between the application and the database. Make sure that the application is using array fetch to optimize network traffic with the database. Also consider using PL/SQL packages for bulk processing since these will not need to transfer data outside of the Exadata network.

Database Design for Exadata

The design of your database—table structure, indexing schemes, and so forth—has more influence on your application performance than almost any other factor. The optimizer tries hard to find the best plan, but the solution space of all possible plans is dictated by the physical implementation of data into tables and indexes. These decisions are typically made early on—often before any application code is written—and are difficult to change later.

The fundamental principles of database design are the same in Exadata as in other Oracle systems. We start by creating a "normalized" form of the data in which all redundancy is removed. We then add indexes and sometimes redundancy (denormalization) to the model for performance reasons.

Indexing decisions in Exadata can, however, be influenced by some of the unique aspects of the Exadata architecture:

- Exadata has greater potential parallelism than many comparable architectures. This means that some SQL statements that might otherwise need indexes to achieve a certain execution time might be able to use brute-force parallelism instead.

- Smart Scans reduce the amount of data that needs to be processed in the Compute Nodes during certain full scan operations. This changes the relative cost of an indexed-based plan when compared to a full table scan.
- Storage Indexes furthermore can provide very good performance for certain queries that might otherwise require traditional indexing.
- Index-based execution plans may be able to take better advantage of the Exadata Smart Flash Cache (see Chapter 15). Table scans can take only limited advantage of the Exadata Smart Flash Cache while index blocks are likely to be more heavily cached.

The first three factors tend to decrease the cost of full scan execution plans and decrease the need for indexes. The fourth factor—the Exadata Smart Flash Cache—provides more performance boost to indexed plans.

Storage Indexes

Storage Indexes store minimum and maximum values—and flag the existence of null values—for certain columns within a Storage Cell's 1MB storage unit. Storage Indexes exist within the memory of the cell and have no persistence in the event of a cell reboot.

Oracle automatically maintains Storage Indexes for a maximum of eight columns in each cell storage unit. The indexes are created during initial query execution, so they are very sensitive to the initial workload of the application. Furthermore, it's possible though unlikely that a different set of eight columns might be indexed on different storage units. The effect of Storage Indexes is therefore somewhat unpredictable.

Currently index-organized tables and clustered tables are not eligible for Storage Indexes.

Offloading

Offloading is how Exadata arranges for processing that would normally occur on the Database Node to be performed on the Storage Cell. Smart Scans implement Offloading, which occurs when the cell does one of the following:

- Performs predicate filtering, returning only virtual blocks matching the WHERE clause of a query
- Uses column projection to return only those columns in the SELECT list
- Computes and creates virtual columns
- Performs function offloading by executing certain function results at the cell level

Unlike Storage Indexes, Offloading is fairly predictable. If all the following conditions are met, Offloading occurs:

- The operation is a full table or index scan.
- There is a WHERE clause predicate with a straightforward comparison operation (=, >, etc.).
- The operation is a direct path read operation.

Note
There are some exceptions. For instance, in-memory parallel query execution is dependent on system load and may sporadically suppress Smart Scans because it does not employ direct path I/O. See Chapter 4 for more information.

Although predictable, Smart Scans do not always occur when you expect them. Smart Scans reduce the overhead of large table scans. However, the Oracle Optimizer does not always take this reduction in full table scan overhead into account when comparing various plans. As a result, the optimizer might choose to use an index-based plan when a Smart Scan is possible and might be preferable.

Exadata Smart Flash Cache and Indexes

The Exadata Smart Flash Cache can accelerate both scans and indexed SQL executions, but by default it does not cache blocks retrieved via full or Smart Scans. Chapter 15 covers this in more detail, but it's generally true to say that the Exadata Smart Flash Cache is intended mainly to accelerate the sort of OLTP workloads that are typical of indexed queries.

A typical index lookup involves four to five logical I/Os: three or four to traverse the B*-tree index, and one I/O to retrieve the table block from disk. The header and branch blocks of the index tend to cache very effectively. Indeed, it's typical for these blocks to be resident in the buffer cache of the Database Nodes.

We can encourage the caching of index blocks by applying the CELL_FLASH_ CACHE KEEP clause to the index, as in this example:

```
ALTER INDEX customers_pk
   STORAGE (CELL_FLASH_CACHE KEEP)
```

Regardless of whether or not you apply the KEEP clause, be aware that while Smart Scans and Storage Indexes may optimize full table scans, the Exadata Smart Flash Cache optimizes index lookups. In both cases, the optimizer is generally unaware of the optimizations, so making sure the right plan is chosen may require manual intervention.

Index Design for New Applications

The methodology for designing indexes in a new application should be as follows:

1. Identify the key queries that are response time critical.
2. Identify the set of indexes that might be needed to support all those queries.
3. Eliminate any redundant indexes—select a minimum set of concatenated indexes.
4. Benchmark the application with various combinations of indexes to determine the optimal set, remembering that every index adds overhead to DML operations.

It is a sad reality that the final benchmarking step almost never occurs! The effort required to do exhaustive benchmarking may seem excessive in the early stages of application development but will usually be repaid by reduced performance tuning overhead when the application is in production.

When designing indexes for Exadata, the methodology is no different. However, for each index-based query that is considered, you should ask two additional questions:

- Could a Smart Scan–based plan be equally effective?
- Is it possible that a Storage Index would be effective?

It's probable or at least possible that when designing indexes for an Exadata application you end up with fewer indexes overall, but the ultimate answer can be determined only through benchmarking. For a given SQL you would want to compare the performance for the following:

- An index-based plan
- A traditional full table scan
- An offloaded Smart Scan
- A scan that exploits Storage Indexes
- An index scan accelerated by the Exadata Smart Flash Cache

As well as looking at execution plans and overall wait statistics (see Chapter 4), you could monitor the statistics in V$SYSSTAT or V$SESSTAT to see if either Storage Indexes or Smart Scans have been effective, as shown in Listing 13.3 (Offloading_ etc.sql).

Listing 13.3   Monitoring Offloading, Storage Indexes, and Flash Activity

```
SQL> 1
  1 SELECT name, VALUE
  2    FROM v$sysstat where name in ('cell flash cache read hits',
  3      'cell physical IO bytes saved by storage index',
  4      'cell physical IO bytes eligible for predicate offload',
  5      'cell scans'
  6    )
  7* order by name
SQL> /

NAME                                        VALUE
------------------------------------  ----------
cell flash cache read hits              8.5225E+10
cell physical IO bytes eligible for pred 4.8860E+16
icate offload
cell scans                                 1630285
cell physical IO bytes saved by storage 5448777728
index
```

These statistics are incremented when the Storage Cells perform Smart Scans, save I/O through the use of Storage Indexes, or find relevant data in the Flash Cache. Chapters 4 and 15 contain more details.

Indexing Strategy for Existing Applications

Often Exadata is used to host a number of existing applications as part of a workload consolidation program. In this scenario, the existing index set may or may not have been optimal for the original platform but will probably not be optimal for Exadata. When Exadata was initially gaining awareness in the Oracle community, the idea that you could "drop all the indexes" in an Exadata configuration gained some initial traction. Of course, this is far from a good idea—only a subset of SQLs in a typical application are satisfied with plans optimized with Smart Scan or Storage Indexes.

Therefore, a sensible strategy involves incrementally disabling indexes and testing the impact after each operation. Oracle's "invisible index" capability makes it easy to quickly disable and reenable specific indexes for this purpose.

Here is the general procedure:

1. Identify redundant and disused indexes.
2. Identify indexes that may be unnecessary in Exadata.
3. Make individual indexes "invisible."
4. Measure the impact on performance.
5. Restore or delete the index.

Identifying Redundant and Disused Indexes

Identifying redundant and disused indexes isn't an Exadata-specific activity, but it's one that is highly recommended whenever reviewing indexes.

Unused indexes can be identified in a number of ways. The V$SQL_PLAN table reveals indexes that do not appear in any cached SQL, as shown in Listing 13.4 (Indexes_without_plan.sql).

Listing 13.4 Finding Indexes That Do Not Appear in a Cached Plan

```
SELECT table_name, index_namen
  FROM user_indexes i
WHERE uniqueness <> 'UNIQUE'
  AND index_name NOT IN
(SELECT DISTINCT object_name
        FROM v$sql_plan
        WHERE operation LIKE '%INDEX%'
        AND object_owner = USER)
```

It's also possible to identify an unused index by applying the MONITORING clause to the index, and then later examining the table, as shown in Listing 13.5 (Index_monitoring.sql).

Listing 13.5 Monitoring for Disused Indexes

```
-- Turn monitoring on for all indexes:

BEGIN
    FOR r IN (SELECT index_name FROM user_indexes)
    LOOP
        EXECUTE IMMEDIATE 'ALTER INDEX ' || r.index_name || ' MONITORING USAGE';
    END LOOP;
END;
/

-- Later run this query

SELECT index_name,
       table_name,
       used,
       start_monitoring
  FROM v$object_usage
WHERE MONITORING = 'YES';
```

Warning

Remember, indexes that are used to enforce uniqueness or reduce locking on foreign keys may appear to be unused. However, they are anything but! Make sure you do not inadvertently drop indexes implementing a constraint or optimizing foreign key locking.

Identifying Indexes That May Be Unnecessary under Exadata

Smart Scans and Storage Indexes are unlikely to help when an index is being used for a primary or unique key index. They are much more likely to help when an index lookup has the following characteristics:

- It is being used for a MAX/MIN lookup.

- It is being used for a nonselective range scan or equality lookup—the sort of index scan that is on the edge of being eligible for a full table scan.

- It is not being used for a unique lookup (since it will almost certainly degrade if the index is removed).

- It is not being used for a full index scan (since a full index scan can be offloaded).

Making Individual Indexes Invisible

Indexes that meet the preceding criteria can be quickly disabled by using the Oracle invisible indexing feature. Invisible indexes are still kept up-to-date during DML operations but are disregarded by the optimizer as candidates for query plans—unless the OPTIMIZER_USE_INVISIBLE_INDEXES parameter is set to TRUE.

Following is an example query that makes use of an index to retrieve data only for those with an IQ above 150. Statistically this constitutes less than one-tenth of 1% of the population, and in normal Oracle an index would absolutely be the correct way to optimize the query:

```
1  SELECT MAX (rating)
2    FROM exa_txn_data e
3* WHERE iq > 150

MAX
---
KDC

Elapsed: 00:00:00.76

Execution Plan

---------------------------------------------------------------------
|Operation                       | Name          | Cost (%CPU)| Time     |
|---------------------------------------------------------------------
|SELECT STATEMENT                 |               |  132   (0)| 00:00:02 |
| SORT AGGREGATE                  |               |           |          |
|  TABLE ACCESS BY INDEX ROWID| EXA_TXN_DATA  |  132   (0)| 00:00:02 |
|   INDEX RANGE SCAN              | EXA_IQ_IDX    |    3   (0)| 00:00:01 |
---------------------------------------------------------------------
```

The query has an elapsed time of 0.76 seconds and an optimizer cost of 132. Can we drop this index in Exadata and still get OK performance? Let's see:

```
1* ALTER INDEX exa_iq_idx INVISIBLE

Index altered.

Elapsed: 00:00:00.38
  1  SELECT MAX (rating)
  2    FROM exa_txn_data e
  3* WHERE iq > 150

MAX
---
KDC

Elapsed: 00:00:00.99

Execution Plan
---------------------------------------------------------
----------------------------------------------------------------------
| Operation                 | Name        | Cost (%CPU)| Time     |
----------------------------------------------------------------------
| SELECT STATEMENT          |             | 10056  (1) | 00:02:01 |
|  SORT AGGREGATE           |             |            |          |
|   TABLE ACCESS STORAGE FULL| EXA_TXN_DATA | 10056  (1) | 00:02:01 |
----------------------------------------------------------------------


Predicate Information (identified by operation id):
---------------------------------------------------
   6 - storage("IQ">150)
       filter("IQ">150)
```

From the optimizer's point of view the cost has increased dramatically—from 132 to 10,056! But the elapsed time has increased by only .23 seconds. If we want to look further, we can see that the new query takes advantage of Storage Indexes as well as Smart Scan Offloading:

```
  1  SELECT name, VALUE
  2    FROM v$statname JOIN v$mystat USING (statistic#)
  3   WHERE name IN
       ('cell physical IO bytes eligible for predicate offload',
  4     'cell physical IO interconnect bytes returned by smart scan',
  5*    'cell physical IO bytes saved by storage index')

NAME                                                            VALUE
---------------------------------------------------------- ----------
cell physical IO bytes eligible for predicate offload       299040768
cell physical IO bytes saved by storage index               129155072
cell physical IO interconnect bytes returned by smart scan      52160
```

If this query was the only query depending on the EXA_IQ_IDX, we could make the rational decision to drop the index. Exadata Smart Scan and Storage Index optimization deliver almost all the advantages offered by the index.

Of course there will often be many queries to evaluate and overall application workloads to consider. In an ideal world, each change to an index would be evaluated using some form of application-specific benchmark, perhaps using benchmarking tools such as Dell's Toad Benchmark Factory or Oracle Real Application Testing.

We generally don't live in an ideal world in which every application change can be fully benchmarked. But at least if we are able to selectively disable indexes using the `INVISIBLE` method, we can incrementally adjust indexing on an Exadata system and monitor each change as best we can before finally deciding either to keep or to drop the index.

Choosing Compression Levels

Exadata offers unique options for database compression. Standard Oracle allows you to compress data within the traditional database storage system. The data within a row is compressed, but the row structure itself remains unchanged.

Traditional compression saves storage within the database and possibly improves or degrades performance for accessing the data. Load times are almost always increased by compression, but read time *might* improve if the majority of the read elapsed time involves physical I/O. Since the compressed table is smaller, it requires less I/O to scan, so full table scan time might actually improve.

Exadata adds Exadata Hybrid Columnar Compression (EHCC), and we've devoted a chapter to that topic (Chapter 5). In summary, though:

- The ARCHIVE HIGH setting is an extreme compression that sacrifices performance to squeeze out the maximum possible storage savings. Don't use the ARCHIVE HIGH setting if you have any concern at all for performance.

- ARCHIVE LOW compression has minimal overhead for full scan operations—typically the cost of compressing and decompressing is compensated for by the reduction in table size and consequent reduction in I/O overhead.

- ARCHIVE levels of compression, however, do degrade single-row lookups, since the row must be reconstructed from the hybrid columnar structure. If single-block lookups are important, use COMPRESS FOR QUERY or possibly consider non-EHCC compression such as COMPRESS FOR OLTP (or no compression at all).

SQL Tuning for Exadata

In Oracle performance tuning we often warn against "silver bullet" thinking. There are very few simple changes that have almost magical performance advantages.

Exadata does, however, offer very significant performance improvements that resemble silver bullets. For SQL statements that can benefit from Offloading or that fully leverage the Flash storage, orders-of-magnitude improvements may be observed. This has led to some superficial perceptions of Exadata as a silver bullet for SQL performance.

The problem with silver bullet thinking is that it encourages us to look for simple solutions to complex problems. Exadata does not cure bad SQL, and all of the normal disciplines of SQL tuning apply equally to Exadata as to any Oracle Database. It's just that we have a few extra factors to consider—most notably the unique execution properties of the Exadata system.

The most significant aspect of Exadata-specific SQL tuning is to make sure that the Exadata-specific optimizations that we expect and desire actually occur.

The specific situations in which Offloading occurs were outlined earlier in this chapter and elsewhere within this book. To recap a few of the situations that might suppress Offloading:

- The optimizer chooses an index plan instead of a scan, and this results in the step being ineligible for Offloading.

- The operation does not perform direct path reads but instead reads from the buffer cache, again disabling Offloading.

- The WHERE clause is too complex to be offloaded to the Storage Cell.

Consequently, when trying to persuade Oracle to employ Offloading:

- Eliminate the temptation for an indexed plan by removing the indexes concerned. Obviously this can have side effects! We discussed this in detail earlier in the chapter.

- Collect better statistics, especially if there is a lack of histograms or system statistics, or extended statistics is allowing the optimizer to calculate an unrealistically low cost for an indexed plan. DBMS_STATS includes a special EXADATA mode that helps the optimizer understand the relatively better full table scan performance of the Exadata system:

```
dbms_stats.gather_system_stats('EXADATA');
```

- Use a NOINDEX hint. This might not be possible if the SQL cannot be edited, and it limits the optimizer's ability to use an index that might be useful in the future. But it has the advantage of at least being restricted in scope to the current SQL statement.

- Use (or hack) a stored outline or manipulate a SQL baseline to achieve a fixed plan that performs Offloading. This is a fairly extreme measure to achieve a specific plan when you are unable to edit the SQL to add a hint. It has similar drawbacks to using a hint and is less transparent—and therefore harder on subsequent DBAs who might try to work out why the SQL plan won't change.

Note

The outline technique is described in Oracle Support Note ID 730062.1. The baseline technique involves swapping baselines using DBMS_SPM.LOAD_PLANS_FROM_CURSOR_CACHE().

- Change database parameters to increase optimizer costing for indexed plans, specifically optimizer_index_caching and optimizer_index_cost_adj. While these parameters will influence the optimizer's calculation of index costs, and might in a single case change an index plan to a scan, the unintended consequences of adjusting these parameters has led most experts to argue against this technique.
- Force a direct path with the _SERIAL_DIRECT_READ=TRUE parameter.
- Change the PARALLEL_DEGREE_POLICY parameter to MANUAL or LIMITED to avoid an in-memory parallel query (which may be suppressing direct path reads).

Exadata RAC Tuning

Exadata is primarily a RAC-based database machine, and ensuring that the cluster database is tuned correctly is of primary importance in achieving optimum performance.

Note

It is possible, though unusual, to create single-instance databases on Exadata. However, for the purposes of this discussion we'll assume that the database is a RAC database.

Understanding how instances in the cluster communicate is critical to understanding RAC performance. Exadata's optimized I/O capabilities—Exadata Smart Flash Cache, Storage Indexes, and Smart Scans—allow it to service I/O more effectively than an "average" Oracle Database configuration. Nevertheless, we want to avoid disk I/O whenever possible, primarily by keeping frequently accessed data in memory.

Global Cache Basics

In a RAC configuration, the data we want might be in the memory of one of the other instances. In this case, RAC uses the cluster interconnect to obtain the required data from another instance that has it in memory, rather than reading it from disk. Each request across the interconnect is referred to as a **Global Cache** (GC) request.

Note that these interconnect requests occur only for buffered reads. Direct path reads do not attempt to read from the local buffer cache or from the Global Cache. In practice, this means that most Global Cache activity is from single-block read requests (since full scans are mostly direct path).

To coordinate these inter-instance block transfers, Oracle assigns each block to a master instance. This instance is essentially responsible for keeping track of which instance has last accessed a particular block of data.

Whenever an Oracle instance wants a block of data that is not in its buffer cache, it asks the master instance for the block. If the master instance has the data concerned, it sends it back across the interconnect; this is recorded as a **2-way** wait.

If the master instance does not have the block in memory, but has a record of another instance accessing the block, it forwards the block request to this third instance. The third instance then returns the block to the requesting instance; this is recorded as a **3-way** wait.

If no instance has the block in memory, the master advises the requesting instance to retrieve the block from disk: this is recorded as a **grant**.

Regardless of which instance wants the block, which instance has the block, and which instance is mastering the block, the number of instances involved in the transfer will never be more than three. This means that the performance penalty as additional instances are added is minimized. However, as we increase the number of instances, the ratio of 3-way waits to 2-way waits increases, and some reduction in Global Cache performance should be expected. What this means in practice is that we need to pay particular attention to Global Cache traffic as we increase the number of Compute Nodes in our Exadata system if we still expect to achieve scalability.

RAC Tuning Principles

The RAC architecture outlined in the previous section leads directly to the general principles of RAC performance. RAC performs well, and scales well, if the following are true:

- The time taken to request a block across the interconnect (Global Cache requests) is much lower—say, ten times less—than the time to retrieve a block from the disk. Global Cache requests are intended to avoid the necessity of a disk read, and sometimes the disk read must occur even after the Global Cache request. If the Global Cache request time is anywhere near the time it takes to read from disk, the approach backfires. Luckily, optimal Global Cache requests are quick—typically ten to 100 times faster than disk read time.

▪ The cluster is well balanced, or at least there are no overloaded instances in the cluster. Since so many RAC operations involve two or three instances, an overloaded instance might cause problems for its neighbors as well as itself. Indeed, an overloaded CPU on a remote instance is one of the most common causes for long Global Cache wait times on an otherwise idle local instance.

▪ The overhead incurred through cluster activities is a small proportion of the total database time. We want our RAC database to be a database first, and a cluster second. If the proportion of time spent performing Global Cache activities is high in proportion to other activities, we may need to look at ways of reducing the Global Cache traffic.

Cluster Overhead

Above anything else, we want to make sure that a RAC cluster is able to perform database activities without being impeded by cluster-related overheads. In a healthy cluster, the time spent in cluster-related activities is mainly determined by the average time to make a Global Cache request (Global Cache latency) multiplied by the number of Global Cache requests that must be made:

Cluster time = Average GC latency x GC requests

It therefore follows that reducing cluster overhead is mainly a process of minimizing the Global Cache latency and eliminating any unnecessary Global Cache requests. The importance of those optimizations depends upon the relative time spent in cluster-related activities.

We can see the overall contribution of cluster-related waits in comparison to other high-level time categories in the query in Listing 13.6 (Top_level_waits.sql).

Listing 13.6 Summary of Wait Categories Showing Cluster Overhead

```
SQL> SELECT wait_class time_cat,
  2          ROUND((time_secs),2) time_secs,
  3          ROUND((time_secs) * 100 / SUM(time_secs)
  4              OVER (), 2) pct
  5  FROM (SELECT wait_class wait_class,
  6               SUM(time_waited_micro)/1000000 time_secs
  7        FROM gv$system_event
  8        WHERE wait_class <> 'Idle' AND time_waited > 0
  9        GROUP BY wait_class
 10        UNION
 11        SELECT 'CPU', ROUND((SUM(VALUE)/1000000),2) time_secs
 12        FROM gv$sys_time_model
```

```
13       WHERE stat_name IN ('background cpu time', 'DB CPU'))
14   ORDER BY time_secs DESC;
```

		Time
Time category	Time (s)	pct
User I/O	721,582.92	41.61
System I/O	459,658.69	26.51
CPU	389,056.04	22.44
Other	124,291.97	7.17
Cluster	18,341.66	1.06
Concurrency	11,545.14	.67
Application	6,503.29	.38
Commit	2,433.27	.14
Configuration	525.96	.03
Network	87.24	.01
Administrative	82.90	.00
Scheduler	2.53	.00

As a rule of thumb, we might expect that cluster-related waits constitute less than 10% of total database time. Cluster wait times greater than 10 to 20% of total database time probably warrant investigation.

We can drill into individual cluster waits using Enterprise Manager or with a query such as the one shown in Listing 13.7 (Cluster_waits.sql).

Listing 13.7 Breakdown of Cluster Waits

```
SQL> WITH system_event AS
  2      (SELECT CASE
  3               WHEN wait_class = 'Cluster' THEN event
  4               ELSE wait_class
  5             END  wait_type, e.*
  6        FROM gv$system_event e)
  7   SELECT wait_type,  ROUND(total_waits/1000,2) waits_1000 ,
  8         ROUND(time_waited_micro/1000000/3600,2) time_waited_hours,
  9         ROUND(time_waited_micro/1000/total_waits,2) avg_wait_ms ,
 10         ROUND(time_waited_micro*100
 11             /SUM(time_waited_micro) OVER(),2) pct_time
 12   FROM (SELECT wait_type, SUM(total_waits) total_waits,
 13             SUM(time_waited_micro) time_waited_micro
 14           FROM system_event e
 15          GROUP BY wait_type
 16          UNION
 17          SELECT 'CPU',   NULL, SUM(VALUE)
 18            FROM gv$sys_time_model
 19           WHERE stat_name IN ('background cpu time', 'DB CPU'))
 20   WHERE wait_type <> 'Idle'
 21   ORDER BY  time_waited_micro  DESC;
```

	Waits	Time	Avg Wait	Pct of
Wait Type	\1000	Hours	Ms	Time
CPU		6.15		43.62
Other	38,291	1.76	.17	12.50
Application	32	1.41	157.35	10.00
User I/O	822	.97	4.25	6.88
System I/O	995	.96	3.46	6.78
gc current multi block request	**9,709**	**.87**	**.32**	**6.15**
gc cr multi block request	**16,210**	**.48**	**.11**	**3.37**

Commit	300	.44	5.31	3.13
gc current block 2-way	5,046	.37	.26	2.59
gc current block 3-way	2,294	.28	.43	1.97
gc cr block busy	984	.16	.58	1.11

Here are descriptions of some of the more important Global Cache wait events:

- **gc cr/current block 2-way**—These are waits for Global Cache block requests involving only two instances. As outlined at the beginning of the chapter, this occurs when the block master instance is able to forward a block directly to the requesting instance.

- **gc cr/current block 3-way**—These waits occur when the block master does not have the block concerned and forwards the request to a third instance.

- **gc cr/current multi block request**—A wait that occurs when requesting multiple blocks in a single request. This is typically associated with full table or index scans.

- **gc cr/current grant 2-way**—The block master informs the requesting instance that the requested block is not available from another instance. The requesting instance then performs a disk I/O to retrieve the block.

- **gc cr/current block busy**—The requesting instance must wait for the instance that holds the block to complete some other operation before the block can be forwarded. This can happen because the block concerned is under heavy contention or because the requesting instance must flush undo records to the redo log before shipping a consistent copy.

- **gc cr/current block congested**—This wait can be reported when CPU or memory pressure prevents the LMS process from keeping up with requests. It may occur because one of the instances in the Exadata cluster is overloaded.

- **gc cr/current block lost**—Lost block waits occur when a block that has been transmitted is not received. Moderate rates might suggest that the interconnect is overloaded. High rates probably indicate network hardware issues.

Reducing Global Cache Latency

The RAC architecture requires and expects instances to fetch data blocks across the interconnect as an alternative to reading those blocks from disk. The performance of Exadata is therefore very sensitive to the time it takes to retrieve a block from the Global Cache, which we call **Global Cache latency**.

Some documents and presentations suggest that Global Cache latency is primarily or exclusively **interconnect latency**: the time it takes to send the block across the interconnect network. Interconnect latency is certainly an important part of overall Global Cache latency, but it's not the only part. Indeed, given the high-performance InfiniBand network integrated into Exadata interconnect, latency is rarely an issue.

However, Global Cache latency can increase when Oracle processes such as the Global Cache Service (LMS) have to perform a significant amount of CPU-intensive processing when a block is transferred. In certain circumstances non-CPU operations—such as flushing redo entries to disk—also contribute to Global Cache latency.

To measure Global Cache latency, we use the wait interface as exposed by GV$SYSTEM_EVENT. The query in Listing 13.8 (Gc_latency.sql) reports on average times for each of the Global Cache request types as well as cell single-block read time (for comparison).

Listing 13.8 Breakdown of Cluster Waits

```
SQL> SELECT event, SUM(total_waits) total_waits,
  2          ROUND(SUM(time_waited_micro) / 1000000, 2)
  3          time_waited_secs,
  4          ROUND(SUM(time_waited_micro) / 1000 /
  5          SUM(total_waits), 2) avg_ms
  6  FROM gv$system_event
  7  WHERE       event LIKE 'gc%block%way'
  8       OR event LIKE 'gc%multi%'
  9       OR event LIKE 'gc%grant%'
 10       OR event LIKE 'cell single%'
 11  GROUP BY event
 12  HAVING SUM(total_waits) > 0
 13  ORDER BY event;

                                       Total       Time  Avg Wait
Wait event                             Waits      (secs)     (ms)
-----------------------------------  ----------- ---------- --------
cell single block physical rea       58,658,569   343,451    5.86
gc cr block 2-way                     1,226,123       133     .11
gc cr grant 2-way                     3,557,547       329     .09
gc cr grant congested                    33,230         3     .10
gc cr multi block request             1,867,799     2,716    1.45
gc current block 2-way                4,245,674       449     .11
gc current grant 2-way                1,885,528       166     .09
gc current grant busy                   656,165       145     .22
gc current grant congested               17,004         2     .10
gc current multi block request           10,996         2     .18
```

When Global Cache waits are high, we should first determine if the latency is primarily the result of interconnect network waits. It is unlikely that physical interconnect issues will be predominant given the Exadata engineered architecture, but it is always good practice to systematically eliminate it as a root cause.

You can determine the private IP address for the interconnect by querying the view GV$CLUSTER_INTERCONNECTS. We can then ping that IP address from another node in the cluster to determine average latency. We use the -s 8192 flag to set an 8K packet size so as to align with the block size of this Oracle Database:

```
$ ping -c 5 -s 8192 192.168.10.2
PING 192.168.10.2 (192.168.10.2) 8192(8220) bytes of data.
8200 bytes from 192.168.10.2: icmp_seq=1 ttl=64 time=0.103 ms
8200 bytes from 192.168.10.2: icmp_seq=2 ttl=64 time=0.097 ms
8200 bytes from 192.168.10.2: icmp_seq=3 ttl=64 time=0.101 ms
8200 bytes from 192.168.10.2: icmp_seq=4 ttl=64 time=0.111 ms
8200 bytes from 192.168.10.2: icmp_seq=5 ttl=64 time=0.108 ms
```

In addition to high latencies—as exposed by the ping command—interconnect issues can show up as "lost" or congested blocks.

Lost blocks occur when a block is transmitted but never received. The query in Listing 13.9 (gc_lost_blocks.sql) shows the number of blocks lost compared to the number sent and received.

Listing 13.9   Identifying Lost Blocks

```
SQL> SELECT name, SUM (VALUE)
  2      FROM gv$sysstat
  3      WHERE    name LIKE 'gc%lost'
  4          OR name LIKE 'gc%received'
  5          OR name LIKE 'gc%served'
  6  GROUP BY name
  7* ORDER BY name

NAME                                               SUM(VALUE)
-------------------------------------------------- ----------
gc blocks lost                                              0
gc claim blocks lost                                        0
gc cr blocks received                                 1492713
gc cr blocks served                                   1492713
gc current blocks received                            7834472
gc current blocks served                              7834472
```

Time spent waiting for lost block retransmission is recorded in the wait events gc cr request retry, gc cr block lost, and gc current block lost. The times associated with these waits should be low: typically less than 1% of the total when compared to the total number of blocks recorded in the gc cr/current blocks received/served statistics.

If there are very high lost block counts (relative to blocks received)—or if the time associated with lost blocks becomes significant compared to total database time—the most likely cause is a network hardware issue: possibly faults in the network cards or cabling.

LMS Latency

Interconnect network performance is at the heart of Global Cache latency, but high Global Cache latencies are often the result of delays in the Oracle software layers. The LMS service on the remote instances contributes most of the non-network latency to Global Cache requests; it is responsible for constructing and returning the requested blocks (although LMS historically stands for Lock Management Service, it is usually more correctly described as the Global Cache Service). The query in Listing 13.10 (lms_latency.sql) shows LMS latencies for each instance for current and consistent read requests.

Listing 13.10 LMS Latency per Instance

```
SQL> WITH sysstats AS (
  2      SELECT instance_name,
  3             SUM(CASE WHEN name LIKE 'gc cr%time'
  4                      THEN VALUE END) cr_time,
  5             SUM(CASE WHEN name LIKE 'gc current%time'
  6                      THEN VALUE END) current_time,
  7             SUM(CASE WHEN name LIKE 'gc current blocks served'
  8                      THEN VALUE END) current_blocks_served,
  9             SUM(CASE WHEN name LIKE 'gc cr blocks served'
 10                      THEN VALUE END) cr_blocks_served
 11        FROM gv$sysstat JOIN gv$instance
 12        USING (inst_id)
 13       WHERE name IN
 14                 ('gc cr block build time',
 15                  'gc cr block flush time',
 16                  'gc cr block send time',
 17                  'gc current block pin time',
 18                  'gc current block flush time',
 19                  'gc current block send time',
 20                  'gc cr blocks served',
 21                  'gc current blocks served')
 22    GROUP BY instance_name)
 23  SELECT instance_name , current_blocks_served,
 24         ROUND(current_time*10/current_blocks_served,2) avg_current_ms,
 25         cr_blocks_served,
 26         ROUND(cr_time*10/cr_blocks_served,2) avg_cr_ms
 27    FROM sysstats;

            Current Blks      Avg      CR Blks     Avg
Instance          Served   CU ms       Served   Cr ms
-----------  -----------  ------  -----------  ------
Node2          3,997,991     .28      636,299     .14
Node1          3,838,045     .21      856,684     .15
```

If the network is responsive and fast, but LMS latency is high, one of the following might be implicated:

- An overloaded instance is unable to respond fast enough to Global Cache requests. In particular, the LMS processes might be overloaded with requests or starved for CPU.

- I/O bottlenecks—particularly for redo log I/O—are slowing down the response to Global Cache requests.

The overloaded instance phenomenon is often the result of an imbalanced cluster: if any instance in the cluster is significantly overloaded, Global Cache response times on the idle instances suffer. The best solution is to try to achieve a better cluster balance (see the section "Balancing an Exadata RAC Database" later in this chapter).

The other typical cause of high latencies is when the LMS process must flush uncommitted changes to the redo log prior to sending the block back to the requesting instance. If the application design is such that uncommitted blocks are often in demand across instances in the cluster, these redo log flushes might become common. If there are bottlenecks in the redo log devices, the I/O waits are magnified.

We can measure the impact on LMS response time by leveraging the timing information in GV$SYSTAT and the FLUSHES statistic in GV$CR_BLOCK_SERVER. Putting the two together, we can calculate the proportion of blocks that required flushing and the proportion of LMS time spent performing the flush, as shown in Listing 13.11 (Flush_time.sql).

Listing 13.11   LMS Flush Time Calculation

```
SQL> WITH sysstat AS (
  2          SELECT SUM(CASE WHEN name LIKE '%time'
  3                          THEN VALUE END) total_time,
  4                 SUM(CASE WHEN name LIKE '%flush time'
  5                          THEN VALUE END) flush_time,
  6                 SUM(CASE WHEN name LIKE '%served'
  7                          THEN VALUE END) blocks_served
  8          FROM gv$sysstat
  9          WHERE name IN
 10                         ('gc cr block build time',
 11                          'gc cr block flush time',
 12                          'gc cr block send time',
 13                          'gc current block pin time',
 14                          'gc current block flush time',
 15                          'gc current block send time',
 16                          'gc cr blocks served',
 17                          'gc current blocks served')),
 18          cr_block_server as (
 19          SELECT SUM(flushes) flushes,
 20                 SUM(data_requests) data_requests
 21          FROM gv$cr_block_server    )
 22   SELECT ROUND(flushes*100/blocks_served,2) pct_blocks_flushed,
 23          ROUND(flush_time*100/total_time,2) pct_lms_flush_time
 24    FROM sysstat CROSS JOIN cr_block_server;

PCT_BLOCKS_FLUSHED PCT_LMS_FLUSH_TIME
------------------ ------------------
              1.13              39.97
```

Note how even a vanishingly small proportion of block flushes can still account for a large proportion of total LMS time.

Balancing an Exadata RAC Database

Achieving balance between the instances that constitute an Exadata RAC database cluster is important for scalability, manageability, and performance. While some variation in workload across the cluster is to be expected, in an unbalanced cluster the following undesirable situations can arise:

- **Sessions on busy instances get poor service time.** Even though there may be spare capacity in the cluster as a whole, sessions on busy instances are unable to use that capacity and experience poor performance.

- **Sessions on idle instances wait for blocks from busy instances.** Because a lot of operations result in requests to remote instances, an overloaded instance can cause performance problems across the entire cluster. A session on an "idle" instance may experience high Global Cache wait times waiting on blocks from the busy instance.

- **Benefits of adding new instances may not be realized.** If some of the instances in the cluster are subject to a higher workload, these instances may become bottlenecks to overall database throughput. As instances are added to the cluster, expected performance improvements might be unattainable.

- **Tuning is harder because each instance has different symptoms.** In an unbalanced cluster, sessions on busy instances may experience high CPU waits while sessions on less busy instances experience high Global Cache waits. Troubleshooting performance problems on an unbalanced cluster can therefore be more challenging because of the mixed symptoms.

We can assess cluster balance fairly easily. The query in Listing 13.12 (Cluster_balance.sql) reports on CPU, DB time, and logical reads on each instance within the database since startup.

Listing 13.12 Cluster Balance

```
SQL> WITH sys_time AS (
   2      SELECT inst_id, SUM(CASE stat_name WHEN 'DB time'
   3                        THEN VALUE END) db_time,
   4             SUM(CASE WHEN stat_name IN ('DB CPU', 'background cpu time')
   5                 THEN  VALUE  END) cpu_time
   6        FROM gv$sys_time_model
   7      GROUP BY inst_id          )
   8  SELECT instance_name,
   9         ROUND(db_time/1000000,2) db_time_secs,
  10         ROUND(db_time*100/SUM(db_time) over(),2) db_time_pct,
  11         ROUND(cpu_time/1000000,2) cpu_time_secs,
  12         ROUND(cpu_time*100/SUM(cpu_time) over(),2)  cpu_time_pct
  13     FROM     sys_time
  14     JOIN gv$instance USING (inst_id);
```

Instance Name	DB Time (secs)	Pct of DB Time	CPU Time (secs)	Pct of CPU Time
Node1	1,209,611.63	73.65	309,136.54	72.20
Node2	432,728.60	26.35	119,025.94	27.80

In this example it is clear that Node1 is being subjected to a disproportionate level of CPU load. If this is not addressed, increasing cluster workload will almost certainly lead to performance degradation as Node1 becomes the bottleneck for the entire cluster.

Listing 13.12 summarizes performance since the instances in the cluster were started. You can see a comparison in real time and historical load on each instance in the server in the Instances tab on the Enterprise Manager performance page as shown in Figure 13.3.

An imbalance in RAC load can be due to a single session—or just a few sessions—placing a heavy load on specific instances. These imbalances might be unavoidable,

Figure 13.3   Examining cluster balance in Enterprise Manager

although parallelizing operations across the cluster can often help balance the load. Other possible causes include

- Sessions directly connecting to individual instances in the cluster. This might happen if the TNSNAMES.ORA file contains entries for individual instances as well as cluster entries.
- Out-of-date TNSNAMES.ORA files on clients or on the servers that are causing RAC load balancing to fail.
- Unbalanced services configuration resulting in specific services placing excessive load on a subset of the instances in the cluster.

Remember as well that load on a particular database may be balanced, but more than one database may coexist on the cluster. For load to be balanced across all nodes of the cluster, all databases need to be balanced.

Balancing Workloads with IORM and DBRM

In the previous section we looked at how to balance the workload of a single RAC database across an Exadata system. However, database consolidation is one of the key drivers for Exadata adoption, and many or most Exadata systems host multiple databases. In some cases, the aggregate power of the Exadata system is sufficient to meet the peak demands of all these databases. But if not, we need a way to ensure that resources are shared fairly among the databases or alternatively that resources are allocated to the highest-priority workloads.

Exadata I/O Resource Management (IORM) gives us a mechanism for controlling the allocation of I/O resources across all the databases that access the Storage Nodes. Additionally, Database Resource Management (DBRM) can be used to control the allocation of CPU on the Compute Nodes using Instance Caging.

These techniques are discussed in depth in Chapter 14. The following sections briefly summarize the key concepts. IORM and DBRM are your primary tools to ensure equitable and balanced resource utilization within your Exadata Database Machine.

Prioritizing I/O

IORM resource plans are established at the Storage Cell level using the CellCLI ALTER IORMPLAN command. The IORM ALLOCATION clause specifies a relative percentage of I/O capacity that is applied to individual instances when the Storage Cell is saturated. Once the Storage Cell I/O capacity is reached, I/O requests from individual instances are queued in such a way as to meet the relative allocations specified in the IORM plan.

The IORM LIMIT clause creates an absolute limit on I/O for individual instances which applies even when the Storage Cell is not saturated. This allows you to prevent individual instances from ever exceeding a particular proportion of Storage Cell I/O.

IORM plans can also be applied to DBRM consumer group categories. This allows you to specify I/O limits for specific workload categories that span individual databases. This allows high-priority workloads to get I/O precedence regardless of the database from which they originate.

See Chapter 14 for more details on IORM.

Prioritizing CPU

While IORM can be used to achieve fine-grained control over I/O, our options for controlling CPU between instances are more limited.

The CPU_COUNT parameter controls the number of CPU cores that an instance will leverage when calculating degrees of parallelism and other multithreaded operations. It is also the basis by which DBRM limits CPU utilization—DBRM throttles activity to prevent an instance from exceeding the CPU utilization implied by CPU_COUNT. Therefore, by manipulating CPU_COUNT, we can modify the balance of CPU consumption from specific databases as well as control the allocation of those CPU resources within individual databases. This technique is known as **Instance Caging**.

See Chapter 14 for more on Instance Caging.

Optimizing Exadata I/O

It's generally regarded as good practice to tune I/O last in the systematic tuning methodology. The load placed on the I/O subsystem is often magnified by suboptimal SQL and constrained by contention points such as locks and latches. Therefore, you can't be sure of the correct I/O load until you have addressed these concerns.

This advice applies as much to Exadata as to any other Oracle Database. You should avoid heroic I/O tuning efforts—and certainly hardware upgrades such as adding Storage Cells—until you have normalized the workload through SQL tuning and contention management.

When you do come to Exadata I/O tuning, however, you have far more limited options than in a traditional system. In a "build it yourself" Oracle Database you have the option to add or upgrade disk drives and radically change the distribution of data on the disks. In an Exadata engineered system you have far fewer such options. You can upgrade from a Half Rack to a Full Rack—or even add an Exadata Storage Expansion Rack—to increase your I/O bandwidth, but you can't rip out the drives and replace them all with faster disks.

The following sections cover some options you do have if you determine that your I/O performance in a default configuration is inadequate.

Leveraging Flash More Effectively

We'll see in Chapter 16 how to set up ASM disk groups based on Exadata Flash drives as a complement to the Exadata Smart Flash Cache. Disk groups composed completely of Flash can provide much better performance for tables that are small enough to fit within the relatively smaller capacity of the Flash disk group, since you can be sure that these tables will never need to generate I/Os from magnetic disk.

Configuring the Write-Back Facility

It's possible—especially if you are running on an older Exadata system—that the Flash Cache is running in write-through mode in which all I/O writes must complete synchronously to disk. Enabling the write-back cache can improve performance if you are suffering from a write bottleneck. Chapter 16 explains in detail how this can be achieved.

Configuring ASM

Even though you can't change the number or types of disks in your cluster, you can modify the way in which these disks are allocated to ASM disk groups and hence to segments, temporary tablespaces, and redo.

The default ASM configuration contains three disk groups: one for data files (DATA), one for redo and flashback recovery files (RECO), and one for the database file system (DBFS_DG). This default configuration can be modified to further isolate I/O by creating dedicated disk groups for temporary tablespaces or for specific table or index segments.

ASM also offers several specific configuration options that can influence the performance of the disk group:

- Optimal disk placement can be specified by associating a file with an ASM template in which the Primary Extent Zone is set to HOT. These files are stored in the "faster" outermost tracks of the disk and experience greater throughput and reduced latency.

  ### Note
  In a spinning disk, more data passes below the read/write head on the outer portions of the disk because of the greater circumference. Hence overall throughput is improved. If all the data is on the outermost segments, seek latency may reduce as well, since the read/write head moves across a shorter arc.

- You may configure ASM disk groups using either coarse-grained or fine-grained striping. Coarse-grained striping uses a stripe size equal to the allocation unit for the disk group: 1MB by default. Fine-grained striping uses a stripe size of

128K. Coarse-grained striping is probably the best configuration for database files, whereas fine-grained striping might be more suitable for redo, flashback, and archive logs because it might allow for smaller I/Os to be parallelized across multiple requests.

- The ASM attribute `cell.smart_scan_capable` is set to `TRUE` by default on an Exadata system. You can set this attribute to `FALSE` to selectively disable Smart Scans, though it's more common to use session parameters or hints to achieve this outcome. It may also be necessary to set this parameter to `FALSE` if you wish to share an ASM disk group with a non-Exadata system.

Changing the Block Size

Changing the database block size is a polarizing topic in the Oracle community—with passionate opinions on both sides. Theoretically, increasing the block size reduces the number of physical I/Os required to perform table or index scans, although Oracle's multiblock read capability generally achieves the same result. Higher block sizes may reduce B*-tree index depth as well, which might reduce the number of I/Os required to satisfy an index lookup.

On the other hand, lower block sizes can create greater buffer cache effectiveness, reduce latch and lock contention on "hot" blocks, and improve interconnect efficiency—in theory.

Anecdotal and experimental results can demonstrate either of these effects. But because the effects of changing block size are so workload dependent, the only way to be sure is to try multiple block sizes and measure the performance. If you don't have benchmark evidence showing that a different block size is superior for your application, you should probably leave the block size at the default.

Summary

Most of the traditional Oracle tuning techniques apply equally to Exadata. However, the unique performance characteristics of Exadata do create additional performance challenges and opportunities.

Storage Indexes, Smart Scans, and the high parallelism incorporated within the Exadata architecture generally tend to make full scan execution plans more attractive on Exadata when compared to indexed paths. The Exadata Smart Flash Cache meanwhile accelerates index lookups. You may find that *some* of your application indexes are unnecessary in Exadata—follow a systematic approach to rationalizing indexes by interactively turning indexes "invisible" and measuring the impact.

Other key components of Exadata tuning include optimizing the RAC database configuration and prioritizing workloads using IORM.

14

Database Consolidation on Exadata

In traditional models, business applications are bound to a particular infrastructure, resulting in low efficiency, utilization, and flexibility. Recently, there has been a big movement in the IT industry to rationalize, simplify, and standardize IT resources. There are many drivers for this movement; not surprisingly, the key motivation is cost reduction. Cost reduction comes in many forms, such as a decrease in server footprint, minimizing cooling costs, reduction in management overhead, and even the requirement for higher utilization. Lowering expenses—both capital and operating—is the key benefit of consolidating workloads onto a shared infrastructure.

An example of this cost reduction movement is the server consolidation crusade that has been going on for a number of years. With the advent of revolutionary virtualization technologies, consolidation has become a very streamlined approach.

This chapter focuses on how the Exadata system can be used as an ideal consolidation platform. It describes the consolidation approach including planning, setup, and management.

Database Consolidation Models

There are different forms of database consolidation. Database consolidation can be accomplished using virtualization technologies. For example:

- Hypervisor-based consolidation, such as VMware, Oracle VM, or Hyper-V.

- Consolidating a group of database instances on shared infrastructure. This is referred to as **database instance consolidation**.
- Commingling many applications in separate schemas in a single database is referred to as **schema consolidation**.

Many DBAs will implement a hybrid of these three configurations. Each technology and option has its own merits and issues. Customers are often reluctant to migrate to build their consolidation platform based on a virtualization. This is partly due to the virtualization overhead and its impact on overall performance. This is especially key for applications that are latency sensitive. But truthfully, it is becoming less of a technology (latency or throughput) issue and more of an Oracle Database licensing issue.

In this chapter, database instance consolidation and schema consolidation are the main focal points. In addition, the new Oracle Database 12c feature Pluggable Database is covered to round out the topic.

Exadata Consolidation Planning

There are key planning areas for consolidating onto the Exadata. A consolidation effort is executed well only if there is a consolidation and standardization steering committee in place. The consolidation effort must also be driven by senior executives. Not doing so makes the exercise a very IT-driven, narrowly focused initiative, which typically does not get much traction.

Here are the main goals and objectives of this consolidation steering committee:

- Define eligible applications for consolidation.
- Determine how many applications or databases will be consolidated, and also define the fullness factor, that is, the threshold number of consolidated databases that will be comfortably supported on Exadata.
- Drive how the Exadata platform should be configured. This includes the size of the Exadata that should be employed.
- Evaluate consolidation success factors.
- Determine a placement policy and/or evaluate whether an application will employ a database consolidation model or schema consolidation.
- Define a plan for migrating existing applications as well as new applications to the Exadata consolidated platform.
- Define outliers or applications that cannot or should not be consolidated. For example, some applications may require extreme response time or have sizing requirements that are not conducive to a consolidated environment.

Grouping Applications

It is very important to group applications together according to business or functional requirements and also based on similar SLAs. The following example illustrates this grouping:

- **Business**—Build separate server pools for lines of business or departments. Or create separate server pools for different application service levels or governance compliance.

- **Functional**—Build a server pool for similarly functioning applications (for example, internal-facing versus external-facing applications).

- **Technical**—Build separate server pools based on OS type, database version, or isolation requirements; or for applications with complementary workloads; or around specific high-availability goals.

These SLAs should be based on availability, serviceability, or even response time. An obvious example of an incorrect consolidation model would be consolidating QA environments with production, but a less obvious example could be where business-critical applications are housed together with applications that have no defined performance or availability objectives.

Server Pools

A **consolidation server pool** (or simply server pool) is a set of servers or even a collection of Exadata Database Machine systems that is used as the target consolidation platform. For a large-scale consolidation, an Exadata Half Rack, which consists of a four-node cluster, is the recommended minimum server pool size. For smaller or more targeted consolidations (for example, for a specific business unit), a smaller server pool such as an Exadata X5-2 Quarter Rack or Eighth Rack can be used. This option is even more viable if a standby database on a separate Exadata is deployed.

Server pools can be built for specific configurations and support specific business requirements. For example, administrators can build one server pool based on regulatory data requirements (PCI, PII, HIPAA, and so on) and another for their business-critical 11gR2 applications. It is a best practice for applications with similar SLA requirements to coexist in a consolidated environment; in other words, do not mix mission-critical applications with noncritical applications in the same server pool.

Before applications are even considered for consolidation, the respective business units should define key HA requirements, such as application target recovery time or RTO, the application's maximum data loss tolerance, or RPO. Additionally, the tolerance for different planned maintenance windows should also be inspected. Some applications can tolerate occasional planned outages, whereas others cannot. A key aspect of consolidation is that users benefit from the inherent elasticity and agility of shared resources. However, the loss of availability is also shared across applications. This unavailability can come in the form of planned or unplanned outages. Thus, loss of availability has to be mitigated or made transparent to users.

Warning

When availability, performance, or security is scarified in a shared platform, most application owners inevitably shift back toward their comfort zone; that is, they turn to a nonshared, nonconsolidation configuration. Thus, the consolidation venture must be executed correctly the first time.

Chargeback

Database as a Service (DBaaS) is a new paradigm where end users, such as DBAs or developers, can request and consume database services. DBaaS is a self-service model for provisioning database resources and provides a shared, consolidated platform. DBaaS is generally tied to chargeback based on database usage.

Chargeback is used to associate the costs of IT resources with the people or organizations that consume these resources. Chargeback enables the administrator to track the use of business-critical resources or metrics by the application owner or consuming entities and then report the usage charges to these entities. It is not simply an allotment of resources; it serves as a means of accountability—that is, consumers are more accountable for their consumption when there is a chargeback mechanism in place. Departments can accurately share or report costs with business users or business units, commensurate with the usage of the resources.

Chargeback has three basic metrics against which to compute resource consumption: CPU usage, memory, and storage allocation. These metrics constitute a charge plan that can be applied to any target type configured for chargeback. Many IT organizations also extend their chargeback plans to include deployment architectures. For example, chargeback plans can be aligned to the degree of high availability, business continuity, or even the number of change requests required.

Adopting a metering and chargeback model can deliver significant benefits to both IT and business units. For example, providers and consumers understand the cost of the services delivered and establish accountability for the consumption of resources. Additionally, metering gives visibility into how the environment is being used and provides the opportunity to make improvements in the environment and service catalog offerings.

Following are examples of chargeback plans:

- **Gold package**—eight CPUs, 40GB aggregate SGA (across four-node RAC), Data Guard deployment
- **Silver package**—four CPUs, 20GB aggregate SGA (across four-node RAC)
- **Bronze package**—two CPUs, 8GB aggregate SGA (across four-node RAC)
- **Entry-level package**—two CPUs, 2GB SGA on RAC one node

Evaluating Sizing Requirements

The number of applications that can be consolidated depends on size, resource consumption, and the SLAs of the applications that will be consolidated. Furthermore, a predefined threshold of the system resource usage also dictates how much can be consolidated. Often organizations purchase an Exadata, then determine consolidation density; however, an alternative and more successful method is to scope the consolidation density, then acquire the appropriate Exadata based on the scoping study.

Sizing applications that are placed in the Exadata consolidated platform depend on the state of the application, that is, whether it is a new or existing application. For new applications, initial sizing is the same as for any current capacity-planning exercise: determine the expected load, test in development and QA environments, and define growth. For existing applications, leverage tools such as AWR reports, vmstat, and iostat to determine consumption. OEM 12c Consolidation Planner provides a streamlined approach for gathering this dataset.

Poor or inconsistent performance in a consolidated environment can affect SLAs, or even cause outages, and is typically a consequence of mixing noncomplementary, or antagonistic, workloads. Thus, the key aspect of any successful Exadata consolidation is to ensure that only complementary workloads are co-located.

When reviewing complementary workloads, ensure that the consolidated workloads' peak CPU utilization does not greatly exceed the average CPU utilization. The gap between peak and average should be kept to a minimum, which ensures that the CPUs are being utilized as fully as possible. This is an incremental approach; that is, for every application that is consolidated, a review process must be performed. For example, when evaluating candidate applications and workloads, determine what impact the new workload will have on peak and average CPU utilization. A complementary workload causes the average load to increase more than the peak. An optimal situation would be where the peak usage remains unchanged, while the average increases.

Administrators can then use Consolidation Planner to run different scenarios for redistributing workloads onto existing systems or new environments (using a what-if capability) and determine if this will result in SLA violations. Consolidation Planner provides a guided migration path for consolidation, and the advice is based on both technical and business reasons. Running Consolidation Planner against Exadata configurations is very streamlined, since Exadata (target) configurations are well known.

Setting Up Exadata for Consolidation

It is no secret that the main resources consumed by databases are I/O, memory, and CPU. Thus, CPU and resources of candidate applications must be thoroughly reviewed. This section describes the metrics and data points to look for before consolidating.

Storage and I/O Settings

It is recommended that you review existing applications' storage usage before consolidation. Databases in silo configurations are typically provisioned with more storage than they use, so one of the key items to review is how much of the allocated storage is actually in use, that is, how much is free and how much contains data. Be watchful of systems that use thin provisioned storage, as this can be misleading with respect to provisioned storage. Systems that have grossly overallocated storage provide administrators a good opportunity to consolidate storage space. Before migrating applications onto the consolidated platform, application owners should ensure that obsolete or unneeded data is cleansed or archived. This not only improves storage efficiency but also improves overall migration time.

Storage IOPS is probably the most overlooked area in database consolidation. After all, consolidating databases is essentially the aggregation of IOPS. DBAs should look at average and peak IOPS for each database to be consolidated as part of the consolidation planning exercise.

Use AWR reports to collect the following I/O metrics:

IOPS = Physical reads total I/O requests + Physical writes total I/O requests

MBytes/s = Physical reads total bytes + Physical writes total bytes

These metrics help determine the storage throughput needed to support the application. Aggregate the IOPS or MBytes/s for all nodes if the existing application is running on RAC. Keep in mind that each layer in the I/O stack should be able to sustain this I/O load as well as future consolidated loads.

Note

As of this writing, there is no mechanism for applying database-specific space management quotas within a disk group.

The following scripts aid in capturing and gauging the appropriate number of IOPS.

First we need a table to hold the data captured between snapshots, so we create the SUPER_TIMER table as shown in Listing 14.1.

Listing 14.1 Create a Timer Table

```
-- TIMER_CREATE.SQL
drop table super_timer;
create table super_timer
(
    timer_name      varchar2(40)    not null primary key,
    timer_start     date            not null,
    timer_stop      date            null,
    lrg_reads1      number          not null,
    lrg_writes1     number          not null,
    sma_reads1      number          not null,
    sma_writes1     number          not null,
    tby_reads1      number          not null,
    tby_writes1     number          not null,
    lrg_reads2      number          null,
    lrg_writes2     number          null,
    sma_reads2      number          null,
    sma_writes2     number          null,
    tby_reads2      number          null,
    tby_writes2     number          null
);
```

Once we've created the timer table, we simply call the timer start and stop scripts as follows before and after our workload runs, respectively. Note that you pass a name to reference the timer.

```
-- TIMER_START.SQL
set verify off
insert into super_timer
SELECT upper('&1'), sysdate, null,
    sum(decode(name,'physical read total multi block requests',value,0)),
    sum(decode(name,'physical write total multi block requests',value,0)),
    sum
(decode(name,'physical read total IO requests',value,0)-
decode(name,'physical read total multi block requests',value,0)),
    sum
(decode(name,'physical write total IO requests',value,0)-
decode(name,'physical write total multi block requests',value,0)),
    sum(decode(name,'physical read total bytes',value,0)),
    sum(decode(name,'physical write total bytes',value,0)),
    null, --null, null,
    null, null, null, null, null
FROM v$sysstat;
commit;
```

```
-- TIMER_STOP.SQL
set verify off
update super_timer
set (timer_stop, lrg_reads2, lrg_writes2, sma_reads2,
sma_writes2, tby_reads2, tby_writes2)
=
(
 SELECT sysdate,
    sum(decode(name,'physical read total multi block requests',value,0)),
    sum(decode(name,'physical write total multi block requests',value,0)),
    sum(
decode(name,'physical read total IO requests',value,0)-
decode(name,'physical read total multi block requests',value,0)),
    sum
(decode(name,'physical write total IO requests',value,0)-
decode(name,'physical write total multi block requests',value,0)),
    sum(decode(name,'physical read total bytes',value,0)),
    sum(decode(name,'physical write total bytes',value,0))
 FROM v$sysstat
)
where timer_name = upper('&1');
commit;
```

Now all that's left is to display the runtime and IOPS via the `TIMER_RESULTS.SQL`
script shown next. Note that you may decide to skip the second and third queries
which show the small and large sizes, instead just using the first query for the
overall results. We included them for completeness. Feel free to comment out or
delete what you don't want.

```
-- TIMER_RESULTS.SQL
set verify off

set linesize 256
set trimout on
set trimspool on

column timer_name     format a20          heading 'TIMER NAME'
column run_time       format a8           heading 'RUN TIME|HH:MM:SS'

column tby_read       format 999,999.999  heading 'TOTAL|READ|MB'
column tby_writes     format 999,999.999  heading 'TOTAL|WRITE|MB'
column tr_mbps        format 999,999.999  heading 'TOTAL|READ|MB/S'
column tw_mbps        format 999,999.999  heading 'TOTAL|WRITE|MB/S'
column tr_iops        format 999,999.999  heading 'TOTAL|READ|IOPS'
column tw_iops        format 999,999.999  heading 'TOTAL|WRITE|IOPS'
column tot_iops       format 999,999.999  heading 'TOTAL|R/W|IOPS'

column sma_reads      format 999,999,999  heading 'SMALL|READ|COUNT'
column sma_writes     format 999,999,999  heading 'SMALL|WRITE|COUNT'
column sma_total      format 999,999,999  heading 'SMALL|TOTAL|COUNT'
column sr_iops        format 999,999,999  heading 'SMALL|READ|IOPS'
column sw_iops        format 999,999,999  heading 'SMALL|WRITE|IOPS'
column st_iops        format 999,999,999  heading 'SMALL|TOTAL|IOPS'

column lrg_reads      format 999,999,999  heading 'LARGE|READ|COUNT'
column lrg_writes     format 999,999,999  heading 'LARGE|WRITE|COUNT'
column lrg_total      format 999,999,999  heading 'LARGE|TOTAL|COUNT'
column lr_iops        format 999,999,999  heading 'LARGE|READ|IOPS'
column lw_iops        format 999,999,999  heading 'LARGE|WRITE|IOPS'
column lt_iops        format 999,999,999  heading 'LARGE|TOTAL|IOPS'
```

```
select timer_name,
       floor((timer_stop-timer_start )*24)
       || ':' ||
       mod(floor((timer_stop-timer_start )*24*60),60)
       || ':' ||
       mod(floor((timer_stop-timer_start)*24*60*60),60) run_time,
       ROUND((tby_reads2-tby_reads1)/1048576,3)          tby_read,
       ROUND((tby_writes2-tby_writes1)/1048576,3)         tby_writes,
       ROUND((tby_reads2-tby_reads1)/1048576/
(timer_stop-timer_start)/86400,3)    tr_mbps,
       ROUND((tby_writes2-tby_writes1)/1048576/
(timer_stop-timer_start)/86400,3) tw_mbps,
       ROUND(((sma_reads2-sma_reads1)+(lrg_reads2-lrg_reads1))/
(timer_stop-timer_start)/86400,3)    tr_iops,
       ROUND(((sma_writes2-sma_writes1)+(lrg_writes2-lrg_writes1))/
(timer_stop-timer_start)/86400,3) tw_iops,
       ROUND(((sma_reads2-sma_reads1)+(sma_writes2-sma_writes1)+
              (lrg_reads2-lrg_reads1)+(lrg_writes2-lrg_writes1))/
(timer_stop-timer_start)/86400,3) tot_iops
from super_timer
where timer_name = upper('&1');

select timer_name,
       floor((timer_stop-timer_start )*24)
       || ':' ||
       mod(floor((timer_stop-timer_start )*24*60),60)
       || ':' ||
       mod(floor((timer_stop-timer_start)*24*60*60),60) run_time,
       sma_reads2-sma_reads1                        sma_reads,
       sma_writes2-sma_writes1                      sma_writes,
       (sma_reads2-sma_reads1)+(sma_writes2-sma_writes1) sma_total,
       ROUND((sma_reads2-sma_reads1)/(timer_stop-timer_start)/86400,3)   sr_iops,
       ROUND((sma_writes2-sma_writes1)/(timer_stop-timer_start)/86400,3) sw_iops,
       ROUND(((sma_reads2-sma_reads1)+(sma_writes2-sma_writes1))/
(timer_stop-timer_start)/86400,3) st_iops
from super_timer
where timer_name = upper('&1');

select timer_name,
       floor((timer_stop-timer_start )*24)
       || ':' ||
       mod(floor((timer_stop-timer_start )*24*60),60)
       || ':' ||
       mod(floor((timer_stop-timer_start)*24*60*60),60) run_time,
       lrg_reads2-lrg_reads1                        lrg_reads,
       lrg_writes2-lrg_writes1                      lrg_writes,
       (lrg_reads2-lrg_reads1)+(lrg_writes2-lrg_writes1) lrg_total,
       ROUND((lrg_reads2-lrg_reads1)/(timer_stop-timer_start)/86400,3)   lr_iops,
       ROUND((lrg_writes2-lrg_writes1)/(timer_stop-timer_start)/86400,3) lw_iops,
       ROUND(((lrg_reads2-lrg_reads1)+
(lrg_writes2-lrg_writes1))/(timer_stop-timer_start)/86400,3) lt_iops
from super_timer
where timer_name = upper('&1');
```

The following is an example execution of these four scripts. We execute and measure a Cartesian join query. Note that we must name the timer being referenced, so we passed ISHAN to the timer SQL script calls.

```
-- TIMER_TEST.SQL
@timer_create

@timer_start ISHAN
```

```
select count(*) from all_objects a, all_objects;

@timer_stop ISHAN

@timer_results ISHAN
```

Memory Settings

There are a number of parameters that need to be modified on the OS in order for Exadata to support and scale a consolidation configuration. If parameters or settings are not configured appropriately, the OS may require reboots, or other outages may occur to accommodate incremental consolidation.

A key aspect of consolidation is the efficient use of memory. This is especially true of database instance consolidation, where many database instances are running in a server pool. A large part of consolidation planning is determining how many database instances will be consolidated.

Table 14.1 describes the Exadata Linux recommendations.

Table 14.1   Exadata Linux Recommendations

OS Parameters	Recommendation	Comment
HugePages	HugePages is recommended if PageTables in /proc/meminfo is more than 2% of physical memory. HugePages should equal the sum of the shared memory segments used by all the database instances on that server.	When all the database instances are running, the amount of shared memory being used can be calculated by analyzing the output from the `ipcs -m` command. The HugePages setting must be recalculated before any of the database's SGA_TARGET settings is increased or if additional databases are consolidated. The USE_LARGE_PAGES=ONLY init.ora parameter on each consolidated instance prevents any instance from starting unless sufficient HugePages are available.
kernel.shmmni	kernel.shmmni should be greater than the number of projected databases.	The kernel.shmmni OS parameter defines the number of shared memory segments.
kernel.shmmax	kernel.shmmax should be set to 85% of the server physical memory size.	The kernel.shmmax OS parameter defines the maximum shared memory segment size.

Table 14.1   Exadata Linux Recommendations (*Continued*)

OS Parameters	Recommendation	Comment
kernel.semmns	kernel.semmns should be greater than the sum or projected sum of all database processes, as specified by the database PROCESSES parameter.	kernel.semmns sets the maximum total number of system semaphores.
kernel.semmsl	kernel.semmsl should be set to greater than the largest database PROCESSES parameter of any instance.	kernel.semmsl defines the maximum number of semaphores in a semaphore set.

CPU Settings

As stated earlier, system stability is of the utmost importance in consolidated configurations, since many applications can be affected by an unplanned event or even a planned outage.

Two primary reasons for instability in a configuration are excessive memory and CPU consumption. Excessive memory consumption can potentially induce system swapping, which eventually leads to key Clusterware and database instance processes being swapped out, resulting in an eviction of the node. In the case of excessive CPU consumption, similarly, key Clusterware and database instance processes cannot get CPU cycles, leading to node evictions.

To mitigate these issues, users should adhere to the guidelines discussed in the following section.

Instance Caging and Database Resource Management

In nonconsolidated environments, the CPU_COUNT database parameter is not a relevant setting; however, in a consolidation configuration, CPU_COUNT is of paramount importance. This is because, in the absence of the CPU_COUNT setting, each database instance detects all of the CPUs on the server. For example, on a ten-core quad-socket server (totaling 40 CPUs), with 30 running database instances, without the CPU_COUNT setting, there would be an aggregate CPU detection of 120 CPUs, which is a 30x oversubscription.

One mechanism to effectively limit or contain CPU resources per database instance is to leverage the Oracle Database feature Instance Caging, which has been available since 11.2.0.1. Instance Caging relies on the Oracle Database Resource Manager (DBRM) feature. DBRM is a feature of the Oracle Database and is also integrated with the Oracle Clusterware QoS feature. DBRM provides granular control of system resources between workloads and databases. This makes DBRM a critical feature for consolidated systems, as it is used to manage CPU, disk I/O, and parallel execution (PQ operations).

DBRM distinctly supports the two primary Exadata consolidation models described earlier. For example, DBRM can be used for managing resource utilization and contention between applications for schema consolidation, and managing resource utilization and contention between database instances for database consolidation.

For schema consolidation, DBAs can create a consumer group for each consolidated schema application. The resource plan directive associates the resource consumer group with a resource plan and specifies how CPU and I/O are to be allocated to the consumer group.

The following PL/SQL block creates a simple resource plan with three user-specified consumer groups:

```
BEGIN
  DBMS_RESOURCE_MANAGER.CREATE_SIMPLE_PLAN(SIMPLE_PLAN => 'NISHADB_PLAN',
  CONSUMER_GROUP1 => 'APPLICATION_A', GROUP1_PERCENT => 70,
  CONSUMER_GROUP2 => ' APPLICATION_B', GROUP2_PERCENT => 20)
  CONSUMER_GROUP3 => ' APPLICATION_C', GROUP3_PERCENT => 10)
;
END;
/
ALTER SYSTEM SET RESOURCE_MANAGER_PLAN = 'NISHADB_PLAN' SID='*' SCOPE='BOTH';
```

In the database consolidation model, DBRM controls and monitors CPU usage and contention through Instance Caging and the DBRM resource plan. Additionally, DBRM in conjunction with IORM controls disk I/O usage and contention through IORM's inter-database resource plans. The key ingredient here is the inter-database IORM plans, which enable the I/O resources (across Exadata cells) against multiple databases. IORM is covered in the next section. We focus on the Instance Caging feature here.

There are two steps to enabling the Instance Caging feature.

First, for each consolidated instance, set the resource plan for CPU directives to enable Instance Caging. Assign the DBRM resource plan by setting the RESOURCE_MANAGER_PLAN initialization parameter. In most cases, users can simply set RESOURCE_MANAGER_PLAN to DEFAULT_PLAN, if the management of workloads within a database is not needed:

```
ALTER SYSTEM SET RESOURCE_MANAGER_PLAN = 'DEFAULT_PLAN' SID='*' SCOPE='BOTH';
```

Or, using the earlier example:

```
ALTER SYSTEM SET RESOURCE_MANAGER_PLAN = 'NISHADB_PLAN' SID='*' SCOPE='BOTH';
```

Keep in mind that although there are possibilities to create complex DBRM resource plans using nested consumer groups, it is best to keep it simple using a single level.

Second, set the CPU_COUNT initialization parameter to the maximum number of CPUs the instance should use at any time. By default, CPU_COUNT is set to the total number of CPUs on the server and includes hyperthreaded CPUs (CPU threads). Since the CPU_COUNT is a dynamic parameter, its value can be altered as needed.

Note that the CPU_COUNT parameter implicitly influences many Oracle parameters and internal structures, such as parallelism, buffer cache, and latch structure allocations. It is recommended that the minimum value for CPU_COUNT be set to 2, since there are situations where setting CPU_COUNT to 1 causes database instances to be susceptible to hangs or poor performance. Additionally, avoid making several rapid changes to CPU_COUNT as this has been known to be problematic.

I/O Resource Management

Managing CPU resources is a cornerstone feature of DBRM; however, to fully manage and control I/O resources requires the enablement of the I/O Resource Management (IORM) feature. IORM, along with the Exadata Offloading capabilities, are marquee features that separate Exadata from all other converged systems. It is important to note that the IORM is defined and set at the Exadata Storage Server layer and thus is a feature of Exadata server software.

IORM manages the Exadata cell I/O resources on a per-Exadata cell basis. To understand how IORM works, one needs to follow the process flow for IORM: When the database issues an I/O, it sends the I/O request via an iDB message packet to the Exadata Storage Cells. This message packet contains tagged payload information such as the consumer group and resource category (if used). These I/O requests are then placed on the CELLSRV I/O queues and processed by IORM, where the resource plan is evaluated. IORM evaluates the individual I/O requests for each of the consumer groups and databases, validates their priority against the defined resource plans, and finally schedules or places the I/O request onto the cell disk queues. Databases and consumer groups with higher allocations are scheduled more frequently than those with lower allocations. Note that when the Exadata cell's I/O rate is within the predefined threshold, IORM does not queue or intervene on foreground (user) I/O requests.

When creating an IORM plan, first evaluate the workload characteristics of the consolidated databases. If all or a majority of the workload is geared toward lower latency, such as OLTP, a plan directive should reflect this allocation. The same is true of data warehouse (throughput-based) consolidated configurations. When mixed workloads are consolidated (for example, data warehouse and transactional OLTP), careful consideration has to be made of how I/O capacity is used. The following examples illustrate IORM for OLTP, data warehouse, and mixed-configuration workloads.

In the first example, the following IORM directive plan is used to support the
management of I/O resources of two high-priority OLTP-based databases and other
consolidated databases. The po database and oe database have differing I/O pri-
orities, but both have higher priority than the remaining consolidated databases:

```
cellcli> alter iormplan dbplan = -
 ((name=po, level=1, allocation=50), -
  (name=oe, level=1, allocation=40), -
  (name=other, level=1, allocation=10)));
```

Although not necessary, we can explicitly set the low latency objective for IORM to
ensure the lowest latency of I/O:

```
alter iormplan objective=low_latency;
```

In the following scenario, we review the IORM plan for data-warehouse-based
consolidation. There are three key high-throughput databases in this example:
edw, etl, and stage. Databases edw and etl are the most important databases on
the system; the Informatica stage database is less critical. Any additional consolidated databases configured on the system fall into the other bucket.

```
cellcli> alter iormplan dbplan = -
 ((name=edw, level=1, allocation=40), -
  (name=etl, level=1, allocation=40), -
  (name=stage, level=1, allocation=10), -
  (name=other, level=1, allocation=10)));
```

This IORM directive indicates that when there is disk contention, edw and etl get
equal disk bandwidth and each also gets four times the bandwidth of stage.
    A more complex multilevel directive can also be created if a certain resource
management effect is desired. For example, if edw needed a certain level of bandwidth higher than etl, and etl had higher requirements than stage and the
other consolidated databases, the following could be defined:

```
cellcli> alter iormplan dbplan = -
((name=edw, level=1, allocation=60),
 (name=etl, level=1, allocation=40),
 (name=stage, level=2, allocation=100),
 (name=odi_test, level=3, allocation=50),
 (name=other, level=3, allocation=50)),
catplan=' '
```

However, as stated before, IORM works best when it is kept to a simple single-level plan.
    The preceding examples specify standard resource allocations; however, IORM
also has the capability to set a hard limit on the disk utilization for each database.

This is enabled using the `limit` attribute in the directive. Note that when `limit` is specified, excess I/O capacity cannot be used by other consolidated databases. Thus, the `limit` attribute essentially provides more predictable and consistent database performance at the expense of not leveraging underutilized I/O capacity. Nevertheless, the `limit` attribute becomes an important feature when chargeback is based on I/O bandwidth consumption. The following IORM plan illustrates the usage of the `limit` attribute:

```
ALTER IORMPLAN dbplan= -
((name=po, level=1, allocation=50, limit=50), -
(name=oe, level=1, allocation=40, limit=50), -
(name=other, level=1, allocation=10, limit=30));
```

This final example illustrates defining an appropriate plan for mixed-workload databases in a consolidated environment. In this example we have the critical OLTP databases, `po` and `oe`, along with the two business-critical data warehouse databases, `edw` and `etl`. For these mixed-workload consolidations, it is important to define which workload has the higher priority. Note that you cannot guarantee both throughput and low latency at the same time; that is, one must be sacrificed. In most cases low latency generally trumps.

In the following example, low latency implicitly takes precedence based on allocations of the OLTP-based databases. Using this directive, IORM automatically optimizes for low latency. If the data warehouse databases need higher priority, those databases need greater allocations set than the OLTP databases.

```
cellcli> alter iormplan dbplan = -
((name=po, level=1, allocation=40),
(name=oe, level=1, allocation=30),
(name=etl, level=1, allocation=10),
(name=edw, level=1, allocation=10),
(name=other, level=1, allocation=10);
```

To enforce high throughput on the Exadata storage, the following can be set:

```
alter iormplan objective=high throughput;
```

For a balance between latency and throughput, the following can be set:

```
alter iormplan objective=balanced;
```

When IORM is enabled in its "basic" mode, it automatically manages and prioritizes critical background I/Os such as log file syncs and control file reads. On Exadata cells on versions 11.2.3.2 and above, IORM is enabled by default to guard against excessively high latencies for small I/Os, using the `basic` objective. User-defined resource manager plans are not enforced in this mode. To enable IORM for user-defined resource manager plans, the objective must be set to `auto`. Use the following CellCLI command to change the objective:

```
alter iormplan objective=auto;
```

To switch back IORM to the default `basic` objective setting, use the following CellCLI command:

```
alter iormplan objective=basic;
```

With the release of 11.2.3.1 and higher, Exadata Storage Server software IORM now supports new inter-database plans based on shares, as opposed to previous versions, which used percentages. A share is a relative distribution of the I/O resources. In addition, the new default directive specifies the default value for all databases that are not explicitly named in the database plan.

Category resource management is an advanced feature. It allows you to allocate resources primarily by the category of the work being done. For example, suppose all databases have three categories of workloads: OLTP, reports, and maintenance. To allocate the I/O resources based on these workload categories, you would use category resource management.

With inter-database IORM plans, you can also specify the following for each database:

- **Flashcache**—enables or disables the usage of Flash Cache for a particular database. Available in Exadata software version 11.2.2.3.0 and higher.
- **Flashlog**—enables or disables usage of Flash Log for a database.
- **Limit**—limits each database's maximum possible disk utilization to 50%.

Please note that the ALTER IORMPLAN Flash Cache attribute can be set to `off` to prevent a database from using the Flash Cache. This allows Flash Cache to be reserved for mission-critical databases. You should disable Flash Cache usage only if you are sure it is affecting the Flash Cache hit rate of critical databases. Disabling Flash Cache has the negative side effect of increasing disk I/O load.

Once the appropriate IORM plan is created, you can activate it using the `active` command; conversely, the `inactive` command can be used to disable the IORM plans (note that this command needs to be performed on a per-cell basis; thus dcli is used to execute across the cells and ensure consistency):

```
CellCLI> alter iormplan active
```

To list the IORM objective across all cells, the following `dcli` command can be used. Since we ran this on a Quarter Rack Exadata, we get output for three cells:

```
dcli -g cell_group cellcli -e "list iormplan attributes objective"

cell01: auto
cell02: auto
cell03: auto

cellCLI> list iormplan detail
name: exas01cel01_IORMPLAN
catPlan:
dbPlan: name=po,level=1,allocation=50,name=oe,level=1,allocation=40,
name=other,level=1,allocation=50
status: active
```

Isolation Management

Isolation requirements between tenants can greatly influence the method or degree of consolidation. Whether you consolidate multiple application schemas in a single database, host multiple databases on a single Exadata platform, or use some combination of both approaches depends on the level of isolation the system demands.

In this deployment model, the consolidated database essentially consists of one or more application schemas running across one or more servers in a hardware pool. Customers who deploy this model typically consolidate 15 to 20 applications (schemas). In the schema consolidation model, the tenancy granularity is the schema. Therefore, the schema needs to have proper isolation.

Although schema consolidation provides the highest level of consolidation, careful consideration and planning must be done to ensure that the consolidated applications can coexist. For example, check for schema namespace collisions and confirm certification of packaged applications to run in these consolidation configurations. The implementation of schema consolidation has become very streamlined with the 12c Pluggable Database feature. However, you'll need to be implementing 12c databases to take advantage of this feature. For 11g databases, users can follow the best practices in this section.

Isolation can be categorized into four areas: fault, operational, resource, and security. Each consolidation model deals with isolation in a slightly different manner. For example, using OS and/or database built-in capabilities, often in combination with advanced features or products, provides a more complete solution, commensurate with the risk.

The following sections focus on considerations for tenant isolation for both database and schema consolidation models on Exadata platforms.

Fault Isolation in Database Consolidation

In the database consolidation model, the multitenancy granularity is the database, so each database (and each database instance) is isolated from the other databases in the hardware pool. Although all the databases may run from the same Oracle Home installation, database faults are generally isolated to a failing instance; that is, fault isolation is maintained by fencing off the offending instance.

For example, if a database instance becomes unresponsive, one of the neighboring node's LMS processes requests Oracle Clusterware's Clusterware Synchronization Service (CSS) component to perform a "member kill" operation against the offending instance. In rare cases, when the unresponsive instance cannot be killed, an invasive operation such as a node reboot is invoked; in these rare cases, other database instances are affected. However, proper application design and implementation of documented best practices can limit the impact of instance or node failure.

For example, the use of RAC features such as Fast Application Notification (FAN), Fast Connection Failover (FCF), or the 12c feature Application Continuity (AC) can provide a faster application reaction against failure event notification, such as node or database instance down events. Allowing the application to reconnect more quickly minimizes the overall impact of the outage.

Fault Isolation in Schema Consolidation

In the fault isolation schema consolidation model, an application fault in one schema does not cause other applications to fail. However, login storms or improperly configured application or mid-tiers can impact other consolidated applications. To minimize the impact of login storms, configure mid-tier connection pools appropriately. In some cases, login-rate limiters can be defined for the Oracle Listener. Poorly written database resident code, such as PL/SQL, can also affect other unrelated applications. A thorough testing of the application as well as code review is necessary to prevent application faults.

Operational Isolation in Database Consolidation

Operational isolation ensures that any management or maintenance performed on a database or its operating environment does not affect other running databases in the pool, including startup and shutdown of instances, patching, and backup and recovery.

Startup and Shutdown

In most consolidation configurations, the number of Oracle Homes is kept to a minimum, and typically one Oracle Home is used for all the consolidated databases. To provide operational isolation, create named users for each cloud DBA for the database, and add those users to the password file (needs REMOTE_LOGIN_PASSWORDFILE to be set to EXCLUSIVE). Then grant SYSDBA privileges to those named users. By having different password files for each database, users can gain SYSDBA privileges only to their database.

To perform operational functions, such as startup or shutdown, the DBA should connect to the appropriate database user with the SYSDBA privilege. Typically this is performed via OEM; therefore, the necessary database credentials need to be established in OEM.

Patching

Patching databases in a consolidated environment involves two tasks: planning for the patch application (logistics) and executing the actual patch. When you're building consolidated environments on Exadata, downtime SLAs and appropriate expectations need be set with application owners regarding scheduled or unscheduled patching. Frequent requests, by application owners, for database patching is not efficient and should be discouraged, as the patching not only impacts all databases, it may even adversely affect some databases.

A schedule for patch application should be predefined and acknowledged by all participating tenants. For example, a schedule for Oracle PSUs should be well defined. One-off patches should be evaluated for priority and relevance with respect to the entire database consolidated community. When patches need to be applied, the most efficient method is to stage the patch, which involves cloning the Oracle Home, applying the patch to the cloned Home, and finally switching the Oracle Home. Rolling patch applications should be leveraged where possible.

If the patch management logistics across databases are not practical or if sharing of SYSDBA across databases is not desired, a separate Oracle Home for a group of databases can be an alternative. For these cases, each Oracle Home should use a distinct username and OSDBA. However, running database instances from different Oracle Homes does increase complexity and affects overall efficiency.

Operational Isolation in Schema Consolidation

Since there is a single database in the schema consolidation model, operational isolation essentially becomes an exercise in minimizing the impact of the recovery and restoration of lost data or patch management.

For the most efficient data restore possible, a careful design of the backup policy is needed. The backup method should include the restore granularity appropriate for the application. Typically for schema consolidation, nightly backups as well as Data Pump exports of the schema are needed. If data is lost or deleted, features such as Flashback Table, Flashback Query, and Flashback Transaction should be used to provide the least invasive approach for restore. In Oracle Database 12c, RMAN includes the capability to restore an individual table level. Determine how many applications and databases will be consolidated, and also define the fullness factor.

The patching issues in schema consolidation are similar to those in database consolidation.

Resource Isolation in Database Consolidation

Resource isolation deals with the allocation and segregation of system resources. In database consolidation, the competing resources include memory, CPU, and I/O (storage capacity as well as IOPS):

- **Memory**—Appropriate sga_target and sga_max_target values need to be set on a per-instance basis for each node and must be maintained consistently across all instances of the same database. Note that prior to Oracle 12c, there was no capability to enforce and control the PGA size via the pre-12c PGA_AGGREGATE_TARGET initialization parameter. Oracle Database 12c now provides the capability to set a hard limit on PGA by enabling automatic PGA management, which requires the repurposed PGA_AGGREGATE_LIMIT parameter settings. It is therefore recommended that you set a hard limit on PGA to avoid excessive PGA usage:

  ```
  SQL> ALTER SYSTEM SET PGA_AGGREGATE_LIMIT=2G;
  ```

- **CPU**—Like memory settings, the CPU values should be set appropriately. As discussed in the previous section, this can be done by setting CPU_COUNT to a specific value or by enabling the Instance Caging feature. The latter is recommended because it also enforces a DBRM resource plan, providing better control of CPU consumption. Follow the best practices outlined in the earlier "CPU Settings" section.

- **I/O**—I/O containment and resource management come in the form of IORM. This is covered in detail in the earlier "I/O Resource Management" section.

Resource Isolation in Schema Consolidation

In the resource isolation in the schema consolidation model, multiple applications contend for the same database and system resources; thus resource management is a necessity for schema consolidation. Oracle Database resource profile limits provide basic "knobs" to control consumption and can be supplemented with Oracle DBRM along with Oracle QoS. Applications can be put into consumer groups with an appropriate resource plan directive mapping with a resource plan. This specifies how CPU, I/O, and parallel server resources are allocated to the consumer group.

For storage-capacity-related issues, DBAs can cap the storage consumed by applications using tablespace quotas. There should be close monitoring of tablespace usage by each schema so that growth patterns and thresholds can be managed.

Security Isolation in Database Consolidation

In any consolidated environment, a security implementation should use the "least privileges" approach to hardening the environment. In most cases, a single Oracle Home is used by all database instances on a given node. If several databases are sharing the same Oracle Home, any user who is part of the OSDBA group for that Oracle Home has SYSDBA access to all database instances running from that Home. This is a good approach to reduce manageability overhead; however, it does open security issues.

It is recommended that you implement the following best practices for this type of configuration:

- Minimize access to the database server (that is, SQL*Net pipe-only access).
- Use named user accounts for DBAs with sudo access for privileged commands.
- Implement and enable Database Vault to provide role separation to control user data access:
  - To protect application and schema data from unauthorized access, employ Database Vault using Realms. The security admin should enable Realms for each application upon provisioning the database.
  - For E-Business Suite, Siebel, and PeopleSoft users, deploy the redefined Data Vault Realms.
  - Encrypt data where necessary.

Security Isolation in Schema Consolidation

Security isolation between schemas is one of the most important aspects of consolidation. The out-of-the-box Oracle Database profiles can be used to limit access to data. However, many times deeper security measures and policies must be put in place. These may include protecting data at rest, giving granular access control, as well as performing security auditing. For these cases, encryption should be implemented where necessary, via Advanced Security, Realms-based access control,

Database Vault, and Audit Vault for runtime audit management. The following are other security best practices for schema consolidation:

- Give access to SYSDBA, SYSOPER, and SYSASM only to DBAs.
- Give guest DBAs only schema-level access and V$ view access.
- Ensure use of private synonyms.
- Use strong database user passwords.
- Set appropriate values for PASSWORD_LOCK_TIME and FAILED_LOGIN_ATTEMPTS.

12c Pluggable Database

There is nothing Exadata specific with respect to Pluggable Databases (PDBs) from a deployment perspective; however, Exadata's engineered system model, along with the PDB feature, provides a rich environment for implementing a DBaaS strategy. Therefore, for completeness (in this consolidation discussion), we introduce Pluggable Database at a high level.

Prior to Oracle Database 12c, the schema consolidation model offered the most efficient and highest level of consolidation. However, this model required careful consideration and planning to ensure that the consolidated applications could coexist with respect to performance, security, and manageability. Additionally, tasks such as schema namespace collisions had to be evaluated. Thus, schema consolidation was not the easiest to implement, though it provided the highest ROI.

With the advent of Oracle Database 12c, a new architecture for consolidation was introduced. This new feature is called Oracle Multitenant and is commonly known as Pluggable Database (PDB). This feature greatly simplifies consolidation of multiple applications onto a shared database environment and removes the limitations of the previous versions. PDB allows for the deployment of a multitenant container database (CDB) which can contain one or more PDBs. PDB removes the key barriers to adopting schema-based consolidation and removes the ongoing operational problems that come with that approach.

The feature is a dramatic change in the Oracle architecture, and thus virtually every Oracle component and feature has been modified and improved to support PDB, including DBRM, Advanced Security, and RAC, without sacrificing performance. For example, Oracle Database 12c Resource Manager is extended with specific functionality to instantly control the competition between the PDBs within a CDB.

Creating multiple PDBs in a single CDB allows for sharing of memory and background processes. This inherently allows you to operate many more PDBs on a particular server platform than when deploying dedicated single-instance databases.

This is similar to the benefit that schema consolidation brings. However, PDBs combine the best of all the other consolidation models and thus should be considered as the primary mode for consolidation in 12c Exadata.

A key aspect of PDB is its portability or mobility. PDB can be unplugged from one CDB and plugged into another. Alternatively, you can clone a PDB within the same CDB, or from one CDB to another. These operations, together with creating a PDB, are done with new SQL commands and take just seconds.

Summary

Today's business world is an ever-changing environment of increasing complexity and challenges, requiring corporations to build agility and flexibility into their IT infrastructure to swiftly adapt to changes in the marketplace. An IT organization's key initiatives include consolidating systems, standardizing business processes, moving to shared services, and meeting corporate compliance. Consolidation is one of the major strategies that organizations are pursuing to achieve greater efficiencies in their operations.

Consolidation becomes an eventual outcome and action as a result of rationalization, simplification, and standardization. However, database consolidation has been considered the "last frontier" of virtualization or consolidation.

Engineered systems like Exadata are a key component of consolidation and DBaaS. Many Exadata features are geared toward multi-workload and multi-application support, as well as proper isolation from noisy neighbor issues.

This is partly because of territorial or political obstacles, a lack of motivation, or even a lack of understanding of the available technologies. In this chapter we reviewed planning and best practices for database consolidation on Exadata.

## 15

Exadata Smart Flash Cache in Depth

The Exadata Database Machine combines Flash solid-state disks with more traditional magnetic disks in order to achieve economic storage of large datasets together with the ability to achieve low latency and high throughput. In this chapter we review the architecture of Exadata Flash solid-state disk and examine in detail how Exadata Smart Flash Cache and Exadata Smart Flash Logging allow you to transparently leverage this Flash I/O.

Solid-State Disk Technology

To understand how Flash technology contributes to Exadata system performance and how best to exploit that technology, let's start by comparing the performance and economics of Flash and spinning-disk technology.

Limitations of Disk Technology

Magnetic disks have been a continuous component of mainstream computer equipment for generations of IT professionals. First introduced in the 1950s, the fundamental technology has remained remarkably constant: one or more **platters** contain magnetic charges that represent bits of information. These magnetic charges are read and written by an **actuator arm**, which moves across the disk to a specific position on the radius of the platter, and then waits for the platter to rotate to the

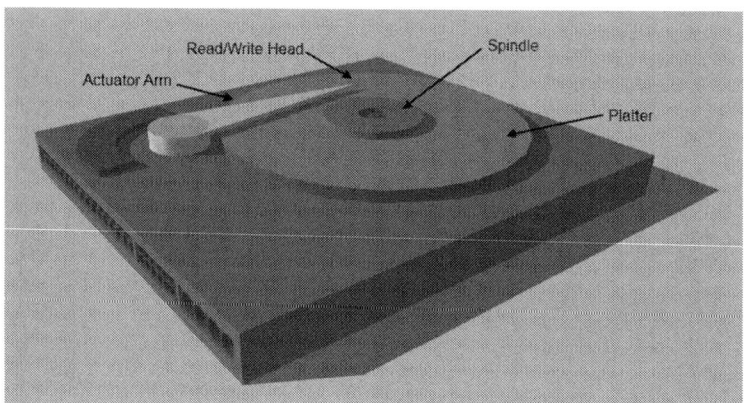

Figure 15.1   Magnetic disk architecture

appropriate location (see Figure 15.1). The time taken to read an item of information is the sum of the time taken to move the head into position (**seek time**), the time taken to rotate the item into place (**rotational latency**), and the time taken to transmit the item through the disk controller (**transfer time**).

Moore's Law—first articulated by Intel founder Gordon Moore—observes that transistor density doubles every 18 to 24 months. In its broadest interpretation, Moore's Law reflects the exponential growth that is commonly observed in almost all electronic components, influencing CPU speed, RAM, and disk storage capacity.

While this exponential growth is observed in almost all electronic aspects of computing—including hard disk densities—it does not apply to mechanical technologies such as those underlying magnetic disk I/O. For instance, had Moore's Law been in effect for the rotational speed of disk devices, disks today should be rotating about 100 million times faster than in the early 1960s; in fact they are rotating only eight times faster.

Note

If an 8-inch disk rotating at 2800 RPM in 1962 was subject to Moore's Law, by now the velocity on the outside of the disk would be about ten times the speed of light. As Scotty from *Star Trek* would say, "Ye canna change the laws of physics!"

So while the other key components of computer performance have been advancing exponentially, magnetic disk drives have been improving only incrementally. There have been some significant technical innovations—Perpendicular Magnetic Recording, for instance—but these in general have led to improved capacity and reliability rather than speed. Consequently, disk drives are slower today (when compared to other components or even their own storage capacity) than in the past. Consequently, disk I/O has increasingly limited the performance of database systems, and the practice of database performance tuning has largely become a process of avoiding disk I/O whenever possible.

The Rise of Solid-State Flash Disks

Heroic efforts have been made over the years to avoid the increasingly onerous bottleneck of the magnetic disk drive. The most prevalent, and until recently most practical, solution has been to "short stroke" and "stripe" magnetic disks: essentially installing more disks than are necessary for data storage in order to increase total I/O bandwidth. This increases the overall I/O capacity of the disk subsystem but has a limited effect on latency for individual I/O operations.

Note

Short stroking involves limiting the amount of data stored on a disk so that all of the data is concentrated on the perimeter of the disk. This can improve I/O seek latency by reducing the average distance the actuator arm needs to move across the disk and by concentrating data in the outer sectors of the platter where the overall rotational speed is highest. A short-stroked disk drive may deliver maybe twice the throughput of a drive that is at full capacity, depending on how much of the storage capacity is discarded.

In contrast to a magnetic disk, solid-state disks (SSDs) contain no moving parts and provide tremendously lower I/O latencies. Commercial SSDs are currently implemented using either DDR RAM—effectively a battery-backed RAM device—or NAND Flash. NAND Flash is an inherently nonvolatile storage medium and almost completely dominates today's SSD market. NAND Flash is the technology used for Exadata SSD.

Flash SSD Latency

Performance of Flash SSD is orders of magnitude superior to that of magnetic disk devices, especially for read operations. Figure 15.2 compares the read latency of various types of SSDs and traditional magnetic disks (note that these are approximate and vary markedly depending on the drive make and configuration).

Economics of Solid-State Disks

The promise of solid-state disks has led some to anticipate a day when all magnetic disks are replaced by solid-state disks. While this might someday come to pass, in the short term the economics of storage and the economics of I/O are at

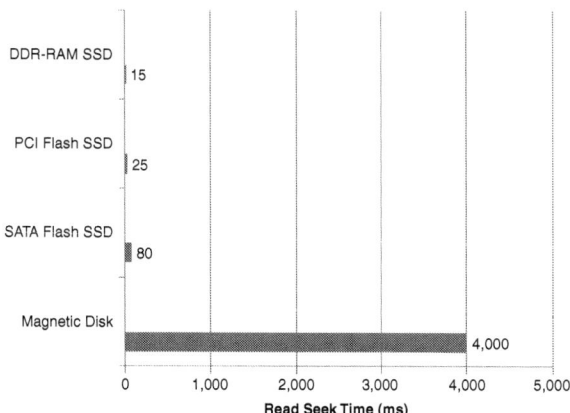

Figure 15.2   Seek times for various drive technologies

odds—magnetic disk provides a more economical medium per unit of storage, while Flash provides a more economical medium for delivering high I/O rates and low latencies.

Figure 15.3 illustrates the two competing trends: while the cost of I/O is reduced with solid-state technology, the cost per terabyte increases. Various flavors of SSD (PCI/SATA and MLC/SLC) offer different price and performance characteristics

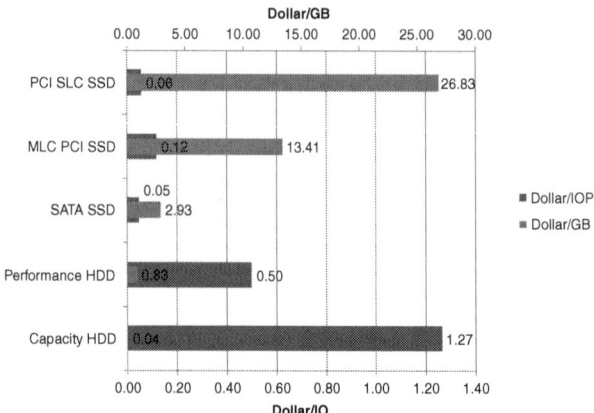

Figure 15.3   Economics of storage for solid-state and magnetic disks

compared to magnetic disks (15K versus 7K RPM, for instance). The SSD devices that offer good economics of I/O offer poorer economics for mass storage. Of course the cost per gigabyte for SSD is dropping rapidly, but no faster than the falling cost of magnetic disks or the growth in database storage demand—especially in the era of Big Data.

Since most databases include both hot and cold data—small amounts of frequently accessed data as well as large amounts of idle data—most databases will experience the best economic benefit by combining both solid-state and traditional magnetic disk technologies. This is why Exadata combines both magnetic disks and Flash disks to provide the optimal balance between storage economics and performance. If Exadata contained only magnetic disks, it could not provide superior OLTP performance; if it contained only SSDs, it could not offer compelling economical storage for large databases.

Flash SSD Architecture and Performance

The performance differences between solid-state drives and magnetic disks involve more than simply a reduction in read latency. Just as the fundamental architecture of magnetic disks favors certain I/O operations, the architecture of solid-state drives favors specific and different types of I/O. Understanding how an SSD handles the different types of operations helps us make the best decisions when choosing configuration options.

SLC, MLC, and TLC Disks

Flash-based solid-state disks have a three-level hierarchy of storage. Individual bits of information are stored in **cells**. In a single-level cell (SLC) SSD, each cell stores only a single bit. In a multilevel cell (MLC), each cell may store 2 or more bits of information. MLC SSD devices consequently have greater storage densities, but lower performance and reliability. However, because of the economic advantages of MLC, Flash storage vendors have been working tirelessly to improve the performance and reliability of MLC Flash, and it is now generally possible to get excellent performance from an MLC-based device.

Until recently, MLC SSDs contained only 2 bits of information per cell. However, triple-level cache (TLC) SSDs are now becoming available: these are MLC devices that can store 3 bits of information. In theory, higher-density MLCs may appear in the future. However, increasing the number of bits in each cell reduces the longevity and performance of the cell. So far, Exadata systems have used only SLC or two-level MLC devices.

Cells are arranged in pages—typically 4K or 8K in size—and pages into blocks of between 128K and 1M, as shown in Figure 15.4.

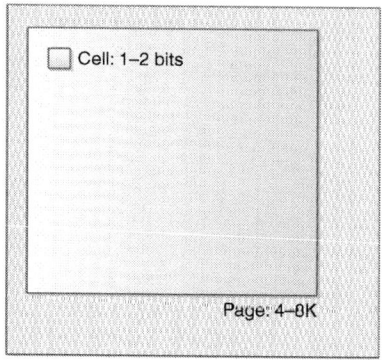

Figure 15.4 SSD storage hierarchy (logarithmically scaled)

Write Performance and Endurance

The page and block structure is particularly significant for Flash SSD performance because of the special characteristics of write I/O in Flash technology. Read operations, and initial write operations, require only a single-page I/O. However, changing the contents of a page requires an erase and overwrite of a complete block. Even the initial write can be significantly slower than a read, but the block erase operation is particularly slow—around 2 milliseconds.

Figure 15.5 shows the approximate times for a page seek, page write, and block erase.

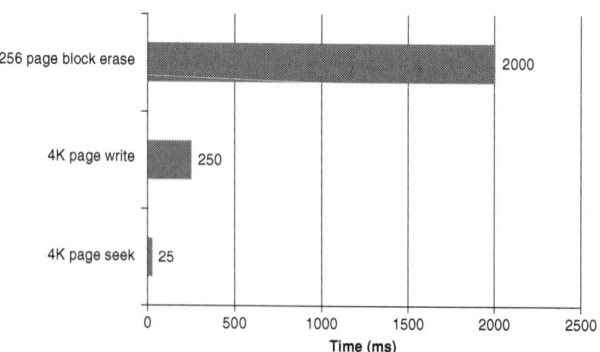

Figure 15.5 Flash SSD performance characteristics

Write I/O has another consequence in Flash solid-state drives: after a certain number of writes, a cell may become unusable. This write endurance limit differs among drives but is typically between 10,000 cycles for a low-end MLC device and up to 1,000,000 cycles for a high-end SLC device. SSDs generally "fail safe" when a cell becomes unwritable, marking the page as bad and moving the data to a new page.

Garbage Collection and Wear Leveling

Enterprise SSD manufacturers make great efforts to avoid the performance penalty of the erase operation and the reliability concerns raised by write endurance. Sophisticated algorithms are used to ensure that erase operations are minimized and that writes are evenly distributed across the device.

Erase operations are avoided through the use of **free lists** and **garbage collection**. During an update, the SSD marks the block to be modified as invalid and copies the updated contents to an empty block, retrieved from a "free list." Later, garbage collection routines recover the invalid block, placing it on a free list for subsequent operations. Some SSDs maintain storage above the advertised capacity of the drive to ensure that the free list does not run out of empty blocks for this purpose. This is known as **overprovisioning**.

Note

Microsoft Windows includes a TRIM command, which allows the operating system to inform the SSD when entire files are deleted and can therefore be moved to the free block pool. However, since we almost never delete Oracle Database files in production systems, this command has little effect for Oracle Databases.

Figure 15.6 illustrates a simplified SSD update algorithm. In order to avoid a time-consuming ERASE operation, the SSD controller marks a block to be updated as invalid (1), then takes an empty block from the free list (2) and writes the new data to that block (3). Later on, when the disk is idle, the invalid blocks are garbage collected by erasing the invalidated block.

Wear leveling is the algorithm that ensures that no particular block is subjected to a disproportionate number of writes. It may involve moving the contents of hot blocks to blocks from the free list and eventually marking overused blocks as unusable.

Wear leveling and garbage collection algorithms in the disk controller are what separate the men from the boys in SSDs. Without effective wear leveling and garbage collection we would expect SSD drives to exhibit performance degradation and a reduced effective life. With the sophisticated algorithms employed by Oracle (Sun) and other SSD vendors these issues are rarely significant.

However, the implications of garbage collection and wear leveling do influence what we expect from a database system that uses Flash SSDs. Sustained heavy sequential write I/O, or write operations that concentrate on a small number of

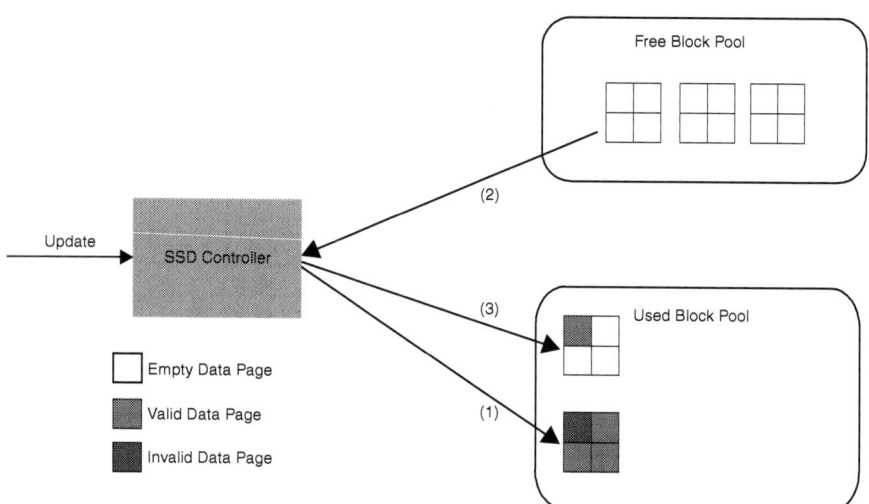

Figure 15.6 Flash SSD garbage collection

hot pages, may not allow the garbage collection and wear leveling algorithms time to clean up invalid pages or distribute hot pages between operations. As a result, SSDs subject to these sorts of workloads may exhibit performance or storage capacity degradation. This may influence decisions around the use of Flash SSD for sequential write-intensive workloads such as those involved in redo log operations.

SATA versus PCIe SSD

Flash SSD drives come in two fundamental types: SATA and PCIe. A SATA SSD connects to the computer using the SATA interface employed by most magnetic disks. A PCIe drive connects directly to the PCI bus, familiar to most of us as the slot in our home computers to which graphics cards are attached.

SATA SSDs are convenient, because they can be attached wherever a traditional magnetic SATA disk is found. Unfortunately, the SATA interface was designed for magnetic disks, which have latencies in the order of milliseconds. When a Flash SSD—which has latencies in the order of microseconds—uses a SATA interface, the overhead of SATA becomes significant and may account for as much as two-thirds of the total read latency.

The PCIe interface was designed for extremely low-latency devices such as graphics adapters and allows these devices to interact directly with the computer's processor bus. Consequently, PCIe SSD devices have much lower latencies than SATA SSDs—read latencies on the order of 25 microseconds versus perhaps 75 microseconds for a typical SATA SSD (see Figure 15.2).

The Oracle Database Flash Cache

Although Exadata systems do not use the Oracle Database Flash Cache (DBFC), any discussion of the Exadata Smart Flash Cache (ESFC) inevitably invites comparisons with the DBFC. So before we dig deeply into Exadata Flash, let's quickly review how the Oracle Database Flash Cache works. The DBFC is available from Oracle RDBMS 11*g* Release 2 on Oracle operating systems (Solaris and Oracle Enterprise Linux).

The Database Flash Cache serves as a secondary cache to the Oracle buffer cache. Oracle manages data blocks in the buffer cache using a modified least recently used (LRU) algorithm. Simplistically speaking, blocks age out of the buffer cache if they have not been accessed recently. When the DBFC is present, blocks that age out of the data cache are not discarded but are instead written (by the Database Writer, DBWR) to the Flash device. Should the blocks be required in the future, they can be read from the Flash Cache instead of from slower magnetic-disk-based database files.

Figure 15.7 shows the Oracle Database Flash Cache architecture. An Oracle server process reads blocks from the database files and stores them in the buffer cache (1). Subsequent reads can obtain the data blocks from the buffer cache without having to access the database file (2). When the block ages out of the buffer

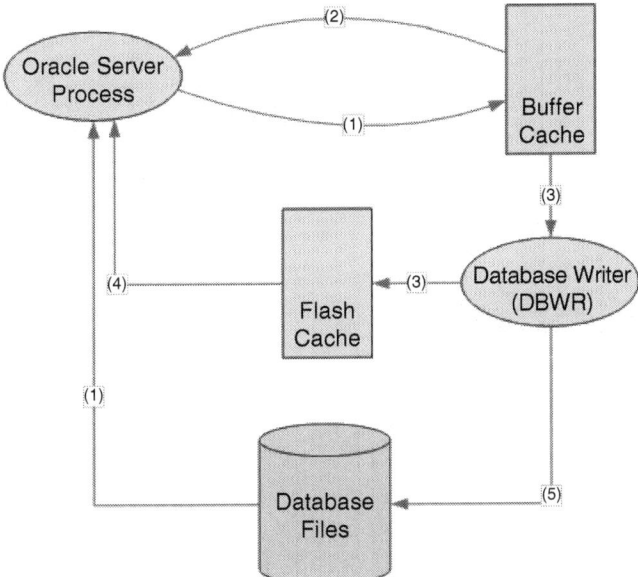

Figure 15.7   Oracle Database Flash Cache architecture

cache, the database writer loads it into the Flash Cache (3), but only if doing so does not interfere with writing modified blocks to disk (5). Subsequent reads may now find a block in either the Flash Cache (4) or the buffer cache (2).

Note

The Oracle DBFC allows non-Exadata systems to benefit from Flash SSD. However, the DBFC is not included in any Exadata configurations and should not be confused with the Exadata Smart Flash Cache (ESFC).

Exadata Flash Hardware

Now that we have thoroughly reviewed Flash SSD technology and the Database Flash Cache, let's look at how Flash SSD is incorporated into the Exadata architecture. In an Exadata system, Flash SSD is contained in the Storage Cells only. There is no SSD configured within the Compute Nodes.

Each Storage Cell contains four PCIe Flash SSD drives. The exact configuration depends on the Exadata version:

- On an X2 system, each cell contains four 96GB Sun F20 SLC PCI Flash cards. That's 384GB total per Storage Cell for a total of 5.2TB of Flash in a full Exadata rack.

- On an X3 system, each cell contains four 400GB Sun F40 MLC PCI Flash cards. That is 1.6TB of Flash per cell and a total of 22.4TB of Flash for a full Exadata rack.

- On an X4 system, each cell contains four 800GB Sun F80 MLC PCI Flash cards. That's 3.2TB of Flash per cell and a total of 44.8TB of Flash for a full Exadata rack!

Note that the increase in capacity between X-2, X-3, and X-4 has been achieved not by adding more Flash SSD cards, but by increasing the capacity of each drive.

Also note that the increase in capacity in X-3 was achieved primarily by moving from SLC to MLC cards. While it's true that SLC is inherently more durable and offers lower latencies than MLC, it's also true that in the years since the F20 was introduced MLC technology has improved significantly. Oracle claims the MLC F40 cards, shown in Figure 15.8, actually have twice the raw throughput of the SLC F20 cards.

Note

Oracle claims 101,000 4K reads per second for an F20 card, while claiming a rate of 190,000 8K reads per second for the F40. Given that most Flash SSD accesses are 8K blocks, we can expect the throughput of an F40 to be three to four times that of an F20 for OLTP workloads.

Figure 15.8   Oracle Sun F40 PCIe Flash SSD

Exadata Smart Flash Cache

The default configuration in an Exadata system is to use all of the Flash on the system as cache—in the Exadata Smart Flash Cache (ESFC). We'll see in the next chapter how we can allocate that Flash for other purposes, but out of the box, it's the ESFC that will deliver most of the Flash advantage.

The ESFC has a similar architecture to the Database Flash Cache that we looked at earlier in this chapter. However, there are some significant differences that you'll want to be aware of, so avoid the mistake of assuming that the ESFC is just the Database Flash Cache for Exadata.

Exadata Smart Flash Cache Architecture

The ESFC is managed by the Exadata Storage Cell Server software **CELLSRV**. In general, when a Database Node requests a block of data from an ASM disk, the CELLSRV software issues asynchronous requests to the ESFC and to the grid disks that underlie the ASM disk group. If the data is in the Flash Cache, this is satisfied from the cache, and if not, from the grid disk. After forwarding the block to the Database Node, CELLSRV then stores any blocks retrieved from the grid disks into the Flash Cache—provided that the blocks are "eligible."

Eligibility for caching is determined by metadata sent to the Storage Cell by the database server. This includes the size and type of I/O, as well as the segment's CELL_FLASH_CACHE storage clause.

While it's possible to configure an Oracle Database on Exadata as a single instance, most Exadata databases are configured as RAC clusters. In normal circumstances, therefore, the request arrives at the Storage Cell only when the block has not been found in the buffer cache of the requesting node, or in another node in the cluster.

Figure 15.9 represents the data flow for simple Exadata reads:

1. The database looks for the blocks in the local cache.
2. If not found in local cache, the database uses Cache Fusion to find the block in the Global Cache across the cluster.
3. If not found in the Global Cache, the database requests the block from the storage server.
4. The storage server reads the block from both the Flash and the disk system.
5. The storage server returns the block from whichever source satisfies the request faster.
6. The storage server places the block into the Exadata Smart Flash Cache, if it was not already present.

Note

Remember that regardless of the number of Database Nodes in the Exadata system, the number of instances involved in such a Global Cache request can never be more than three. At most the requesting instance contacts the instance mastering the particular block, which then forwards that request to the last known instance to access the block.

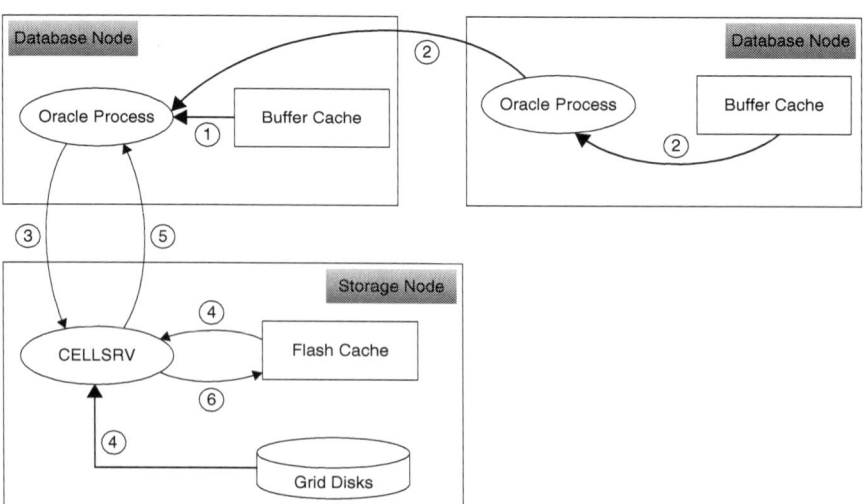

Figure 15.9   Exadata read I/O lifecycle

It may seem unnecessary to belabor the Global Cache architecture of RAC in conjunction with our description of ESFC. However, the relationship between ESFC and the RAC Global Cache is critical to setting our expectations for ESFC performance. The ESFC is actually a third-level cache, resorted to only when Oracle fails to find the required data in the local buffer cache and in the global RAC cache. In some circumstances, the effectiveness of the local buffer cache and the Global Cache are so great that the additional caching of the ESFC offers only incremental advantage.

What the Exadata Smart Flash Cache Stores

Not everything that is sent from the Storage Cell to the database server gets placed in the Flash Cache. The storage server software can differentiate between different types of I/O requests—backup, Data Pump, archive logs, and so on. Only data file and control file blocks are cached in the ESFC. The CELLSRV also differentiates between database blocks accessed via single-block reads and those retrieved via full or Smart table scans.

By default Exadata stores only small I/Os in the Exadata Smart Flash Cache. Small I/Os in most cases are single-block reads. During a full table scan Oracle requests blocks in multiblock lumps (by default 16 blocks), and these are not stored in the Exadata Smart Flash Cache unless you change the CELL_FLASH_CACHE clause for the segment.

Flash Cache Compression

The F40 and F80 Flash SSD devices—provided on Exadata X-3 and X-4 machines respectively—can provide hardware-expedited compression of data within the Flash Cache. Depending on the nature of the data being stored in the cache, this can increase the effective capacity from two to four times. The compression is implemented in the Flash drives so it places virtually no load on the system. The feature requires the Advanced Compression option.

The Flash Cache compression is not enabled by default and is enabled by issuing an ALTER CELL flashCacheCompress=TRUE command and (on an X3 system) ALTER CELL flashCacheCompX3Support=TRUE. These commands must be issued before the Flash Cache is created, so you need to drop and re-create the Flash Cache to take advantage of this feature. See Oracle Support Note ID 1664257.1 for full details.

CELL_FLASH_CACHE Storage Clause

The segment STORAGE clause CELL_FLASH_CACHE controls prioritization of blocks within the ESFC and also the treatment of Smart Scan blocks. It has three possible settings:

- If set to NONE, no blocks for the segment are ever stored in the Exadata Smart Flash Cache.
- If set to DEFAULT, small I/Os (single-block reads) are stored in the Exadata Smart Flash Cache.
- If set to KEEP, Smart Scan and full table scan blocks are stored in the Exadata Smart Flash Cache. Furthermore, when the storage server needs to evict blocks from the ESFC, blocks with the setting KEEP are evicted last.

We can examine the current settings for the CELL_FLASH_CACHE clause by querying USER_SEGMENTS or DBA_SEGMENTS:

```
SQL> l
  1* SELECT segment_name,segment_type,cell_flash_cache
       FROM user_segments where segment_name like 'EXA%'
SQL> /

SEGMENT_NAME             SEGMENT_TYPE        CELL_FLASH_CACHE
-----------------------  ------------------  ----------------
EXA_TXN_DATA             TABLE               KEEP
EXA_TXN_DATA_EIGHT_PK    INDEX               KEEP
EXA_TXN_DATA_EIGTH       TABLE               KEEP
EXA_TXN_DATA_HALF        TABLE               NONE
EXA_TXN_DATA_HALF_PK     INDEX               KEEP
EXA_TXN_DATA_PK          INDEX               DEFAULT
EXA_TXN_DATA_SAS         TABLE               KEEP
```

We can adjust the setting for CELL_FLASH_CACHE during a CREATE TABLE or CREATE INDEX statement or after the fact using ALTER TABLE or ALTER INDEX:

```
SQL> ALTER TABLE exa_txn_data STORAGE (CELL_FLASH_CACHE none);

Table altered.
```

Flash Cache KEEP Expiration

Some Oracle documentation describes the KEEP clause as pinning blocks into the ESFC, but this is not completely accurate. The KEEP clause prioritizes blocks but does not guarantee that all of an object's blocks will be in ESFC. Oracle at the most reserves only 80% of the Exadata Smart Flash Cache for KEEP blocks. KEEP blocks are less likely to be aged out than DEFAULT, but eventually they will leave the cache if they are not accessed and other blocks are introduced—especially if more KEEP blocks are introduced.

Additionally, blocks marked for the KEEP segment of the cache are not privileged indefinitely; by default, a block's KEEP privilege expires after 24 hours. You can observe this behavior by issuing a LIST FLASHCACHECONTENT command.

Here we see blocks in the Exadata Smart Flash Cache introduced as part of a scan of a table that had the CELL_FLASH_CACHE KEEP attribute:

```
CellCLI> list flashcachecontent where objectNumber=139536 detail
              cachedKeepSize:        2855739392
              cachedSize:            2855936000
              dbID:                  325854467
              dbUniqueName:
              hitCount:              0
              hoursToExpiration:     24
              missCount:             2729
              objectNumber:          139536
              tableSpaceNumber:      5
```

About 2.8GB of data is shown as both cachedSize and cachedKeepSize. HoursToExpiration shows how long the KEEP attribute is maintained. After 24 hours the entry for this object looks like this:

```
list flashcachecontent where objectNumber=139536 detail
              cachedKeepSize:        0
              cachedSize:            2855936000
              dbID:                  325854467
              dbUniqueName:
              hitCount:              0
              missCount:             2729
              objectNumber:          139536
              tableSpaceNumber:      5
```

After the expiration period, blocks are still in the cache but are no longer marked as KEEP and can be evicted to make way for other non-KEEP blocks that may be introduced.

Monitoring Exadata Smart Flash Cache

In Chapter 16, we'll look in detail at Exadata Smart Flash Cache monitoring using CellCLI statistics and other tools. But since these techniques are fairly complex—more suited to benchmarking and research projects than day-to-day practical tuning—let's look at some simpler ways of determining the effectiveness of the Exadata Smart Flash Cache.

Clearly, the bottom line for any Flash technology is the reduction in overall I/O time. Therefore, the most effective technique is to alternate between various CELL_FLASH_CACHE settings and measure the difference in observed execution time and wait times in V$SYSTEM_EVENT and V$SESSION_EVENT. However, changing

CELL_FLASH_CACHE on a production system is going to be somewhat disruptive, and you're not always going to be able to perform side-by-side tests of different options. V$SYSSTAT and V$SESSSTAT contain two statistics that provide quick insight into Exadata Smart Flash Cache performance:

- **Cell Flash Cache read hits**—This records the number of read requests that found a match in the Exadata Smart Flash Cache.

- **Physical read requests optimized**—This records the number of read requests that were "optimized" either by the Exadata Smart Flash Cache or through Storage Indexes. While this is less directly applicable to the Exadata Smart Flash Cache than the cell flash cache read hits statistic, it has the advantage of having an analogue column in V$SQL as we will see below.

Comparing these statistics to the physical read total IO requests statistic gives us some indication, as shown in Listing 15.1, of how many I/Os are being optimized (esfc_sessstat_qry.sql).

Listing 15.1   Optimized Cell I/O Statistics

```
SQL> 1
  1      SELECT name, VALUE
  2        FROM v$mystat JOIN v$statname
  3             USING (statistic#)
  4       WHERE name IN ('cell flash cache read hits',
  5                      'physical read requests optimized',
  6*                     'physical read total IO requests')
SQL> /

NAME                                         VALUE
----------------------------------------- -------------
physical read total IO requests            117,246
physical read requests optimized            58,916
cell flash cache read hits                  58,916
```

V$SQL records optimized read requests—Flash Cache and/or Storage Index I/O—in the column optimized_phy_read_requests. Therefore we can identify the SQLs cached that have the highest amount of optimized I/O and therefore are likely the heaviest users of the Exadata Smart Flash Cache. Listing 15.2 (esfc_vsql.sql) shows the top five SQLs in terms of optimized I/O.

Listing 15.2   Top Five Optimized I/O SQL Statements

```
SQL> 1
  1  SELECT sql_id,
  2         sql_text,
  3         optimized_phy_read_requests,
  4         physical_read_requests,
  5         optimized_hit_pct,
  6         pct_total_optimized
```

```
 7    FROM ( SELECT sql_id,
 8                  substr(sql_text,1,40) sql_text,
 9                  physical_read_requests,
10                  optimized_phy_read_requests,
11                  optimized_phy_read_requests * 100
12                       / physical_read_requests
13                    AS optimized_hit_pct,
14                  optimized_phy_read_requests
15                  * 100
16                  / SUM (optimized_phy_read_requests)
17                       OVER ()
18                  pct_total_optimized,
19                  RANK () OVER (ORDER BY
20                            optimized_phy_read_requests DESC)
21                    AS optimized_rank
22            FROM v$sql
23          WHERE optimized_phy_read_requests > 0
24        ORDER BY optimized_phy_read_requests DESC)
25*  WHERE optimized_rank <= 5
SQL> /

                   Optimized     Total Optimized Pct Total
SQL_ID             Read IO     Read IO   Hit Pct Optimized
---------------    -----------  ----------- --------- --------
77kphjxam5akb        270,098      296,398    91.13    12.19
4mnz7k87ymgur        269,773      296,398    91.02    12.18
8mw2xhnu943jn        176,596      176,596   100.00     7.97
4xt8y8qs3gcca        117,228      117,228   100.00     5.29
bnypjf1kb37p1        117,228      117,228   100.00     5.29
```

Exadata Smart Flash Cache Performance

The performance gains you can expect from the ESFC vary depending on your workload and configuration. Let's look at a few examples.

Exadata Smart Flash Cache and Smart Scans

As mentioned earlier, Smart Scans are generally not cached in the Flash Cache, unless the CELL_FLASH_CACHE STORAGE setting is set to KEEP. Figure 15.10 illustrates this

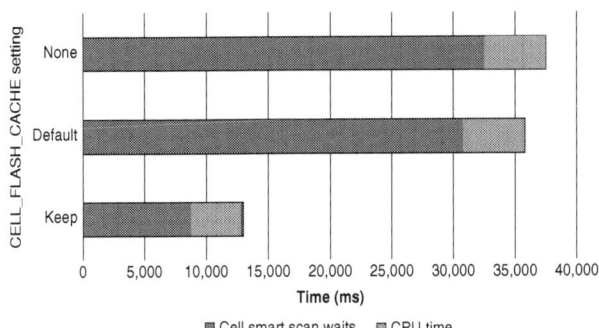

Figure 15.10   Effect of CELL_FLASH_CACHE storage setting on Exadata Smart Scans

effect: successive scan operations on a large (50-million-row) table (using exactly the same SELECT and WHERE clauses) are unaffected by the Flash Cache, unless the table is associated with the CELL_FLASH_CACHE KEEP clause.

Full (Not So Smart) Scans

Full table scans are treated very similarly to Smart Scans by the Exadata Smart Flash Cache. Consider the full table scan process: we read the first batch of blocks from the table, place them in the Flash Cache, read the next blocks and cache, and repeat until all the blocks have been read. Now, by the time we reach the end of the table, the first blocks in the table have been pushed down the least-recently-used chain and are now relatively "cold." Indeed, by the time the last blocks have been read, the first blocks may have already aged out.

If this has happened, when we read the table again we find few or no blocks in the cache. Even worse, we've "polluted" the cache by filling it with large numbers of blocks from the full table scan that may never be read again. This is one of the reasons Oracle over time has almost completely eliminated caching of table scan blocks from the buffer cache and why by default Exadata does not cache full table scan blocks in the Exadata Smart Flash Cache.

Figure 15.11 illustrates exactly this phenomenon. When a large (50-million-row) full table scan is repeated with DEFAULT Flash Caching, it finds few blocks present in the Flash Cache and observes essentially no performance advantage over the case in which table storage is defined as CELL_FLASH_CACHE NONE. When the table has the CELL_FLASH_CACHE KEEP clause applied, its blocks are prioritized for retention in the ESFC, and as a result a very high Flash hit rate is obtained and consequently there is a large reduction in scan time.

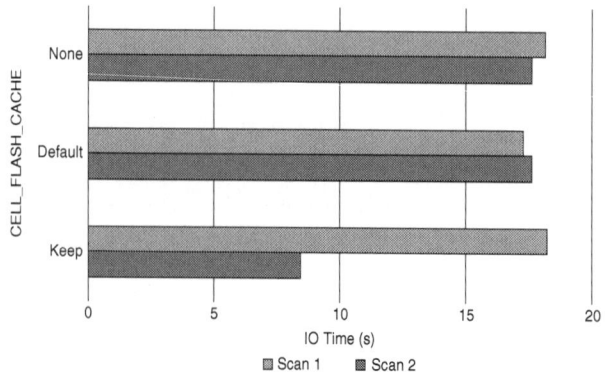

Figure 15.11   Example of ESFC on a large full (non-Smart) table scan

So, then, how should we set CELL_FLASH_CACHE for segments subjected to frequent full table scans? Again, it depends on your workload and transaction priority, but a setting of KEEP is probably a good idea for tables that are small enough to fit into the Exadata Smart Flash Cache without difficulty, which are subject to full scans at frequent intervals and when you are motivated to optimize those scans. Typical candidates may be smaller tables involved with joins, profile and authentication tables, or anything else that is read constantly via full table scan.

Smart Flash Cache KEEP Overhead

We've been trained to regard the cost of storing data in a cache as negligible. After all, it takes only nanoseconds to store data in a RAM-based cache, and that's the sort of cache we're most used to—as in the Oracle Database buffer cache. However, the performance dynamics are substantially different for a Flash-based cache. Adding an element to the Exadata Smart Flash Cache is normally faster than writing to disk, but it's a *lot* slower than writing to memory (about 95 microseconds versus 10 nanoseconds).

As we discussed earlier in this chapter, write latency for Flash devices can degrade significantly if garbage collection algorithms cannot keep up with a high rate of block updates. In a worst-case scenario, write operations can experience an order-of-magnitude degradation when entire pages of Flash storage require an erase operation prior to a new write. This situation is most likely to occur when large sequential writes are applied to Flash devices.

When we apply the CELL_FLASH_CACHE KEEP clause in order to optimize a full table scan or Smart Scan, we are effectively asking the Flash Cache to store the entire contents of a potentially very large table. The first time this happens we need to apply a large number of potentially sequential writes to the Flash Cache, and this can incur substantial overhead.

Figure 15.12 illustrates this overhead in practice. The first two bars represent the repeatable profile for full scan with a default value for CELL_FLASH_CACHE. When an ALTER TABLE statement is issued setting CELL_FLASH_CACHE to KEEP, performance initially worsens markedly as shown in the third bar. The additional time represents the time it takes the Storage Cell to populate the Exadata Smart Flash Cache with the entire contents of the table being scanned.

Subsequent scans—as represented in the fourth bar—show a performance improvement since they can be satisfied from data held in the Smart Flash Cache. However, we might anticipate from time to time that the table might age out of the cache and that consequently a costly repopulation of the Exadata Smart Flash Cache would be required.

The overhead of initially populating the Exadata Smart Flash Cache varies depending on the version of Exadata (and hence the version of Flash hardware) but is additive to the overhead of reading from disk. In other words, the first full table

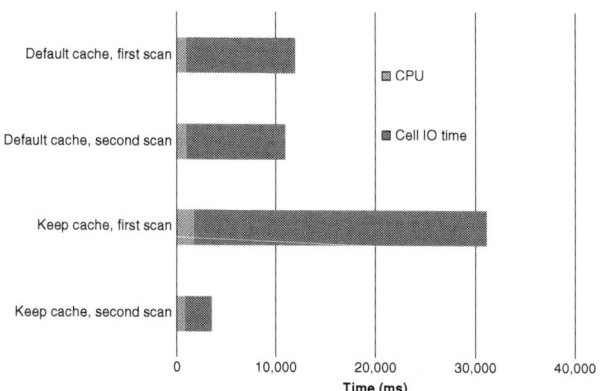

Figure 15.12 Overhead of full scans with `CELL_FLASH_CACHE` set to `KEEP`

scan with `CELL_FLASH_CACHE` set to `KEEP` is actually *worse* than a full table scan with `CELL_FLASH_CACHE` set to `NONE`.

Weigh this possibility—and the possibility of pushing other more promising blocks out of the smart cache—before setting `CELL_FLASH_CACHE` to `KEEP` for a large table. You should apply the `CELL_FLASH_CACHE KEEP` setting very judiciously.

Index Lookups and the ESFC

Index lookups have a completely different pattern of interaction with the ESFC compared to both Smart and "dumb" scans.

First, since indexed single-block reads are subject to caching in the buffer cache of each instance, there's a reduced chance that a disk read will occur at all. Hit rates in the buffer cache of 90% or more are commonplace, so only one in ten logical read requests or fewer might pass through to the storage server.

Second, because Exadata databases are usually RAC databases, the Database Nodes use the RAC interconnect to obtain the required block from another instance that might have the block in its buffer cache if it can't be found in the local buffer cache.

Blocks that cannot be found in the local buffer cache or Global Cache may be found in the Exadata Smart Flash Cache, but given the relatively large amounts of memory available on the Database Nodes, it's quite possible that such a block either never has been requested before or has aged out of the cache anyway.

Nevertheless, for many tables, supplementing the buffer cache and Global Cache with the ESFC leads to substantial improvements by reducing the cost of a buffer or Global Cache "miss." Figure 15.13 shows such a situation. Disabling the ESFC by setting the `CELL_FLASH_CACHE` clause to `NONE` results in a significant increase

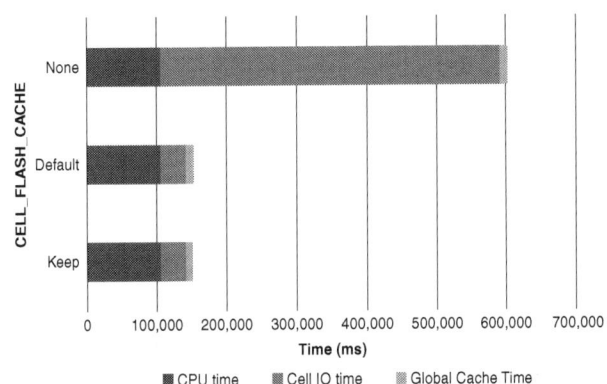

Figure 15.13   ESFC and primary key lookups (500,000 primary key lookups)

in the time taken to perform random single-block reads (500,000 reads over a random range of 500,000 key values in a 100-million-row table).

Setting the CELL_FLASH_CACHE to KEEP is often unnecessary and possibly counterproductive for indexed single-block reads. While KEEP tends to retain the block's read for a longer period (at the expense of other blocks, of course), the LRU aging out of blocks in the DEFAULT cache probably leads to a more effective cache overall. In other words, you may see some small improvement in indexed reads for a specific table if you set CELL_FLASH_CACHE to KEEP, but you'll be doing so at the cost of a less efficient ESFC overall and hurting the performance of queries on segments where CELL_FLASH_CACHE is set to DEFAULT. And remember, KEEP affects the caching of blocks accessed via full scans in such a way as to potentially harm performance (discussed earlier in this chapter).

Exadata Smart Flash Logging

Exadata Storage Software 11.2.2.4 introduced the Smart Flash Logging feature. The intent of this feature is to reduce overall redo log sync times by allowing the Exadata Flash storage to serve as a secondary destination for redo log writes. During a redo log sync, Oracle writes to the disk and Flash simultaneously and allows the redo log sync operation to complete as soon as either device completes its write.

In the event that the Flash Cache wins the race to write, the data need be held for only a short time until the storage server is certain that all writes have made it to the redo log. Since the Smart Flash Log is only a temporary store, only a small amount of Flash storage is required—512MB per cell (out of 3.2TB on an X4, 1.6TB on an X3, or 365GB on an X2 system).

Figure 15.14 illustrates the essential flow of control. Oracle processes performing DML generate redo entries which are written to the redo buffer (1). Periodically
or upon COMMIT the LGWR flushes the buffer (2), resulting in an I/O request to the
CELLSRV process (3). CELLSRV writes to Flash and grid disk simultaneously (4),
and when either I/O completes, it returns control to the LGWR (5).

The use of Flash SSD to optimize redo log operations has been a somewhat con-
tentious topic. Many—including this author—have argued that Flash SSD is a poor
choice for redo log workloads. The nature of sequential redo log I/O tends to favor the
spinning magnetic disk since sequential I/O minimizes seek latency, while penaliz-
ing Flash-based SSD, since the continual overwriting of existing blocks makes the
probability of a block erase very high.

Note

For more information and opinions on how Flash SSD is a poor choice for redo log
workloads, see http://guyharrison.squarespace.com/ssdguide/ and http://kevinclosson
.wordpress.com/2011/11/01/flash-is-fast-provisioning-flash-for-oracle-database-
redo-logging-emc-f-a-s-t-is-flash-and-fast-but-leaves-redo-where-it-belongs/.

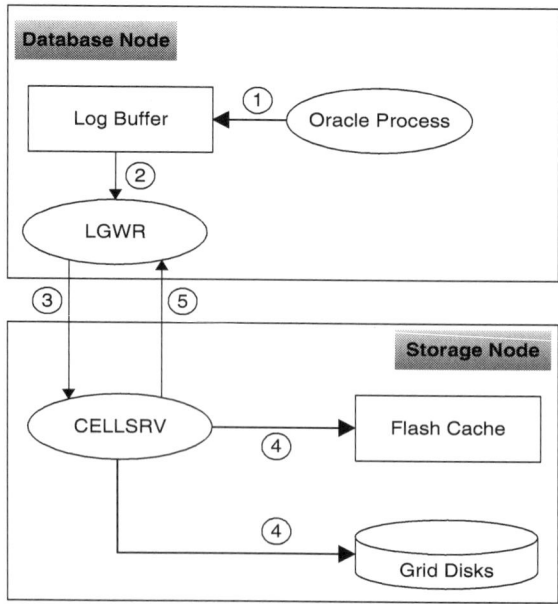

Figure 15.14 Exadata Smart Flash Logging

However, the Exadata Smart Flash Logging feature is not predicated on some theoretical write I/O advantage for Flash SSD. Rather it aims to "smooth out" redo log writes by running redo log writes out through two channels (grid disk and Flash SSD) and allowing the redo log write to complete when either of the two completes.

Redo log sync waits—which occur whenever a COMMIT occurs—generally involve only a couple of milliseconds of wait time since they involve only a small sequential write operation on an (ideally) relatively lightly loaded disk subsystem. Keeping redo logs on separate ASM disk groups from data files helps ensure that heavy data file I/O loads do not affect the time taken for redo operations.

However, it's inevitable that from time to time a redo log sync operation will conflict with some other I/O—an archive read or Data Guard operation, for instance. In these circumstances some redo log sync operations may take a very long time indeed.

Following is some Oracle trace log data that shows some redo log sync waits:

```
WAIT #4..648: nam='log file sync' ela= 710
WAIT #4..648: nam='log file sync' ela= 733
WAIT #4...648: nam='log file sync' ela= 621
WAIT #4...648: nam='log file sync' ela= 507
WAIT #4...648: nam='log file sync' ela= 683
WAIT #4...648: nam='log file sync' ela= 2084
WAIT #4...648: nam='log file sync' ela= 798
WAIT #4...648: nam='log file sync' ela= 1043
WAIT #4...648: nam='log file sync' ela= 2394
WAIT #4...648: nam='log file sync' ela= 932
WAIT #4...648: nam='log file sync' ela= 291780
WAIT #4...648: nam='log file sync' ela= 671
WAIT #4...648: nam='log file sync' ela= 957
WAIT #4...648: nam='log file sync' ela= 852
WAIT #4...648: nam='log file sync' ela= 639
WAIT #4...648: nam='log file sync' ela= 699
WAIT #4...648: nam='log file sync' ela= 819
```

The ela entry shows the elapsed time in microseconds. Most of the waits are less than 1 millisecond (1000 microseconds), but in the middle we see an anomalous wait of 291,780 microseconds (about one-third of a second!).

Occasional very high redo log sync waits like the one just shown might not seem too disturbing until you remember that redo log sync waits are frequently included in the most critical application transactions. Online operations such as saving a shopping cart, confirming an order, and saving a profile change all generally involve some sort of commit operation, and it's well known that today's online consumers rapidly lose patience when operations delay even by fractions of a second. So even occasional high redo log wait times are cause for concern. It's the intent of Exadata Smart Flash Logging to smooth out these disturbing outliers.

Controlling and Monitoring Smart Flash Logging

Exadata Smart Flash Logging is enabled by default and you don't have to do anything specifically to enable it—other than to make sure your Storage Cells are running at least Exadata Storage Software 11.2.2.4.

You can confirm your Flash Log status by issuing a LIST FLASHLOG command at a CellCLI prompt:

```
CellCLI> list flashlog  detail
         name:                   exalcel01_FLASHLOG
         cellDisk:               FD_09_exalcel01,FD_02_exalcel01,
         creationTime:           2012-07-07T06:56:23-07:00
         degradedCelldisks:
         effectiveSize:          512M
         efficiency:             100.0
         id:                     3c08cfe1-ea43-4fde-85c2-0bbd5cbd11ec
         size:                   512M
         status:                 normal
```

You can control the behavior of Exadata Smart Flash Logging by using a resource management plan. This allows you to turn Exadata Smart Flash Logging on or off for individual databases.

So, for instance, this command will turn Exadata Smart Flash Logging off for database GUY and leave it on for all other databases:

```
ALTER IORMPLAN dbplan=((name='GUY',flashLog=false),
                       (name=other,flashlog=on))'
```

You can monitor the behavior of Exadata Smart Flash Logging by using the following CellCLI command:

```
CellCLI> list metriccurrent where objectType='FLASHLOG';
         FL_ACTUAL_OUTLIERS          FLASHLOG      1 IO requests
         FL_BY_KEEP                  FLASHLOG      0
         FL_DISK_FIRST               FLASHLOG      253,540,190 IO requests
           ...... ......
         FL_FLASH_FIRST              FLASHLOG      11,881,503 IO requests
           ...... ......
         FL_PREVENTED_OUTLIERS       FLASHLOG      275,125 IO requests
```

These are probably the most interesting CellCLI metrics generated by this command:

- **FL_DISK_FIRST**—the grid disk log write completed first during the redo log write operation

- **FL_FLASH_FIRST**—the Flash SSD completed first during the redo log write operation

- **FL_PREVENTED_OUTLIERS**—the number of redo log writes that were optimized by the Flash Logging that would otherwise have taken longer than 500 milliseconds to complete

Testing Exadata Smart Flash Logging

Let's look at an example. Say we test Exadata Smart Flash Logging by running 20 concurrent processes, each of which performs 200,000 updates and commits—a total of 4 million redo log sync operations. Now, Exadata Smart Flash Logging is disabled using a resource plan (see the ALTER IORMPLAN statement in the previous section) and the tests are repeated. We capture every redo log sync wait in a DBMS_MONITOR trace file for analysis using the R statistical package.

With Exadata Smart Flash Logging disabled, our key CellCLI metrics look like this:

```
FL_DISK_FIRST            32,669,310 IO requests
FL_FLASH_FIRST            7,318,741 IO requests
FL_PREVENTED_OUTLIERS       774,146 IO requests
```

With Exadata Smart Flash Logging enabled, the metrics look like this:

```
FL_DISK_FIRST            33,201,462 IO requests
FL_FLASH_FIRST            7,337,931 IO requests
FL_PREVENTED_OUTLIERS       774,146 IO requests
```

So for this particular cell the Flash disk "won" only 3.8% of the time (the ratio of FL_FLASH_FIRST and FL_DISK_FIRST) and prevented no outliers. (Outliers are redo log syncs that take longer than 500 milliseconds to complete.) So on the surface, it would seem that very little has been achieved.

However, statistical analysis of the redo log sync times provides a somewhat different interpretation. Table 15.1 summarizes the key statistics for the two tests.

Table 15.1   Effect of Exadata Smart Flash Logging on Redo Log Sync Waits

Smart Flash Logging	Redo Log Sync Time (microseconds)				
	Min	Median	Mean	99%	Max
On	1.0	650	723	1656	75,740
Off	1.0	627	878	4662	291,800

Exadata Smart Flash Logging reduced the mean log file sync wait time by over 15%—and this difference was statistically significant. There was also a significant reduction in the 99th percentile—the minimum wait time for the top 1% of waits was reduced from about 4.6 seconds to 1.6 seconds.

Figure 15.15 shows the distribution of log file sync waits with the Exadata Smart Flash Logging feature enabled and disabled. Turning Exadata Smart Flash Logging on created a strange hump on the high side of what otherwise looks like a normal bell curve distribution. Understanding that hump requires that we take a look at the distribution of very high outlier redo log waits.

Figure 15.16 shows the distribution of the top 10,000 waits. This shows far more clearly how Exadata Smart Flash Logging worked to reduce high outlier log file sync waits. These waits have been pulled back, but to a point that is still above the average wait time for other log file sync waits. This creates the hump in Figure 15.15 and represents a significant reduction in the time taken for outlying redo log waits.

While Flash SSD is not necessarily an ideal storage medium for redo write I/O, Exadata Smart Flash Logging does reduce the impact of very high outlier redo log writes.

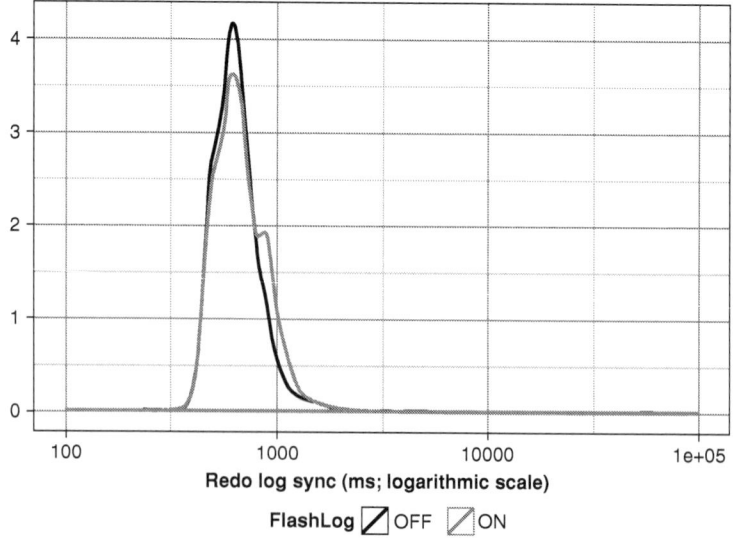

Figure 15.15 Distribution of log file sync waits with Exadata Smart Flash Logging

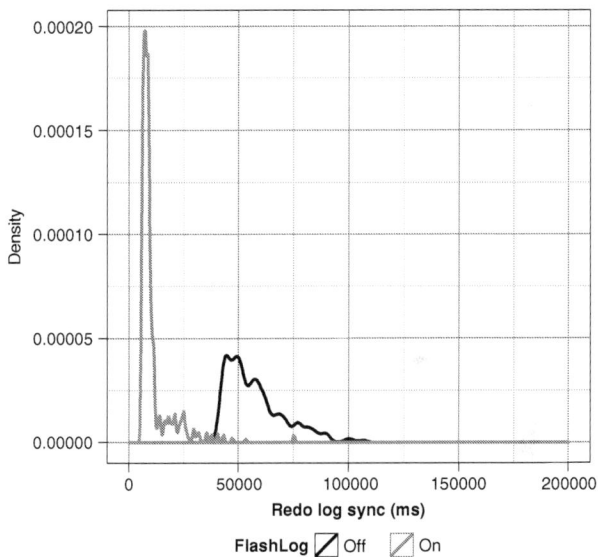

Figure 15.16   Distribution of top 10,000 log file sync waits with Exadata
Smart Flash Logging

Smart Flash Cache WriteBack

Prior to Storage Server Software version 11.2.3.2.0 (associated with Exadata X3) Exadata Smart Flash Cache was a write-through cache, meaning that write operations were applied both to the cache and to the underlying disk devices but were not signaled as complete until the I/O to the disk completed.

Starting with 11.2.3.2.0 of the Exadata Storage Software, Exadata Smart Flash Cache may act as a write-back cache. This means that a write operation is made to the cache initially and de-staged to grid disks at a later time. This can be effective in improving the performance of an Exadata system that is subject to I/O write bottlenecks on the Oracle data files.

Note
Version 11.2.3.2.1 is the recommended minimum for this feature as it contains fixes to significant issues discovered in the initial release.

Data File Write I/O Bottlenecks

As with earlier incarnations of the Exadata Smart Flash Cache, the write-back cache deals primarily only with data file blocks; redo writes are optimized separately by the Exadata Smart Flash Logging function.

Writes to data file generally happen as a background task in Oracle, and most of the time we don't actually wait on these I/Os. That being the case, what advantage can we expect if these writes are optimized? To understand the possible advantages of the write-back cache let's review the nature of data file write I/O in Oracle and the symptoms that occur when write I/O becomes the bottleneck.

When a block in the buffer cache is modified, it is the responsibility of the DBWR to write these "dirty" blocks to disk. The DBWR does this continuously and uses asynchronous I/O processing, so generally sessions do not have to wait for the I/O to occur—the only time sessions wait directly on write I/O is when a redo log sync occurs following a COMMIT.

However, should all the buffers in the buffer cache become dirty, a session may wait when it wants to bring a block into the cache, resulting in a free buffer wait.

Figure 15.17 illustrates the phenomenon. User sessions wishing to bring new blocks into the buffer cache need to wait on free buffer waits until the Database Writer cleans

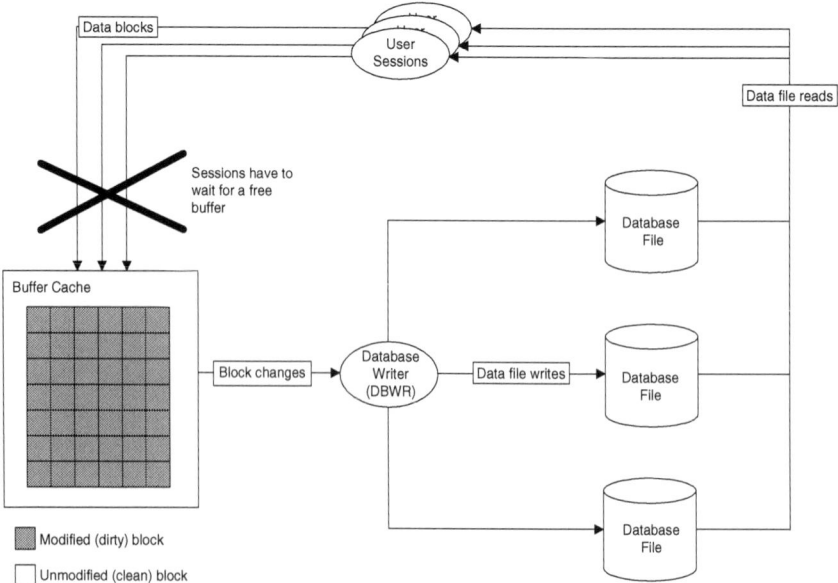

Figure 15.17 Buffer cache operation and free buffer waits

out dirty blocks. Write complete waits may also be observed. These occur when a session tries to access a block that the DBWR is in the process of writing to disk.

Free buffer waits can occur in update-intensive workloads when the I/O bandwidth of the Oracle sessions reading into the cache exceeds the I/O bandwidth of the Database Writer. Because the Database Writer uses asynchronous parallelized write I/O, and because all processes concerned are accessing the same files, free buffer waits usually happen when the I/O subsystem can service reads faster than it can service writes.

There exists just such an imbalance between read and write latency in Exadata. The Exadata Smart Flash Cache accelerates reads by a factor of perhaps four to ten times, while offering no comparable advantage for writes. As a result, a very busy Exadata X2 system could become bottlenecked on free buffer waits. The Exadata Smart Flash Cache write-back cache provides acceleration to data file writes as well as reads and therefore reduces the chance of free buffer wait bottlenecks.

Write-Back Cache Architecture

Figure 15.18 illustrates the Exadata Smart Flash Cache write-back architecture. An Oracle process modifies a database block which is then dirty (1). The DBWR

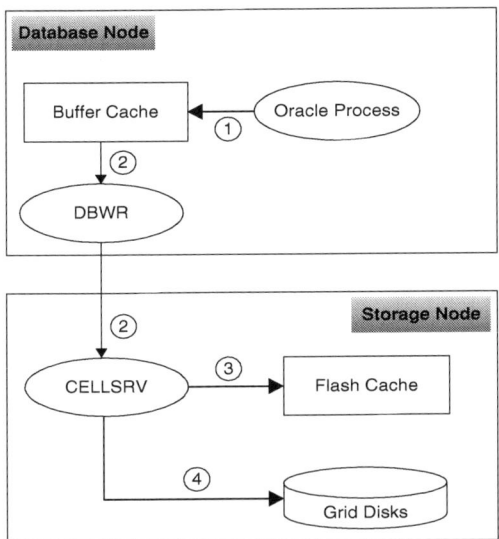

Figure 15.18   Exadata Smart Flash Cache write-back architecture

periodically sends these blocks to the Storage Cell for write (2). For eligible blocks (almost all blocks in the buffer cache will be eligible) the Storage Cell CELLSRV process writes the dirty blocks to the Flash Cache (3) and returns control to the DBWR. Later the CELLSRV writes the dirty block to the database files on the grid disk (4).

There's no particular urgency in the CELLSRV flushing blocks to grid disk, since any subsequent reads will be satisfied by the Flash Cache.

Furthermore, since the Exadata Smart Flash Cache is a persistent cache, there's no reason to be concerned about data loss in the event of power failure. The write-back cache is also subject to the same redundancy policies as the underlying ASM-controlled grid disks, so even in the event of a catastrophic cell failure the data will be preserved.

Enabling and Disabling the Write-Back Cache

You can check if you have the write-back cache enabled by issuing the command `list cell attributes flashcachemode`. The `flashcachemode` variable returns `writeThrough` if the write-back cache is disabled and `writeBack` if it is not:

```
CellCLI> list cell attributes flashcachemode detail
        flashCacheMode:        writeback
```

Enabling the cache is described in Oracle Support Note ID 1500257.1. For good reason, the Storage Cells need to be idled during the process so that writes can be quiesced before being channeled through the cache. This can be done one cell at a time in a rolling procedure, or during a complete shutdown of all databases and ASM instances.

The non-rolling method involves issuing the following commands on each cell while all database and ASM services on the system are shut down:

```
DROP FLASHCACHE
ALTER CELL SHUTDOWN SERVICES CELLSRV
ALTER CELL FLASHCACHEMODE=WRITEBACK
ALTER CELL STARTUP SERVICES CELLSRV
CREATE FLASHCACHE ALL
```

The rolling method is similar but involves some extra steps to ensure that grid disks are not in use. See Oracle Support Note ID 1500257.1 for the detailed procedure.

Write-Back Cache Performance

Figure 15.19 illustrates the effectiveness of the write-back cache for workloads that encounter free buffer waits. The workload used to generate Figure 15.19 was

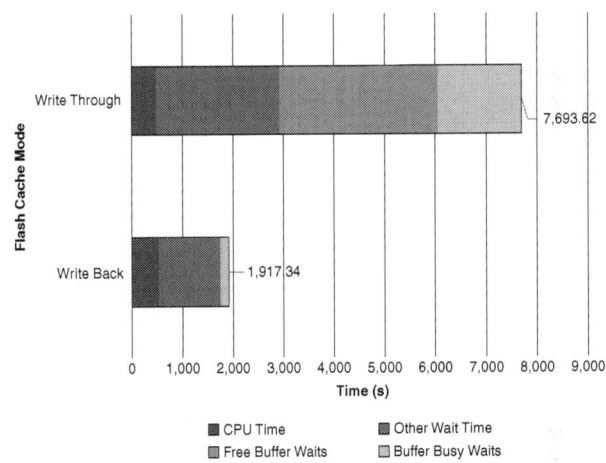

Figure 15.19 Effect of write-back cache performance on free buffer waits

heavily write intensive with very little read I/O overhead (all the necessary read data was in cache). As a result, it experienced a very high degree of free buffer waits and some associated buffer busy waits. Enabling the write-back cache completely eliminated the free buffer waits by effectively accelerating the write I/O bandwidth of the database writer. As a result, throughput increased fourfold.

However, don't be misled into thinking that the write-back cache is a silver bullet for all workloads. Only workloads that are experiencing free buffer waits are likely to see this sort of performance gain. Workloads where the dominant waits are for CPU, read I/O, Global Cache coordination, log writes, and so on are unlikely to see any substantial benefit from the write-back cache.

Summary

SSD provides far greater I/O capacity and far lower I/O latencies than traditional magnetic disk.

The default configuration for Exadata Flash SSD is as in the Exadata Smart Flash Cache. The primary purpose of the Exadata Smart Flash Cache is to accelerate read I/O for database files by configuring Flash as a cache over the grid disks that service data file read I/O. By default the Exadata Smart Flash Cache does not accelerate Smart or full table scans, but you can configure CELL_FLASH_CACHE KEEP to alter this behavior.

Exadata Smart Flash Logging allows the Flash Cache to participate in redo log write operations. This helps alleviate the occasional very high redo write "outliers."

The Exadata Smart Flash Cache can also operate as a write-back cache, allowing it to satisfy write requests as well as read requests; this can improve performance on systems that are experiencing data file write I/O bottlenecks—as evidenced by free buffer waits.

## 16

Advanced Exadata Flash Configuration

In this chapter we look at more advanced techniques for exploiting Exadata Flash disk. By default Exadata configures all Flash disk as Exadata Smart Flash Cache. This configuration provides performance improvements for a wide variety of workloads and requires very little configuration on behalf of the Exadata administrator. However, it is also possible to configure Exadata Flash disks as grid disks and allocate these to ASM disk groups, which can then be used to directly support tablespaces or redo logs. In this chapter we'll see how to create such a configuration and see how it performs for various workloads.

Using Flash as Grid Disks

Exadata systems contain an incredible amount of Flash disk—up to 44TB of Flash disk on a fully configured X4 machine. This Flash contributes substantially to the overall price of an Exadata system, and you really want to make sure that you're getting the best possible value from it!

The default configuration—using all the Exadata Flash storage as cache—is a "no configuration required" option. It doesn't require much in the way of setup, and it gives immediate benefit across a wide range of workloads. However, it's not necessarily the most effective use of your Flash resources.

It's possible to reconfigure all or some of your Flash disk as grid disk, which can then be made available to ASM and used as the basis for data files or redo logs. In many cases, this results in superior performance.

Why would we want to create Flash-based grid disks? There are a few compelling reasons:

- If a table is small enough to fit entirely into Flash, *every* I/O to that table is Flash accelerated. With the Exadata Smart Flash Cache, read I/O is accelerated only if the block concerned happens to be in Flash.

- Exadata Smart Flash Cache optimizes single-block reads very effectively but does not by default optimize Smart or full table scans. Using the CELL_ FLASH_CACHE KEEP storage setting has some undesirable side effects that we can avoid by placing the table completely within Flash.

- Not all database I/O is covered by the Exadata Smart Flash Cache—I/O to temporary segments and to redo logs, for instance. By creating grid disks we have the possibility of accelerating those I/Os as well.

Grid Disks, Cell Disks, and the Flash Cache

The Exadata storage system is of course created from physical disk devices, either High Performance or High Capacity SAS magnetic disks together with Flash SSDs. These physical disks are generically known as **cell disks**.

By default SAS disks are mapped as grid disks, which are exposed to the Database Nodes as LUNs and can be used to create ASM disk groups.

We can expose each of these layers by issuing CellCLI and sqlplus commands. LIST CELLDISK exposes all the disks—Flash or SAS (described in the output as HardDisk)—on the system:

```
CellCLI> LIST celldisk ATTRIBUTES name,devicename, size ,diskType
         CD_00_exa1cel01          /dev/sda        1832.59375G    HardDisk
         CD_01_exa1cel01          /dev/sdb        1832.59375G    HardDisk
         CD_03_exa1cel01          /dev/sdc        1861.703125G   HardDisk
         CD_04_exa1cel01          /dev/sdd        1861.703125G   HardDisk
                                      ........
         FD_12_exa1cel01          /dev/sdu        22.875G        FlashDisk
         FD_13_exa1cel01          /dev/sdv        22.875G        FlashDisk
         FD_14_exa1cel01          /dev/sdw        22.875G        FlashDisk
         FD_15_exa1cel01          /dev/sdx        22.875G        FlashDisk
```

LIST GRIDDISK shows how the cell disks are mapped to grid disks:

```
CellCLI> LIST griddisk ATTRIBUTES name,cellDisk,diskType
         DATA_EXA1_CD_00_exa1cel01    CD_00_exa1cel01        HardDisk
```

```
DATA_EXA1_CD_01_exa1cel01          CD_01_exa1cel01          HardDisk
DATA_EXA1_CD_02_exa1cel01          CD_02_exa1cel01          HardDisk
                          ..........
DATA_EXA1_CD_09_exa1cel01          CD_09_exa1cel01          HardDisk
DATA_EXA1_CD_10_exa1cel01          CD_10_exa1cel01          HardDisk
DATA_EXA1_CD_11_exa1cel01          CD_11_exa1cel01          HardDisk
```

Grid disks show up to ASM as logical disks in the format *o/cell_ip_address/ GridDiskName*:

```
SQL> l
  1      SELECT label , PATH, header_status
  2      FROM v$asm_disk
  3* ORDER BY name
SQL> /

LABEL                 PATH                            HEADER_STATU
-------------------   -----------------------------   ------------
DATA_EXA1_CD_00_EXA1  o/192.168.10.3/DATA_EXA1_CD_00  MEMBER
CEL01                 _exa1cel01

DATA_EXA1_CD_00_EXA1  o/192.168.10.4/DATA_EXA1_CD_00  MEMBER
CEL02                 _exa1cel02

DATA_EXA1_CD_00_EXA1  o/192.168.10.5/DATA_EXA1_CD_00  MEMBER
CEL03                 _exa1cel03
```

By default Flash disks are configured as Exadata Smart Flash Cache and are not visible to the Database Nodes. You can see the cell disks that make up the Flash Cache by using the LIST FLASHCACHE command:

```
CellCLI> list flashcache detail
        name:              exa1cel01_FLASHCACHE
        cellDisk:          FD_07_exa1cel01,FD_09_exa1cel01,FD_02_exa1cel01,FD_05_
exa1cel01,FD_15_exa1cel01,FD_00_exa1cel01,FD_04_exa1cel01,FD_08_exa1cel01,FD_01_
exa1cel01,FD_11_exa1cel01,FD_10_exa1cel01,FD_14_exa1cel01,FD_12_exa1cel01,FD_13_
exa1cel01,FD_06_exa1cel01,FD_03_exa1cel01
        creationTime:      2013-12-31T17:55:30-08:00
        degradedCelldisks:
        effectiveCacheSize: 287.5G
        id:                7989f434-c89c-4c6e-8d62-f299824da633
        size:              287.5G
        status:            normal
```

Figure 16.1 shows the mapping of cell disks, grid disks, Flash Cache, and ASM in a default Exadata configuration. All of the SAS hard disks are mapped to grid disks, which in turn are used to create the ASM disk groups supporting the database. All the Flash disks are used to create the Exadata Smart Flash Cache.

Figure 16.2 shows the configuration of an Exadata system in which some of the Flash disk is allocated to grid disk, and some to the Exadata Smart Flash Cache.

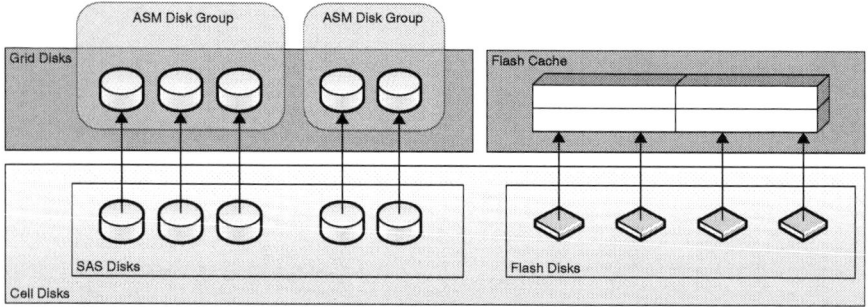

Figure 16.1   Default mapping of cell and grid disks in Exadata

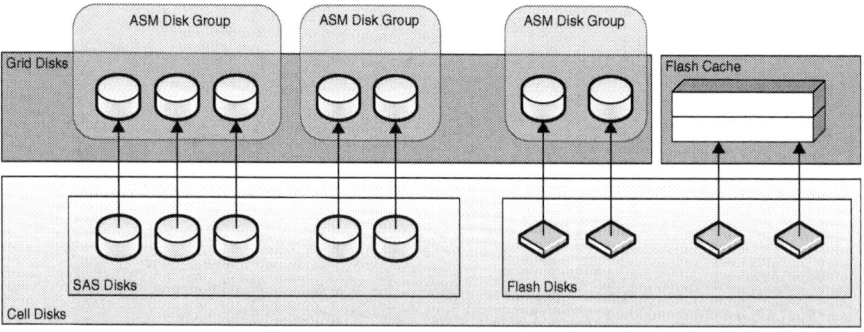

Figure 16.2   Defining Exadata Flash disks as both Flash Cache and grid disks

Creating a Flash-Based ASM Disk Group

If we want to use the Exadata Flash disks for something other than the Exadata Smart Flash Cache, we need to remove some of the Flash disks from the Flash Cache and allocate them as grid disks. Then these grid disks can be used to create an ASM disk group to house data files or redo logs.

Reallocating all of the Flash disks to grid disks is not advisable; the performance benefits of the Exadata Smart Flash Cache are compelling, and the Oracle engineered machine architecture assumes the presence of a Flash Cache in order to balance performance. So generally we allocate only some of the Flash disks as grid disks and leave the remainder as a smaller Exadata Smart Flash Cache.

Here's the procedure:

1. Drop the existing Exadata Smart Flash Cache.
2. Create a smaller Flash Cache.
3. Create grid disks from the remaining Flash disks.
4. Create an ASM disk group from these grid disks.

Creating the Grid Disks

First we must remove some of the Flash disks from the Exadata Smart Flash Cache. On each storage server, drop the Flash Cache and create a new Flash Cache of a smaller size:

```
CellCLI> drop flashcache
Flash cache exa1cel01_FLASHCACHE successfully dropped
CellCLI> create flashcache all size=288g
Flash cache exa1cel01_FLASHCACHE successfully created
```

Now, we can create grid disks from the remaining Flash disks:

```
CellCLI> create griddisk all flashdisk prefix=ssddisk
```

On the X2 system on which these commands were run, there was 384GB of Flash on each Storage Cell, so the preceding commands create about 96GB of SSD grid disk.

We can see the grid disks that have been created using the LIST GRIDDISK command:

```
CellCLI> LIST griddisk ATTRIBUTES name,cellDisk,size
where diskType='FlashDisk'
         ssddisk_FD_00_exa1cel01        FD_00_exa1cel01        4.828125G
         ssddisk_FD_01_exa1cel01        FD_01_exa1cel01        4.828125G
         ssddisk_FD_02_exa1cel01        FD_02_exa1cel01        4.828125G
         ssddisk_FD_03_exa1cel01        FD_03_exa1cel01        4.828125G
         ssddisk_FD_04_exa1cel01        FD_04_exa1cel01        4.828125G
         ssddisk_FD_05_exa1cel01        FD_05_exa1cel01        4.828125G
         ssddisk_FD_06_exa1cel01        FD_06_exa1cel01        4.828125G
         ssddisk_FD_07_exa1cel01        FD_07_exa1cel01        4.828125G
```

The size of the grid disks we have created corresponds to the physical configuration of the Flash accelerator cards. On an X2 system, the Flash Cards (Sun F20) are composed of four Flash Modules, each of which contains eight 4GB Flash units. Each of the grid disks corresponds to one of these Flash units.

Creating a Flash Disk Group

Grid disks show up as ASM disks with the following format: *o*/*cellIPAddress*/ *GridDiskName*. The prefix specified when you created the grid disks can be used to distinguish between hard grid disks and Flash grid disks. In the case of our example, all our Flash grid disks were prefixed with `ssddisk` as specified in the `CREATE GRIDDISK` command. Therefore, the following command creates an ASM disk group from all unallocated Flash-based grid disks:

```
SQL>
  1  create diskgroup DATA_SSD normal redundancy disk 'o/*/ssddisk*'
  2  attribute 'compatible.rdbms'='11.2.0.0.0',
  3  'compatible.asm'='11.2.0.0.0',
  4  'cell.smart_scan_capable'='TRUE',
  5* 'au_size'='4M'
```

Of course you can use the database control for the ASM instance to create the new disk groups. Your new Flash disks should show up as candidate disks, as shown in Figure 16.3.

Once the ASM disk group is created, you can use it as the basis for a tablespace, redo logs, or any other item that can be managed by ASM.

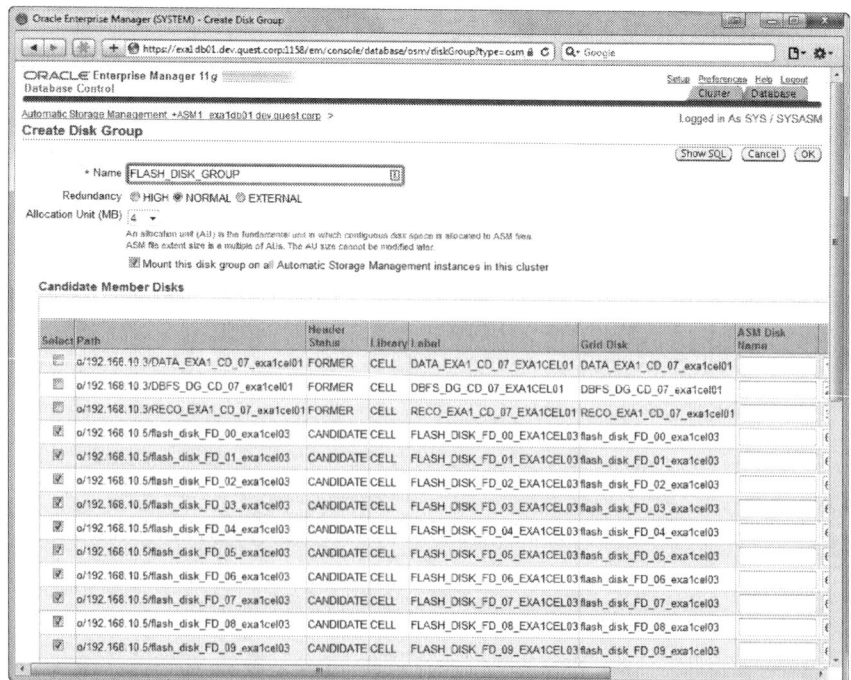

Figure 16.3   Creating a Flash-based ASM disk group in Enterprise Manager

Flash Tablespace versus Flash Cache

Let's see how the performance of a Flash-based tablespace compares with the performance of the Exadata Smart Flash Cache.

Index Fetch Performance

As noted in the previous chapter, the performance benefits of the Exadata Smart Flash Cache are greatest when performing single-block random reads typical of indexed primary key lookups.

Figure 16.4 compares the elapsed time for 500,000 primary key lookups across a 500,000-row range of key values. The first bar shows the performance with CELL_FLASH_CACHE set to NONE. The next two bars show the performance when CELL_FLASH_CACHE is set to DEFAULT or KEEP. Performance is significantly improved with a reduction in elapsed time of about 32%.

However, placing the entire segment (and its indexes) on the SSD tablespace reduced elapsed time by about 70% and I/O time by 93%, as shown in the final three bars in Figure 16.4. In this case placing the segment on an SSD-based tablespace gave far better performance than the Exadata Smart Flash Cache.

The performance advantage of the Flash tablespace over Flash Cache depends heavily on the data access patterns. When the hit rate in the Exadata Smart Flash Cache is very high, the Flash Cache might approach the performance of the Flash

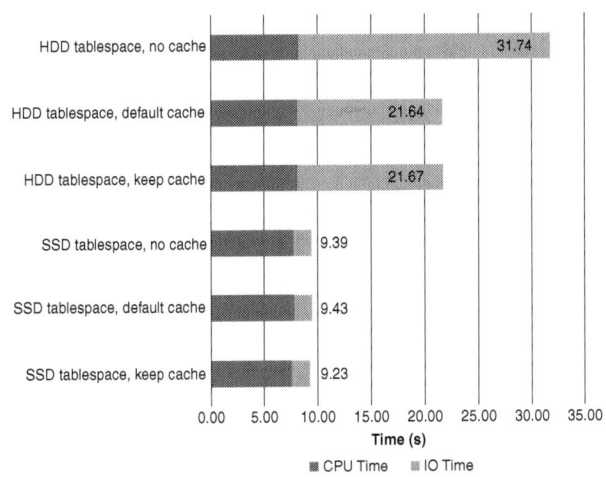

Figure 16.4   Index lookups comparing Flash Cache to Flash tablespace

tablespace. However, it always remains true that for a block to be accelerated by the Exadata Smart Flash Cache there has to be an initial SAS disk read to get the block into the cache. When the segment is stored directly on SSD, this initial hard disk I/O never occurs.

Furthermore, the Exadata Smart Flash Cache can be less predictable than a Flash tablespace solution. If the cache is "cold" or if the segment has not been accessed recently, performance may be unusually bad. With an SSD tablespace we won't get any intermittent performance degradation from a cold Flash Cache.

On the other hand, the Exadata Smart Flash Cache can accelerate I/O for tables that are far too massive to fit into Flash in their entirety. Placing a segment on a Flash tablespace requires that we have enough Flash storage for the entire segment. Of course, partitioning such a table may provide a mechanism for us to overcome this obstacle, and we'll examine that solution later in this chapter.

A final point from the data in Figure 16.4: there is no effective difference in performance for the SSD tablespace with the various CELL_FLASH_CACHE options. It's of no use to try to cache data already in SSD in the Exadata Smart Flash Cache since for a cache to be effective, it has to offer better performance than the underlying storage. So when storing a table in a Flash tablespace, set the CELL_FLASH_CACHE clause to NONE.

Scan Performance

As we saw in Chapter 15, the Exadata Smart Flash Cache does not by default store blocks processed as part of a full or Smart table scan. It is possible to use the CELL_FLASH_CACHE KEEP setting to instruct the Exadata Smart Flash Cache to store scanned blocks, but there are some problems with doing this.

First, loading a large segment into the Exadata Smart Flash Cache can actually degrade performance during the initial scan. Second, loading up a large segment into the cache might push out more deserving blocks from the cache, hurting the performance of other queries. Third, if the table is very large, the initial blocks loaded might expire from the cache before the scan completes. Finally, blocks introduced into the KEEP area of the Exadata Smart Flash Cache expire after 24 hours, so if a table is scanned infrequently, the Exadata Smart Flash Cache may fail to optimize these scans.

If we are certain that we want to optimize full or Smart Scans against a segment, it might therefore be better to house that segment directly on Flash, rather than disturbing Exadata Smart Flash Cache performance by setting CELL_FLASH_CACHE to KEEP.

Figure 16.5 compares the scan times for identical tables on SAS and Flash-based tablespaces with the Exadata Smart Flash Cache enabled or disabled. The first pair of bars represents the baseline performance for a scan without any Flash

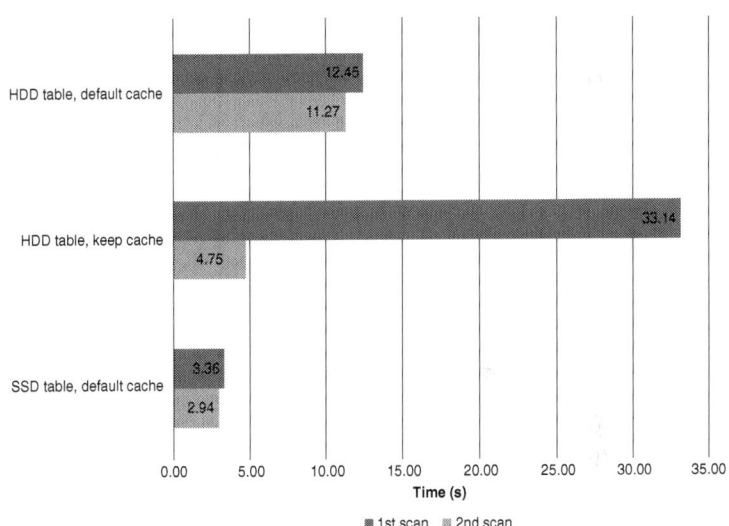

Figure 16.5 Scan performance for SAS and Flash-based tables

acceleration. The second set of bars shows the effect of setting `CELL_FLASH_CACHE` `KEEP`—the initial scan is degraded because of the overhead of storing the table into Flash, though subsequent scans are accelerated.

The final two sets of bars in Figure 16.5 show the performance when the table is stored on a Flash tablespace. Scans are fully optimized regardless of the setting for `CELL_FLASH_CACHE`, and the initial degradation involved with loading Exadata Smart Flash Cache is avoided.

Creating a Flash Temporary Tablespace

The Exadata Smart Flash Cache can cache blocks associated with segments: tables, indexes, and partitions. For index lookups and simple table scans the I/Os associated with scanning these segments will dominate SQL I/O wait time. However, for complex SQLs that involve hash joins, sorts, or `GROUP BY` operations, the I/O associated with temporary segments can become significant and may dominate overall performance.

When a sort or hash operation is required, Oracle allocates an area of private memory from the Program Global Area (PGA). The total amount of PGA memory available for all sessions is generally determined by either `MEMORY_TARGET` or `PGA_AGGREGATE_TARGET`.

When insufficient memory is available for a sort or hash operation, Oracle must read and write to temporary segments during the operation. In a one-pass operation, Oracle needs to write out and read back only a single segment. In a multipass operation, Oracle needs to write and read back many temporary table segments. The more passes required, the more I/O is involved and the slower the operation becomes.

The I/O required for a sort or hash operation grows rapidly as the number of passes increases and usually becomes the overwhelming factor in SQL performance as the number of passes increases.

Figure 16.6 shows the relationship between the amount of PGA memory available for a sort operation and the execution time for the statement. As memory becomes constrained, temporary tablespace I/O increases and eventually dominates SQL statement performance.

On Oracle Databases using directly attached PCI Flash, using Flash as the basis for a temporary tablespace can result in significant reductions in temporary tablespace I/O. Figure 16.7 demonstrates this effect.

Unfortunately, these results could not be replicated on an Exadata system. Figure 16.8 shows how performance of a disk sort operation responds to varying amounts

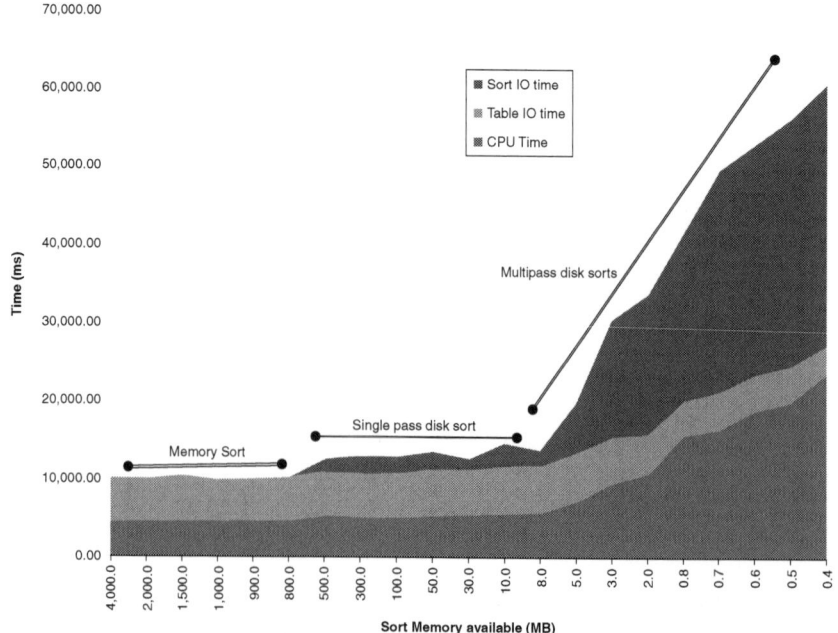

Figure 16.6 Relationship between sort memory and execution time

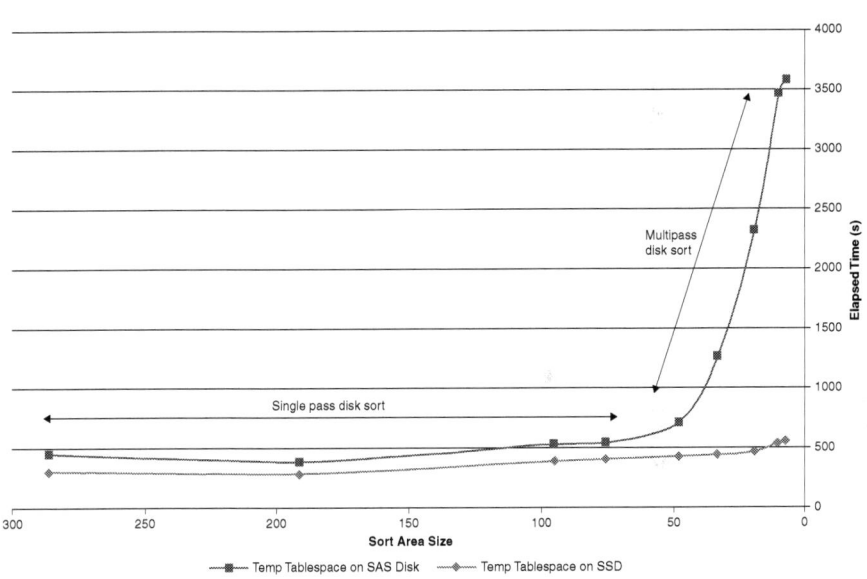

Figure 16.7   Reduction in temporary tablespace I/O on a non-Exadata system

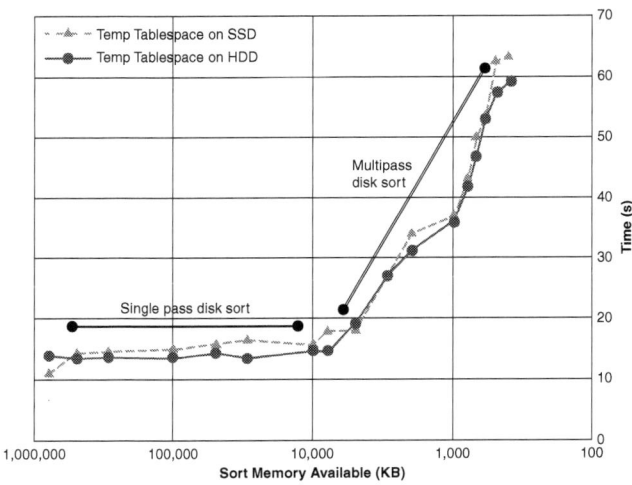

Figure 16.8   Performance of Flash-based temporary tablespace on Exadata X2

of PGA memory with both a Flash-based and SAS-based temporary tablespace. Performance for each option was virtually identical.

A detailed examination of wait times for each option revealed that although performance for temporary tablespace reads was somewhat optimized by the use of a Flash temporary tablespace, write operations to the Flash tablespace were significantly poorer than those to the SAS-based tablespace. Consequently, no overall optimization was achieved. Your results might vary depending on the version of Exadata hardware and your specific workloads.

Using Flash for Redo Logs

Since time immemorial (well, since the late eighties anyway) the Oracle architecture has been designed to avoid waits on I/O. The buffer cache serves to avoid disk reads, and disk writes are written asynchronously to the data files by the DBWR in the background. The idea has been to avoid requiring sessions to wait on I/O whenever possible.

The one I/O you cannot avoid is the I/O that occurs when a COMMIT statement is issued. Atomic-Consistent-Independent-Durable (ACID) transactions *must* write to some form of persistent (or redundant) storage so that they are not lost in the event of a system failure. When a COMMIT is issued, the redo log entries are flushed from memory to the redo log files on disk. Consequently redo log I/O—exposed to us as redo log sync waits—is an important part of a transactional system's I/O overhead.

Since redo log I/O is an unavoidable part of application I/O, and since SSDs provide faster I/O, it's not surprising to find that many in the community have proposed accelerating redo I/O using SSD. However, experiments (and theory) have generally demonstrated that redo log I/O is not a perfect candidate for Flash acceleration.

Redo log file I/O involves almost completely uninterrupted sequential write operations. These sorts of I/O are optimal for magnetic disk architecture, since the read/write head does not need to move between write requests, thus eliminating seek latency. On the other hand, the I/Os involved are least optimal for a Flash SSD, since the circular nature of the redo log files (blocks are continuously being overwritten) puts a very heavy load on the garbage collection algorithms. The chance is very high that when writing continuously to redo logs, erase operations will eventually be required and therefore write performance will be poor.

Figure 16.9 compares the performance of a transaction workload involving 100,000 update and commit transactions specifically designed to generate redo log sync waits. The redo logs were created with a 4096 block size, and Exadata Smart Flash Logging was disabled.

These results match similar findings on other systems which show that redo log performance is not improved—and may well suffer—when logs are placed on SSD.

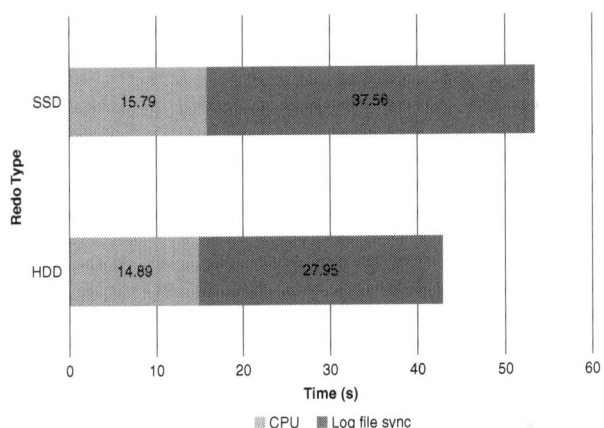

Figure 16.9 Relative performance for redo log based on SSD versus redo on HDD

Note

There's a bug in some early versions of the CellCLI software (without doubt it is present in 112.2.3.2) that results in the default redo log block size being set to 512 bytes with fairly disastrous performance consequences. You can specify the block size in the ALTER DATABASE ADD LOGFILE command. See http://guyharrison.squarespace.com/blog/2011/12/6/using-ssd-for-redo-on-exadata-pt-2.html for more information.

There are some credible reports of redo log performance improving on SSD when rather than the small transactions used in the workload that generated Figure 16.9, we instead write large amounts of redo with each COMMIT. To see if Exadata Flash could accelerate large redo operations, let's take a look at what happens when we execute a large number of COMMITs with varying amounts of redo.

The results of this redo size test are shown in Figure 16.10. Rather than improving with increasing redo log entry size, the SSDs actually degraded faster than SSD. These results only serve to reinforce the recommendation not to place redo logs on SSD in Exadata. Most benchmarks have found that placing redo logs on SSD storage at best confers no benefit to raw redo write time and at worst creates significant performance penalty.

Note

The "sawtooth" pattern of the data in Figure 16.10 reveals the dynamics of the log buffer in action. The log buffer buffers redo writes and on this database was 1MB in size. Consequently, redo writes slightly over 1MB performed slightly better than those under 1MB because the redo buffer had recently been flushed to disk when the COMMIT occurred. See http://guyharrison.squarespace.com/blog/2013/9/17/redo-log-sync-time-vs-redo-size.html for more information.

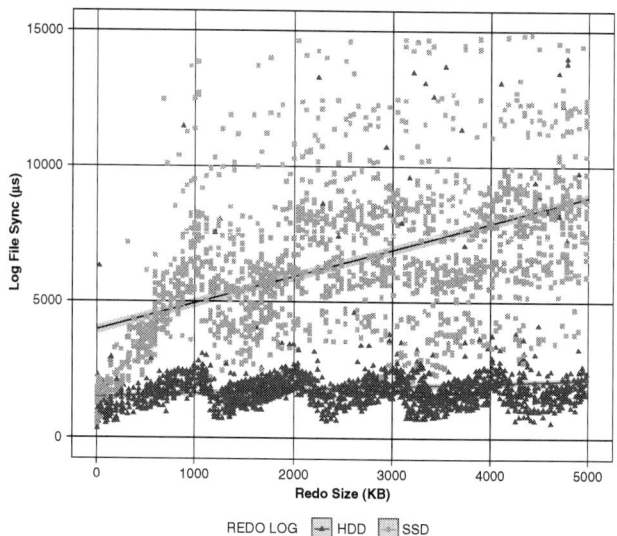

Figure 16.10   Effect of varying redo size on log file sync time

Storage Tiering Solutions

Placing a segment on an SSD tablespace can provide greater optimization and greater predictability than using the Exadata Smart Flash Cache. But one of the killer advantages of the Exadata Smart Flash Cache is that it can optimize tables and indexes that are too large to be hosted on Flash disk.

The challenge of dealing with storage subsystems is not specific to Exadata. Indeed, there are two megatrends involved:

- Increasing data volumes (Big Data) require solutions that provide economical storage of masses of data. This essentially requires systems that incorporate magnetic disk.

- Increasing transaction rates and exponential increases in CPU capacity require solutions that provide economical provision of IOPS and minimize latency. This is the province of solid-state disk and in-memory solutions.

For many or even most databases, the only way to balance these trends is to "tier" various forms of storage, including RAM, SSD, and magnetic disk. The Oracle Database provides a variety of mechanisms that allow you to move data between the tiers to balance IOPS and storage costs and maximize performance. The key capabilities that you should consider are

- Partitioning, which allows an object (table or index) to be stored across various forms of storage and allows data to be moved online from one storage medium to another
- Compression, which can be used to reduce the storage footprint (but may increase the retrieval time)
- Oracle 12 Automatic Database Optimization (ADO), which allows policy-based compression of data based on activity or movement of segments to alternative storage based on free space

Using Partitions to Tier Data

Almost any tiered storage solution requires that a table's data be spread across multiple tiers. Typically, the most massive tables contain data that has been accumulated over time. Also, the most recently collected data typically has the greatest activity, while data created further in the past tends to have less activity.

Oracle partitioning allows a table's data to be stored in multiple segments (e.g., partitions), and those partitions can be stored within separate tablespaces. It is therefore the cornerstone of any database tiering solution.

A complete discussion of all of the Oracle partitioning capabilities is beyond the scope of this chapter. However, let's consider a scheme that could work to spread the contents of a table across two tiers of storage in an Exadata system. The hot tier is stored on a Flash-based tablespace, and the cold tier is stored on an SAS-based tablespace.

Interval partitioning allows us to nominate a default partition for new data while selecting specific storage for older data.

Listing 16.1 provides an example of an interval partitioned table. New data inserted into this table is stored in partitions on the SSD_TS tablespace, and data older than July 1, 2013, is stored on the SAS_TS tablespace.

Listing 16.1 Interval Partitioned Table

```
CREATE TABLE ssd_partition_demo
(
    id              NUMBER PRIMARY KEY,
    category        VARCHAR2 (1) NOT NULL,
    rating          VARCHAR2 (3) NOT NULL,
    insert_date     DATE NOT NULL
)
PARTITION BY RANGE (insert_date)
    INTERVAL ( NUMTOYMINTERVAL (1, 'month') )
    STORE IN (ssd_ts)
```

```
(PARTITION cold_data VALUES LESS THAN
    (TO_DATE ('2013-07-01', 'SYYYY-MM-DD'))
    TABLESPACE sas_ts);
```

After some data is loaded into the table, we can see how new data is stored on the SSD-based tablespace (SSD_TS), while older data is stored on the SAS-based tablespace (SAS_TS):

```
SQL> l
  1  SELECT partition_name, high_value, tablespace_name
  2    FROM user_tab_partitions
  3* WHERE table_name = 'SSD_PARTITION_DEMO'
SQL> /

PARTITION HIGH_VALUE                                    TABLESPACE
--------- -------------------------------------------- ----------
COLD_DATA TO_DATE(' 2013-07-01 00:00:00', 'SYYYY-M      SAS_TS
          M-DD HH24:MI:SS', 'NLS_CALENDAR=GREGORIA
SYS_P68   TO_DATE(' 2013-11-01 00:00:00', 'SYYYY-M      SSD_TS
          M-DD HH24:MI:SS', 'NLS_CALENDAR=GREGORIA
SYS_P69   TO_DATE(' 2013-12-01 00:00:00', 'SYYYY-M      SSD_TS
          M-DD HH24:MI:SS', 'NLS_CALENDAR=GREGORIA
SYS_P70   TO_DATE(' 2013-10-01 00:00:00', 'SYYYY-M      SSD_TS
          M-DD HH24:MI:SS', 'NLS_CALENDAR=GREGORIA
SYS_P71   TO_DATE(' 2013-09-01 00:00:00', 'SYYYY-M      SSD_TS
          M-DD HH24:MI:SS', 'NLS_CALENDAR=GREGORIA
SYS_P72   TO_DATE(' 2013-08-01 00:00:00', 'SYYYY-M      SSD_TS
          M-DD HH24:MI:SS', 'NLS_CALENDAR=GREGORIA
SYS_P73   TO_DATE(' 2014-01-01 00:00:00', 'SYYYY-M      SSD_TS
          M-DD HH24:MI:SS', 'NLS_CALENDAR=GREGORIA
SYS_P74   TO_DATE(' 2014-02-01 00:00:00', 'SYYYY-M      SSD_TS
          M-DD HH24:MI:SS', 'NLS_CALENDAR=GREGORIA
```

This configuration is initially suitable, but of course as data ages, we expect less access and we'll want to move it from the SSD tablespace to an SAS-based tablespace. To do this we issue an ALTER TABLE MOVE PARTITION statement.

For instance, the PL/SQL in Listing 16.2 moves all partitions with a HIGH_VALUE of more than 90 days ago from the SSD_TS tablespace to the SAS_TS tablespace.

Listing 16.2 PL/SQL to Move Old Partitions from SSD to SAS Tablespace

```
DECLARE
    num_not_date           EXCEPTION;
    PRAGMA EXCEPTION_INIT (NUM_NOT_DATE, -932);
    invalid_identifier     EXCEPTION;
    PRAGMA EXCEPTION_INIT (invalid_identifier, -904);

    l_highdate             DATE;
BEGIN
    FOR r IN (SELECT table_name,
                     partition_name,
                     high_value
                FROM user_tab_partitions
               WHERE tablespace_name <> 'SSD_TS')
```

```
LOOP
   BEGIN
      -- pull the highvalue out as a date
      EXECUTE IMMEDIATE 'SELECT ' || r.high_value || ' from dual'
         INTO l_highdate;

      IF l_highdate < SYSDATE - 90
      THEN
         EXECUTE IMMEDIATE
               'alter table '
            || r.table_name
            || ' move partition "'
            || r.partition_name
            || '" tablespace sas_ts';
      END IF;
   EXCEPTION
      WHEN num_not_date OR invalid_identifier   -- max_value not a date
      THEN
         NULL;
   END;
   END LOOP;
END;
```

In 11*g*, this operation blocks DML on each partition during the move (or fails with error ORA-00054 if the partition can't be locked). In 12*c*, you may specify the ONLINE clause to allow transactions on the affected partition to continue. After the move, local indexes corresponding to the moved partition and all global indexes are marked as unusable unless you specify the UPDATE INDEXES or UPDATE GLOBAL INDEXES clause.

The 12*c* syntax for moving partitions online is simple and effective, but in 11*g* we can achieve the same result albeit in a more complex manner. Using the DBMS_ REDEFINITION package, we can create an interim table in the target tablespace, synchronize all changes between that interim table and the original partition, and then effectively exchange that interim table for the original partition.

Listing 16.3 provides an example of using DBMS_REDEFINITION. We create a distinct interim table in the target tablespace, which is synchronized with the existing partition. When the FINISH_REDEF_TABLE method is called, all transactions that may have been applied to the partition are guaranteed to have been applied to the interim table, and the table is exchanged with the partition concerned. The interim table—which is now mapped to the original partition segment—can now be removed.

Listing 16.3 Using DBMS_REDEFINITION to Move a Tablespace Online

```
-- Enable/ Check that table is eligible for redefinition
BEGIN
  DBMS_REDEFINITION.CAN_REDEF_TABLE(
    uname        => USER,
    tname        => 'SSD_PARTITION_DEMO',
    options_flag => DBMS_REDEFINITION.CONS_USE_ROWID,
```

```
    part_name    => 'SYS_P86');
END;
/
-- Create interim table in the tablespace where we want to move to
CREATE TABLE interim_partition_storage TABLESPACE sas_ts
AS SELECT * FROM ssd_partition_demo PARTITION (sys_p86) WHERE ROWNUM <1;

-- Begin redefinition
BEGIN
  DBMS_REDEFINITION.START_REDEF_TABLE(
    uname       => USER,
    orig_table  => 'SSD_PARTITION_DEMO',
    int_table   => 'INTERIM_PARTITION_STORAGE',
    col_mapping => NULL,
    options_flag => DBMS_REDEFINITION.CONS_USE_ROWID,
    part_name   => 'SYS_P86');
END;
/
-- If there are any local indexes create them here
-- Synchronize
BEGIN
  DBMS_REDEFINITION.SYNC_INTERIM_TABLE(
    uname       => USER,
    orig_table  => 'SSD_PARTITION_DEMO',
    int_table   => 'INTERIM_PARTITION_STORAGE',
    part_name   => 'SYS_P86');
END;
/

-- Finalize the redefinition (exchange partitions)
BEGIN
  DBMS_REDEFINITION.FINISH_REDEF_TABLE(
    uname       => USER,
    orig_table  => 'SSD_PARTITION_DEMO',
    int_table   => 'INTERIM_PARTITION_STORAGE',
    part_name   => 'SYS_P86');
END;
/
```

Using DBMS_REDEFINITION is cumbersome, but generally it is the best approach in 11g when you expect that the partition being moved may be subject to ongoing transactions. In 12c the ONLINE clause of MOVE PARTITION is far easier.

12c ILM and ADO

Oracle Database 12c introduced Information Lifecycle Management (ILM) and Automatic Data Optimization (ADO). These features are designed to help you manage data throughout its lifecycle. The lifecycle of a data element might involve storing it initially on low-latency storage such as SSD, compressing it and/or moving it to slower storage as it ages, and eventually archiving it to a separate segment.

For instance, ADO allows you to create a policy that compresses data that has not been accessed for some time. This is pretty cool, but it doesn't directly help us with storage tiering. However, the ADO syntax also contains a TIER TO clause which at first glance might seem to allow us to manage data movement between tablespaces.

For instance, the initial Oracle 12*c* SQL language reference implies that the following statement should be legal:

```
ALTER TABLE ssd_partition_demo ADD POLICY ssd_policy
    TIER TO ssd_ts AFTER 1 MONTH OF NO ACCESS;
```

Alas, in existing releases of 12*c*, this syntax is not supported. The TIER TO clause can be used to define a secondary storage destination for a segment, but this tiering occurs only when a tablespace runs low on free space and cannot be coupled with an activity filter. A future release of Oracle Database software may provide us with more functionality, but for now this capability does not allow us to selectively move rows or partitions between SSD- and SAS-based storage.

Summary

The Exadata Smart Flash Cache makes effective use of the Exadata Flash disks for a wide variety of workloads and requires little configuration. However, with a little bit of effort we can create ASM disk groups based entirely on Flash storage and use these to selectively optimize hot segments, or experiment with placing temporary tablespaces or redo logs on Flash storage. Creating a Flash-based disk group can allow superior performance for specific workloads, though it definitely requires more effort than simply configuring the Exadata Smart Flash Cache.

Consider creating a Flash ASM disk group to hold relatively small "hot" segments, especially relatively small segments subject to periodic time-critical full table scans. Using partitioning, we can create a tiered storage solution for Exadata by storing hot partitions on Flash and colder partitions on SAS disk.

## 17

Exadata Tools and Utilities

The Oracle Exadata Database Machine is converged hardware built upon standard commodity components but with a lot of customization engineered into the solution. Exadata uses Oracle Enterprise Linux on commodity Sun hardware using Intel x86 64-bit processors, using Oracle Grid Infrastructure for clustering, and running the standard Oracle Database software (Enterprise Edition). Not having any proprietary OS or software makes the transition that much easier, reducing the amount of proprietary command sets the administrator needs to be aware of and understand.

This chapter covers some commands and utilities specific to Exadata as well as some existing tools to manage and administer the Exadata Database Machine. It does not cover the standard command set or toolkit that comes with RAC or with Linux, as that should be base knowledge.

Exadata Diagnostic Tools

Oracle has a fairly comprehensive toolset related to diagnostics on the Exadata Database Machine platform and is always improving these or adding more tools to assist with diagnostics and improve the resolution time on their flagship hardware platform. The toolset includes

- Exachk
- Trace File Analyzer (TFA) Collector

- ExaWatcher
- SunDiag

In addition, there are standard utilities that apply to all Oracle Database and platform infrastructure, such as

- OSWatcher
- RDA
- RACcheck

We go into further detail about the Exadata-specific utilities in this section.

SunDiag

The SunDiag utility is used to collect the data and log files required for debugging and troubleshooting hardware issues on the Exadata Database Machine platform. Since this utility is always being enhanced, you should periodically check for and download the latest version and also review the latest instructions. These can be found in Oracle Support Note ID 761868.1.

`Sundiag.pl` is already installed on the Exadata servers, but if you need to reinstall or update your current version, the procedure is as follows:

1. Download the latest version from Oracle Support, which is in a .zip file.
2. Unzip the .zip file contents to a staging directory such as /tmp.
3. Copy the latest version to all the remaining nodes, including the Compute Nodes and cells.

SunDiag is executed via the shell script `/opt/oracle.SupportTools/sundiag.sh`. This script is executed on each Storage Cell and Compute Node. When completed, we will be left with a zipped file in /tmp, which contains the results and may be uploaded to Oracle Support.

Using the `dcli` command utility, we can execute this from a Compute Node with SSH equivalency across all the cells and Compute Nodes.

There are multiple modes for executing SunDiag:

- To collect hardware diagnostic information only, execute the `sundiag.sh` script without any additional parameters.
- To collect hardware diagnostic information as well the OSWatcher utility data, execute the `sundiag` script called but include an additional argument of `osw`.

- To collect hardware diagnostic information as well as ILOM data, execute the `sundiag` script but include an additional argument of either `snapshot` or `ilom`. Both arguments will first attempt to collect ILOM snapshot information. The `snapshot` option uses the host's root ID password to execute the ILOM snapshot and then transfer it over the network. With this option, the `ilom` option gathers user-level ILOM data via the Intelligent Platform Management Interface (IPMI)_ interface.

The SunDiag utility collects kernel, disk partitioning, and PCI bus information, as well as physical disk status and kernel log files. In addition, on Storage Cells, SunDiag also gathers information about the cell and the disks under it, using CellCLI commands to gather information about the cells, physical disks, LUNs, cell disks, grid disks, and Flash Cache. Additionally, at an OS level, it captures information about the PCI Flash Modules as well as system log files specific to Storage Cells.

Exachk: Exadata Health Check

Oracle's Exadata-specific Exachk utility validates the Exadata configuration and performance information based on best practices and known issues. The Exachk utility collects data regarding key software, hardware, firmware, and configurations; assesses the current installation; and delivers a report of its findings and evaluation. The output assists customers in reviewing and cross-referencing current collected data against supported version levels and recommended Oracle Exadata best practices.

Note

You will also find references to Oracle HealthCheck for Exadata. HealthCheck is the earlier incarnation of Exachk and is now frozen and retained only for backward compatibility to the first generation of Exadata—HP Oracle Database Machine.

Since this utility is always being enhanced, you should periodically check your version using the following code. If it is outdated, download the latest version and also review the latest instructions. The current version can be found in Oracle Support Note ID 1070954.1. Once downloaded, Exachk should be placed under the /opt/oracle.SupportTools/exachk directory.

```
[oracle@oe01db02 exachk]$ pwd
/opt/oracle.SupportTools/exachk
[oracle@oe01db02 exachk]$ ./exachk -v

EXACHK VERSION: 2.2.5_20140530
```

To understand how to use Exachk, we could execute exachk -h, which provides a very comprehensive list of the options available and their usage:

```
./exachk -h
Usage :  ./exachk [-abvhpfmsuSo:c:t:]
         -h      Prints this page.
-a All (Perform best practice check and recommended patch check)
-b Best Practice check only. No recommended patch check
-v Show version
-p Patch check only
-m exclude checks for Maximum Availability Architecture (MAA)
scorecards(see user guide for more details)
-u
Run exachk to check pre-upgrade or post-upgrade best practices for
11.2.0.3 and above
         -o pre or -o post is mandatory with -u option like ./exachk -u -o pre
-f Run Offline. Checks will be performed on data already collected from
the system
-o Argument to an option. if -o is followed by v,V,Verbose,VERBOSE or
Verbose, it will print checks which pass on the screen
if -o option is not specified, it will print only failures on screen. For
eg: exachk -a -o v
-clusternodes
Pass comma separated node names to run exachk only on subset of nodes.
-dbnames
Pass comma separated database names to run exachk only on subset of
databases
-localonly
Run exachk only on local node.
-debug
Run exachk in debug mode. Debug log will be generated.
-dbnone
Do not prompt database selection and skip all database related checks.
-dball
Do not prompt database selection and run database related checks on all
 databases discovered on system.
-c Used only under the guidance of Oracle support or development to
override default components
-upgrade
Used to force upgrade the version of exachk being run.
```

Some of the additional features available in the latest version of Exachk include

- Comparing differences between two individual Exadata reports
- Comparing collections from two different runs
- Enhancements to the self-updating feature
- Running Exachk as the root user, which is especially useful in cases where role and duty separation is used
- Support for the new Zero Data Loss Recovery Appliance

Under normal operations, Exachk is interactive in nature, asking for confirmation of options and choices and prompting for passwords. However, Exachk can be run in "silent" mode as well. This makes it easy to schedule Exachk to run on a periodic basis and send results over email. This configuration has certain prerequisites that need to be met:

- Configure SSH equivalency for the Oracle user ID to all Compute Nodes.
- Configure password-less sudo privileges for Oracle users to execute the commands as root.
- If password-less sudo cannot be configured for security reasons, another method is to use the -S option which excludes root-level checks.

Another new feature with Exachk that can be useful is its ability to load the results into a repository. (For specifics, look at Oracle Support Note ID 1602329.1, which covers the Collection Manager for ORAchk and Exachk.) This is useful for customers with a large number of systems. They can upload the results of Exachk and ORAchk to see the results of the audit checks in a repository for historical comparison and reporting.

The following are needed in order to use the Collection Manager for Exachk:

- A table created with a specific structure, the name of which is user defined. The table structure can potentially change between different releases of Exachk; therefore, you should get the script to create the table from the Exachk user's guide for the specific release.
- The following specific environment variables which drive the upload:
  - **RAT_UPLOAD_CONNECT_STRING**—the database connection string
  - **RAT_UPLOAD_TABLE**—the table name into which the details are uploaded
  - **RAT_UPLOAD_USER**—the schema owner for the table
  - **RAT_UPLOAD_PASSWORD**—the password for the schema that owns the table
  - **RAT_UPLOAD_ORACLE_HOME**—the path for the Oracle Home to use for the upload

InfiniBand Network Diagnostic Tools

On the InfiniBand switches, there is a subnet manager software layer called OpenSM. This is started with the switch as a daemon, and we can check the status of the service using the standard Linux command:

```
[root@oe01sw-iba0 ~]# chkconfig --list opensmd
opensmd         0:off   1:off   2:off   3:off   4:off   5:off   6:off
[root@oe01sw-iba0 ~]# service opensmd status
opensm (pid 7147) is running...
[root@oe01sw-iba0 ~]#
```

This service can be enabled or disabled using the enable_sm and disable_sm commands.

Every Exadata configuration will have at least two InfiniBand switches, with the exception of a Full Rack having three InfiniBand switches. When we connect multiple racks, the number of switches in play increases. Each InfiniBand switch is running a subnet manager. However, only one switch takes on the role of subnet master.

The subnet priority across all the switches in the InfinBand network is used to identify the master and slave switches in the configuration. By setting a subnet manager to a higher priority than other subnet managers, we are declaring that particular subnet manager as the master in the InfiniBand network. If there are multiple subnet managers set at the same priority, the first subnet manager to identify itself as the master takes over the role. If the current master subnet manager becomes unavailable, another subnet manager will take over the role based on the same rules.

A Full Rack on a multirack configuration has two leaf switches and a spine switch. The subnet manager on the spine switch is always configured to be at a higher priority than the two leaf switches. Therefore, by default the subnet manager on the spine switch is always the master in the InfiniBand network.

The command setsmpriority sets the subnet manager priority. The command getmaster identifies the current master of the InfiniBand subnet. Listing 17.1 is an example of these commands on a Quarter Rack with two InfiniBand switches.

Listing 17.1   Sample Configuration on a Quarter Rack with Two InfiniBand Switches

```
[root@oe01sw-iba0 ~]# uname -a
Linux oe01sw-iba0.at-rockside.lab 2.6.27.13-nm2 #1 SMP Thu Feb 5 20:25:23
CET 2009 i686 i686 i386 GNU/Linux
[root@oe01sw-iba0 ~]# cat /etc/opensm/opensm.conf  | grep priority
# SM priority used for deciding who is the master
# Range goes from 0 (lowest priority) to 15 (highest).
sm_priority 5
[root@oe01sw-iba0 ~]# getmaster
Local SM enabled and running, state STAND BY
20140627 14:52:51 Master SubnetManager on sm lid 1 sm guid
0x2128f56921a0a0 : SUN DCS 36P QDR oe01sw-ibb0 172.17.33.14

[root@oe01sw-ibb0 ~]# uname -a
Linux oe01sw-ibb0.at-rockside.lab 2.6.27.13-nm2 #1 SMP Thu Feb 5 20:25:23
CET 2009 i686 i686 i386 GNU/Linux
[root@oe01sw-ibb0 ~]# cat /etc/opensm/opensm.conf  | grep priority
# SM priority used for deciding who is the master
# Range goes from 0 (lowest priority) to 15 (highest).
sm_priority 5
[root@oe01sw-ibb0 ~]# getmaster
Local SM enabled and running, state MASTER
20140627 14:42:15 Master SubnetManager on sm lid 1 sm guid
0x2128f56921a0a0 : SUN DCS 36P QDR oe01sw-ibb0 172.17.33.14
```

To check the InfiniBand routing tables we can use the `ibroute` command. The argument to pass to `ibroute` is the port lid for the switch that we wish to query. Sample output from a Quarter Rack is included here:

```
[root@oe01db01 ~]# ibroute 1
Unicast lids [0x0-0xe] of switch Lid 1 guid 0x002128f56921a0a0 (SUN DCS
36P QDR oe01sw-ibb0 172.17.33.14):
  Lid  Out    Destination
       Port   Info
0x0001 000 : (Switch portguid 0x002128f56921a0a0: 'SUN DCS 36P QDR oe01sw-
ibb0 172.17.33.14')
0x0002 017 : (Switch portguid 0x002128f56b22a0a0: 'SUN DCS 36P QDR oe01sw-
iba0 172.17.33.13')
0x0003 018 : (Channel Adapter portguid 0x0021280001fc6307: 'oe01db02 S
192.168.10.2 HCA-1')
0x0004 010 : (Channel Adapter portguid 0x0021280001fc6308: 'oe01db02 S
192.168.10.2 HCA-1')
0x0005 015 : (Channel Adapter portguid 0x0021280001fc6c6b: 'oe01db01 S
192.168.10.1 HCA-1')
0x0006 007 : (Channel Adapter portguid 0x0021280001fc6c6c: 'oe01db01 S
192.168.10.1 HCA-1')
0x0007 014 : (Channel Adapter portguid 0x0021280001fc57b3: 'oe01cel02 C
192.168.10.4 HCA-1')
0x0008 001 : (Channel Adapter portguid 0x0021280001fc57b4: 'oe01cel02 C
192.168.10.4 HCA-1')
0x0009 016 : (Channel Adapter portguid 0x0021280001fc4be3: 'oe01cel03 C
192.168.10.5 HCA-1')
0x000a 004 : (Channel Adapter portguid 0x0021280001fc4be4: 'oe01cel03 C
192.168.10.5 HCA-1')
0x000d 013 : (Channel Adapter portguid 0x0021280001fc6267: 'oe01cel01 C
192.168.10.3 HCA-1')
0x000e 002 : (Channel Adapter portguid 0x0021280001fc6268: 'oe01cel01 C
192.168.10.3 HCA-1')
12 valid lids dumped
 [root@oe01db01 ~]# ibroute 2
Unicast lids [0x0-0xe] of switch Lid 2 guid 0x002128f56b22a0a0 (SUN DCS
36P QDR oe01sw-iba0 172.17.33.13):
  Lid  Out    Destination
       Port   Info
0x0001 017 : (Switch portguid 0x002128f56921a0a0: 'SUN DCS 36P QDR oe01sw-
ibb0 172.17.33.14')
0x0002 000 : (Switch portguid 0x002128f56b22a0a0: 'SUN DCS 36P QDR oe01sw-
iba0 172.17.33.13')
0x0003 010 : (Channel Adapter portguid 0x0021280001fc6307: 'oe01db02 S
192.168.10.2 HCA-1')
0x0004 018 : (Channel Adapter portguid 0x0021280001fc6308: 'oe01db02 S
192.168.10.2 HCA-1')
0x0005 007 : (Channel Adapter portguid 0x0021280001fc6c6b: 'oe01db01 S
192.168.10.1 HCA-1')
0x0006 015 : (Channel Adapter portguid 0x0021280001fc6c6c: 'oe01db01 S
192.168.10.1 HCA-1')
0x0007 001 : (Channel Adapter portguid 0x0021280001fc57b3: 'oe01cel02 C
192.168.10.4 HCA-1')
0x0008 014 : (Channel Adapter portguid 0x0021280001fc57b4: 'oe01cel02 C
192.168.10.4 HCA-1')
0x0009 004 : (Channel Adapter portguid 0x0021280001fc4be3: 'oe01cel03 C
192.168.10.5 HCA-1')
0x000a 016 : (Channel Adapter portguid 0x0021280001fc4be4: 'oe01cel03 C
192.168.10.5 HCA-1')
0x000d 002 : (Channel Adapter portguid 0x0021280001fc6267: 'oe01cel01 C
192.168.10.3 HCA-1')
0x000e 013 : (Channel Adapter portguid 0x0021280001fc6268: 'oe01cel01 C
192.168.10.3 HCA-1')
12 valid lids dumped
```

To check the overall health of the InfiniBand switch, on the Exadata switch itself, we can run the env_test command as follows. This command performs a series of hardware tests, which include power, voltage, fan speed, temperature, and so on, and reports back the status of these tests. Sample output is included here:

```
[root@oe01sw-iba0 ~]# env_test
Environment test started:
Starting Environment Daemon test:
Environment daemon running
Environment Daemon test returned OK
Starting Voltage test:
Voltage ECB OK
Measured 3.3V Main = 3.27 V
Measured 3.3V Standby = 3.37 V
Measured 12V = 11.97 V
Measured 5V = 4.99 V
Measured VBAT = 3.10 V
Measured 2.5V = 2.49 V
Measured 1.8V = 1.78 V
Measured I4 1.2V = 1.22 V
Voltage test returned OK
Starting PSU test:
PSU 0 present OK
PSU 1 present OK
PSU test returned OK
Starting Temperature test:
Back temperature 26
Front temperature 28
SP temperature 50
Switch temperature 41, maxtemperature 42
Temperature test returned OK
Starting FAN test:
Fan 0 not present
Fan 1 running at rpm 12208
Fan 2 running at rpm 12099
Fan 3 running at rpm 11772
Fan 4 not present
FAN test returned OK
Starting Connector test:
Connector test returned OK
Starting Onboard ibdevice test:
Switch OK
All Internal ibdevices OK
Onboard ibdevice test returned OK
Starting SSD test:
SSD test returned OK
Environment test PASSED
[root@oe01sw-iba0 ~]#
```

Verifying InfiniBand Topology

Oracle created a script called verify_topology that validates the topology of the InfiniBand network based upon your configuration. This script is located on the Compute Nodes under /opt/oracle/SupportTools/ibdiagtools. Following are the command-line options and switches that can be passed when executing verify_topology:

```
[root@oe01db01 ibdiagtools]# ./verify-topology --help
    Usage: ./verify-topology [-v|--verbose] [-r|--reuse (cached maps)] [-m|--mapfile]
    [-ibn|--ibnetdiscover (specify location of ibnetdiscover output)]
```

```
[-ibh|--ibhosts (specify location of ibhosts output)]
[-ibs|--ibswitches (specify location of ibswitches output)]
[-t|--topology [torus | quarterrack ] default is fattree]
[-a|--additional [interconnected_quarterrack]
[-factory|--factory non-exadata machines are treated as error]
[-ssc|--ssc to test ssc on fake hardware as if on t4-4]
[-t5ssc|--t5ssc to test ssc on fake hardware as if on t5-8]
[-m6ssc|--m6ssc to test ssc on fake hardware as if on m6-32]
```

The most important options to understand are -t and -a, as they basically define
the expected InfiniBand network topology to use as a baseline. The topology of the
network depends on the number of racks being interconnected and the size of each
of the Exadata racks in the network. Following are the possible arguments that go
along with the -t option:

- **-torus**—A torus network is a special network architecture that is used
  mostly in high-performance computing labs, where the switches form a non-
  cyclic ring. The specifics of a torus network are out of scope for this book.

- **fattree (default option)**—A fattree topology is one where there are
  multiple root-level nodes in a hierarchical network topology. This option
  applies to a Full Rack or a multirack cabling configuration.

- **quarterrack**—This is a specific case of a fattree topology where there is
  no particular root-level switch in the configuration. This would apply in the
  case of an Eighth Rack, Quarter Rack, or Half Rack, since we have only two
  InfiniBand switches in all three cases.

- **-a interconnected_quarterrack**—This is a special case of a fattree
  topology with multirack cables that do not fall into the fattree option. The
  exception is when the two racks are interconnected at Eighth or Quarter
  Racks.

Following is sample output from a verify_topology script for an Exadata Eighth
Rack:

```
[root@oe01db01 ibdiagtools]# ./verify-topology -t quarterrack
[ DB Machine Infiniband Cabling Topology Verification Tool ]
             [Version IBD VER 2.d ]
-------------- Quarter Rack Exadata V2 Cabling Check---------
Check if all hosts have 2 CAs to different switches........... [SUCCESS]
Leaf switch check: cardinality and even distribution ......... [SUCCESS]
Check if each rack has an valid internal ring ................ [SUCCESS]
```

infinicheck

Oracle provides a utility called infinicheck that takes validation of the InfiniBand
network one step further than topology and physical port-level connections. From

an InfiniBand network perspective, this should be the starting point of any validation and debugging that need to happen.

The infinicheck utility can be found on the Compute Nodes under the /opt/
oracle.SupportTools/ibdiagtools directory. infinicheck requires SSH equivalency
for the root user from the executing node to all the Storage Cells as well as to the
Compute Nodes. infinicheck tests and verifies the following and ensures that
the results of these tests are within the expected and acceptable ranges:

- Connectivity and communication tests from all Compute Nodes to all cells
- Connectivity and communication tests from all Compute Nodes to all other
  Compute Nodes
- Performance tests from Compute Nodes to cells
- Performance tests from Compute Nodes to Compute Nodes

Following is an example of the basic infinicheck command run against a Quarter Rack:

```
[root@oe01db01 ibdiagtools]# ./infinicheck
                        INFINICHECK
            [Network Connectivity, Configuration and Performance]
                        [Version IBD VER 2.d ]
Verifying User Equivalance of user=root to all hosts.
(If it isn't setup correctly, an authentication prompt will appear to push
keys to all the nodes)
Verifying User Equivalance of user=root to all cells.
(If it isn't setup correctly, an authentication prompt will appear to push
keys to all the nodes)
                    ####  CONNECTIVITY TESTS  ####
                    [COMPUTE NODES -> STORAGE CELLS]
                        (30 seconds approx.)
[SUCCESS]..............Results OK
[SUCCESS]....... All  can talk to all storage cells
        Verifying Subnet Masks on all nodes
[SUCCESS] ......... Subnet Masks is same across the network
        Prechecking for uniformity of rds-tools on all nodes
[SUCCESS].... rds-tools version is the same across the cluster
        Checking for bad links in the fabric
[SUCCESS].......... No bad fabric links found
                    [COMPUTE NODES -> COMPUTE NODES]
                        (30 seconds approx.)
[SUCCESS]..............Results OK
[SUCCESS]....... All hosts can talk to all other nodes
                    ####  PERFORMANCE TESTS  ####
                    [(1) Storage Cell to Compute Node]
                        (195 seconds approx)
[SUCCESS]..............Results OK
                    [(2) Every COMPUTE NODE to another COMPUTE NODE]
                        (135 seconds approx)
[SUCCESS]..............Results OK
                    [(3) Every COMPUTE NODE to ALL STORAGE CELLS]
                        (looking for SymbolErrors)
                        (195 seconds approx)
[SUCCESS]..............Results OK
[SUCCESS]....... No port errors found
```

```
INFINICHECK REPORTS SUCCESS FOR NETWORK CONNECTIVITY and PERFORMANCE
----------DIAGNOSTICS -----------
Hosts found: 192.168.10.2 | 192.168.10.1 |
3 Cells found: ..
192.168.10.3    | 192.168.10.4    | 192.168.10.5    |
2 Host ips found: ..
192.168.10.2    | 192.168.10.1    |
#########   Host to Cell Connectivity   ##########
Analyzing cells_conntest.log...
[SUCCESS]..... All nodes can talk to all other nodes
Now Analyzing Compute Node-Compute Node connectivity
#########   Inter-Host Connectivity   ##########
Analyzing hosts_conntest.log...
[SUCCESS]..... All hosts can talk to all its peers
#########   Performance Diagnostics   ##########
###   [(1) STORAGE CELL to COMPUTE NODE    ######
Analyzing perf_cells.log.* logfile(s)....
         --------Throughput results using rds-stress --------
         2300 MB/s and above is expected for runs on quiet machines
192.168.10.2( 192.168.10.2 ) to oe01cel01( 192.168.10.3 ) : 3421 MB/s...OK
192.168.10.2( 192.168.10.2 ) to oe01cel01( 192.168.10.3 ) : 3736 MB/s...OK
192.168.10.1( 192.168.10.1 ) to oe01cel02( 192.168.10.4 ) : 3460 MB/s...OK
192.168.10.1( 192.168.10.1 ) to oe01cel02( 192.168.10.4 ) : 3741 MB/s...OK
192.168.10.2( 192.168.10.2 ) to oe01cel03( 192.168.10.5 ) : 3320 MB/s...OK
192.168.10.2( 192.168.10.2 ) to oe01cel03( 192.168.10.5 ) : 3739 MB/s...OK
#########   Performance Diagnostics   ##########
####     [(2) Every DBNODE to its PEER       ######
Analyzing perf_hosts.log.* logfile(s)....
         --------Throughput results using rds-stress --------
         2300 MB/s and above is expected for runs on quiet machines
192.168.10.2( 192.168.10.2 ) to 192.168.10.1( 192.168.10.1):3137 MB/s...OK
192.168.10.2( 192.168.10.2 ) to 192.168.10.1( 192.168.10.1):3735 MB/s...OK
------------------------
```

Other Useful Exadata Commands

The Exadata components this section focuses on are the InfiniBand network layer and the Storage Cells.

The Storage Cells and the aspects related to monitoring and debugging at the storage level have been covered in earlier chapters. The following sections just cover the commands required to identify the storage software version to ensure that they are synchronized.

First we'll go into further detail with respect to the InfiniBand network layer. We'll see how to dig deeper and debug and troubleshoot issues that are reported by the IB layer validation and reporting tools.

imageinfo and imagehistory

Apart from the standard OEL kernel, each cell and Compute Node also runs an Exadata Storage Server–specific software image which is a key integration point. This applies to both the Compute Nodes and the Storage Cells, albeit the image running on a Compute Node is considerably smaller than what is running on the cells.

To see the software images that are currently running on the compute and storage servers we use the imageinfo command. To see the various options one can pass to the command, execute Imageinfo -help and Imagehistory -help. Following is sample output from a Compute Node for imageinfo:

```
[root@oe01db01 ~]# imageinfo --all-options
Kernel version: 2.6.39-400.128.1.el5uek #1 SMP Wed Oct 23 15:32:53 PDT 2013 x86_64
Image version: 12.1.1.1.0.131219
Image created: 2013-12-19 04:13:36 -0800
Image activated: 2014-07-08 23:28:49 -0400
Image type: production
Image status: success
Image label: OSS_12.1.1.1.0_LINUX.X64_131219
Node type: COMPUTE
System partition on device: /dev/mapper/VGExaDb-LVDbSys2
```

And the following is sample output for imageinfo from a Storage Cell:

```
[root@oe01cel01 ~]# imageinfo --all-options
Kernel version: 2.6.39-400.128.1.el5uek #1 SMP Wed Oct 23 15:32:53 PDT 2013 x86_64
Cell version: OSS_12.1.1.1.0_LINUX.X64_131219
Cell rpm version: cell-12.1.1.1.0_LINUX.X64_131219-1

Active image version: 12.1.1.1.0.131219
Active image created: 2013-12-19 04:44:32 -0800
Active image activated: 2014-07-08 16:37:52 -0400
Active image type: production
Active image status: success
Active image label: OSS_12.1.1.1.0_LINUX.X64_131219
Active node type: STORAGE
Active system partition on device: /dev/md6
Active software partition on device: /dev/md8
In partition rollback: Impossible

Cell boot usb partition: /dev/sdm1
Cell boot usb version: 12.1.1.1.0.131219

Inactive image version: 11.2.3.3.0.131014.1
Inactive image created: 2013-10-14 17:56:23 -0700
Inactive image activated: 2014-07-03 17:16:58 -0400
Inactive image type: production
Inactive image status: success
Inactive image label: OSS_11.2.3.3.0_LINUX.X64_131014.1
Inactive node type: STORAGE
Inactive system partition on device: /dev/md5
Inactive software partition on device: /dev/md7
Boot area has rollback archive for the version: 11.2.3.3.0.131014.1
Rollback to the inactive partitions: Possible
```

InfiniBand Network–Related Commands

This section covers some of the basic command sets available on the Exadata machine that specifically manage the InfiniBand network that exists within Exadata.

There are certain acronyms used specifically to describe InfiniBand networks that we will see in use throughout this section. These are

- **CA**—channel adapters. These are the actual PCIe cards that provide InfiniBand connectivity.

- **LID**—local identifier. An InfiniBand LID address is assigned to uniquely identify each device on the fabric. LIDs are used to deliver layer 2 switching functionality. Depending on the command, the device-specific LID would be identified as either `base lid` or `lid`.

ibstat

The `ibstat` command displays basic information retrieved from the local InfiniBand driver. This can be run on the Compute Nodes as well as the Storage Nodes. Following is sample output for `ibstat`:

```
[root@oedb01 ~]# ibstat --verbose
CA 'mlx4_0'
        CA type: MT26428
        Number of ports: 2
        Firmware version: 2.11.2010
        Hardware version: b0
        Node GUID: 0x0021280001fc6266
        System image GUID: 0x0021280001fc6269
        Port 1:
                State: Active
                Physical state: LinkUp
                Rate: 40
                Base lid: 13
                LMC: 0
                SM lid: 1
                Capability mask: 0x02510868
                Port GUID: 0x0021280001fc6267
                Link layer: IB
        Port 2:
                State: Active
                Physical state: LinkUp
                Rate: 40
                Base lid: 14
                LMC: 0
                SM lid: 1
                Capability mask: 0x02510868
                Port GUID: 0x0021280001fc6268
                Link layer: IB
```

ibhosts

The `ibhosts` command is a script that discovers the InfiniBand topology. It can also use the existing topology file to extract the channel adapter nodes of the endpoint in the topology, namely, both the Storage Cells and Compute Nodes but not the switches. Following is sample output for `ibhosts`:

```
root@oe01db01 ~]# ibhosts
Ca  : 0x0021280001fc6c6a ports 2 "oe01db01 S 192.168.10.1 HCA-1"    COMPUTE NODE
Ca  : 0x0021280001fc6306 ports 2 "oe01db02 S 192.168.10.2 HCA-1"    COMPUTE NODE
Ca  : 0x0021280001fc4be2 ports 2 "oe01cel03 C 192.168.10.5 HCA-1"   STORAGE CELL
Ca  : 0x0021280001fc57b2 ports 2 "oe01cel02 C 192.168.10.4 HCA-1"   STORAGE CELL
Ca  : 0x0021280001fc6266 ports 2 "oe01cel01 C 192.168.10.3 HCA-1"   STORAGE CELL
```

ibswitches

The `ibswitches` command is a script that discovers the InfiniBand fabric topology or uses an existing topology file to extract the switch nodes. Following is sample output for `ibswitches`:

```
[root@oe01db01 ~]# ibswitches
Switch  : 0x002128f56921a0a0 ports 36 "SUN DCS 36P QDR oe01sw-ibb0
172.17.33.14" enhanced port 0 lid 1 lmc 0
Switch  : 0x002128f56b22a0a0 ports 36 "SUN DCS 36P QDR oe01sw-iba0
172.17.33.13" enhanced port 0 lid 2 lmc 0
```

ibnodes

The `ibnodes` command is a script that discovers the InfiniBand fabric topology or uses the existing topology file to extract the InfiniBand nodes of the channel adapters, switches, and routers. Following is sample output for `ibnodes`. The S after the device name identifies the device as a Compute Node server, and the C after the device name identifies a Storage Cell.

```
[root@oe01db01 ~]# ibnodes
Ca     : 0x0021280001fc6306 ports 2 "oe01db02 S 192.168.10.2 HCA-1"
Ca     : 0x0021280001fc4be2 ports 2 "oe01cel03 C 192.168.10.5 HCA-1"
Ca     : 0x0021280001fc6266 ports 2 "oe01cel01 C 192.168.10.3 HCA-1"
Ca     : 0x0021280001fc57b2 ports 2 "oe01cel02 C 192.168.10.4 HCA-1"
Ca     : 0x0021280001fc6c6a ports 2 "oe01db01 S 192.168.10.1 HCA-1"
Switch : 0x002128f56921a0a0 ports 36 "SUN DCS 36P QDR oe01sw-ibb0 172.17.33.14" enhanced
port 0 lid 1 lmc 0
Switch : 0x002128f56b22a0a0 ports 36 "SUN DCS 36P QDR oe01sw-iba0
172.17.33.13" enhanced
port 0 lid 2 lmc 0
```

ibstatus

The `ibstatus` command displays basic information retrieved from the local InfiniBand driver on the server. The following is sample output for `ibstatus` from a Compute Node:

```
[root@oe01db01 ~]# ibstatus
Infiniband device 'mlx4_0' port 1 status:
        default gid:     fe80:0000:0000:0000:0021:2800:01fc:6c6b
        base lid:        0x5
        sm lid:          0x1
        state:           4: ACTIVE
        phys state:      5: LinkUp
        rate:            40 Gb/sec (4X QDR)
        link_layer:      IB

Infiniband device 'mlx4_0' port 2 status:
        default gid:     fe80:0000:0000:0000:0021:2800:01fc:6c6c
        base lid:        0x6
        sm lid:          0x1
        state:           4: ACTIVE
        phys state:      5: LinkUp
        rate:            40 Gb/sec (4X QDR)
        link_layer:      IB
```

The following sample output is for `ibstatus` from a Storage Cell:

```
[root@oe01cel02 ~]# ibstatus
Infiniband device 'mlx4_0' port 1 status:
    default gid:    fe80:0000:0000:0000:0021:2800:01fc:57b3
    base lid:       0x7
    sm lid:         0x1
    state:          4: ACTIVE
    phys state:     5: LinkUp
    rate:           40 Gb/sec (4X QDR)
    link_layer:     IB

Infiniband device 'mlx4_0' port 2 status:
    default gid:    fe80:0000:0000:0000:0021:2800:01fc:57b4
    base lid:       0x8
    sm lid:         0x1
    state:          4: ACTIVE
    phys state:     5: LinkUp
    rate:           40 Gb/sec (4X QDR)
    link_layer:     IB
```

ibping

The `ibping` command can be used to verify connectivity to the various nodes within the InfiniBand network. The "ping" test is not based on IP addresses but rather at a layer below that in the networking stack. The `ping` target is based on the LIDs. In order to test connectivity, we need to run `ibping` in server mode on the target server and then in client mode to ping the specific LID on the server:

```
##Run "ibping" in server mode on db node:
[root@oe01db01 ~]# ibping -S

## Run "ibping" from a storage cell in Client Mode
[root@oe01cel01 ~]# ibping --verbose --count 4 --Lid 5
Pong from oe01db01.at-rockside.lab.(none) (Lid 5): time 0.099 ms
Pong from oe01db01.at-rockside.lab.(none) (Lid 5): time 0.055 ms
Pong from oe01db01.at-rockside.lab.(none) (Lid 5): time 0.056 ms
Pong from oe01db01.at-rockside.lab.(none) (Lid 5): time 0.050 ms

--- oe01db01.at-rockside.lab.(none) (Lid 5) ibping statistics ---
4 packets transmitted, 4 received, 0% packet loss, time 4000 ms
rtt min/avg/max = 0.050/0.065/0.099 ms
```

iblinkinfo

The `iblinkinfo` command reports link information for each port in an InfiniBand fabric, node by node. This is useful for debugging performance issues due to links going bad or shutting down. Wherever the link is active and connected, the server is also identified. Furthermore, this InfiniBand link information is shown from the perspective of all the switches in the IB network. This is clearly evident from the following example:

```
[root@oe01db01 ~]# iblinkinfo --verbose
Switch: 0x002128f56921a0a0 SUN DCS 36P QDR oe01sw-ibb0 172.17.33.14:
          1    1[  ] ==( 4X          10.0 Gbps Active/  LinkUp)==>
    8     2[  ] "oe01cel02 C 192.168.10.4 HCA-1" ( )
          1    2[  ] ==( 4X          10.0 Gbps Active/  LinkUp)==>
```

```
14    2[  ] "oe01cel01 C 192.168.10.3 HCA-1" ( )
        1    3[  ] ==(                        Down/ Polling)==>                    [
] "" ( )
        1    4[  ] ==( 4X              10.0 Gbps Active/  LinkUp)==>
10    2[  ] "oe01cel03 C 192.168.10.5 HCA-1" ( )
        1    5[  ] ==(                        Down/ Polling)==>                    [
] "" ( )
        1    6[  ] ==(                        Down/ Polling)==>                    [
] "" ( )
        1    7[  ] ==( 4X              10.0 Gbps Active/  LinkUp)==>
6    2[  ] "oe01db01 S 192.168.10.1 HCA-1" ( )
        1    8[  ] ==(                        Down/ Polling)==>                    [
] "" ( )
        1    9[  ] ==(                        Down/ Polling)==>                    [
] "" ( )
        1   10[  ] ==( 4X              10.0 Gbps Active/  LinkUp)==>
4    2[  ] "oe01db02 S 192.168.10.2 HCA-1" ( )
        1   11[  ] ==(                        Down/Disabled)==>                    [
] "" ( )
        1   12[  ] ==(                        Down/ Polling)==>                    [
] "" ( )
        1   13[  ] ==( 4X              10.0 Gbps Active/  LinkUp)==>
2   14[  ] "SUN DCS 36P QDR oe01sw-iba0 172.17.33.13" ( )
        1   14[  ] ==( 4X              10.0 Gbps Active/  LinkUp)==>
2   13[  ] "SUN DCS 36P QDR oe01sw-iba0 172.17.33.13" ( )
        1   15[  ] ==( 4X              10.0 Gbps Active/  LinkUp)==>
2   16[  ] "SUN DCS 36P QDR oe01sw-iba0 172.17.33.13" ( )
        1   16[  ] ==( 4X              10.0 Gbps Active/  LinkUp)==>
2   15[  ] "SUN DCS 36P QDR oe01sw-iba0 172.17.33.13" ( )
        1   17[  ] ==( 4X              10.0 Gbps Active/  LinkUp)==>
        2   18[  ] "SUN DCS 36P QDR oe01sw-iba0 172.17.33.13" ( )
        1   18[  ] ==( 4X              10.0 Gbps Active/  LinkUp)==>
2   17[  ] "SUN DCS 36P QDR oe01sw-iba0 172.17.33.13" ( )
        1   19[  ] ==(                        Down/Disabled)==>                    [
] "" ( )
...
        1   31[  ] ==( 4X              10.0 Gbps Active/  LinkUp)==>
2   31[  ] "SUN DCS 36P QDR oe01sw-iba0 172.17.33.13" ( )
        1   32[  ] ==(                        Down/Disabled)==>                    [
] "" ( )
...
        1   36[  ] ==(                        Down/Disabled)==>                    [
] "" ( )
CA: oe01db02 S 192.168.10.2 HCA-1:
        0x0021280001fc6307      3    1[  ] ==( 4X              10.0 Gbps Active/
LinkUp)==>      2   10[  ] "SUN DCS 36P QDR oe01sw-iba0 172.17.33.13" ( )
        0x0021280001fc6308      4    2[  ] ==( 4X              10.0 Gbps Active/
LinkUp)==>      1   10[  ] "SUN DCS 36P QDR oe01sw-ibb0 172.17.33.14" ( )
CA: oe01cel03 C 192.168.10.5 HCA-1:
        0x0021280001fc4be3      9    1[  ] ==( 4X              10.0 Gbps Active/
LinkUp)==>      2    4[  ] "SUN DCS 36P QDR oe01sw-iba0 172.17.33.13" ( )
        0x0021280001fc4be4     10    2[  ] ==( 4X              10.0 Gbps Active/
LinkUp)==>      1    4[  ] "SUN DCS 36P QDR oe01sw-ibb0 172.17.33.14" ( )
CA: oe01cel01 C 192.168.10.3 HCA-1:
        0x0021280001fc6267     13    1[  ] ==( 4X              10.0 Gbps Active/
LinkUp)==>      2    2[  ] "SUN DCS 36P QDR oe01sw-iba0 172.17.33.13" ( )
        0x0021280001fc6268     14    2[  ] ==( 4X              10.0 Gbps Active/
LinkUp)==>      1    2[  ] "SUN DCS 36P QDR oe01sw-ibb0 172.17.33.14" ( )
CA: oe01cel02 C 192.168.10.4 HCA-1:
        0x0021280001fc57b3      7    1[  ] ==( 4X              10.0 Gbps Active/
LinkUp)==>      2    1[  ] "SUN DCS 36P QDR oe01sw-iba0 172.17.33.13" ( )
        0x0021280001fc57b4      8    2[  ] ==( 4X              10.0 Gbps Active/
LinkUp)==>      1    1[  ] "SUN DCS 36P QDR oe01sw-ibb0 172.17.33.14" ( )
Switch: 0x002128f56b22a0a0 SUN DCS 36P QDR oe01sw-iba0 172.17.33.13:
        2    1[  ] ==( 4X              10.0 Gbps Active/  LinkUp)==>
7    1[  ] "oe01cel02 C 192.168.10.4 HCA-1" ( )
        2    2[  ] ==( 4X              10.0 Gbps Active/  LinkUp)==>
```

```
13    1[  ]  "oe01cel01 C 192.168.10.3 HCA-1" ( )
      2    3[  ]  ==(                    Down/ Polling)==>                [
] "" ( )
      2    4[  ]  ==( 4X          10.0 Gbps Active/  LinkUp)==>
9     1[  ]  "oe01cel03 C 192.168.10.5 HCA-1" ( )
      2    5[  ]  ==(                    Down/ Polling)==>                [
] "" ( )
      2    6[  ]  ==(                    Down/ Polling)==>                [
] "" ( )
      2    7[  ]  ==( 4X          10.0 Gbps Active/  LinkUp)==>
5     1[  ]  "oe01db01 S 192.168.10.1 HCA-1" ( )
      2    8[  ]  ==(                    Down/ Polling)==>                [
] "" ( )
...
      2   10[  ]  ==( 4X          10.0 Gbps Active/  LinkUp)==>
3     1[  ]  "oe01db02 S 192.168.10.2 HCA-1" ( )
      2   11[  ]  ==(                    Down/Disabled)==>                [
] "" ( )
      2   12[  ]  ==(                    Down/ Polling)==>                [
] "" ( )
      2   13[  ]  ==( 4X          10.0 Gbps Active/  LinkUp)==>
1    14[  ]  "SUN DCS 36P QDR oe01sw-ibb0 172.17.33.14" ( )
      2   14[  ]  ==( 4X          10.0 Gbps Active/  LinkUp)==>
1    13[  ]  "SUN DCS 36P QDR oe01sw-ibb0 172.17.33.14" ( )
      2   15[  ]  ==( 4X          10.0 Gbps Active/  LinkUp)==>
1    16[  ]  "SUN DCS 36P QDR oe01sw-ibb0 172.17.33.14" ( )
      2   16[  ]  ==( 4X          10.0 Gbps Active/  LinkUp)==>
1    15[  ]  "SUN DCS 36P QDR oe01sw-ibb0 172.17.33.14" ( )
      2   17[  ]  ==( 4X          10.0 Gbps Active/  LinkUp)==>
1    18[  ]  "SUN DCS 36P QDR oe01sw-ibb0 172.17.33.14" ( )
      2   18[  ]  ==( 4X          10.0 Gbps Active/  LinkUp)==>
1    17[  ]  "SUN DCS 36P QDR oe01sw-ibb0 172.17.33.14" ( )
      2   19[  ]  ==(                    Down/Disabled)==>                [
] "" ( )
...
      2   31[  ]  ==( 4X          10.0 Gbps Active/  LinkUp)==>
1    31[  ]  "SUN DCS 36P QDR oe01sw-ibb0 172.17.33.14" ( )
      2   32[  ]  ==(                    Down/Disabled)==>                [
] "" ( )
...
      2   36[  ]  ==(                    Down/Disabled)==>         [  ] "" ( )
CA: oe01db01 S 192.168.10.1 HCA-1:
      0x0021280001fc6c6b       5     1[  ]  ==( 4X          10.0 Gbps Active/
LinkUp)==>      2    7[  ]  "SUN DCS 36P QDR oe01sw-iba0 172.17.33.13" ( )
      0x0021280001fc6c6c       6     2[  ]  ==( 4X          10.0 Gbps Active/
LinkUp)==>      1    7[  ]  "SUN DCS 36P QDR oe01sw-ibb0 172.17.33.14" ( )
```

ibcheckstate

The ibcheckstate command scans the InfiniBand fabric to validate the port logical and physical state and reports any ports that have a logical state other than active or a physical state other than LinkUp.

The information is represented from the perspective of all endpoints in the IB network, which includes switches as well as the servers. The endpoints are identified by the GUID. This can be correlated with the output of ibnodes to map the GUIDs to the actual server or switch.

Following is sample output for ibcheckstate:

```
[root@oe01cel01 ~]# ibcheckstate -v
# Checking Switch: nodeguid 0x002128f56921a0a0
Node check lid 1: OK
```

```
Port check lid 1 port 1:   OK
Port check lid 1 port 2:   OK
Port check lid 1 port 4:   OK
Port check lid 1 port 7:   OK
Port check lid 1 port 10:  OK
Port check lid 1 port 13:  OK
Port check lid 1 port 14:  OK
Port check lid 1 port 15:  OK
Port check lid 1 port 16:  OK
Port check lid 1 port 17:  OK
Port check lid 1 port 18:  OK
Port check lid 1 port 31:  OK

# Checking Switch: nodeguid 0x002128f56b22a0a0
Node check lid 2:  OK
Port check lid 2 port 1:   OK
Port check lid 2 port 2:   OK
Port check lid 2 port 4:   OK
Port check lid 2 port 7:   OK
Port check lid 2 port 10:  OK
Port check lid 2 port 13:  OK
Port check lid 2 port 14:  OK
Port check lid 2 port 15:  OK
Port check lid 2 port 16:  OK
Port check lid 2 port 17:  OK
Port check lid 2 port 18:  OK
Port check lid 2 port 31:  OK

# Checking Ca: nodeguid 0x0021280001fc6306
Node check lid 3:  OK
Port check lid 3 port 1:   OK
Port check lid 3 port 2:   OK

# Checking Ca: nodeguid 0x0021280001fc6c6a
Node check lid 5:  OK
Port check lid 5 port 1:   OK
Port check lid 5 port 2:   OK

# Checking Ca: nodeguid 0x0021280001fc4be2
Node check lid 9:  OK
Port check lid 9 port 1:   OK
Port check lid 9 port 2:   OK

# Checking Ca: nodeguid 0x0021280001fc57b2
Node check lid 7:  OK
Port check lid 7 port 1:   OK
Port check lid 7 port 2:   OK

# Checking Ca: nodeguid 0x0021280001fc6266
Node check lid 13:  OK
Port check lid 13 port 1:   OK
Port check lid 13 port 2:   OK

## Summary: 7 nodes checked, 0 bad nodes found
##          34 ports checked, 0 ports with bad state found
```

ibcheckerrors

The ibcheckerrors command is a script that clears the Performance Manager agent error counters in port counters by either discovering the InfiniBand fabric topology or using an existing topology file. Following is sample output for ibcheckerrors:

```
[root@oe01db01 ~]# ibcheckerrors -v

# Checking Switch: nodeguid 0x002128f56921a0a0
Node check lid 1:  OK
Error check on lid 1 (SUN DCS 36P QDR oe01sw-ibb0 172.17.33.14) port all:  OK

# Checking Switch: nodeguid 0x002128f56b22a0a0
Node check lid 2:  OK
Error check on lid 2 (SUN DCS 36P QDR oe01sw-iba0 172.17.33.13) port all:  OK

# Checking Ca: nodeguid 0x0021280001fc6306
Node check lid 3:  OK
Error check on lid 3 (oe01db02 S 192.168.10.2 HCA-1) port 1:  OK
Node check lid 4:  OK
Error check on lid 4 (oe01db02 S 192.168.10.2 HCA-1) port 2:  OK

# Checking Ca: nodeguid 0x0021280001fc4be2
Node check lid 9:  OK
Error check on lid 9 (oe01cel03 C 192.168.10.5 HCA-1) port 1:  OK
Node check lid 10:  OK
Error check on lid 10 (oe01cel03 C 192.168.10.5 HCA-1) port 2:  OK

# Checking Ca: nodeguid 0x0021280001fc6266
Node check lid 13:  OK
Error check on lid 13 (oe01cel01 C 192.168.10.3 HCA-1) port 1:  OK
Node check lid 14:  OK
Error check on lid 14 (oe01cel01 C 192.168.10.3 HCA-1) port 2:  OK

# Checking Ca: nodeguid 0x0021280001fc57b2
Node check lid 7:  OK
Error check on lid 7 (oe01cel02 C 192.168.10.4 HCA-1) port 1:  OK
Node check lid 8:  OK
Error check on lid 8 (oe01cel02 C 192.168.10.4 HCA-1) port 2:  OK

# Checking Ca: nodeguid 0x0021280001fc6c6a
Node check lid 5:  OK
Error check on lid 5 (oe01db01 S 192.168.10.1 HCA-1) port 1:  OK
Node check lid 6:  OK
Error check on lid 6 (oe01db01 S 192.168.10.1 HCA-1) port 2:  OK

## Summary: 7 nodes checked, 0 bad nodes found
##          34 ports checked, 0 ports have errors beyond threshold
```

If the command reports errors, you can further investigate them using the following commands:

- **ibcheckerrors**—scans the InfiniBand fabric to validate the connectivity and reports errors from the port counters

- **ibqueryerrors**—queries and reports nonzero IB port counters

- **ibchecknet**—scans the InfiniBand fabric to validate the connectivity and reports errors from the port counters

- **ibchecknode**—checks node connectivity and performs a simple check to verify the functionality of the specified node

- **ibcheckport**—checks port connectivity and performs simple sanity checks for the specified port

Once the issue has been diagnosed and rectified, we can reset the counters using the following commands:

- `ibclearerrors`—clears the Performance Manager agent port counters by either discovering the InfiniBand fabric topology or using an existing topology file
- `ibclearcounters`—clears the Performance Manager agent error counters in port counters

Monitoring Exadata Storage Cells

In addition to the tools and utilities previously described for general monitoring and administration purposes, we can also use Oracle Enterprise Manager or Dell/Quest Spotlight to monitor various aspects of the Exadata.

Dell Software Tools for Exadata

Dell is a household name when it comes to laptops and desktop computers and has been a major provider of servers and storage servers for Oracle Databases for more than a decade. Dell also became a major provider of software tools for Oracle Database administration and development when it acquired Quest Software in 2012. Quest Software was best known in Oracle circles as the creator of Toad. Toad is an administration and development tool for Oracle Databases as well as for other database systems. Dell claims there are more than 3 million users of Toad worldwide.

Dell software group also provides a variety of other Oracle-related products including SharePlex, which provides high-speed replication between Oracle Databases, and Foglight, which provides monitoring and performance management for all types of databases, application servers, and application infrastructure.

All Dell software products are certified on Oracle Databases on the Exadata platform. In addition, Dell offers a specific version of the Toad DBA suite for Exadata management. This version of Toad includes Spotlight on Oracle Exadata, which is a version of the popular Spotlight on Oracle product which provides specific diagnostics for Exadata systems.

Spotlight on Oracle Exadata provides a diagrammatic representation of Exadata status as shown in Figure 17.1.

This screen shows the normal representation of an Oracle RAC database: Global Cache performance, interconnect, and cluster balance. It also provides key statistics from the Exadata Storage Cells relating to total cell load, Smart Scan activity and efficiency, Exadata Smart Flash Cache hit rate and time savings, and Exadata Hybrid Columnar Compression activity. Clicking on any of these icons takes the user to a page in which detailed activity for the Exadata component can be examined. It's also possible to examine CellCLI statistics aggregated across the system. Figure 17.2 provides an example of the Exadata Smart Flash Cache details screen.

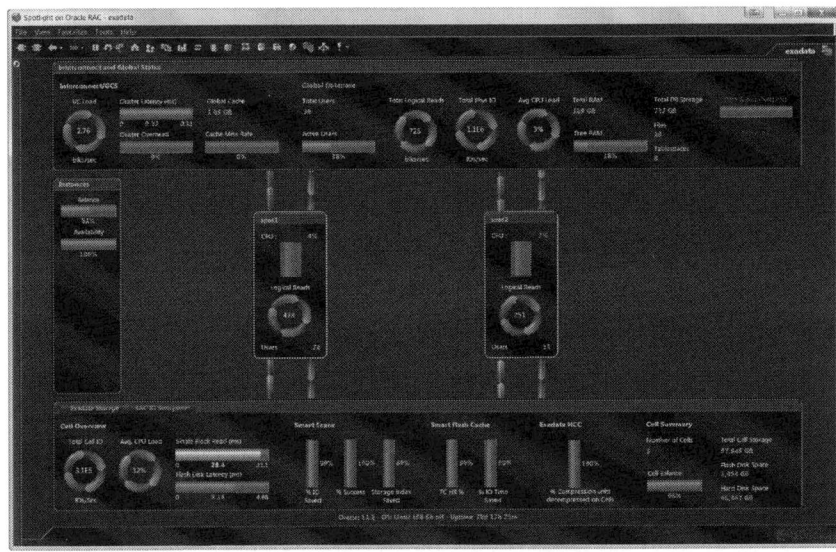

Figure 17.1 Quest Spotlight DBA suite for Oracle Exadata edition

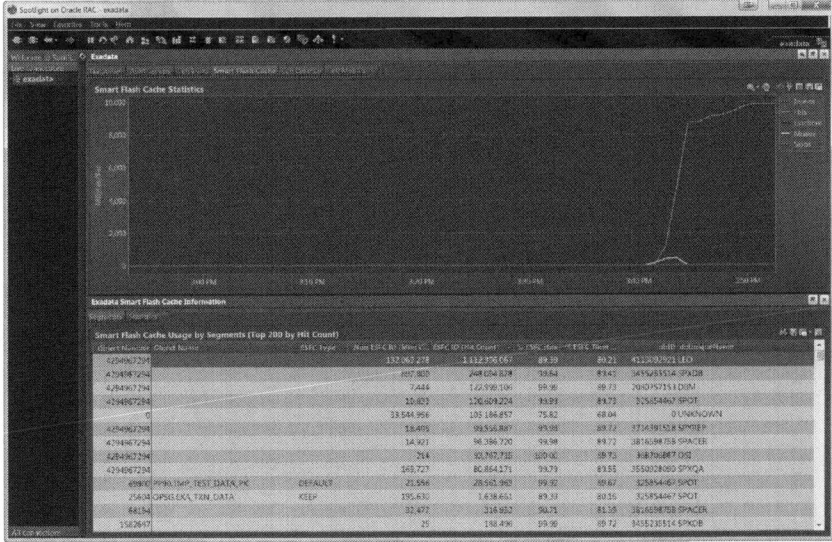

Figure 17.2 Toad for Oracle Exadata Smart Flash Cache monitoring

Dell's Toad suite also includes SQL Optimizer, which is a tool that uses an artificial intelligence engine to generate rewrites for any given SQL and determines the rewrites that generate the best performance improvement. The product incorporates many Exadata-specific improvements, including

- Highlighting of Smart Scan or Bloom filter operations
- SQL rewrite rules that support enabling or disabling Smart Scan and Bloom filter operations and determining the query impact
- Intelligent rewrite of embedded SQL clauses to encourage offloading of entire subquery operations to the storage server
- Integrated Plan Control module that uses Oracle plan baselines to improve SQL performance by enabling and disabling Smart Scan and Bloom filter operations without the need to modify source code

Examples of these can be seen in Figures 17.3 and 17.4.

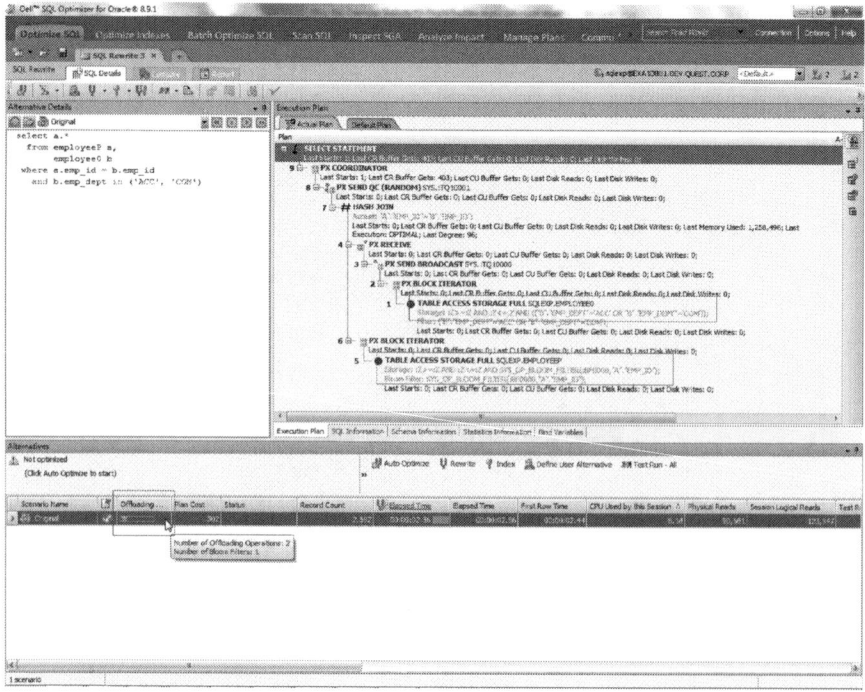

Figure 17.3   Toad's Exadata-aware SQL Optimizer—SQL plan with Bloom filter

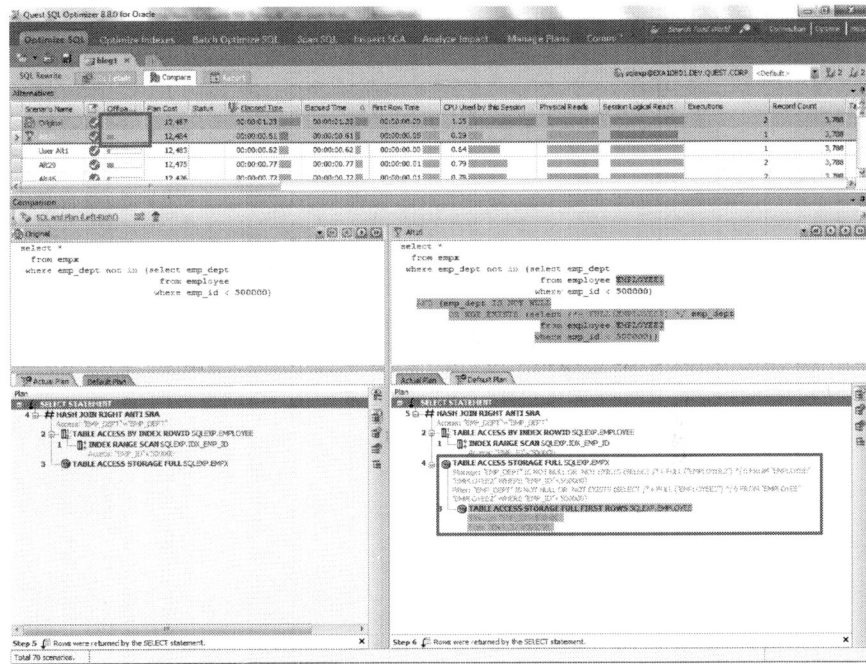

Figure 17.4   Toad's Exadata-aware SQL Optimizer—SQL rewrite

Monitoring the Cell with Enterprise Manager

Oracle Enterprise Manager (OEM) can be used to collect statistics from the Storage Cells once they have been set up appropriately as OEM targets. There are certain tasks that need to be performed beyond the plug installation and target discovery; these are covered in the following sections.

Setting Up the OEM Target

Setting up password-less connections between all of the Compute and Storage Nodes is required before OEM can collect Storage Cell statistics. The procedure is documented in the online help for Enterprise Manager. The short script shown in Listing 17.2 (`setup_ssh_root.sh`) partially automates the procedure.

Listing 17.2   Setting Up Password-Less SSH (Cluster_balance.sql)

```
ssh-keygen -t dsa
while [ $# -gt 0 ]; do
    export remoteHost=$1

    # Root user
    scp ~/.ssh/id_dsa.pub root@${remoteHost}:
    ssh root@${remoteHost} 'mkdir .ssh;chmod 700 .ssh; cat ~/id_dsa.pub
>>~/.ssh/authorized_keys;chmod 600 ~/.ssh/authorized_keys '


    #cellmonitor
    ssh root@${remoteHost} 'mkdir ~cellmonitor/.ssh;
        chmod 700 ~cellmonitor/.ssh;
        cat  ~/id_dsa.pub >>~cellmonitor/.ssh/authorized_keys;
        chmod 600 ~cellmonitor/.ssh/authorized_keys;
        chown cellmonitor ~cellmonitor/.ssh;
        chown cellmonitor ~cellmonitor/.ssh/authorized_keys'
    shift
done
```

On each Compute Node, run the script with the names of all the Storage Nodes provided as arguments:

```
bash set_ssh_root.sh exa1cel01 exa1cel02 exa1cel03
```

Then you will be prompted with various SSH messages about passphrases, and so on. Just hit Return or Y if prompted, except when asked for passwords. You'll have to enter the password for each Storage Cell twice to get everything set up. After that you should be able to SSH to the Storage Cells without being prompted for a password.

To set up Enterprise Manager monitoring of the cells, choose Add Exadata Cell Targets from the Related Links section of the database Home page (Figure 17.5).

The next page explains some of the prerequisites for adding a storage server target, including the creation of a password-less SSH configuration. From there, we find the page for adding a storage server as shown in Figure 17.6.

Now we can see the Exadata cells show up in the Exadata Cells section of the Cluster Database page (Figure 17.7).

Now that the cells are being monitored, we can see historical and real-time views for any cell statistics. To do this, drill into the cell from the link shown in Figure 17.7, then select the specific property. Figure 17.8 shows an example.

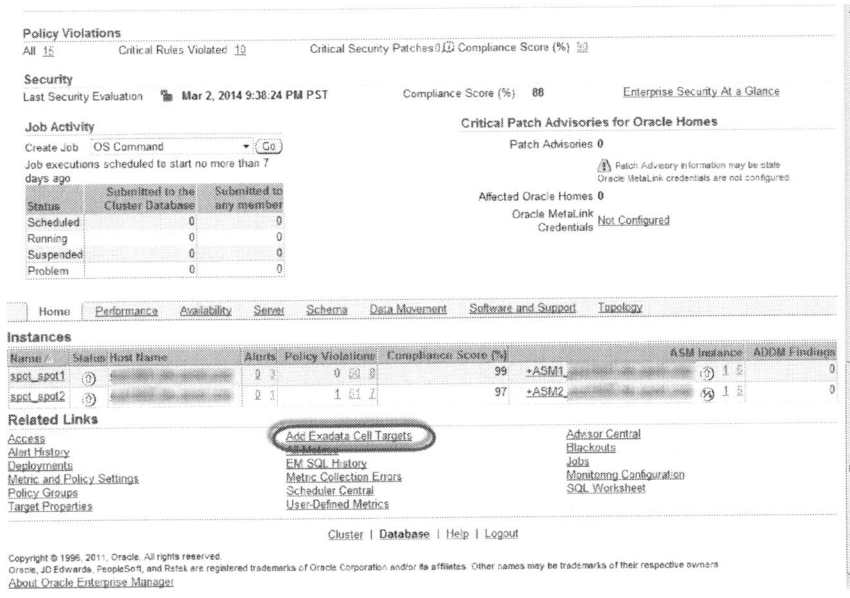

Figure 17.5   Initiating Add Exadata Cell Targets process

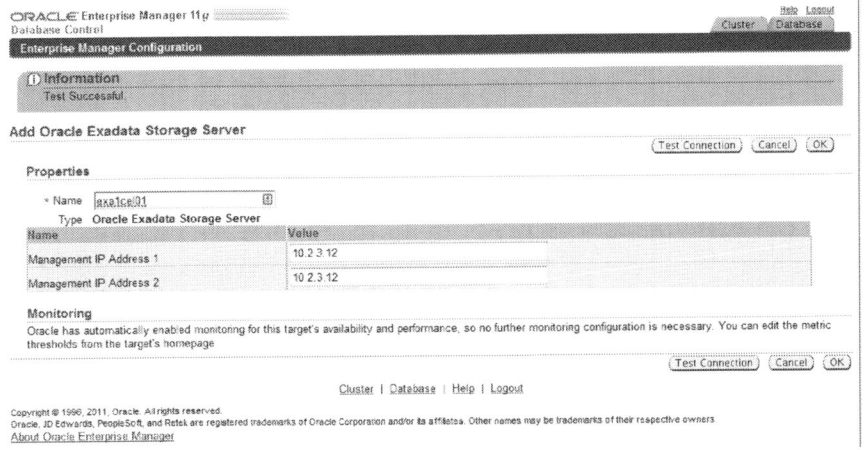

Figure 17.6   Testing connectivity to Exadata cells

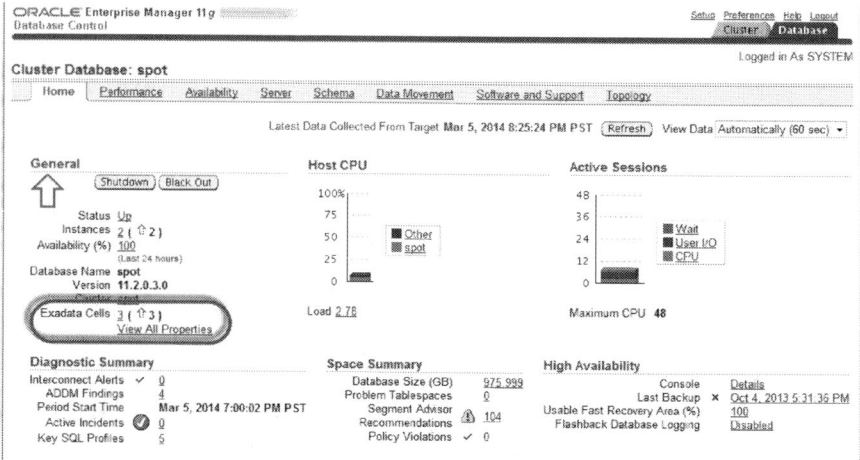

Figure 17.7   Exadata Cells link active in Enterprise Manager

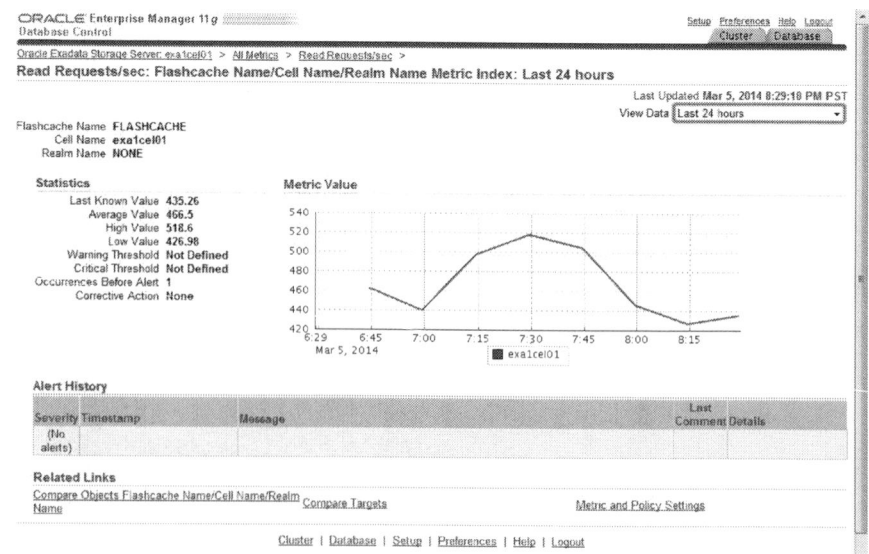

Figure 17.8   Tracking a cell metric in Enterprise Manager

Collating CellCLI Statistics across Nodes

At some time you might need to calculate ratios for CellCLI statistics across all nodes. This can be pretty tedious, even when you use dcli to run the same command on all nodes. Guy Harrison wrote a Perl utility to collate statistics across all nodes. This is described at his blog (http://guyharrison.squarespace.com/blog/2011/7/31/a-perl-utility-to-improve-exadata-cellcli-statistics.html). Using this script we can easily get collated statistics for various CellCLI metrics:

```
$ perl cellcli.pl --hosts exa1cel01,exa1cel02,exa1cel03   --mask FL_.*FIRST --desc

Name             Description                                      Sum
---------------  -----------------------------------------  -----------
FL_DISK_FIRST    no of redo writes first completed to disk  2.27974e+08
FL_FLASH_FIRST   no of redo writes first completed to flash 7.22336e+06
```

Summary

As we have seen, the Oracle Exadata Database Machine is a unique solution that combines hardware technologies with intelligent application-aware software. As a result, Oracle has developed various utilities that allow us to manage and monitor this unique hardware.

Oracle's Enterprise Manager is now fully integrated into the administration, management, and monitoring aspects of Exadata. Apart from OEM, Oracle has provided other Exadata-specific tools as well, such as Exachk (Exadata-specific health check), TFA (Trace File Analyzer), and SunDiag to collect diagnostic and debugging information from a database perspective as well as from a hardware perspective.

The InfiniBand network is a key component of the Exadata architecture, in terms of delivering a platform capable of exceptional levels of availability, reliability, and performance. Oracle has provided utilities like verify_topology and infinicheck that allow you to monitor and validate the InfiniBand network.

A testament to the fact that Exadata is a mature platform is the fact that major third-party database software vendors are now making their tools and utilities Exadata aware. Dell/Quest Spotlight is a good example of this trend.

Index

493

informIT.com THE TRUSTED TECHNOLOGY LEARNING SOURCE

PEARSON InformIT is a brand of Pearson and the online presence for the world's leading technology publishers. It's your source for reliable and qualified content and knowledge, providing access to the leading brands, authors, and contributors from the tech community.

Addison-Wesley   **Cisco Press**   **IBM** Press.   Microsoft Press

PEARSON IT CERTIFICATION   **PRENTICE HALL**   **QUE**   **SAMS**   **vmware PRESS**

LearnIT at InformIT

Looking for a book, eBook, or training video on a new technology? Seeking timely and relevant information and tutorials. Looking for expert opinions, advice, and tips? **InformIT has a solution.**

- Learn about new releases and special promotions by subscribing to a wide variety of monthly newsletters. Visit **informit.com/newsletters**.

- FREE Podcasts from experts at **informit.com/podcasts**.

- Read the latest author articles and sample chapters at **informit.com/articles**.

- Access thousands of books and videos in the Safari Books Online digital library. **safari.informit.com**.

- Get Advice and tips from expert blogs at **informit.com/blogs**.

Visit **informit.com** to find out all the ways you can access the hottest technology content.

Are you part of the IT crowd?

Connect with Pearson authors and editors via RSS feeds, Facebook, Twitter, YouTube and more! Visit **informit.com/socialconnect**.

20622872R00300

Printed in Great Britain
by Amazon